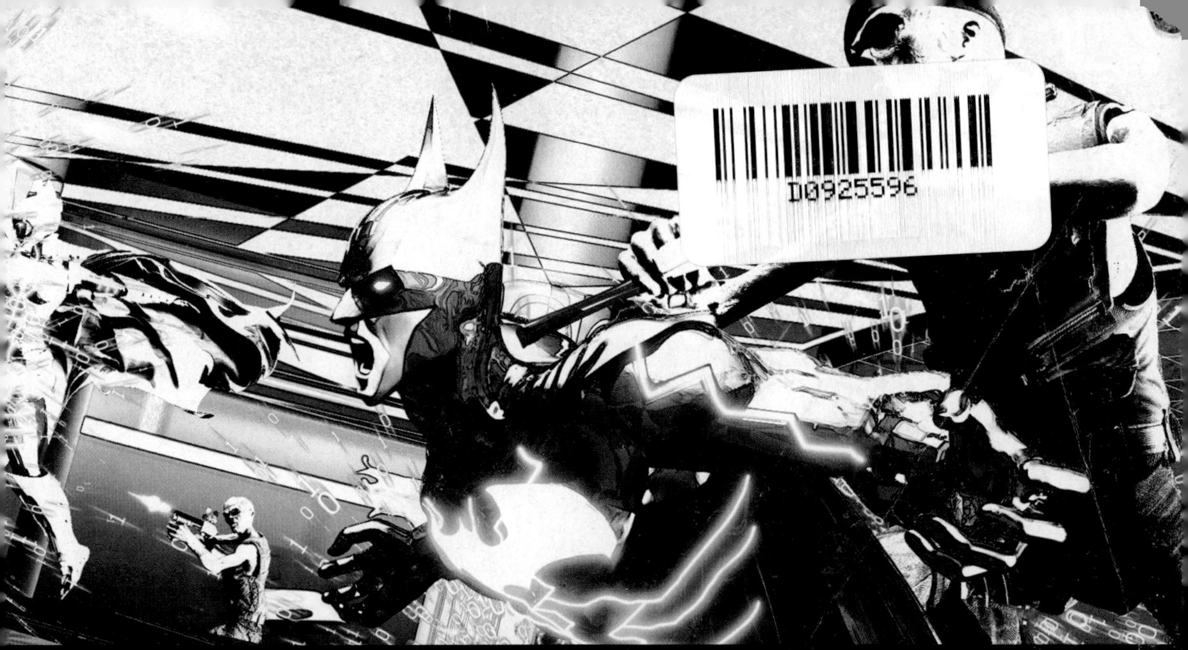

BATMAN, INCORPORATED

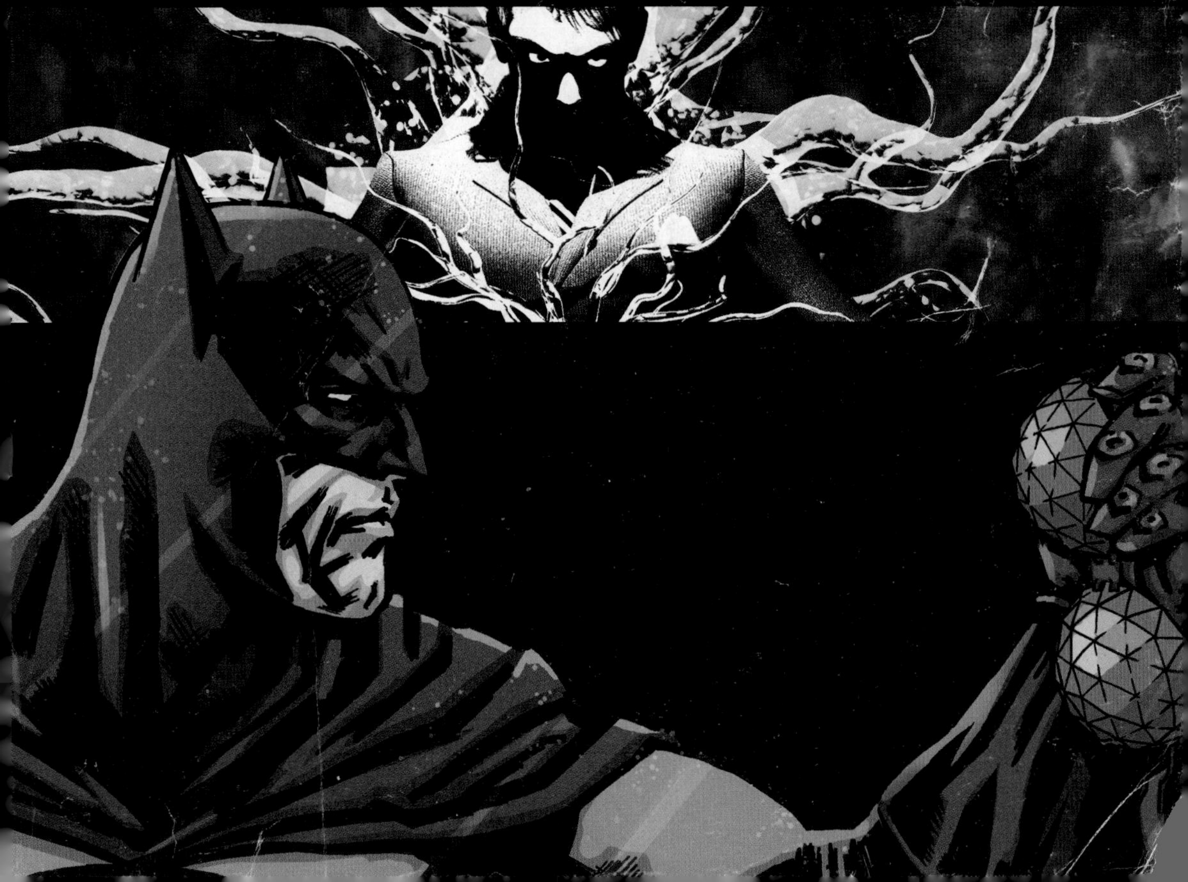

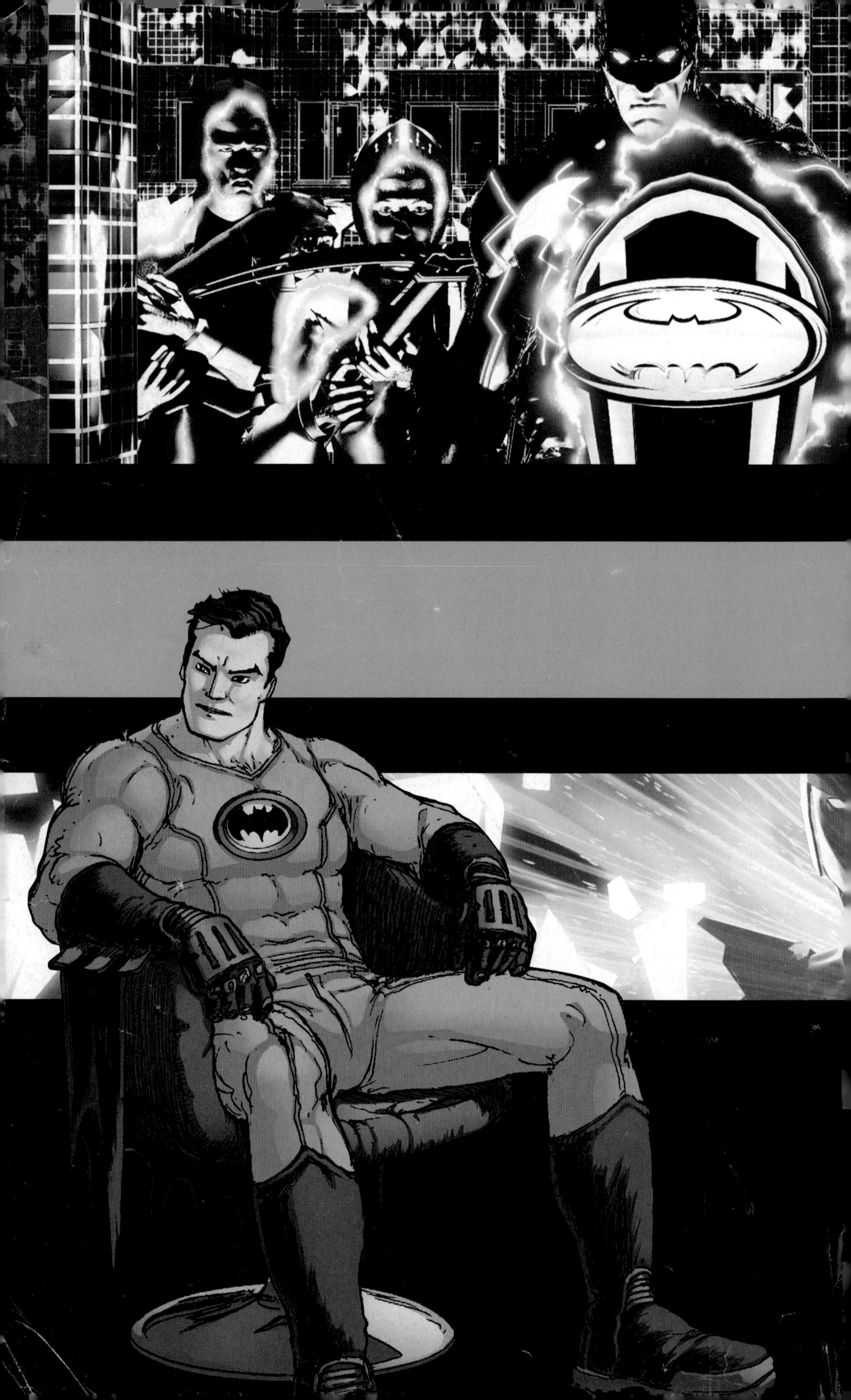

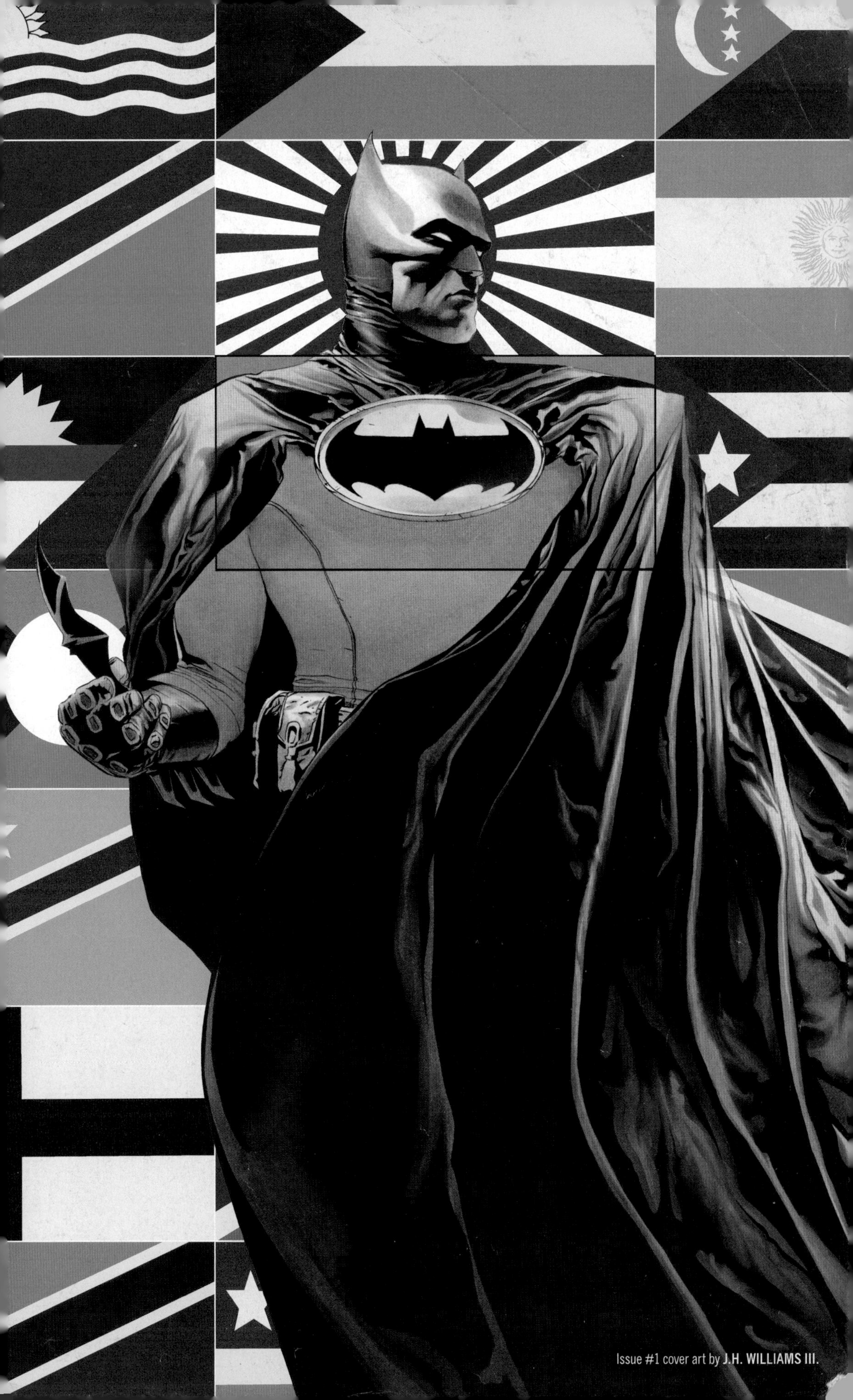

Issue #1 cover art by **J.H. WILLIAMS III.**

Issue #1 variant cover art by **YANICK PAQUETTE** and **MICHEL LACOMBE** (color by **NATHAN FAIRBAIRN**).

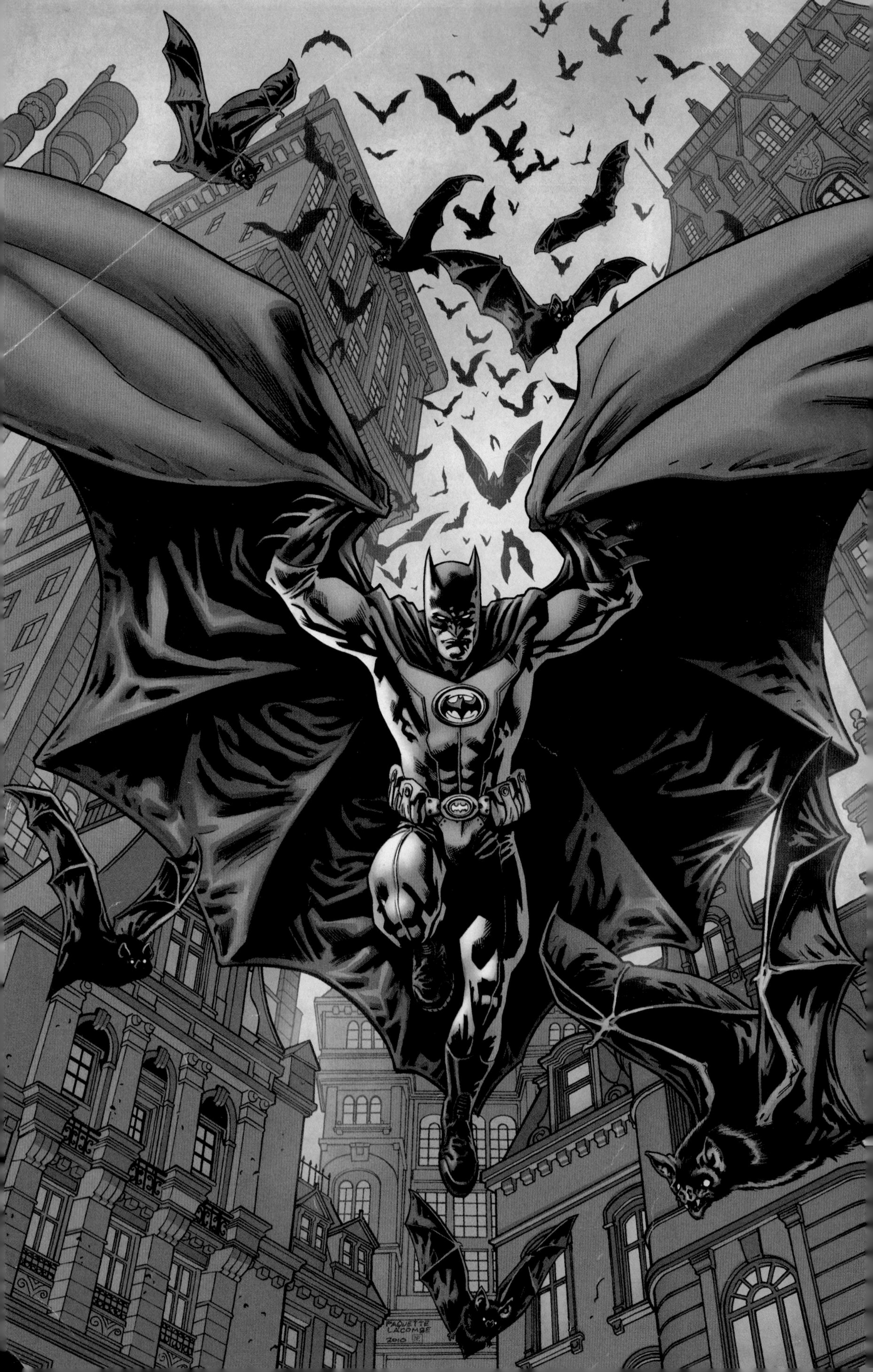
PAQUETTE
LACOMBE
2010

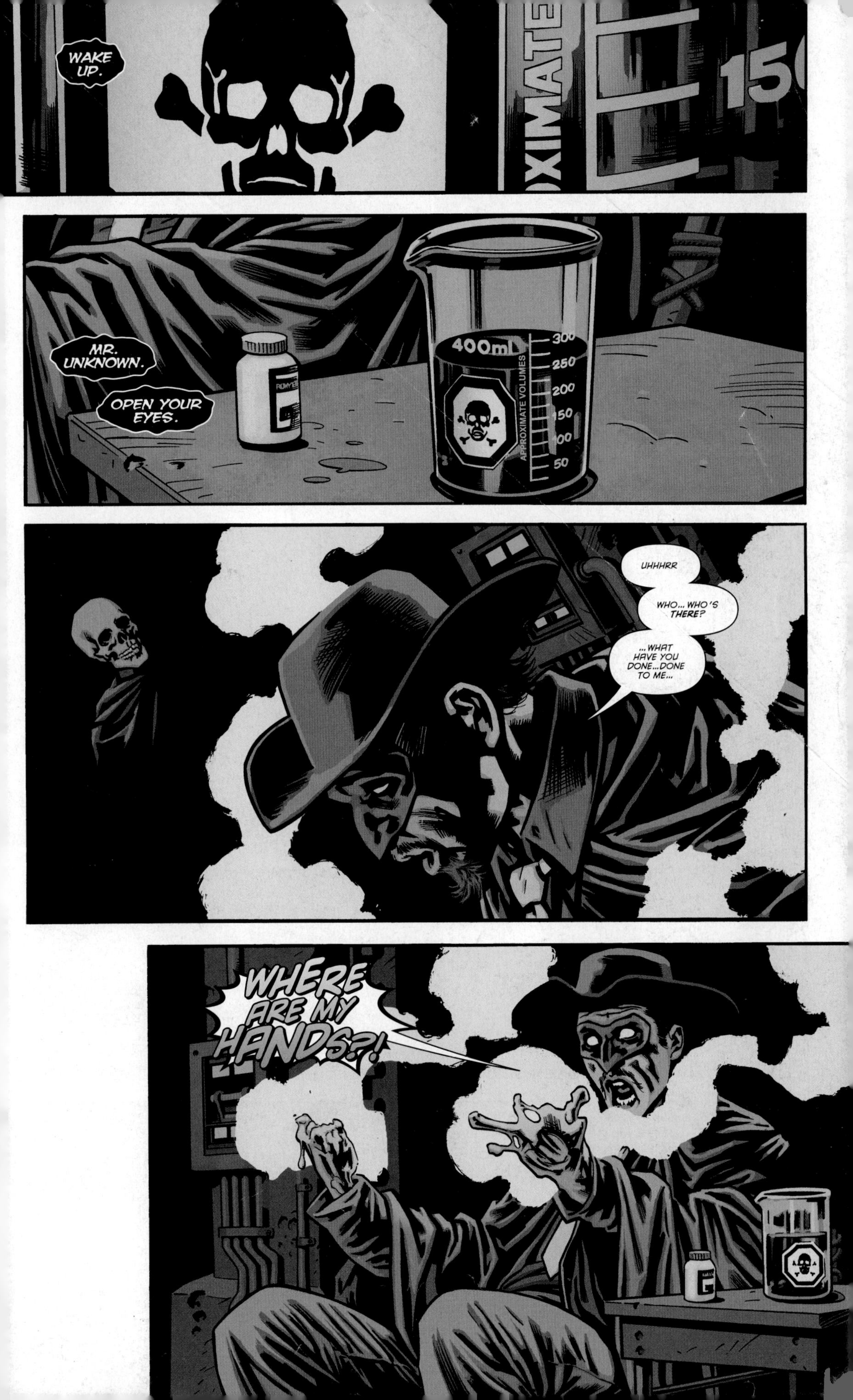
WAKE UP.
OXIMATE
150
MR. UNKNOWN.
OPEN YOUR EYES.
400ml
APPROXIMATE VOLUMES
300
250
200
150
100
50
UHHHRR
WHO... WHO'S THERE?
...WHAT HAVE YOU DONE...DONE TO ME...
WHERE ARE MY HANDS?!

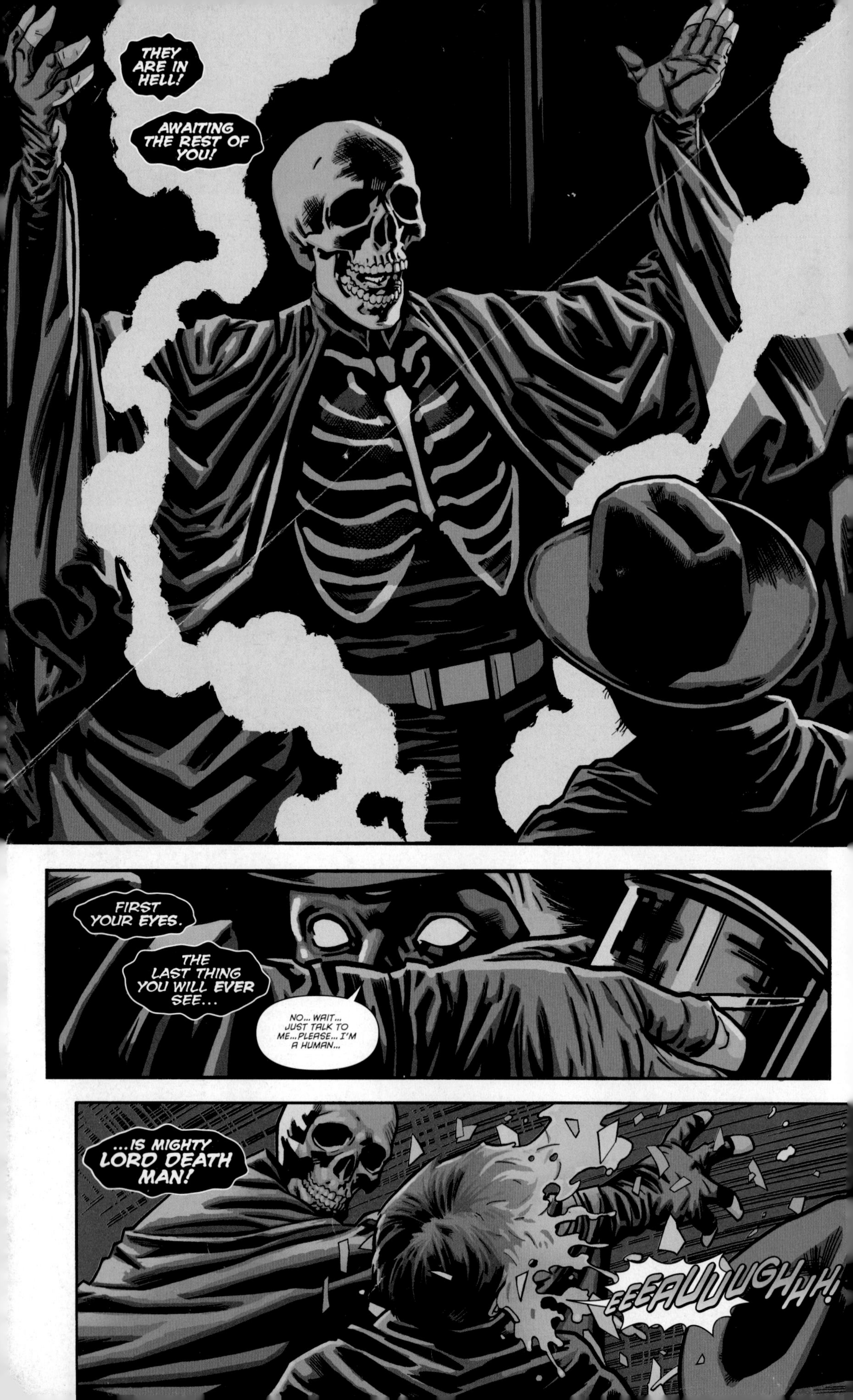
THEY ARE IN HELL!
AWAITING THE REST OF YOU!
FIRST YOUR EYES.
THE LAST THING YOU WILL EVER SEE...
NO... WAIT... JUST TALK TO ME... PLEASE... I'M A HUMAN...
...IS MIGHTY LORD DEATH MAN!
EEEAUUUGHHH!

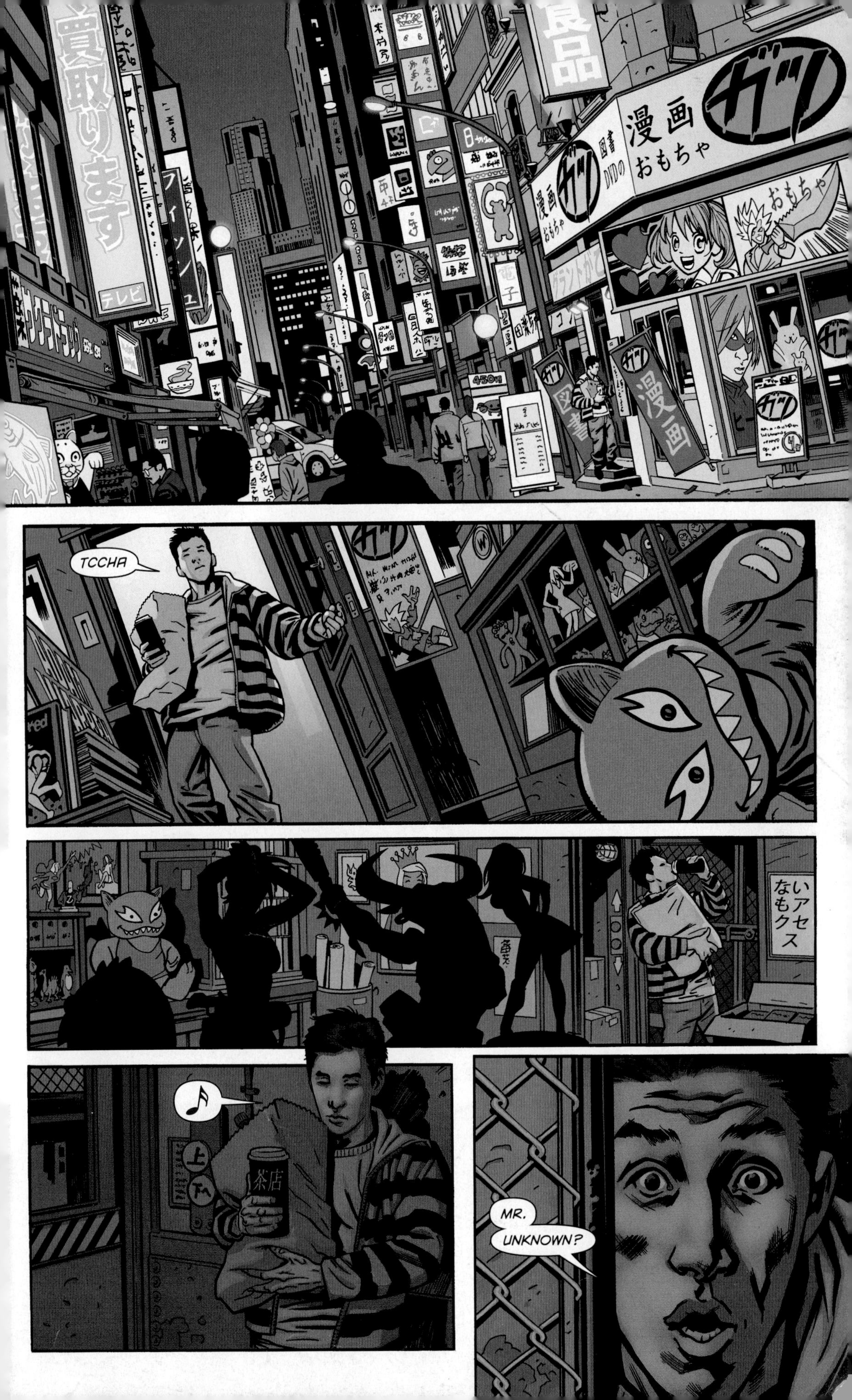
買取ります
テレビ
良品
漫画
おもちゃ
図書
DVDの
電子
漫画
図書
TCCHA
茶店
MR. UNKNOWN?

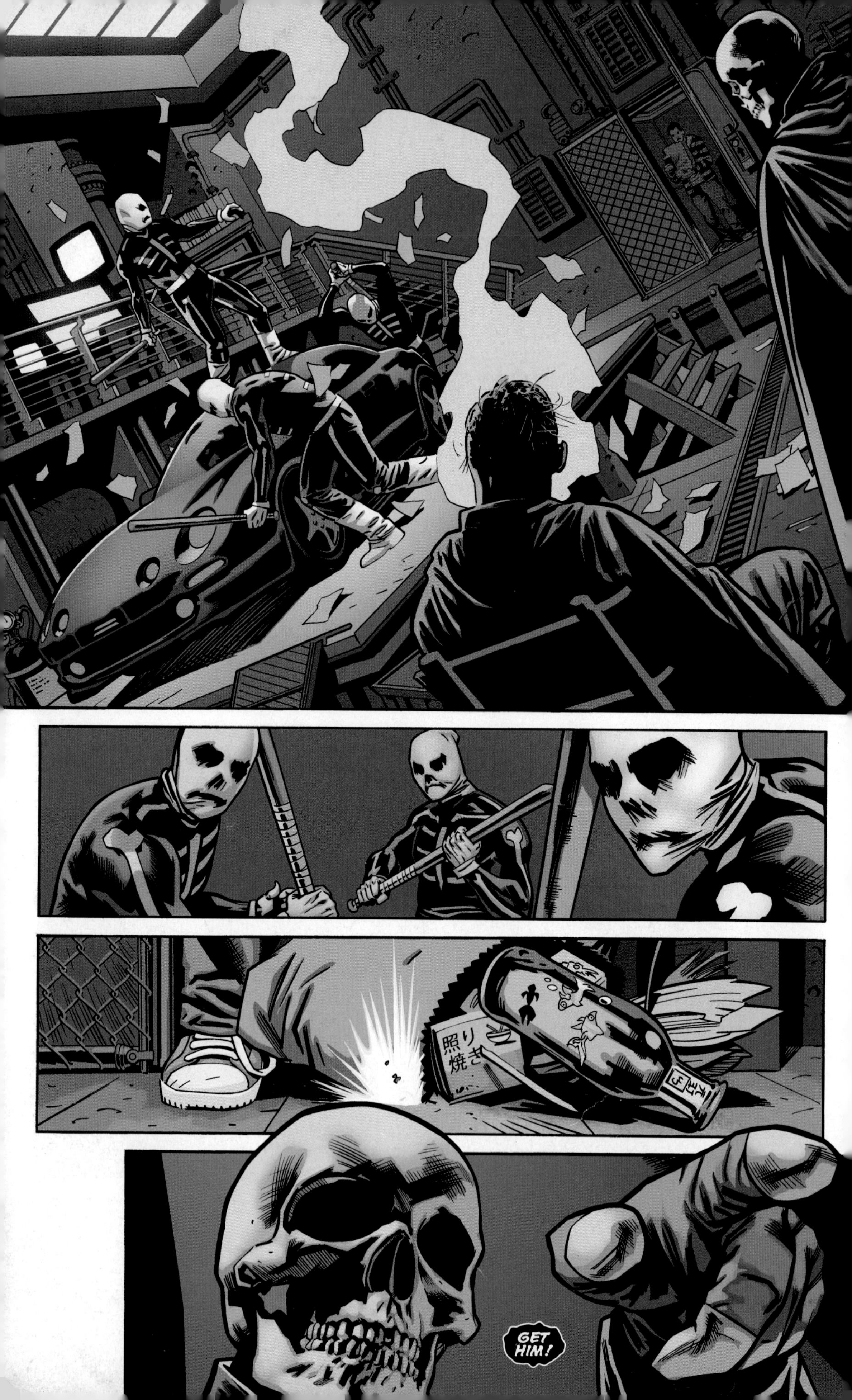
照り焼き
GET HIM!

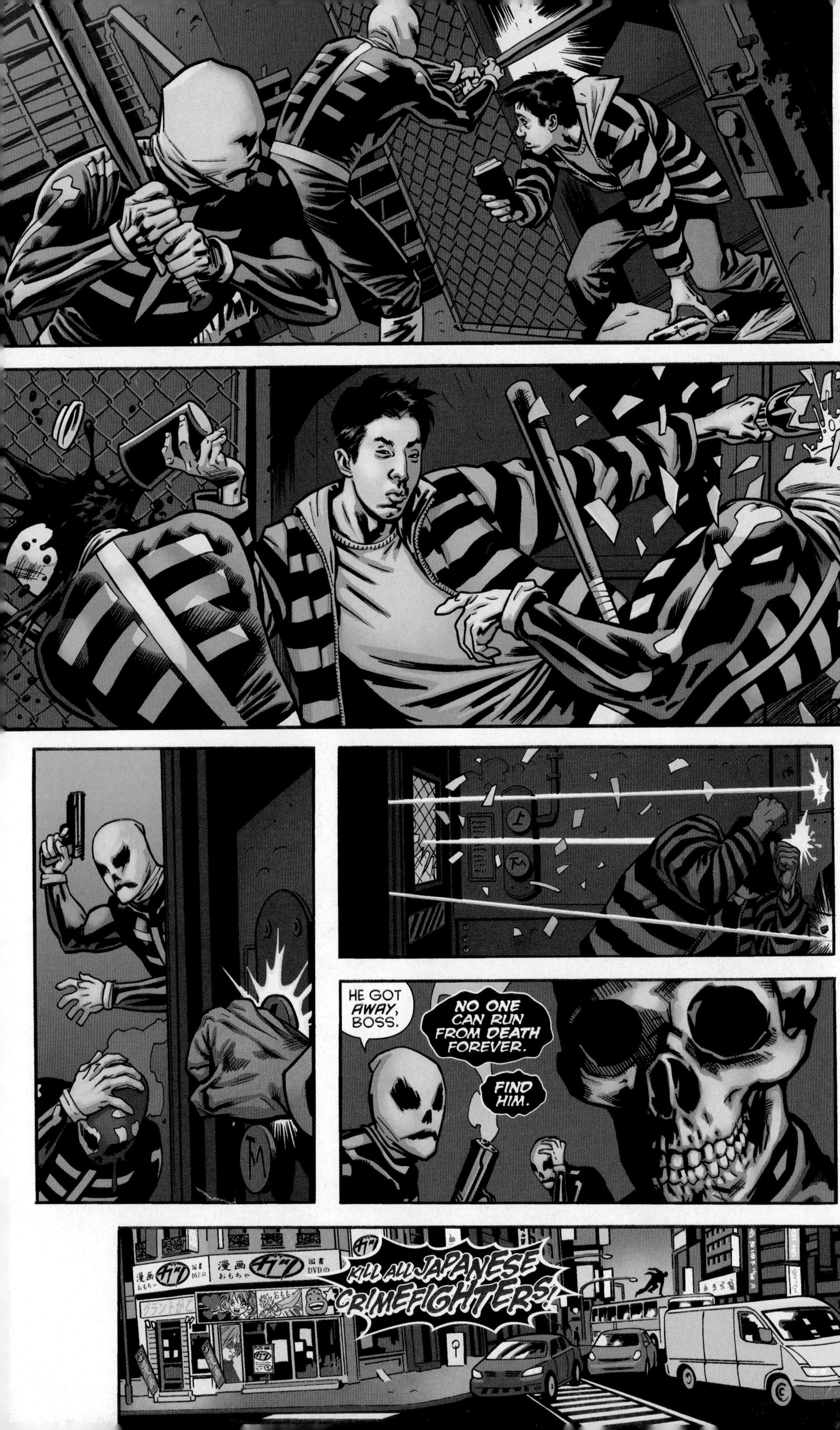
HE GOT AWAY, BOSS.
NO ONE CAN RUN FROM DEATH FOREVER.
FIND HIM.
KILL ALL JAPANESE CRIMEFIGHTERS!

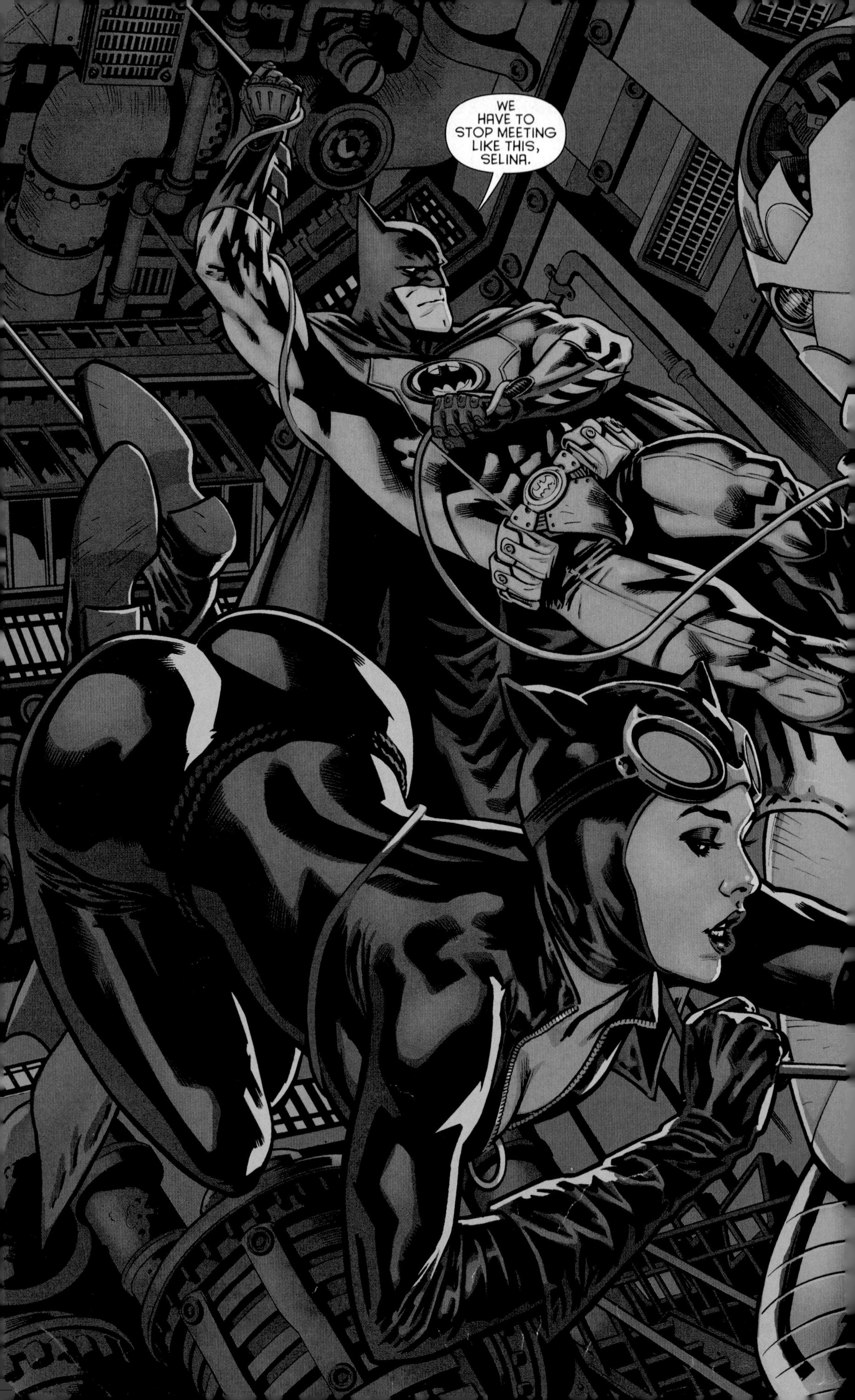
WE HAVE TO STOP MEETING LIKE THIS, SELINA.

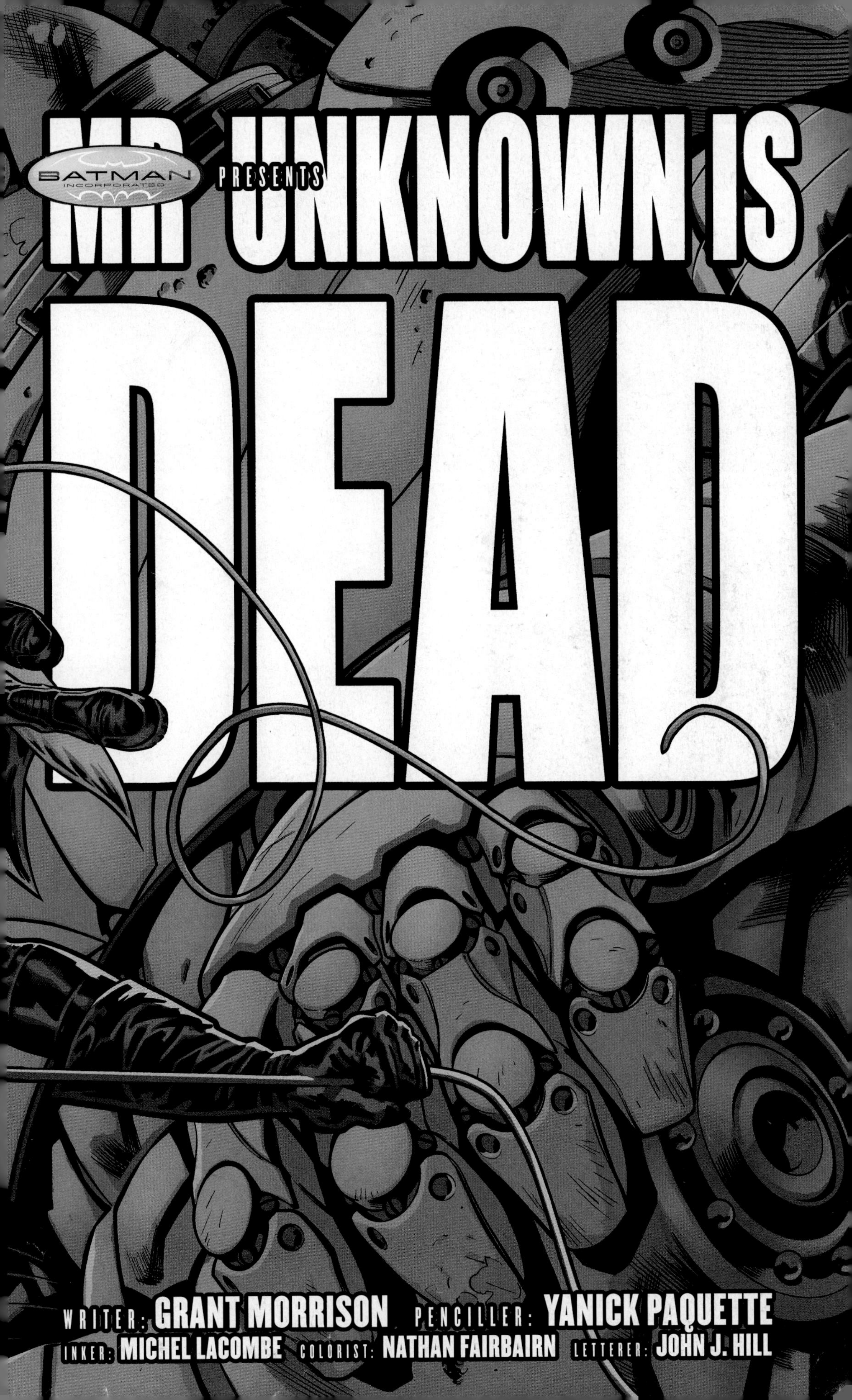
BATMAN INCORPORATED
PRESENTS
MR UNKNOWN IS
DEAD
WRITER: GRANT MORRISON PENCILLER: YANICK PAQUETTE
INKER: MICHEL LACOMBE COLORIST: NATHAN FAIRBAIRN LETTERER: JOHN J. HILL

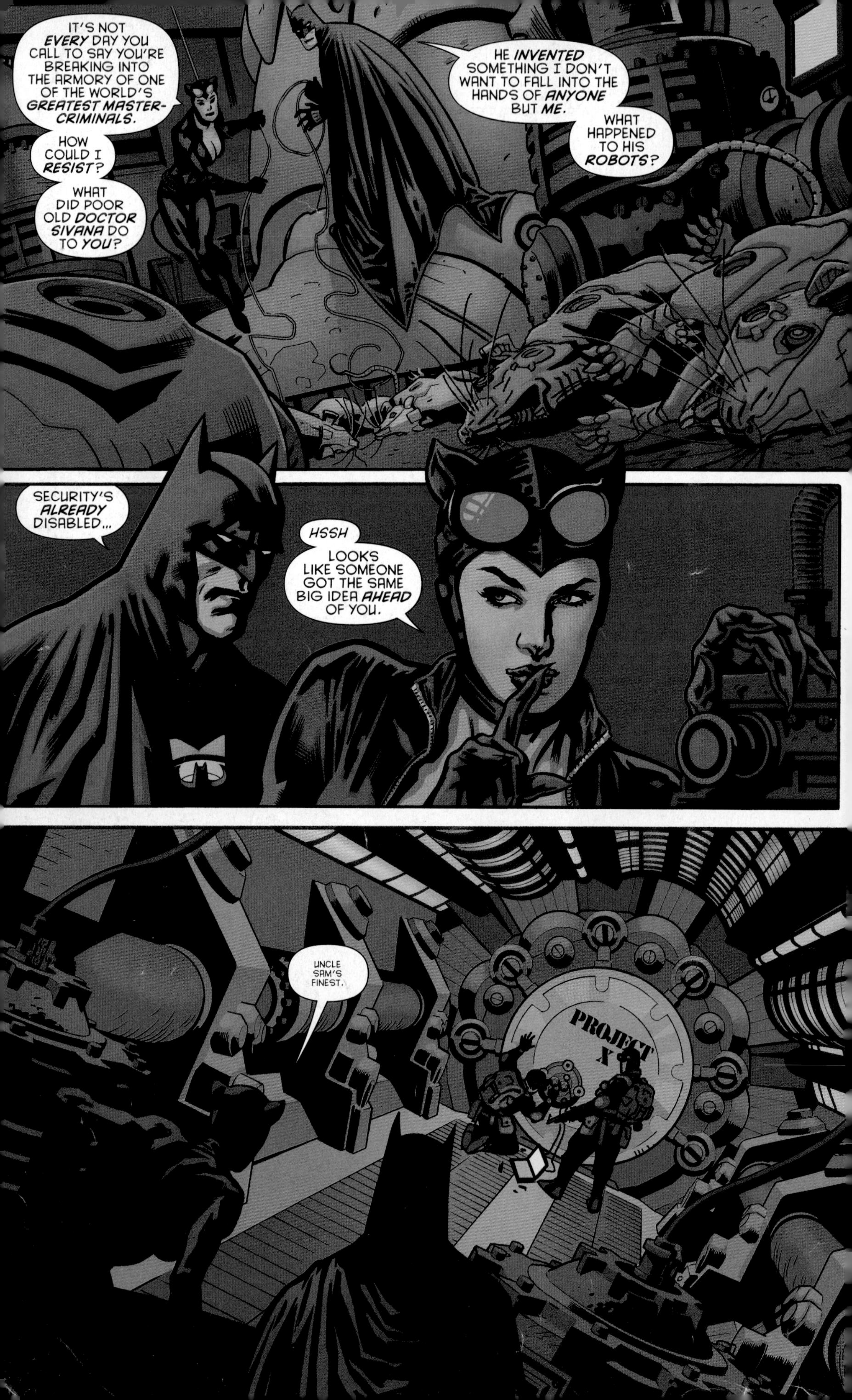
IT'S NOT EVERY DAY YOU CALL TO SAY YOU'RE BREAKING INTO THE ARMORY OF ONE OF THE WORLD'S GREATEST MASTER-CRIMINALS.
HOW COULD I RESIST?
WHAT DID POOR OLD DOCTOR SIVANA DO TO YOU?
HE INVENTED SOMETHING I DON'T WANT TO FALL INTO THE HANDS OF ANYONE BUT ME.
WHAT HAPPENED TO HIS ROBOTS?
SECURITY'S ALREADY DISABLED...
HSSH
LOOKS LIKE SOMEONE GOT THE SAME BIG IDEA AHEAD OF YOU.
UNCLE SAM'S FINEST.
PROJECT X

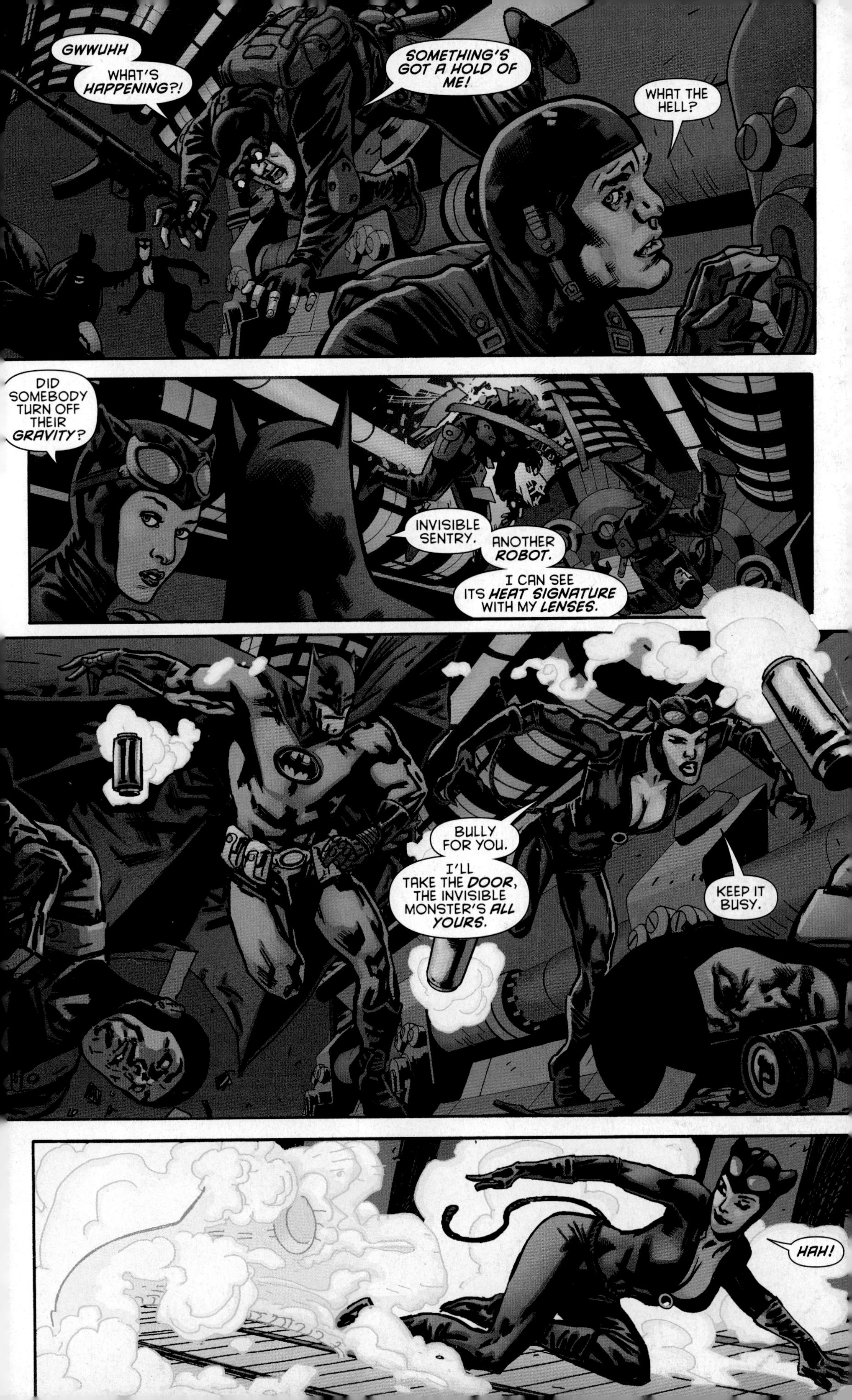

GWWUHH
WHAT'S HAPPENING?!
SOMETHING'S GOT A HOLD OF ME!
WHAT THE HELL?
DID SOMEBODY TURN OFF THEIR GRAVITY?
INVISIBLE SENTRY.
ANOTHER ROBOT.
I CAN SEE ITS HEAT SIGNATURE WITH MY LENSES.
BULLY FOR YOU.
I'LL TAKE THE DOOR, THE INVISIBLE MONSTER'S ALL YOURS.
KEEP IT BUSY.
HAH!

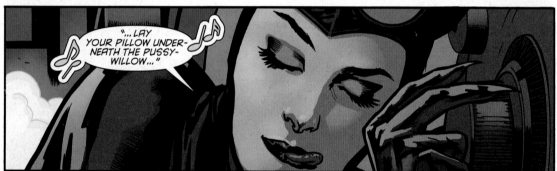
"...LAY YOUR PILLOW UNDERNEATH THE PUSSY-WILLOW..." ♪♫

YOU DONE YET? I MIGHT NEED A *FEW MORE* MINUTES HERE.

RROWRR *THERE* YOU ARE!

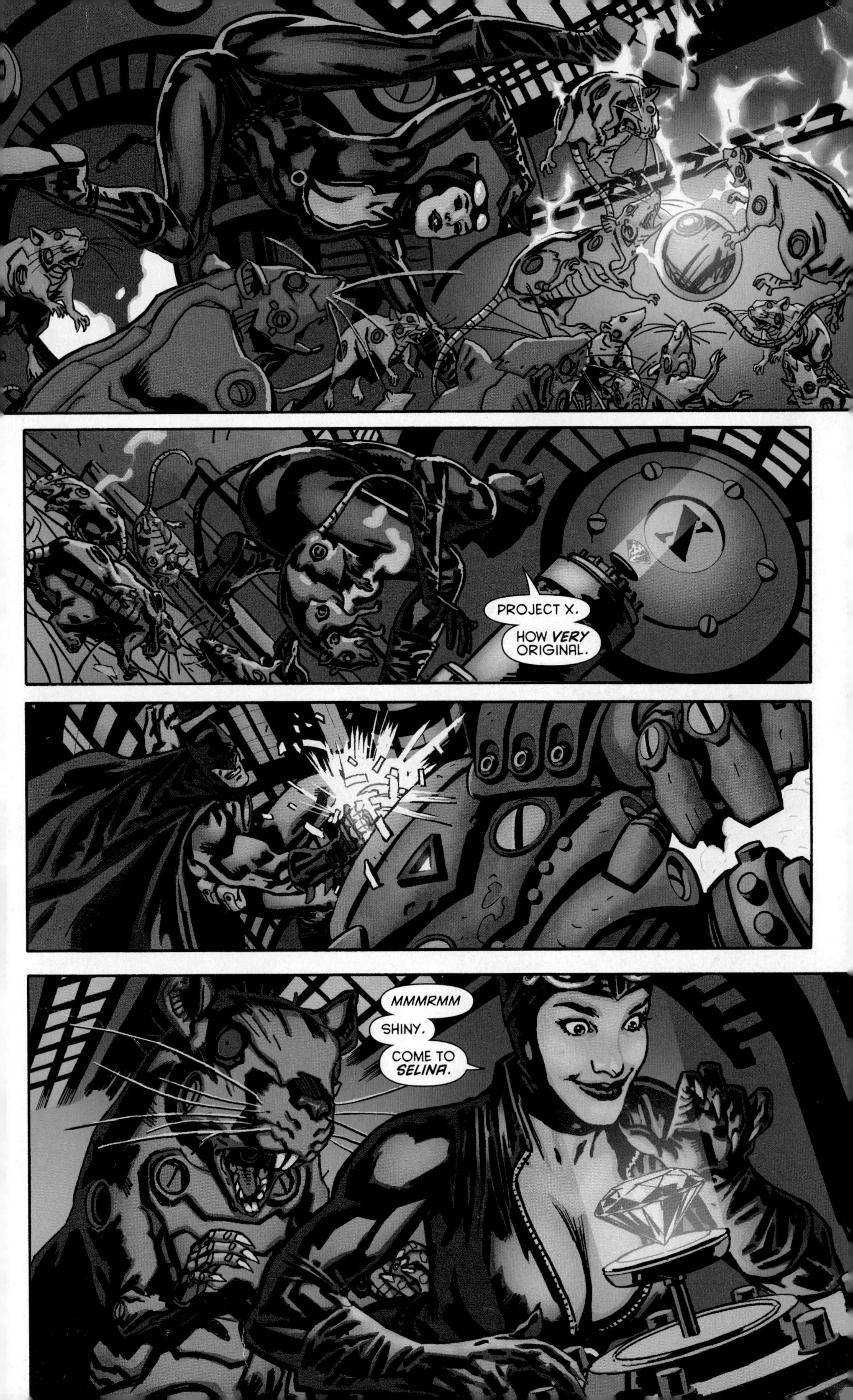
PROJECT X.
HOW VERY ORIGINAL.
MMMRMM
SHINY.
COME TO SELINA.

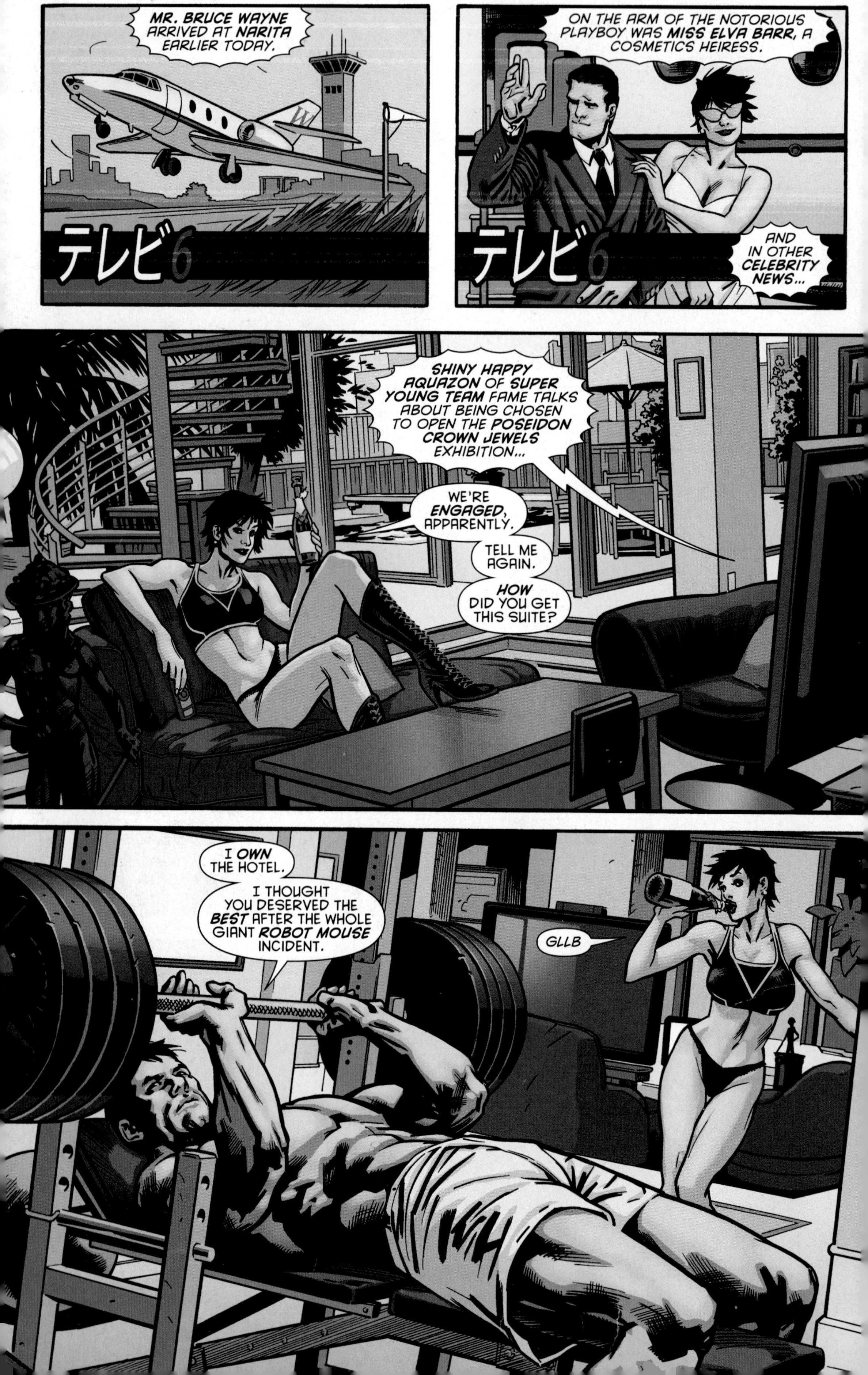

MR. BRUCE WAYNE ARRIVED AT NARITA EARLIER TODAY.
テレビ6
ON THE ARM OF THE NOTORIOUS PLAYBOY WAS MISS ELVA BARR, A COSMETICS HEIRESS.
テレビ6
AND IN OTHER CELEBRITY NEWS...
SHINY HAPPY AQUAZON OF SUPER YOUNG TEAM FAME TALKS ABOUT BEING CHOSEN TO OPEN THE POSEIDON CROWN JEWELS EXHIBITION...
WE'RE ENGAGED, APPARENTLY.
TELL ME AGAIN.
HOW DID YOU GET THIS SUITE?
I OWN THE HOTEL.
I THOUGHT YOU DESERVED THE BEST AFTER THE WHOLE GIANT ROBOT MOUSE INCIDENT.
GLLB

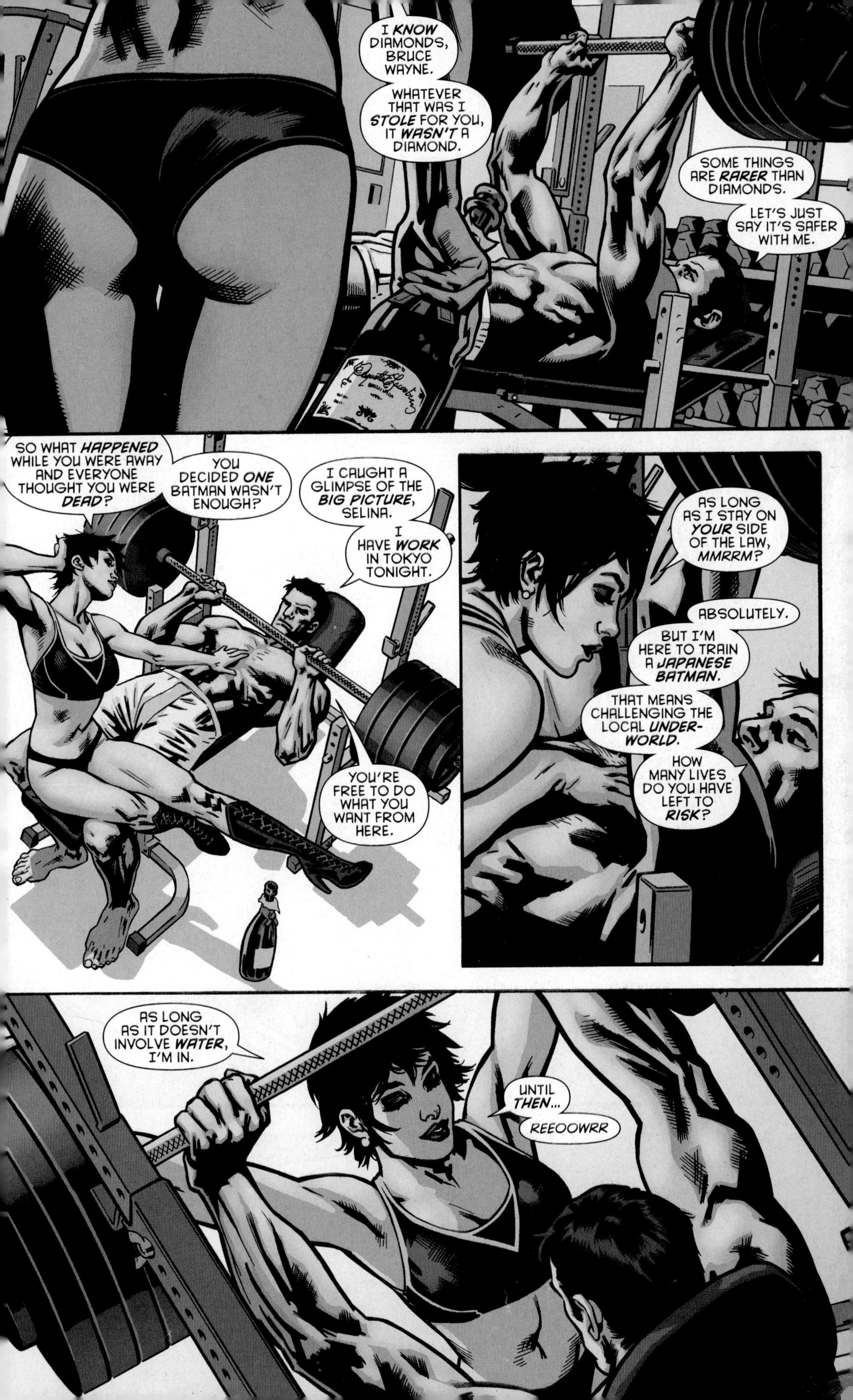
I KNOW DIAMONDS, BRUCE WAYNE.
WHATEVER THAT WAS I STOLE FOR YOU, IT WASN'T A DIAMOND.
SOME THINGS ARE RARER THAN DIAMONDS.
LET'S JUST SAY IT'S SAFER WITH ME.
SO WHAT HAPPENED WHILE YOU WERE AWAY AND EVERYONE THOUGHT YOU WERE DEAD?
YOU DECIDED ONE BATMAN WASN'T ENOUGH?
I CAUGHT A GLIMPSE OF THE BIG PICTURE, SELINA.
I HAVE WORK IN TOKYO TONIGHT.
YOU'RE FREE TO DO WHAT YOU WANT FROM HERE.
AS LONG AS I STAY ON YOUR SIDE OF THE LAW, MMRRM?
ABSOLUTELY.
BUT I'M HERE TO TRAIN A JAPANESE BATMAN.
THAT MEANS CHALLENGING THE LOCAL UNDER-WORLD.
HOW MANY LIVES DO YOU HAVE LEFT TO RISK?
AS LONG AS IT DOESN'T INVOLVE WATER, I'M IN.
UNTIL THEN...
REEOOWRR

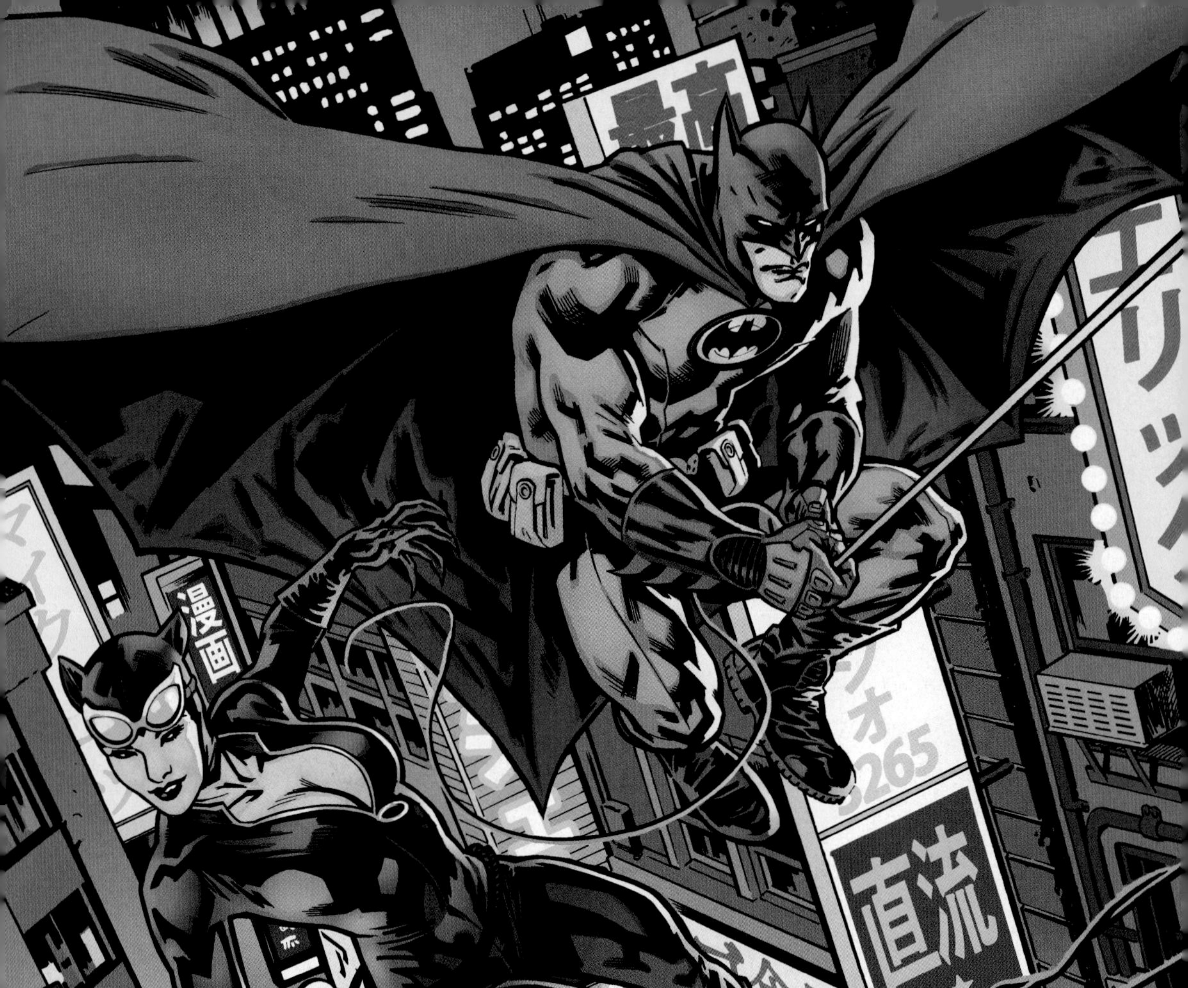
漫画
直流
食品
モリソン
色
猫

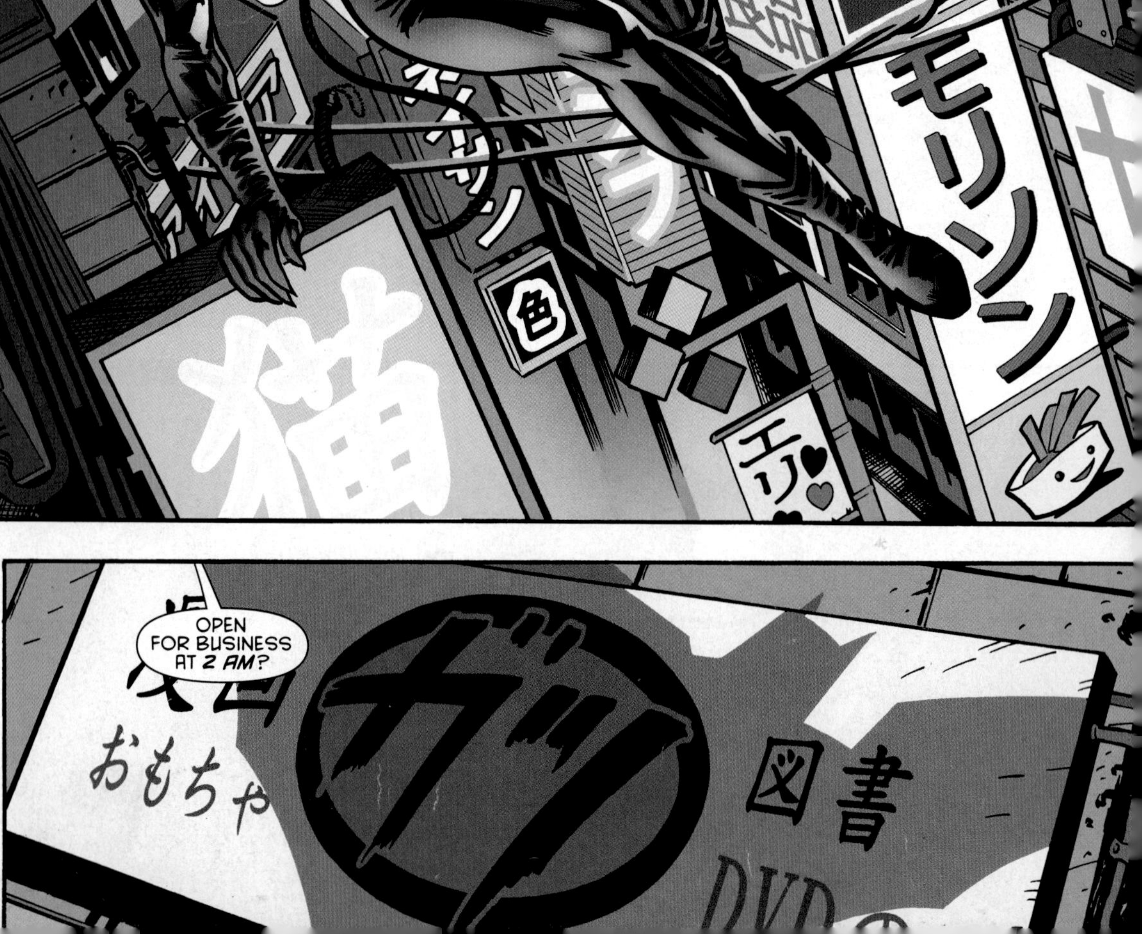
OPEN FOR BUSINESS AT 2 AM?
おもちゃ
図書

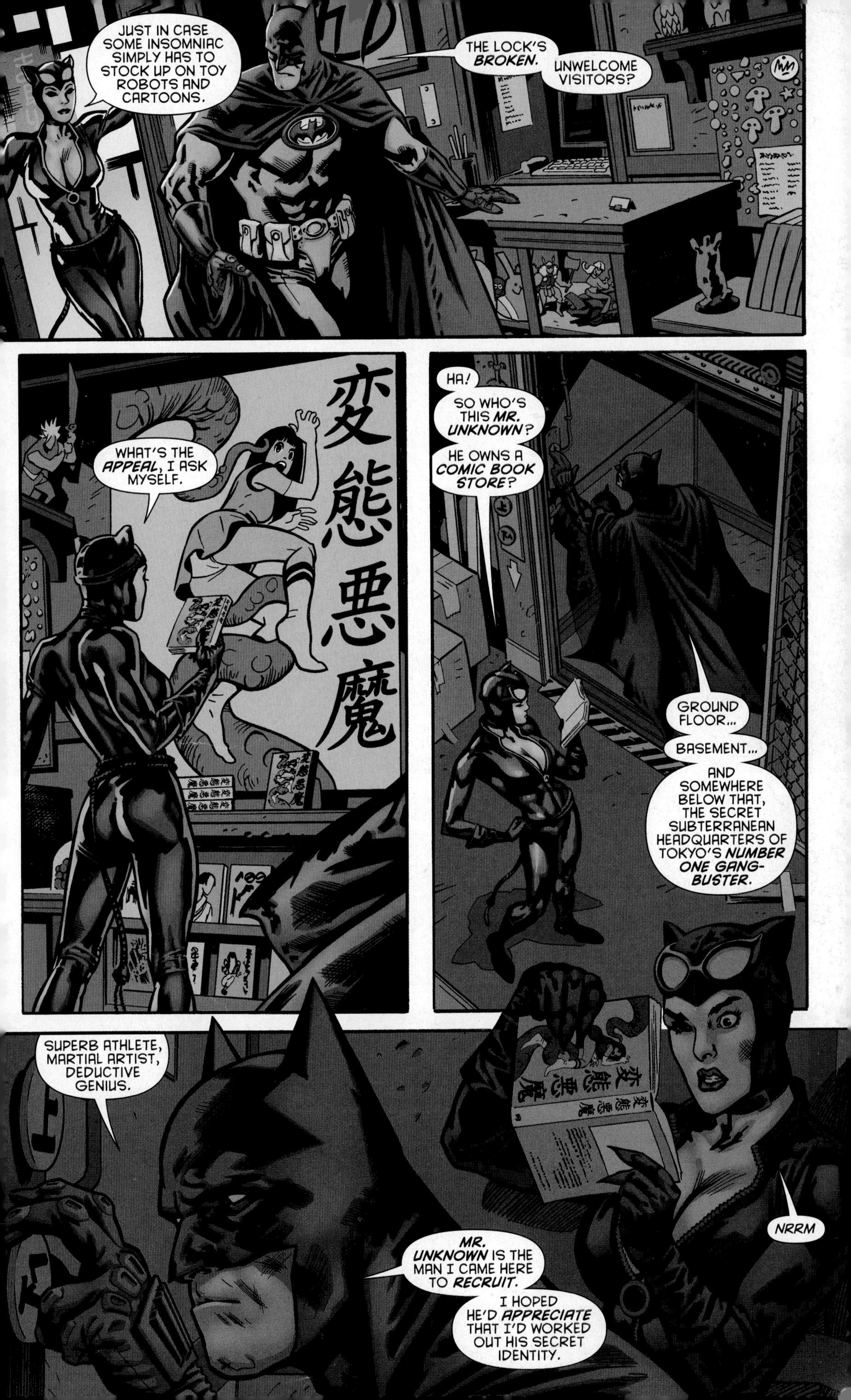

JUST IN CASE SOME INSOMNIAC SIMPLY HAS TO STOCK UP ON TOY ROBOTS AND CARTOONS.
THE LOCK'S *BROKEN.*
UNWELCOME VISITORS?
WHAT'S THE *APPEAL*, I ASK MYSELF.
変態悪魔
HA!
SO WHO'S THIS *MR. UNKNOWN*?
HE OWNS A *COMIC BOOK STORE*?
GROUND FLOOR...
BASEMENT...
AND SOMEWHERE BELOW THAT, THE SECRET SUBTERRANEAN HEADQUARTERS OF TOKYO'S *NUMBER ONE GANG-BUSTER.*
SUPERB ATHLETE, MARTIAL ARTIST, DEDUCTIVE GENIUS.
MR. UNKNOWN IS THE MAN I CAME HERE TO *RECRUIT*.
I HOPED HE'D *APPRECIATE* THAT I'D WORKED OUT HIS SECRET IDENTITY.
NRRM

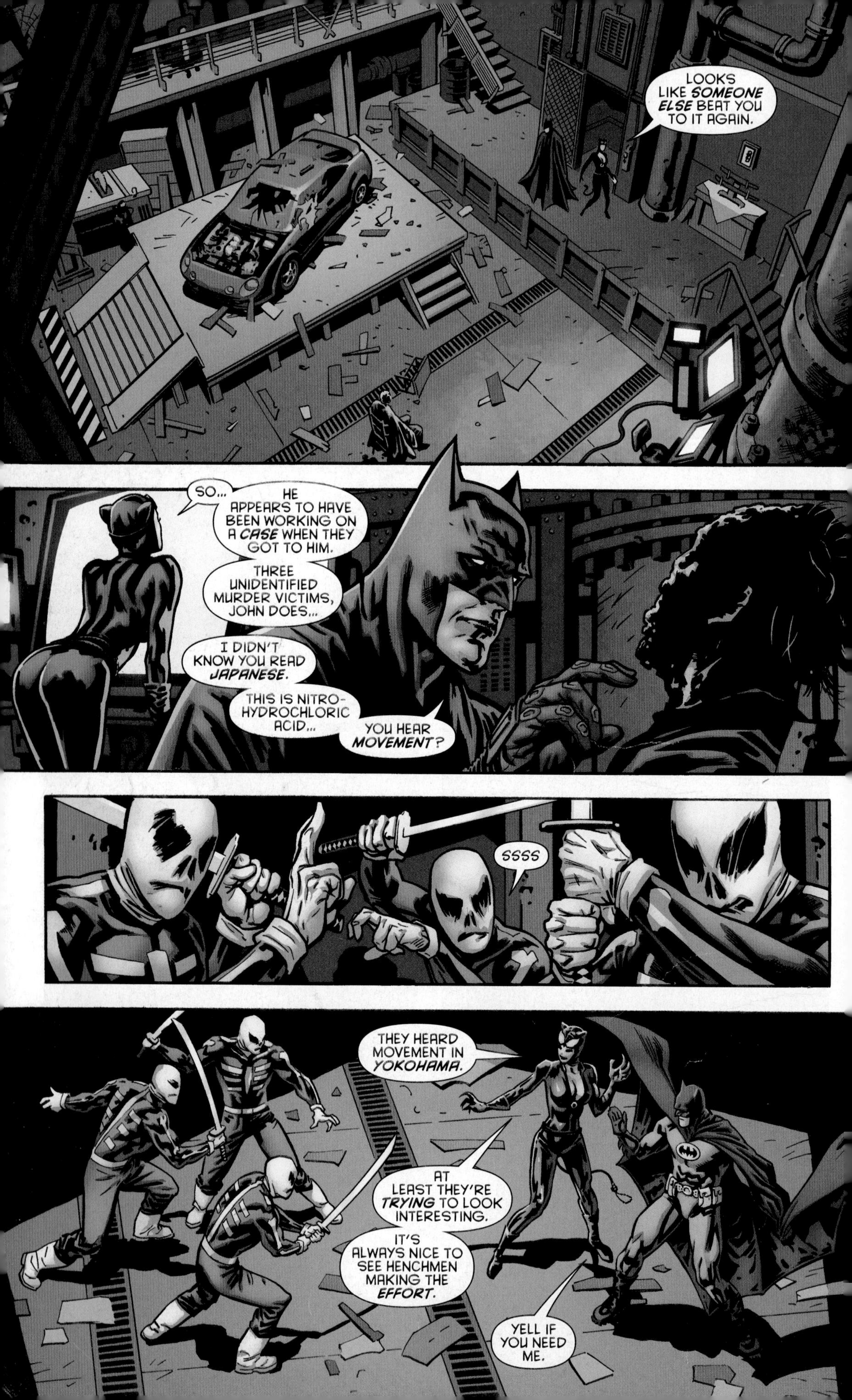
LOOKS LIKE SOMEONE ELSE BEAT YOU TO IT AGAIN.
SO...
HE APPEARS TO HAVE BEEN WORKING ON A CASE WHEN THEY GOT TO HIM.
THREE UNIDENTIFIED MURDER VICTIMS, JOHN DOES...
I DIDN'T KNOW YOU READ JAPANESE.
THIS IS NITRO-HYDROCHLORIC ACID...
YOU HEAR MOVEMENT?
SSSS
THEY HEARD MOVEMENT IN YOKOHAMA.
AT LEAST THEY'RE TRYING TO LOOK INTERESTING.
IT'S ALWAYS NICE TO SEE HENCHMEN MAKING THE EFFORT.
YELL IF YOU NEED ME.

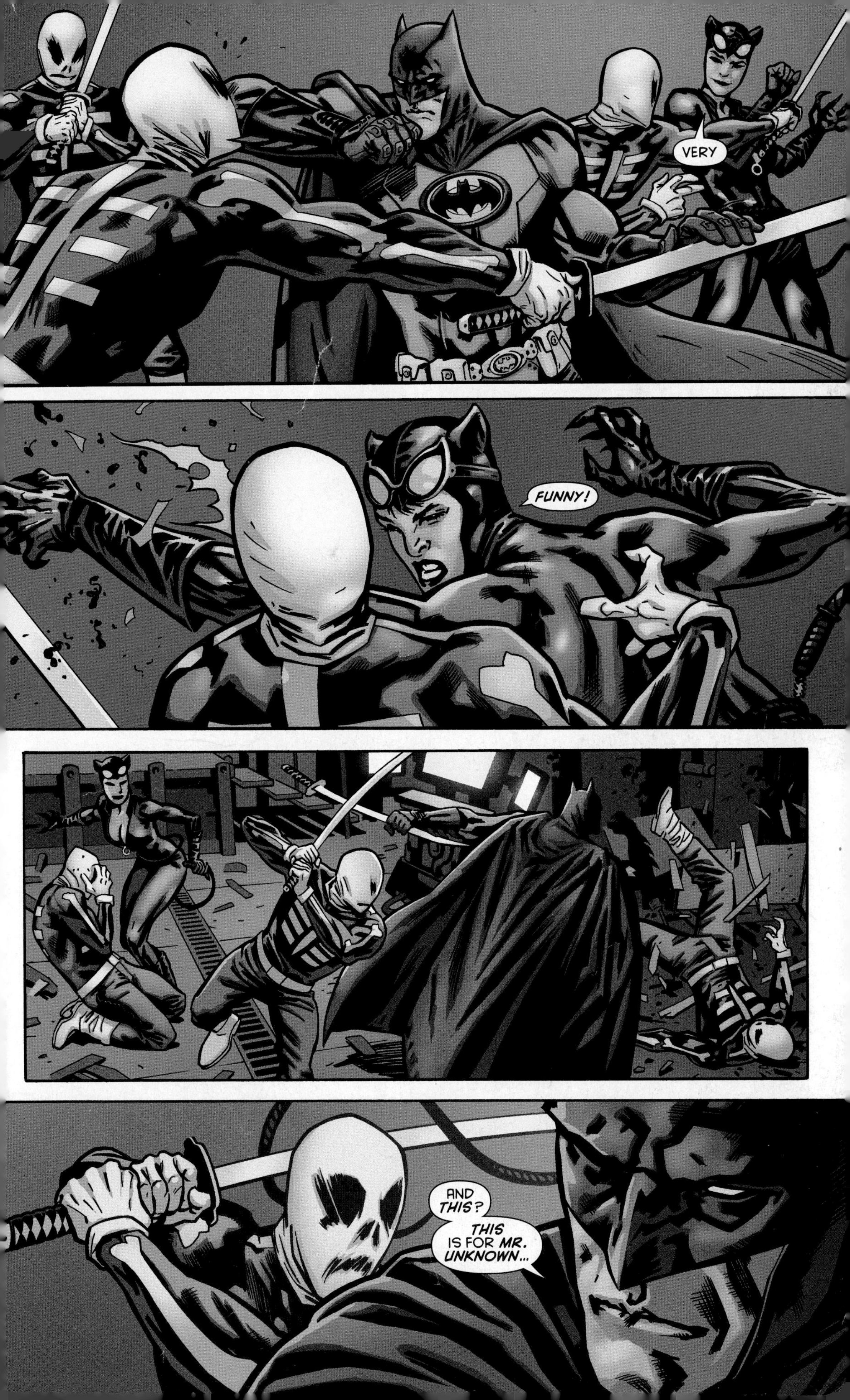
VERY
FUNNY!
AND THIS?
THIS IS FOR MR. UNKNOWN...

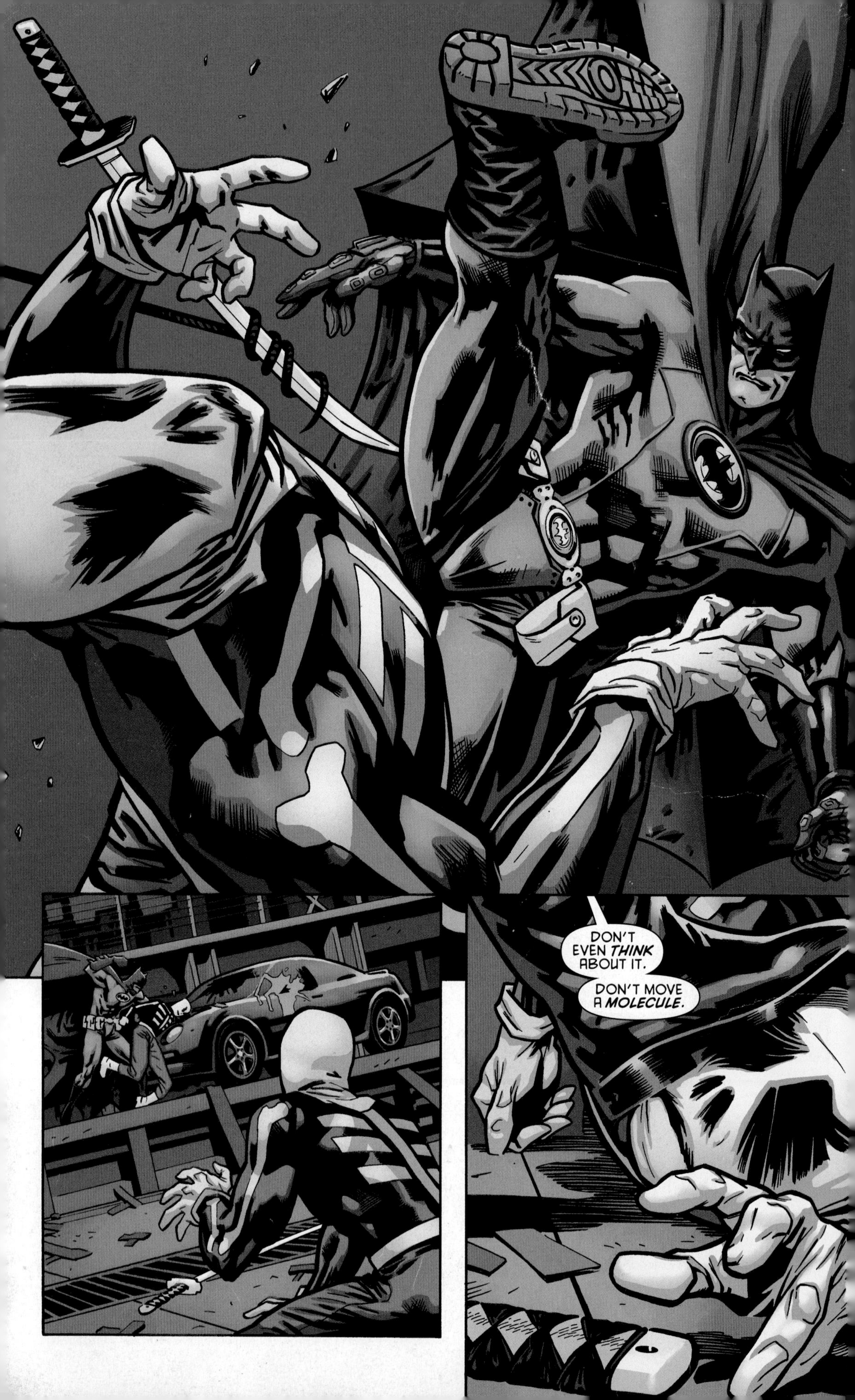
DON'T EVEN THINK ABOUT IT.
DON'T MOVE A MOLECULE.

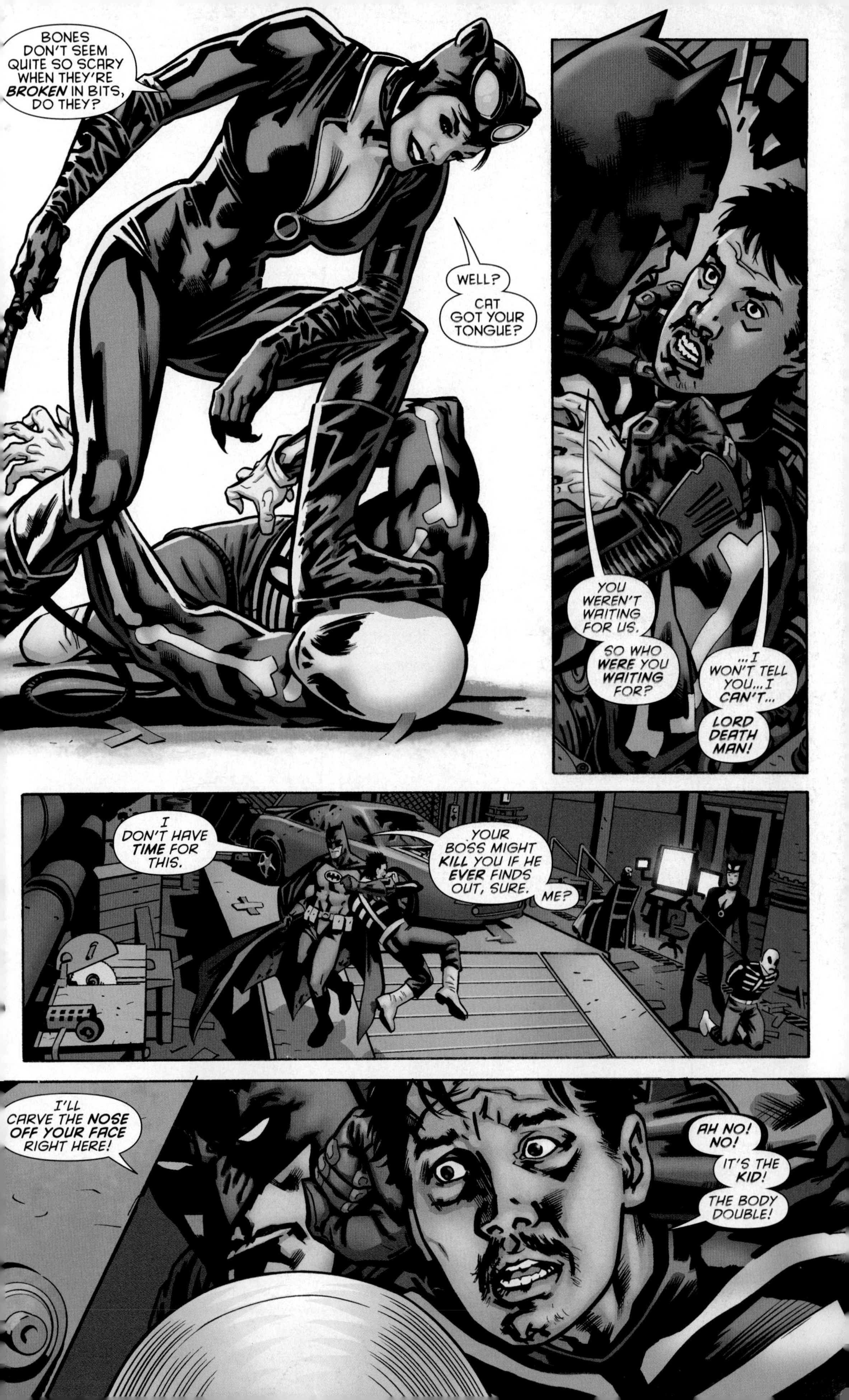
BONES DON'T SEEM QUITE SO SCARY WHEN THEY'RE BROKEN IN BITS, DO THEY?
WELL?
CAT GOT YOUR TONGUE?
YOU WEREN'T WAITING FOR US.
SO WHO WERE YOU WAITING FOR?
...I WON'T TELL YOU...I CAN'T...
LORD DEATH MAN!
I DON'T HAVE TIME FOR THIS.
YOUR BOSS MIGHT KILL YOU IF HE EVER FINDS OUT, SURE.
ME?
I'LL CARVE THE NOSE OFF YOUR FACE RIGHT HERE!
AH NO! NO!
IT'S THE KID!
THE BODY DOUBLE!

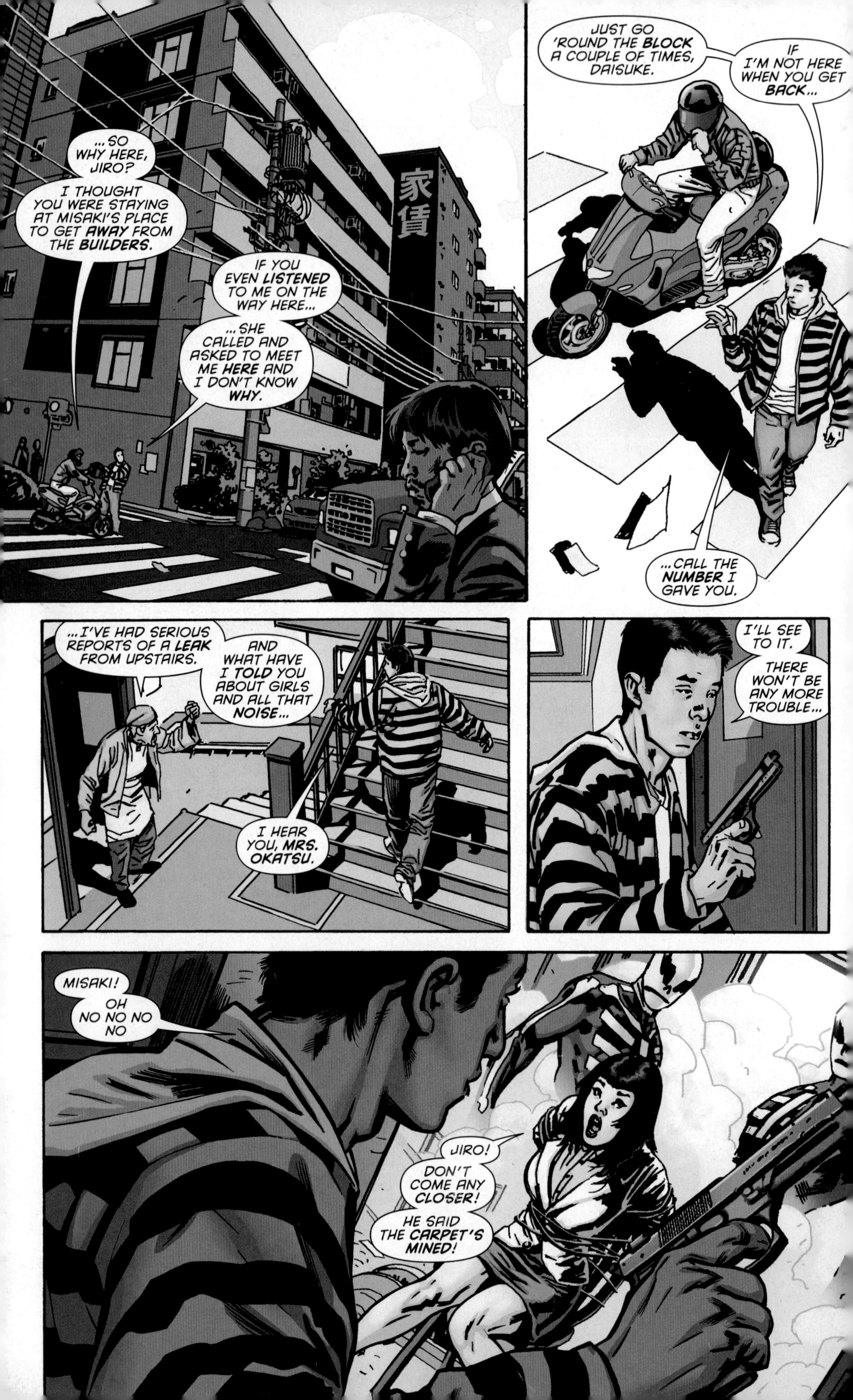

...SO WHY HERE, JIRO?
I THOUGHT YOU WERE STAYING AT MISAKI'S PLACE TO GET AWAY FROM THE BUILDERS.
IF YOU EVEN LISTENED TO ME ON THE WAY HERE...
...SHE CALLED AND ASKED TO MEET ME HERE AND I DON'T KNOW WHY.
家
賃
JUST GO 'ROUND THE BLOCK A COUPLE OF TIMES, DAISUKE.
IF I'M NOT HERE WHEN YOU GET BACK...
...CALL THE NUMBER I GAVE YOU.
...I'VE HAD SERIOUS REPORTS OF A LEAK FROM UPSTAIRS.
AND WHAT HAVE I TOLD YOU ABOUT GIRLS AND ALL THAT NOISE...
I HEAR YOU, MRS. OKATSU.
I'LL SEE TO IT.
THERE WON'T BE ANY MORE TROUBLE...
MISAKI!
OH NO NO NO NO
JIRO!
DON'T COME ANY CLOSER!
HE SAID THE CARPET'S MINED!

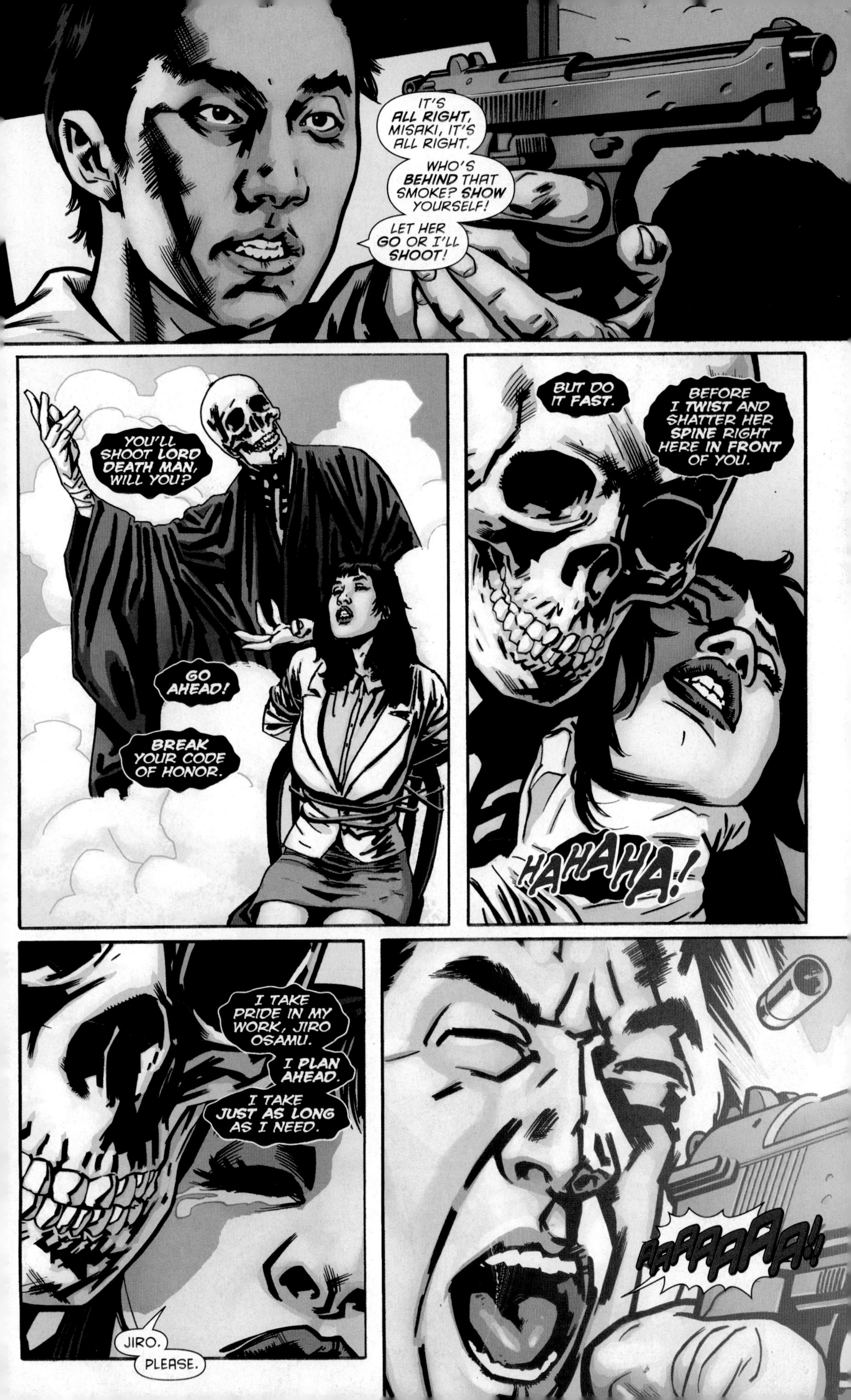
IT'S ALL RIGHT, MISAKI, IT'S ALL RIGHT.
WHO'S BEHIND THAT SMOKE? SHOW YOURSELF!
LET HER GO OR I'LL SHOOT!
YOU'LL SHOOT LORD DEATH MAN, WILL YOU?
GO AHEAD!
BREAK YOUR CODE OF HONOR.
BUT DO IT FAST.
BEFORE I TWIST AND SHATTER HER SPINE RIGHT HERE IN FRONT OF YOU.
HAHAHA!
I TAKE PRIDE IN MY WORK, JIRO OSAMU.
I PLAN AHEAD.
I TAKE JUST AS LONG AS I NEED.
JIRO.
PLEASE.
AAAAAAA!

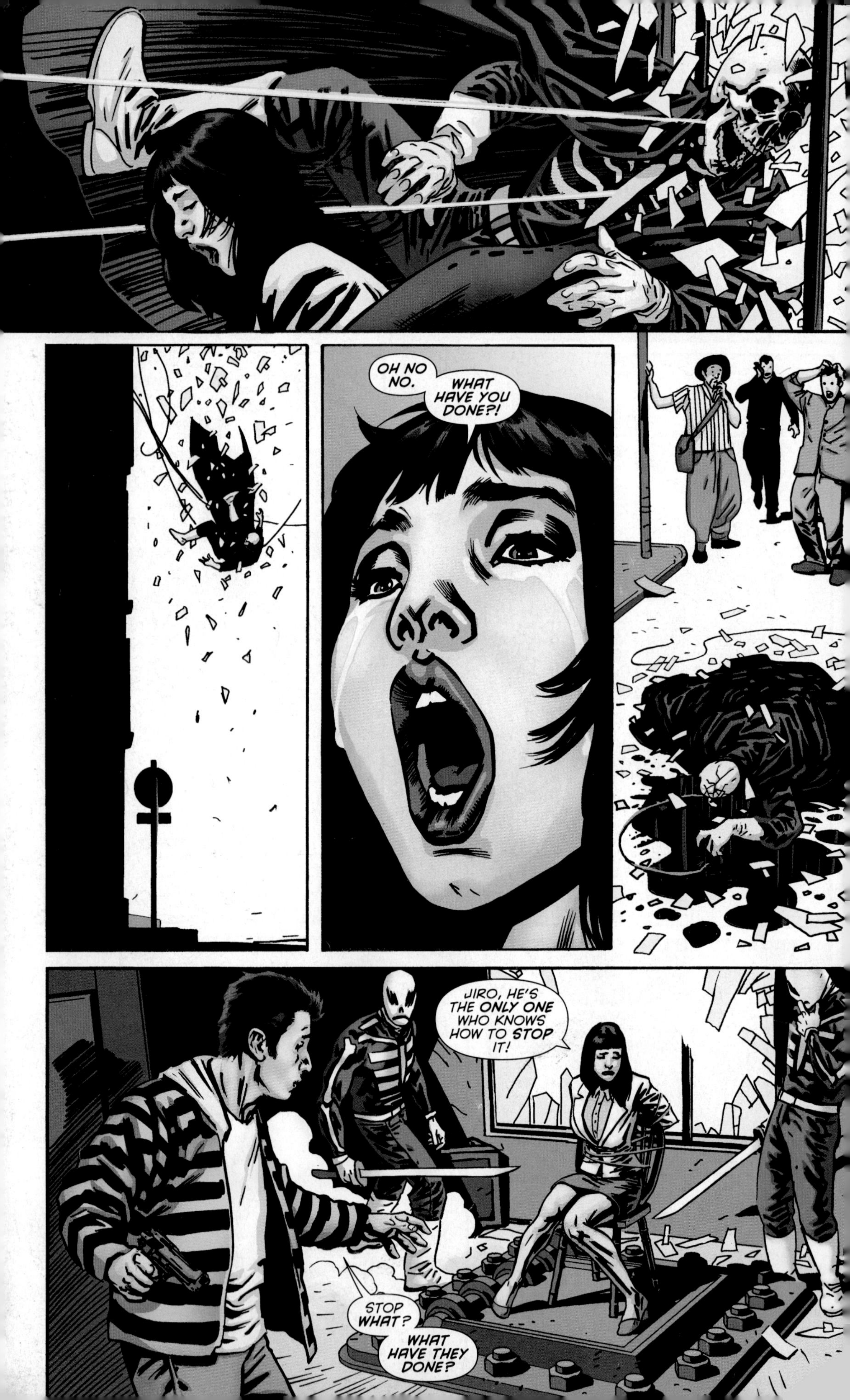
OH NO NO.
WHAT HAVE YOU DONE?!
JIRO, HE'S THE ONLY ONE WHO KNOWS HOW TO STOP IT!
STOP WHAT?
WHAT HAVE THEY DONE?

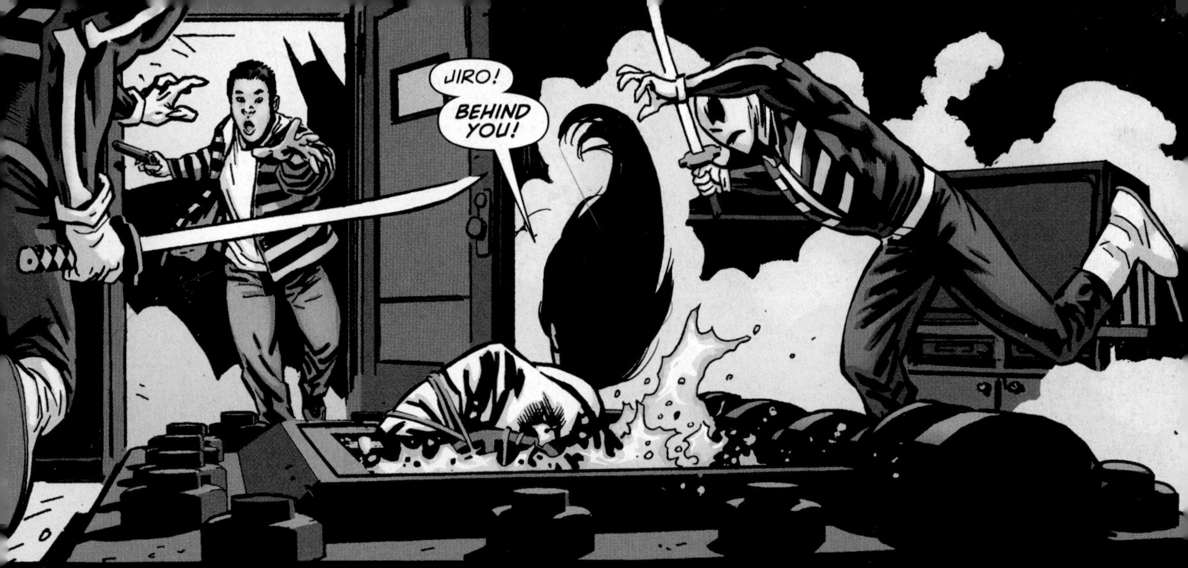
JIRO! BEHIND YOU!

LORD DEATH MAN LIVES TO TAKE LIFE, AND HE'S ONLY JUST BEGUN!

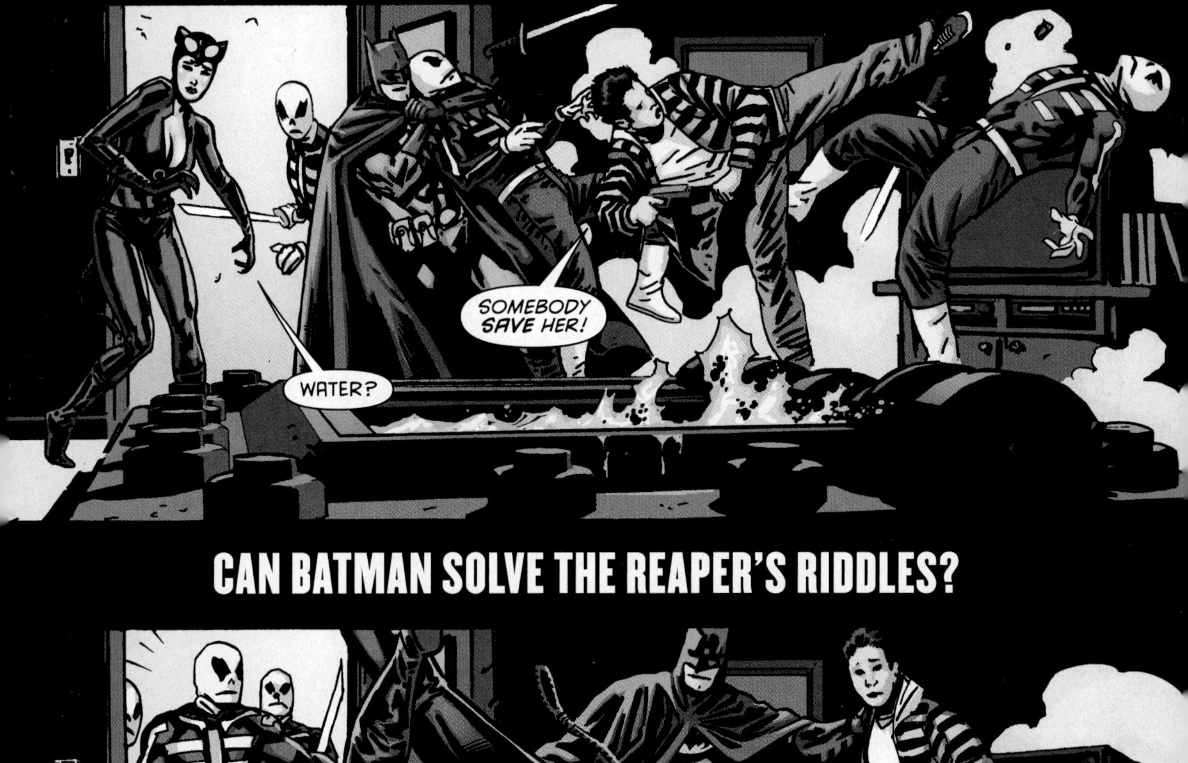
SOMEBODY SAVE HER!
WATER?

CAN BATMAN SOLVE THE REAPER'S RIDDLES?

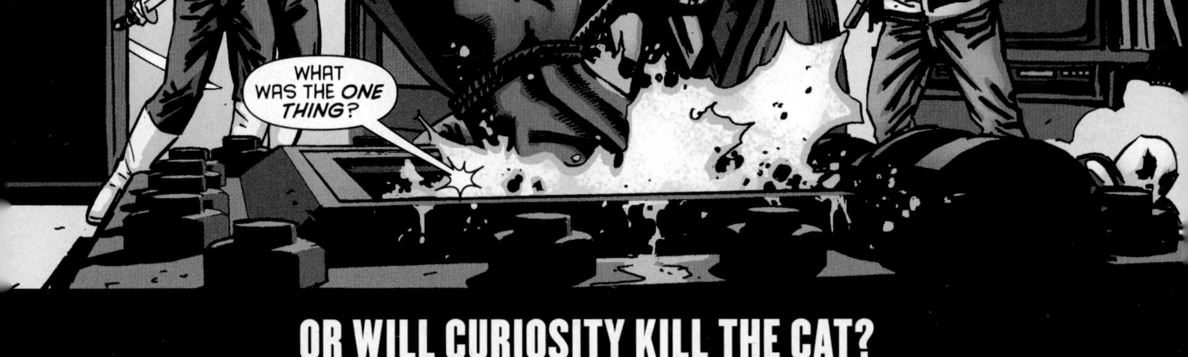
WHAT WAS THE ONE THING?

OR WILL CURIOSITY KILL THE CAT?

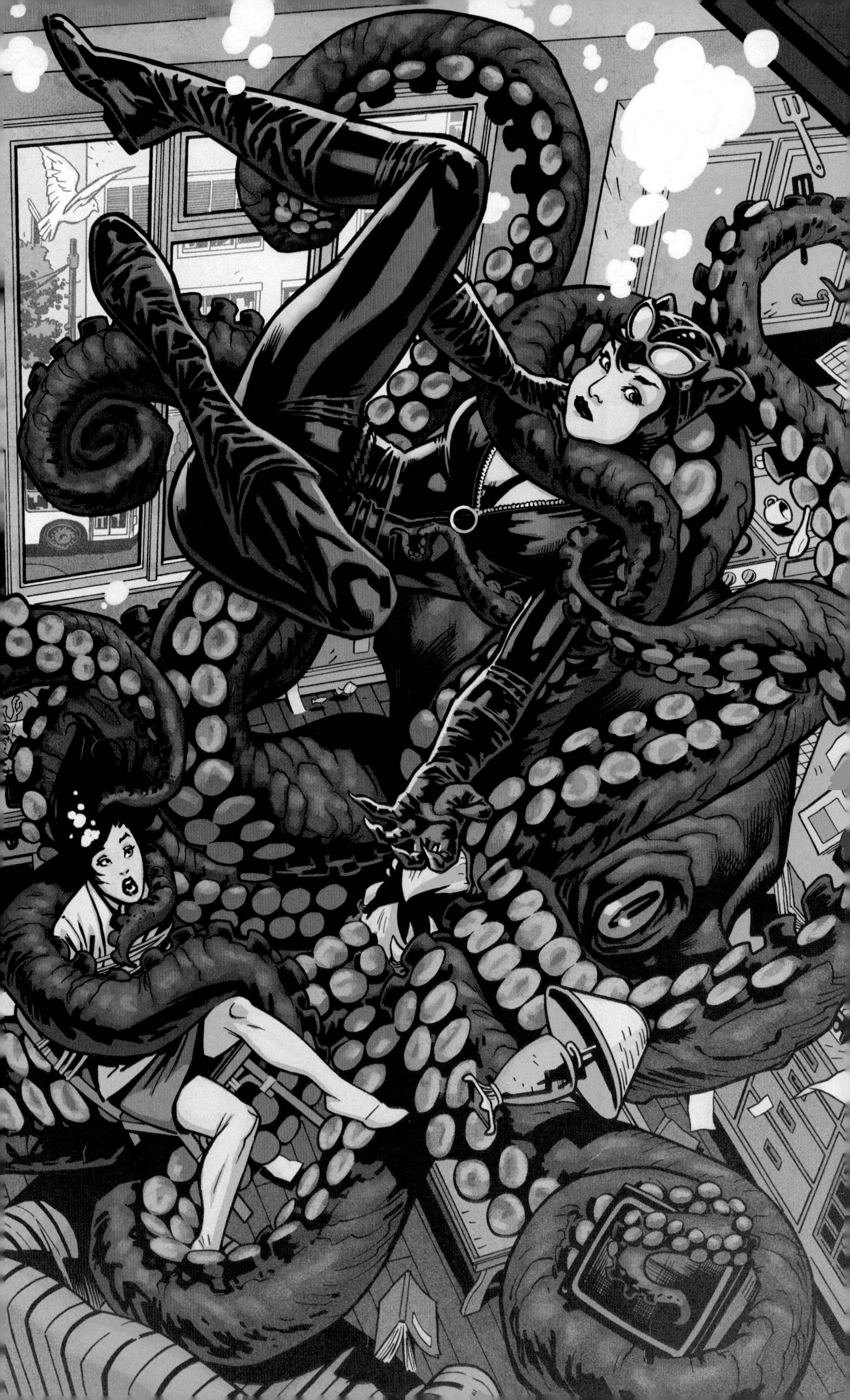

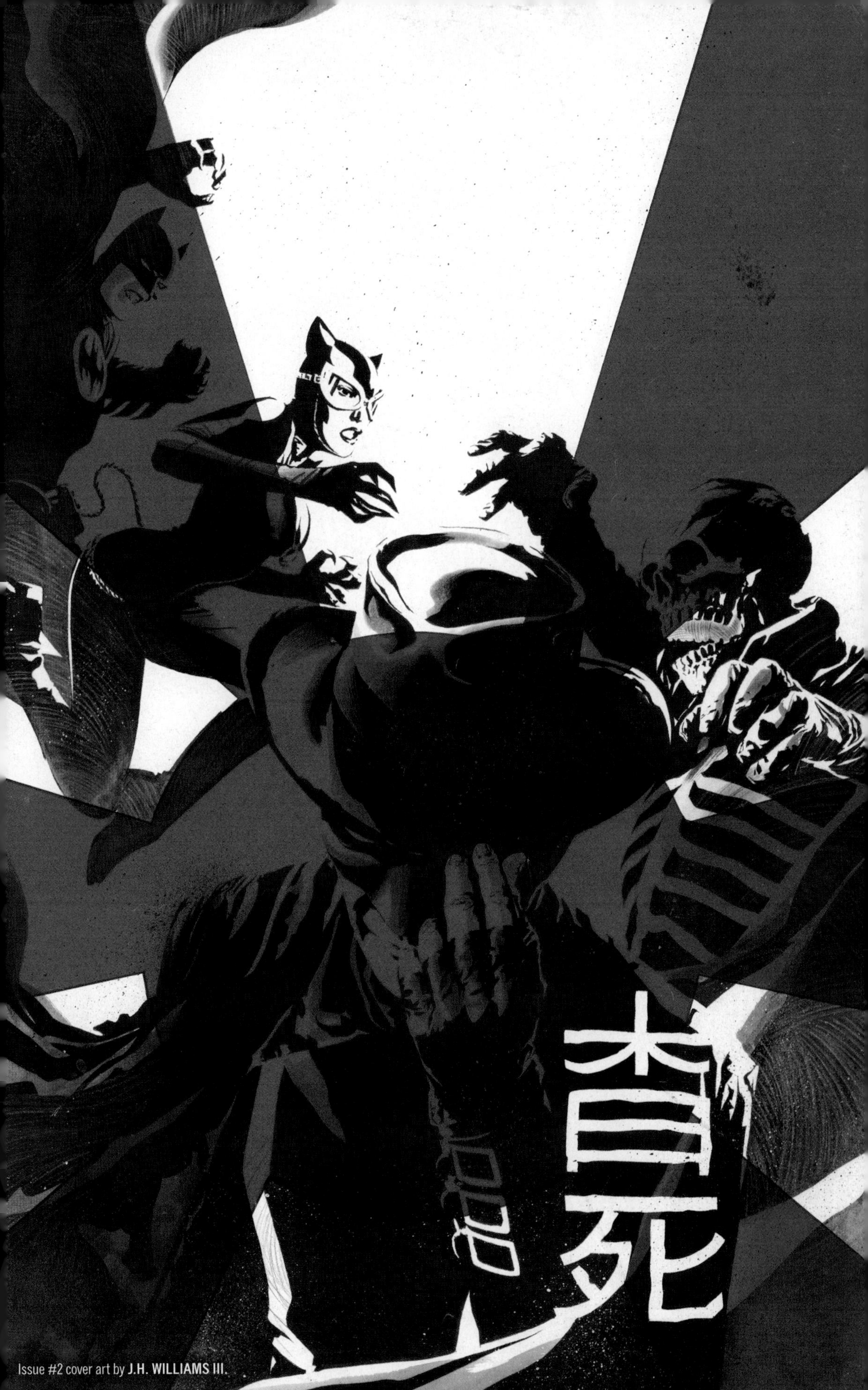

Issue #2 cover art by **J.H. WILLIAMS III.**

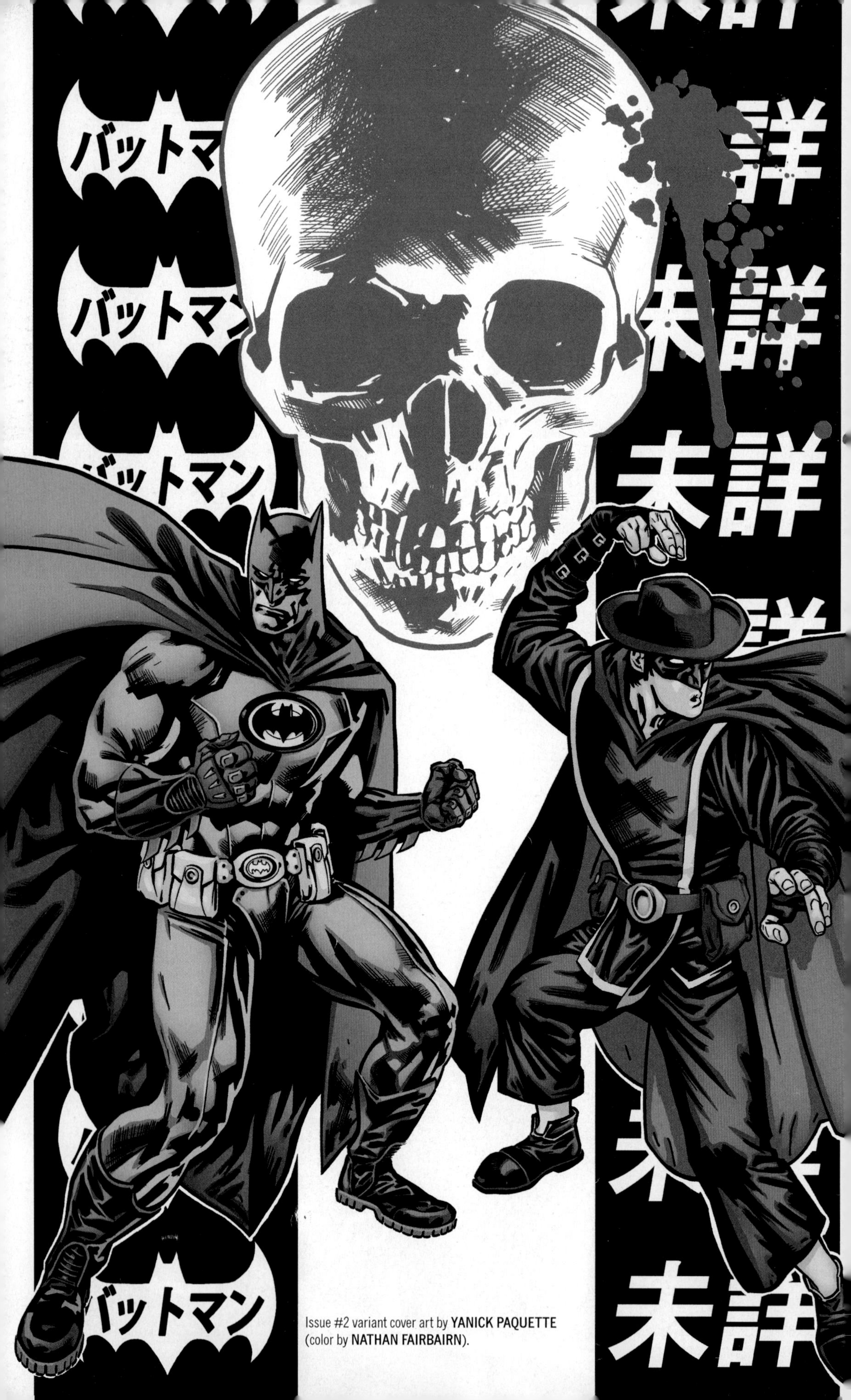
バットマン
バットマン
バットマン
未詳
未詳
Issue #2 variant cover art by **YANICK PAQUETTE**
(color by **NATHAN FAIRBAIRN**).

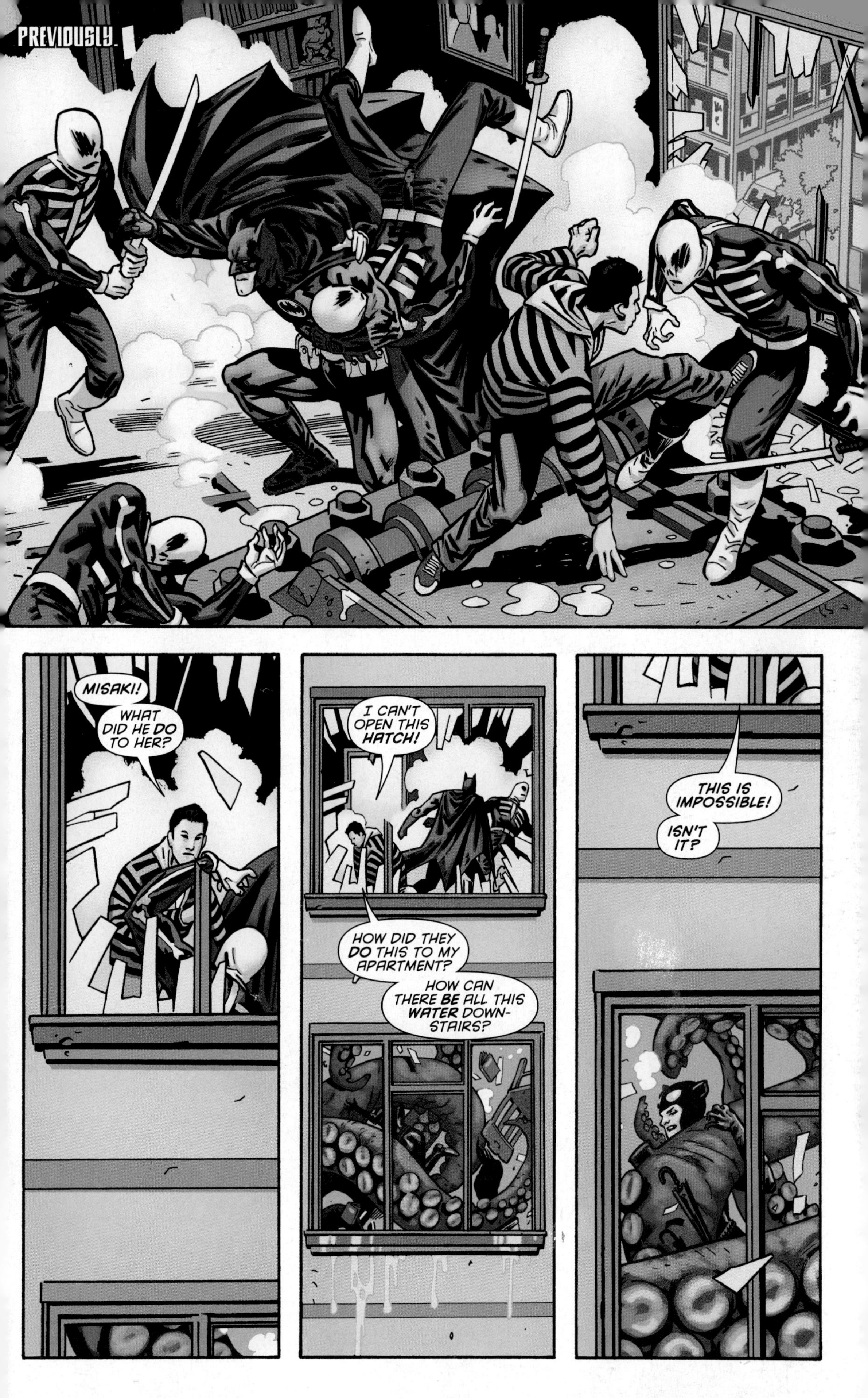
PREVIOUSLY.
MISAKI!
WHAT DID HE DO TO HER?
I CAN'T OPEN THIS HATCH!
HOW DID THEY DO THIS TO MY APARTMENT?
HOW CAN THERE BE ALL THIS WATER DOWN-STAIRS?
THIS IS IMPOSSIBLE!
ISN'T IT?

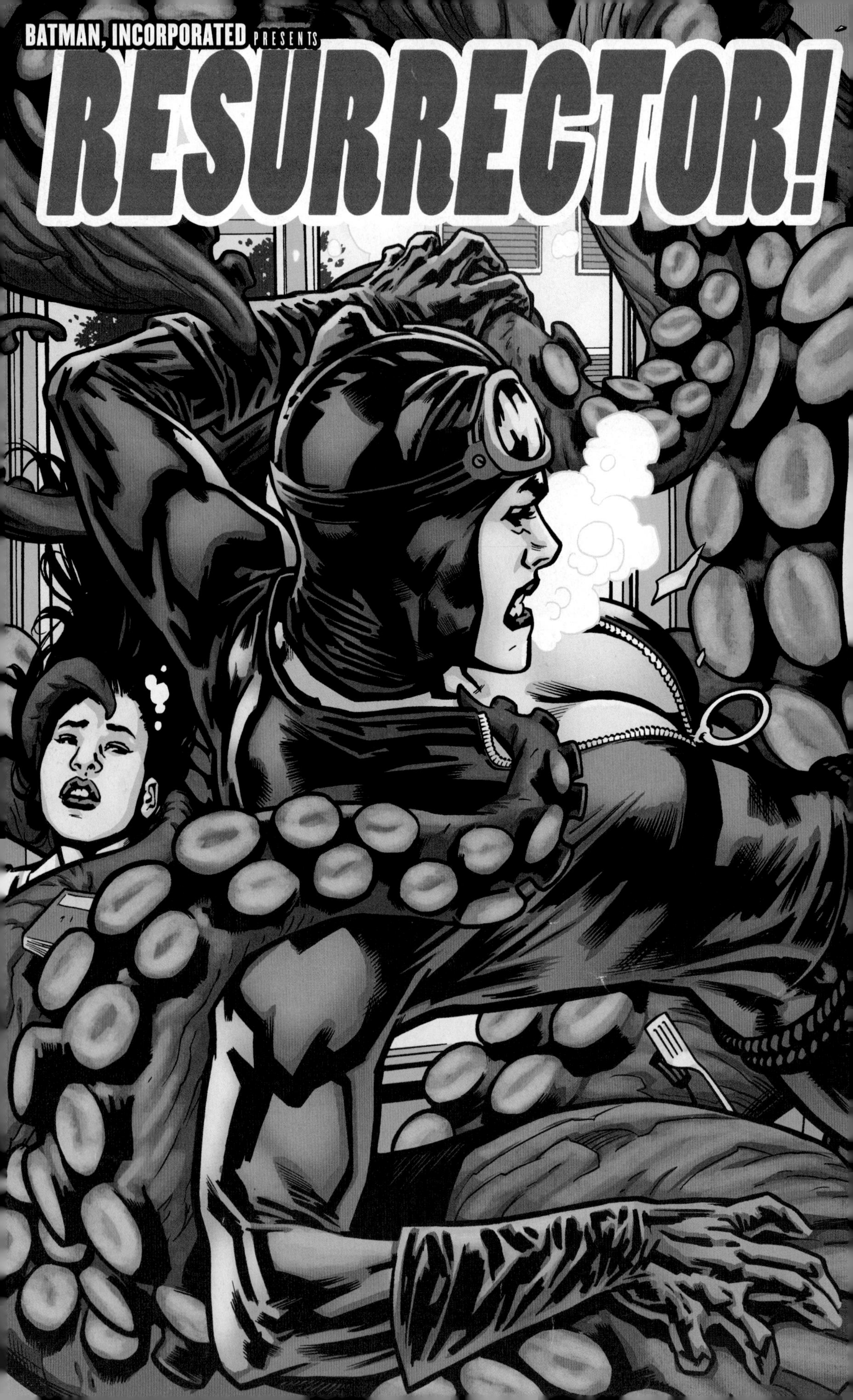
BATMAN, INCORPORATED PRESENTS
RESURRECTOR!

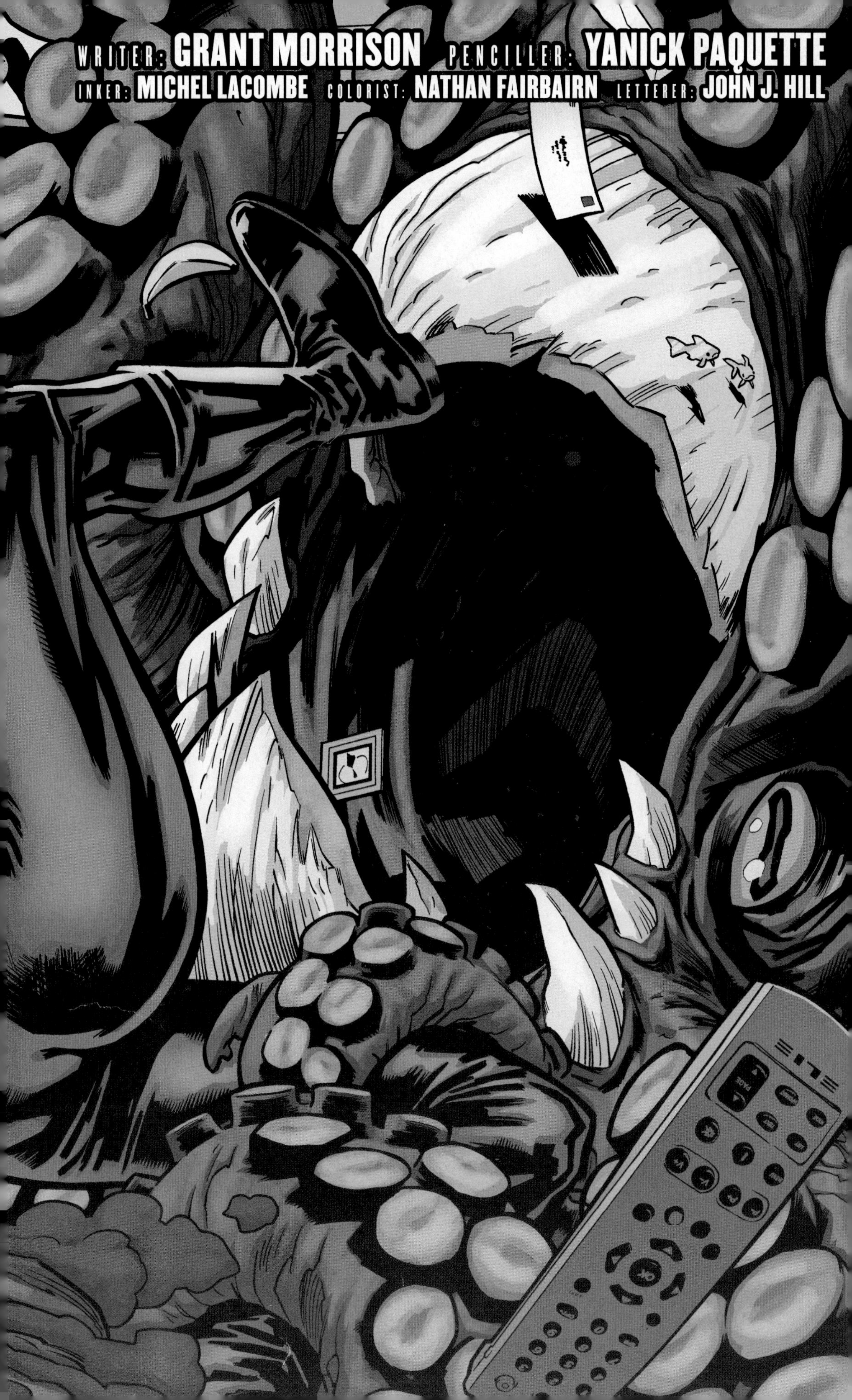
WRITER: GRANT MORRISON PENCILLER: YANICK PAQUETTE
INKER: MICHEL LACOMBE COLORIST: NATHAN FAIRBAIRN LETTERER: JOHN J. HILL

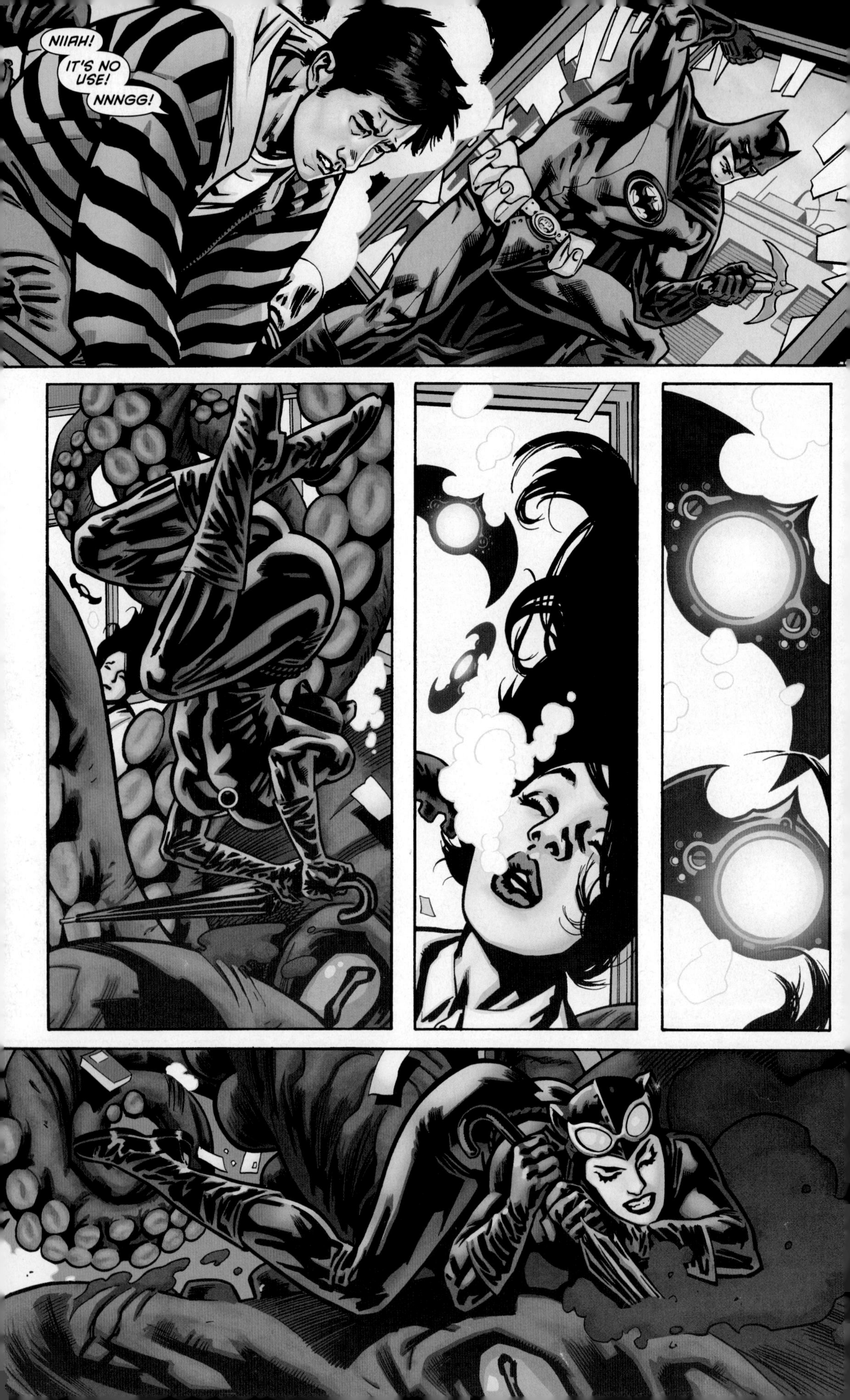
NIIAH!
IT'S NO USE!
NNNGG!

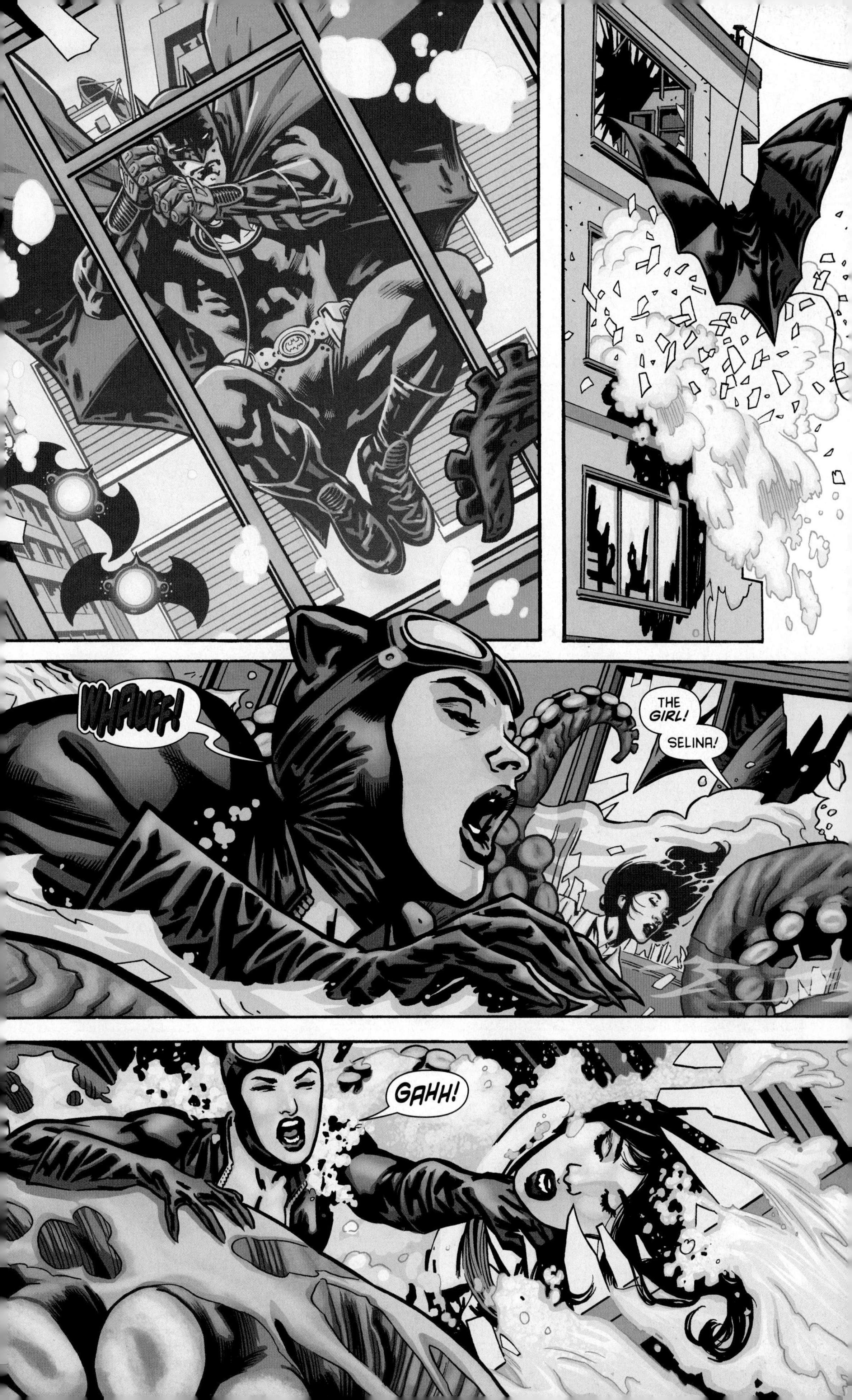
WHAUFF!
THE GIRL!
SELINA!
GAHH!

HOW COULD YOU DO THIS TO US?

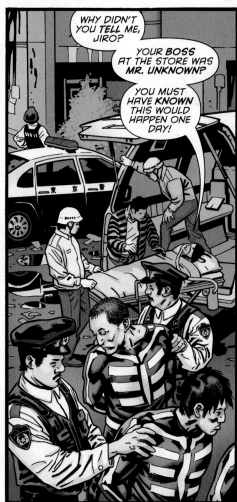

WHY DIDN'T YOU TELL ME, JIRO?

YOUR BOSS AT THE STORE WAS MR. UNKNOWN?

YOU MUST HAVE KNOWN THIS WOULD HAPPEN ONE DAY!

KEEP YOUR VOICE DOWN--PLEASE, MISAKI!

I DIDN'T WANT TO SCARE YOU, THAT'S ALL.

HE HAD A SKULL FOR A HEAD AND CLAMMY FINGERS!

I NEVER WANT TO SEE YOU AGAIN!

東京消防庁
Tokyo Fire Dept

IT'S OVER BETWEEN US, JIRO OSAMU!

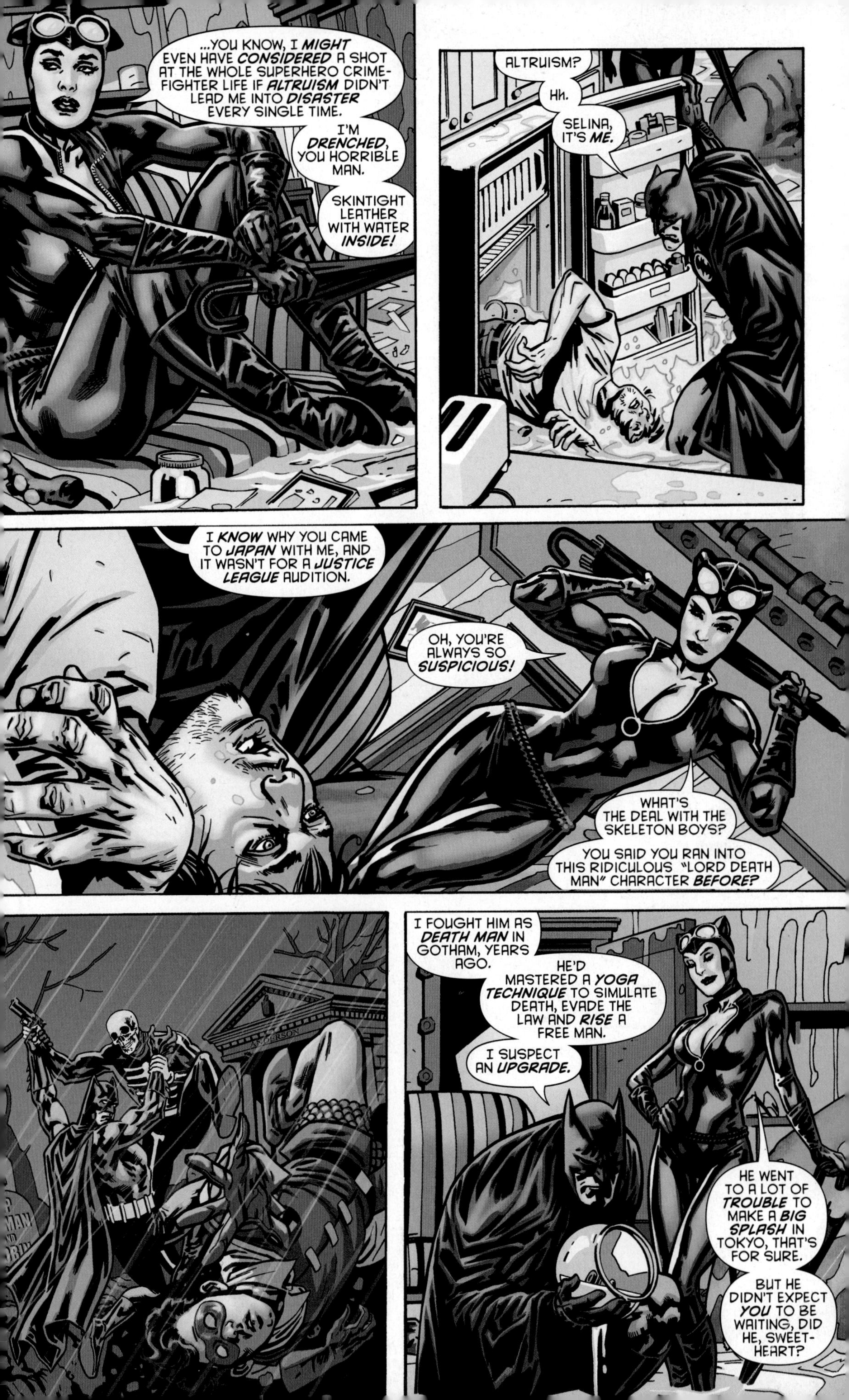
...YOU KNOW, I MIGHT EVEN HAVE CONSIDERED A SHOT AT THE WHOLE SUPERHERO CRIME-FIGHTER LIFE IF ALTRUISM DIDN'T LEAD ME INTO DISASTER EVERY SINGLE TIME.
I'M DRENCHED, YOU HORRIBLE MAN.
SKINTIGHT LEATHER WITH WATER INSIDE!
ALTRUISM?
Hh.
SELINA, IT'S ME.
I KNOW WHY YOU CAME TO JAPAN WITH ME, AND IT WASN'T FOR A JUSTICE LEAGUE AUDITION.
OH, YOU'RE ALWAYS SO SUSPICIOUS!
WHAT'S THE DEAL WITH THE SKELETON BOYS?
YOU SAID YOU RAN INTO THIS RIDICULOUS "LORD DEATH MAN" CHARACTER BEFORE?
ANDERSON
I FOUGHT HIM AS DEATH MAN IN GOTHAM, YEARS AGO.
HE'D MASTERED A YOGA TECHNIQUE TO SIMULATE DEATH, EVADE THE LAW AND RISE A FREE MAN.
I SUSPECT AN UPGRADE.
HE WENT TO A LOT OF TROUBLE TO MAKE A BIG SPLASH IN TOKYO, THAT'S FOR SURE.
BUT HE DIDN'T EXPECT YOU TO BE WAITING, DID HE, SWEET-HEART?

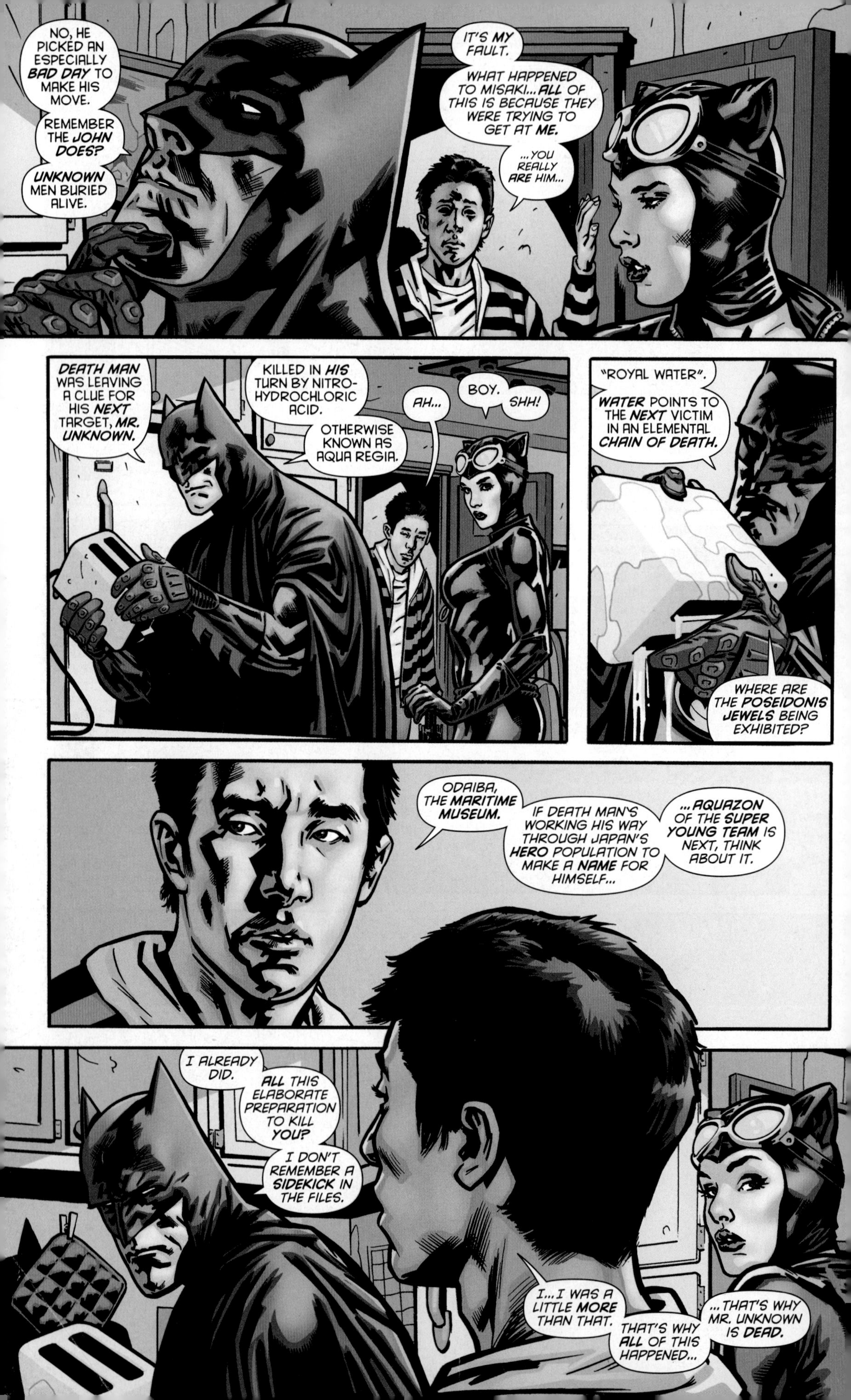

NO, HE PICKED AN ESPECIALLY BAD DAY TO MAKE HIS MOVE.
REMEMBER THE JOHN DOES?
UNKNOWN MEN BURIED ALIVE.
IT'S MY FAULT.
WHAT HAPPENED TO MISAKI... ALL OF THIS IS BECAUSE THEY WERE TRYING TO GET AT ME.
...YOU REALLY ARE HIM...
DEATH MAN WAS LEAVING A CLUE FOR HIS NEXT TARGET, MR. UNKNOWN.
KILLED IN HIS TURN BY NITRO-HYDROCHLORIC ACID.
OTHERWISE KNOWN AS AQUA REGIA.
AH...
BOY.
SHH!
"ROYAL WATER".
WATER POINTS TO THE NEXT VICTIM IN AN ELEMENTAL CHAIN OF DEATH.
WHERE ARE THE POSEIDONIS JEWELS BEING EXHIBITED?
ODAIBA, THE MARITIME MUSEUM.
IF DEATH MAN'S WORKING HIS WAY THROUGH JAPAN'S HERO POPULATION TO MAKE A NAME FOR HIMSELF...
...AQUAZON OF THE SUPER YOUNG TEAM IS NEXT, THINK ABOUT IT.
I ALREADY DID.
ALL THIS ELABORATE PREPARATION TO KILL YOU?
I DON'T REMEMBER A SIDEKICK IN THE FILES.
I... I WAS A LITTLE MORE THAN THAT.
THAT'S WHY ALL OF THIS HAPPENED...
...THAT'S WHY MR. UNKNOWN IS DEAD.

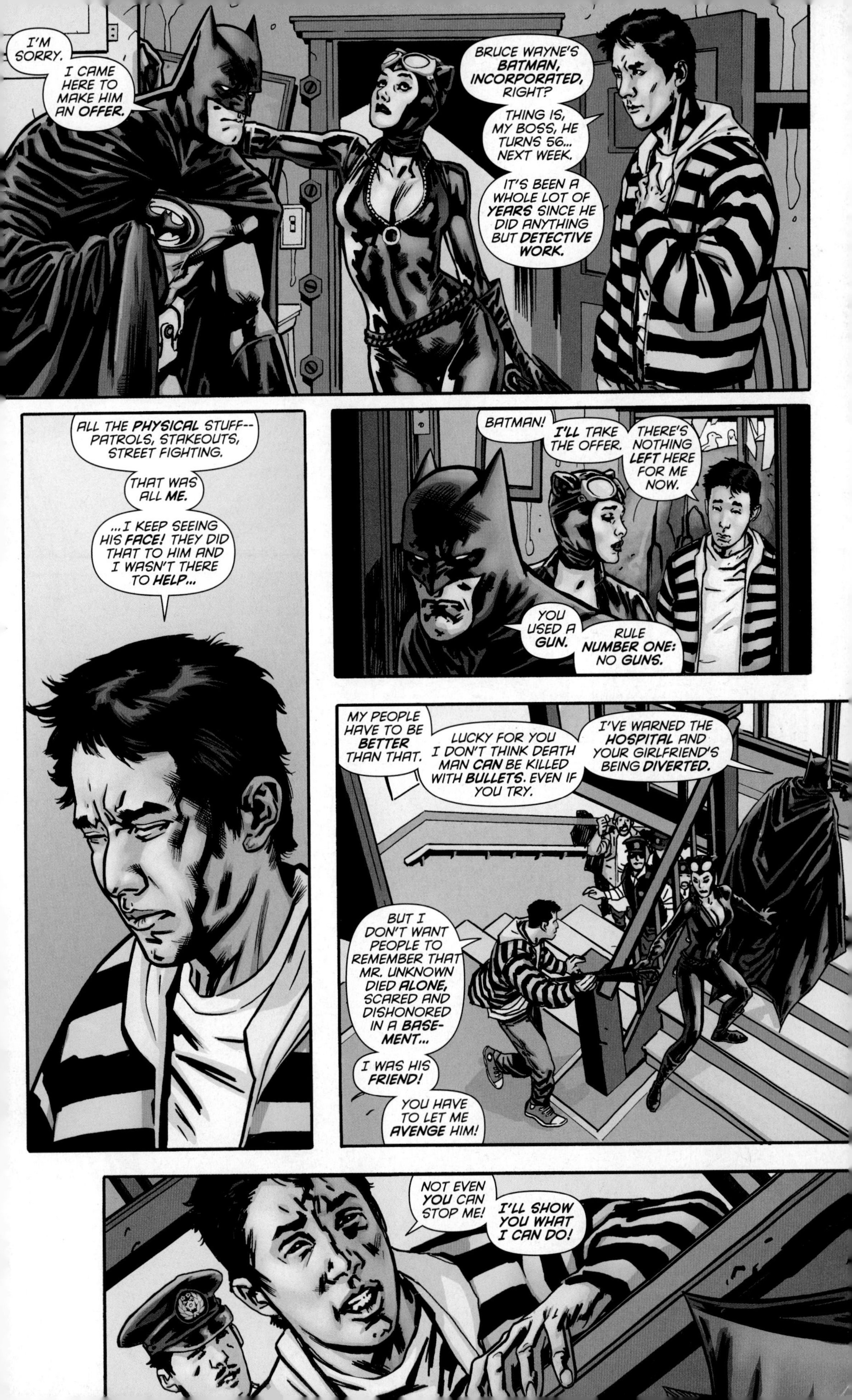
I'M SORRY.
I CAME HERE TO MAKE HIM AN OFFER.
BRUCE WAYNE'S BATMAN, INCORPORATED, RIGHT?
THING IS, MY BOSS, HE TURNS 56... NEXT WEEK.
IT'S BEEN A WHOLE LOT OF YEARS SINCE HE DID ANYTHING BUT DETECTIVE WORK.
ALL THE PHYSICAL STUFF-- PATROLS, STAKEOUTS, STREET FIGHTING.
THAT WAS ALL ME.
...I KEEP SEEING HIS FACE! THEY DID THAT TO HIM AND I WASN'T THERE TO HELP...
BATMAN!
I'LL TAKE THE OFFER.
THERE'S NOTHING LEFT HERE FOR ME NOW.
YOU USED A GUN.
RULE NUMBER ONE: NO GUNS.
MY PEOPLE HAVE TO BE BETTER THAN THAT.
LUCKY FOR YOU I DON'T THINK DEATH MAN CAN BE KILLED WITH BULLETS. EVEN IF YOU TRY.
I'VE WARNED THE HOSPITAL AND YOUR GIRLFRIEND'S BEING DIVERTED.
BUT I DON'T WANT PEOPLE TO REMEMBER THAT MR. UNKNOWN DIED ALONE, SCARED AND DISHONORED IN A BASE-MENT...
I WAS HIS FRIEND!
YOU HAVE TO LET ME AVENGE HIM!
NOT EVEN YOU CAN STOP ME!
I'LL SHOW YOU WHAT I CAN DO!

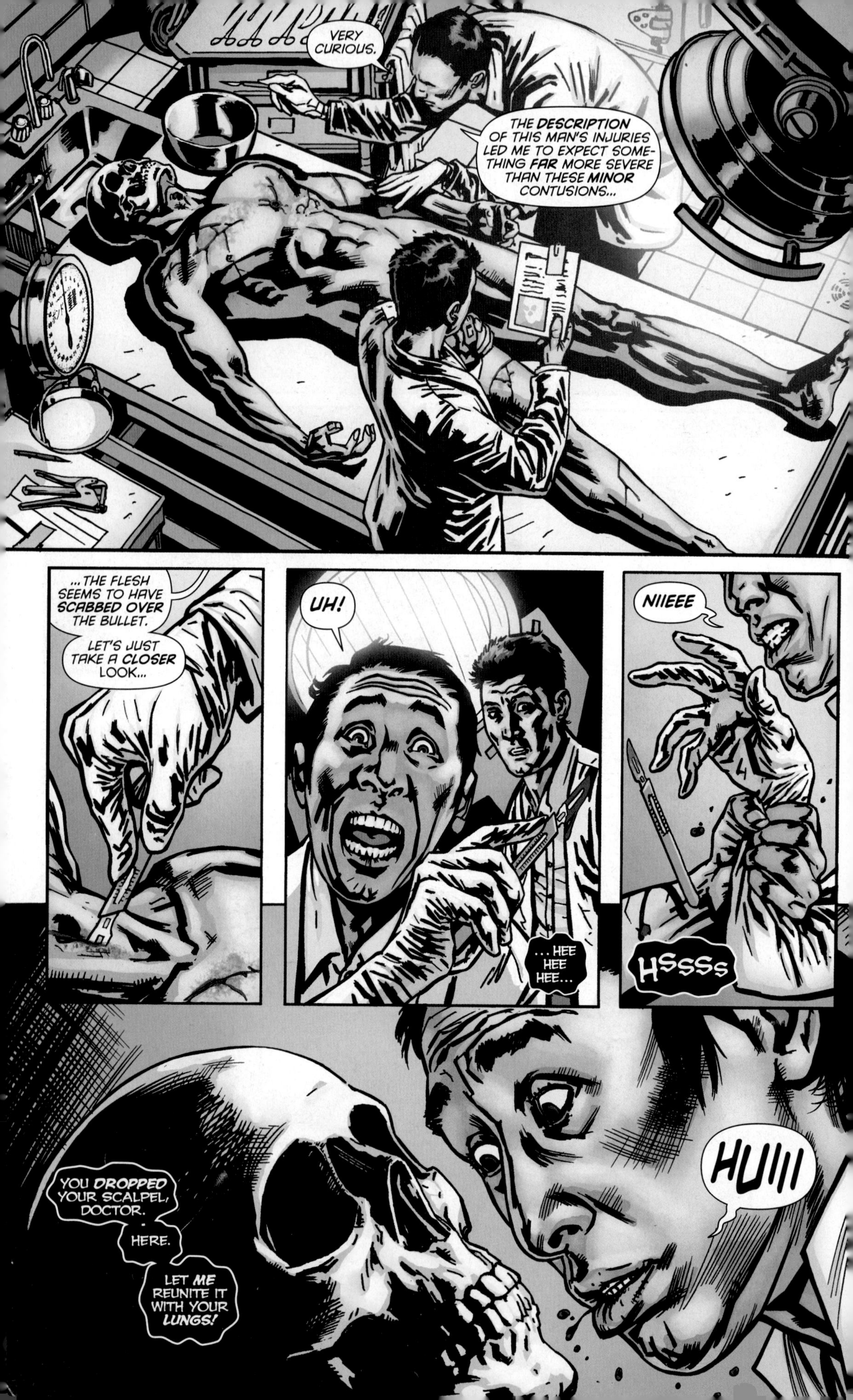
VERY CURIOUS.
THE DESCRIPTION OF THIS MAN'S INJURIES LED ME TO EXPECT SOMETHING FAR MORE SEVERE THAN THESE MINOR CONTUSIONS...
...THE FLESH SEEMS TO HAVE SCABBED OVER THE BULLET.
LET'S JUST TAKE A CLOSER LOOK...
UH!
...HEE HEE HEE...
NIIEEE
HSSSS
YOU DROPPED YOUR SCALPEL, DOCTOR.
HERE.
LET ME REUNITE IT WITH YOUR LUNGS!
HUIII

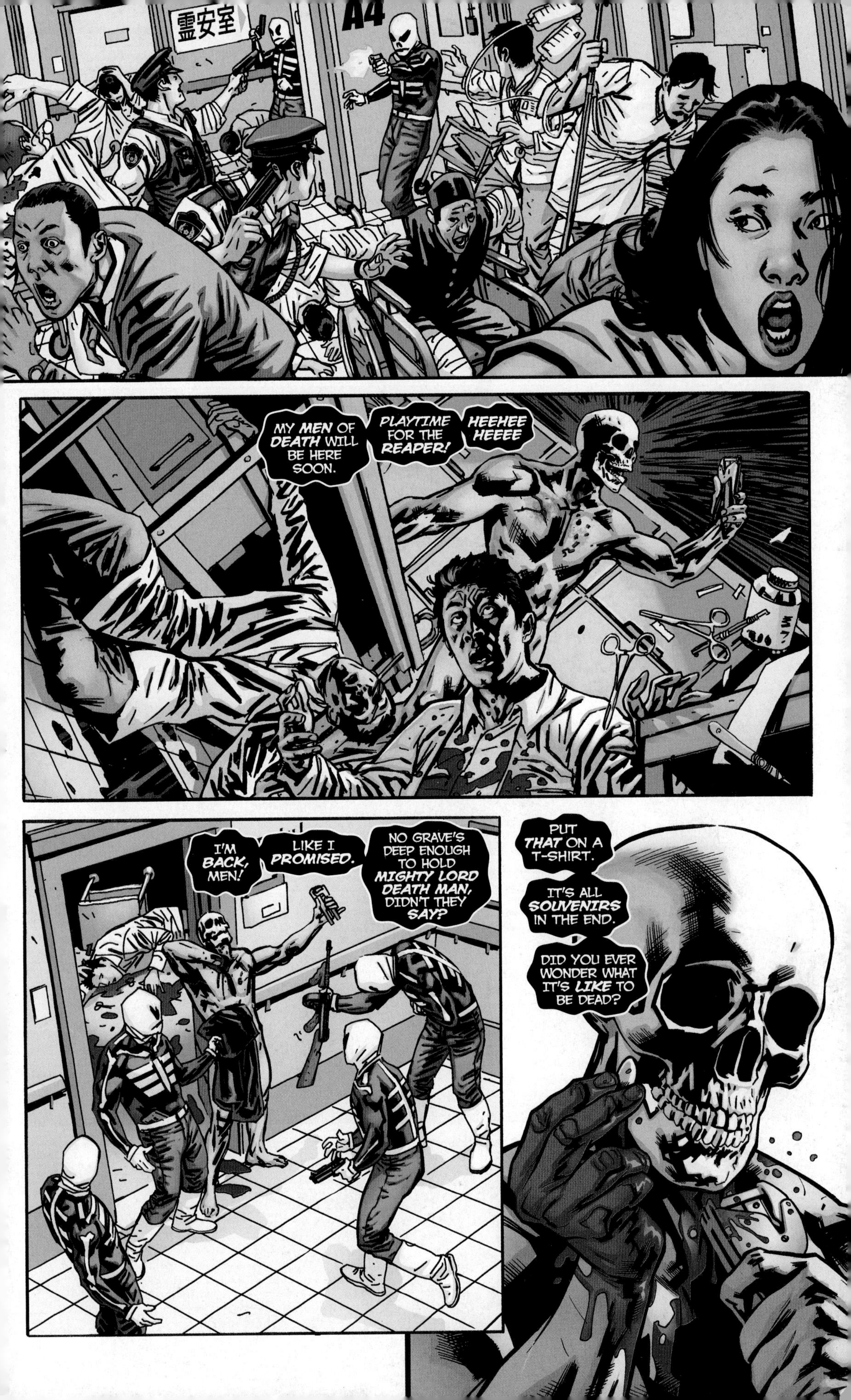

霊安室
A4
MY MEN OF DEATH WILL BE HERE SOON.
PLAYTIME FOR THE REAPER!
HEEHEE HEEEE
I'M BACK, MEN!
LIKE I PROMISED.
NO GRAVE'S DEEP ENOUGH TO HOLD MIGHTY LORD DEATH MAN, DIDN'T THEY SAY?
PUT THAT ON A T-SHIRT.
IT'S ALL SOUVENIRS IN THE END.
DID YOU EVER WONDER WHAT IT'S LIKE TO BE DEAD?

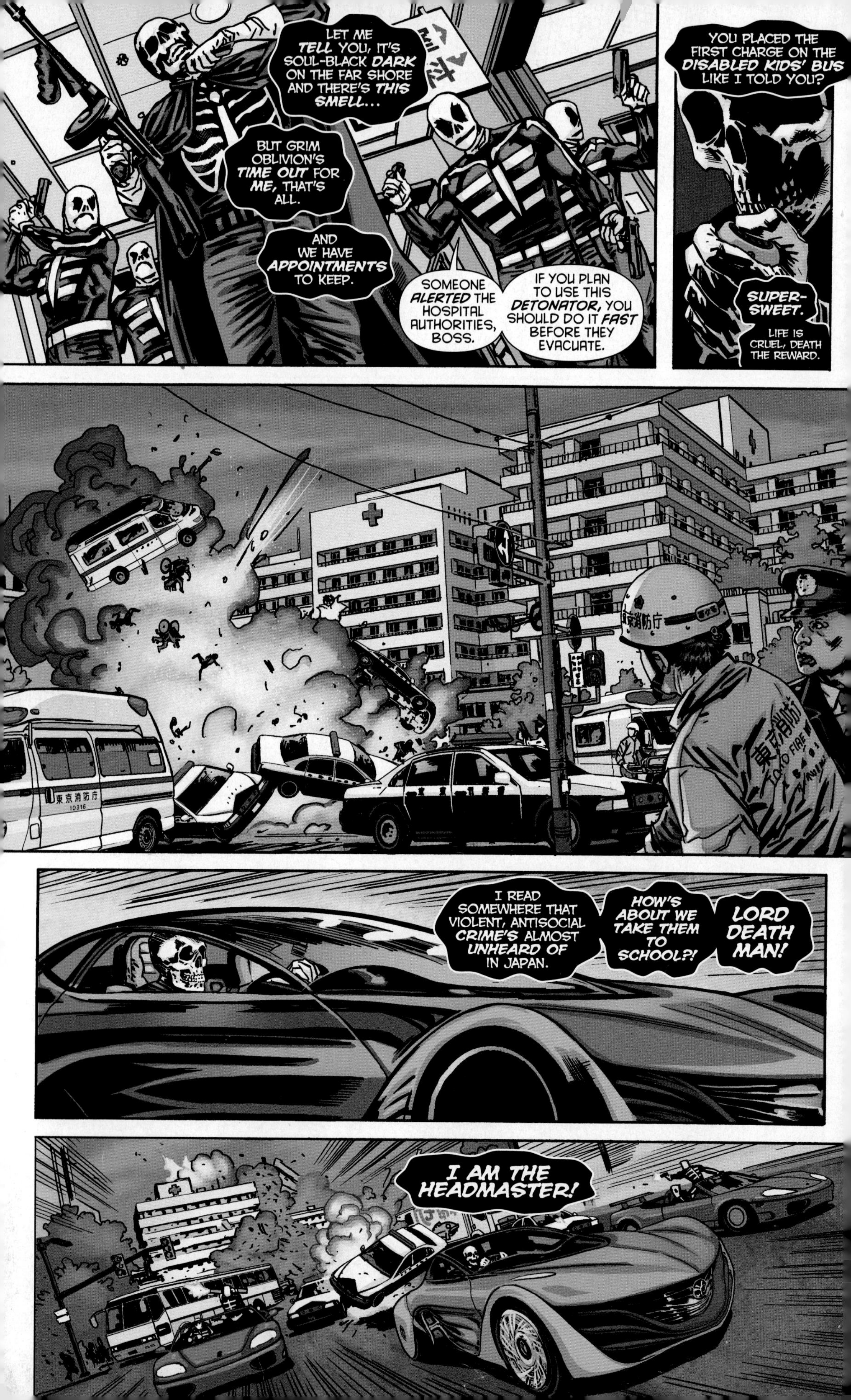

LET ME TELL YOU, IT'S SOUL-BLACK DARK ON THE FAR SHORE AND THERE'S THIS SMELL...
BUT GRIM OBLIVION'S TIME OUT FOR ME, THAT'S ALL.
AND WE HAVE APPOINTMENTS TO KEEP.
SOMEONE ALERTED THE HOSPITAL AUTHORITIES, BOSS.
IF YOU PLAN TO USE THIS DETONATOR, YOU SHOULD DO IT FAST BEFORE THEY EVACUATE.
YOU PLACED THE FIRST CHARGE ON THE DISABLED KIDS' BUS LIKE I TOLD YOU?
SUPER-SWEET.
LIFE IS CRUEL, DEATH THE REWARD.
東京消防庁
10316
I READ SOMEWHERE THAT VIOLENT, ANTISOCIAL CRIME'S ALMOST UNHEARD OF IN JAPAN.
HOW'S ABOUT WE TAKE THEM TO SCHOOL?!
LORD DEATH MAN!
I AM THE HEADMASTER!

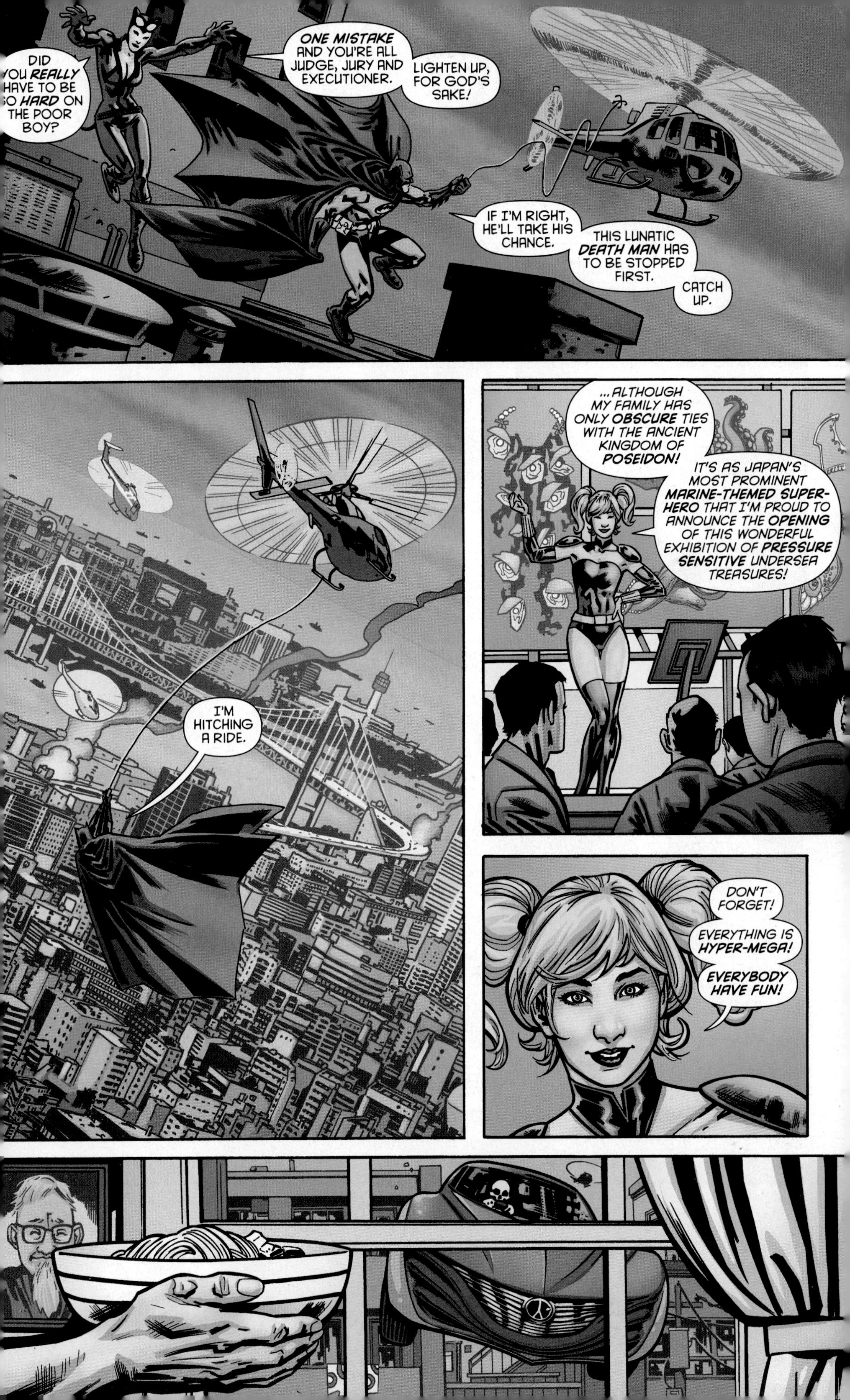
DID YOU REALLY HAVE TO BE SO HARD ON THE POOR BOY?
ONE MISTAKE AND YOU'RE ALL JUDGE, JURY AND EXECUTIONER.
LIGHTEN UP, FOR GOD'S SAKE!
IF I'M RIGHT, HE'LL TAKE HIS CHANCE.
THIS LUNATIC DEATH MAN HAS TO BE STOPPED FIRST.
CATCH UP.
I'M HITCHING A RIDE.
...ALTHOUGH MY FAMILY HAS ONLY OBSCURE TIES WITH THE ANCIENT KINGDOM OF POSEIDON!
IT'S AS JAPAN'S MOST PROMINENT MARINE-THEMED SUPER-HERO THAT I'M PROUD TO ANNOUNCE THE OPENING OF THIS WONDERFUL EXHIBITION OF PRESSURE SENSITIVE UNDERSEA TREASURES!
DON'T FORGET!
EVERYTHING IS HYPER-MEGA!
EVERYBODY HAVE FUN!

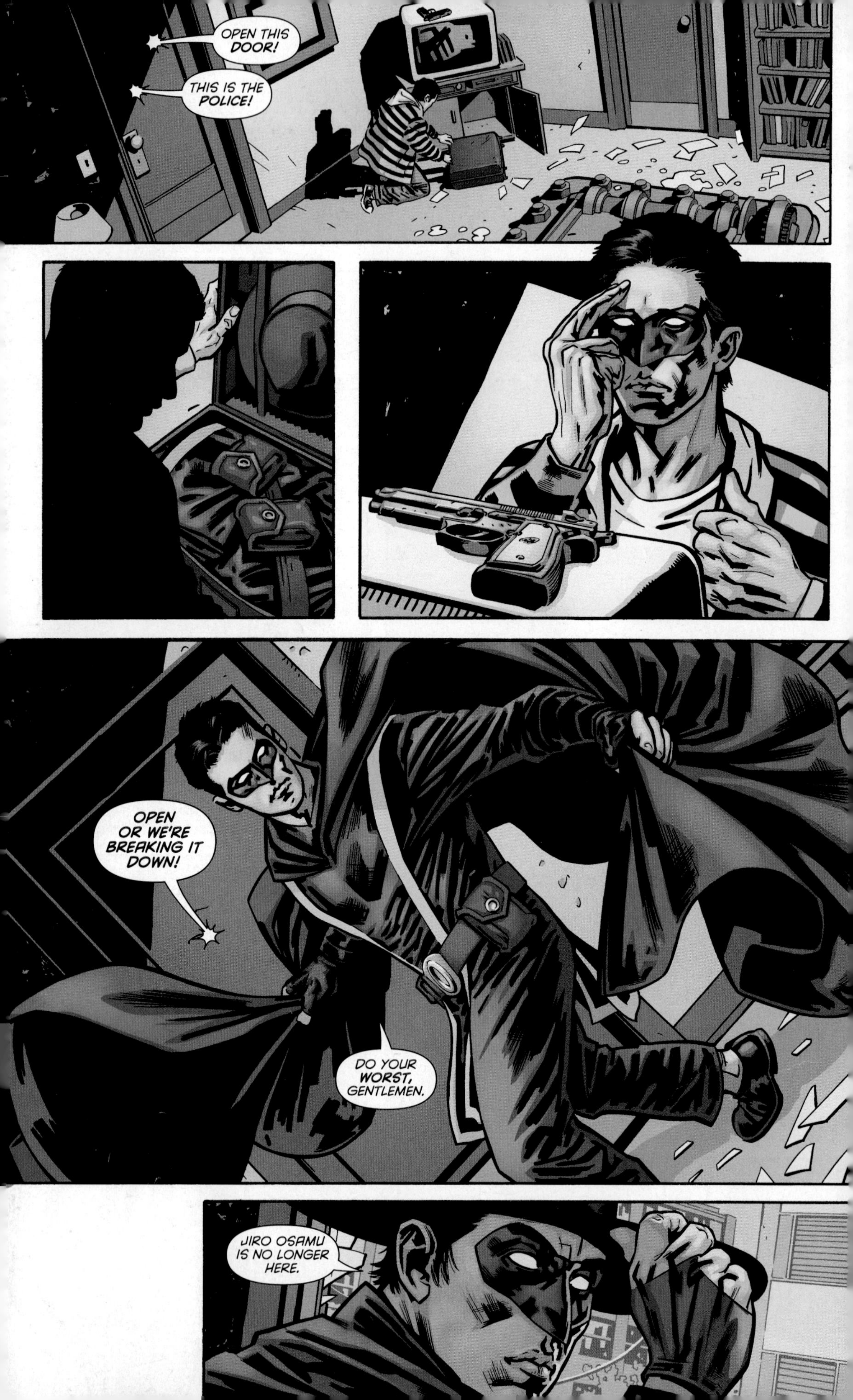
OPEN THIS DOOR!
THIS IS THE POLICE!
OPEN OR WE'RE BREAKING IT DOWN!
DO YOUR WORST, GENTLEMEN.
JIRO OSAMU IS NO LONGER HERE.

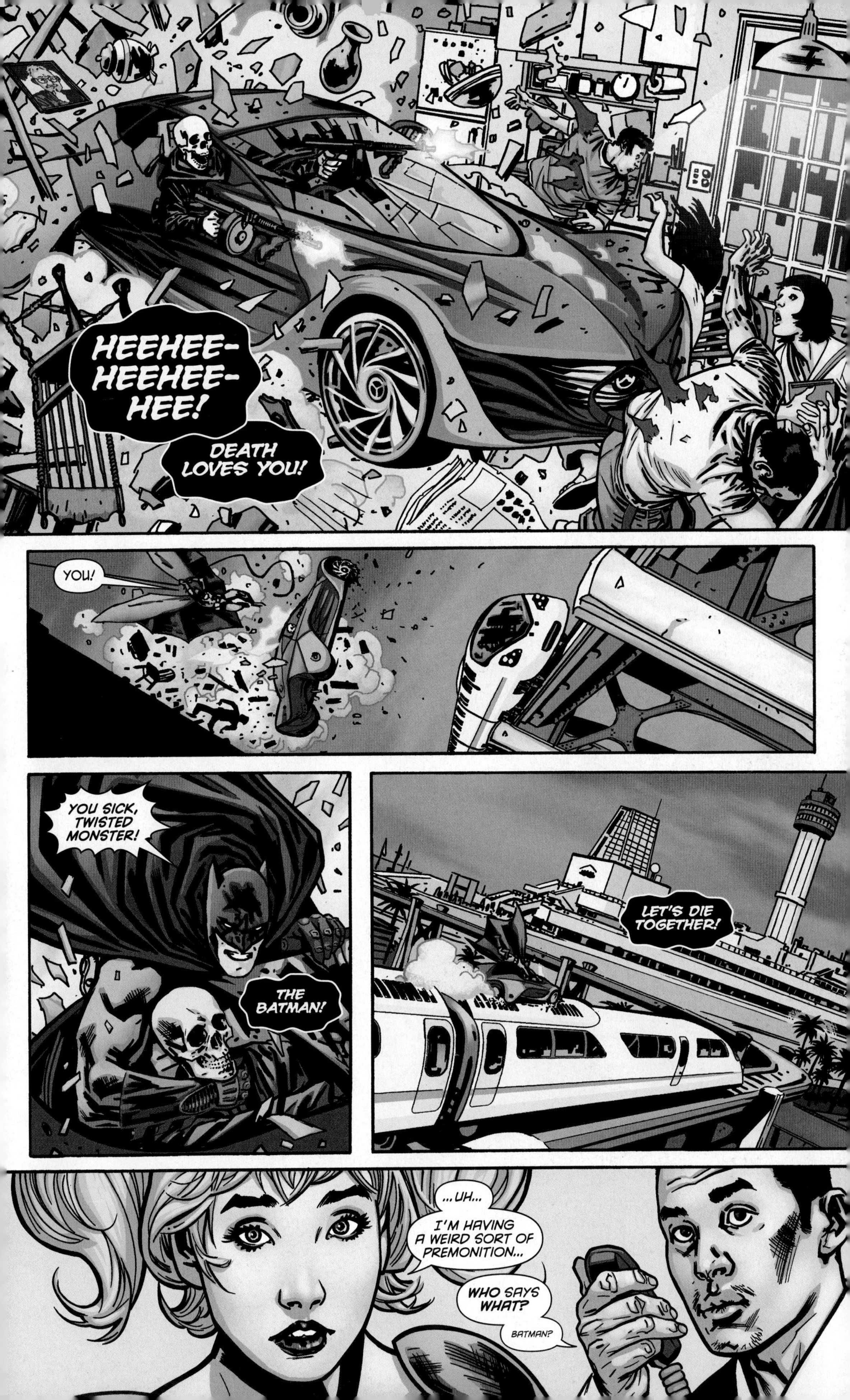
HEEHEE-HEEHEE-HEE!
DEATH LOVES YOU!
YOU!
YOU SICK, TWISTED MONSTER!
THE BATMAN!
LET'S DIE TOGETHER!
...UH...
I'M HAVING A WEIRD SORT OF PREMONITION...
WHO SAYS WHAT?
BATMAN?

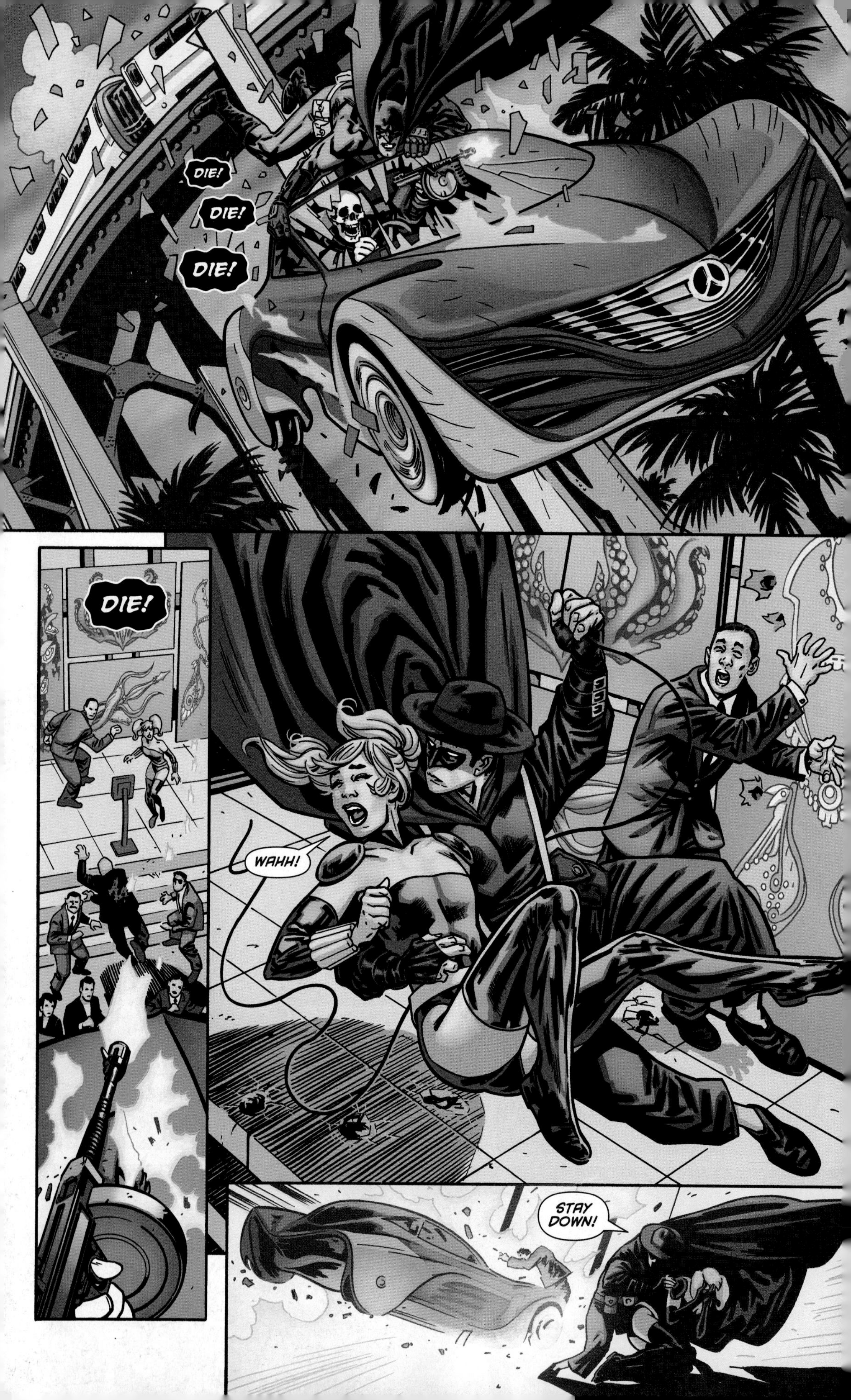
DIE!
DIE!
DIE!
DIE!
WAHH!
STAY DOWN!

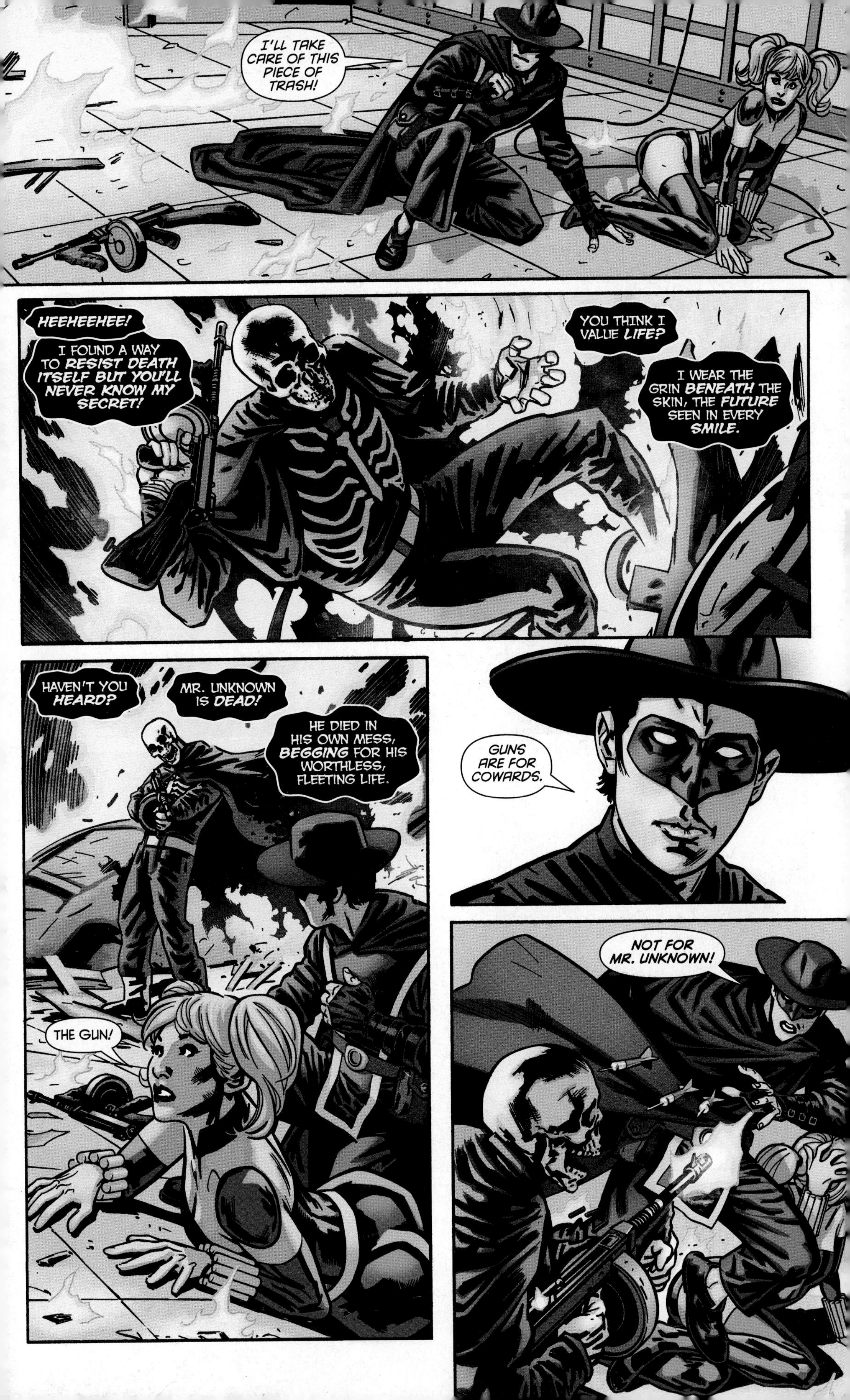
I'LL TAKE CARE OF THIS PIECE OF TRASH!
HEEHEEHEE!
I FOUND A WAY TO RESIST DEATH ITSELF BUT YOU'LL NEVER KNOW MY SECRET!
YOU THINK I VALUE LIFE?
I WEAR THE GRIN BENEATH THE SKIN, THE FUTURE SEEN IN EVERY SMILE.
HAVEN'T YOU HEARD?
MR. UNKNOWN IS DEAD!
HE DIED IN HIS OWN MESS, BEGGING FOR HIS WORTHLESS, FLEETING LIFE.
THE GUN!
GUNS ARE FOR COWARDS.
NOT FOR MR. UNKNOWN!

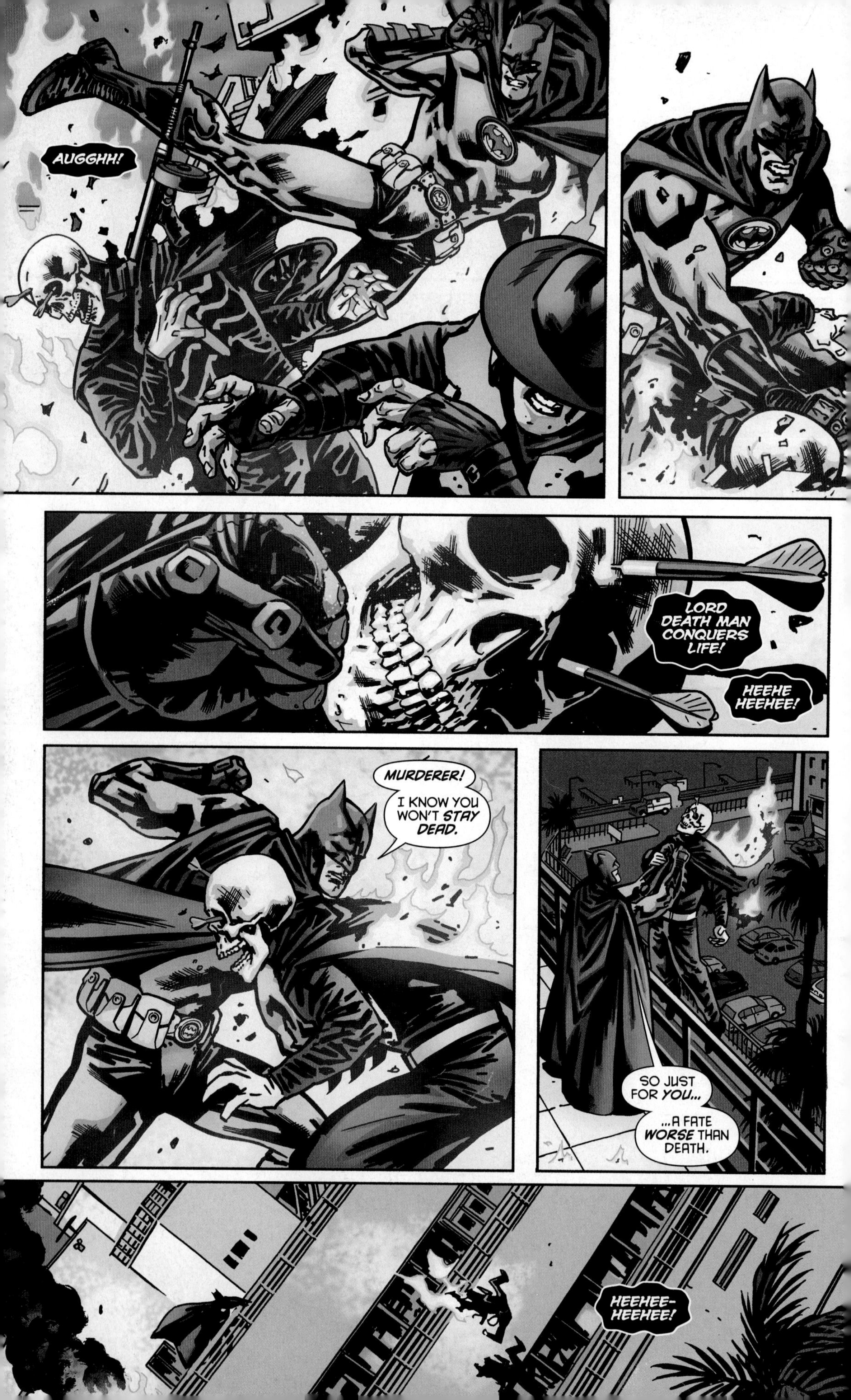
AUGGHH!
LORD DEATH MAN CONQUERS LIFE!
HEEHE HEEHEE!
MURDERER!
I KNOW YOU WON'T STAY DEAD.
SO JUST FOR YOU...
...A FATE WORSE THAN DEATH.
HEEHEE-HEEHEE!

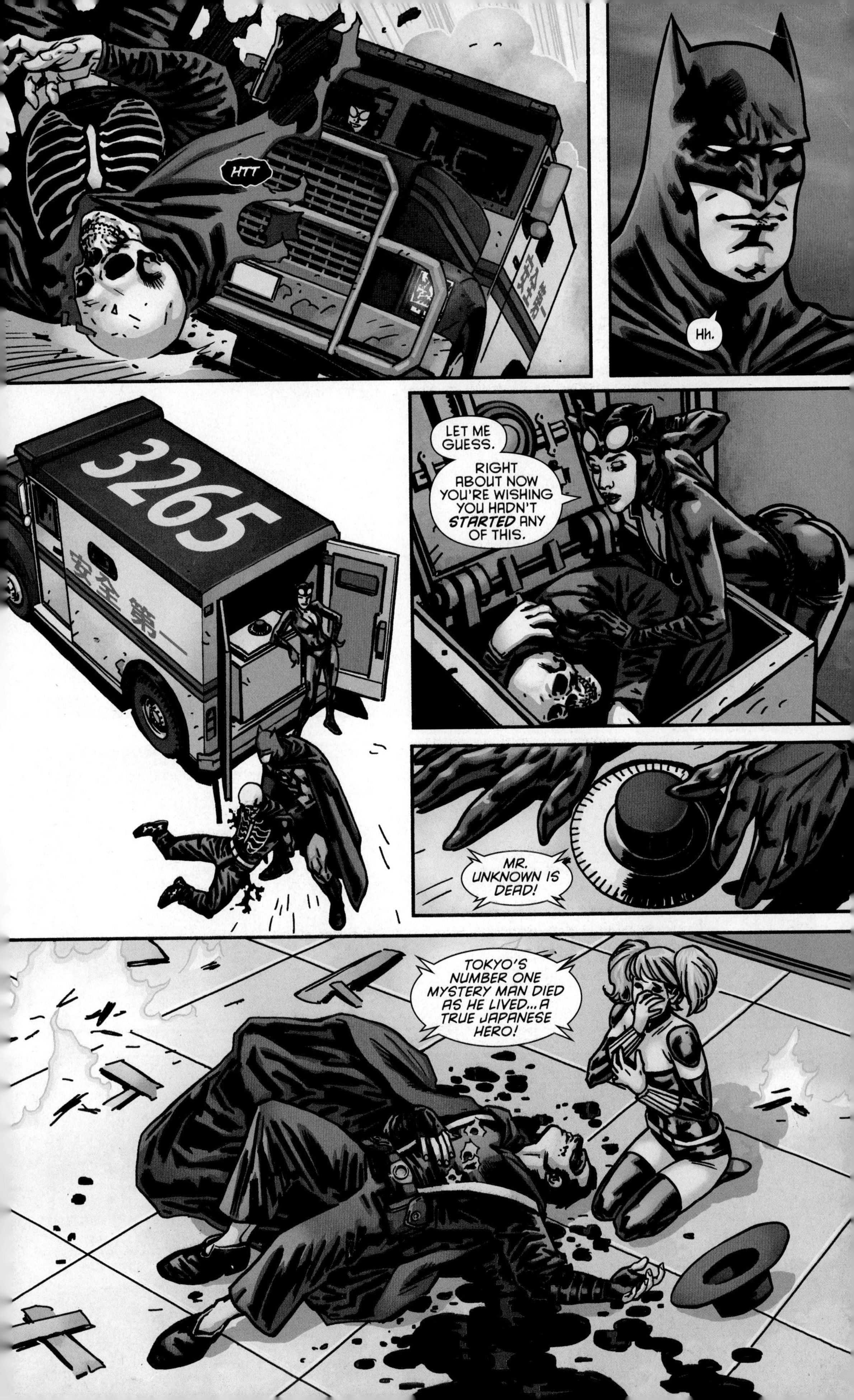
HTT
Hh.
3265
安全第一
LET ME GUESS.
RIGHT ABOUT NOW YOU'RE WISHING YOU HADN'T *STARTED* ANY OF THIS.
MR. UNKNOWN IS DEAD!
TOKYO'S NUMBER ONE MYSTERY MAN DIED AS HE LIVED... A TRUE JAPANESE HERO!

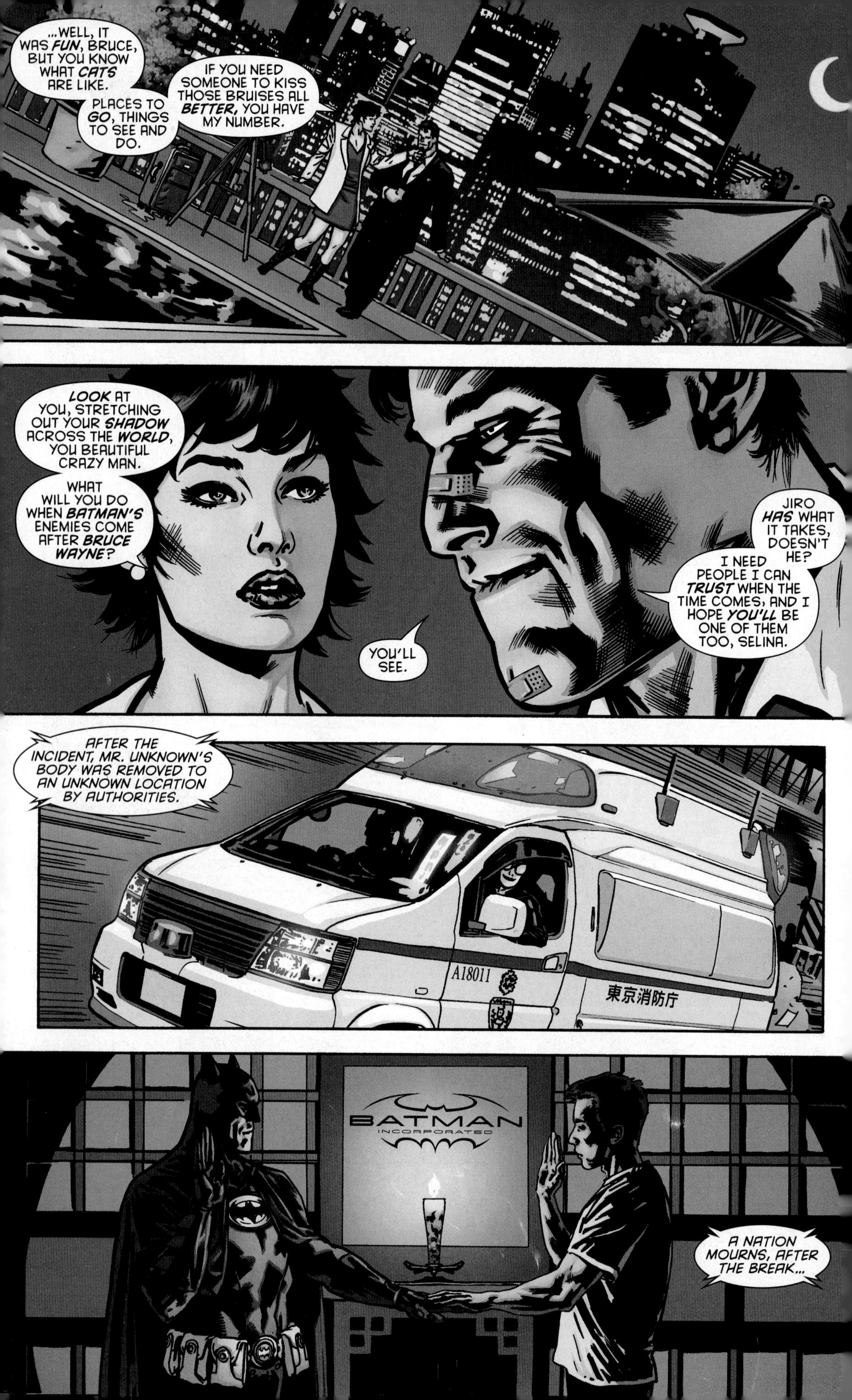
...WELL, IT WAS FUN, BRUCE, BUT YOU KNOW WHAT CATS ARE LIKE.
PLACES TO GO, THINGS TO SEE AND DO.
IF YOU NEED SOMEONE TO KISS THOSE BRUISES ALL BETTER, YOU HAVE MY NUMBER.
LOOK AT YOU, STRETCHING OUT YOUR SHADOW ACROSS THE WORLD, YOU BEAUTIFUL CRAZY MAN.
WHAT WILL YOU DO WHEN BATMAN'S ENEMIES COME AFTER BRUCE WAYNE?
YOU'LL SEE.
JIRO HAS WHAT IT TAKES, DOESN'T HE?
I NEED PEOPLE I CAN TRUST WHEN THE TIME COMES, AND I HOPE YOU'LL BE ONE OF THEM TOO, SELINA.
AFTER THE INCIDENT, MR. UNKNOWN'S BODY WAS REMOVED TO AN UNKNOWN LOCATION BY AUTHORITIES.
A18011
東京消防庁
BATMAN
INCORPORATED
A NATION MOURNS, AFTER THE BREAK...

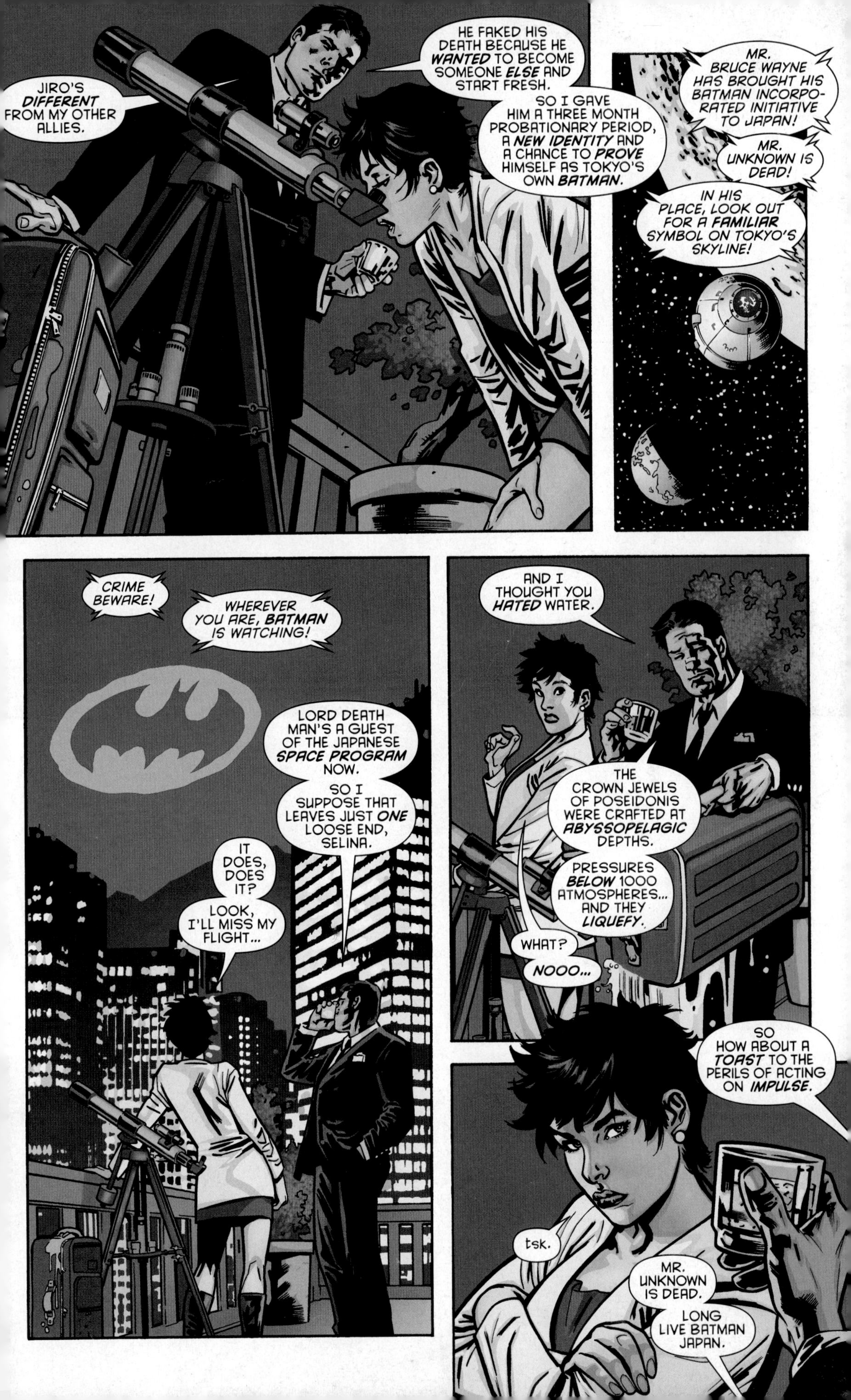
JIRO'S DIFFERENT FROM MY OTHER ALLIES.
HE FAKED HIS DEATH BECAUSE HE WANTED TO BECOME SOMEONE ELSE AND START FRESH.
SO I GAVE HIM A THREE MONTH PROBATIONARY PERIOD, A NEW IDENTITY AND A CHANCE TO PROVE HIMSELF AS TOKYO'S OWN BATMAN.
MR. BRUCE WAYNE HAS BROUGHT HIS BATMAN INCORPORATED INITIATIVE TO JAPAN!
MR. UNKNOWN IS DEAD!
IN HIS PLACE, LOOK OUT FOR A FAMILIAR SYMBOL ON TOKYO'S SKYLINE!
CRIME BEWARE!
WHEREVER YOU ARE, BATMAN IS WATCHING!
LORD DEATH MAN'S A GUEST OF THE JAPANESE SPACE PROGRAM NOW.
SO I SUPPOSE THAT LEAVES JUST ONE LOOSE END, SELINA.
IT DOES, DOES IT?
LOOK, I'LL MISS MY FLIGHT...
AND I THOUGHT YOU HATED WATER.
THE CROWN JEWELS OF POSEIDONIS WERE CRAFTED AT ABYSSOPELAGIC DEPTHS.
PRESSURES BELOW 1000 ATMOSPHERES... AND THEY LIQUEFY.
WHAT?
NOOO...
SO HOW ABOUT A TOAST TO THE PERILS OF ACTING ON IMPULSE.
tsk.
MR. UNKNOWN IS DEAD.
LONG LIVE BATMAN JAPAN.

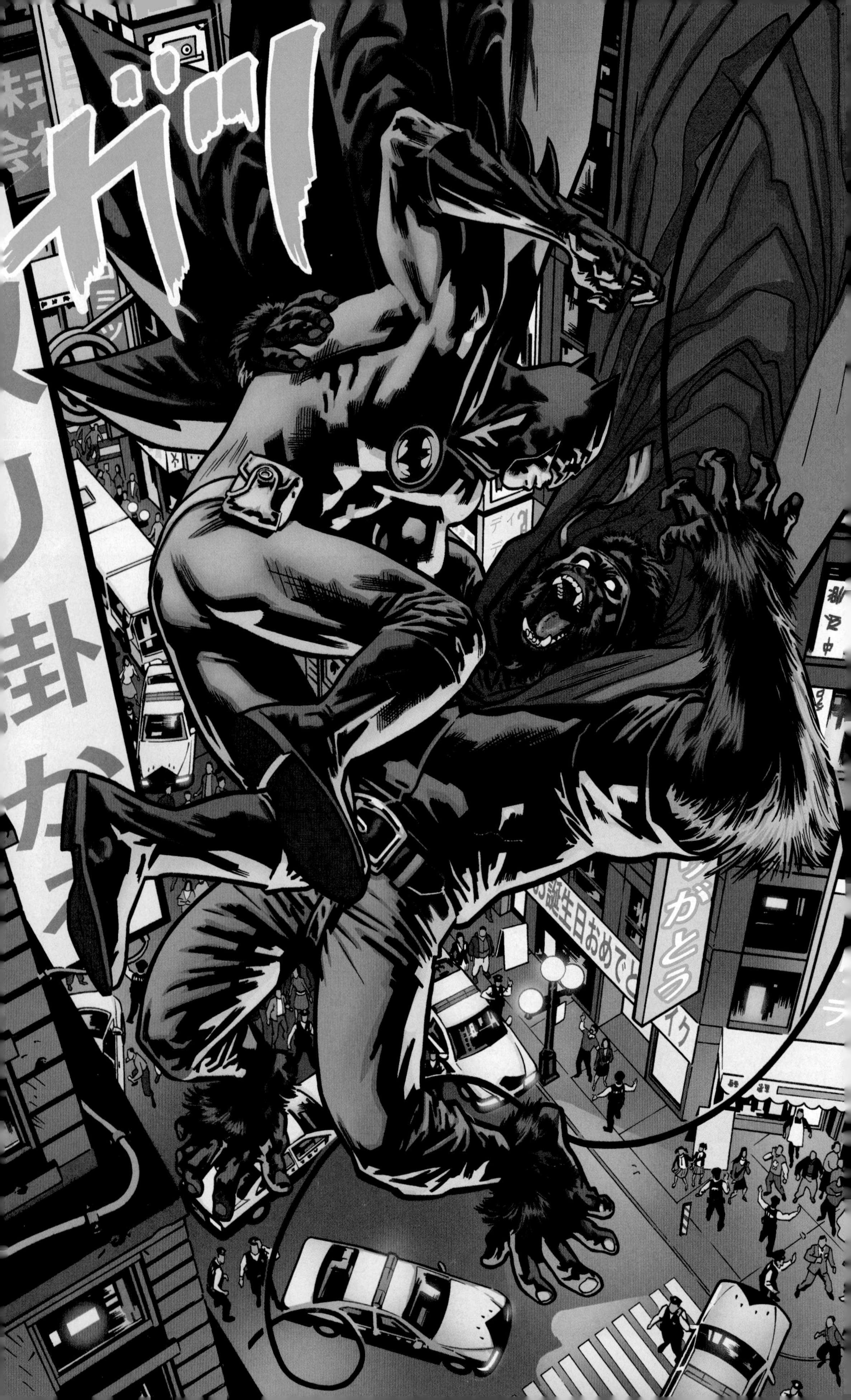
お誕生日おめでと
がとう

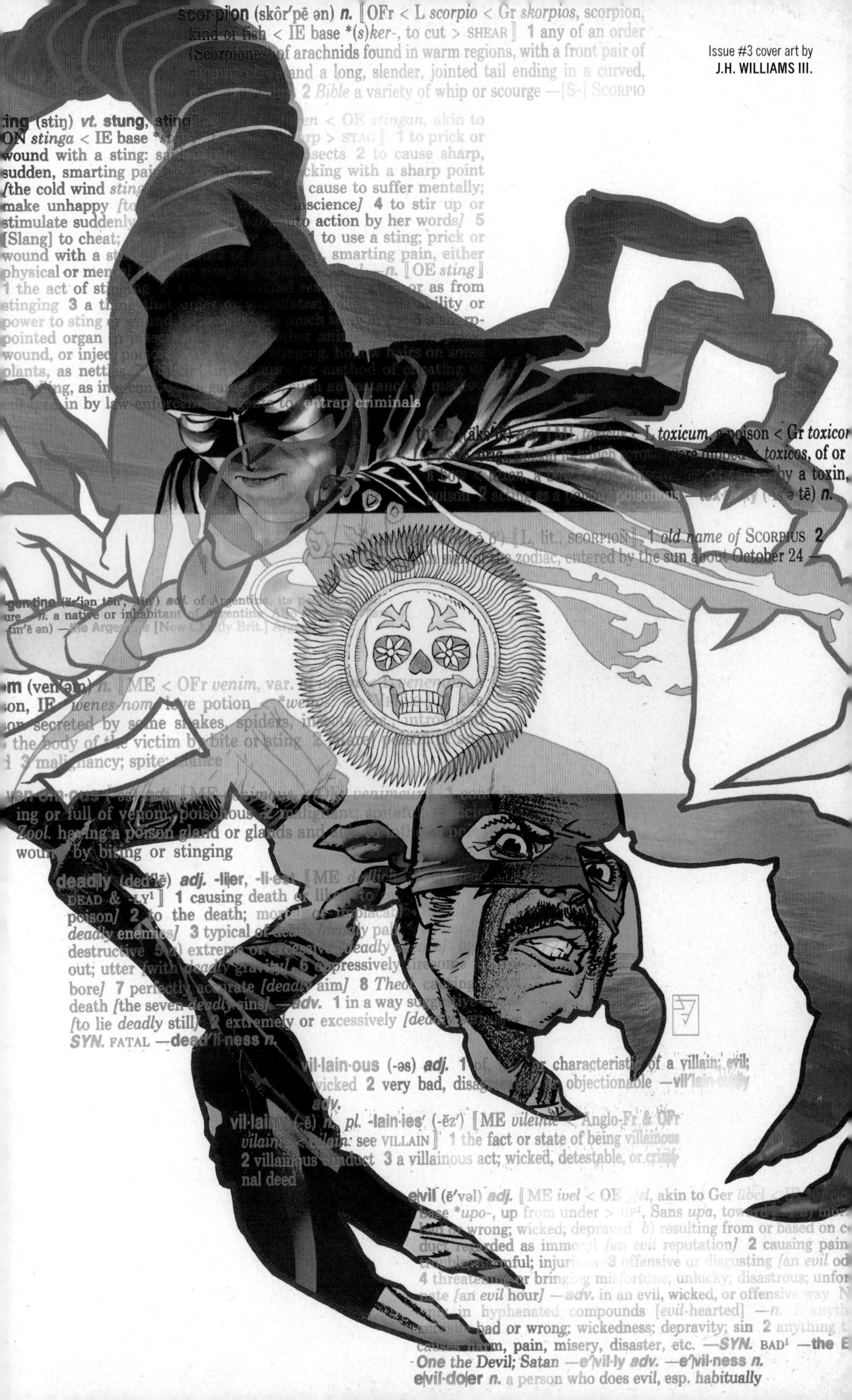
scor·pi·on (skôr′pē ən) n. [OFr < L scorpio < Gr skorpios, scorpion,
kind of fish < IE base *(s)ker-, to cut > SHEAR] 1 any of an order
of arachnids found in warm regions, with a front pair of
and a long, slender, jointed tail ending in a curved,
2 Bible a variety of whip or scourge —[S-] SCORPIO
vil·lain·ous (-əs) adj. 1 of or characteristic of a villain; evil;
wicked 2 very bad, disagreeable, or objectionable
evil (ē′vəl) adj.
One the Devil; Satan —e′vil·ly adv. —e′vil·ness n.
evil·do·er n. a person who does evil, esp. habitually
Issue #3 cover art by
J.H. WILLIAMS III.

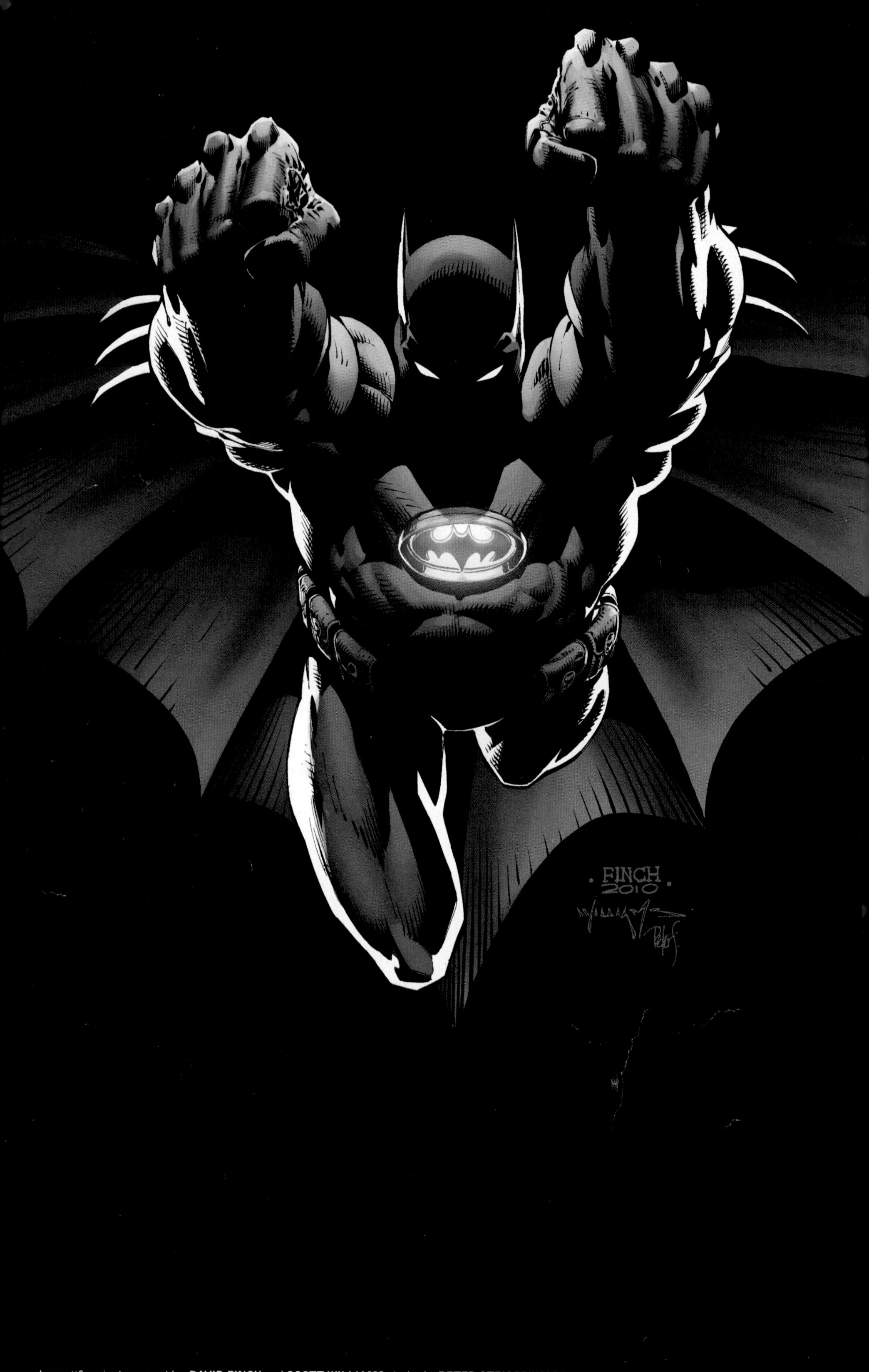
FINCH
2010

Issue #3 variant cover art by **DAVID FINCH** and **SCOTT WILLIAMS** (color by **PETER STEIGERWALD**).

THE NIGHT THE *METALEK* SCOUT TURNED UP IN *DORSET.*

HE WAS THERE.

HE'S *ALWAYS* THERE.

51.9823 S. 58.6062 W

IN TIME OF WAR

STILL HERE?

WHO *AM* I NOW?

WHEN DOES THIS WEAR *OFF?*

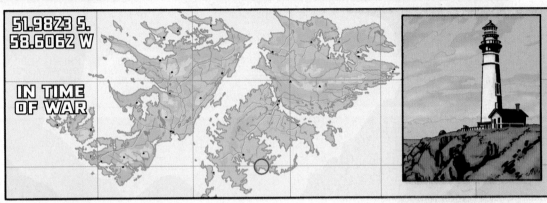

YOU'RE IN THE *CLEAR,* MATE. *VICTORY VS,* REMEMBER?

WHAT THE HELL *HAPPENED* UP THERE?

...DEDALUS... THE NEVER-ENDING *RING...*

HOW CAN I STILL *HEAR* IT?

THE *PAST?*

WE ALL KNOW YOU'RE NOT *ACTUALLY* GAY, *FADAR.*

GIVE IT UP.

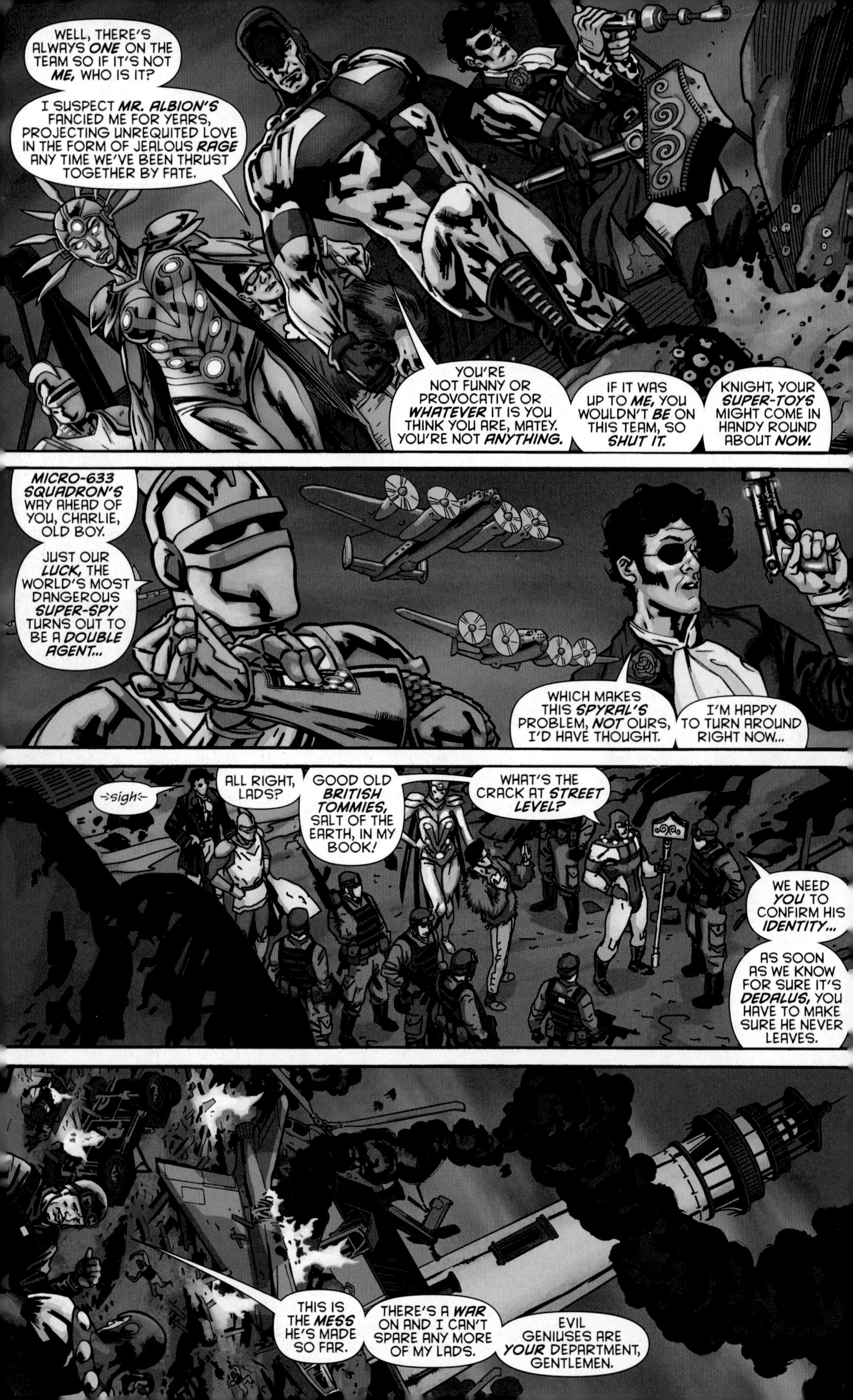
WELL, THERE'S ALWAYS ONE ON THE TEAM SO IF IT'S NOT ME, WHO IS IT?
I SUSPECT MR. ALBION'S FANCIED ME FOR YEARS, PROJECTING UNREQUITED LOVE IN THE FORM OF JEALOUS RAGE ANY TIME WE'VE BEEN THRUST TOGETHER BY FATE.
YOU'RE NOT FUNNY OR PROVOCATIVE OR WHATEVER IT IS YOU THINK YOU ARE, MATEY. YOU'RE NOT ANYTHING.
IF IT WAS UP TO ME, YOU WOULDN'T BE ON THIS TEAM, SO SHUT IT.
KNIGHT, YOUR SUPER-TOYS MIGHT COME IN HANDY ROUND ABOUT NOW.
MICRO-633 SQUADRON'S WAY AHEAD OF YOU, CHARLIE, OLD BOY.
JUST OUR LUCK, THE WORLD'S MOST DANGEROUS SUPER-SPY TURNS OUT TO BE A DOUBLE AGENT...
WHICH MAKES THIS SPYRAL'S PROBLEM, NOT OURS, I'D HAVE THOUGHT.
I'M HAPPY TO TURN AROUND RIGHT NOW...
~sigh~
ALL RIGHT, LADS?
GOOD OLD BRITISH TOMMIES, SALT OF THE EARTH, IN MY BOOK!
WHAT'S THE CRACK AT STREET LEVEL?
WE NEED YOU TO CONFIRM HIS IDENTITY...
AS SOON AS WE KNOW FOR SURE IT'S DEDALUS, YOU HAVE TO MAKE SURE HE NEVER LEAVES.
THIS IS THE MESS HE'S MADE SO FAR.
THERE'S A WAR ON AND I CAN'T SPARE ANY MORE OF MY LADS.
EVIL GENIUSES ARE YOUR DEPARTMENT, GENTLEMEN.

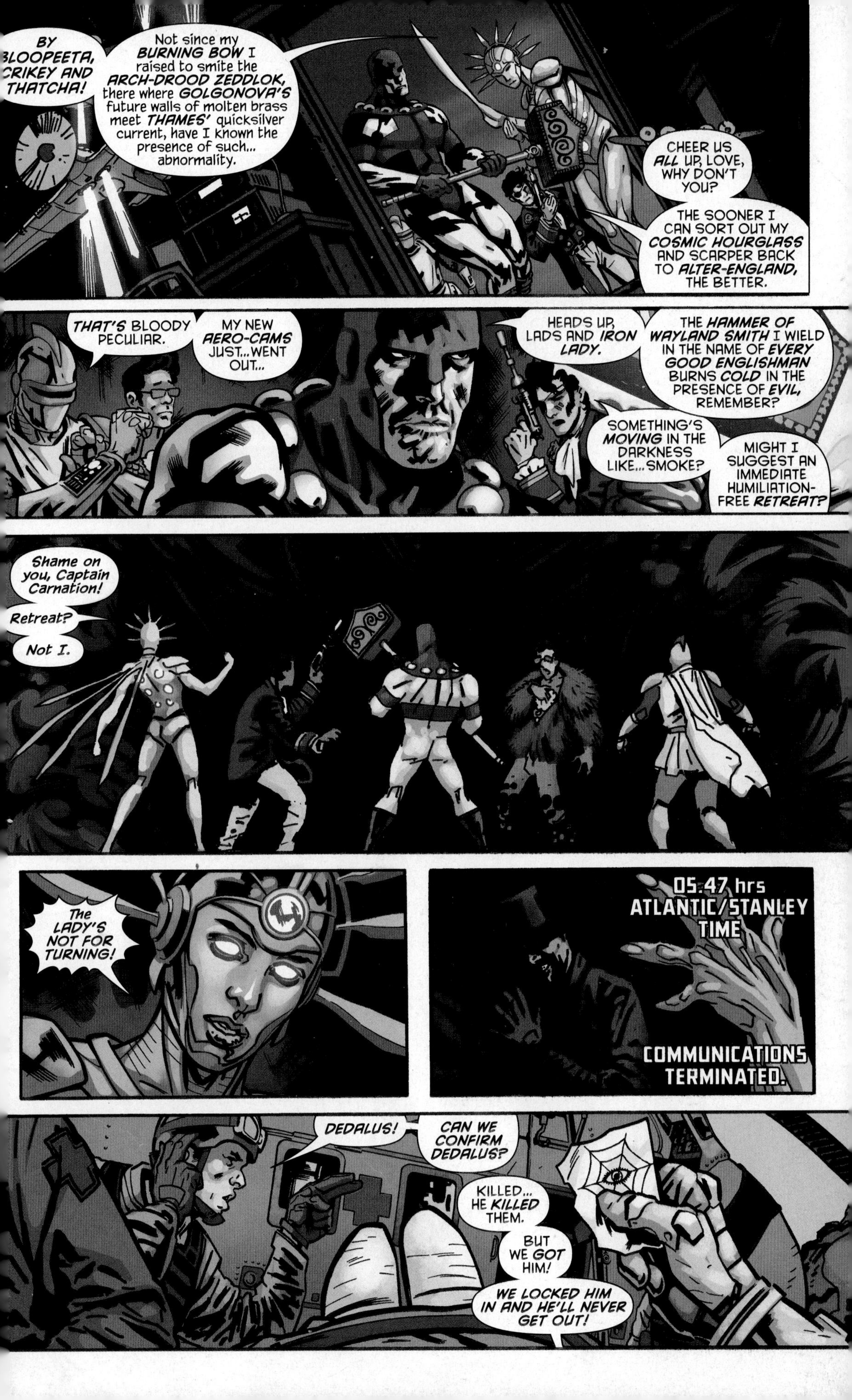

BY BLOOPEETA, CRIKEY AND THATCHA!
Not since my BURNING BOW I raised to smite the ARCH-DROOD ZEDDLOK, there where GOLGONOVA'S future walls of molten brass meet THAMES' quicksilver current, have I known the presence of such... abnormality.
CHEER US ALL UP, LOVE, WHY DON'T YOU?
THE SOONER I CAN SORT OUT MY COSMIC HOURGLASS AND SCARPER BACK TO ALTER-ENGLAND, THE BETTER.
THAT'S BLOODY PECULIAR.
MY NEW AERO-CAMS JUST...WENT OUT...
HEADS UP, LADS AND IRON LADY.
THE HAMMER OF WAYLAND SMITH I WIELD IN THE NAME OF EVERY GOOD ENGLISHMAN BURNS COLD IN THE PRESENCE OF EVIL, REMEMBER?
SOMETHING'S MOVING IN THE DARKNESS LIKE...SMOKE?
MIGHT I SUGGEST AN IMMEDIATE HUMILIATION-FREE RETREAT?
Shame on you, Captain Carnation!
Retreat?
Not I.
The LADY'S NOT FOR TURNING!
05:47 hrs ATLANTIC/STANLEY TIME
COMMUNICATIONS TERMINATED.
DEDALUS!
CAN WE CONFIRM DEDALUS?
KILLED... HE KILLED THEM.
BUT WE GOT HIM!
WE LOCKED HIM IN AND HE'LL NEVER GET OUT!

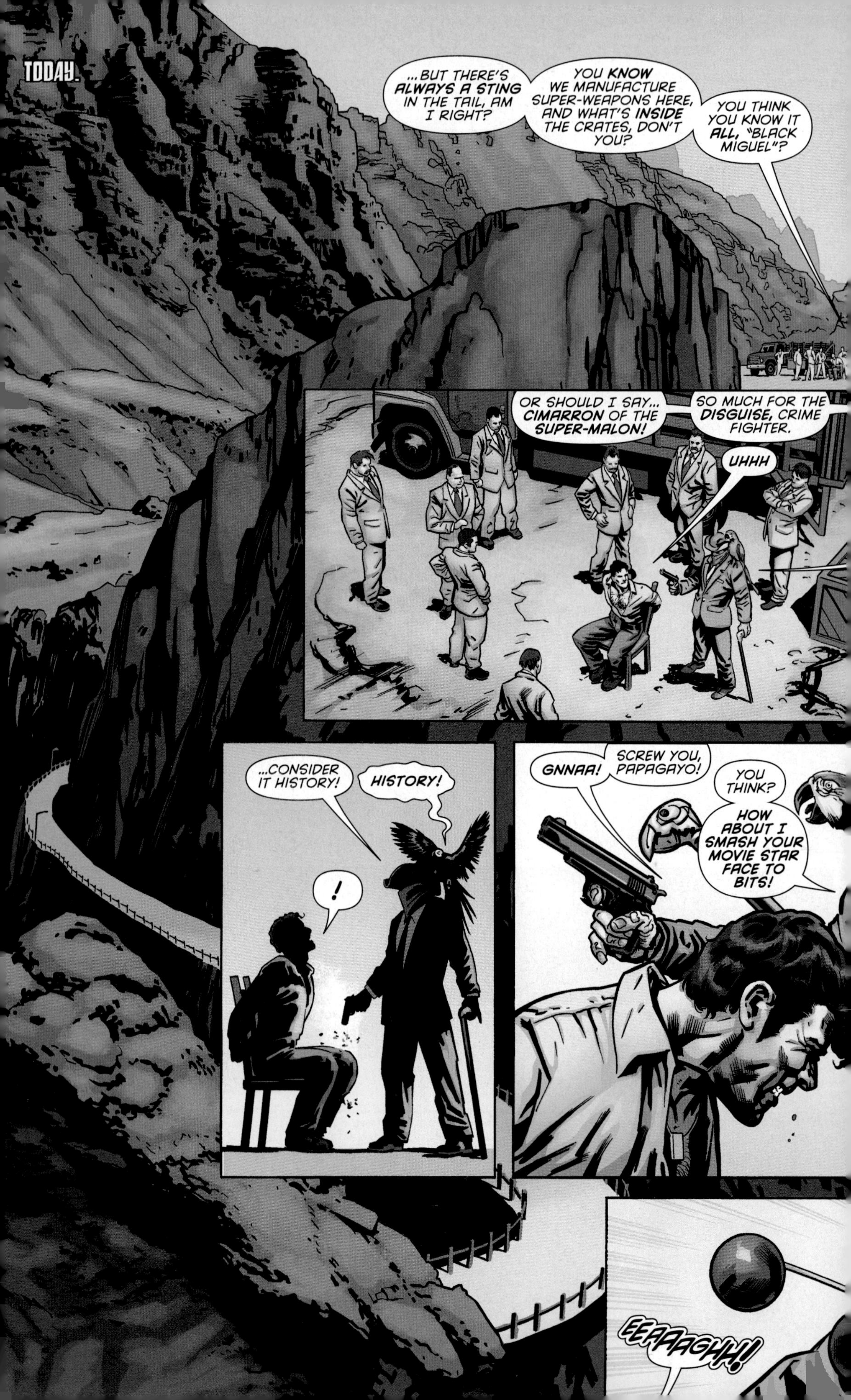

TODAY.
...BUT THERE'S ALWAYS A STING IN THE TAIL, AM I RIGHT?
YOU KNOW WE MANUFACTURE SUPER-WEAPONS HERE, AND WHAT'S INSIDE THE CRATES, DON'T YOU?
YOU THINK YOU KNOW IT ALL, "BLACK MIGUEL"?
OR SHOULD I SAY... CIMARRON OF THE SUPER-MALON!
SO MUCH FOR THE DISGUISE, CRIME FIGHTER.
UHHH
...CONSIDER IT HISTORY!
HISTORY!
!
GNNAA!
SCREW YOU, PAPAGAYO!
YOU THINK?
HOW ABOUT I SMASH YOUR MOVIE STAR FACE TO BITS!
EEAAAGHH!

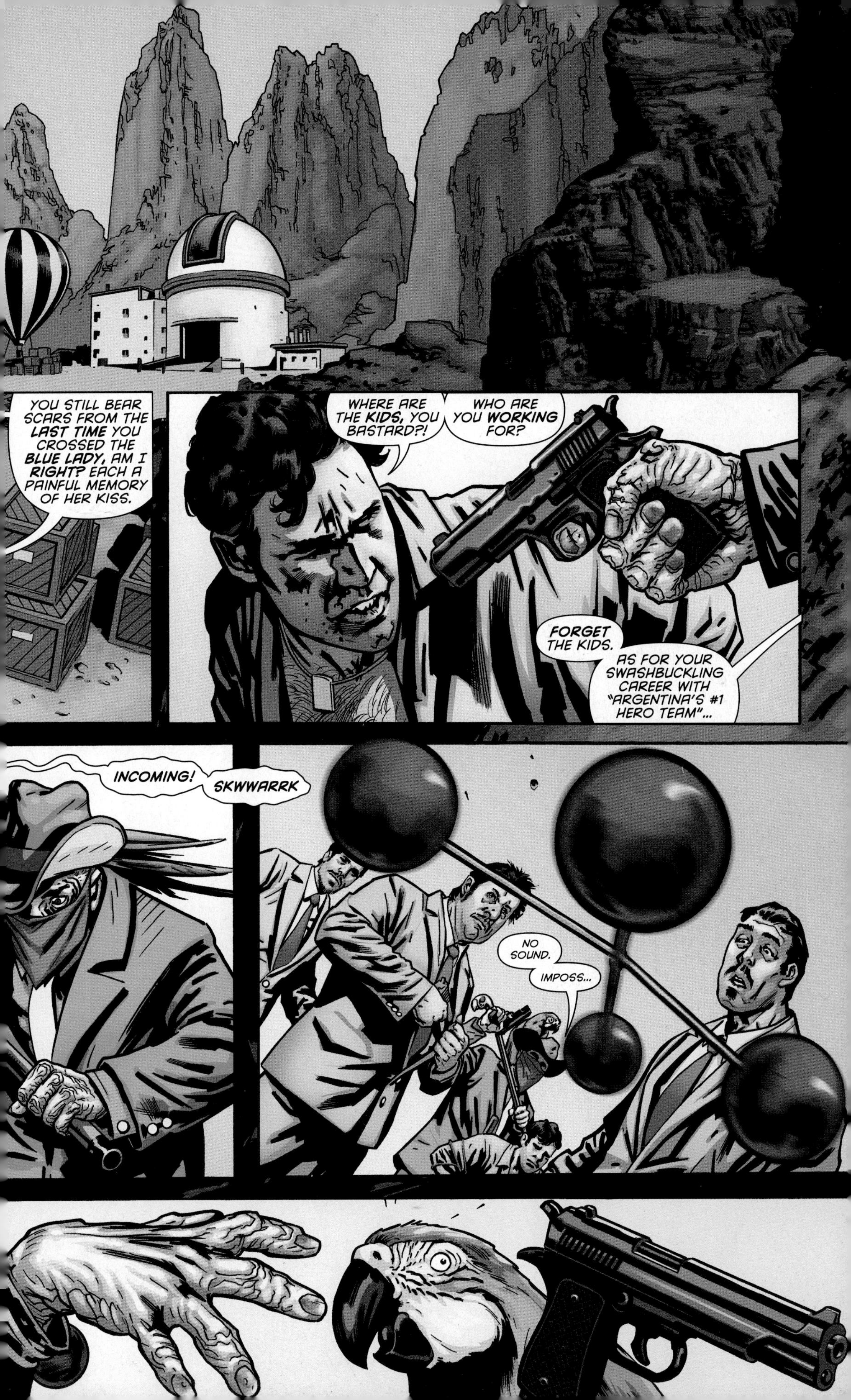
YOU STILL BEAR SCARS FROM THE LAST TIME YOU CROSSED THE BLUE LADY, AM I RIGHT? EACH A PAINFUL MEMORY OF HER KISS.
WHERE ARE THE KIDS, YOU BASTARD?!
WHO ARE YOU WORKING FOR?
FORGET THE KIDS.
AS FOR YOUR SWASHBUCKLING CAREER WITH "ARGENTINA'S #1 HERO TEAM"...
INCOMING!
SKWWARRK
NO SOUND.
IMPOSS...

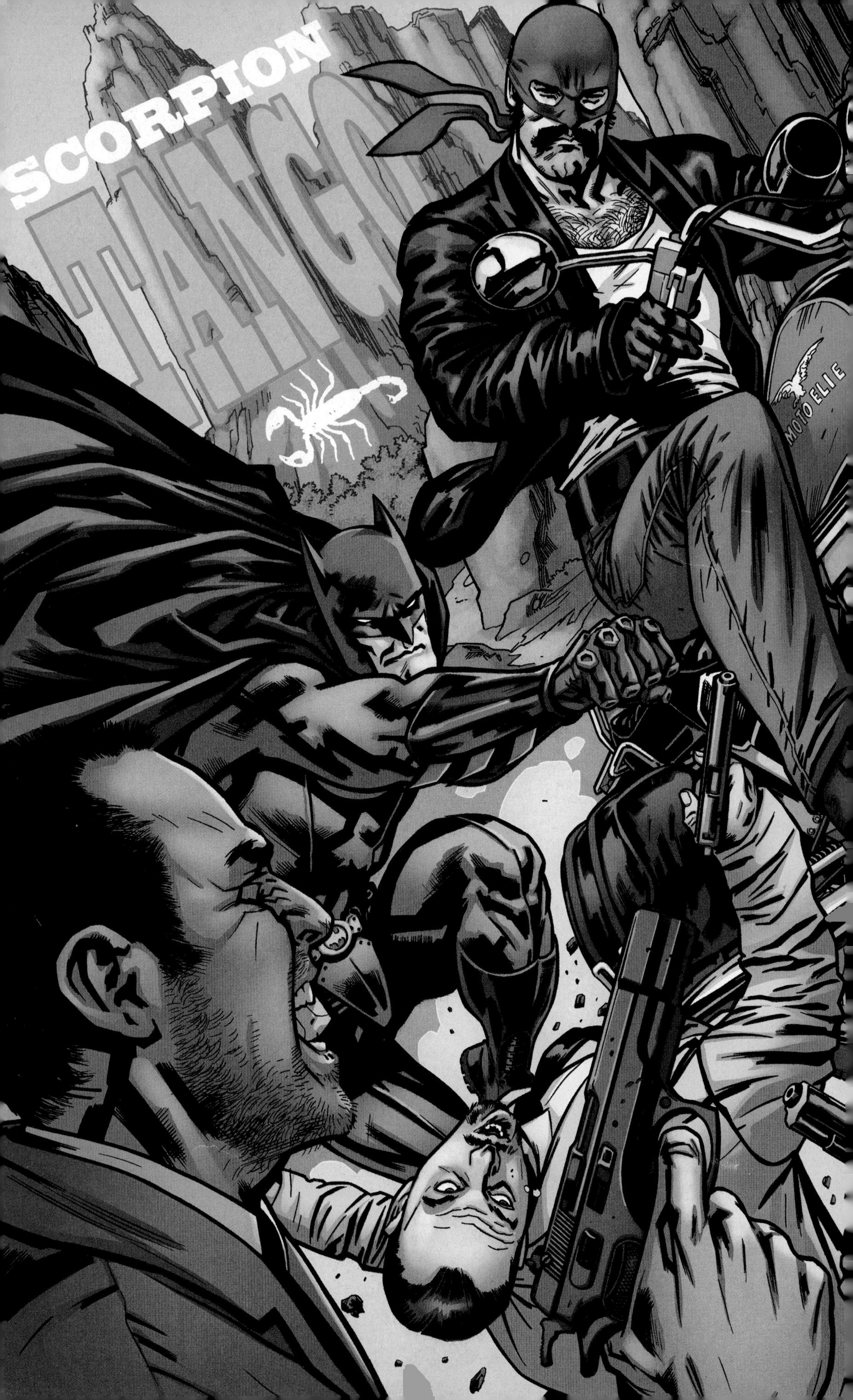
SCORPION

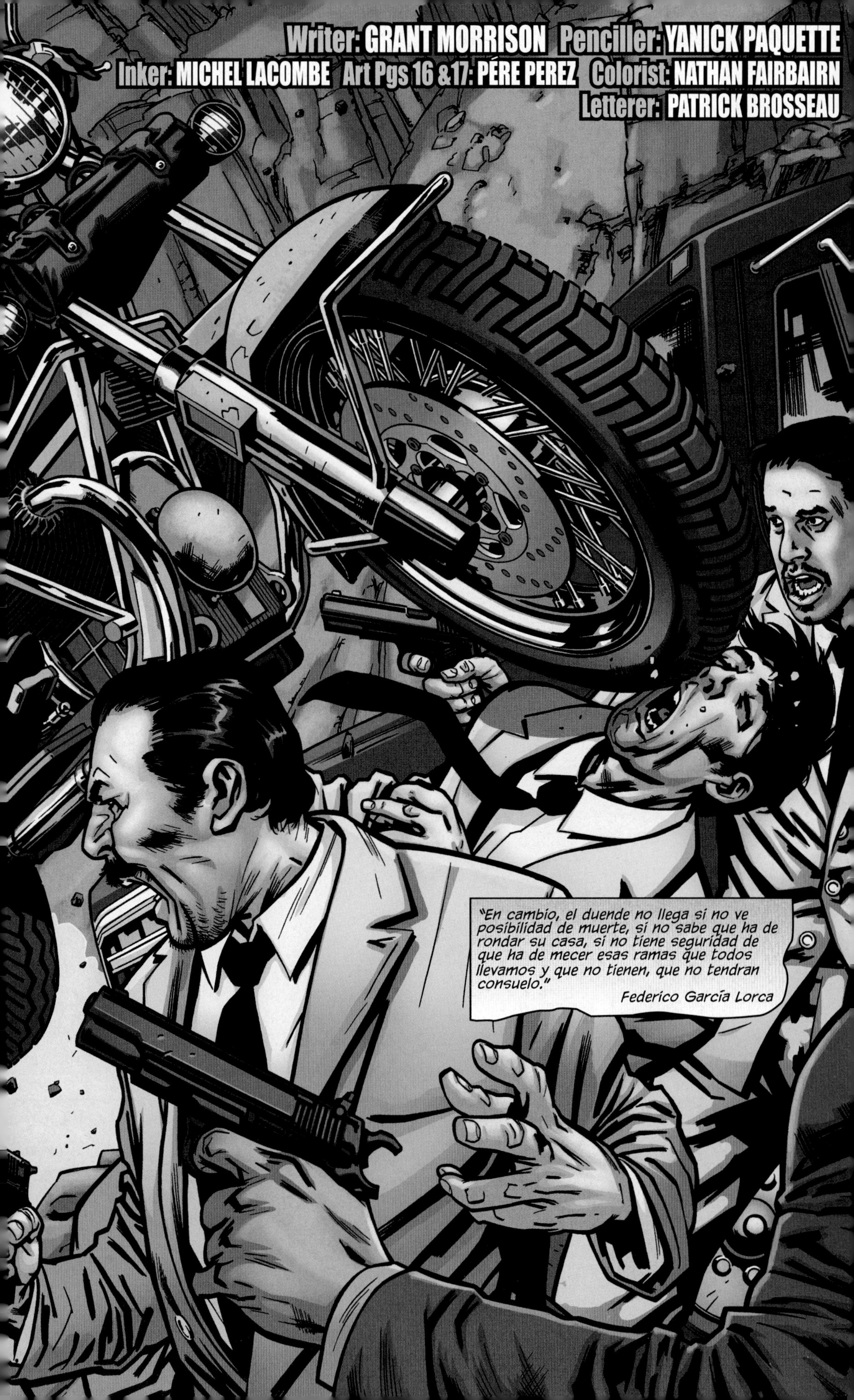
Writer: GRANT MORRISON Penciller: YANICK PAQUETTE
Inker: MICHEL LACOMBE Art Pgs 16 &17: PÉRE PEREZ Colorist: NATHAN FAIRBAIRN
Letterer: PATRICK BROSSEAU
"En cambio, el duende no llega si no ve posibilidad de muerte, si no sabe que ha de rondar su casa, si no tiene seguridad de que ha de mecer esas ramas que todos llevamos y que no tienen, que no tendran consuelo."
Federico García Lorca

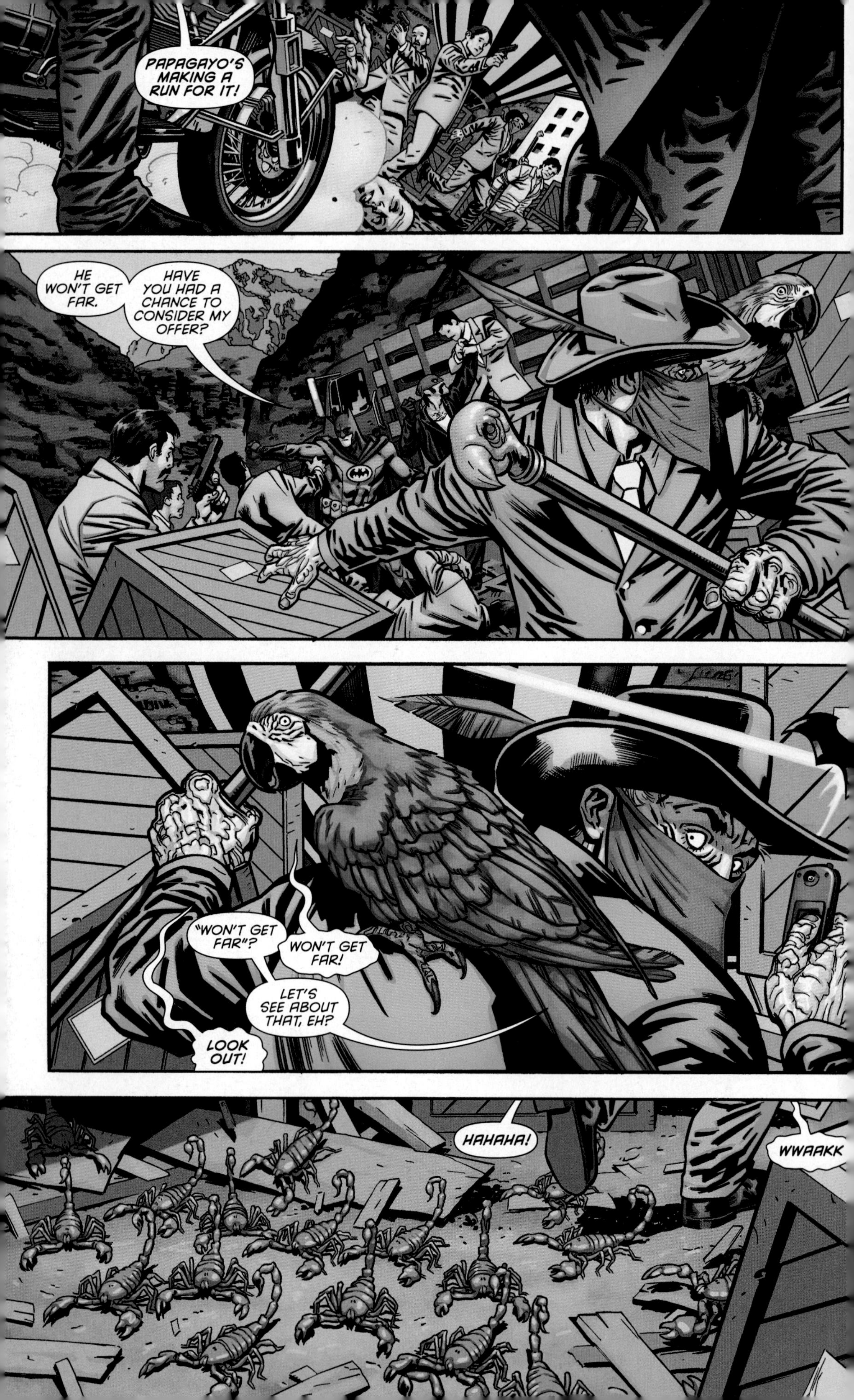
PAPAGAYO'S MAKING A RUN FOR IT!
HE WON'T GET FAR.
HAVE YOU HAD A CHANCE TO CONSIDER MY OFFER?
"WON'T GET FAR"?
WON'T GET FAR!
LET'S SEE ABOUT THAT, EH?
LOOK OUT!
HAHAHA!
WWAAKK

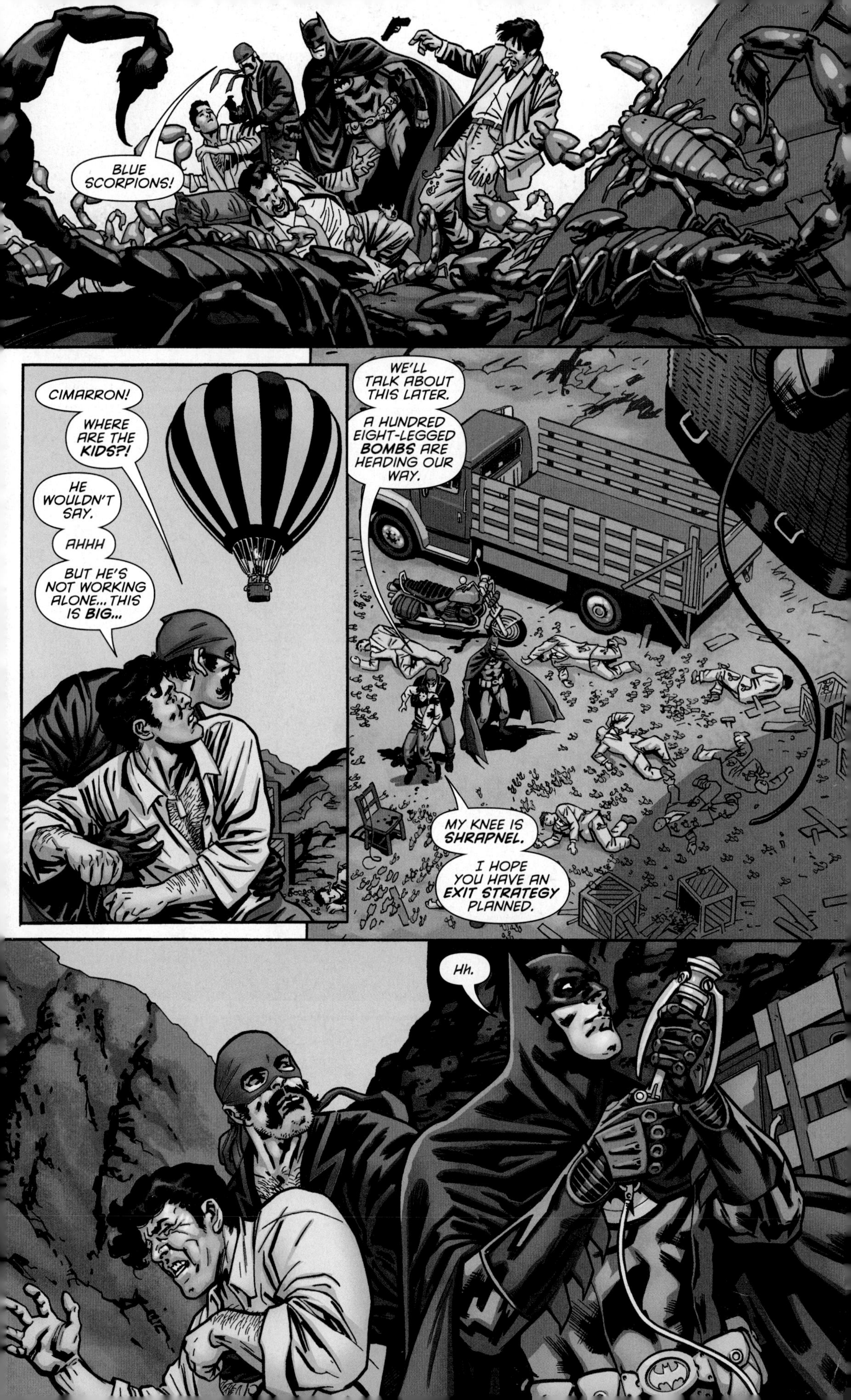
BLUE SCORPIONS!
CIMARRON!
WHERE ARE THE KIDS?!
HE WOULDN'T SAY.
AHHH
BUT HE'S NOT WORKING ALONE... THIS IS BIG...
WE'LL TALK ABOUT THIS LATER.
A HUNDRED EIGHT-LEGGED BOMBS ARE HEADING OUR WAY.
MY KNEE IS SHRAPNEL.
I HOPE YOU HAVE AN EXIT STRATEGY PLANNED.
Hh.

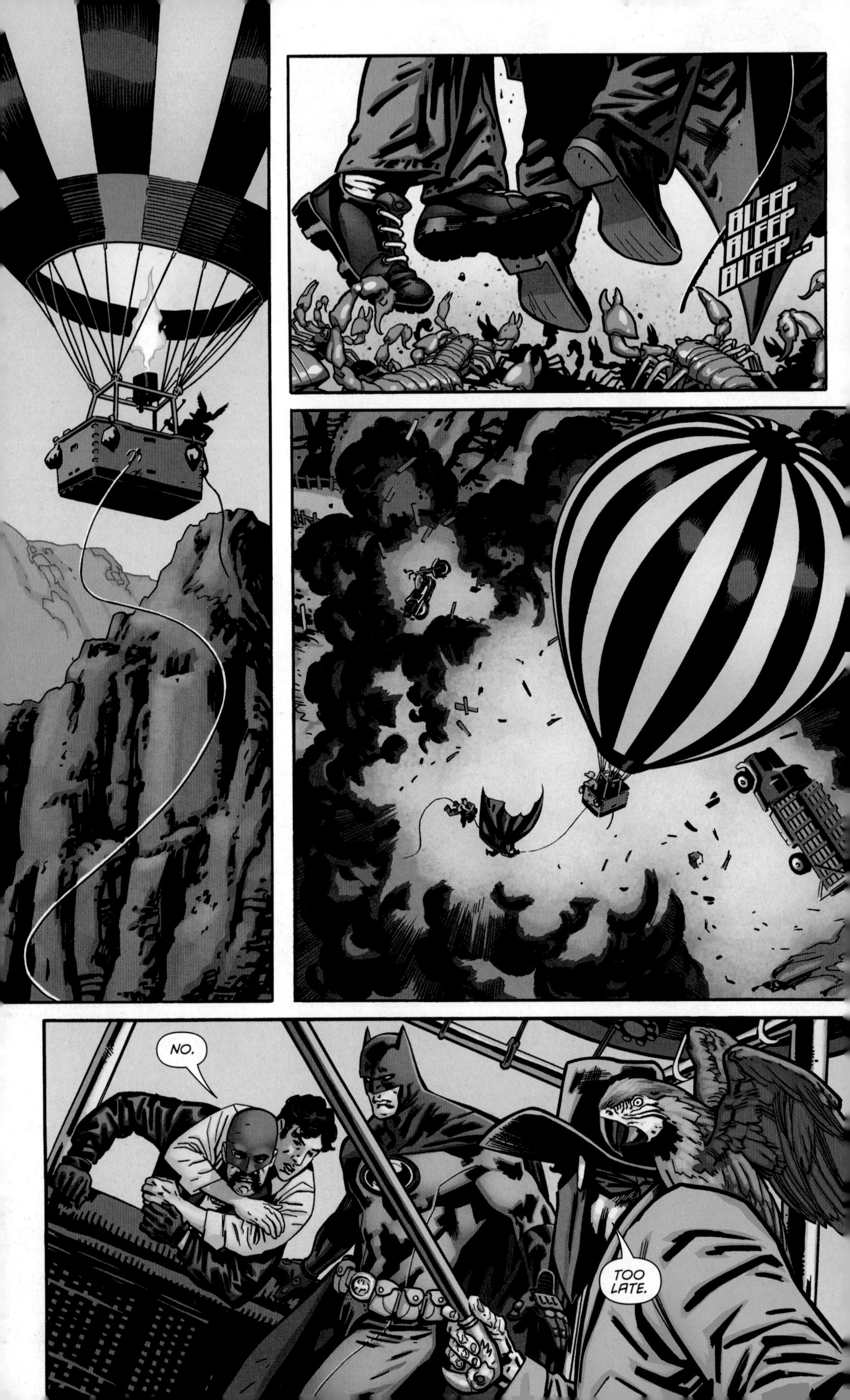
BLEEP BLEEP BLEEP...
NO.
TOO LATE.

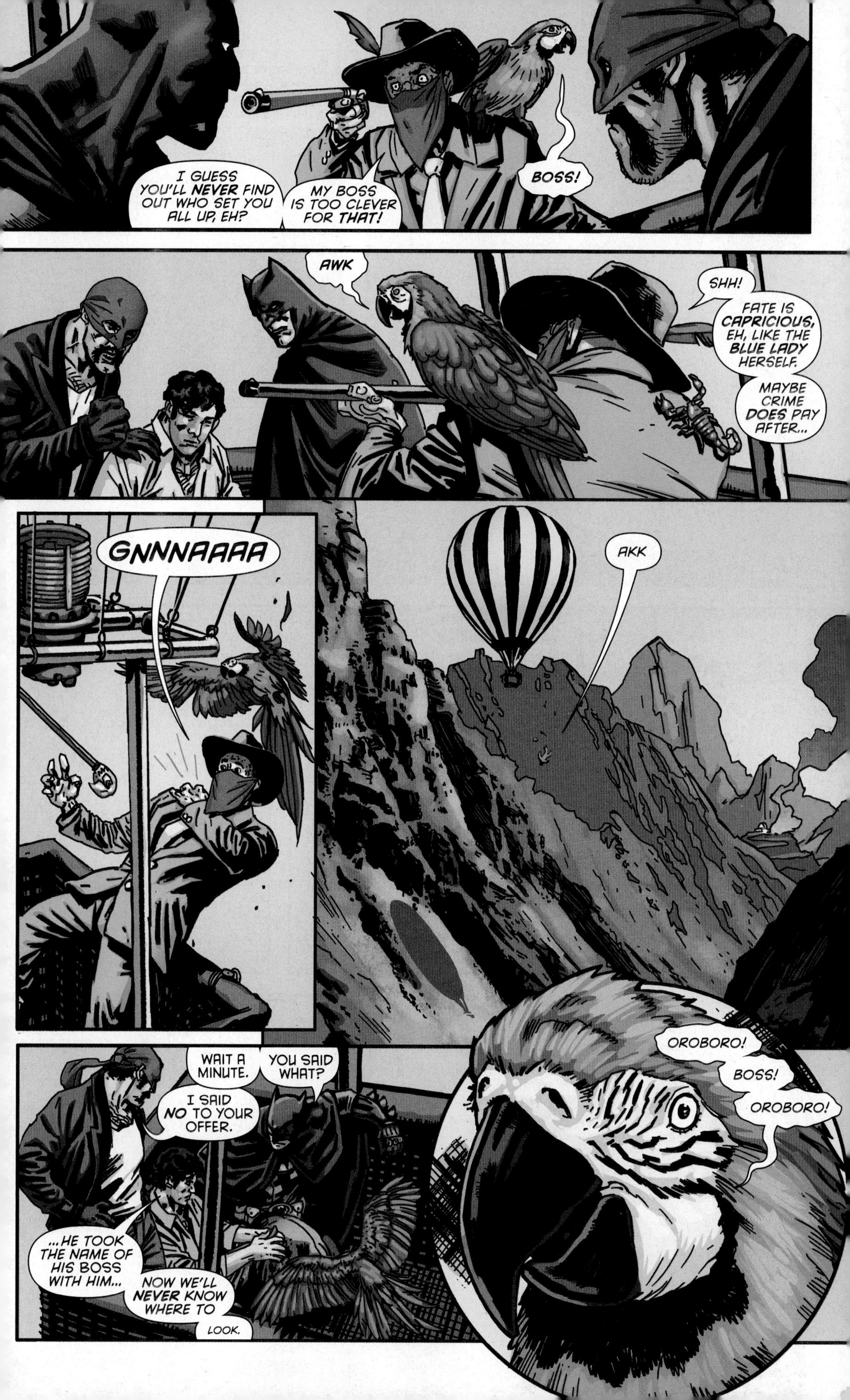
I GUESS YOU'LL NEVER FIND OUT WHO SET YOU ALL UP, EH?
MY BOSS IS TOO CLEVER FOR THAT!
BOSS!
AWK
SHH!
FATE IS CAPRICIOUS, EH, LIKE THE BLUE LADY HERSELF.
MAYBE CRIME DOES PAY AFTER...
GNNNAAAA
AKK
WAIT A MINUTE.
YOU SAID WHAT?
I SAID NO TO YOUR OFFER.
OROBORO!
BOSS!
OROBORO!
...HE TOOK THE NAME OF HIS BOSS WITH HIM...
NOW WE'LL NEVER KNOW WHERE TO
LOOK.

En Buenos Aires, en primavera, el lugar en el que hay que estar es la pista de carreras privada que hay en las espléndidas villas de don Santiago Vargas.

¡Proveedor de milagrosos caballos de carreras a príncipes, jeques y potentados, el soltero más codiciado de Buenos Aires ejerce de anfitrión a un quién es quién de gente guapa supermillonaria!

Don Santiago Vargas!

¡Extravagante!

¡Irresponsable!

¡Enigmático!

EXCUSE ME. I HAVE SOMETHING I NEED TO TAKE CARE OF.

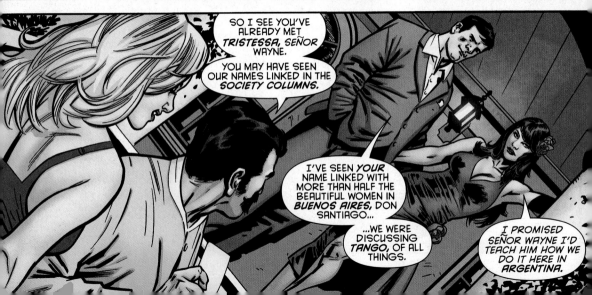

SO I SEE YOU'VE ALREADY MET *TRISTESSA*, SEÑOR *WAYNE*. YOU MAY HAVE SEEN OUR NAMES LINKED IN THE *SOCIETY COLUMNS*.

I'VE SEEN *YOUR* NAME LINKED WITH MORE THAN HALF THE BEAUTIFUL WOMEN IN *BUENOS AIRES*, DON SANTIAGO...

...WE WERE DISCUSSING *TANGO*, OF ALL THINGS.

I PROMISED SEÑOR WAYNE I'D TEACH HIM HOW WE DO IT HERE IN *ARGENTINA*.

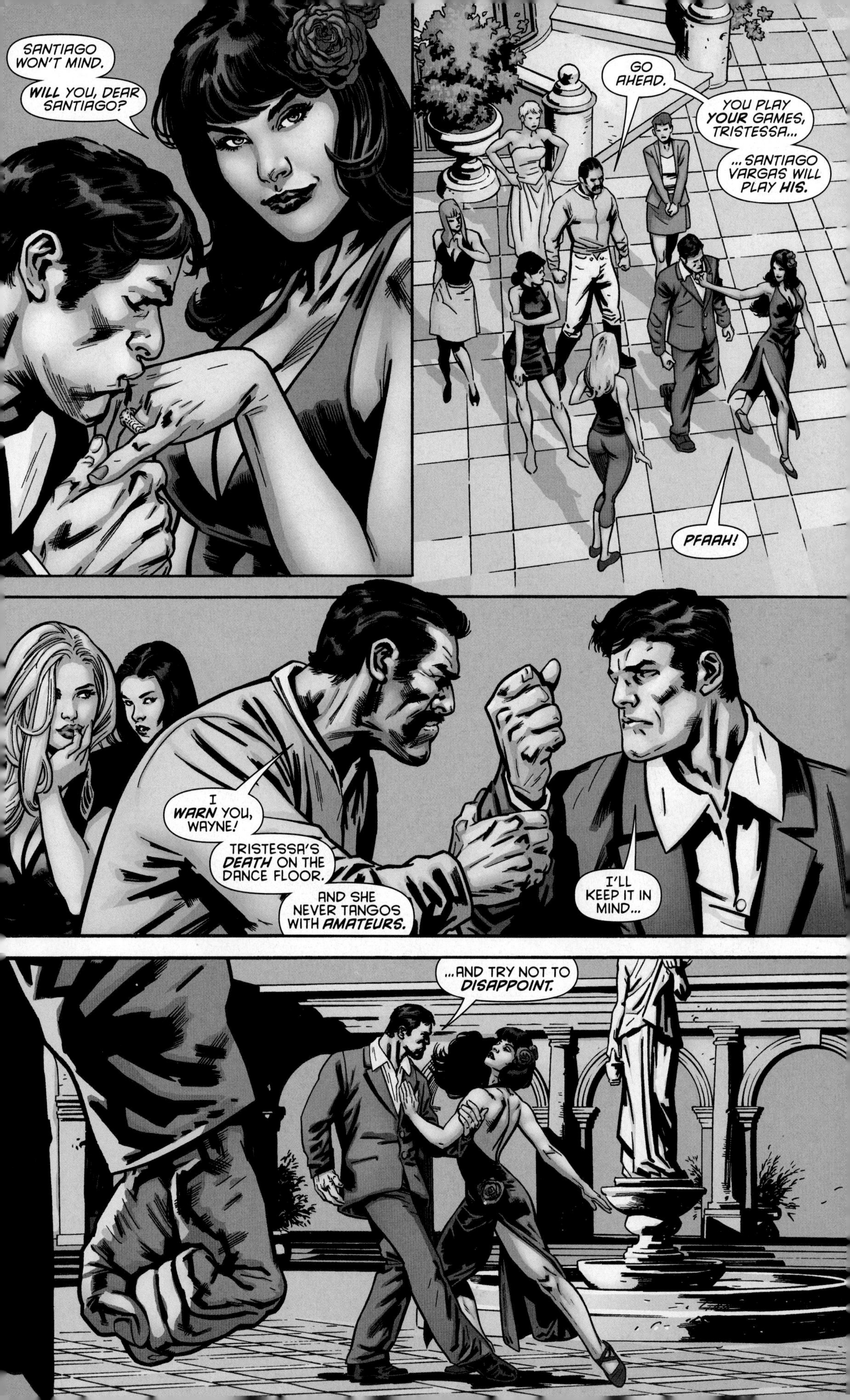
SANTIAGO WON'T MIND.
WILL YOU, DEAR SANTIAGO?
GO AHEAD.
YOU PLAY YOUR GAMES, TRISTESSA...
...SANTIAGO VARGAS WILL PLAY HIS.
PFAAH!
I WARN YOU, WAYNE!
TRISTESSA'S DEATH ON THE DANCE FLOOR.
AND SHE NEVER TANGOS WITH AMATEURS.
I'LL KEEP IT IN MIND...
...AND TRY NOT TO DISAPPOINT.

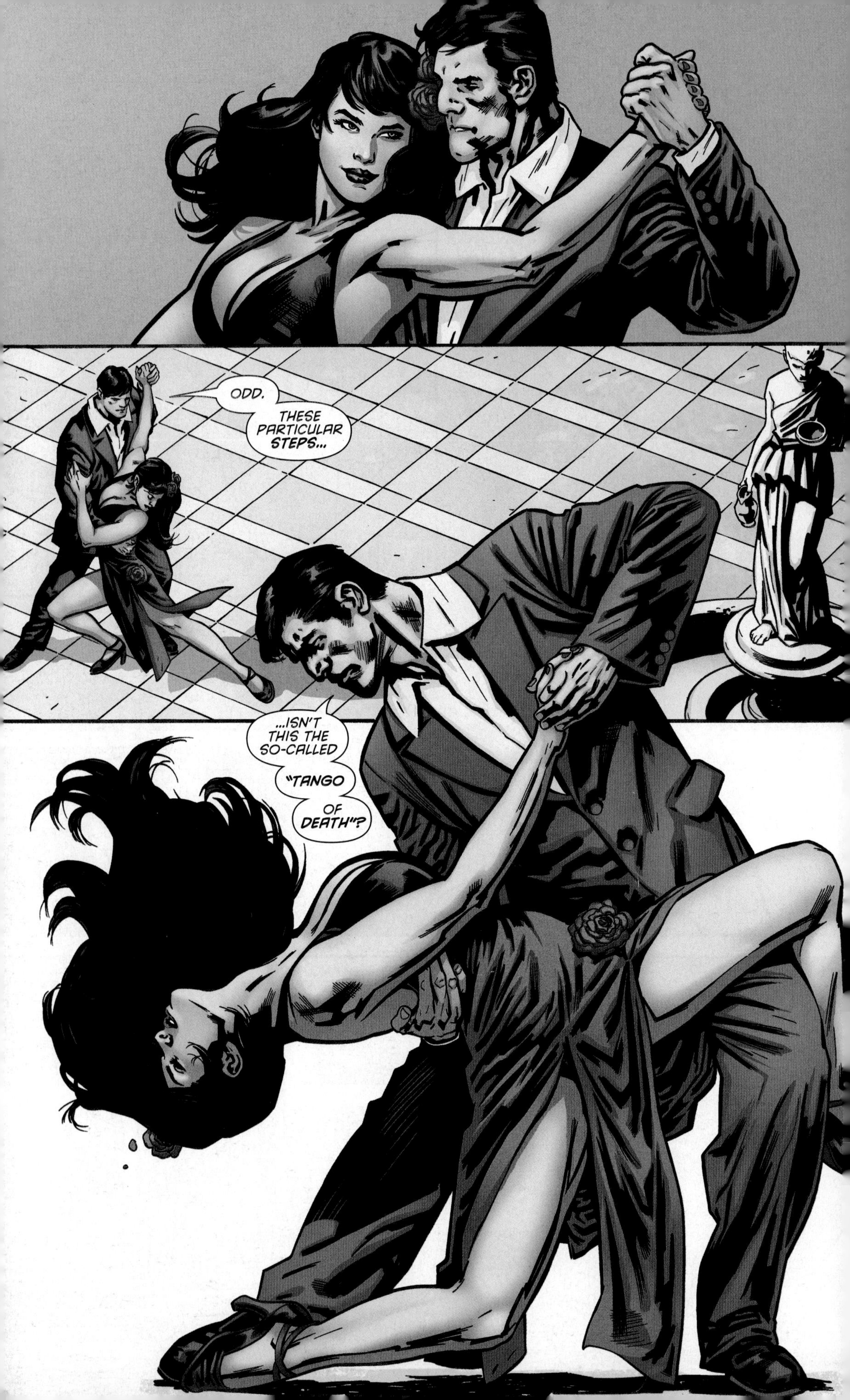
ODD.
THESE PARTICULAR STEPS...
...ISN'T THIS THE SO-CALLED
"TANGO
OF DEATH"?

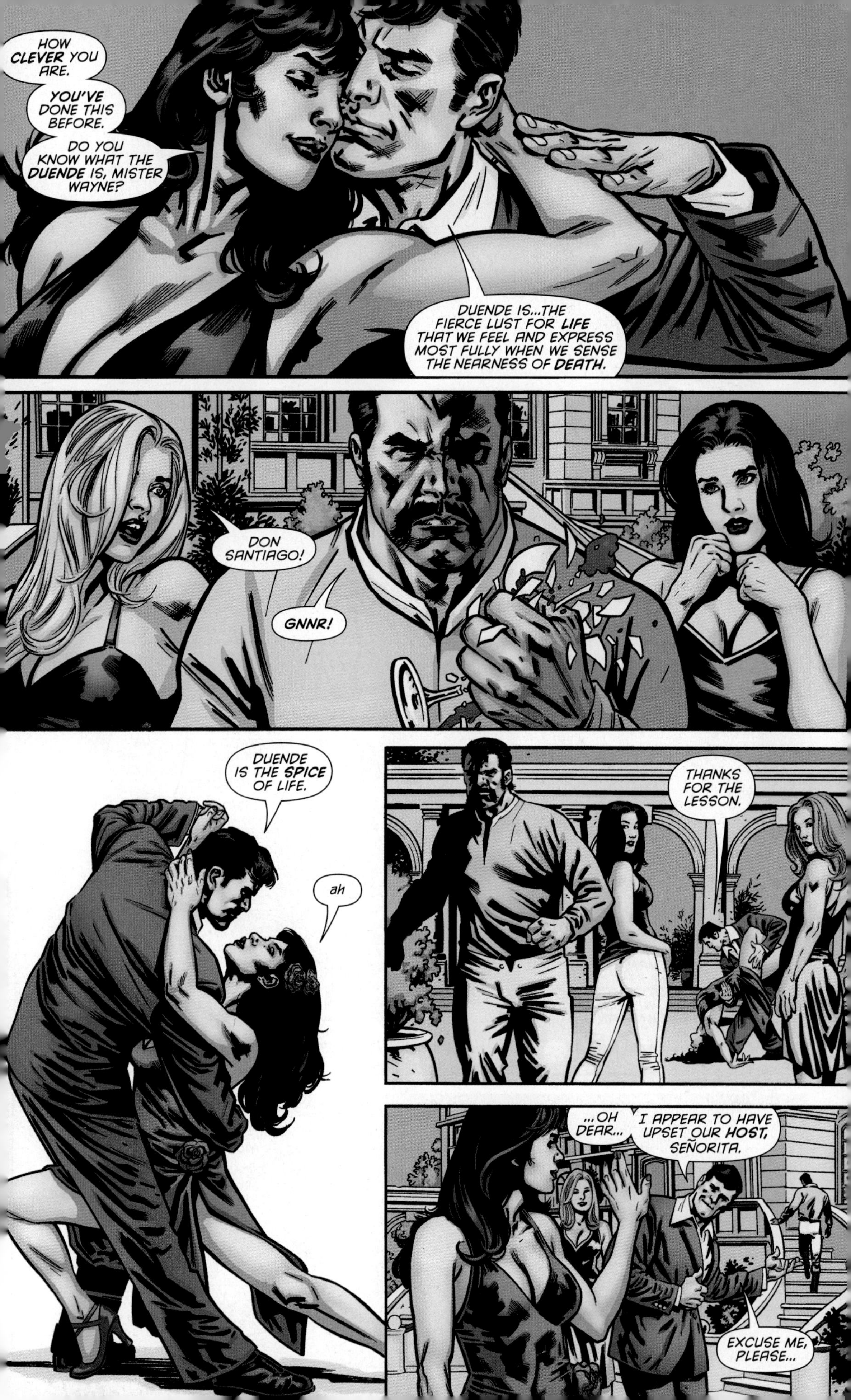
HOW CLEVER YOU ARE.
YOU'VE DONE THIS BEFORE.
DO YOU KNOW WHAT THE DUENDE IS, MISTER WAYNE?
DUENDE IS...THE FIERCE LUST FOR LIFE THAT WE FEEL AND EXPRESS MOST FULLY WHEN WE SENSE THE NEARNESS OF DEATH.
DON SANTIAGO!
GNNR!
DUENDE IS THE SPICE OF LIFE.
ah
THANKS FOR THE LESSON.
...OH DEAR...
I APPEAR TO HAVE UPSET OUR HOST, SEÑORITA.
EXCUSE ME, PLEASE...

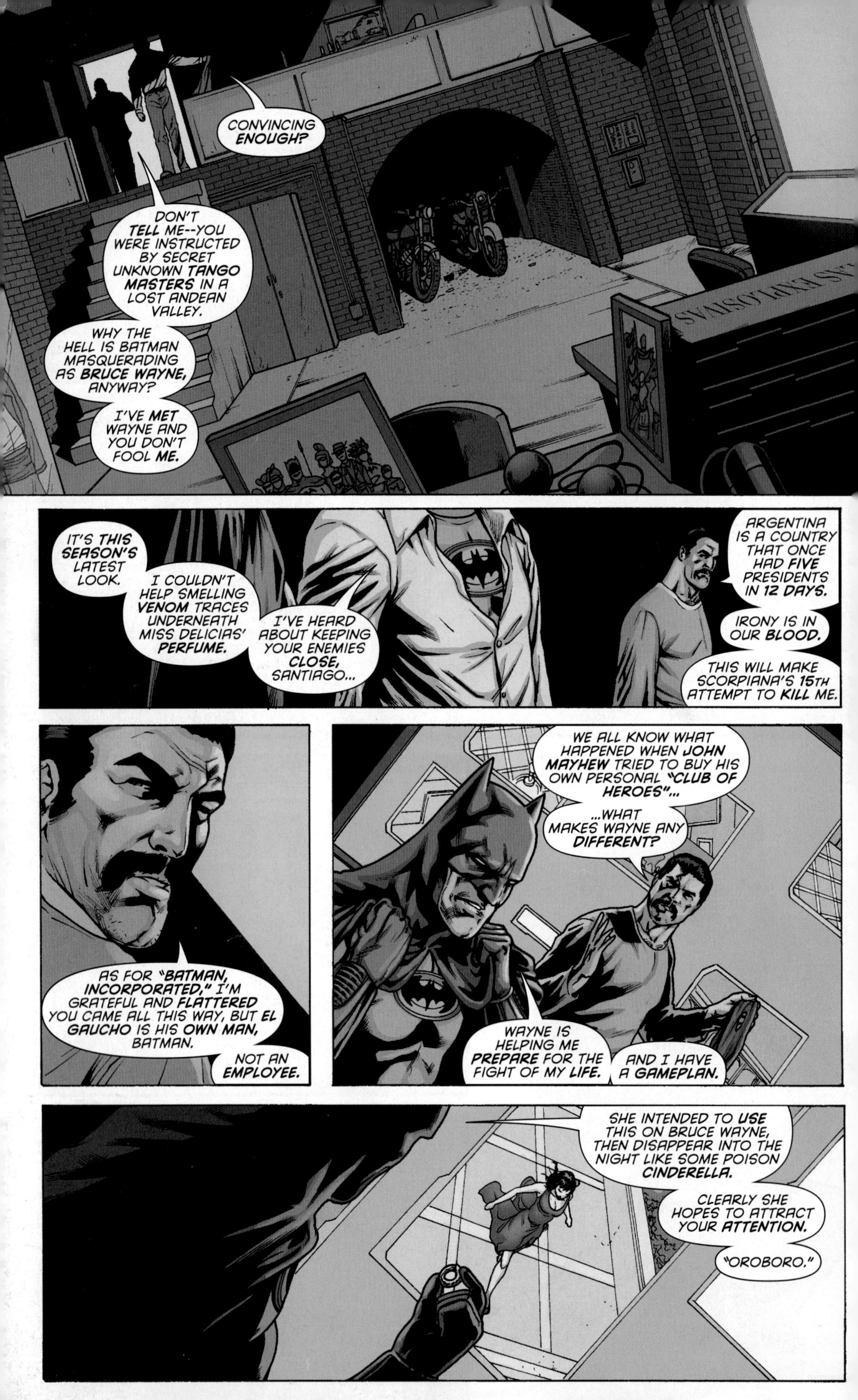
CONVINCING ENOUGH?
DON'T TELL ME--YOU WERE INSTRUCTED BY SECRET UNKNOWN TANGO MASTERS IN A LOST ANDEAN VALLEY.
WHY THE HELL IS BATMAN MASQUERADING AS BRUCE WAYNE, ANYWAY?
I'VE MET WAYNE AND YOU DON'T FOOL ME.
IT'S THIS SEASON'S LATEST LOOK.
I COULDN'T HELP SMELLING VENOM TRACES UNDERNEATH MISS DELICIAS' PERFUME.
I'VE HEARD ABOUT KEEPING YOUR ENEMIES CLOSE, SANTIAGO...
ARGENTINA IS A COUNTRY THAT ONCE HAD FIVE PRESIDENTS IN 12 DAYS.
IRONY IS IN OUR BLOOD.
THIS WILL MAKE SCORPIANA'S 15TH ATTEMPT TO KILL ME.
AS FOR "BATMAN, INCORPORATED," I'M GRATEFUL AND FLATTERED YOU CAME ALL THIS WAY, BUT EL GAUCHO IS HIS OWN MAN, BATMAN.
NOT AN EMPLOYEE.
WE ALL KNOW WHAT HAPPENED WHEN JOHN MAYHEW TRIED TO BUY HIS OWN PERSONAL "CLUB OF HEROES"...
...WHAT MAKES WAYNE ANY DIFFERENT?
WAYNE IS HELPING ME PREPARE FOR THE FIGHT OF MY LIFE.
AND I HAVE A GAMEPLAN.
SHE INTENDED TO USE THIS ON BRUCE WAYNE, THEN DISAPPEAR INTO THE NIGHT LIKE SOME POISON CINDERELLA.
CLEARLY SHE HOPES TO ATTRACT YOUR ATTENTION.
"OROBORO."

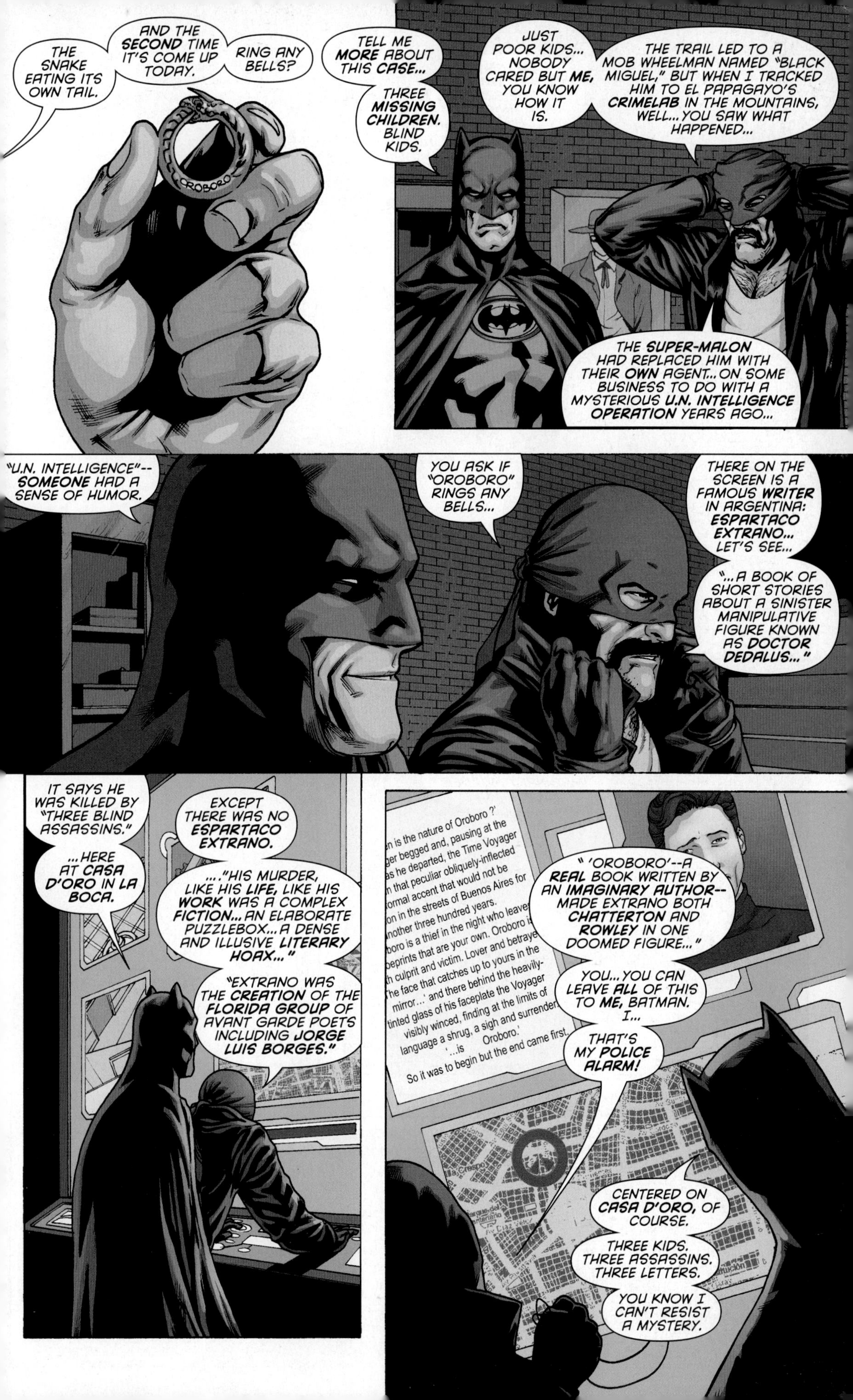

THE SNAKE EATING ITS OWN TAIL.
AND THE SECOND TIME IT'S COME UP TODAY.
RING ANY BELLS?
OROBORO
TELL ME MORE ABOUT THIS CASE...
THREE MISSING CHILDREN. BLIND KIDS.
JUST POOR KIDS... NOBODY CARED BUT ME, YOU KNOW HOW IT IS.
THE TRAIL LED TO A MOB WHEELMAN NAMED "BLACK MIGUEL," BUT WHEN I TRACKED HIM TO EL PAPAGAYO'S CRIMELAB IN THE MOUNTAINS, WELL...YOU SAW WHAT HAPPENED...
THE SUPER-MALON HAD REPLACED HIM WITH THEIR OWN AGENT...ON SOME BUSINESS TO DO WITH A MYSTERIOUS U.N. INTELLIGENCE OPERATION YEARS AGO...
"U.N. INTELLIGENCE"--SOMEONE HAD A SENSE OF HUMOR.
YOU ASK IF "OROBORO" RINGS ANY BELLS...
THERE ON THE SCREEN IS A FAMOUS WRITER IN ARGENTINA: ESPARTACO EXTRANO... LET'S SEE...
"...A BOOK OF SHORT STORIES ABOUT A SINISTER MANIPULATIVE FIGURE KNOWN AS DOCTOR DEDALUS..."
IT SAYS HE WAS KILLED BY "THREE BLIND ASSASSINS."
...HERE AT CASA D'ORO IN LA BOCA.
EXCEPT THERE WAS NO ESPARTACO EXTRANO.
..."HIS MURDER, LIKE HIS LIFE, LIKE HIS WORK WAS A COMPLEX FICTION...AN ELABORATE PUZZLEBOX...A DENSE AND ILLUSIVE LITERARY HOAX..."
"EXTRANO WAS THE CREATION OF THE FLORIDA GROUP OF AVANT GARDE POETS INCLUDING JORGE LUIS BORGES."
" 'OROBORO'--A REAL BOOK WRITTEN BY AN IMAGINARY AUTHOR--MADE EXTRANO BOTH CHATTERTON AND ROWLEY IN ONE DOOMED FIGURE..."
YOU...YOU CAN LEAVE ALL OF THIS TO ME, BATMAN. I...
THAT'S MY POLICE ALARM!
CENTERED ON CASA D'ORO, OF COURSE.
THREE KIDS. THREE ASSASSINS. THREE LETTERS.
YOU KNOW I CAN'T RESIST A MYSTERY.

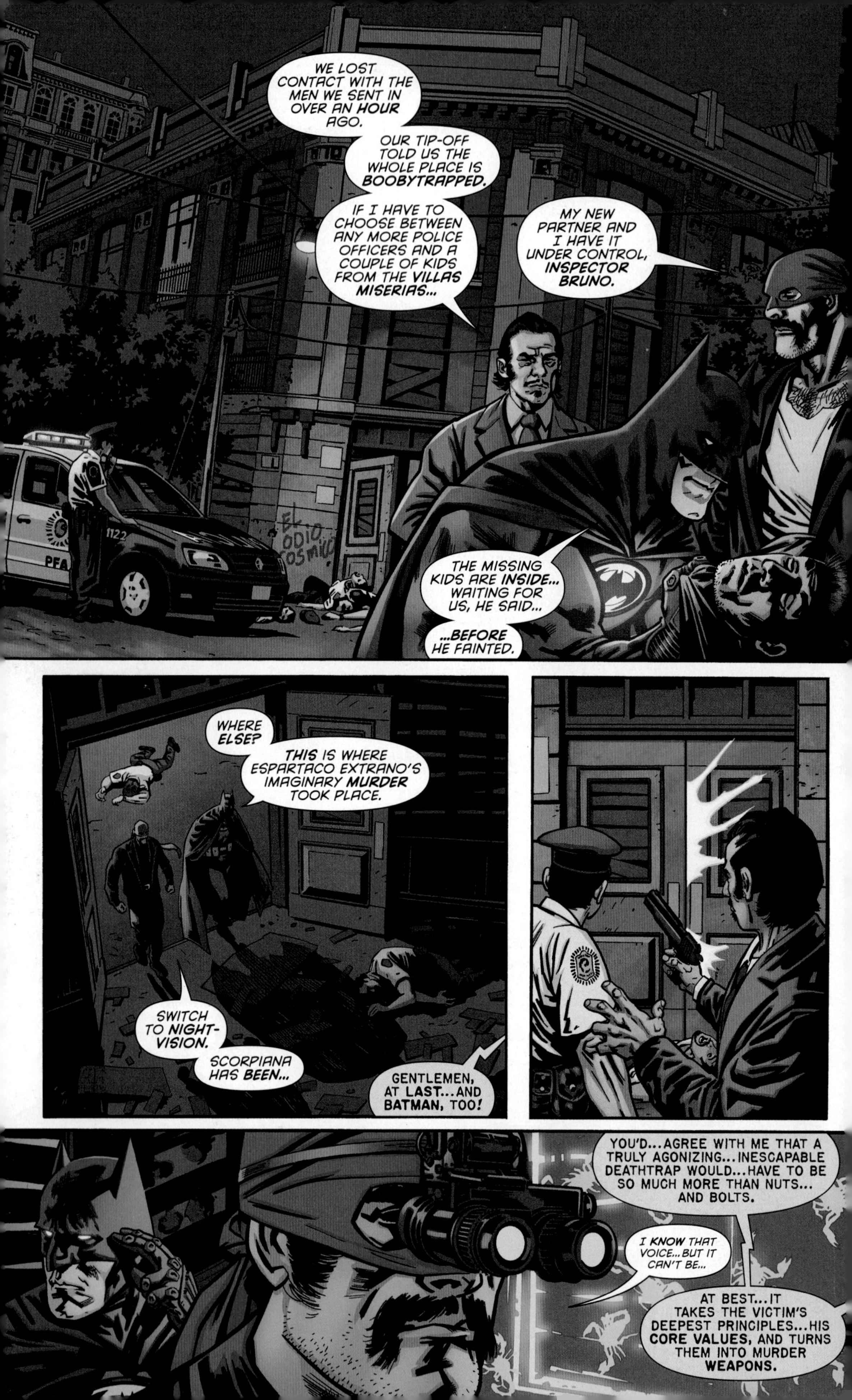

WE LOST CONTACT WITH THE MEN WE SENT IN OVER AN HOUR AGO.
OUR TIP-OFF TOLD US THE WHOLE PLACE IS BOOBYTRAPPED.
IF I HAVE TO CHOOSE BETWEEN ANY MORE POLICE OFFICERS AND A COUPLE OF KIDS FROM THE VILLAS MISERIAS...
MY NEW PARTNER AND I HAVE IT UNDER CONTROL, INSPECTOR BRUNO.
EL ODIO COSMICO
PFA
1122
THE MISSING KIDS ARE INSIDE... WAITING FOR US, HE SAID...
...BEFORE HE FAINTED.
WHERE ELSE?
THIS IS WHERE ESPARTACO EXTRANO'S IMAGINARY MURDER TOOK PLACE.
SWITCH TO NIGHT-VISION.
SCORPIANA HAS BEEN...
GENTLEMEN, AT LAST... AND BATMAN, TOO!
YOU'D... AGREE WITH ME THAT A TRULY AGONIZING... INESCAPABLE DEATHTRAP WOULD... HAVE TO BE SO MUCH MORE THAN NUTS... AND BOLTS.
I KNOW THAT VOICE... BUT IT CAN'T BE...
AT BEST... IT TAKES THE VICTIM'S DEEPEST PRINCIPLES... HIS CORE VALUES, AND TURNS THEM INTO MURDER WEAPONS.

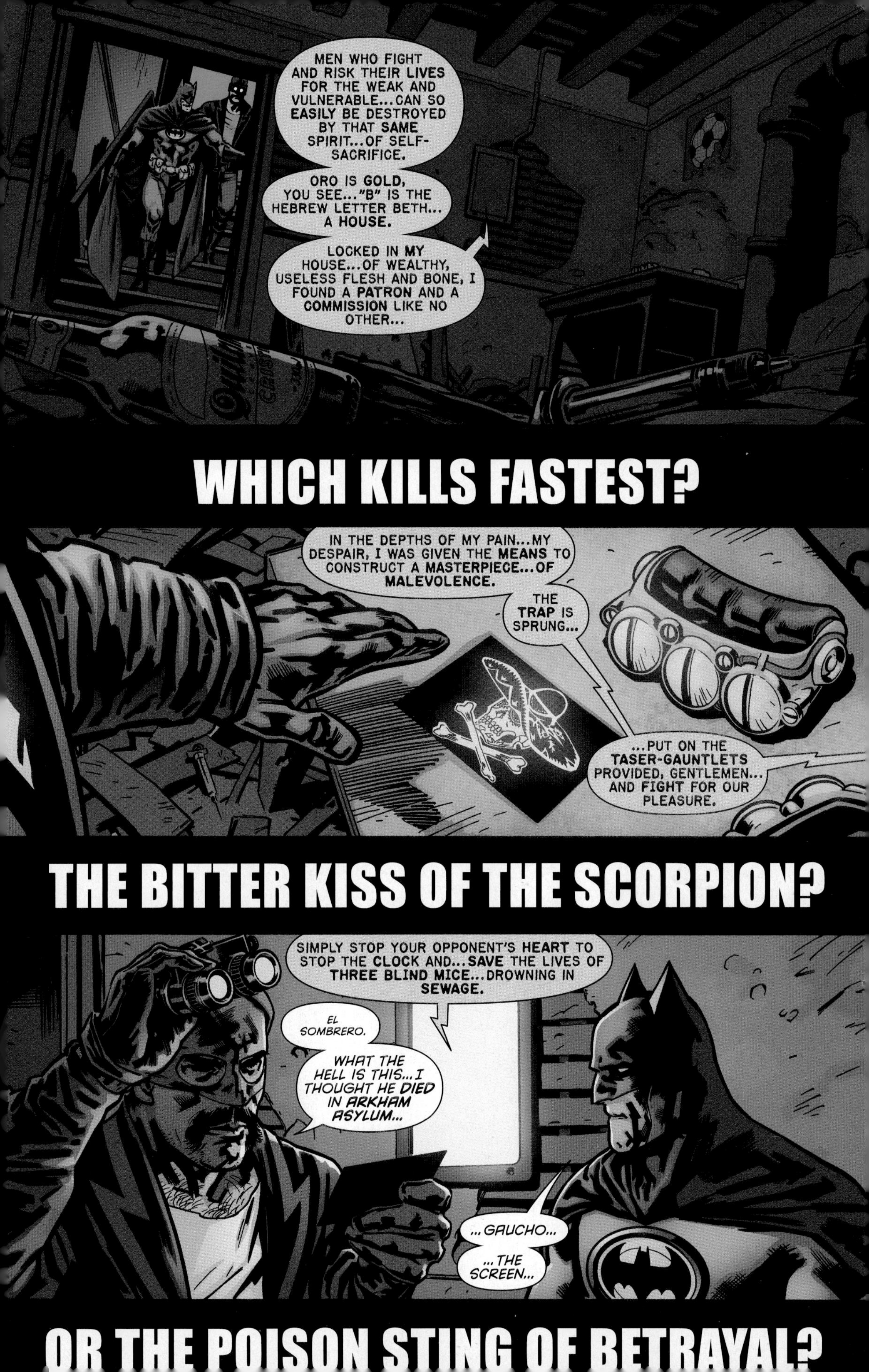
MEN WHO FIGHT AND RISK THEIR LIVES FOR THE WEAK AND VULNERABLE...CAN SO EASILY BE DESTROYED BY THAT SAME SPIRIT...OF SELF-SACRIFICE.
ORO IS GOLD, YOU SEE..."B" IS THE HEBREW LETTER BETH... A HOUSE.
LOCKED IN MY HOUSE...OF WEALTHY, USELESS FLESH AND BONE, I FOUND A PATRON AND A COMMISSION LIKE NO OTHER...
WHICH KILLS FASTEST?
IN THE DEPTHS OF MY PAIN...MY DESPAIR, I WAS GIVEN THE MEANS TO CONSTRUCT A MASTERPIECE...OF MALEVOLENCE.
THE TRAP IS SPRUNG...
...PUT ON THE TASER-GAUNTLETS PROVIDED, GENTLEMEN... AND FIGHT FOR OUR PLEASURE.
THE BITTER KISS OF THE SCORPION?
SIMPLY STOP YOUR OPPONENT'S HEART TO STOP THE CLOCK AND...SAVE THE LIVES OF THREE BLIND MICE...DROWNING IN SEWAGE.
EL SOMBRERO.
WHAT THE HELL IS THIS...I THOUGHT HE DIED IN ARKHAM ASYLUM...
...GAUCHO...
...THE SCREEN...
OR THE POISON STING OF BETRAYAL?

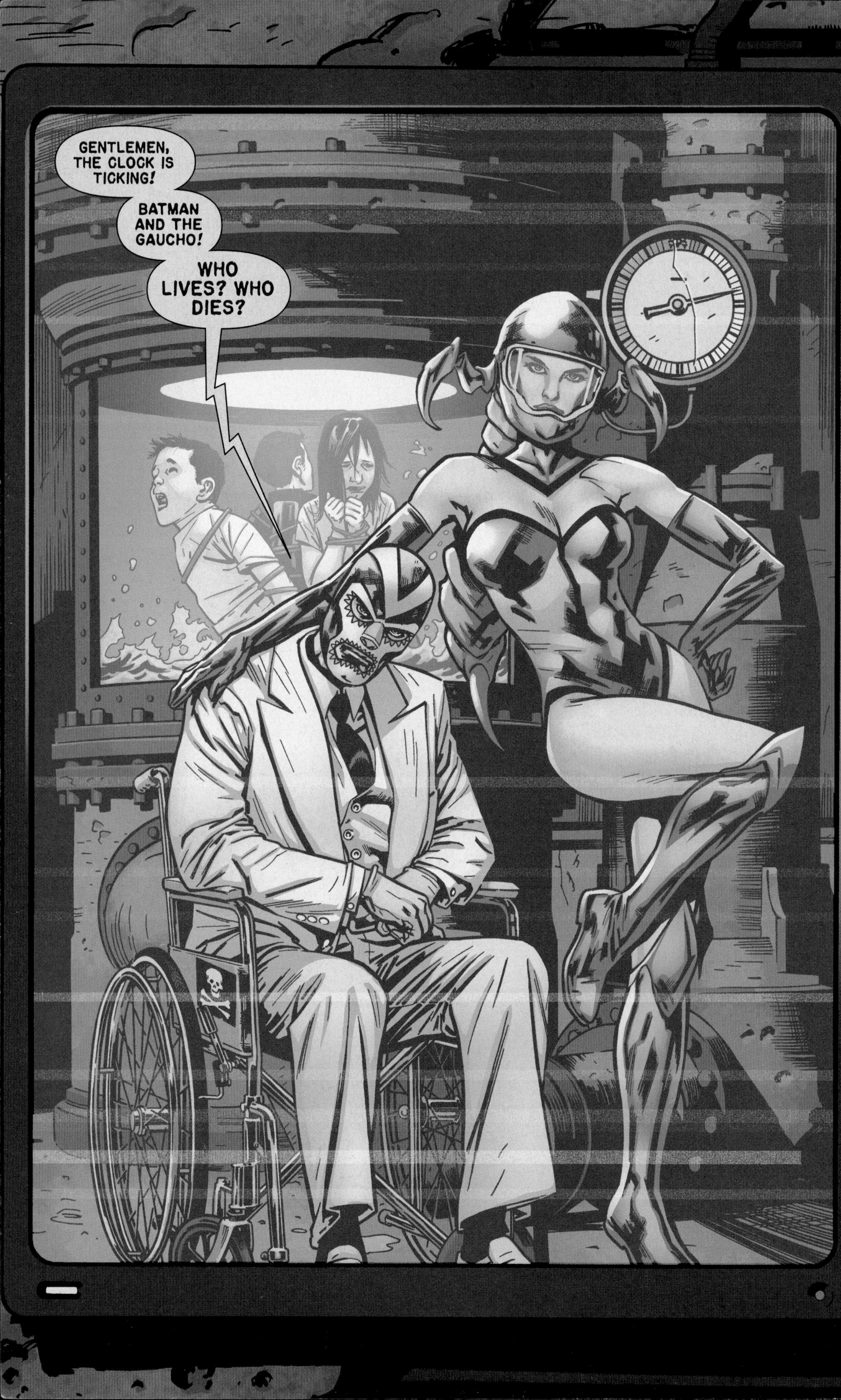
GENTLEMEN, THE CLOCK IS TICKING!
BATMAN AND THE GAUCHO!
WHO LIVES? WHO DIES?

Issue #4 cover art by **J.H. WILLIAMS III.**

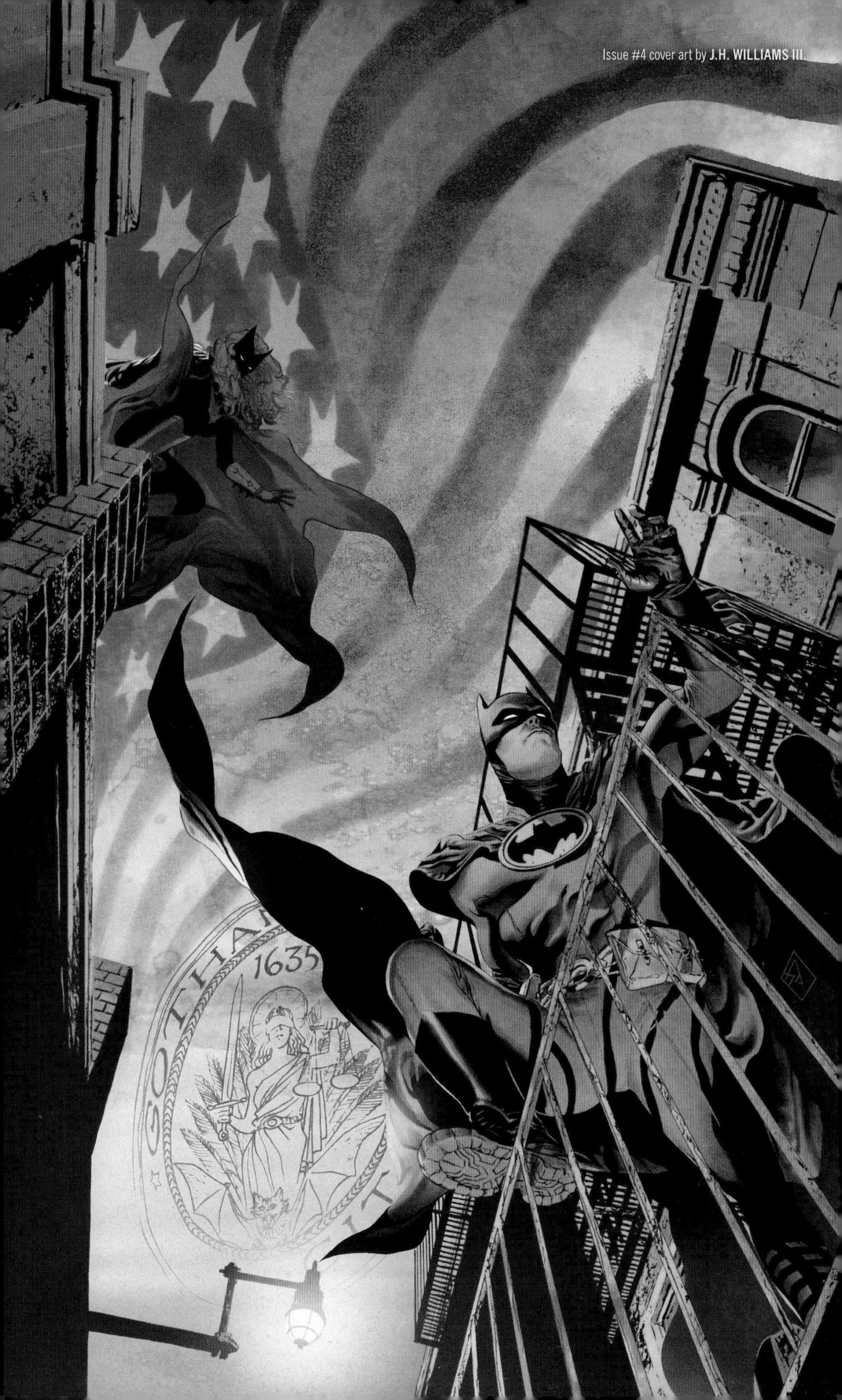
1635

Issue #4 variant cover art by YANICK PAQUETTE (color by NATHAN FAIRBAIRN).

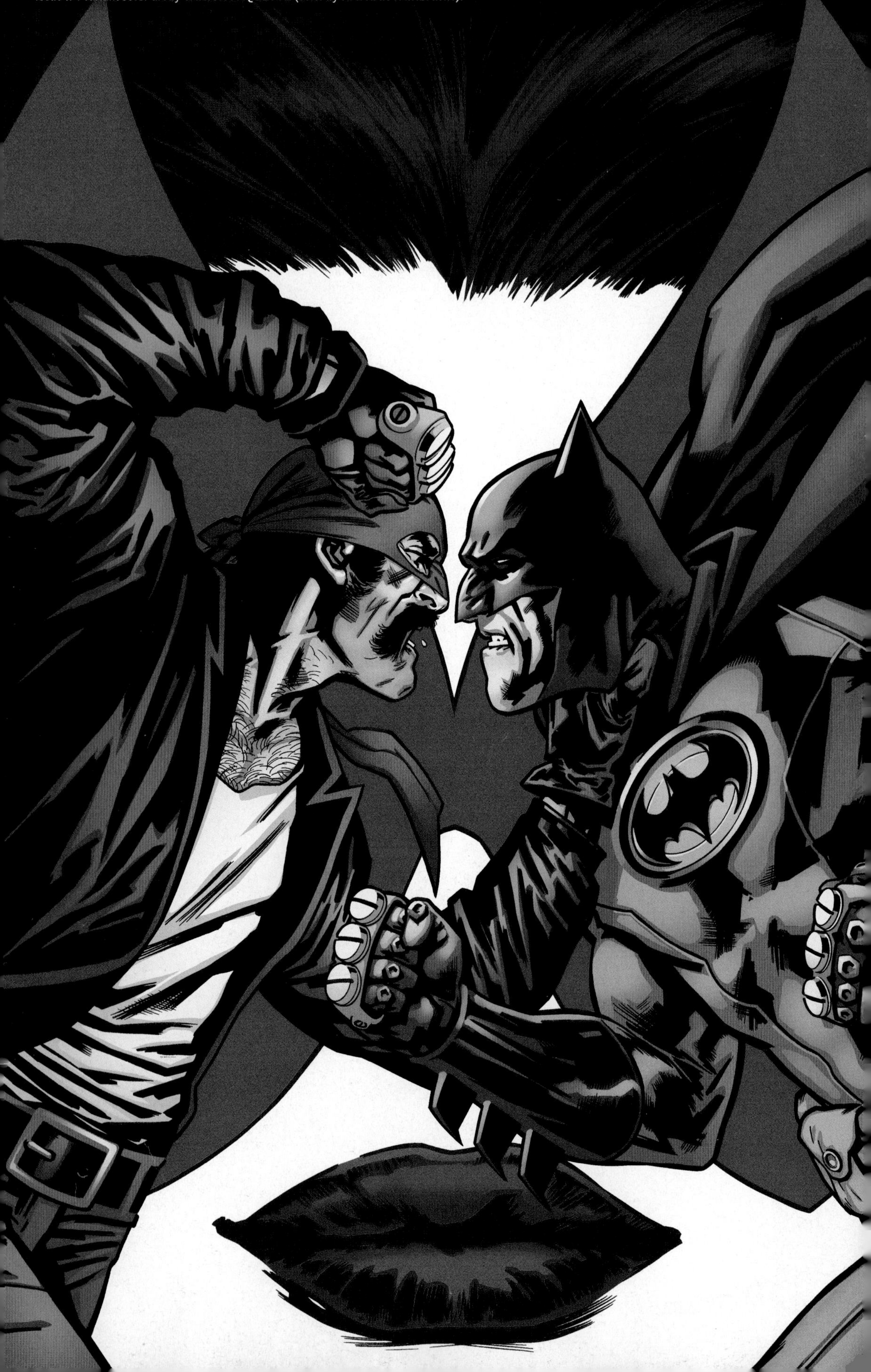

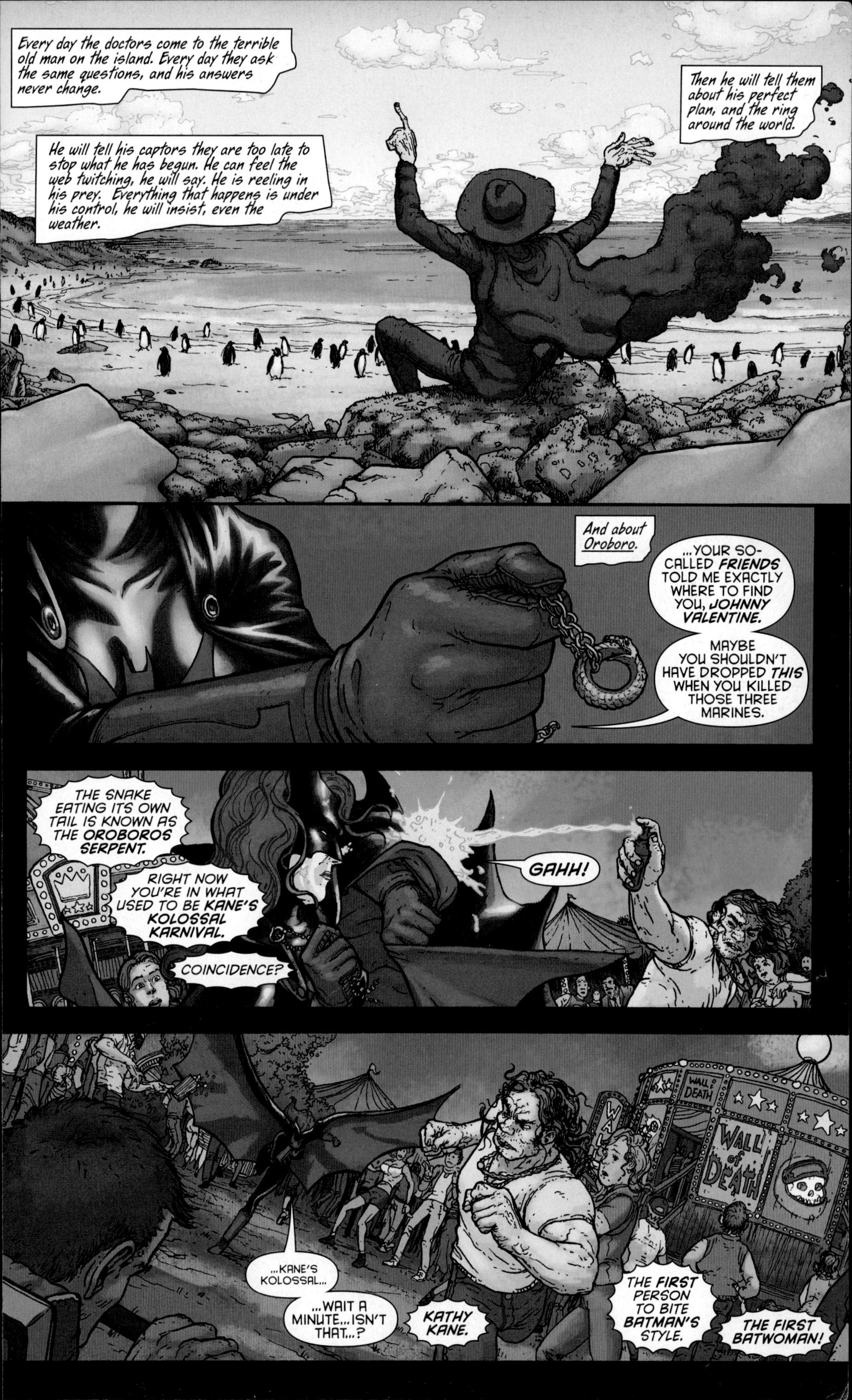

Every day the doctors come to the terrible old man on the island. Every day they ask the same questions, and his answers never change.
He will tell his captors they are too late to stop what he has begun. He can feel the web twitching, he will say. He is reeling in his prey. Everything that happens is under his control, he will insist, even the weather.
Then he will tell them about his perfect plan, and the ring around the world.
And about Oroboro.
...YOUR SO-CALLED FRIENDS TOLD ME EXACTLY WHERE TO FIND YOU, JOHNNY VALENTINE.
MAYBE YOU SHOULDN'T HAVE DROPPED THIS WHEN YOU KILLED THOSE THREE MARINES.
THE SNAKE EATING ITS OWN TAIL IS KNOWN AS THE OROBOROS SERPENT.
RIGHT NOW YOU'RE IN WHAT USED TO BE KANE'S KOLOSSAL KARNIVAL.
COINCIDENCE?
GAHH!
WALL of DEATH
...KANE'S KOLOSSAL...
...WAIT A MINUTE...ISN'T THAT...?
KATHY KANE.
THE FIRST PERSON TO BITE BATMAN'S STYLE.
THE FIRST BATWOMAN!

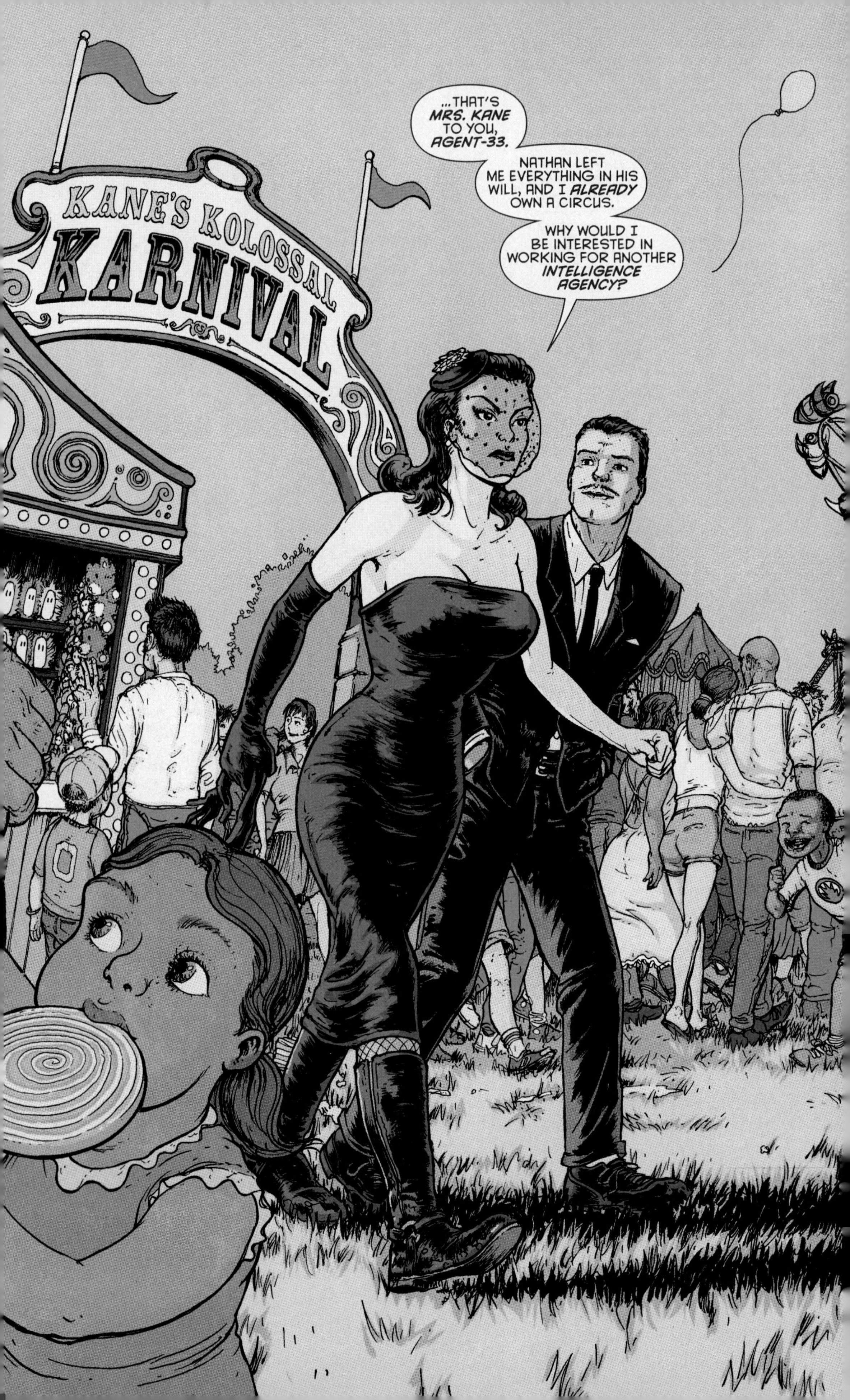
KANE'S KOLOSSAL KARNIVAL
...THAT'S MRS. KANE TO YOU, AGENT-33.
NATHAN LEFT ME EVERYTHING IN HIS WILL, AND I ALREADY OWN A CIRCUS.
WHY WOULD I BE INTERESTED IN WORKING FOR ANOTHER INTELLIGENCE AGENCY?

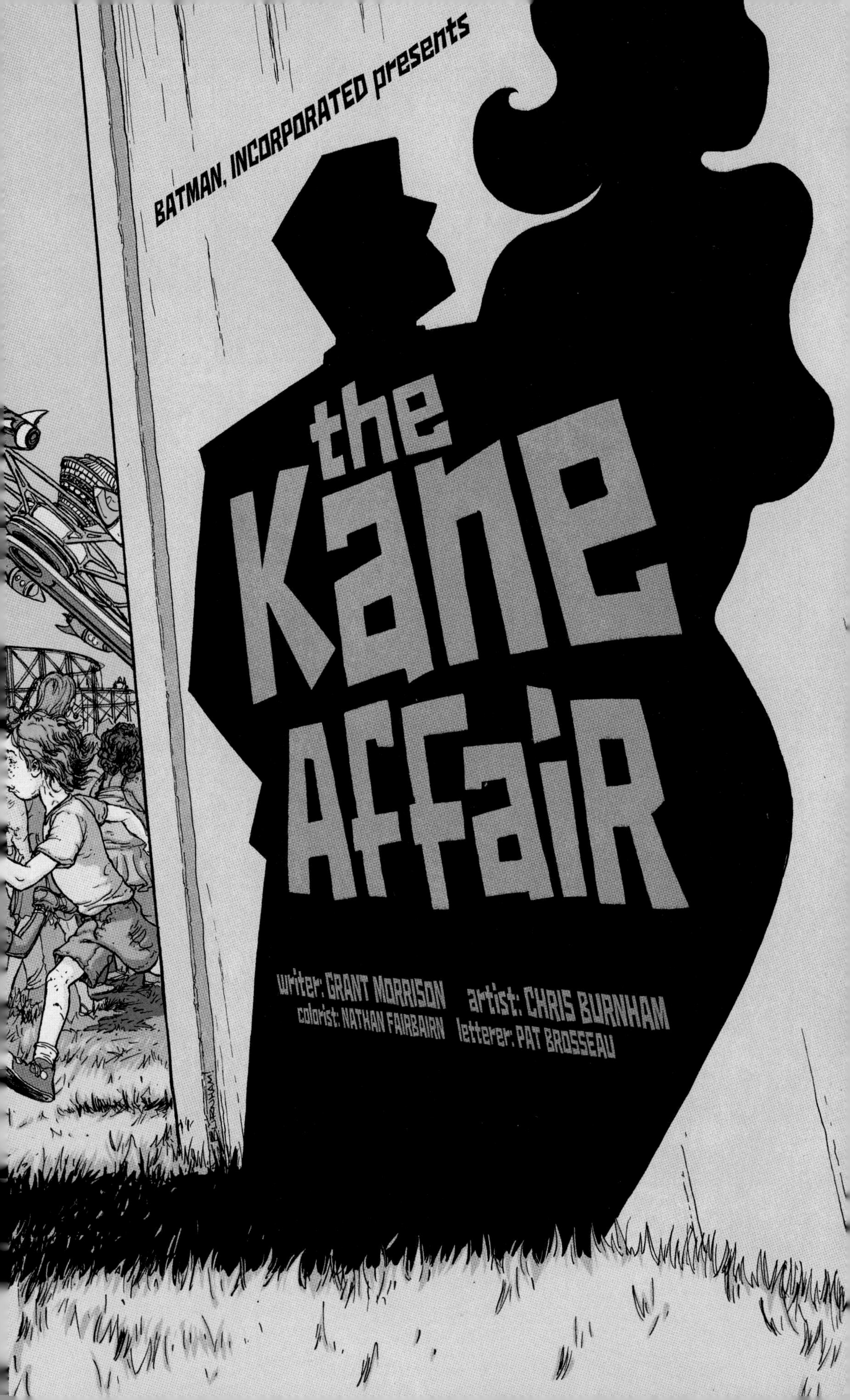
BATMAN, INCORPORATED presents
the Kane Affair
writer: GRANT MORRISON artist: CHRIS BURNHAM
colorist: NATHAN FAIRBAIRN letterer: PAT BROSSEAU
BURNHAM

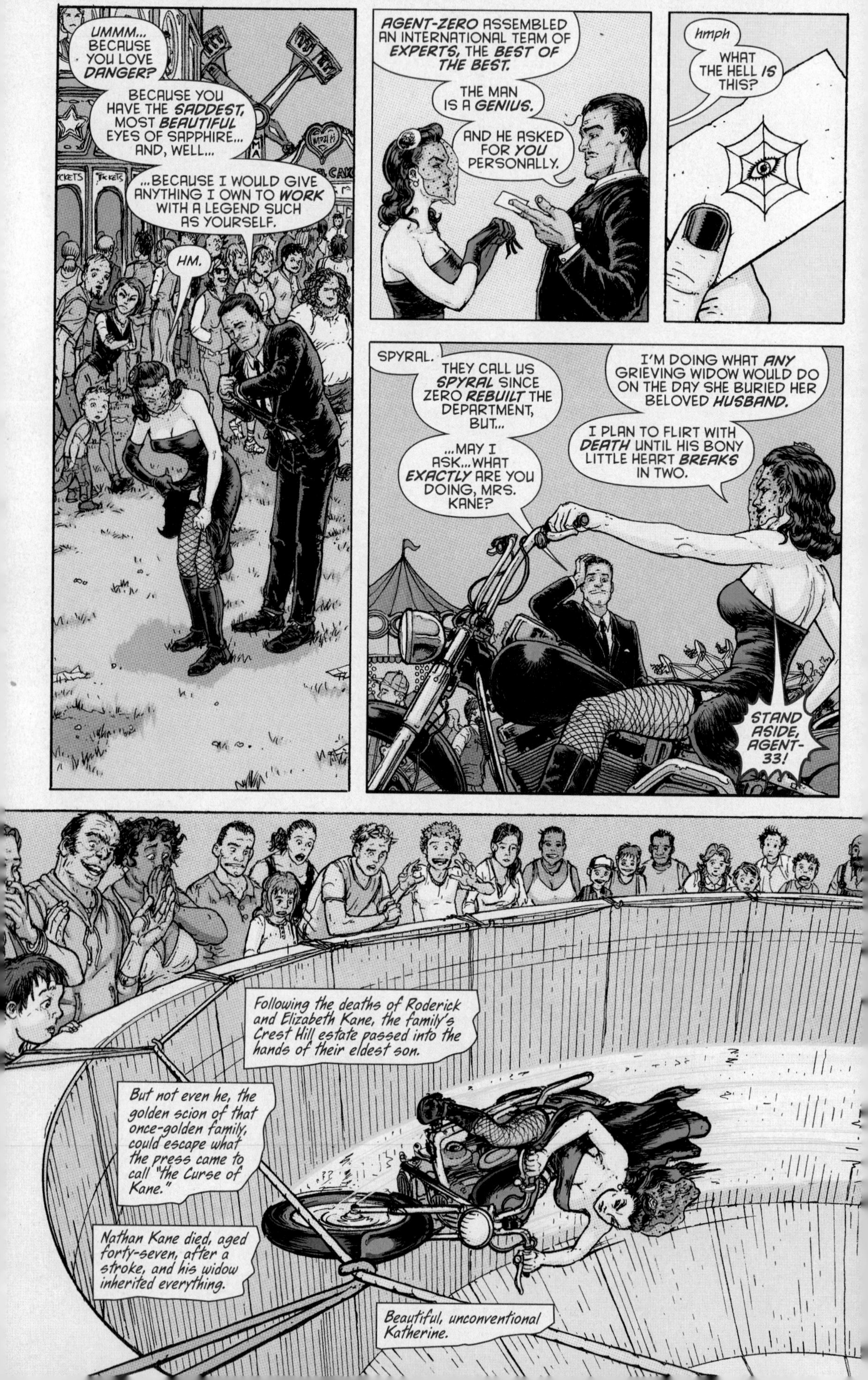
UMMM... BECAUSE YOU LOVE DANGER?
BECAUSE YOU HAVE THE SADDEST, MOST BEAUTIFUL EYES OF SAPPHIRE... AND, WELL...
...BECAUSE I WOULD GIVE ANYTHING I OWN TO WORK WITH A LEGEND SUCH AS YOURSELF.
HM.
AGENT-ZERO ASSEMBLED AN INTERNATIONAL TEAM OF EXPERTS, THE BEST OF THE BEST.
THE MAN IS A GENIUS.
AND HE ASKED FOR YOU PERSONALLY.
hmph
WHAT THE HELL IS THIS?
SPYRAL.
THEY CALL US SPYRAL SINCE ZERO REBUILT THE DEPARTMENT, BUT...
...MAY I ASK...WHAT EXACTLY ARE YOU DOING, MRS. KANE?
I'M DOING WHAT ANY GRIEVING WIDOW WOULD DO ON THE DAY SHE BURIED HER BELOVED HUSBAND.
I PLAN TO FLIRT WITH DEATH UNTIL HIS BONY LITTLE HEART BREAKS IN TWO.
STAND ASIDE, AGENT-33!
Following the deaths of Roderick and Elizabeth Kane, the family's Crest Hill estate passed into the hands of their eldest son.
But not even he, the golden scion of that once-golden family, could escape what the press came to call "the Curse of Kane."
Nathan Kane died, aged forty-seven, after a stroke, and his widow inherited everything.
Beautiful, unconventional Katherine.

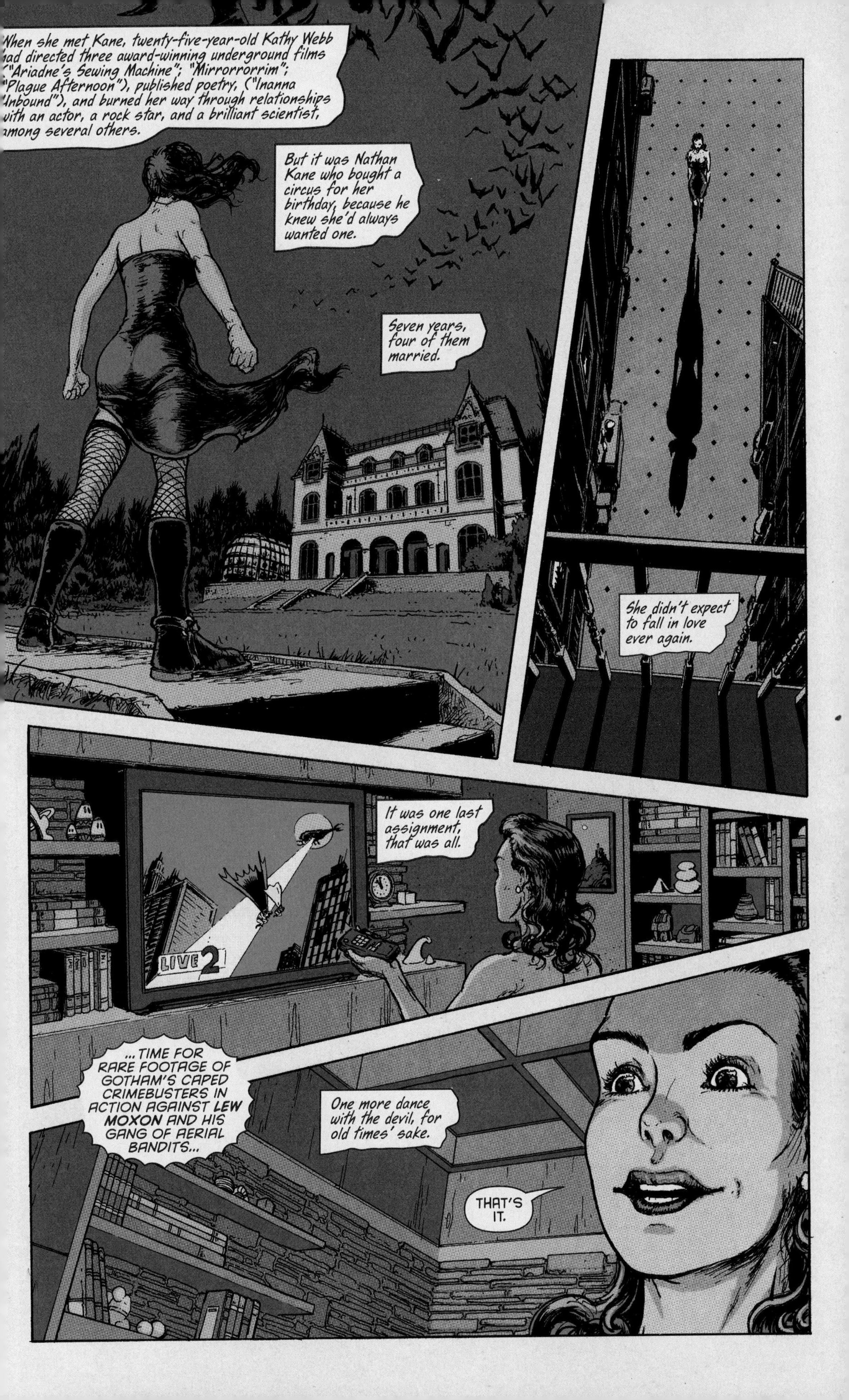
When she met Kane, twenty-five-year-old Kathy Webb had directed three award-winning underground films ("Ariadne's Sewing Machine"; "Mirrorrorrim"; "Plague Afternoon"), published poetry, ("Inanna Unbound"), and burned her way through relationships with an actor, a rock star, and a brilliant scientist, among several others.
But it was Nathan Kane who bought a circus for her birthday, because he knew she'd always wanted one.
Seven years, four of them married.
She didn't expect to fall in love ever again.
It was one last assignment, that was all.
LIVE 2
...TIME FOR RARE FOOTAGE OF GOTHAM'S CAPED CRIMEBUSTERS IN ACTION AGAINST LEW MOXON AND HIS GANG OF AERIAL BANDITS...
One more dance with the devil, for old times' sake.
THAT'S IT.

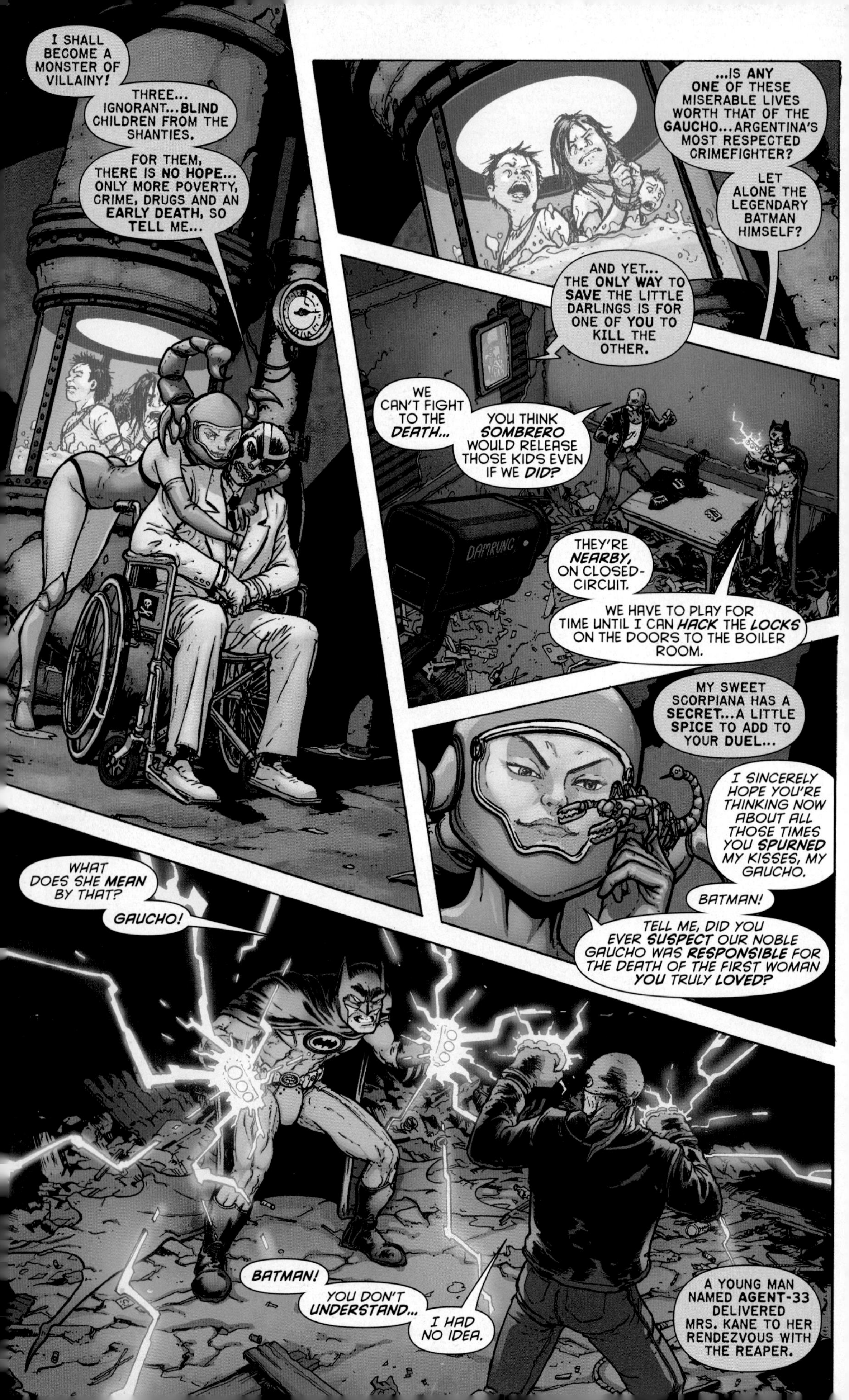

I SHALL BECOME A MONSTER OF VILLAINY!
THREE... IGNORANT...BLIND CHILDREN FROM THE SHANTIES.
FOR THEM, THERE IS NO HOPE... ONLY MORE POVERTY, CRIME, DRUGS AND AN EARLY DEATH, SO TELL ME...
...IS ANY ONE OF THESE MISERABLE LIVES WORTH THAT OF THE GAUCHO...ARGENTINA'S MOST RESPECTED CRIMEFIGHTER?
LET ALONE THE LEGENDARY BATMAN HIMSELF?
AND YET... THE ONLY WAY TO SAVE THE LITTLE DARLINGS IS FOR ONE OF YOU TO KILL THE OTHER.
WE CAN'T FIGHT TO THE DEATH...
YOU THINK SOMBRERO WOULD RELEASE THOSE KIDS EVEN IF WE DID?
DAMRUNG
THEY'RE NEARBY, ON CLOSED-CIRCUIT.
WE HAVE TO PLAY FOR TIME UNTIL I CAN HACK THE LOCKS ON THE DOORS TO THE BOILER ROOM.
MY SWEET SCORPIANA HAS A SECRET...A LITTLE SPICE TO ADD TO YOUR DUEL...
I SINCERELY HOPE YOU'RE THINKING NOW ABOUT ALL THOSE TIMES YOU SPURNED MY KISSES, MY GAUCHO.
BATMAN!
TELL ME, DID YOU EVER SUSPECT OUR NOBLE GAUCHO WAS RESPONSIBLE FOR THE DEATH OF THE FIRST WOMAN YOU TRULY LOVED?
WHAT DOES SHE MEAN BY THAT?
GAUCHO!
BATMAN!
YOU DON'T UNDERSTAND...
I HAD NO IDEA.
A YOUNG MAN NAMED AGENT-33 DELIVERED MRS. KANE TO HER RENDEZVOUS WITH THE REAPER.

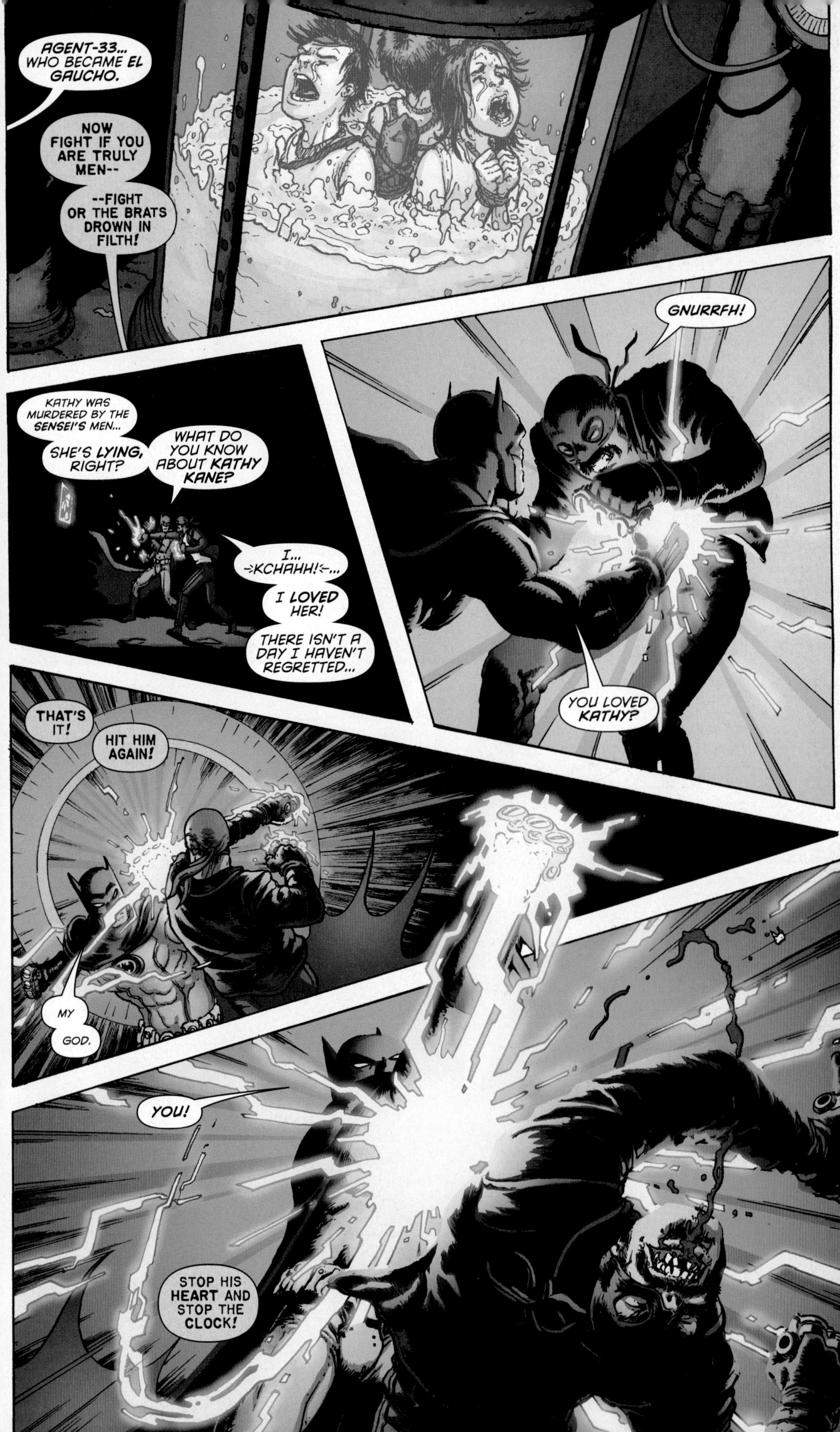
AGENT-33... WHO BECAME EL GAUCHO.
NOW FIGHT IF YOU ARE TRULY MEN--
--FIGHT OR THE BRATS DROWN IN FILTH!
KATHY WAS MURDERED BY THE SENSEI'S MEN...
SHE'S LYING, RIGHT?
WHAT DO YOU KNOW ABOUT KATHY KANE?
I... -KCHAHH!-...
I LOVED HER!
THERE ISN'T A DAY I HAVEN'T REGRETTED...
GNURRFH!
YOU LOVED KATHY?
THAT'S IT!
HIT HIM AGAIN!
MY
GOD.
YOU!
STOP HIS HEART AND STOP THE CLOCK!

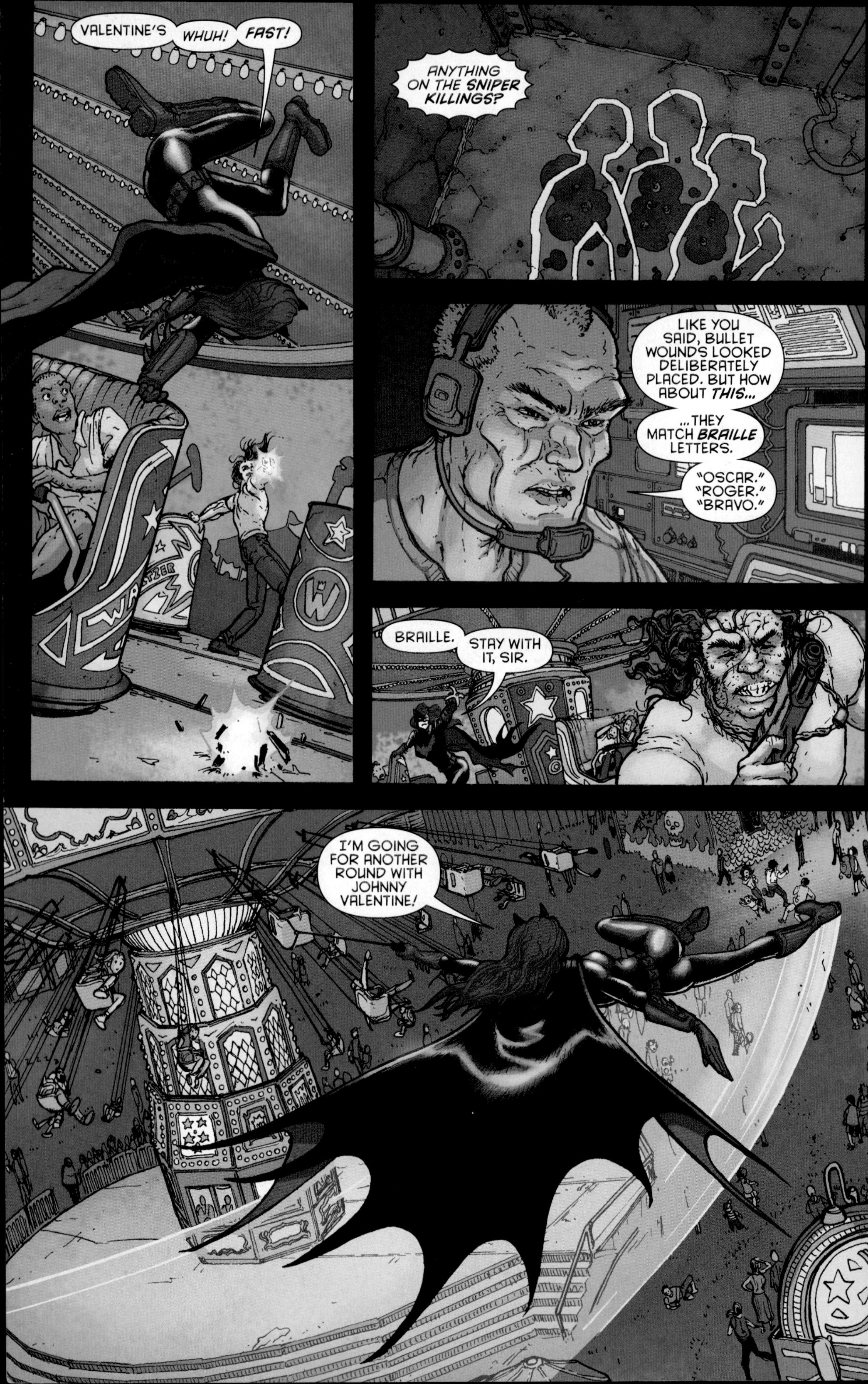
VALENTINE'S
WHUH!
FAST!
ANYTHING ON THE SNIPER KILLINGS?
LIKE YOU SAID, BULLET WOUNDS LOOKED DELIBERATELY PLACED. BUT HOW ABOUT THIS...
...THEY MATCH BRAILLE LETTERS.
"OSCAR." "ROGER." "BRAVO."
BRAILLE.
STAY WITH IT, SIR.
I'M GOING FOR ANOTHER ROUND WITH JOHNNY VALENTINE!

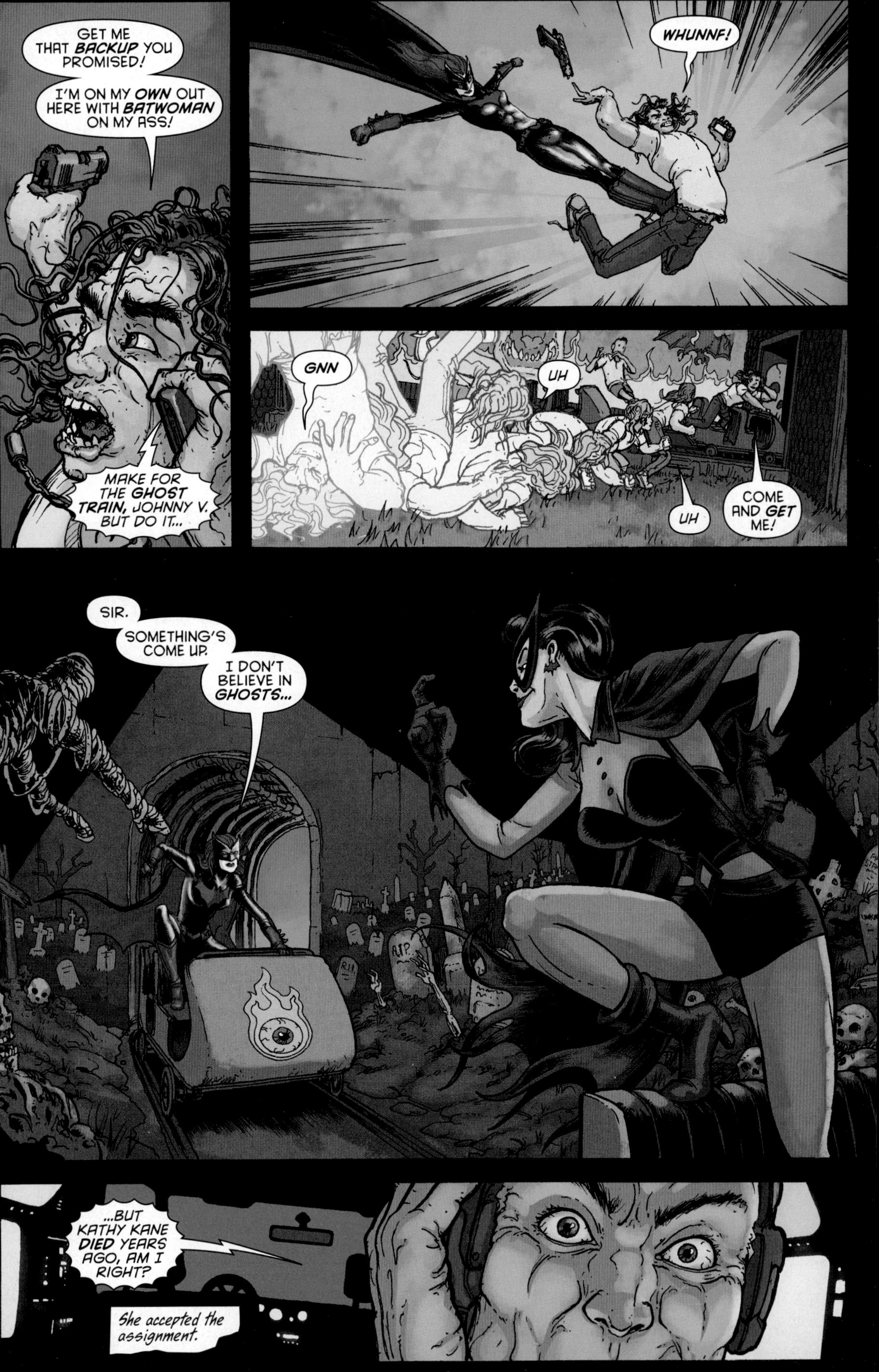
GET ME THAT BACKUP YOU PROMISED!
I'M ON MY OWN OUT HERE WITH BATWOMAN ON MY ASS!
MAKE FOR THE GHOST TRAIN, JOHNNY V. BUT DO IT...
WHUNNF!
GNN
UH
UH
COME AND GET ME!
SIR.
SOMETHING'S COME UP.
I DON'T BELIEVE IN GHOSTS...
...BUT KATHY KANE DIED YEARS AGO, AM I RIGHT?
She accepted the assignment.

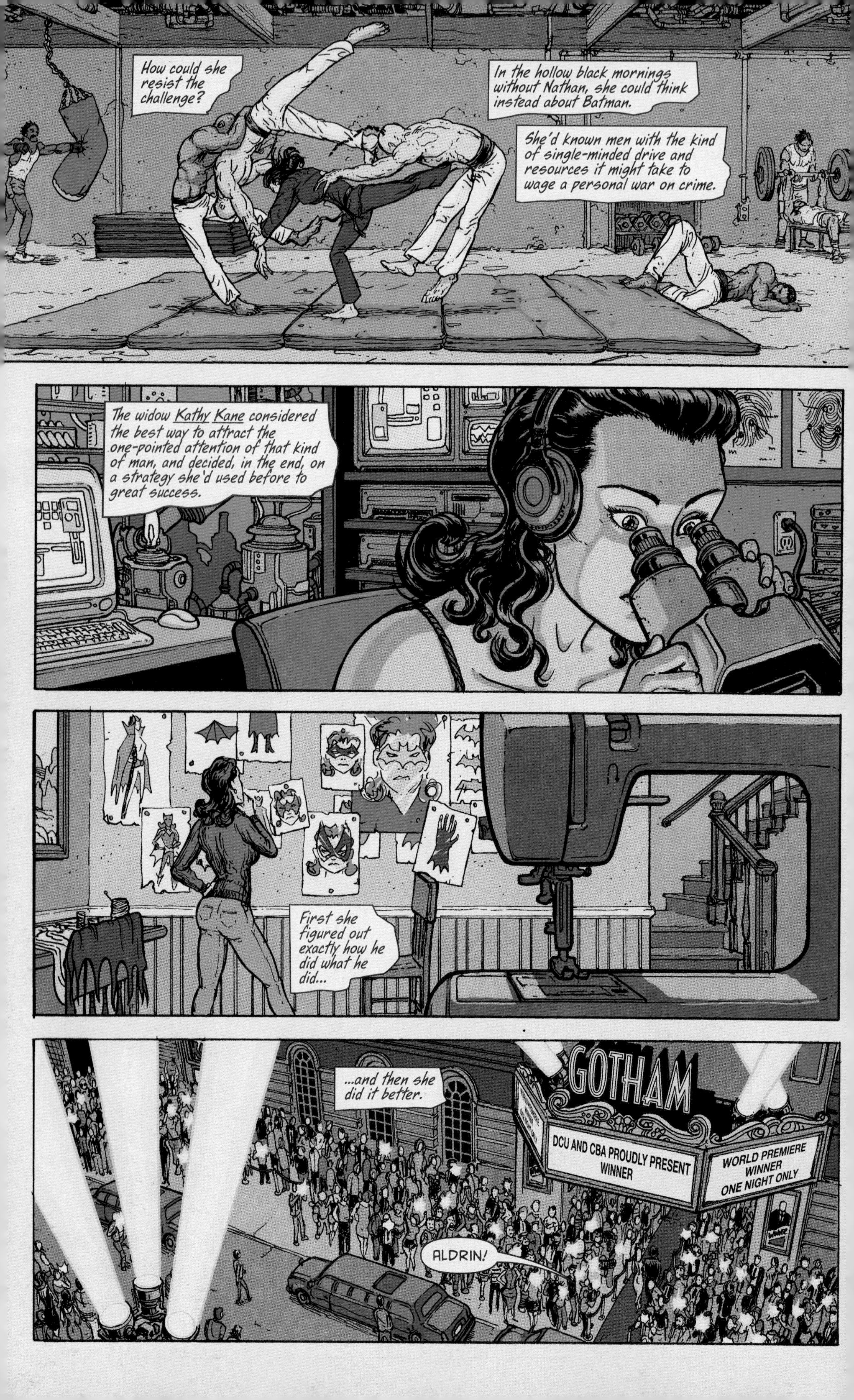
How could she resist the challenge?
In the hollow black mornings without Nathan, she could think instead about Batman.
She'd known men with the kind of single-minded drive and resources it might take to wage a personal war on crime.
The widow Kathy Kane considered the best way to attract the one-pointed attention of that kind of man, and decided, in the end, on a strategy she'd used before to great success.
First she figured out exactly how he did what he did...
...and then she did it better.
GOTHAM
DCU AND CBA PROUDLY PRESENT
WINNER
WORLD PREMIERE
WINNER
ONE NIGHT ONLY
ALDRIN!

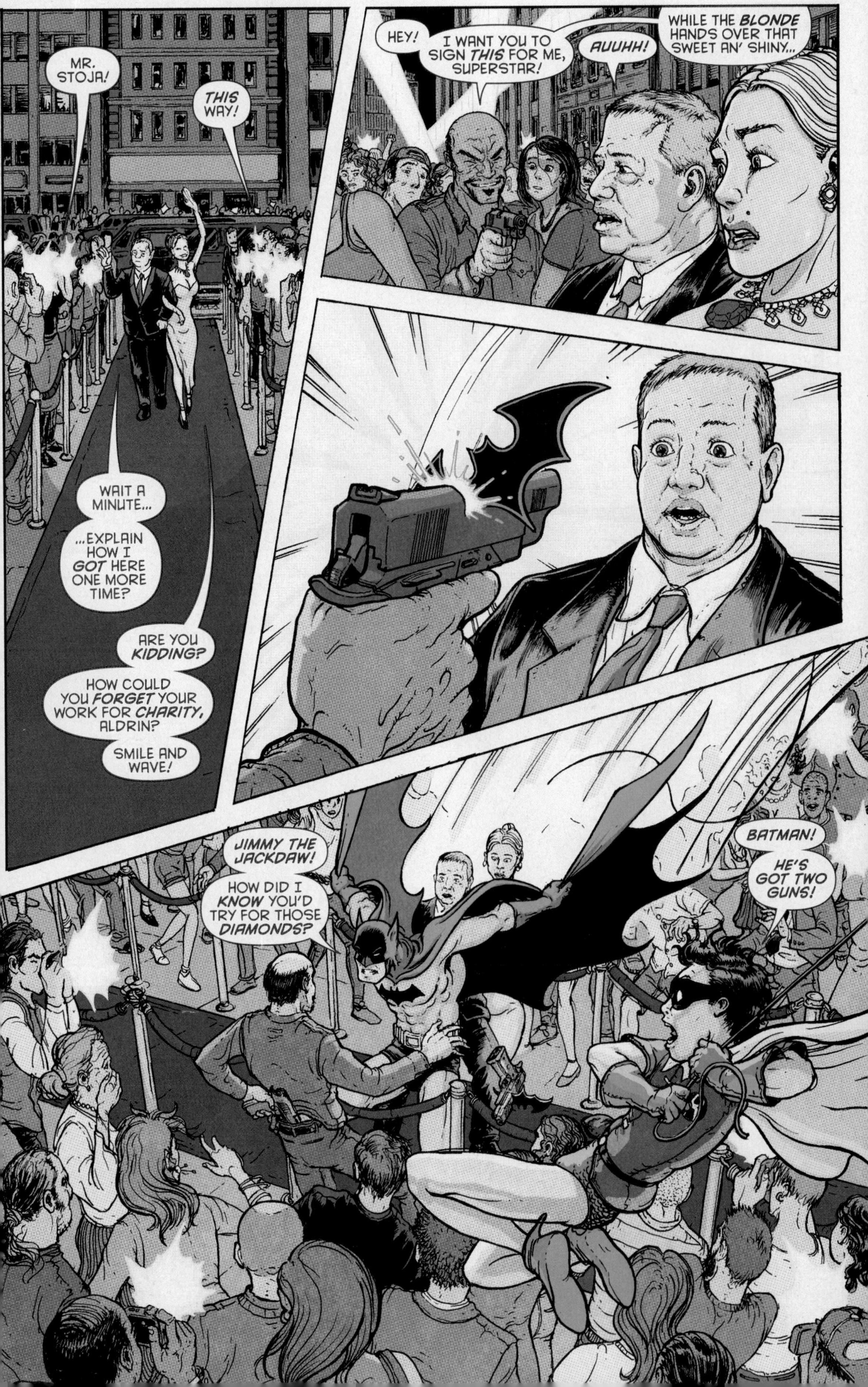
MR. STOJA!
THIS WAY!
WAIT A MINUTE...
...EXPLAIN HOW I GOT HERE ONE MORE TIME?
ARE YOU KIDDING?
HOW COULD YOU FORGET YOUR WORK FOR CHARITY, ALDRIN?
SMILE AND WAVE!
HEY!
I WANT YOU TO SIGN THIS FOR ME, SUPERSTAR!
AUUHH!
WHILE THE BLONDE HANDS OVER THAT SWEET AN' SHINY...
JIMMY THE JACKDAW!
HOW DID I KNOW YOU'D TRY FOR THOSE DIAMONDS?
BATMAN!
HE'S GOT TWO GUNS!

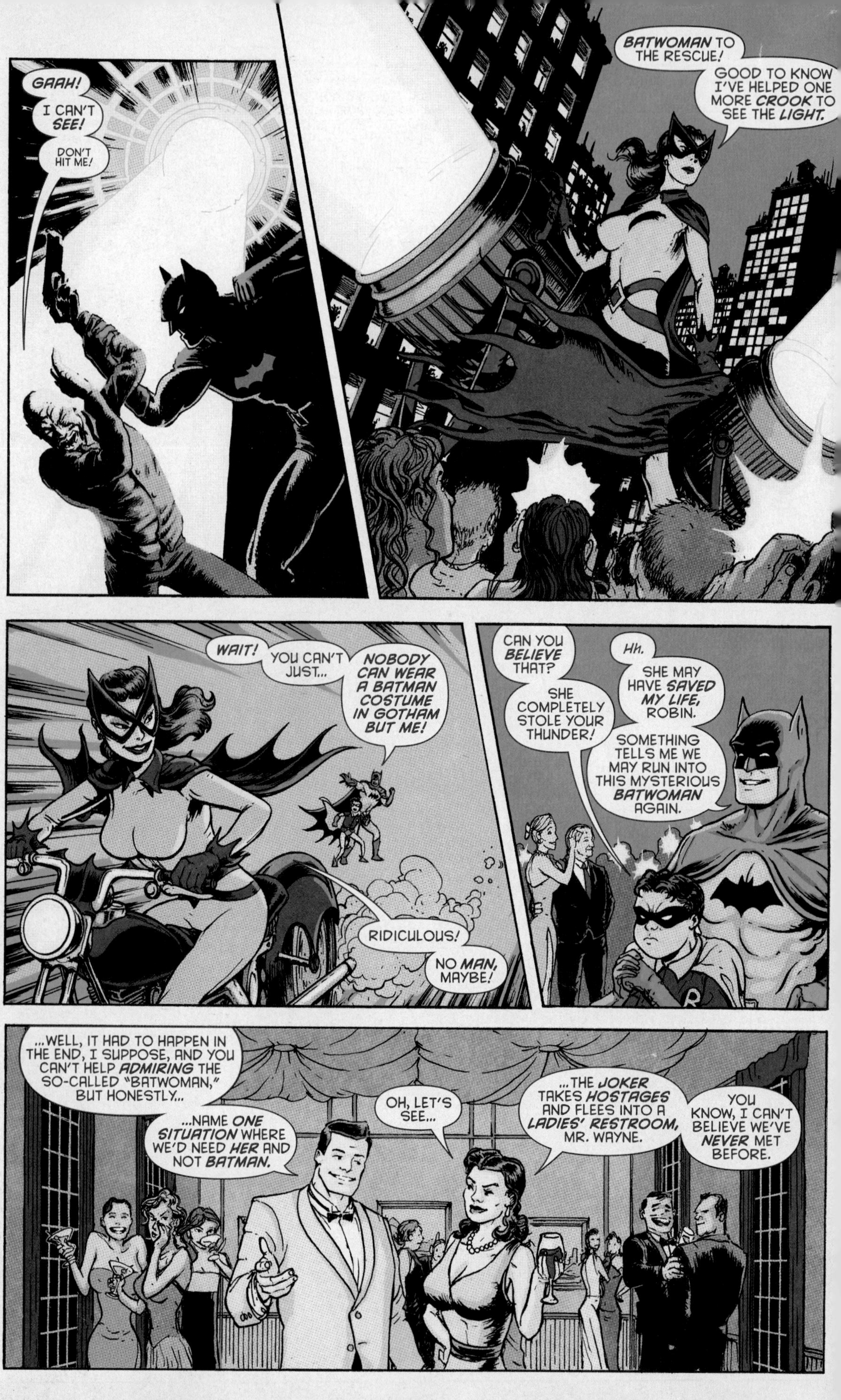
GAAH!
I CAN'T SEE!
DON'T HIT ME!
BATWOMAN TO THE RESCUE!
GOOD TO KNOW I'VE HELPED ONE MORE CROOK TO SEE THE LIGHT.
WAIT!
YOU CAN'T JUST...
NOBODY CAN WEAR A BATMAN COSTUME IN GOTHAM BUT ME!
RIDICULOUS!
NO MAN, MAYBE!
CAN YOU BELIEVE THAT?
SHE COMPLETELY STOLE YOUR THUNDER!
Hh.
SHE MAY HAVE SAVED MY LIFE, ROBIN.
SOMETHING TELLS ME WE MAY RUN INTO THIS MYSTERIOUS BATWOMAN AGAIN.
...WELL, IT HAD TO HAPPEN IN THE END, I SUPPOSE, AND YOU CAN'T HELP ADMIRING THE SO-CALLED "BATWOMAN," BUT HONESTLY...
...NAME ONE SITUATION WHERE WE'D NEED HER AND NOT BATMAN.
OH, LET'S SEE...
...THE JOKER TAKES HOSTAGES AND FLEES INTO A LADIES' RESTROOM, MR. WAYNE.
YOU KNOW, I CAN'T BELIEVE WE'VE NEVER MET BEFORE.

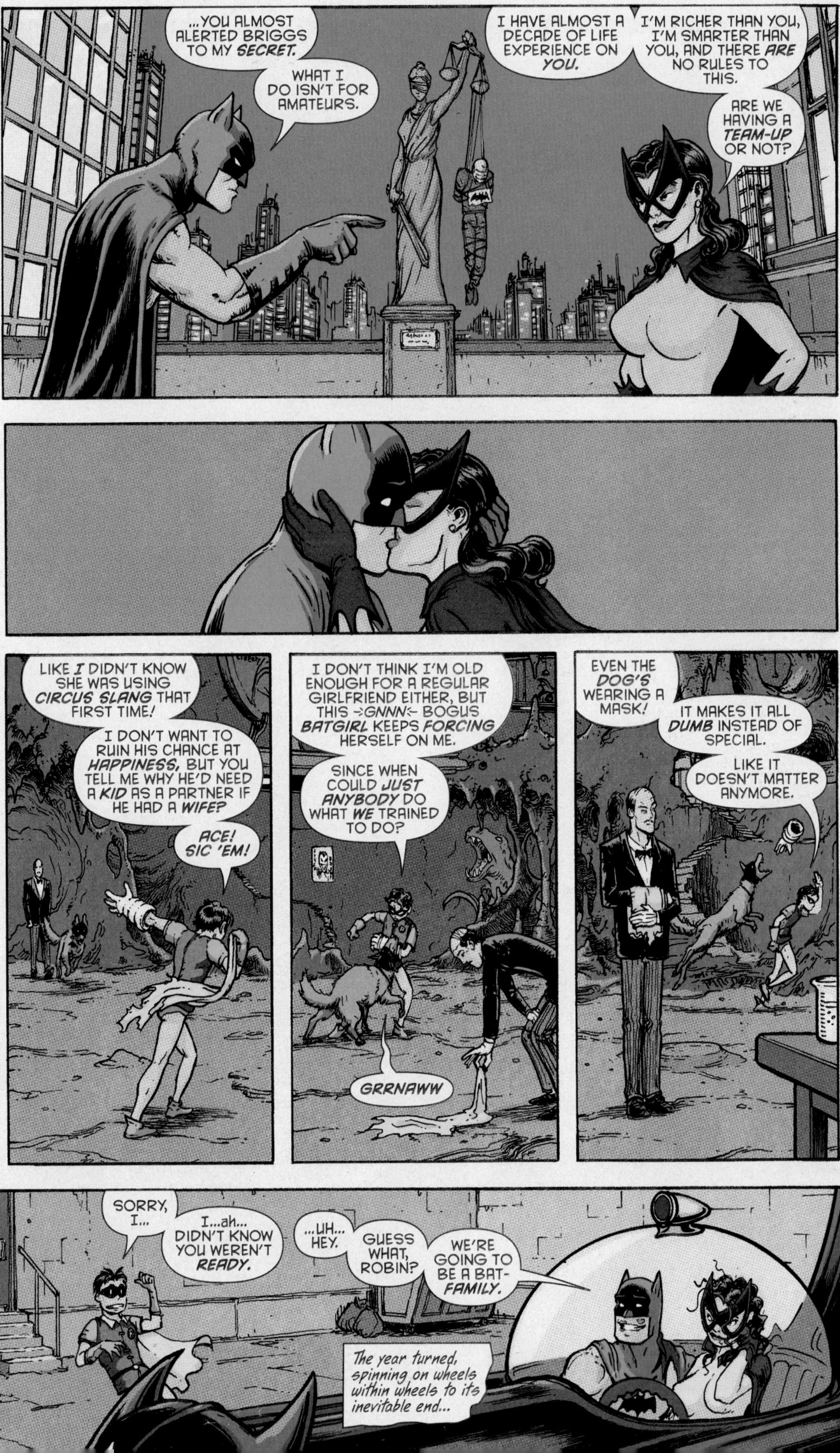
...YOU ALMOST ALERTED BRIGGS TO MY SECRET.
WHAT I DO ISN'T FOR AMATEURS.
I HAVE ALMOST A DECADE OF LIFE EXPERIENCE ON YOU.
I'M RICHER THAN YOU, I'M SMARTER THAN YOU, AND THERE ARE NO RULES TO THIS.
ARE WE HAVING A TEAM-UP OR NOT?
LIKE I DIDN'T KNOW SHE WAS USING CIRCUS SLANG THAT FIRST TIME!
I DON'T WANT TO RUIN HIS CHANCE AT HAPPINESS, BUT YOU TELL ME WHY HE'D NEED A KID AS A PARTNER IF HE HAD A WIFE?
ACE! SIC 'EM!
I DON'T THINK I'M OLD ENOUGH FOR A REGULAR GIRLFRIEND EITHER, BUT THIS ⇒GNNN⇐ BOGUS BATGIRL KEEPS FORCING HERSELF ON ME.
SINCE WHEN COULD JUST ANYBODY DO WHAT WE TRAINED TO DO?
GRRNAWW
EVEN THE DOG'S WEARING A MASK!
IT MAKES IT ALL DUMB INSTEAD OF SPECIAL.
LIKE IT DOESN'T MATTER ANYMORE.
SORRY, I...
I...ah... DIDN'T KNOW YOU WEREN'T READY.
...UH... HEY.
GUESS WHAT, ROBIN?
WE'RE GOING TO BE A BAT-FAMILY.
The year turned, spinning on wheels within wheels to its inevitable end...

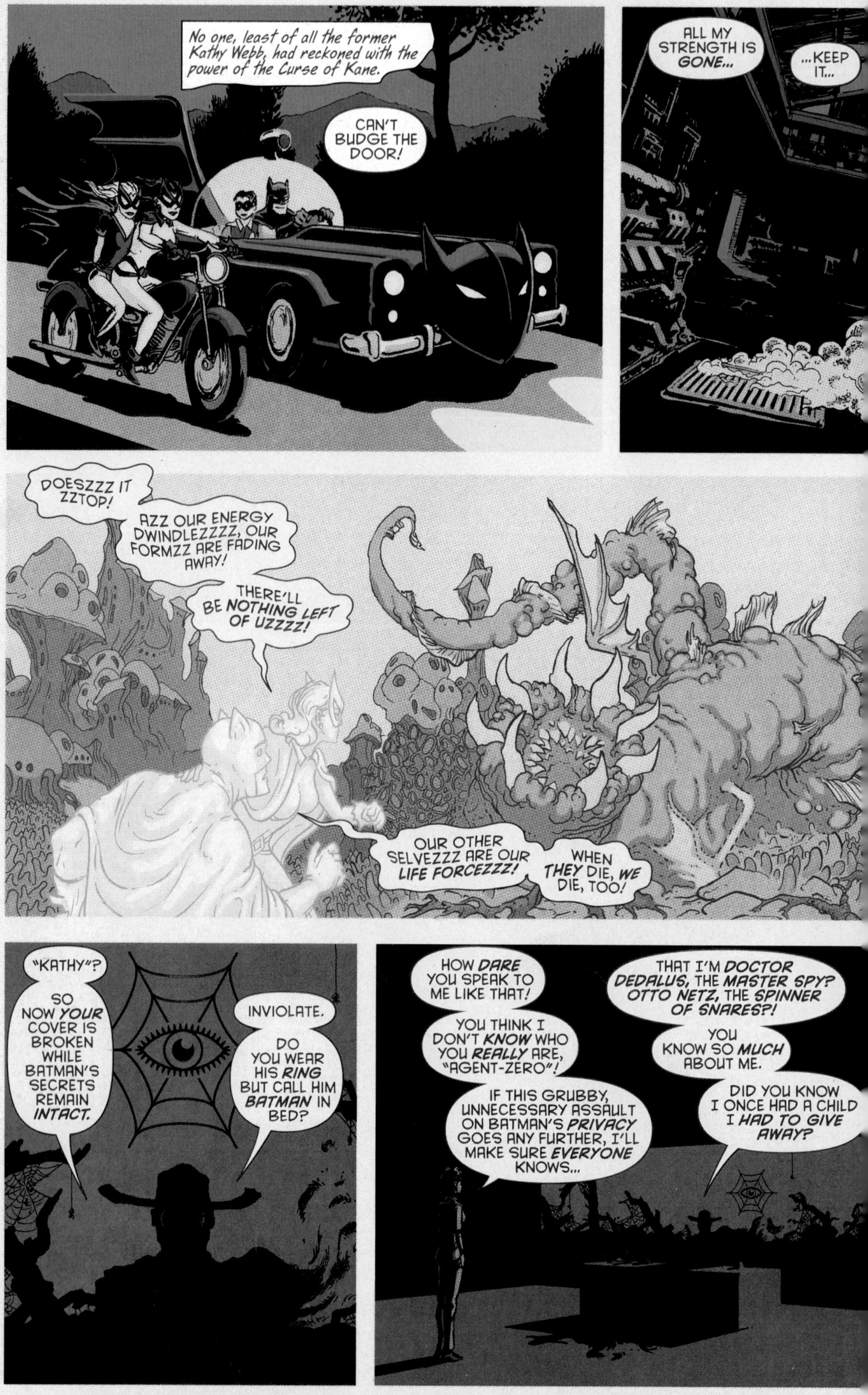
No one, least of all the former Kathy Webb, had reckoned with the power of the Curse of Kane.
CAN'T BUDGE THE DOOR!
ALL MY STRENGTH IS GONE...
...KEEP IT...
DOESZZZ IT ZZTOP!
AZZ OUR ENERGY DWINDLEZZZZ, OUR FORMZZ ARE FADING AWAY!
THERE'LL BE NOTHING LEFT OF UZZZZ!
OUR OTHER SELVEZZZ ARE OUR LIFE FORCEZZZ!
WHEN THEY DIE, WE DIE, TOO!
"KATHY"?
SO NOW YOUR COVER IS BROKEN WHILE BATMAN'S SECRETS REMAIN INTACT.
INVIOLATE.
DO YOU WEAR HIS RING BUT CALL HIM BATMAN IN BED?
HOW DARE YOU SPEAK TO ME LIKE THAT!
YOU THINK I DON'T KNOW WHO YOU REALLY ARE, "AGENT-ZERO"!
IF THIS GRUBBY, UNNECESSARY ASSAULT ON BATMAN'S PRIVACY GOES ANY FURTHER, I'LL MAKE SURE EVERYONE KNOWS...
THAT I'M DOCTOR DEDALUS, THE MASTER SPY? OTTO NETZ, THE SPINNER OF SNARES?!
YOU KNOW SO MUCH ABOUT ME.
DID YOU KNOW I ONCE HAD A CHILD I HAD TO GIVE AWAY?

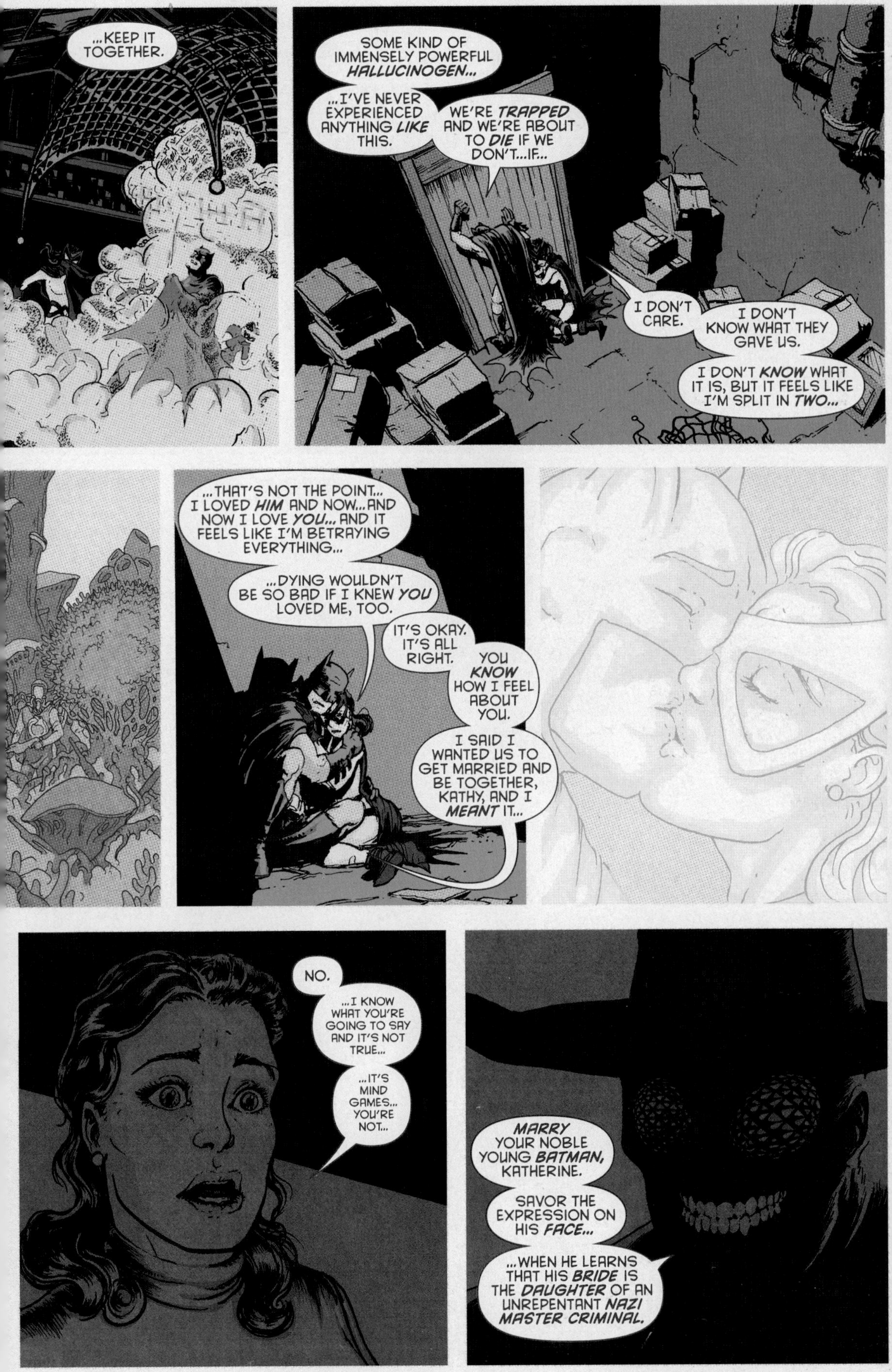
...KEEP IT TOGETHER.
SOME KIND OF IMMENSELY POWERFUL HALLUCINOGEN...
...I'VE NEVER EXPERIENCED ANYTHING LIKE THIS.
WE'RE TRAPPED AND WE'RE ABOUT TO DIE IF WE DON'T...IF...
I DON'T CARE.
I DON'T KNOW WHAT THEY GAVE US.
I DON'T KNOW WHAT IT IS, BUT IT FEELS LIKE I'M SPLIT IN TWO...
...THAT'S NOT THE POINT... I LOVED HIM AND NOW...AND NOW I LOVE YOU... AND IT FEELS LIKE I'M BETRAYING EVERYTHING...
...DYING WOULDN'T BE SO BAD IF I KNEW YOU LOVED ME, TOO.
IT'S OKAY. IT'S ALL RIGHT.
YOU KNOW HOW I FEEL ABOUT YOU.
I SAID I WANTED US TO GET MARRIED AND BE TOGETHER, KATHY, AND I MEANT IT...
NO.
...I KNOW WHAT YOU'RE GOING TO SAY AND IT'S NOT TRUE...
...IT'S MIND GAMES... YOU'RE NOT...
MARRY YOUR NOBLE YOUNG BATMAN, KATHERINE.
SAVOR THE EXPRESSION ON HIS FACE...
...WHEN HE LEARNS THAT HIS BRIDE IS THE DAUGHTER OF AN UNREPENTANT NAZI MASTER CRIMINAL.

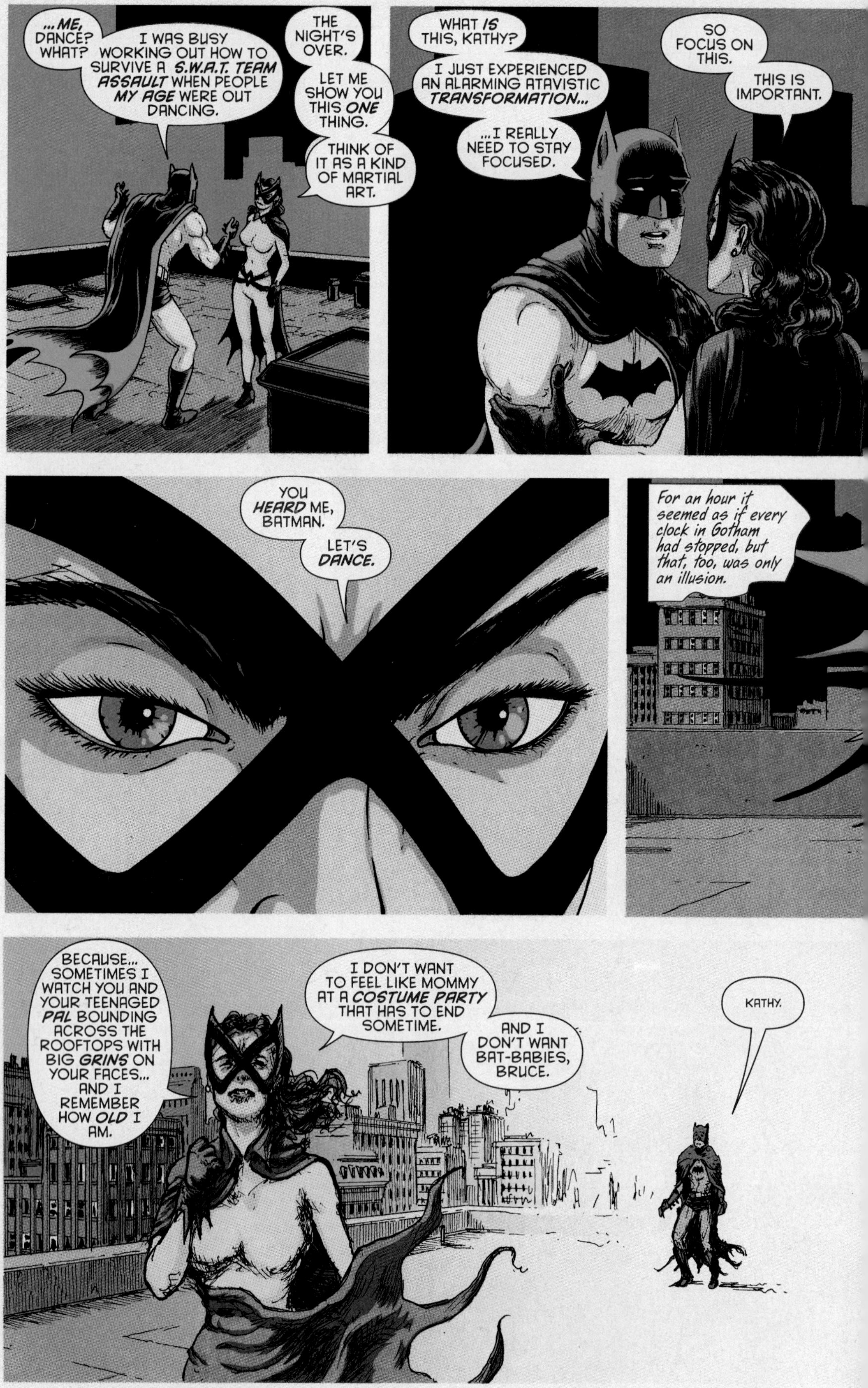
...ME, DANCE? WHAT?
I WAS BUSY WORKING OUT HOW TO SURVIVE A S.W.A.T. TEAM ASSAULT WHEN PEOPLE MY AGE WERE OUT DANCING.
THE NIGHT'S OVER.
LET ME SHOW YOU THIS ONE THING.
THINK OF IT AS A KIND OF MARTIAL ART.
WHAT IS THIS, KATHY?
I JUST EXPERIENCED AN ALARMING ATAVISTIC TRANSFORMATION...
...I REALLY NEED TO STAY FOCUSED.
SO FOCUS ON THIS.
THIS IS IMPORTANT.
YOU HEARD ME, BATMAN.
LET'S DANCE.
For an hour it seemed as if every clock in Gotham had stopped, but that, too, was only an illusion.
BECAUSE... SOMETIMES I WATCH YOU AND YOUR TEENAGED PAL BOUNDING ACROSS THE ROOFTOPS WITH BIG GRINS ON YOUR FACES... AND I REMEMBER HOW OLD I AM.
I DON'T WANT TO FEEL LIKE MOMMY AT A COSTUME PARTY THAT HAS TO END SOMETIME.
AND I DON'T WANT BAT-BABIES, BRUCE.
KATHY.

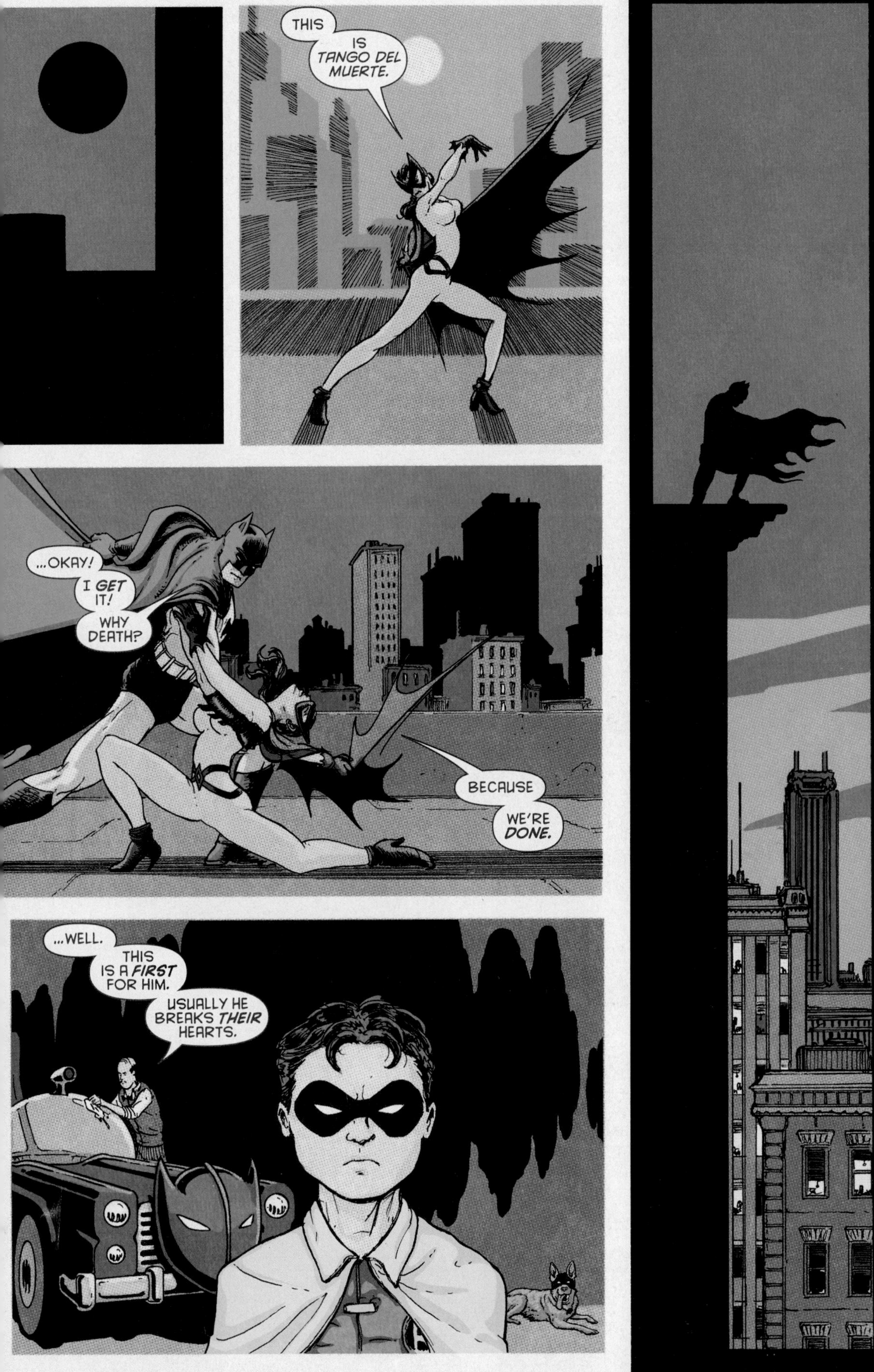
THIS IS TANGO DEL MUERTE.
...OKAY!
I GET IT!
WHY DEATH?
BECAUSE
WE'RE DONE.
...WELL.
THIS IS A FIRST FOR HIM.
USUALLY HE BREAKS THEIR HEARTS.

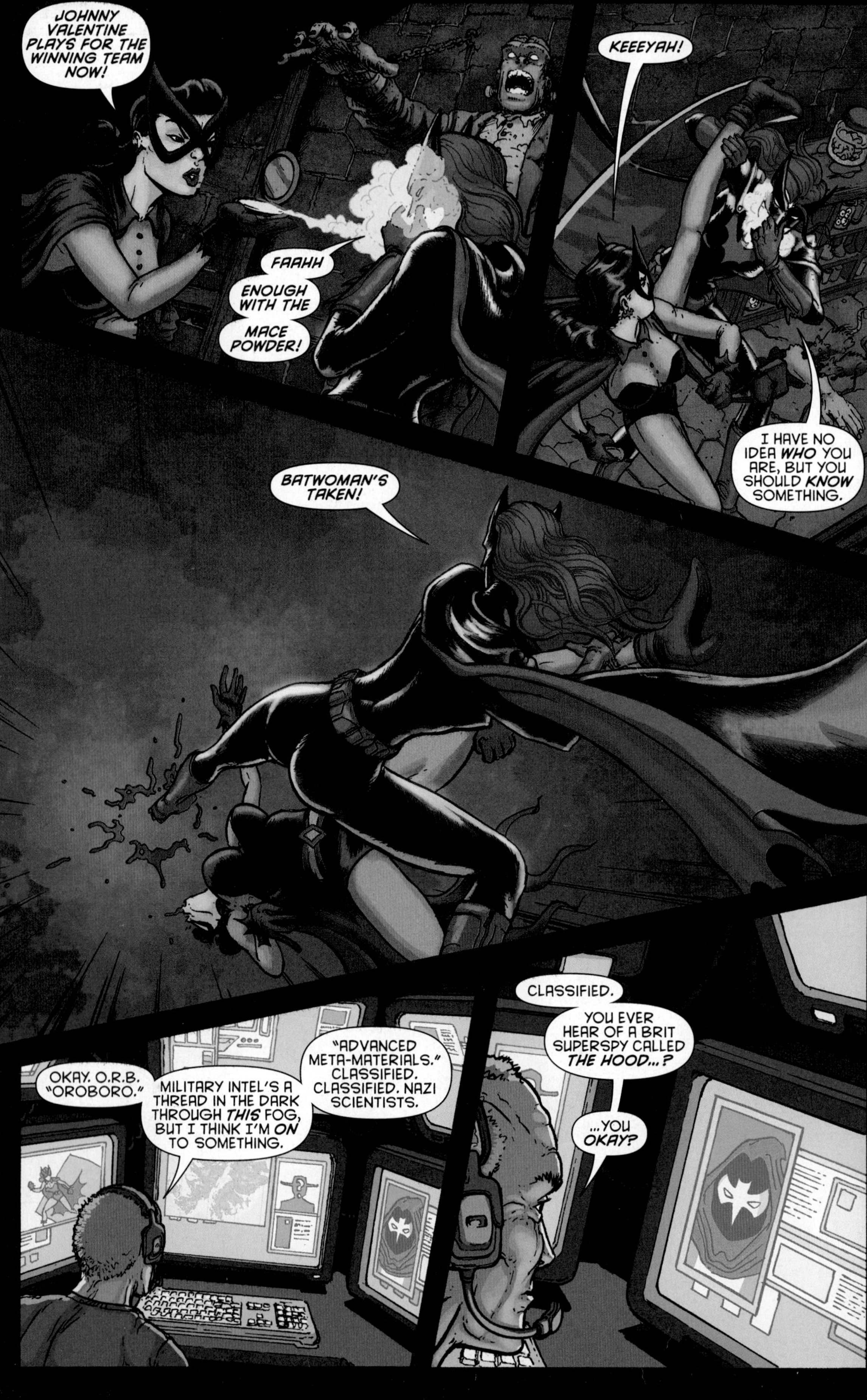
JOHNNY VALENTINE PLAYS FOR THE WINNING TEAM NOW!
FAAHH
ENOUGH WITH THE
MACE POWDER!
KEEEYAH!
I HAVE NO IDEA WHO YOU ARE, BUT YOU SHOULD KNOW SOMETHING.
BATWOMAN'S TAKEN!
OKAY. O.R.B. "OROBORO."
MILITARY INTEL'S A THREAD IN THE DARK THROUGH THIS FOG, BUT I THINK I'M ON TO SOMETHING.
"ADVANCED META-MATERIALS." CLASSIFIED. CLASSIFIED. NAZI SCIENTISTS.
CLASSIFIED.
YOU EVER HEAR OF A BRIT SUPERSPY CALLED THE HOOD...?
...YOU OKAY?

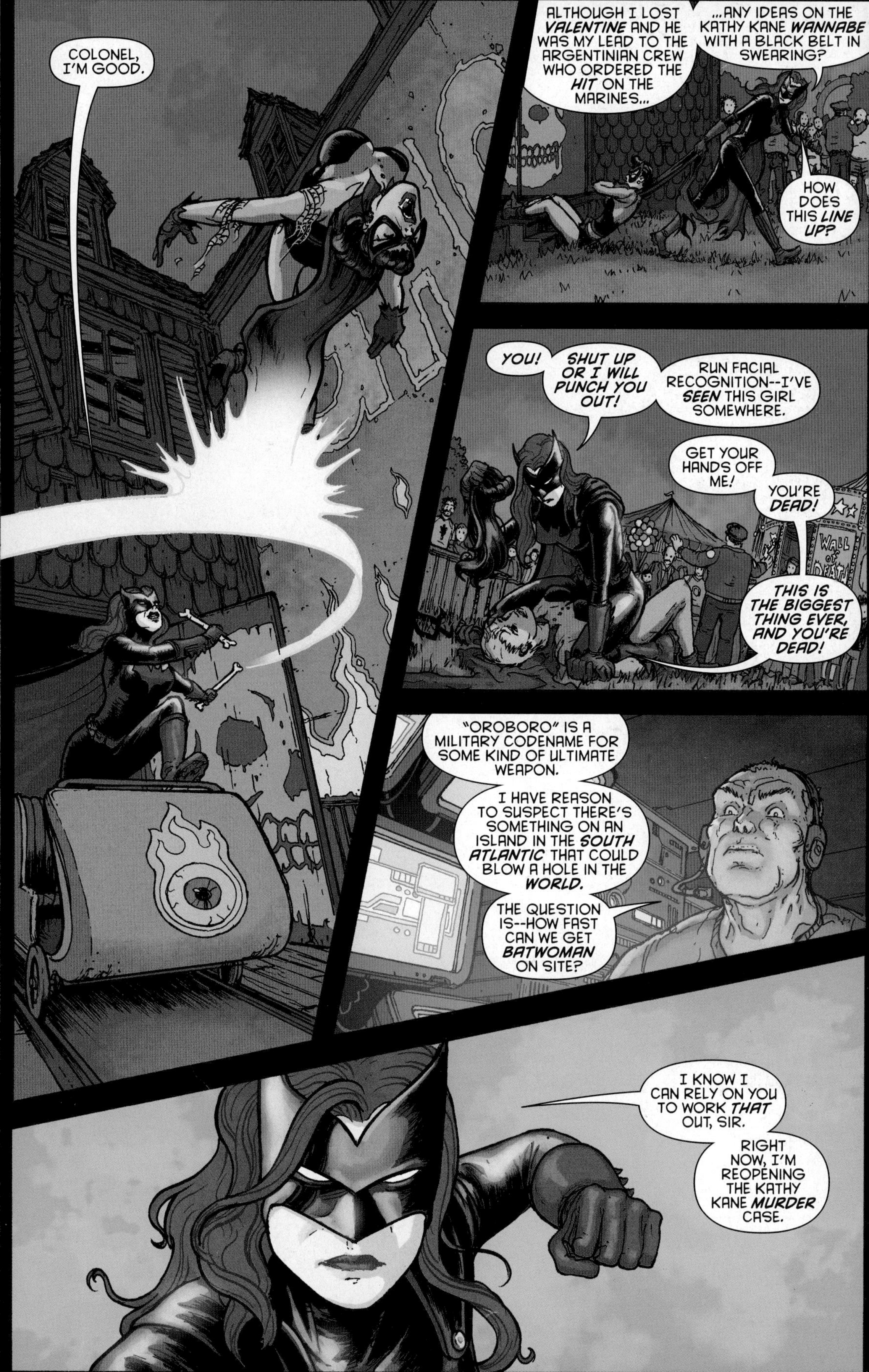
COLONEL, I'M GOOD.
ALTHOUGH I LOST VALENTINE AND HE WAS MY LEAD TO THE ARGENTINIAN CREW WHO ORDERED THE HIT ON THE MARINES...
...ANY IDEAS ON THE KATHY KANE WANNABE WITH A BLACK BELT IN SWEARING?
HOW DOES THIS LINE UP?
YOU!
SHUT UP OR I WILL PUNCH YOU OUT!
RUN FACIAL RECOGNITION--I'VE SEEN THIS GIRL SOMEWHERE.
GET YOUR HANDS OFF ME!
YOU'RE DEAD!
THIS IS THE BIGGEST THING EVER, AND YOU'RE DEAD!
WALL OF DEATH
"OROBORO" IS A MILITARY CODENAME FOR SOME KIND OF ULTIMATE WEAPON.
I HAVE REASON TO SUSPECT THERE'S SOMETHING ON AN ISLAND IN THE SOUTH ATLANTIC THAT COULD BLOW A HOLE IN THE WORLD.
THE QUESTION IS--HOW FAST CAN WE GET BATWOMAN ON SITE?
I KNOW I CAN RELY ON YOU TO WORK THAT OUT, SIR.
RIGHT NOW, I'M REOPENING THE KATHY KANE MURDER CASE.

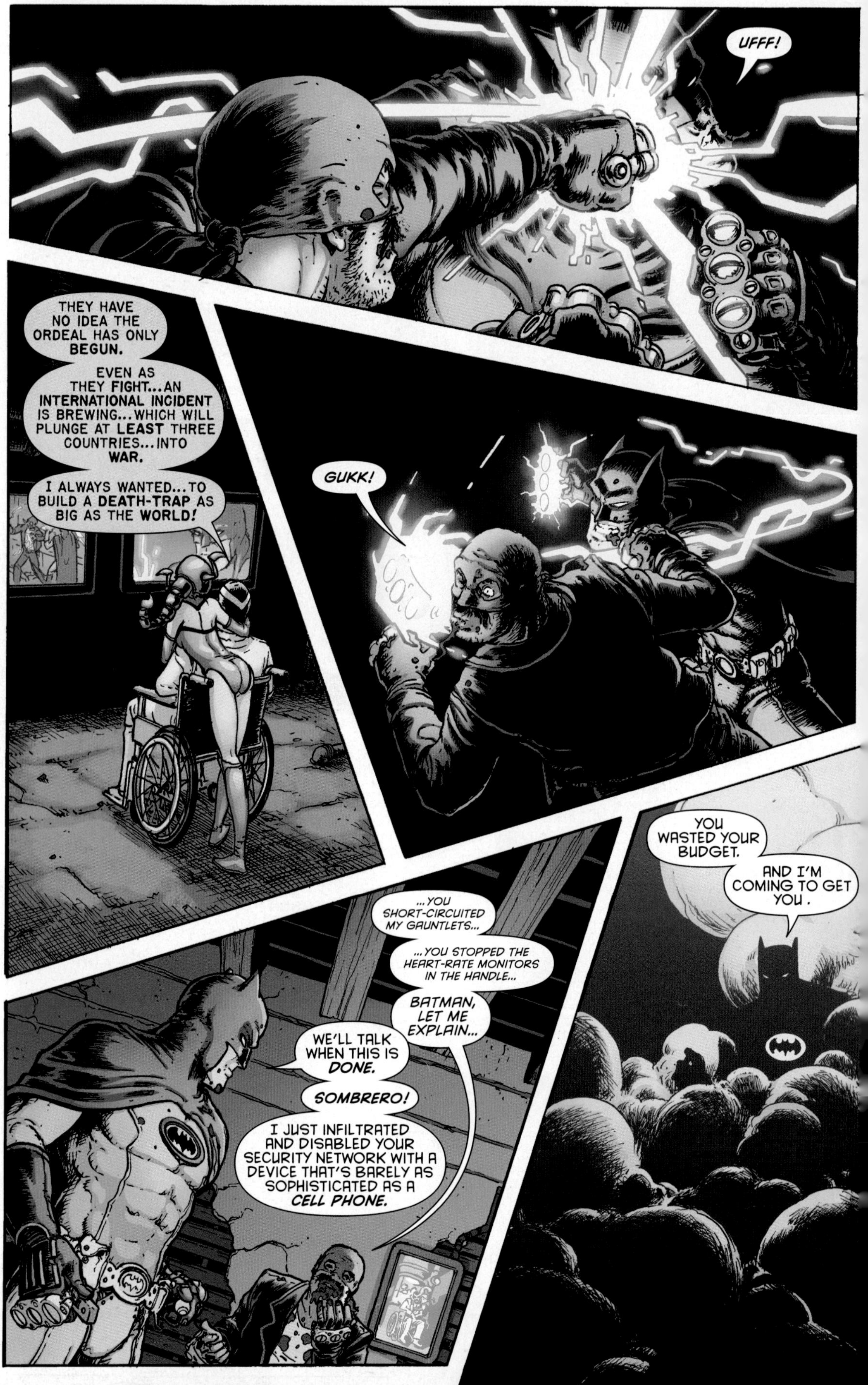
UFFF!
THEY HAVE NO IDEA THE ORDEAL HAS ONLY BEGUN.
EVEN AS THEY FIGHT...AN INTERNATIONAL INCIDENT IS BREWING...WHICH WILL PLUNGE AT LEAST THREE COUNTRIES...INTO WAR.
I ALWAYS WANTED...TO BUILD A DEATH-TRAP AS BIG AS THE WORLD!
GUKK!
...YOU SHORT-CIRCUITED MY GAUNTLETS...
...YOU STOPPED THE HEART-RATE MONITORS IN THE HANDLE...
BATMAN, LET ME EXPLAIN...
WE'LL TALK WHEN THIS IS DONE.
SOMBRERO!
I JUST INFILTRATED AND DISABLED YOUR SECURITY NETWORK WITH A DEVICE THAT'S BARELY AS SOPHISTICATED AS A CELL PHONE.
YOU WASTED YOUR BUDGET.
AND I'M COMING TO GET YOU .

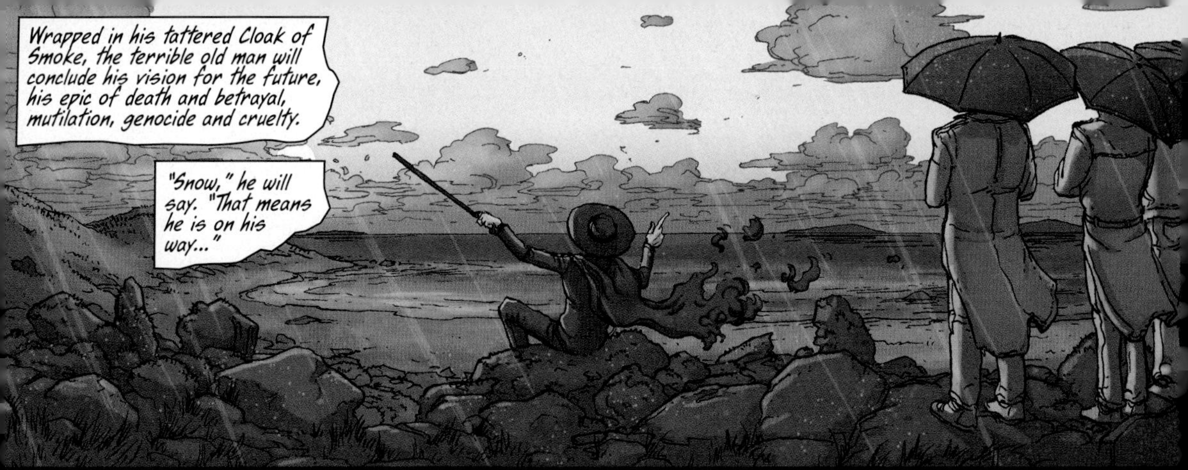
Wrapped in his tattered Cloak of Smoke, the terrible old man will conclude his vision for the future, his epic of death and betrayal, mutilation, genocide and cruelty.
"Snow," he will say. "That means he is on his way..."

THE FLIES ARE IN THE WEB!

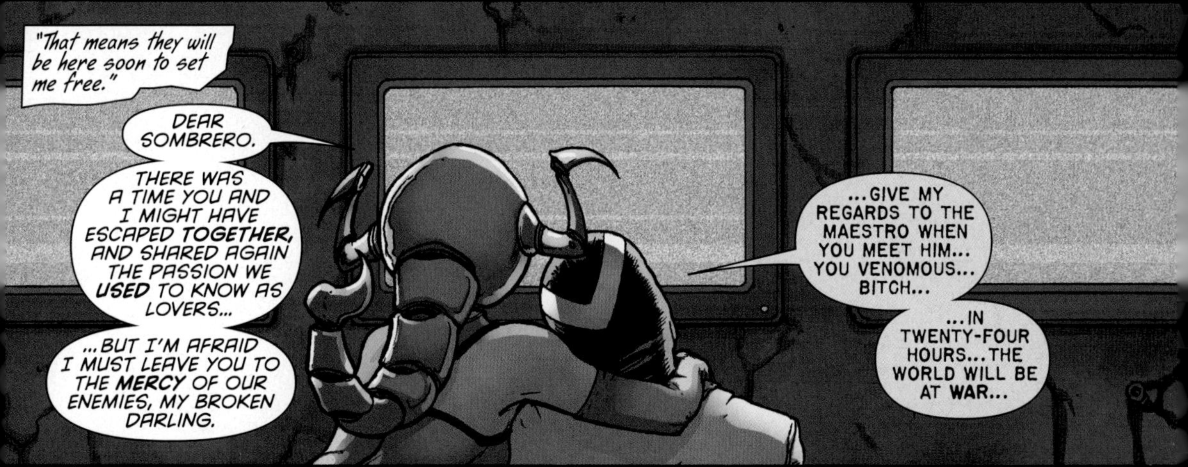
"That means they will be here soon to set me free."
DEAR SOMBRERO.
THERE WAS A TIME YOU AND I MIGHT HAVE ESCAPED TOGETHER, AND SHARED AGAIN THE PASSION WE USED TO KNOW AS LOVERS...
...BUT I'M AFRAID I MUST LEAVE YOU TO THE MERCY OF OUR ENEMIES, MY BROKEN DARLING.
...GIVE MY REGARDS TO THE MAESTRO WHEN YOU MEET HIM... YOU VENOMOUS... BITCH...
...IN TWENTY-FOUR HOURS...THE WORLD WILL BE AT WAR...

THE MONSTER SQUATS IN ITS MAZE OF DEATH!

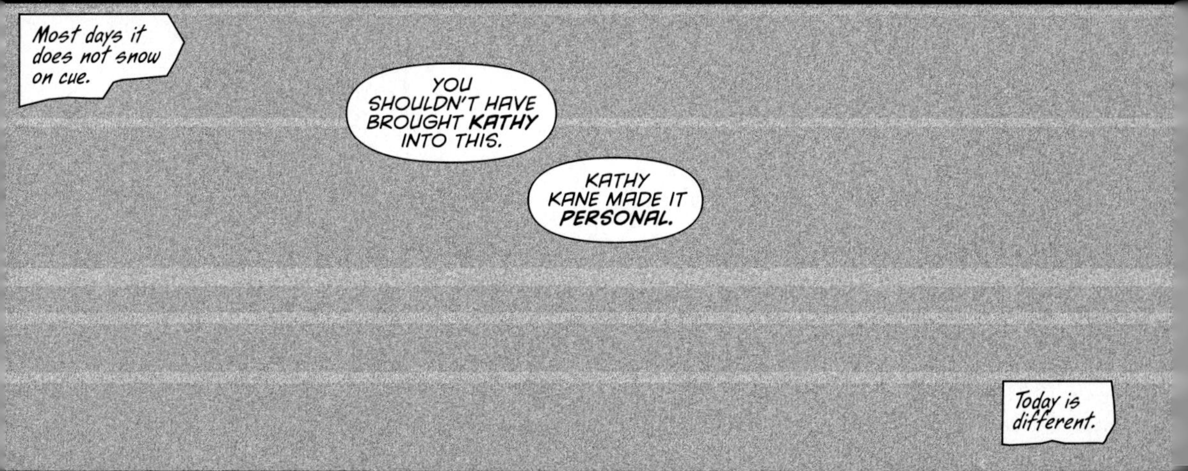
Most days it does not snow on cue.
YOU SHOULDN'T HAVE BROUGHT KATHY INTO THIS.
KATHY KANE MADE IT PERSONAL.
Today is different.

WHAT HORROR LURKS IN THE LABYRINTH OF DOCTOR DEDALUS?

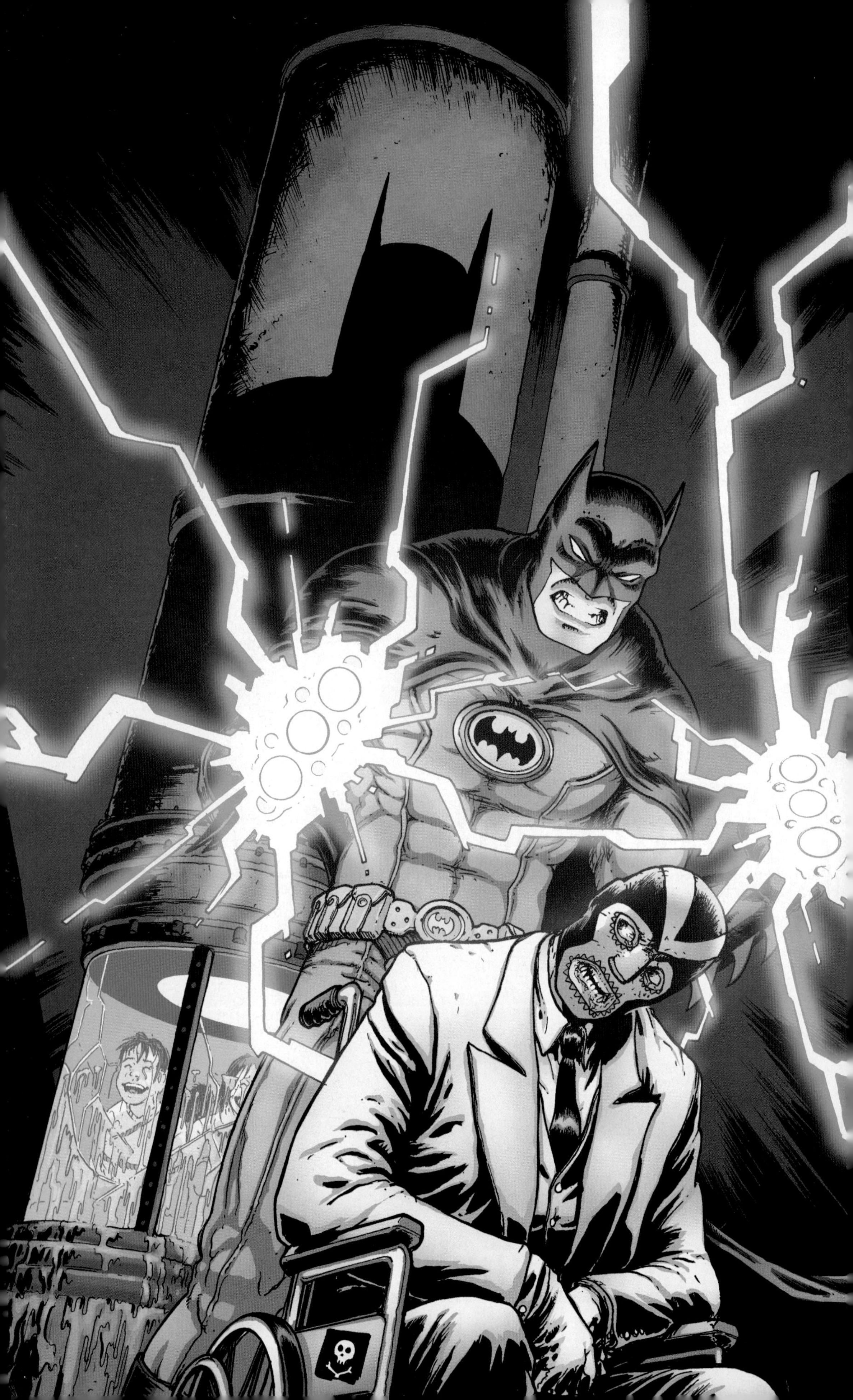

Issue #5 cover art by
J.H. WILLIAMS III.

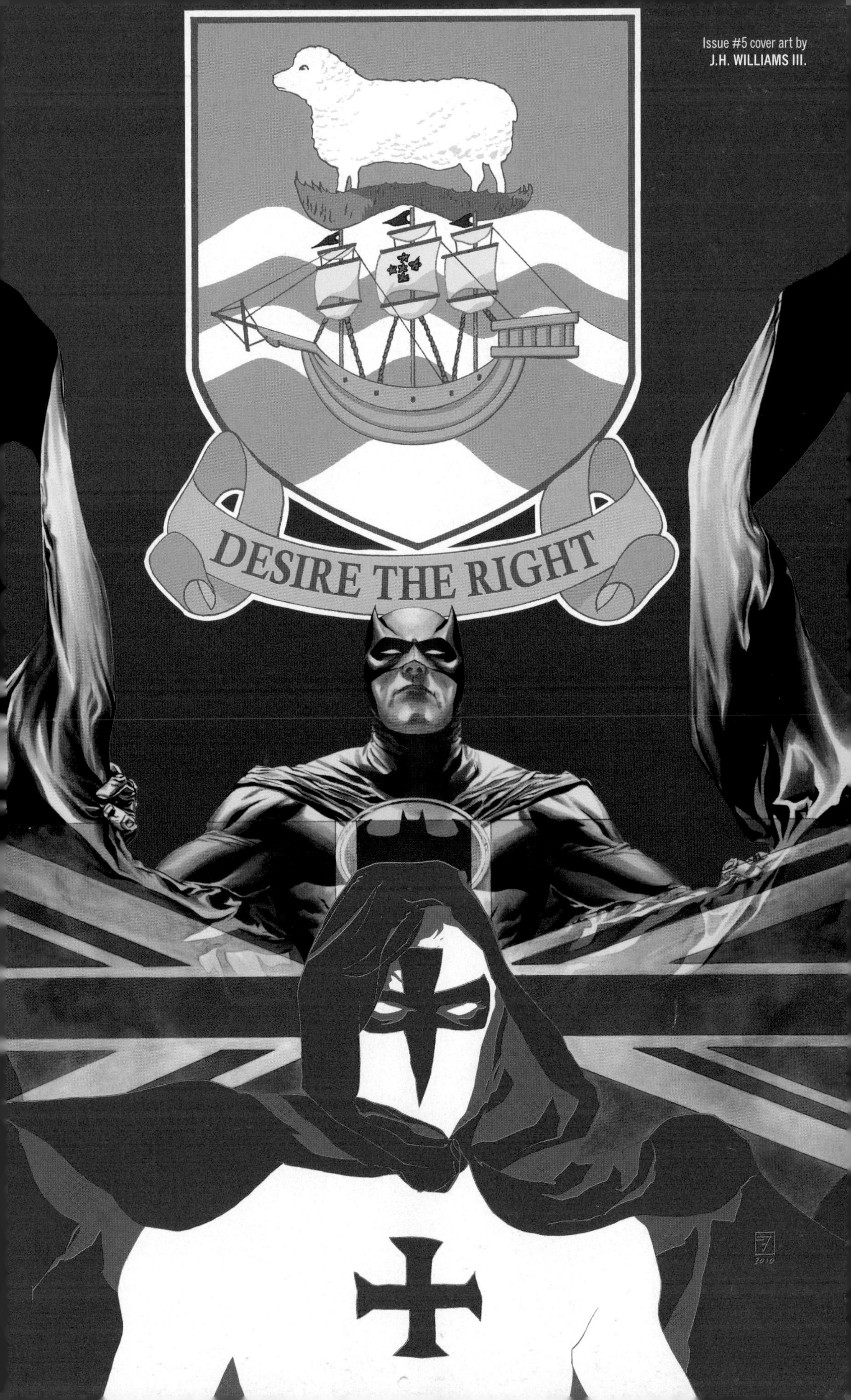
DESIRE THE RIGHT

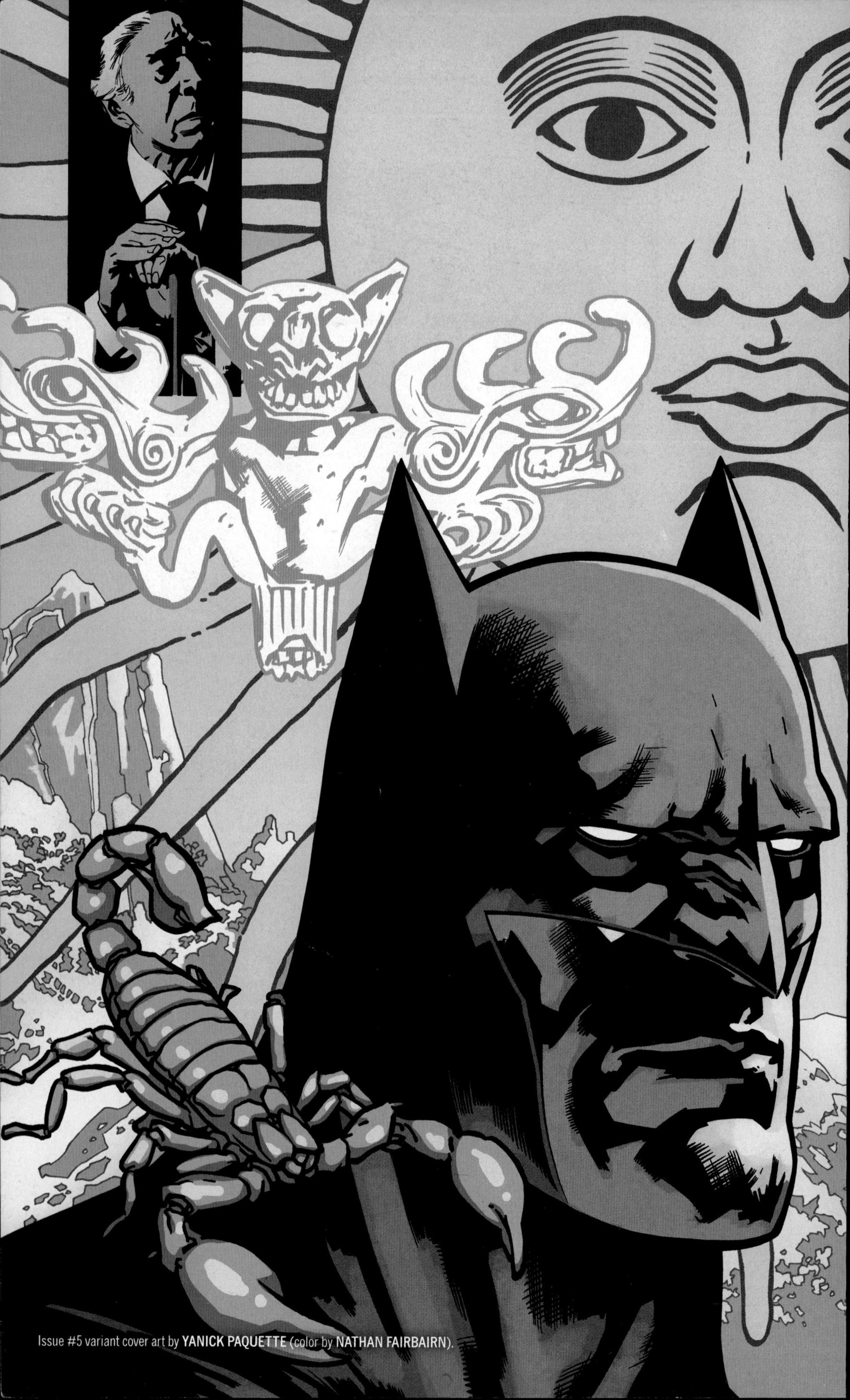

Issue #5 variant cover art by **YANICK PAQUETTE** (color by **NATHAN FAIRBAIRN**).

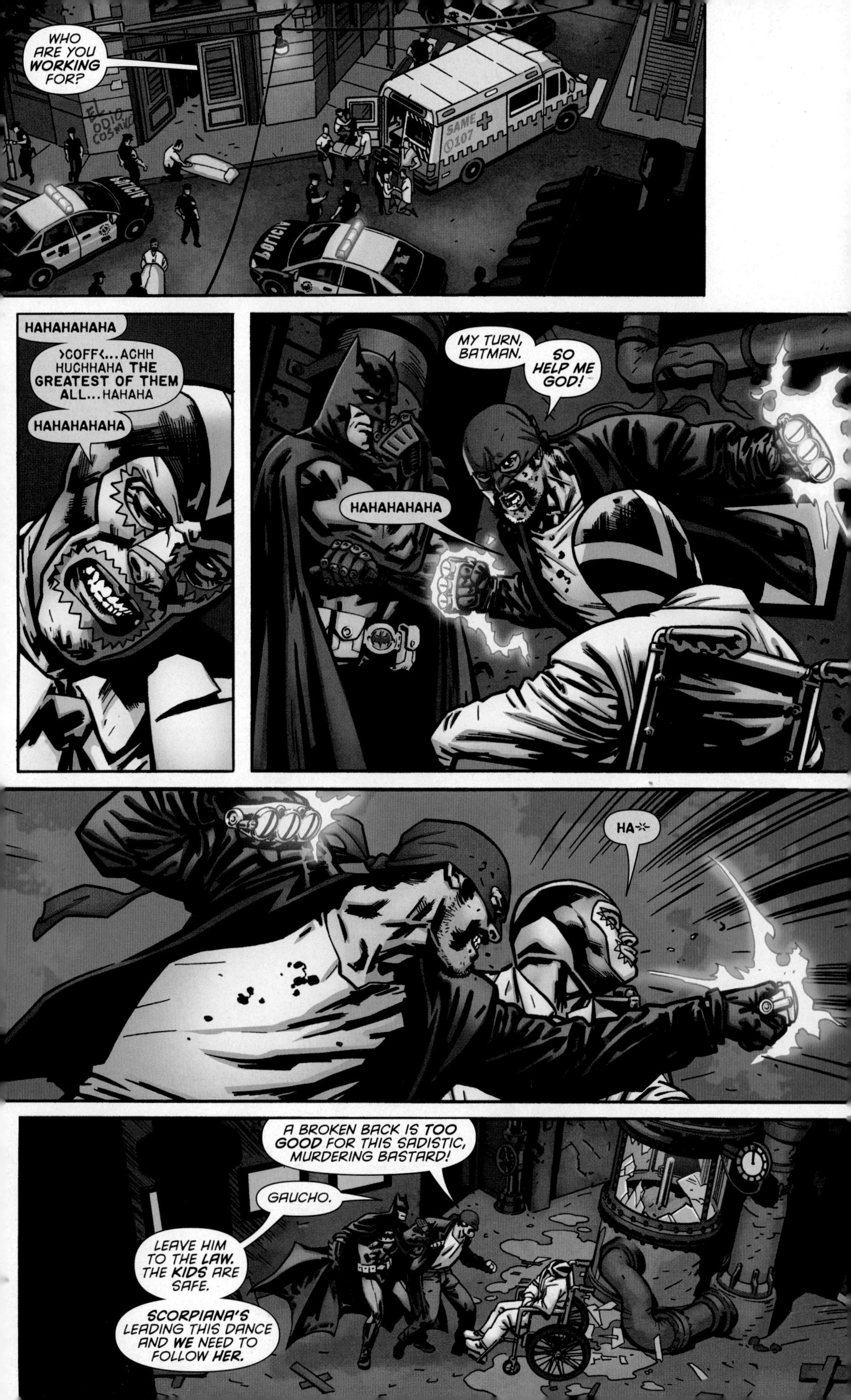

WHO ARE YOU WORKING FOR?
SAME
107
HAHAHAHAHA
>COFF<...ACHH HUCHHAHA THE GREATEST OF THEM ALL...HAHAHA
HAHAHAHAHA
MY TURN, BATMAN.
SO HELP ME GOD!
HAHAHAHAHA
HA-
A BROKEN BACK IS TOO GOOD FOR THIS SADISTIC, MURDERING BASTARD!
GAUCHO.
LEAVE HIM TO THE LAW. THE KIDS ARE SAFE.
SCORPIANA'S LEADING THIS DANCE AND WE NEED TO FOLLOW HER.

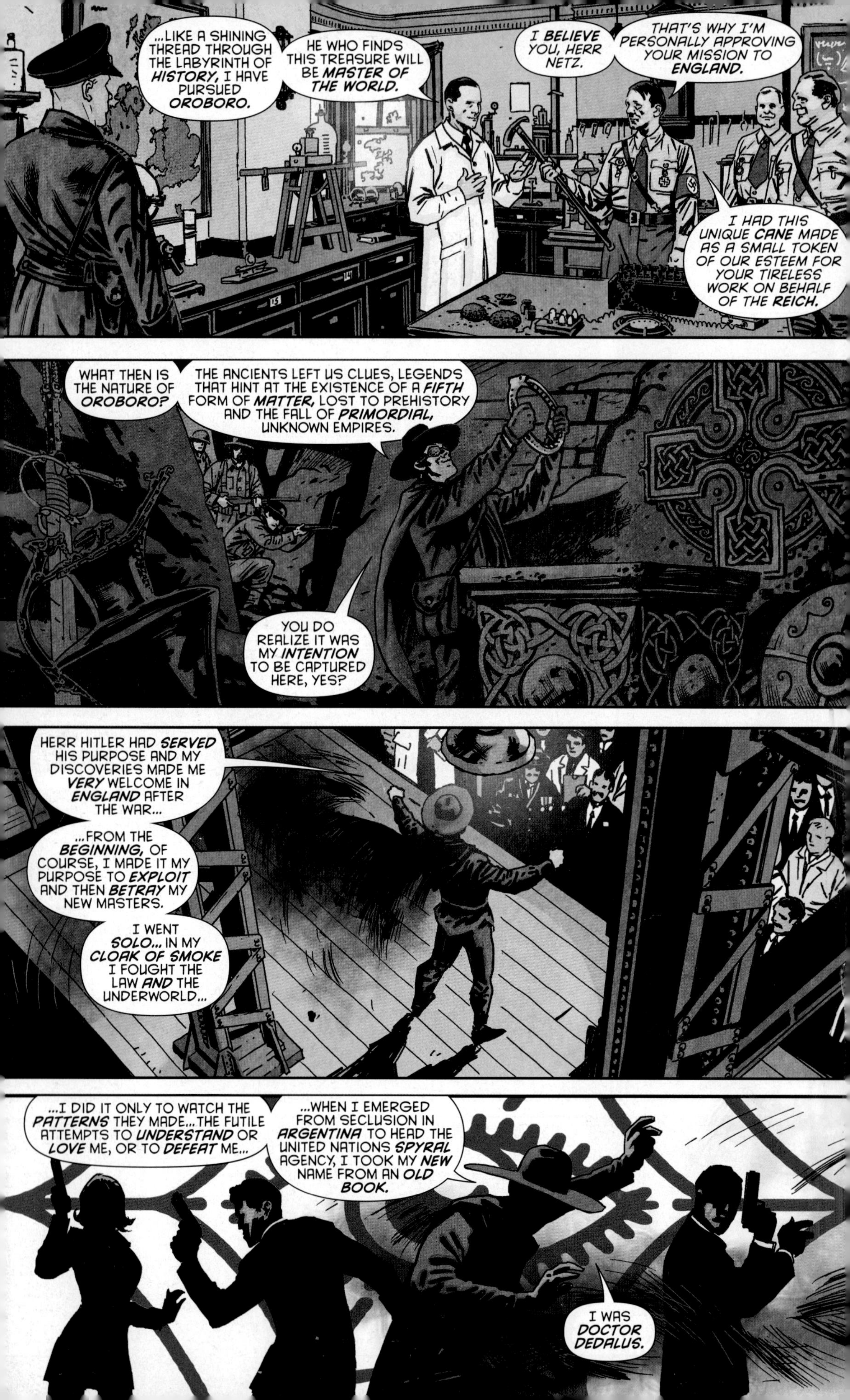
...LIKE A SHINING THREAD THROUGH THE LABYRINTH OF HISTORY, I HAVE PURSUED OROBORO.
HE WHO FINDS THIS TREASURE WILL BE MASTER OF THE WORLD.
I BELIEVE YOU, HERR NETZ.
THAT'S WHY I'M PERSONALLY APPROVING YOUR MISSION TO ENGLAND.
I HAD THIS UNIQUE CANE MADE AS A SMALL TOKEN OF OUR ESTEEM FOR YOUR TIRELESS WORK ON BEHALF OF THE REICH.
WHAT THEN IS THE NATURE OF OROBORO?
THE ANCIENTS LEFT US CLUES, LEGENDS THAT HINT AT THE EXISTENCE OF A FIFTH FORM OF MATTER, LOST TO PREHISTORY AND THE FALL OF PRIMORDIAL, UNKNOWN EMPIRES.
YOU DO REALIZE IT WAS MY INTENTION TO BE CAPTURED HERE, YES?
HERR HITLER HAD SERVED HIS PURPOSE AND MY DISCOVERIES MADE ME VERY WELCOME IN ENGLAND AFTER THE WAR...
...FROM THE BEGINNING, OF COURSE, I MADE IT MY PURPOSE TO EXPLOIT AND THEN BETRAY MY NEW MASTERS.
I WENT SOLO... IN MY CLOAK OF SMOKE I FOUGHT THE LAW AND THE UNDERWORLD...
...I DID IT ONLY TO WATCH THE PATTERNS THEY MADE... THE FUTILE ATTEMPTS TO UNDERSTAND OR LOVE ME, OR TO DEFEAT ME...
...WHEN I EMERGED FROM SECLUSION IN ARGENTINA TO HEAD THE UNITED NATIONS SPYRAL AGENCY, I TOOK MY NEW NAME FROM AN OLD BOOK.
I WAS DOCTOR DEDALUS.

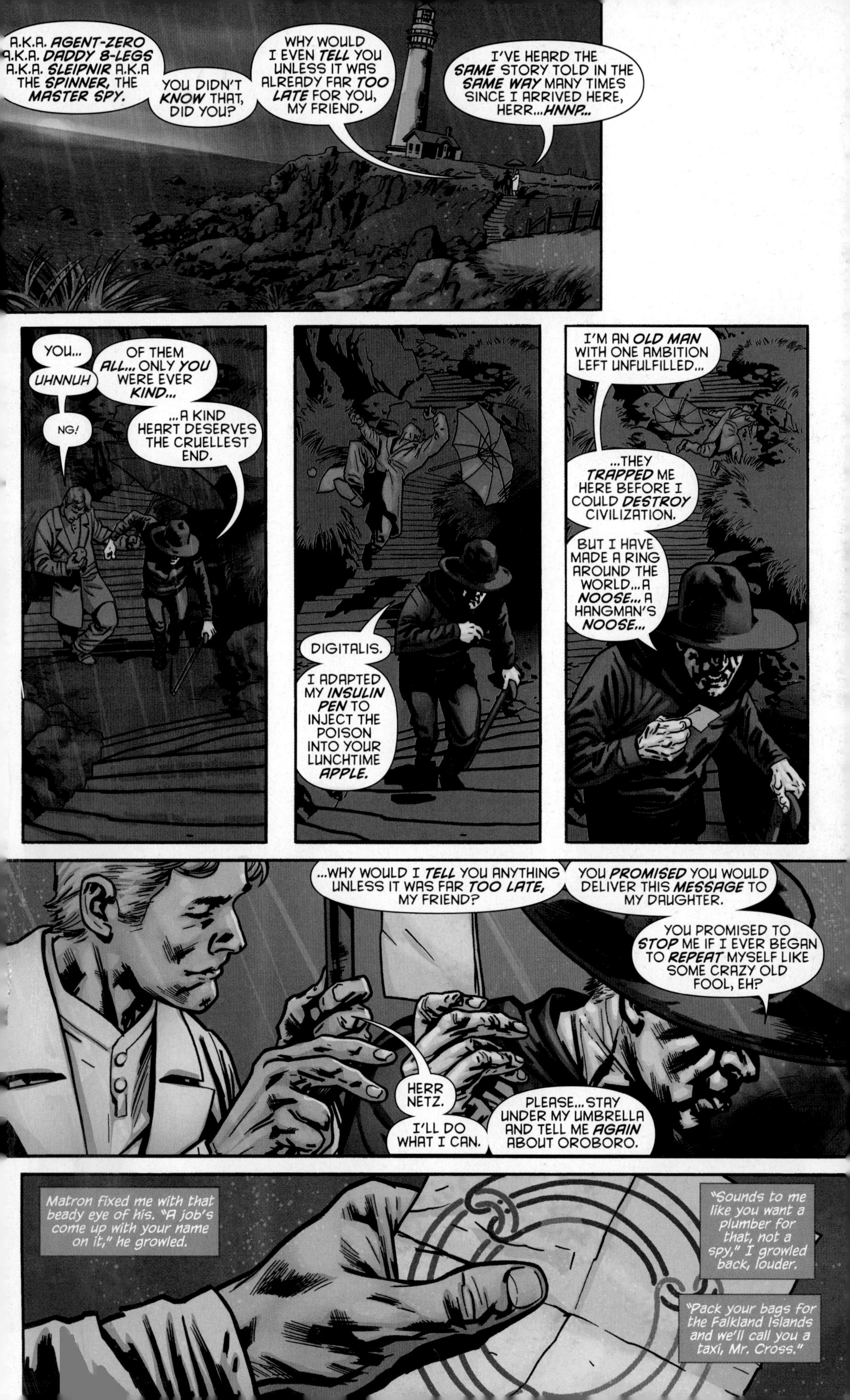

A.K.A. AGENT-ZERO A.K.A. DADDY 8-LEGS A.K.A. SLEIPNIR A.K.A THE SPINNER, THE MASTER SPY.
YOU DIDN'T KNOW THAT, DID YOU?
WHY WOULD I EVEN TELL YOU UNLESS IT WAS ALREADY FAR TOO LATE FOR YOU, MY FRIEND.
I'VE HEARD THE SAME STORY TOLD IN THE SAME WAY MANY TIMES SINCE I ARRIVED HERE, HERR...HNNP...
YOU...
UHNNUH
NG!
OF THEM ALL... ONLY YOU WERE EVER KIND...
...A KIND HEART DESERVES THE CRUELLEST END.
DIGITALIS.
I ADAPTED MY INSULIN PEN TO INJECT THE POISON INTO YOUR LUNCHTIME APPLE.
I'M AN OLD MAN WITH ONE AMBITION LEFT UNFULFILLED...
...THEY TRAPPED ME HERE BEFORE I COULD DESTROY CIVILIZATION.
BUT I HAVE MADE A RING AROUND THE WORLD...A NOOSE... A HANGMAN'S NOOSE...
...WHY WOULD I TELL YOU ANYTHING UNLESS IT WAS FAR TOO LATE, MY FRIEND?
YOU PROMISED YOU WOULD DELIVER THIS MESSAGE TO MY DAUGHTER.
YOU PROMISED TO STOP ME IF I EVER BEGAN TO REPEAT MYSELF LIKE SOME CRAZY OLD FOOL, EH?
HERR NETZ.
I'LL DO WHAT I CAN.
PLEASE...STAY UNDER MY UMBRELLA AND TELL ME AGAIN ABOUT OROBORO.
Matron fixed me with that beady eye of his. "A job's come up with your name on it," he growled.
"Sounds to me like you want a plumber for that, not a spy," I growled back, louder.
"Pack your bags for the Falkland Islands and we'll call you a taxi, Mr. Cross."

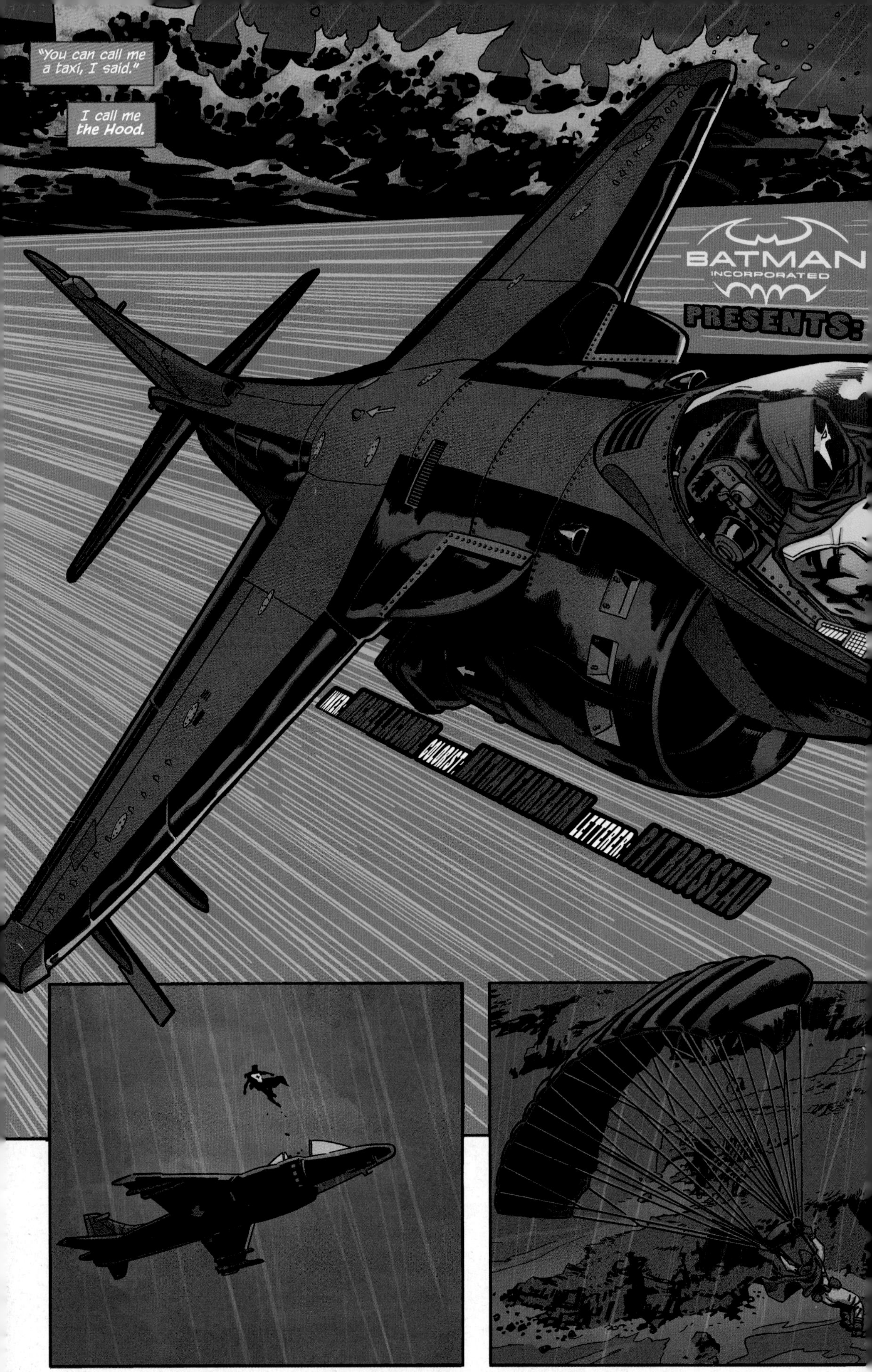

"You can call me a taxi, I said."
I call me the Hood.
BATMAN INCORPORATED
PRESENTS:
INKER:
COLORIST: NATHAN FAIRBAIRN
LETTERER: PAT BROSSEAU

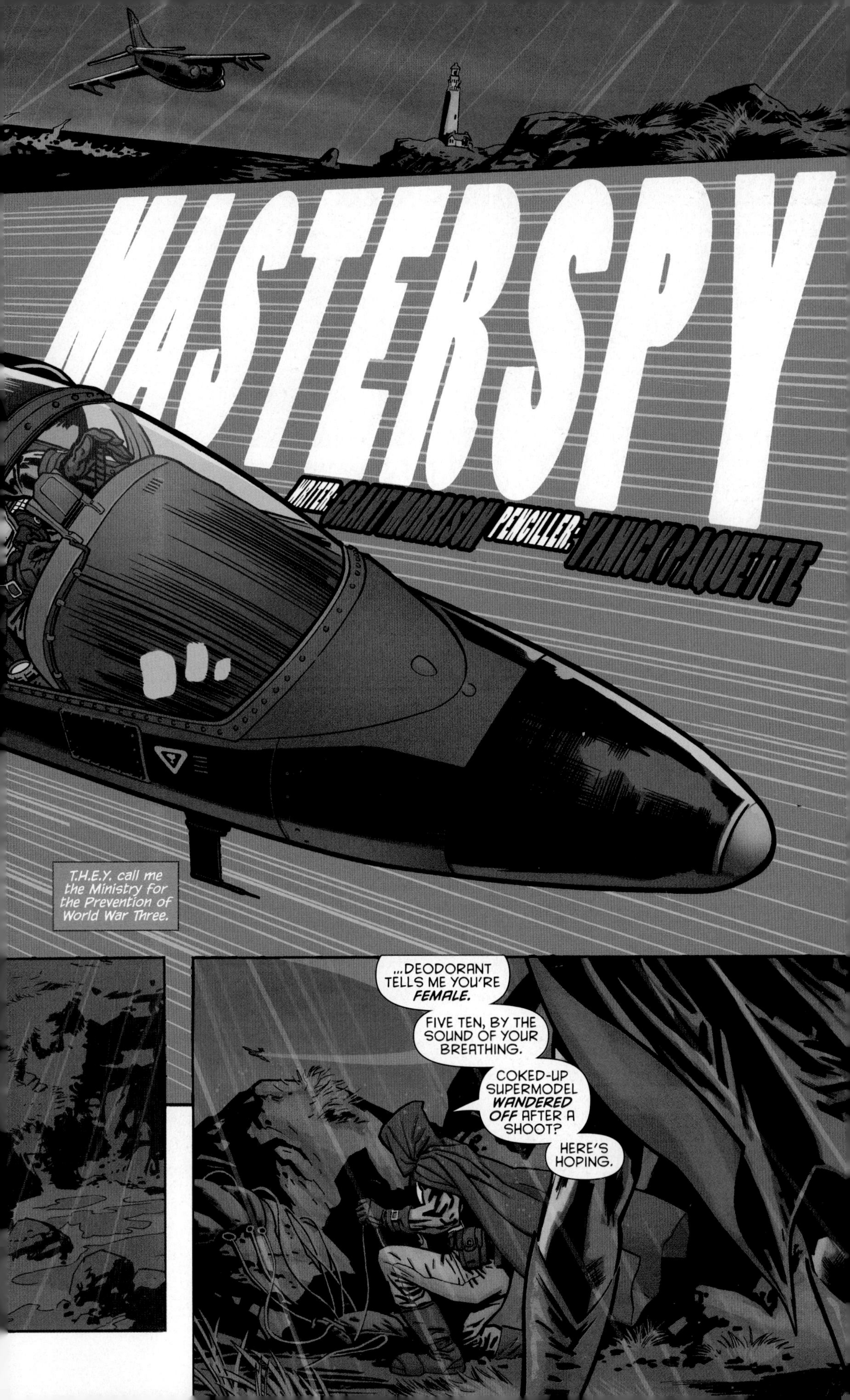
MASTERSPY
WRITER: GRANT MORRISON PENCILLER: YANICK PAQUETTE
T.H.E.Y. call me the Ministry for the Prevention of World War Three.
...DEODORANT TELLS ME YOU'RE FEMALE.
FIVE TEN, BY THE SOUND OF YOUR BREATHING.
COKED-UP SUPERMODEL WANDERED OFF AFTER A SHOOT?
HERE'S HOPING.

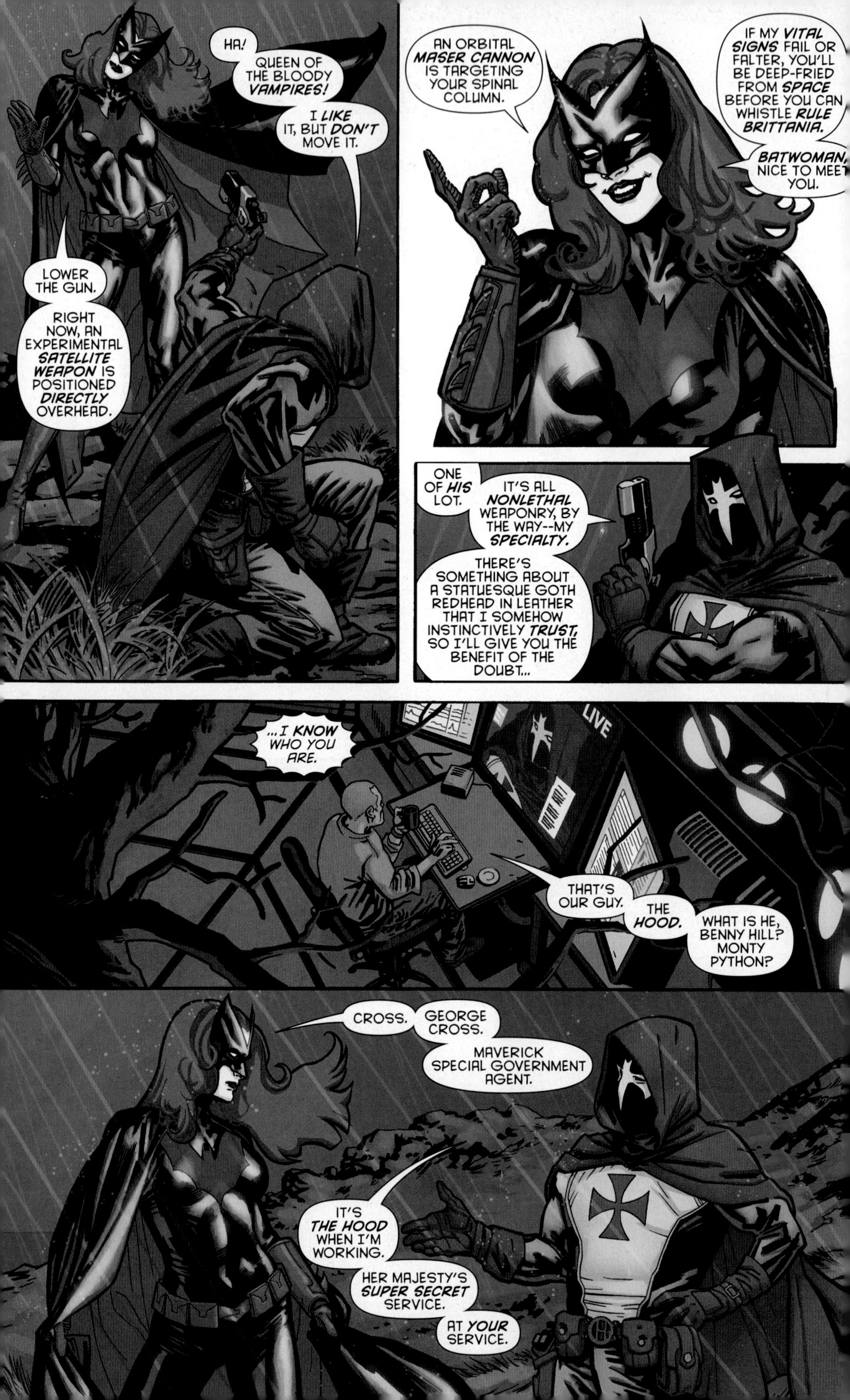
HA!
QUEEN OF THE BLOODY VAMPIRES!
I LIKE IT, BUT DON'T MOVE IT.
LOWER THE GUN.
RIGHT NOW, AN EXPERIMENTAL SATELLITE WEAPON IS POSITIONED DIRECTLY OVERHEAD.
AN ORBITAL MASER CANNON IS TARGETING YOUR SPINAL COLUMN.
IF MY VITAL SIGNS FAIL OR FALTER, YOU'LL BE DEEP-FRIED FROM SPACE BEFORE YOU CAN WHISTLE RULE BRITTANIA.
BATWOMAN. NICE TO MEET YOU.
ONE OF HIS LOT.
IT'S ALL NONLETHAL WEAPONRY, BY THE WAY--MY SPECIALTY.
THERE'S SOMETHING ABOUT A STATUESQUE GOTH REDHEAD IN LEATHER THAT I SOMEHOW INSTINCTIVELY TRUST, SO I'LL GIVE YOU THE BENEFIT OF THE DOUBT...
...I KNOW WHO YOU ARE.
LIVE
THAT'S OUR GUY.
THE HOOD.
WHAT IS HE, BENNY HILL? MONTY PYTHON?
CROSS.
GEORGE CROSS.
MAVERICK SPECIAL GOVERNMENT AGENT.
IT'S THE HOOD WHEN I'M WORKING.
HER MAJESTY'S SUPER SECRET SERVICE.
AT YOUR SERVICE.

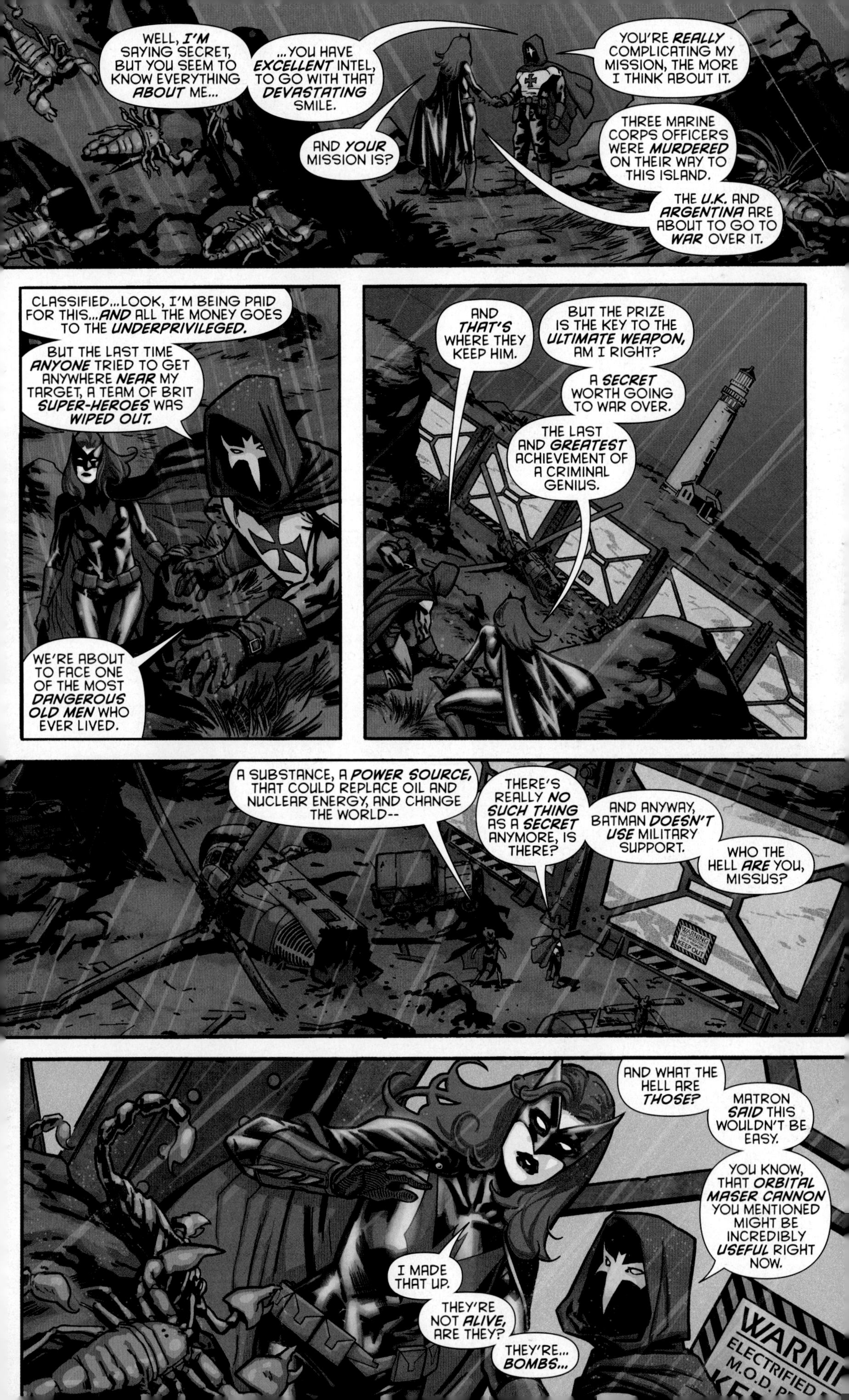

WELL, I'M SAYING SECRET, BUT YOU SEEM TO KNOW EVERYTHING ABOUT ME...
...YOU HAVE EXCELLENT INTEL, TO GO WITH THAT DEVASTATING SMILE.
AND YOUR MISSION IS?
YOU'RE REALLY COMPLICATING MY MISSION, THE MORE I THINK ABOUT IT.
THREE MARINE CORPS OFFICERS WERE MURDERED ON THEIR WAY TO THIS ISLAND.
THE U.K. AND ARGENTINA ARE ABOUT TO GO TO WAR OVER IT.
CLASSIFIED...LOOK, I'M BEING PAID FOR THIS...AND ALL THE MONEY GOES TO THE UNDERPRIVILEGED.
BUT THE LAST TIME ANYONE TRIED TO GET ANYWHERE NEAR MY TARGET, A TEAM OF BRIT SUPER-HEROES WAS WIPED OUT.
WE'RE ABOUT TO FACE ONE OF THE MOST DANGEROUS OLD MEN WHO EVER LIVED.
AND THAT'S WHERE THEY KEEP HIM.
BUT THE PRIZE IS THE KEY TO THE ULTIMATE WEAPON, AM I RIGHT?
A SECRET WORTH GOING TO WAR OVER.
THE LAST AND GREATEST ACHIEVEMENT OF A CRIMINAL GENIUS.
A SUBSTANCE, A POWER SOURCE, THAT COULD REPLACE OIL AND NUCLEAR ENERGY, AND CHANGE THE WORLD--
THERE'S REALLY NO SUCH THING AS A SECRET ANYMORE, IS THERE?
AND ANYWAY, BATMAN DOESN'T USE MILITARY SUPPORT.
WHO THE HELL ARE YOU, MISSUS?
WARNING
KEEP OUT
AND WHAT THE HELL ARE THOSE?
MATRON SAID THIS WOULDN'T BE EASY.
YOU KNOW, THAT ORBITAL MASER CANNON YOU MENTIONED MIGHT BE INCREDIBLY USEFUL RIGHT NOW.
I MADE THAT UP.
THEY'RE NOT ALIVE, ARE THEY?
THEY'RE... BOMBS...
WARNI
ELECTRIFIED
M.O.D.

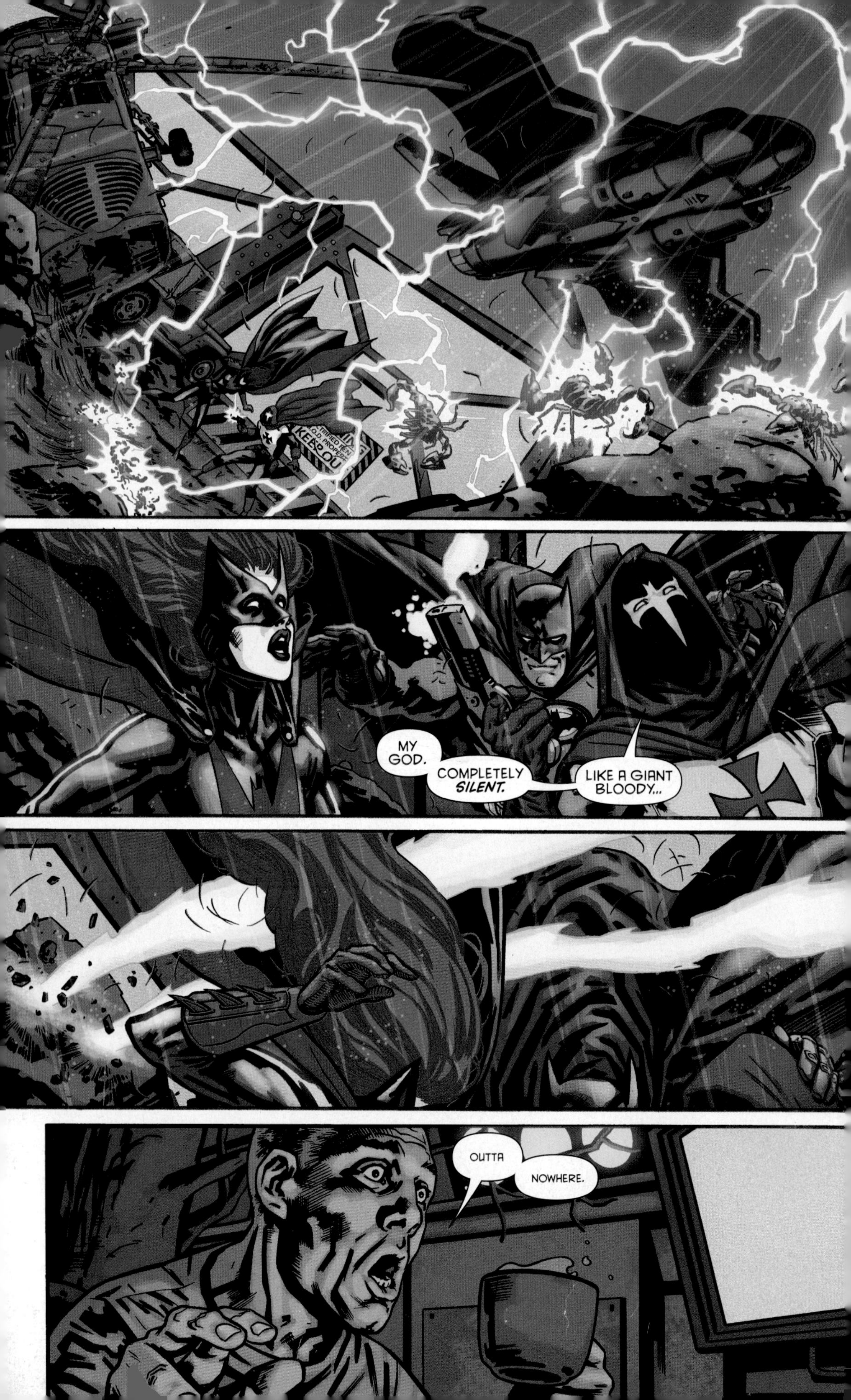
MY GOD.
COMPLETELY *SILENT.*
LIKE A GIANT BLOODY...
OUTTA
NOWHERE.

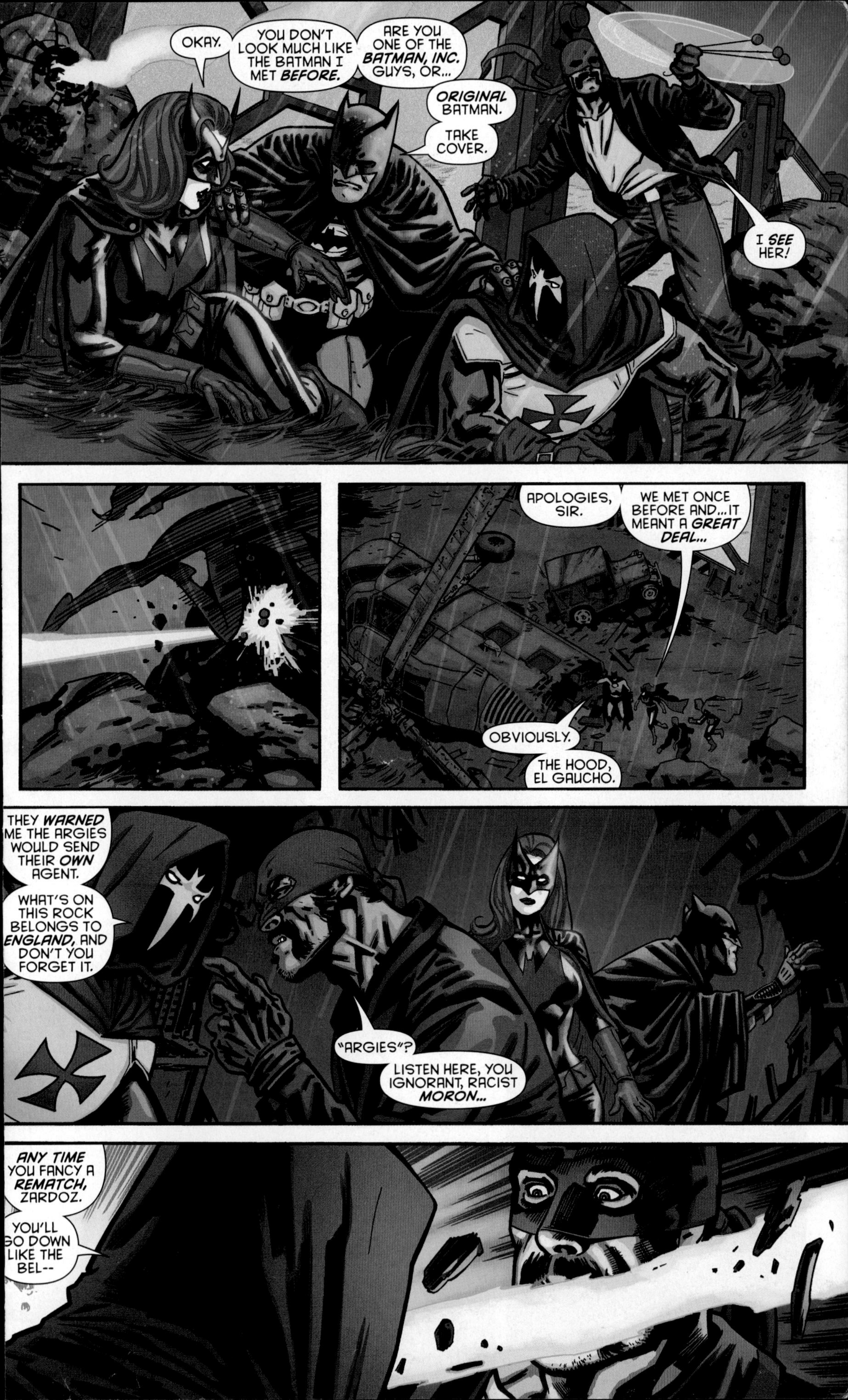
OKAY.
YOU DON'T LOOK MUCH LIKE THE BATMAN I MET BEFORE.
ARE YOU ONE OF THE BATMAN, INC. GUYS, OR...
ORIGINAL BATMAN.
TAKE COVER.
I SEE HER!
APOLOGIES, SIR.
WE MET ONCE BEFORE AND... IT MEANT A GREAT DEAL...
OBVIOUSLY.
THE HOOD, EL GAUCHO.
THEY WARNED ME THE ARGIES WOULD SEND THEIR OWN AGENT.
WHAT'S ON THIS ROCK BELONGS TO ENGLAND, AND DON'T YOU FORGET IT.
"ARGIES"?
LISTEN HERE, YOU IGNORANT, RACIST MORON...
ANY TIME YOU FANCY A REMATCH, ZARDOZ.
YOU'LL GO DOWN LIKE THE BEL--

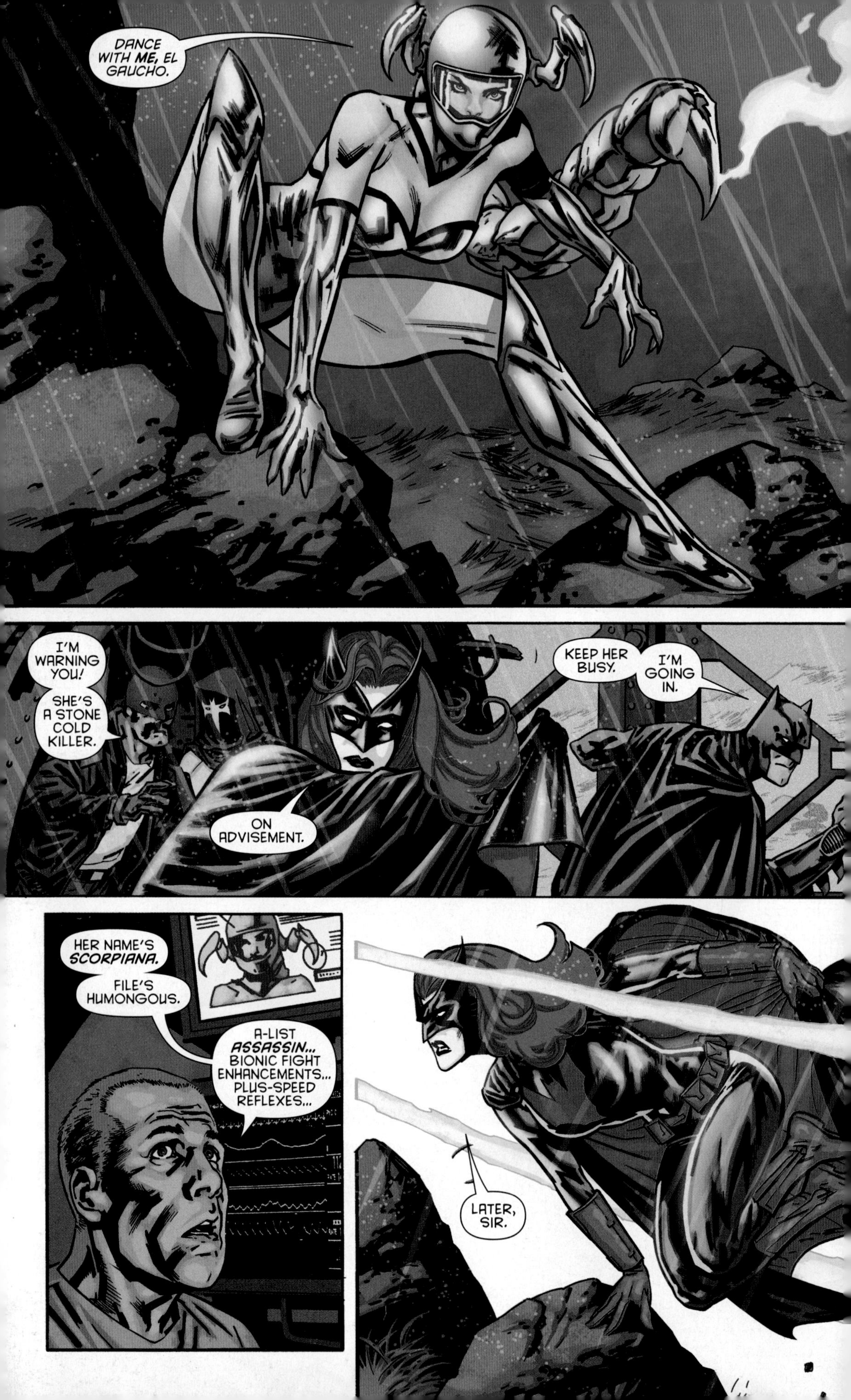
DANCE WITH **ME,** EL GAUCHO.
I'M WARNING YOU!
SHE'S A STONE COLD KILLER.
ON ADVISEMENT.
KEEP HER BUSY.
I'M GOING IN.
HER NAME'S ***SCORPIANA.***
FILE'S HUMONGOUS.
A-LIST ***ASSASSIN...*** BIONIC FIGHT ENHANCEMENTS... PLUS-SPEED REFLEXES...
LATER, SIR.

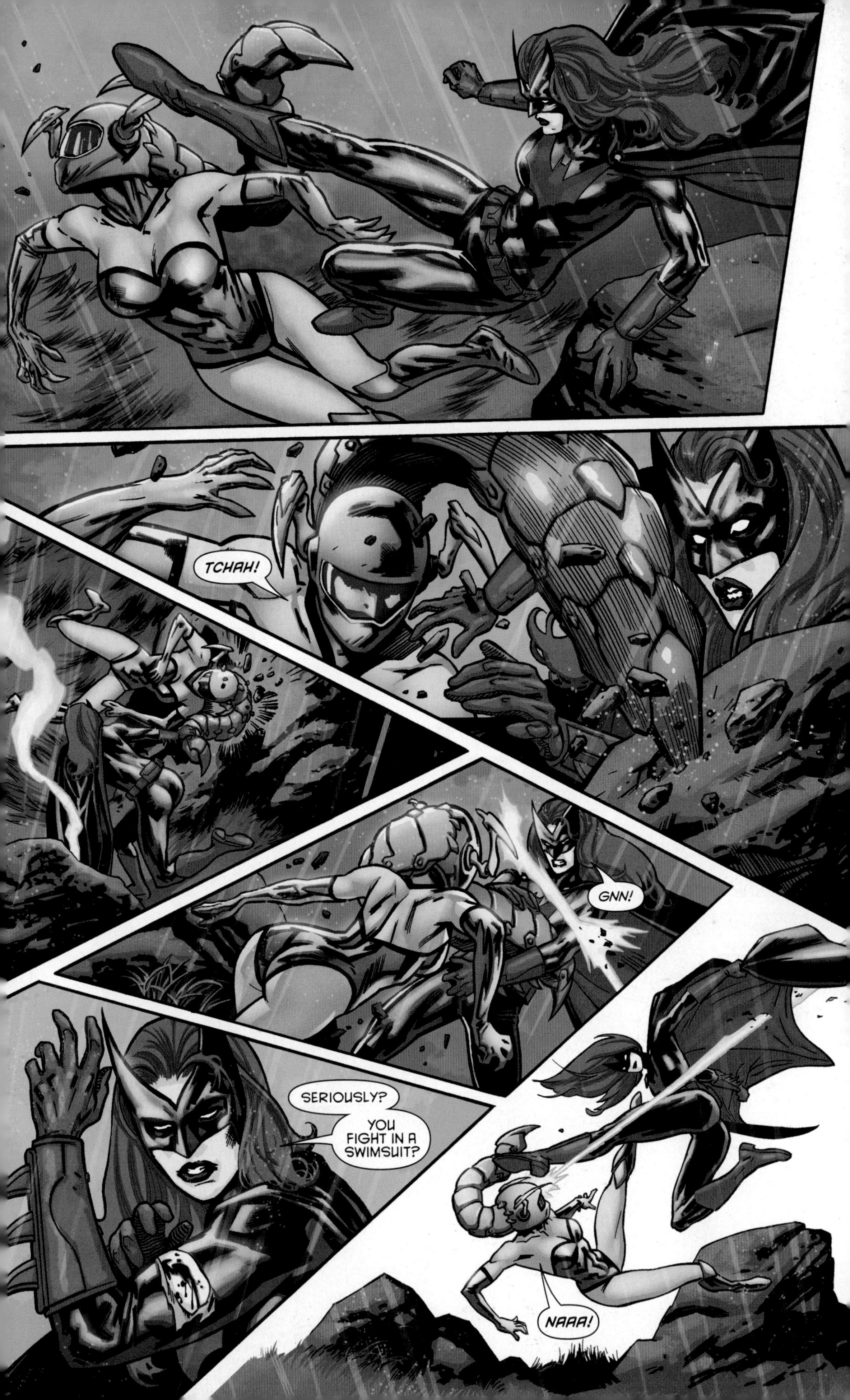
TCHAH!
GNN!
SERIOUSLY?
YOU FIGHT IN A SWIMSUIT?
NAAA!

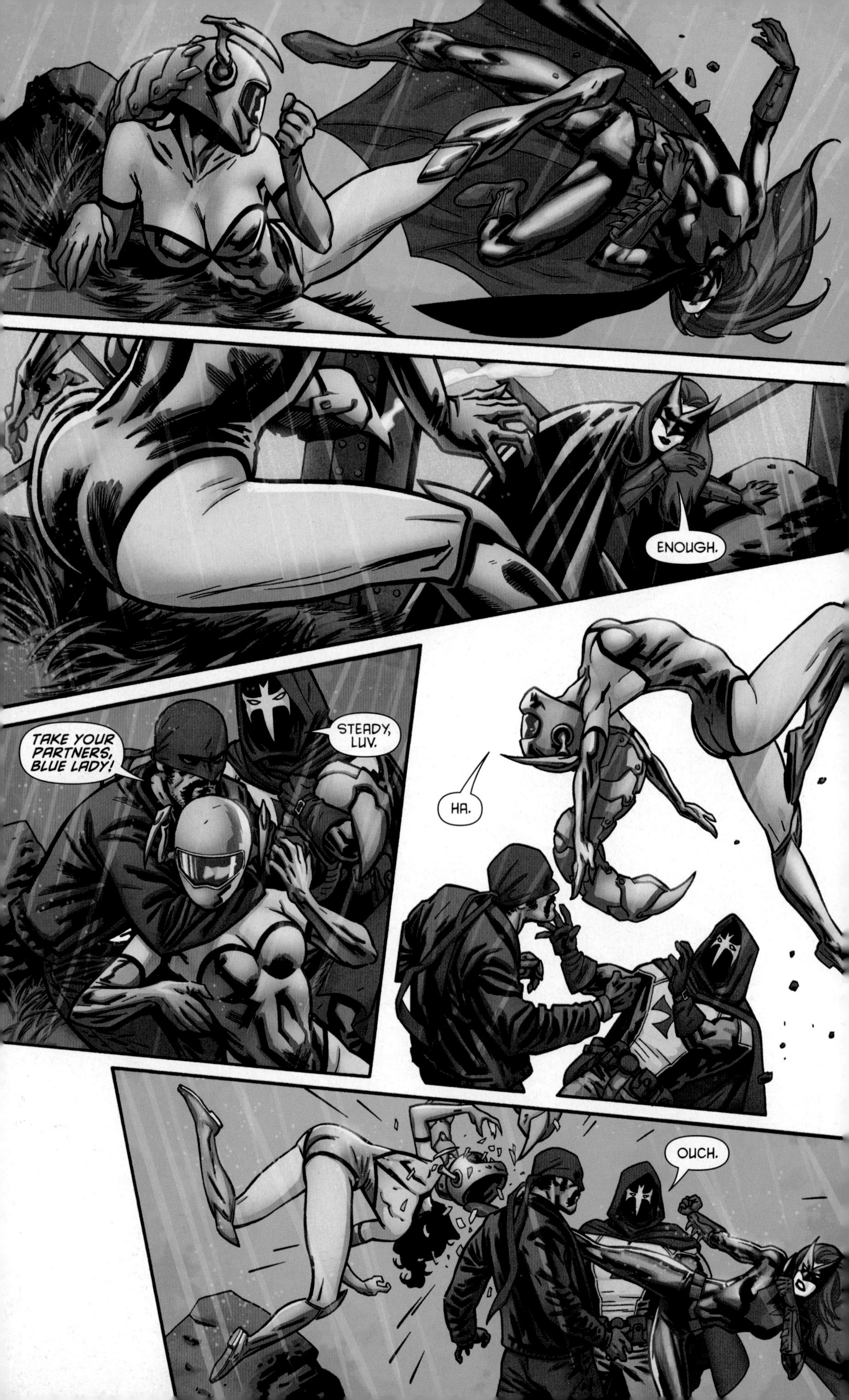
ENOUGH.
TAKE YOUR PARTNERS, BLUE LADY!
STEADY, LUV.
HA.
OUCH.

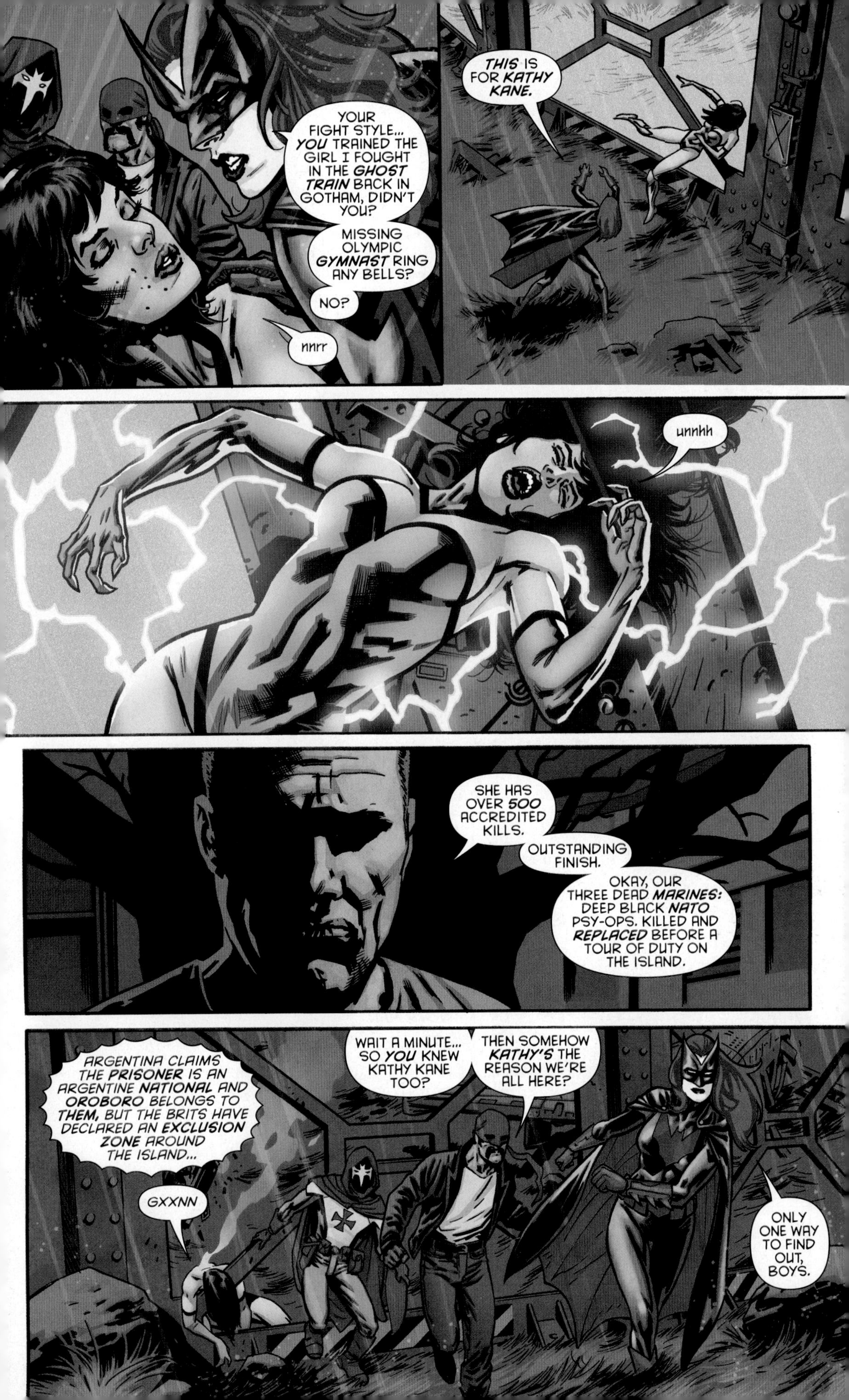
YOUR FIGHT STYLE... YOU TRAINED THE GIRL I FOUGHT IN THE GHOST TRAIN BACK IN GOTHAM, DIDN'T YOU?
MISSING OLYMPIC GYMNAST RING ANY BELLS?
NO?
nnrr
THIS IS FOR KATHY KANE.
unnhh
SHE HAS OVER 500 ACCREDITED KILLS.
OUTSTANDING FINISH.
OKAY, OUR THREE DEAD MARINES: DEEP BLACK NATO PSY-OPS. KILLED AND REPLACED BEFORE A TOUR OF DUTY ON THE ISLAND.
ARGENTINA CLAIMS THE PRISONER IS AN ARGENTINE NATIONAL AND OROBORO BELONGS TO THEM, BUT THE BRITS HAVE DECLARED AN EXCLUSION ZONE AROUND THE ISLAND...
GXXNN
WAIT A MINUTE... SO YOU KNEW KATHY KANE TOO?
THEN SOMEHOW KATHY'S THE REASON WE'RE ALL HERE?
ONLY ONE WAY TO FIND OUT, BOYS.

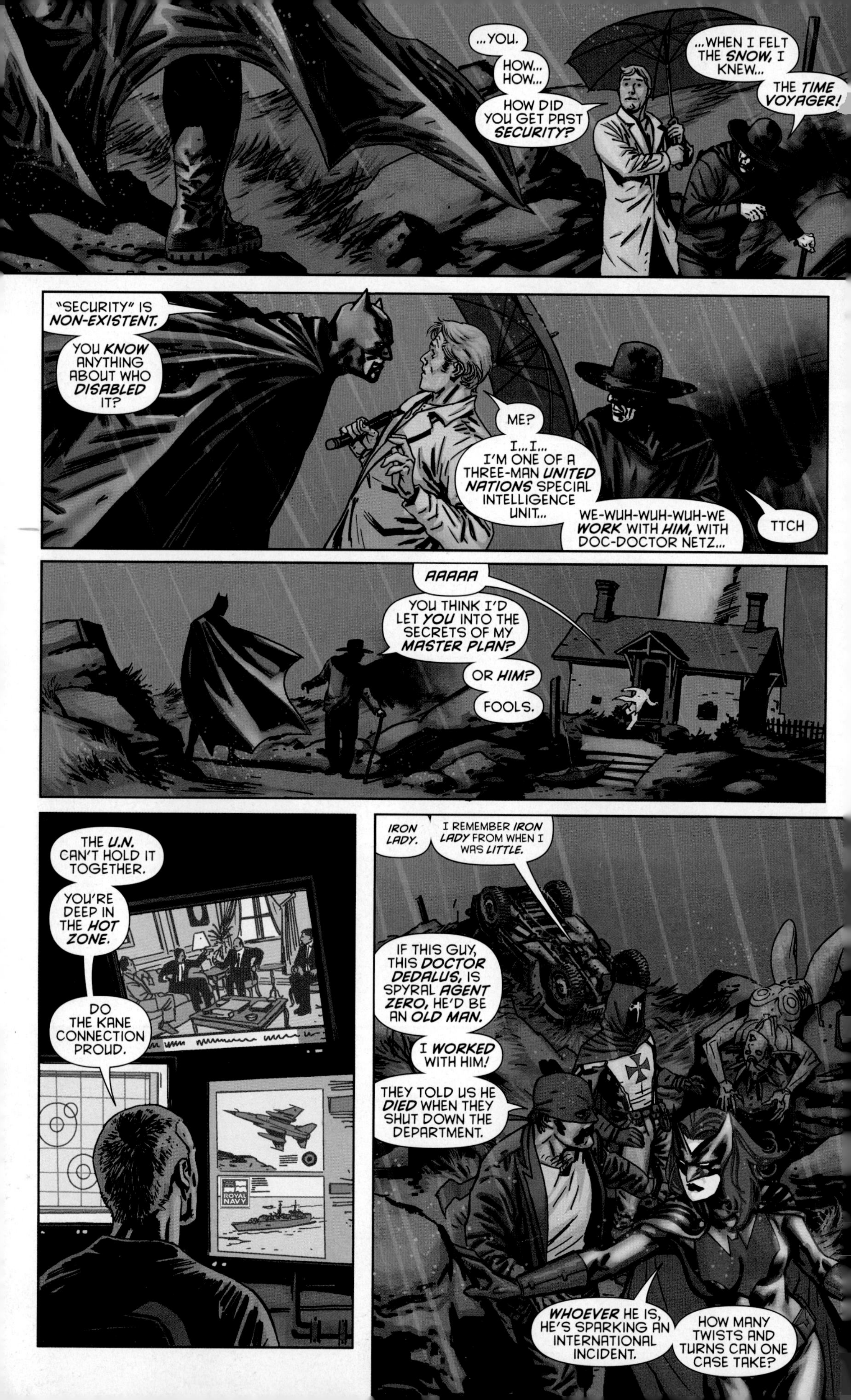

...YOU.
HOW... HOW...
HOW DID YOU GET PAST SECURITY?
...WHEN I FELT THE SNOW, I KNEW...
THE TIME VOYAGER!
"SECURITY" IS NON-EXISTENT.
YOU KNOW ANYTHING ABOUT WHO DISABLED IT?
ME?
I...I... I'M ONE OF A THREE-MAN UNITED NATIONS SPECIAL INTELLIGENCE UNIT...
WE-WUH-WUH-WUH-WE WORK WITH HIM, WITH DOC-DOCTOR NETZ...
TTCH
AAAAA
YOU THINK I'D LET YOU INTO THE SECRETS OF MY MASTER PLAN?
OR HIM?
FOOLS.
THE U.N. CAN'T HOLD IT TOGETHER.
YOU'RE DEEP IN THE HOT ZONE.
DO THE KANE CONNECTION PROUD.
ROYAL NAVY
IRON LADY.
I REMEMBER IRON LADY FROM WHEN I WAS LITTLE.
IF THIS GUY, THIS DOCTOR DEDALUS, IS SPYRAL AGENT ZERO, HE'D BE AN OLD MAN.
I WORKED WITH HIM!
THEY TOLD US HE DIED WHEN THEY SHUT DOWN THE DEPARTMENT.
WHOEVER HE IS, HE'S SPARKING AN INTERNATIONAL INCIDENT.
HOW MANY TWISTS AND TURNS CAN ONE CASE TAKE?

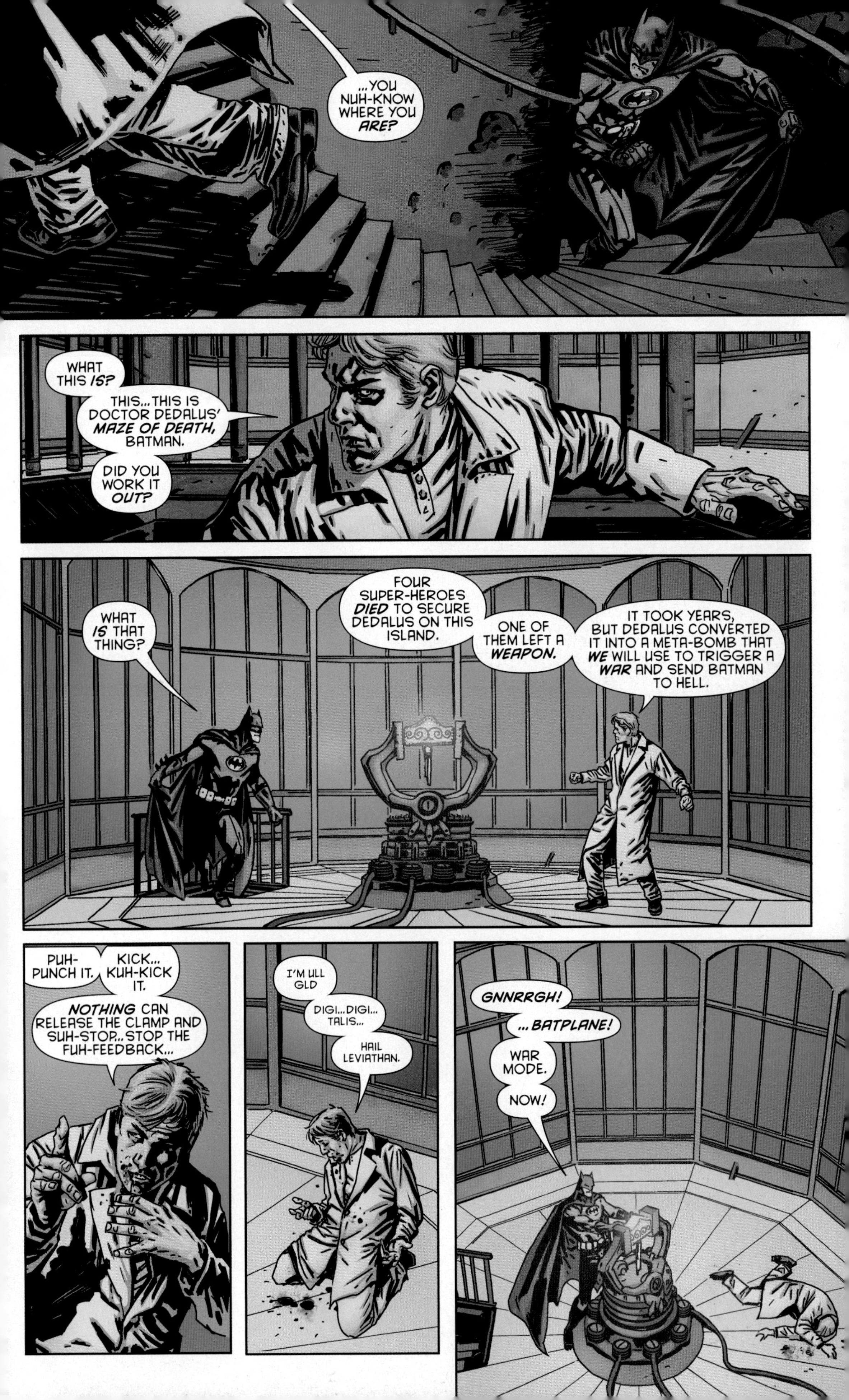
...YOU NUH-KNOW WHERE YOU ARE?
WHAT THIS IS?
THIS... THIS IS DOCTOR DEDALUS' MAZE OF DEATH, BATMAN.
DID YOU WORK IT OUT?
WHAT IS THAT THING?
FOUR SUPER-HEROES DIED TO SECURE DEDALUS ON THIS ISLAND.
ONE OF THEM LEFT A WEAPON.
IT TOOK YEARS, BUT DEDALUS CONVERTED IT INTO A META-BOMB THAT WE WILL USE TO TRIGGER A WAR AND SEND BATMAN TO HELL.
PUH-PUNCH IT.
KICK... KUH-KICK IT.
NOTHING CAN RELEASE THE CLAMP AND SUH-STOP... STOP THE FUH-FEEDBACK...
I'M ULL GLD
DIGI... DIGI... TALIS...
HAIL LEVIATHAN.
GNNRRGH!
...BATPLANE!
WAR MODE.
NOW!

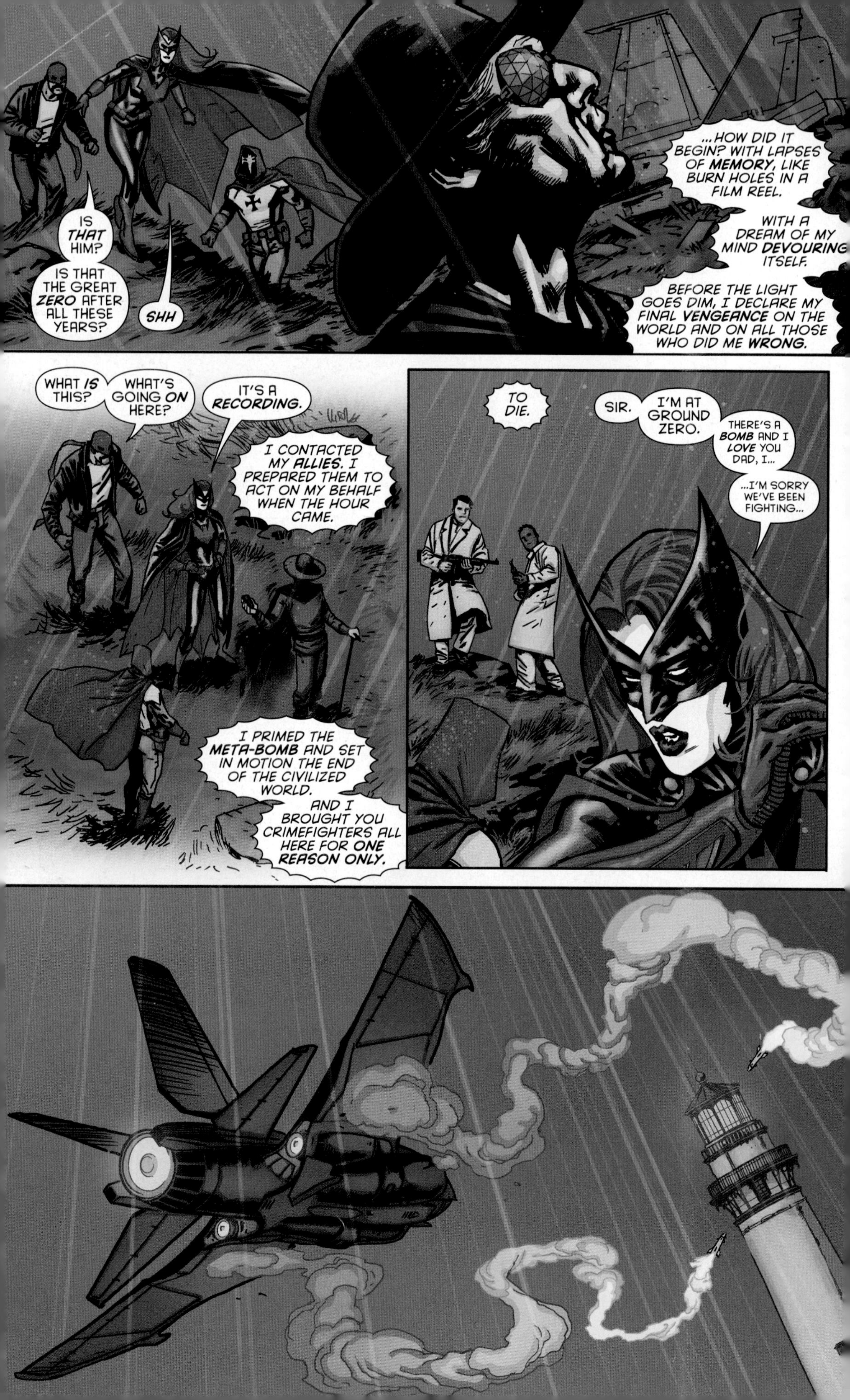

IS THAT HIM?
IS THAT THE GREAT ZERO AFTER ALL THESE YEARS?
SHH
...HOW DID IT BEGIN? WITH LAPSES OF MEMORY, LIKE BURN HOLES IN A FILM REEL.
WITH A DREAM OF MY MIND DEVOURING ITSELF.
BEFORE THE LIGHT GOES DIM, I DECLARE MY FINAL VENGEANCE ON THE WORLD AND ON ALL THOSE WHO DID ME WRONG.
WHAT IS THIS?
WHAT'S GOING ON HERE?
IT'S A RECORDING.
I CONTACTED MY ALLIES. I PREPARED THEM TO ACT ON MY BEHALF WHEN THE HOUR CAME.
I PRIMED THE META-BOMB AND SET IN MOTION THE END OF THE CIVILIZED WORLD.
AND I BROUGHT YOU CRIMEFIGHTERS ALL HERE FOR ONE REASON ONLY.
TO DIE.
SIR.
I'M AT GROUND ZERO.
THERE'S A BOMB AND I LOVE YOU DAD, I...
...I'M SORRY WE'VE BEEN FIGHTING...

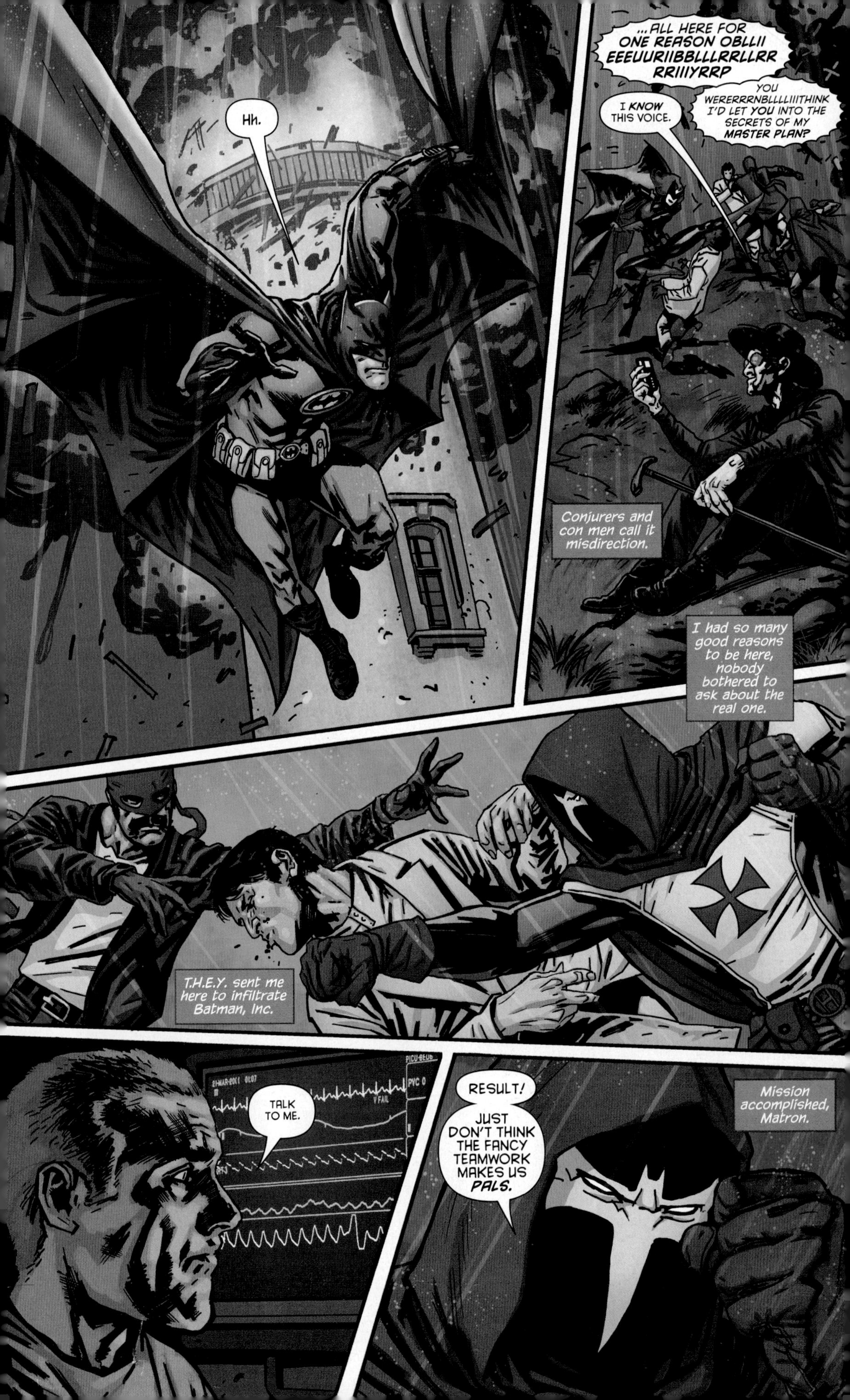
Hh.
...ALL HERE FOR ONE REASON OBLLII EEEUURIIBBLLLRRLLRR RRIIIYRRP
I KNOW THIS VOICE.
YOU WERERRRNBLLLLIIITHINK I'D LET YOU INTO THE SECRETS OF MY MASTER PLAN?
Conjurers and con men call it misdirection.
I had so many good reasons to be here, nobody bothered to ask about the real one.
T.H.E.Y. sent me here to infiltrate Batman, Inc.
TALK TO ME.
RESULT!
JUST DON'T THINK THE FANCY TEAMWORK MAKES US PALS.
Mission accomplished, Matron.

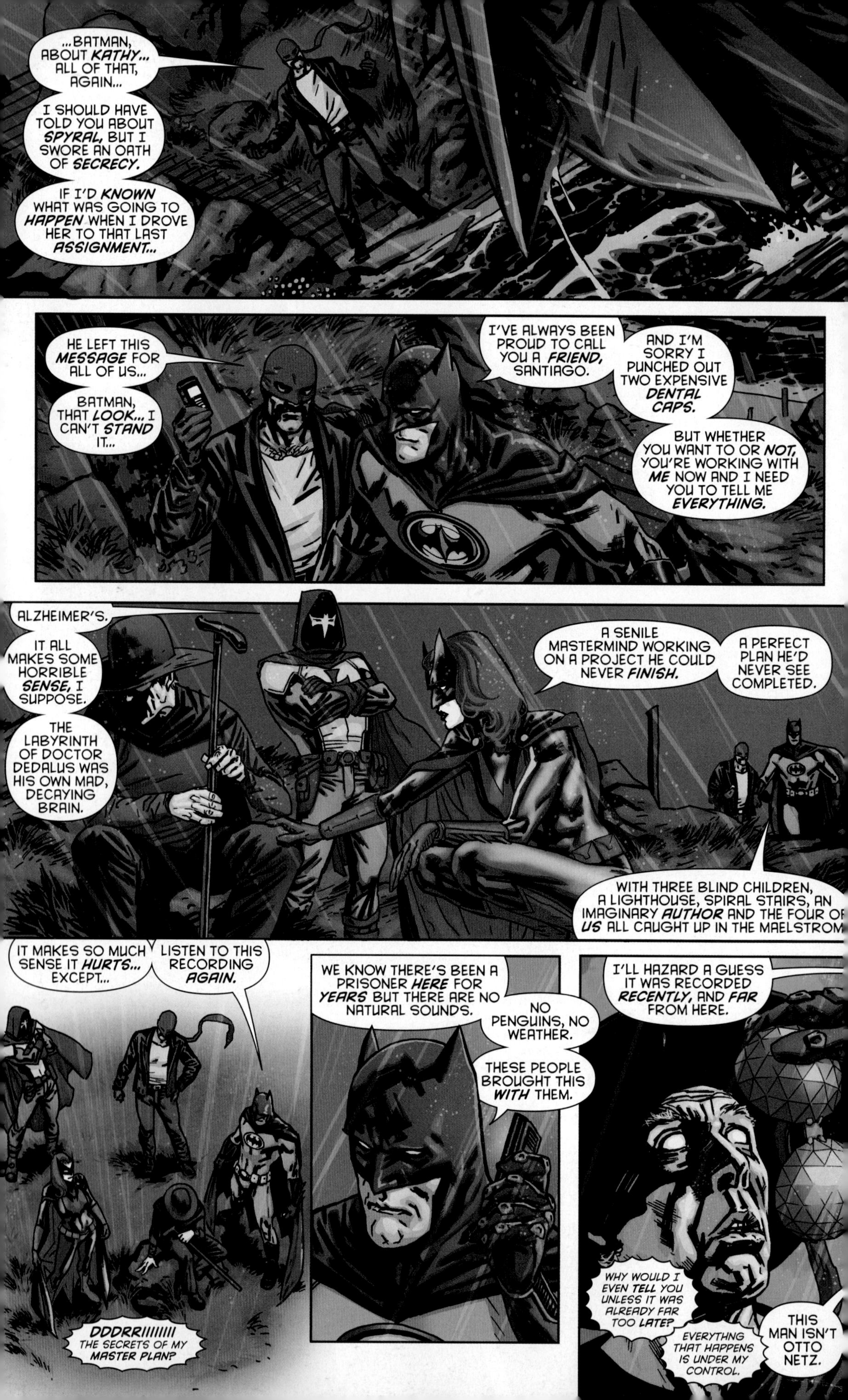
...BATMAN, ABOUT KATHY... ALL OF THAT, AGAIN...
I SHOULD HAVE TOLD YOU ABOUT SPYRAL, BUT I SWORE AN OATH OF SECRECY.
IF I'D KNOWN WHAT WAS GOING TO HAPPEN WHEN I DROVE HER TO THAT LAST ASSIGNMENT...
HE LEFT THIS MESSAGE FOR ALL OF US...
BATMAN, THAT LOOK... I CAN'T STAND IT...
I'VE ALWAYS BEEN PROUD TO CALL YOU A FRIEND, SANTIAGO.
AND I'M SORRY I PUNCHED OUT TWO EXPENSIVE DENTAL CAPS.
BUT WHETHER YOU WANT TO OR NOT, YOU'RE WORKING WITH ME NOW AND I NEED YOU TO TELL ME EVERYTHING.
ALZHEIMER'S.
IT ALL MAKES SOME HORRIBLE SENSE, I SUPPOSE.
THE LABYRINTH OF DOCTOR DEDALUS WAS HIS OWN MAD, DECAYING BRAIN.
A SENILE MASTERMIND WORKING ON A PROJECT HE COULD NEVER FINISH.
A PERFECT PLAN HE'D NEVER SEE COMPLETED.
WITH THREE BLIND CHILDREN, A LIGHTHOUSE, SPIRAL STAIRS, AN IMAGINARY AUTHOR AND THE FOUR OF US ALL CAUGHT UP IN THE MAELSTROM
IT MAKES SO MUCH SENSE IT HURTS... EXCEPT...
LISTEN TO THIS RECORDING AGAIN.
DDDRRIIIIIII THE SECRETS OF MY MASTER PLAN?
WE KNOW THERE'S BEEN A PRISONER HERE FOR YEARS BUT THERE ARE NO NATURAL SOUNDS.
NO PENGUINS, NO WEATHER.
THESE PEOPLE BROUGHT THIS WITH THEM.
I'LL HAZARD A GUESS IT WAS RECORDED RECENTLY, AND FAR FROM HERE.
WHY WOULD I EVEN TELL YOU UNLESS IT WAS ALREADY FAR TOO LATE?
EVERYTHNG THAT HAPPENS IS UNDER MY CONTROL.
THIS MAN ISN'T OTTO NETZ.

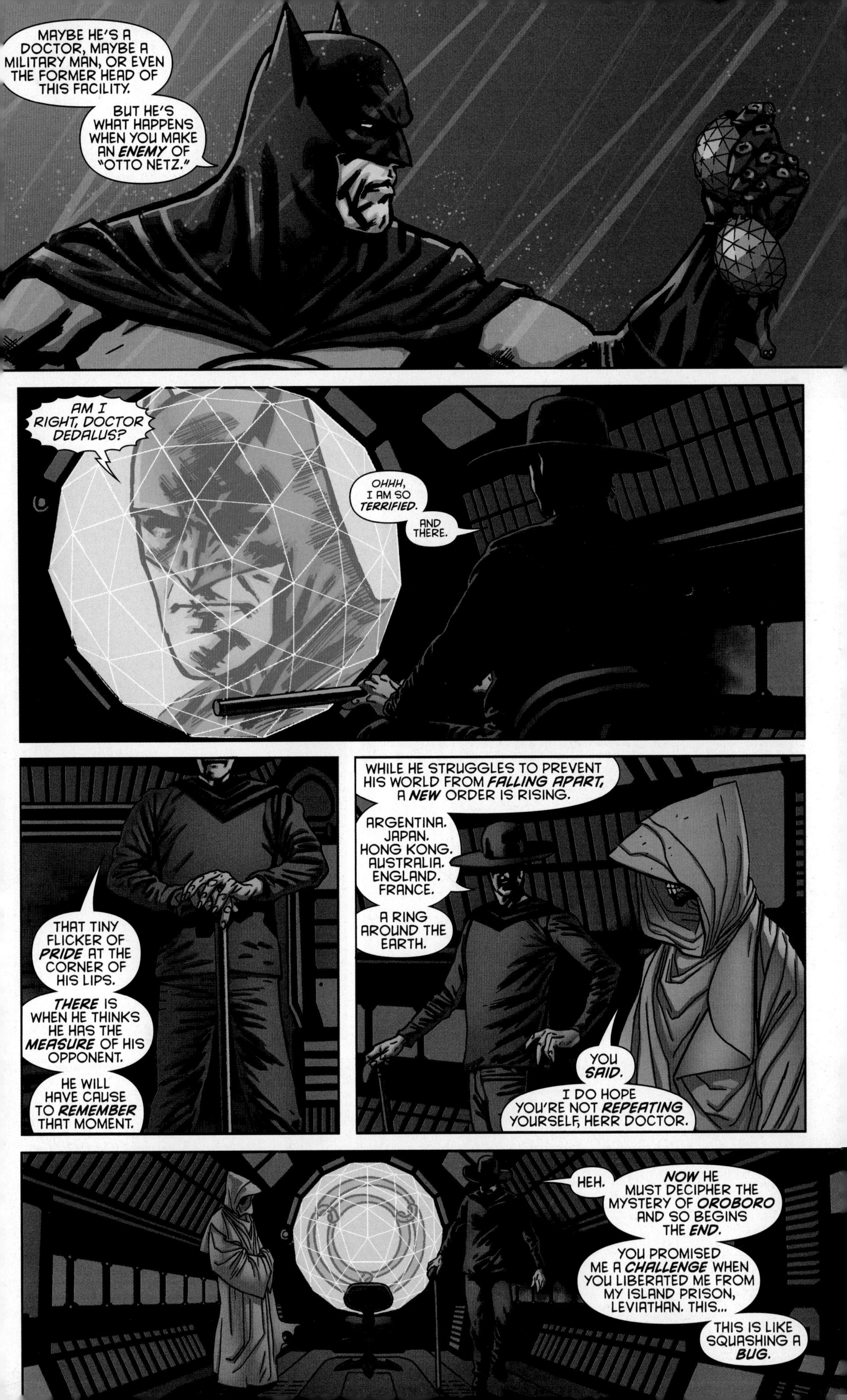
MAYBE HE'S A DOCTOR, MAYBE A MILITARY MAN, OR EVEN THE FORMER HEAD OF THIS FACILITY.
BUT HE'S WHAT HAPPENS WHEN YOU MAKE AN *ENEMY* OF "OTTO NETZ."
AM I RIGHT, DOCTOR DEDALUS?
OHHH, I AM SO *TERRIFIED*.
AND THERE.
THAT TINY FLICKER OF *PRIDE* AT THE CORNER OF HIS LIPS.
THERE IS WHEN HE THINKS HE HAS THE *MEASURE* OF HIS OPPONENT.
HE WILL HAVE CAUSE TO *REMEMBER* THAT MOMENT.
WHILE HE STRUGGLES TO PREVENT HIS WORLD FROM *FALLING APART*, A *NEW* ORDER IS RISING.
ARGENTINA. JAPAN. HONG KONG. AUSTRALIA. ENGLAND. FRANCE.
A RING AROUND THE EARTH.
YOU *SAID*.
I DO HOPE YOU'RE NOT *REPEATING* YOURSELF, HERR DOCTOR.
HEH.
NOW HE MUST DECIPHER THE MYSTERY OF *OROBORO* AND SO BEGINS THE *END*.
YOU PROMISED ME A *CHALLENGE* WHEN YOU LIBERATED ME FROM MY ISLAND PRISON, LEVIATHAN. THIS...
THIS IS LIKE SQUASHING A *BUG*.

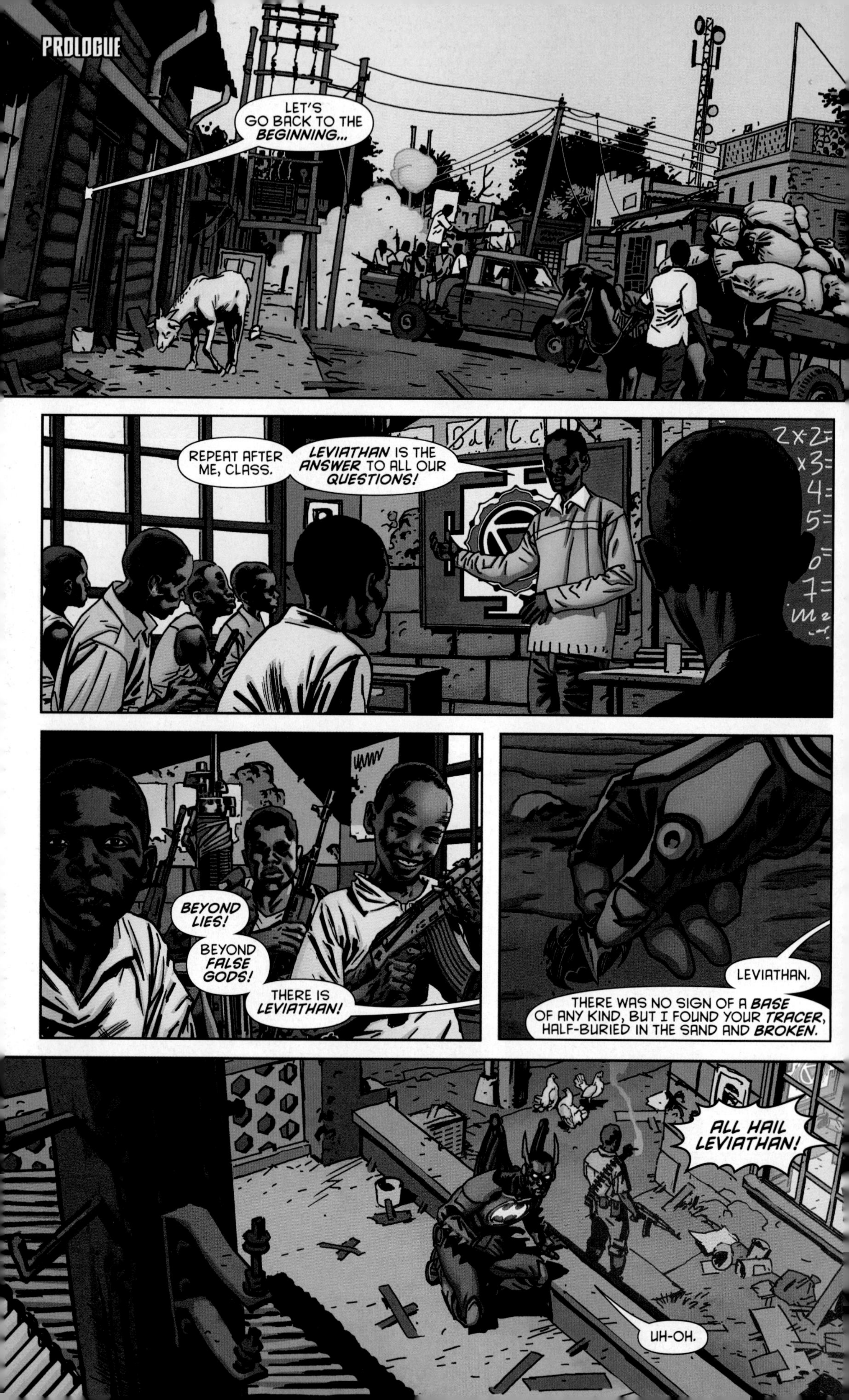
PROLOGUE
LET'S GO BACK TO THE *BEGINNING...*
REPEAT AFTER ME, CLASS.
LEVIATHAN IS THE *ANSWER* TO ALL OUR *QUESTIONS!*
2x2=
x3=
4=
5=
7=
BEYOND LIES!
BEYOND *FALSE GODS!*
THERE IS *LEVIATHAN!*
LEVIATHAN.
THERE WAS NO SIGN OF A *BASE* OF ANY KIND, BUT I FOUND YOUR *TRACER*, HALF-BURIED IN THE SAND AND *BROKEN.*
ALL HAIL LEVIATHAN!
UH-OH.

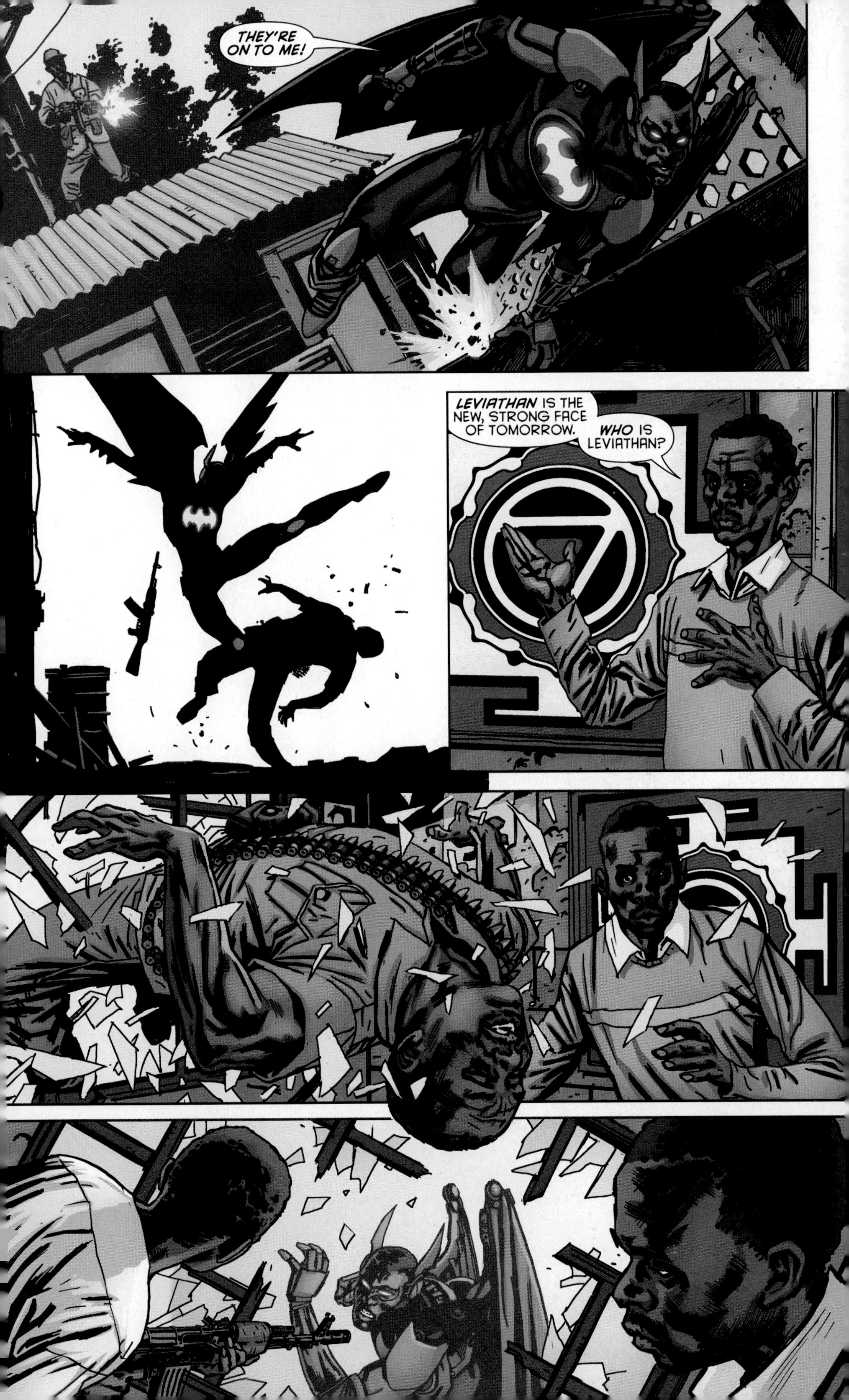
THEY'RE ON TO ME!
LEVIATHAN IS THE NEW, STRONG FACE OF TOMORROW.
WHO IS LEVIATHAN?

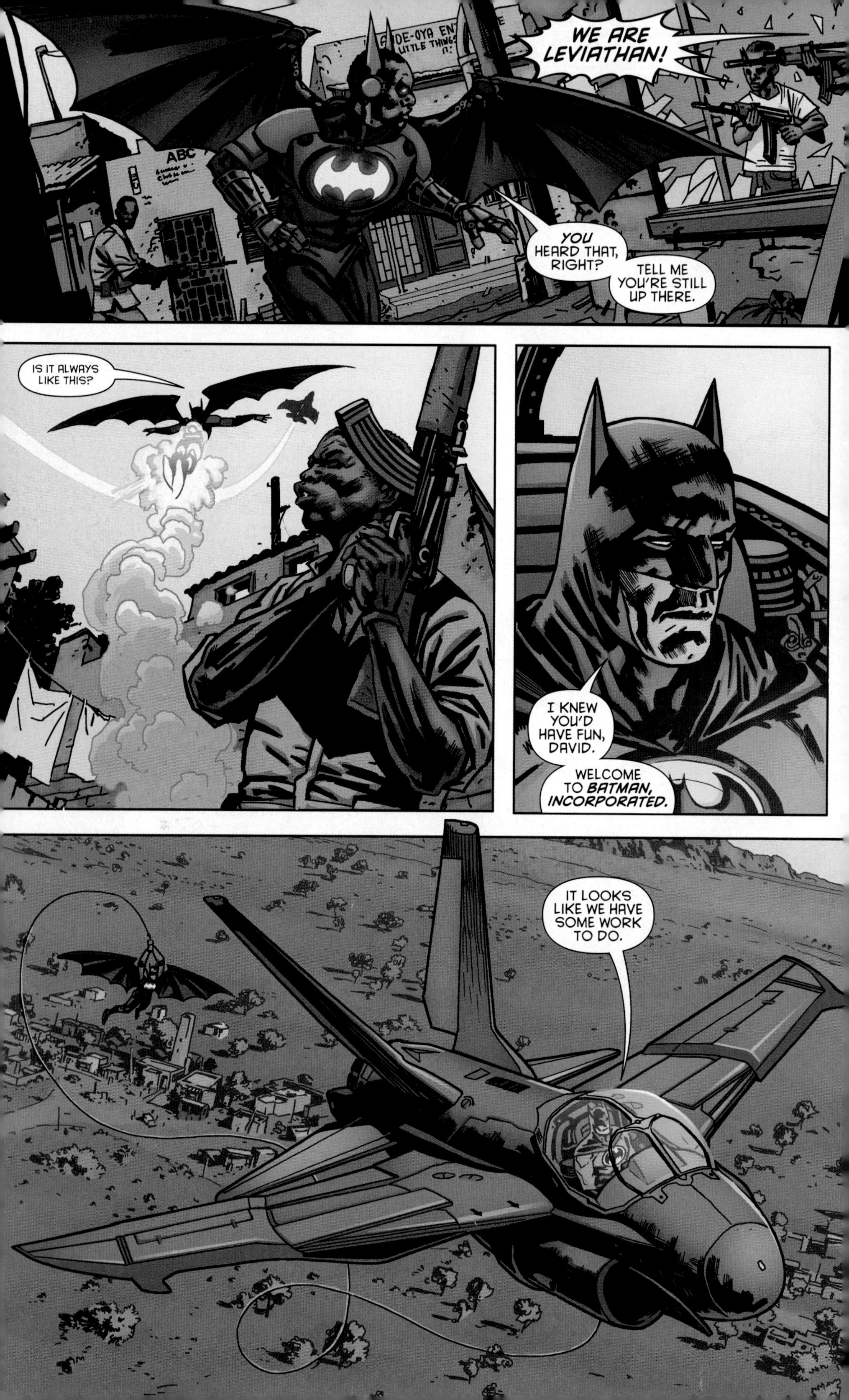

WE ARE LEVIATHAN!
YOU HEARD THAT, RIGHT?
TELL ME YOU'RE STILL UP THERE.
IS IT ALWAYS LIKE THIS?
I KNEW YOU'D HAVE FUN, DAVID.
WELCOME TO BATMAN, INCORPORATED.
IT LOOKS LIKE WE HAVE SOME WORK TO DO.

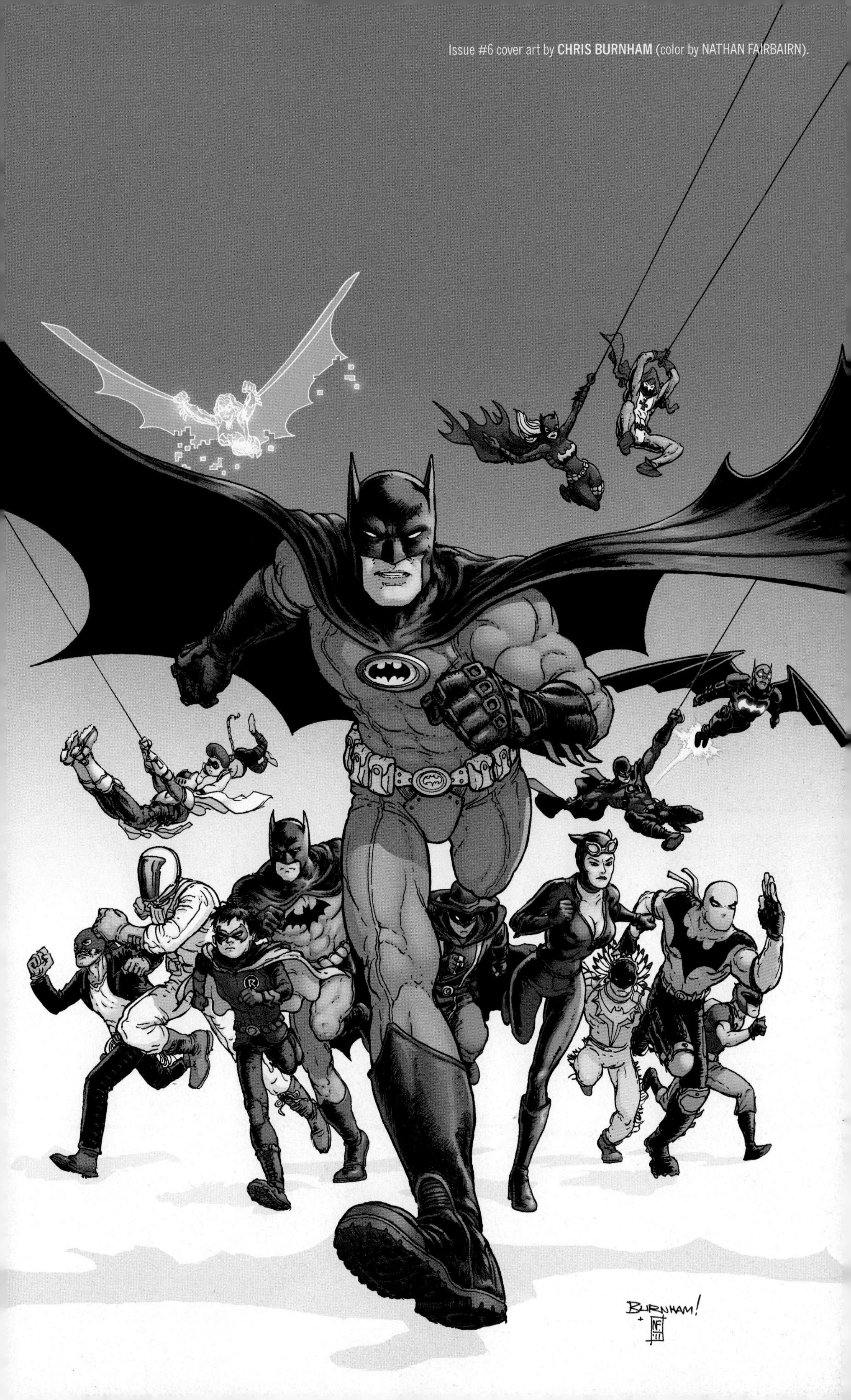
BURNHAM!

Issue #6 cover art by **CHRIS BURNHAM** (color by NATHAN FAIRBAIRN).

Issue #6 variant cover art by **FRAZER IRVING.**

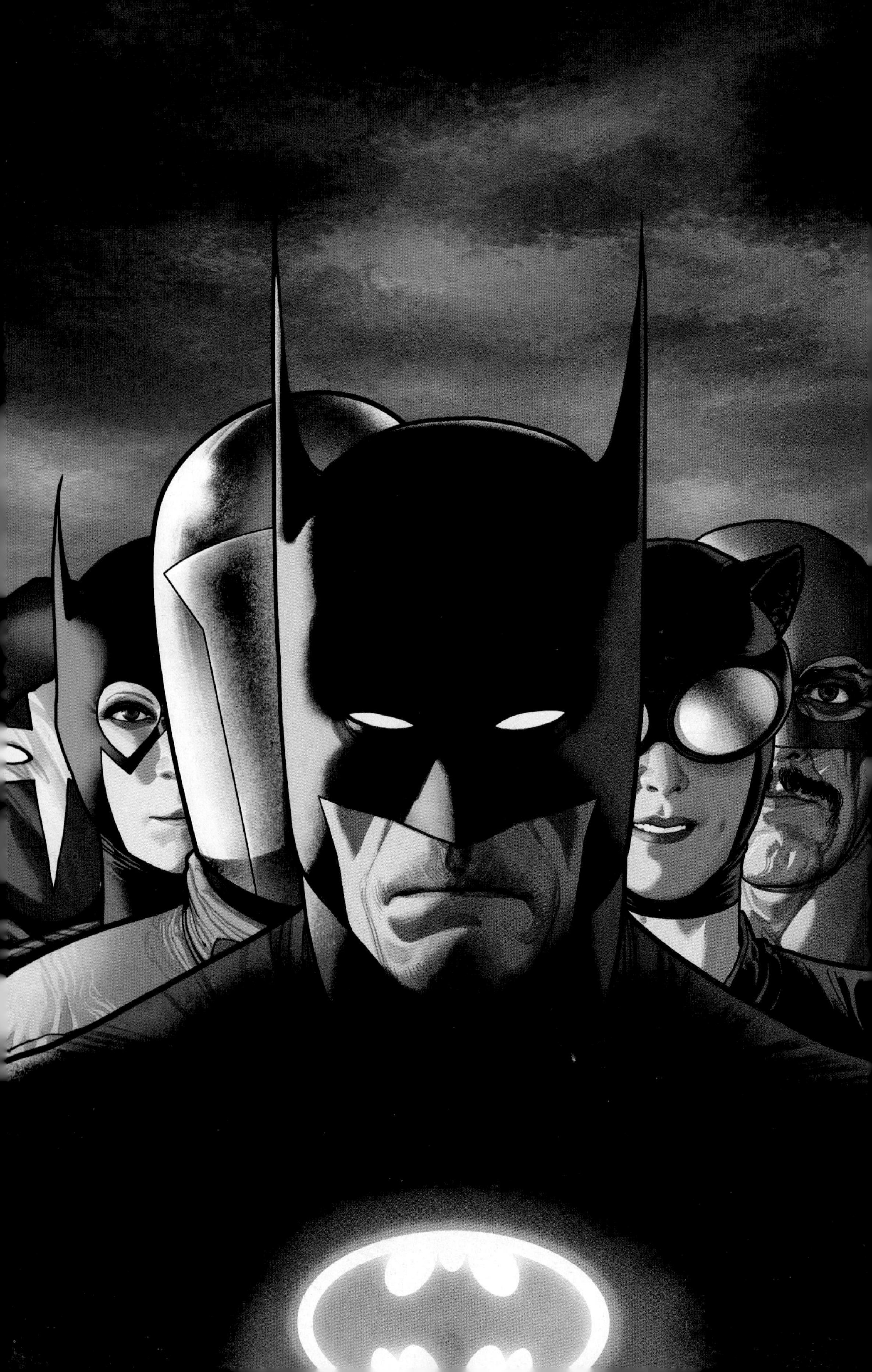

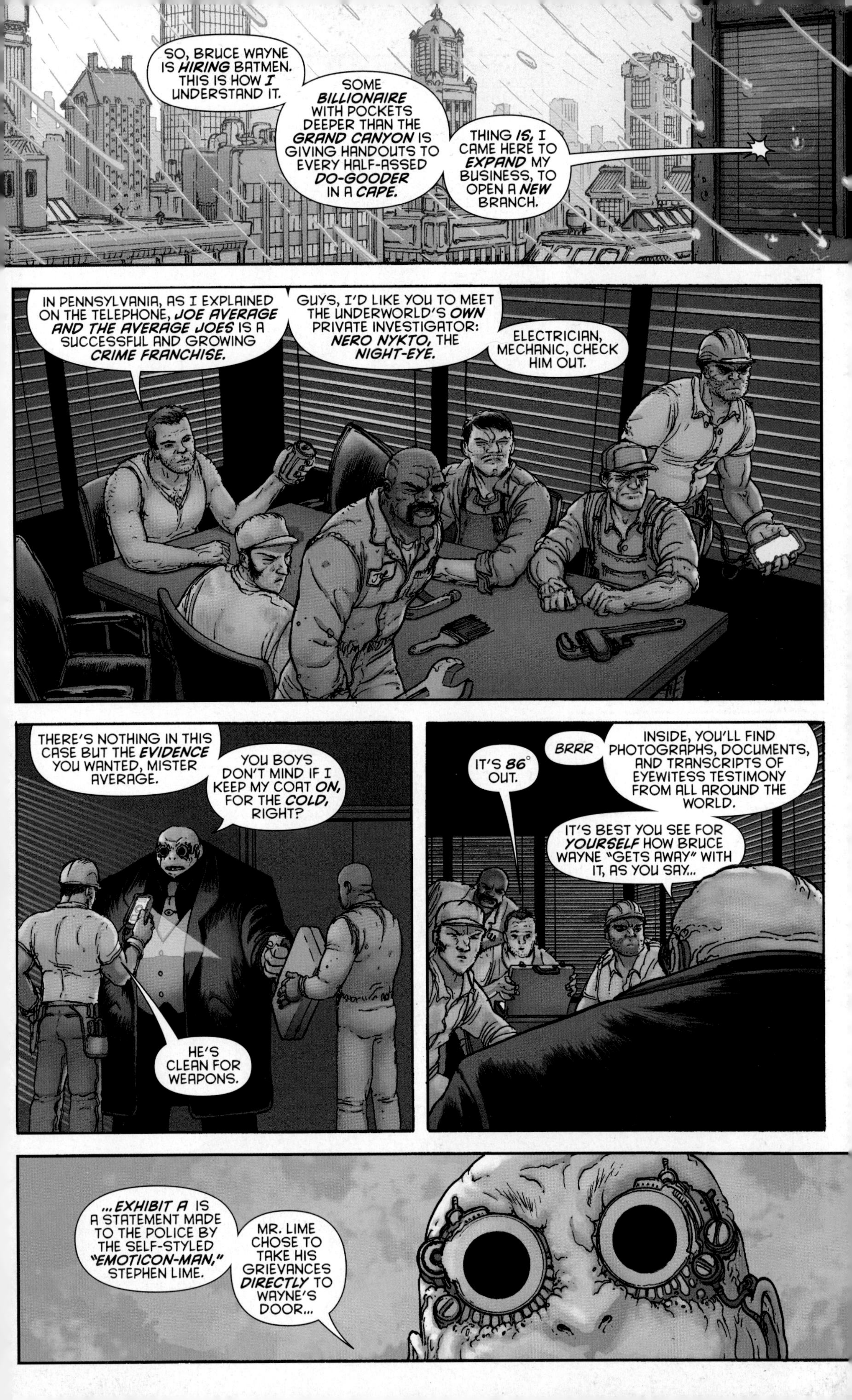
SO, BRUCE WAYNE IS HIRING BATMEN. THIS IS HOW I UNDERSTAND IT.
SOME BILLIONAIRE WITH POCKETS DEEPER THAN THE GRAND CANYON IS GIVING HANDOUTS TO EVERY HALF-ASSED DO-GOODER IN A CAPE.
THING IS, I CAME HERE TO EXPAND MY BUSINESS, TO OPEN A NEW BRANCH.
IN PENNSYLVANIA, AS I EXPLAINED ON THE TELEPHONE, JOE AVERAGE AND THE AVERAGE JOES IS A SUCCESSFUL AND GROWING CRIME FRANCHISE.
GUYS, I'D LIKE YOU TO MEET THE UNDERWORLD'S OWN PRIVATE INVESTIGATOR: NERO NYKTO, THE NIGHT-EYE.
ELECTRICIAN, MECHANIC, CHECK HIM OUT.
THERE'S NOTHING IN THIS CASE BUT THE EVIDENCE YOU WANTED, MISTER AVERAGE.
YOU BOYS DON'T MIND IF I KEEP MY COAT ON, FOR THE COLD, RIGHT?
HE'S CLEAN FOR WEAPONS.
IT'S 86° OUT.
BRRR
INSIDE, YOU'LL FIND PHOTOGRAPHS, DOCUMENTS, AND TRANSCRIPTS OF EYEWITESS TESTIMONY FROM ALL AROUND THE WORLD.
IT'S BEST YOU SEE FOR YOURSELF HOW BRUCE WAYNE "GETS AWAY" WITH IT, AS YOU SAY...
...EXHIBIT A IS A STATEMENT MADE TO THE POLICE BY THE SELF-STYLED "EMOTICON-MAN," STEPHEN LIME.
MR. LIME CHOSE TO TAKE HIS GRIEVANCES DIRECTLY TO WAYNE'S DOOR...

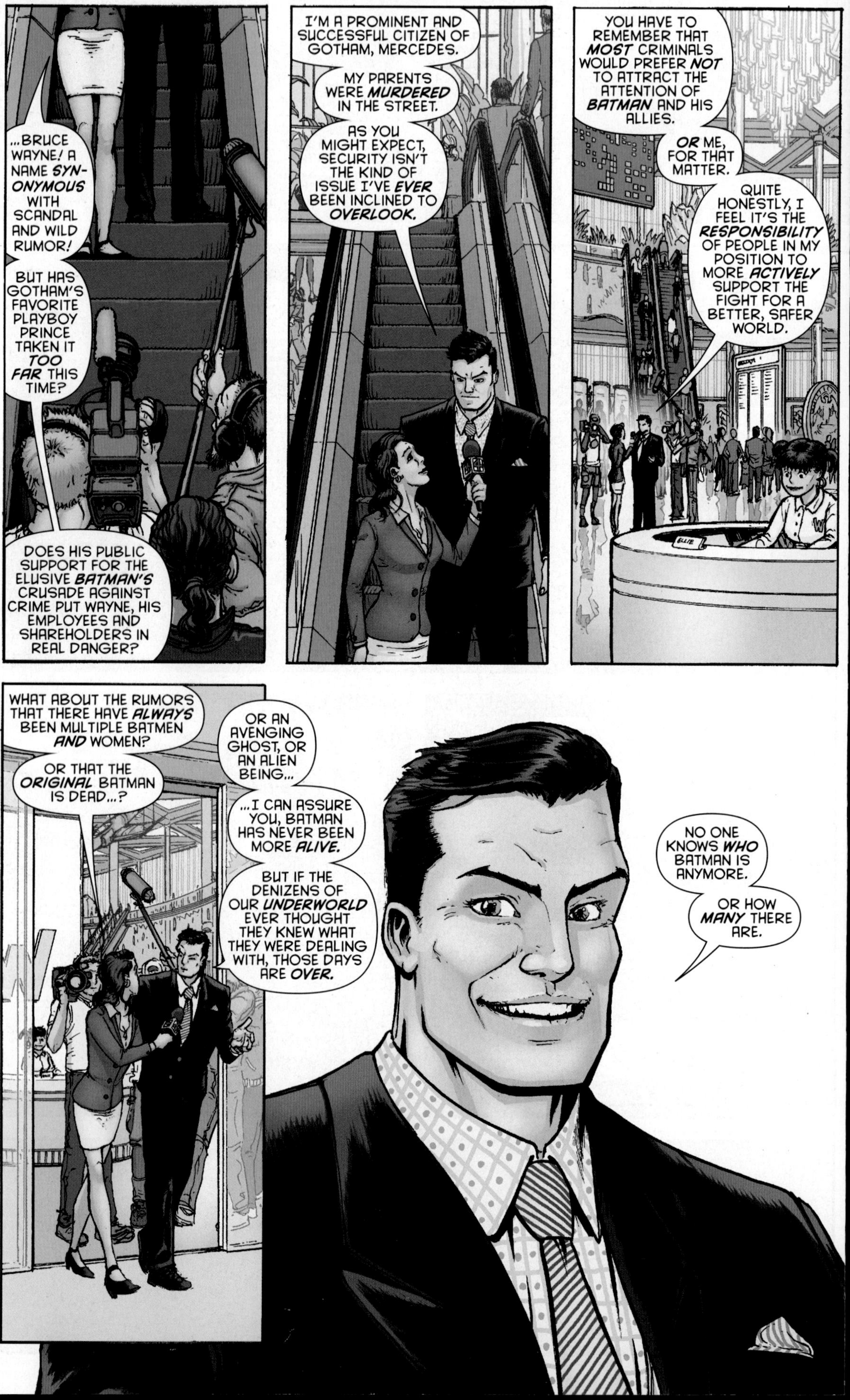
...BRUCE WAYNE! A NAME SYNONYMOUS WITH SCANDAL AND WILD RUMOR!
BUT HAS GOTHAM'S FAVORITE PLAYBOY PRINCE TAKEN IT TOO FAR THIS TIME?
DOES HIS PUBLIC SUPPORT FOR THE ELUSIVE BATMAN'S CRUSADE AGAINST CRIME PUT WAYNE, HIS EMPLOYEES AND SHAREHOLDERS IN REAL DANGER?
I'M A PROMINENT AND SUCCESSFUL CITIZEN OF GOTHAM, MERCEDES.
MY PARENTS WERE MURDERED IN THE STREET.
AS YOU MIGHT EXPECT, SECURITY ISN'T THE KIND OF ISSUE I'VE EVER BEEN INCLINED TO OVERLOOK.
YOU HAVE TO REMEMBER THAT MOST CRIMINALS WOULD PREFER NOT TO ATTRACT THE ATTENTION OF BATMAN AND HIS ALLIES.
OR ME, FOR THAT MATTER.
QUITE HONESTLY, I FEEL IT'S THE RESPONSIBILITY OF PEOPLE IN MY POSITION TO MORE ACTIVELY SUPPORT THE FIGHT FOR A BETTER, SAFER WORLD.
ELLIE
WHAT ABOUT THE RUMORS THAT THERE HAVE ALWAYS BEEN MULTIPLE BATMEN AND WOMEN?
OR THAT THE ORIGINAL BATMAN IS DEAD...?
OR AN AVENGING GHOST, OR AN ALIEN BEING...
...I CAN ASSURE YOU, BATMAN HAS NEVER BEEN MORE ALIVE.
BUT IF THE DENIZENS OF OUR UNDERWORLD EVER THOUGHT THEY KNEW WHAT THEY WERE DEALING WITH, THOSE DAYS ARE OVER.
NO ONE KNOWS WHO BATMAN IS ANYMORE.
OR HOW MANY THERE ARE.

THAT'S *PART* OF THE REASON WHY I BROUGHT YOU OUT *HERE*, AWAY FROM SECURITY TEAMS AND BULLETPROOF WINDOWS.

I ACTUALLY HAVE IT ON GOOD AUTHORITY THAT WE'RE ABOUT TO RECEIVE A *PROTEST VISIT...*

WATCH CAREFULLY.

CRIMINALS USED TO BE AFRAID BECAUSE THEY DIDN'T KNOW *WHERE* BATMAN WAS.

MR. WAYNE...

guhh

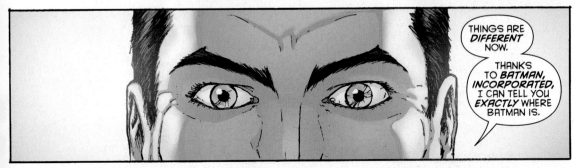

THINGS ARE *DIFFERENT* NOW.

THANKS TO *BATMAN, INCORPORATED,* I CAN TELL YOU *EXACTLY* WHERE BATMAN IS.

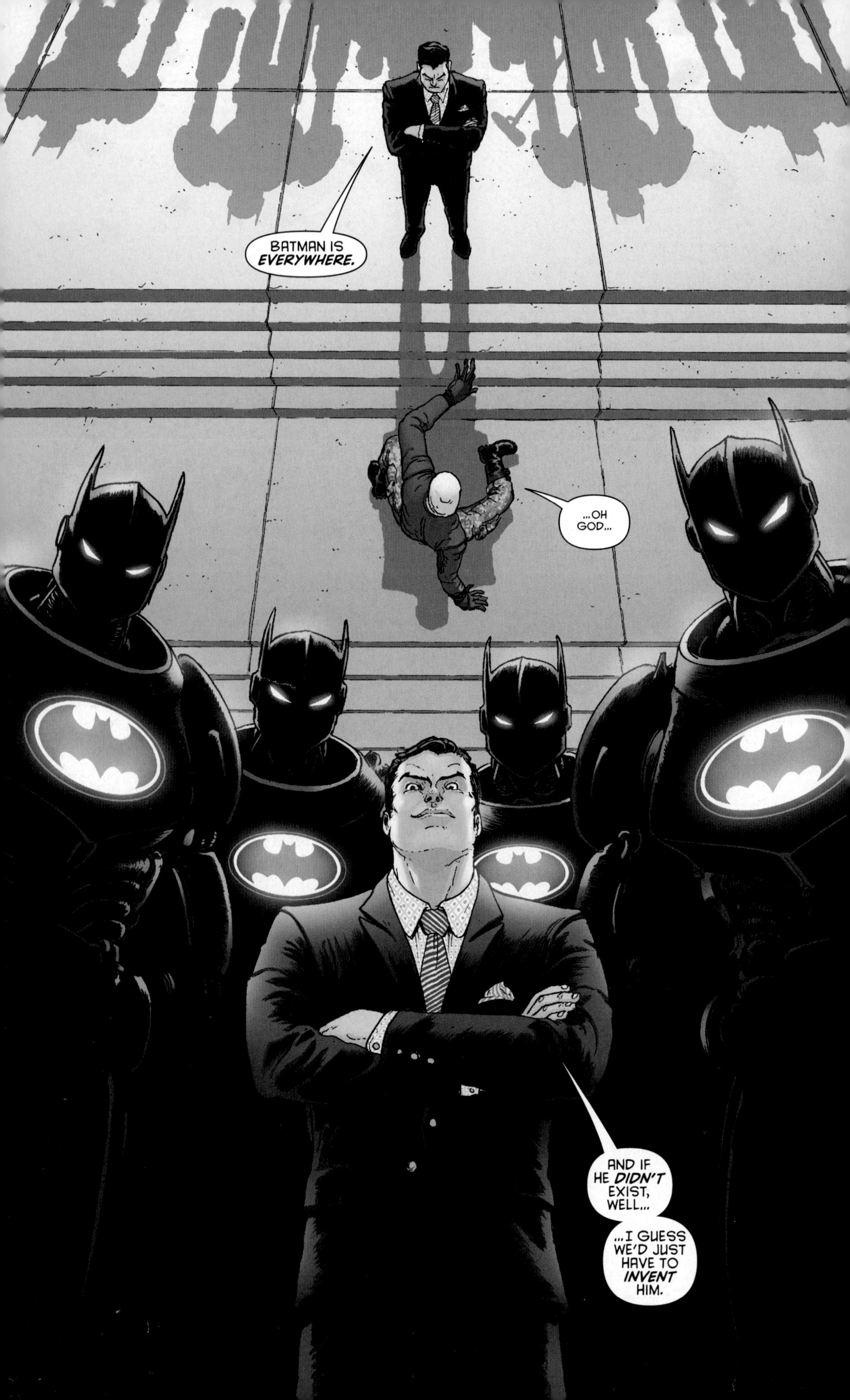
BATMAN IS EVERYWHERE.
...OH GOD...
AND IF HE DIDN'T EXIST, WELL...
...I GUESS WE'D JUST HAVE TO INVENT HIM.

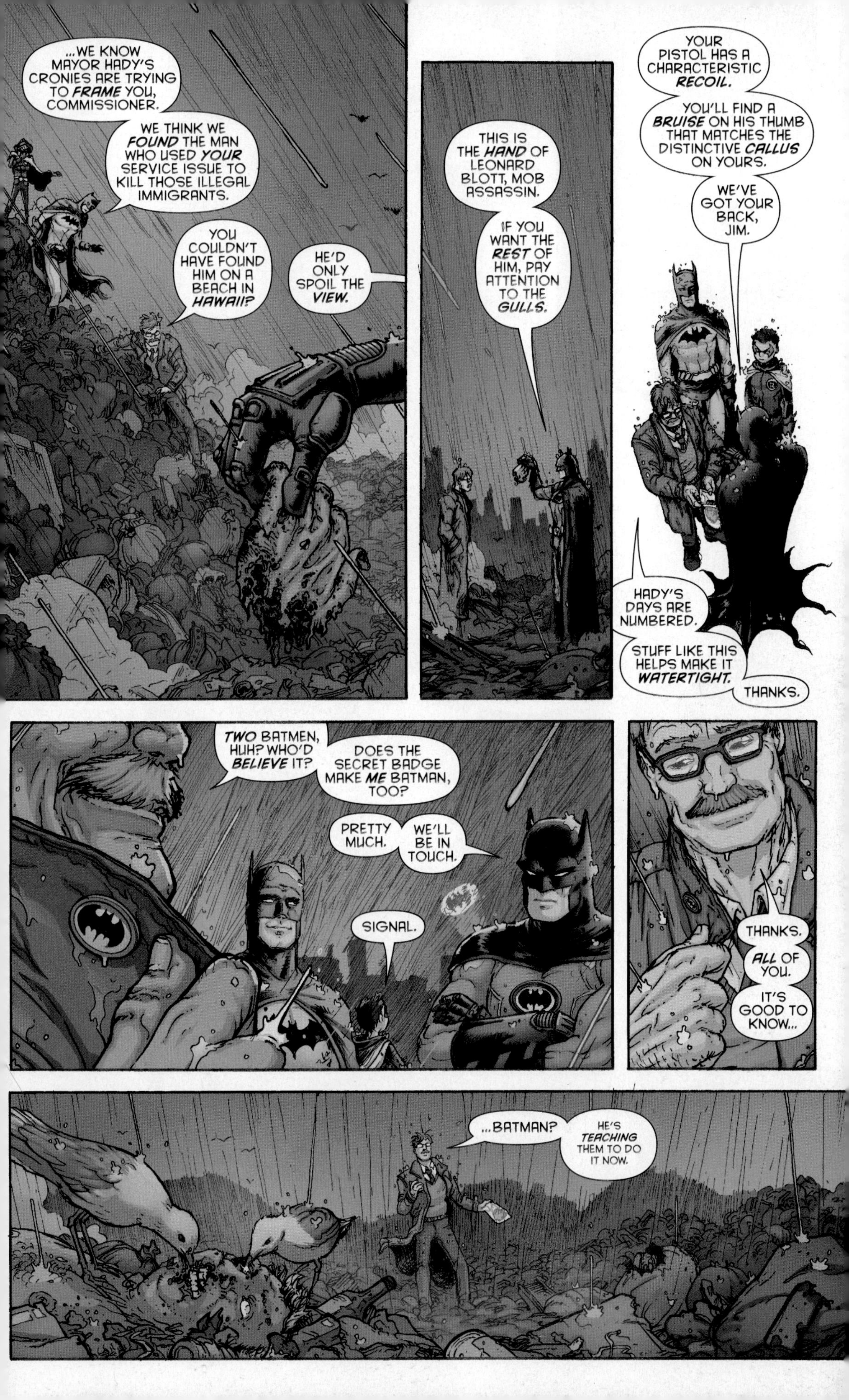
...WE KNOW MAYOR HADY'S CRONIES ARE TRYING TO FRAME YOU, COMMISSIONER.
WE THINK WE FOUND THE MAN WHO USED YOUR SERVICE ISSUE TO KILL THOSE ILLEGAL IMMIGRANTS.
YOU COULDN'T HAVE FOUND HIM ON A BEACH IN HAWAII?
HE'D ONLY SPOIL THE VIEW.
THIS IS THE HAND OF LEONARD BLOTT, MOB ASSASSIN.
IF YOU WANT THE REST OF HIM, PAY ATTENTION TO THE GULLS.
YOUR PISTOL HAS A CHARACTERISTIC RECOIL.
YOU'LL FIND A BRUISE ON HIS THUMB THAT MATCHES THE DISTINCTIVE CALLUS ON YOURS.
WE'VE GOT YOUR BACK, JIM.
HADY'S DAYS ARE NUMBERED.
STUFF LIKE THIS HELPS MAKE IT WATERTIGHT.
THANKS.
TWO BATMEN, HUH? WHO'D BELIEVE IT?
DOES THE SECRET BADGE MAKE ME BATMAN, TOO?
PRETTY MUCH.
WE'LL BE IN TOUCH.
SIGNAL.
THANKS.
ALL OF YOU.
IT'S GOOD TO KNOW...
...BATMAN?
HE'S TEACHING THEM TO DO IT NOW.

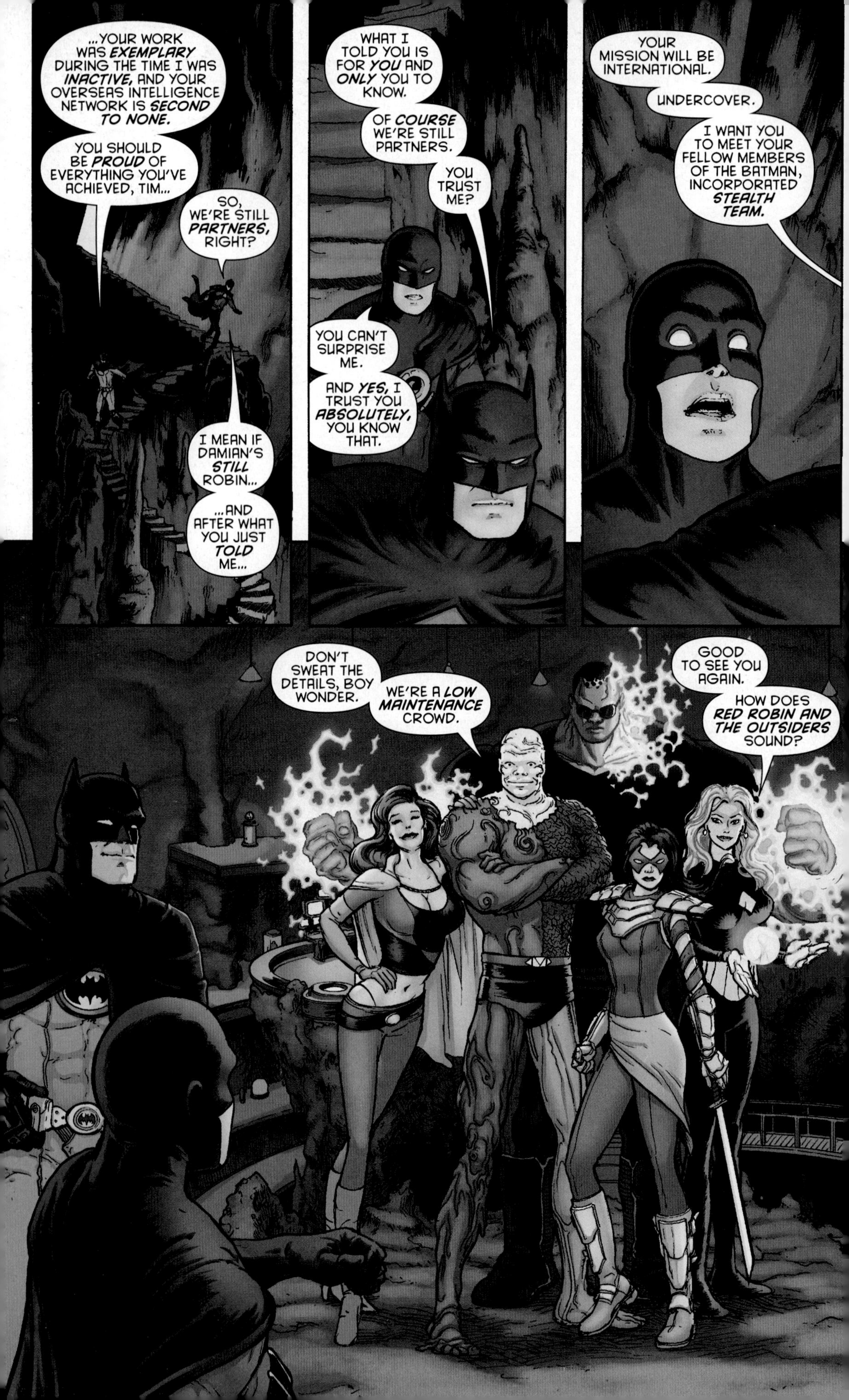
...YOUR WORK WAS EXEMPLARY DURING THE TIME I WAS INACTIVE, AND YOUR OVERSEAS INTELLIGENCE NETWORK IS SECOND TO NONE.
YOU SHOULD BE PROUD OF EVERYTHING YOU'VE ACHIEVED, TIM...
SO, WE'RE STILL PARTNERS, RIGHT?
I MEAN IF DAMIAN'S STILL ROBIN...
...AND AFTER WHAT YOU JUST TOLD ME...
WHAT I TOLD YOU IS FOR YOU AND ONLY YOU TO KNOW.
OF COURSE WE'RE STILL PARTNERS.
YOU TRUST ME?
YOU CAN'T SURPRISE ME.
AND YES, I TRUST YOU ABSOLUTELY, YOU KNOW THAT.
YOUR MISSION WILL BE INTERNATIONAL.
UNDERCOVER.
I WANT YOU TO MEET YOUR FELLOW MEMBERS OF THE BATMAN, INCORPORATED STEALTH TEAM.
DON'T SWEAT THE DETAILS, BOY WONDER.
WE'RE A LOW MAINTENANCE CROWD.
GOOD TO SEE YOU AGAIN.
HOW DOES RED ROBIN AND THE OUTSIDERS SOUND?

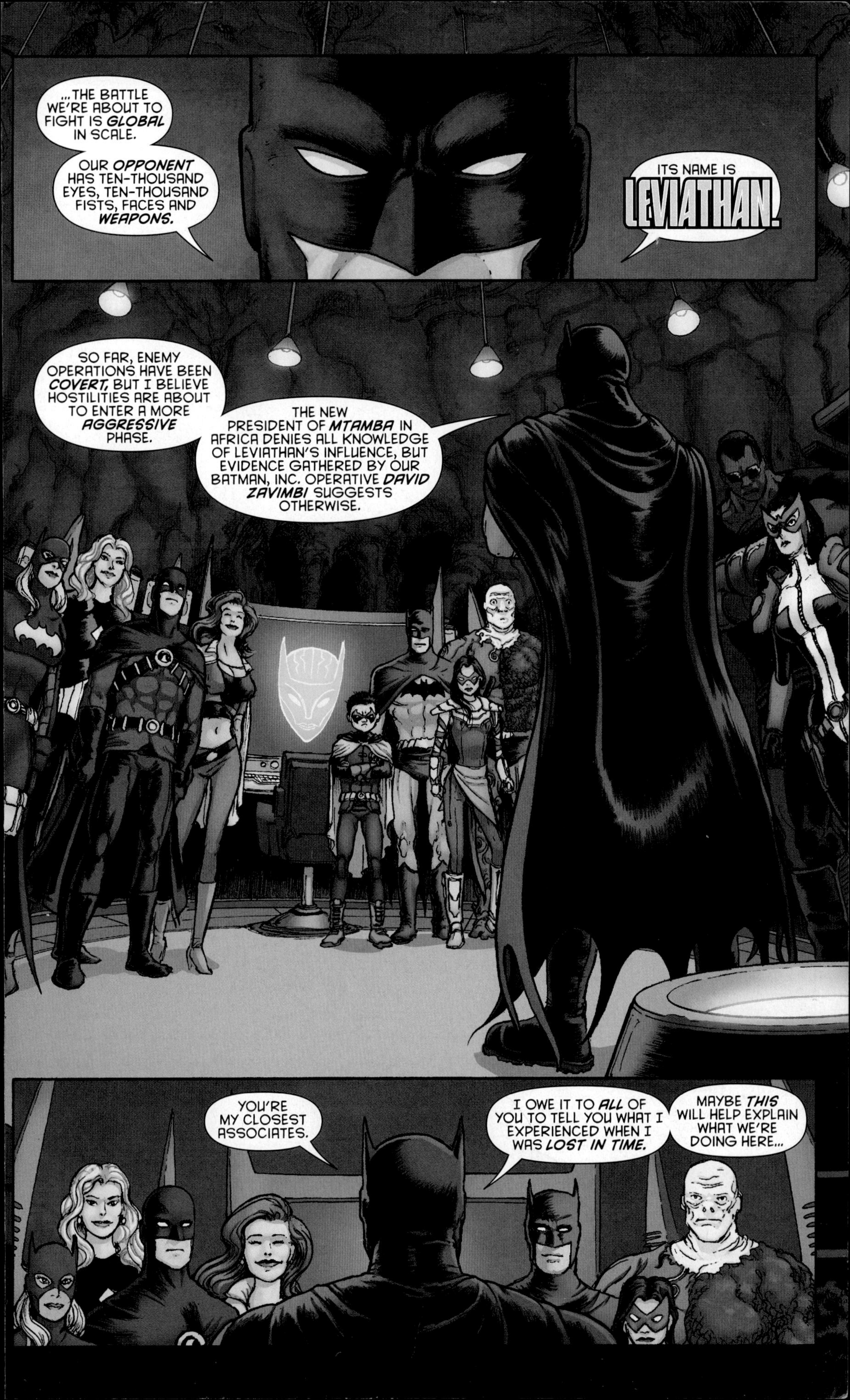
...THE BATTLE WE'RE ABOUT TO FIGHT IS GLOBAL IN SCALE.
OUR OPPONENT HAS TEN-THOUSAND EYES, TEN-THOUSAND FISTS, FACES AND WEAPONS.
ITS NAME IS LEVIATHAN.
SO FAR, ENEMY OPERATIONS HAVE BEEN COVERT, BUT I BELIEVE HOSTILITIES ARE ABOUT TO ENTER A MORE AGGRESSIVE PHASE.
THE NEW PRESIDENT OF MTAMBA IN AFRICA DENIES ALL KNOWLEDGE OF LEVIATHAN'S INFLUENCE, BUT EVIDENCE GATHERED BY OUR BATMAN, INC. OPERATIVE DAVID ZAVIMBI SUGGESTS OTHERWISE.
YOU'RE MY CLOSEST ASSOCIATES.
I OWE IT TO ALL OF YOU TO TELL YOU WHAT I EXPERIENCED WHEN I WAS LOST IN TIME.
MAYBE THIS WILL HELP EXPLAIN WHAT WE'RE DOING HERE...

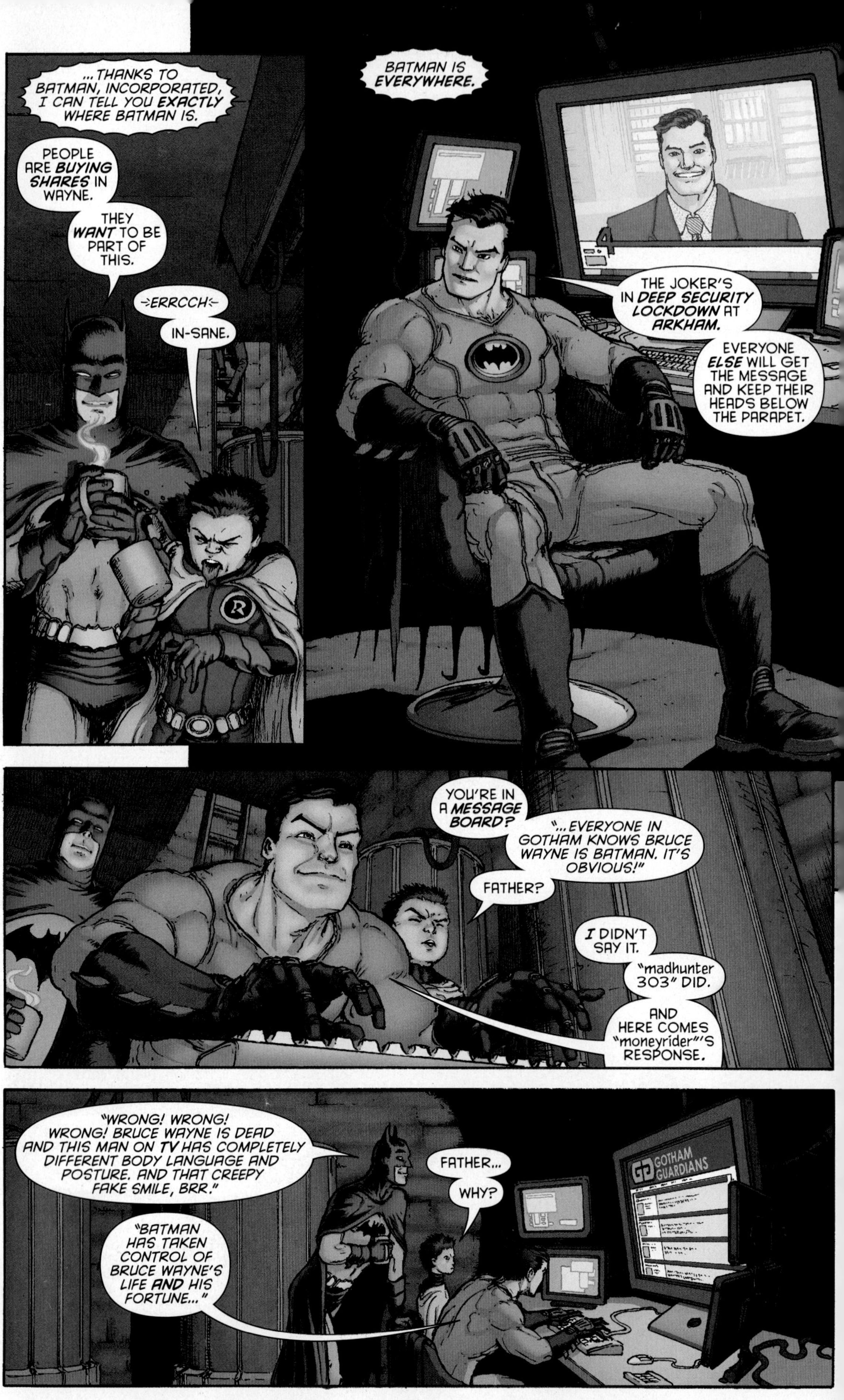

...THANKS TO BATMAN, INCORPORATED, I CAN TELL YOU EXACTLY WHERE BATMAN IS.
PEOPLE ARE BUYING SHARES IN WAYNE.
THEY WANT TO BE PART OF THIS.
ERRCCH
IN-SANE.
BATMAN IS EVERYWHERE.
THE JOKER'S IN DEEP SECURITY LOCKDOWN AT ARKHAM.
EVERYONE ELSE WILL GET THE MESSAGE AND KEEP THEIR HEADS BELOW THE PARAPET.
YOU'RE IN A MESSAGE BOARD?
"...EVERYONE IN GOTHAM KNOWS BRUCE WAYNE IS BATMAN. IT'S OBVIOUS!"
FATHER?
I DIDN'T SAY IT.
"madhunter 303" DID.
AND HERE COMES "moneyrider"'S RESPONSE.
"WRONG! WRONG! WRONG! BRUCE WAYNE IS DEAD AND THIS MAN ON TV HAS COMPLETELY DIFFERENT BODY LANGUAGE AND POSTURE. AND THAT CREEPY FAKE SMILE, BRR."
FATHER...
WHY?
"BATMAN HAS TAKEN CONTROL OF BRUCE WAYNE'S LIFE AND HIS FORTUNE..."
GOTHAM GUARDIANS

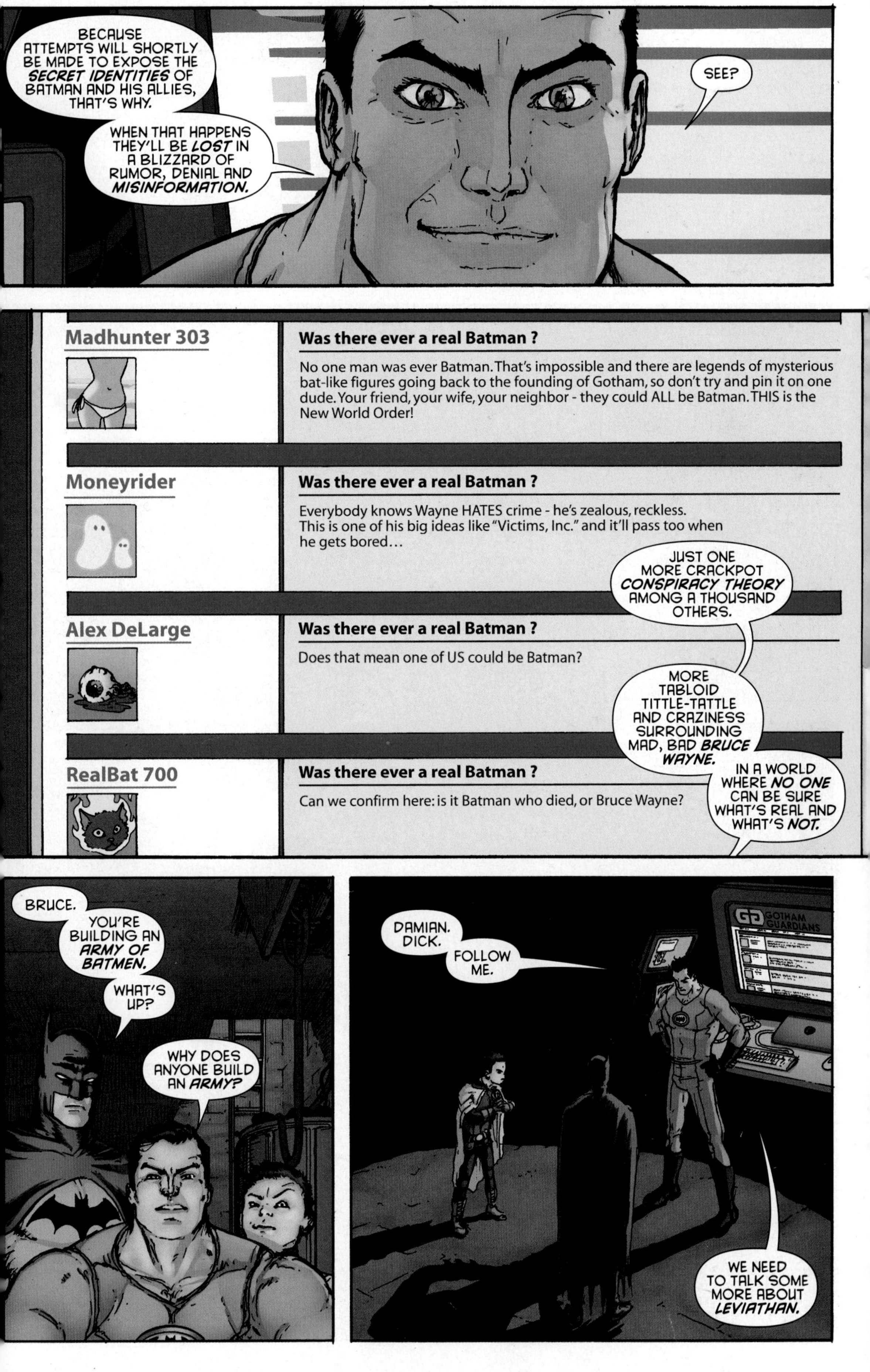
BECAUSE ATTEMPTS WILL SHORTLY BE MADE TO EXPOSE THE *SECRET IDENTITIES* OF BATMAN AND HIS ALLIES, THAT'S WHY.
WHEN THAT HAPPENS THEY'LL BE *LOST* IN A BLIZZARD OF RUMOR, DENIAL AND *MISINFORMATION.*
SEE?
Madhunter 303
Was there ever a real Batman ?
No one man was ever Batman. That's impossible and there are legends of mysterious bat-like figures going back to the founding of Gotham, so don't try and pin it on one dude. Your friend, your wife, your neighbor - they could ALL be Batman. THIS is the New World Order!
Moneyrider
Was there ever a real Batman ?
Everybody knows Wayne HATES crime - he's zealous, reckless. This is one of his big ideas like "Victims, Inc." and it'll pass too when he gets bored…
JUST ONE MORE CRACKPOT *CONSPIRACY THEORY* AMONG A THOUSAND OTHERS.
Alex DeLarge
Was there ever a real Batman ?
Does that mean one of US could be Batman?
MORE TABLOID TITTLE-TATTLE AND CRAZINESS SURROUNDING MAD, BAD *BRUCE WAYNE.*
RealBat 700
Was there ever a real Batman ?
Can we confirm here: is it Batman who died, or Bruce Wayne?
IN A WORLD WHERE *NO ONE* CAN BE SURE WHAT'S REAL AND WHAT'S *NOT.*
BRUCE.
YOU'RE BUILDING AN *ARMY OF BATMEN.*
WHAT'S UP?
WHY DOES ANYONE BUILD AN *ARMY?*
DAMIAN. DICK.
FOLLOW ME.
GOTHAM GUARDIANS
WE NEED TO TALK SOME MORE ABOUT *LEVIATHAN.*

...AND THAT'S IT.

THAT'S AS MUCH AS I *KNOW* SO FAR.

LIKE I SAID, THERE'S NO TIME FOR REHEARSALS, BUT I KNOW *IMPROV* IS SOMETHING YOU'RE BOTH *GOOD* AT.

BRUCE.

YOU SAW THE FUTURE?

IT TURNED OUT OKAY, RIGHT?

WHAT I SAW SEEMS LIKE A *DREAM* NOW.

BUT WE HAVE TO *PREPARE*.

SOMETHING *BIG*, SOMETHING *BAD* IS COMING.

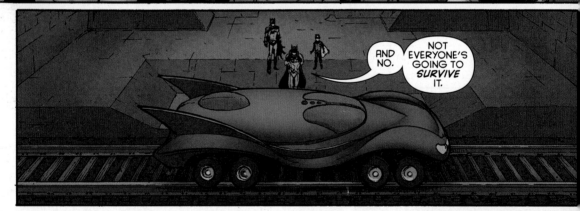

AND NO.

NOT EVERYONE'S GOING TO *SURVIVE* IT.

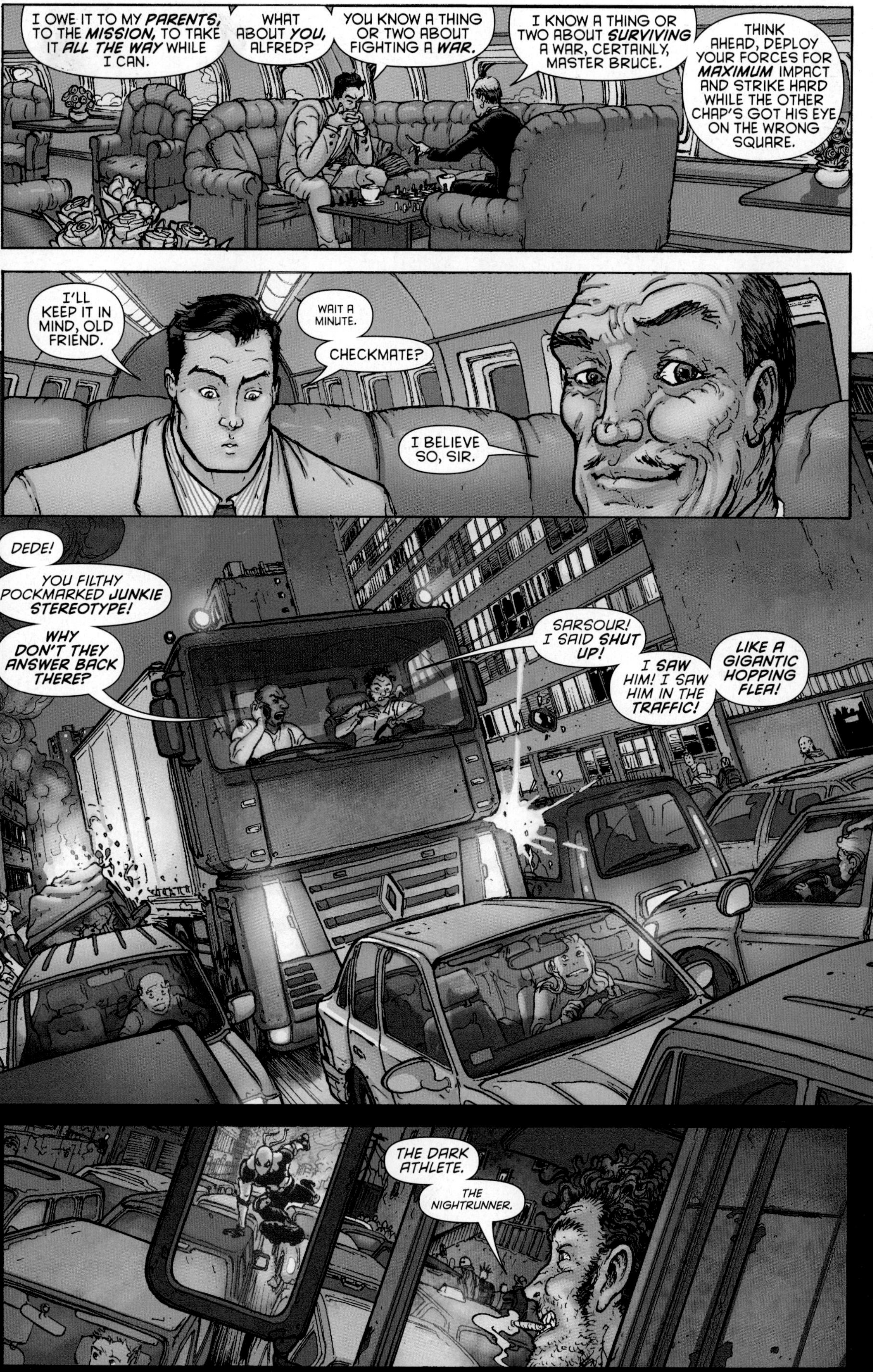
I OWE IT TO MY PARENTS, TO THE MISSION, TO TAKE IT ALL THE WAY WHILE I CAN.
WHAT ABOUT YOU, ALFRED?
YOU KNOW A THING OR TWO ABOUT FIGHTING A WAR.
I KNOW A THING OR TWO ABOUT SURVIVING A WAR, CERTAINLY, MASTER BRUCE.
THINK AHEAD, DEPLOY YOUR FORCES FOR MAXIMUM IMPACT AND STRIKE HARD WHILE THE OTHER CHAP'S GOT HIS EYE ON THE WRONG SQUARE.
I'LL KEEP IT IN MIND, OLD FRIEND.
WAIT A MINUTE.
CHECKMATE?
I BELIEVE SO, SIR.
DEDE!
YOU FILTHY POCKMARKED JUNKIE STEREOTYPE!
WHY DON'T THEY ANSWER BACK THERE?
SARSOUR! I SAID SHUT UP!
I SAW HIM! I SAW HIM IN THE TRAFFIC!
LIKE A GIGANTIC HOPPING FLEA!
THE DARK ATHLETE.
THE NIGHTRUNNER.

SO WHAT HAPPENED NEXT?

READ ON, JOE AVERAGE.

WAYNE ARRIVED IN *PARIS*.

BATMEN SPRUNG UP.

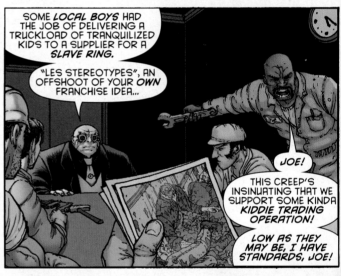

SOME *LOCAL BOYS* HAD THE JOB OF DELIVERING A TRUCKLOAD OF TRANQUILIZED KIDS TO A SUPPLIER FOR A *SLAVE RING*.

"*LES STEREOTYPES*", AN OFFSHOOT OF YOUR *OWN* FRANCHISE IDEA...

JOE! THIS CREEP'S INSINUATING THAT WE SUPPORT SOME KINDA *KIDDIE TRADING OPERATION!*

LOW AS THEY MAY BE, I HAVE *STANDARDS*, JOE!

PLEASE *FORGIVE* THE AVERAGE JOES, THEY KNOW NOT WHAT THEY DO.

MR. NYKTO, GO AHEAD. I'M ALL EARS.

WHAT HAPPENED TO OUR FRIENDS FROM *MARSEILLES?*

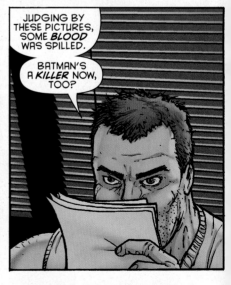

JUDGING BY THESE PICTURES, SOME *BLOOD* WAS SPILLED.

BATMAN'S A *KILLER* NOW, TOO?

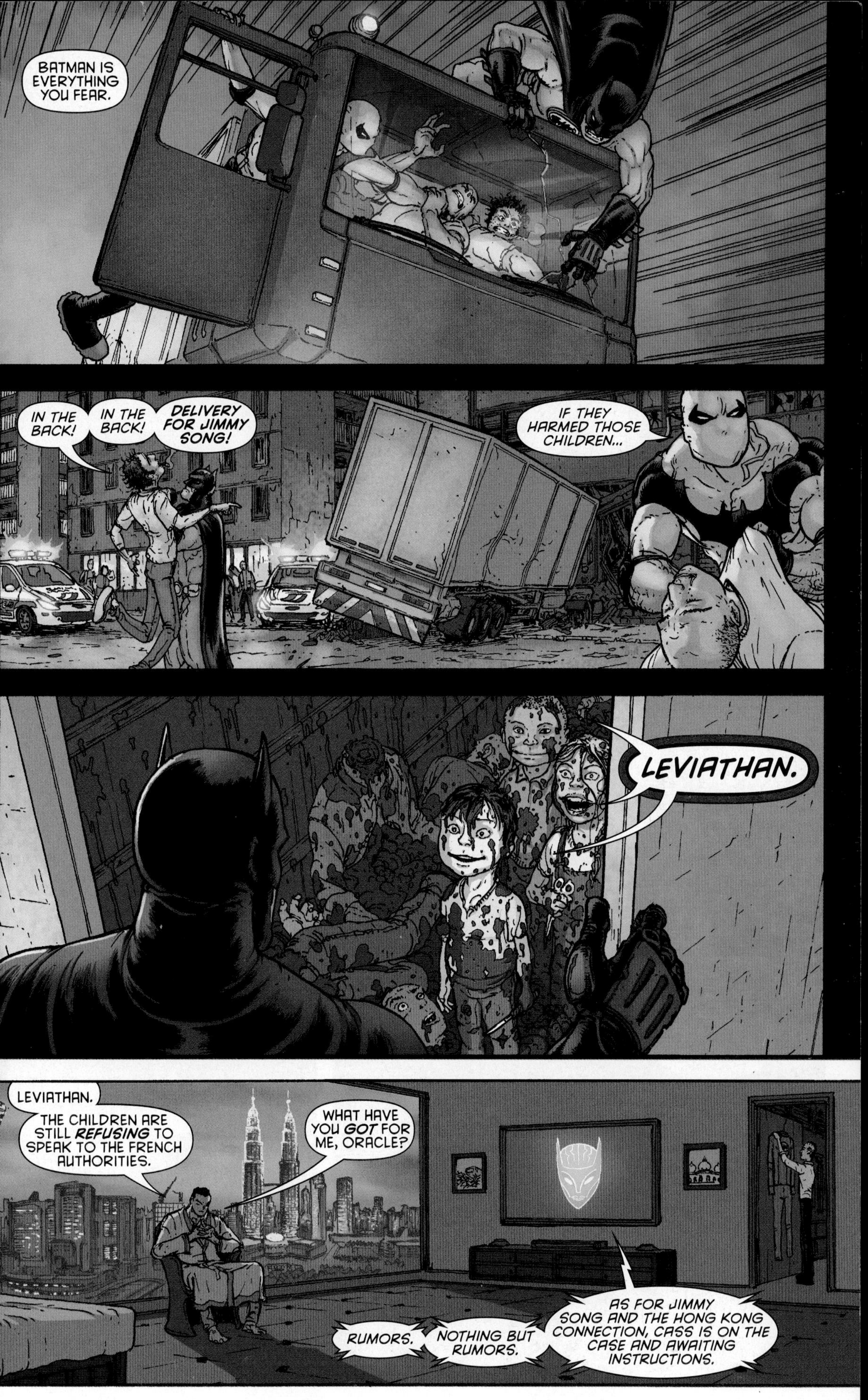
BATMAN IS EVERYTHING YOU FEAR.
IN THE BACK!
IN THE BACK!
DELIVERY FOR JIMMY SONG!
IF THEY HARMED THOSE CHILDREN...
LEVIATHAN.
LEVIATHAN.
THE CHILDREN ARE STILL REFUSING TO SPEAK TO THE FRENCH AUTHORITIES.
WHAT HAVE YOU GOT FOR ME, ORACLE?
RUMORS.
NOTHING BUT RUMORS.
AS FOR JIMMY SONG AND THE HONG KONG CONNECTION, CASS IS ON THE CASE AND AWAITING INSTRUCTIONS.

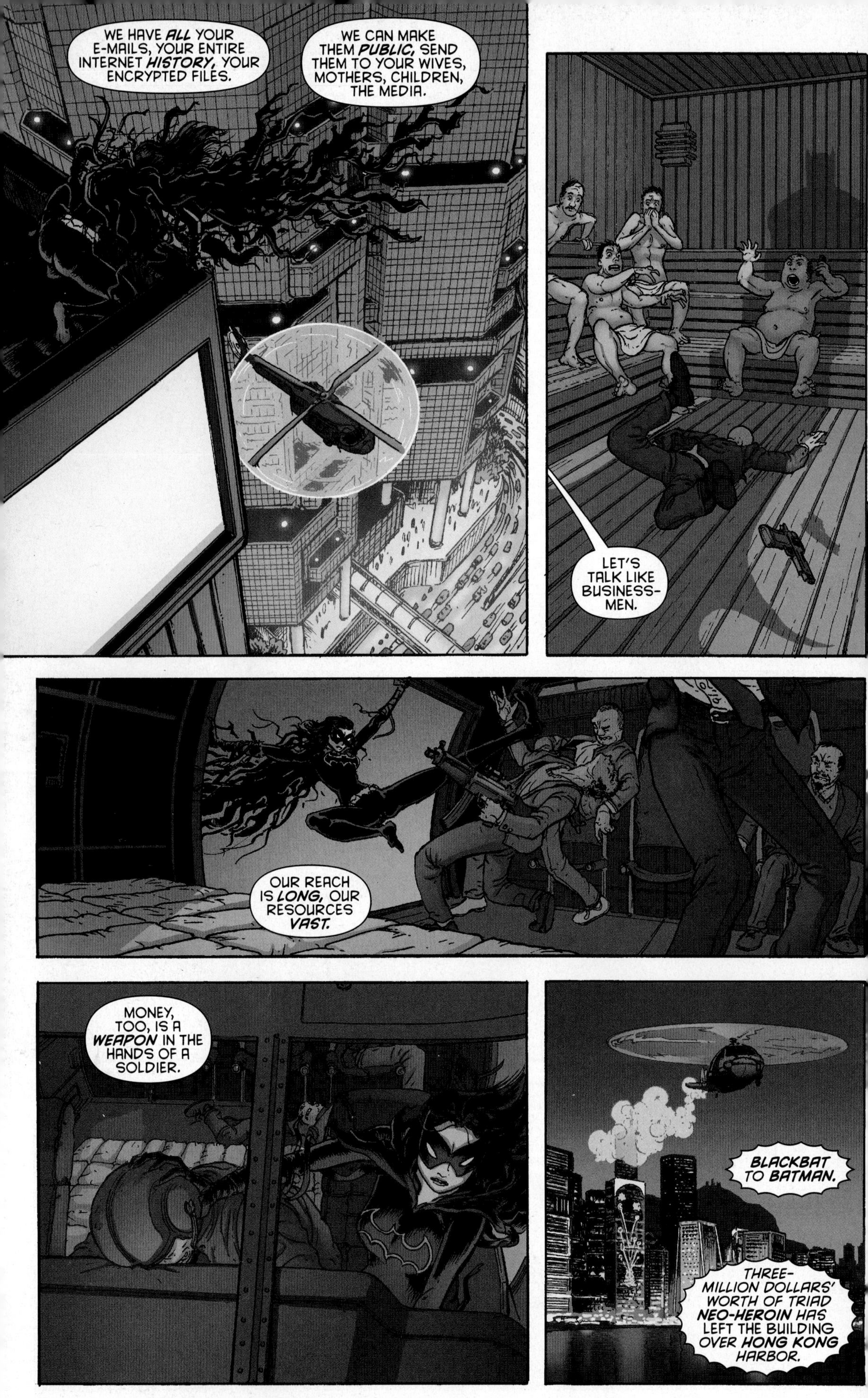
WE HAVE ALL YOUR E-MAILS, YOUR ENTIRE INTERNET HISTORY, YOUR ENCRYPTED FILES.
WE CAN MAKE THEM PUBLIC, SEND THEM TO YOUR WIVES, MOTHERS, CHILDREN, THE MEDIA.
LET'S TALK LIKE BUSINESS-MEN.
OUR REACH IS LONG, OUR RESOURCES VAST.
MONEY, TOO, IS A WEAPON IN THE HANDS OF A SOLDIER.
BLACKBAT TO BATMAN.
THREE-MILLION DOLLARS' WORTH OF TRIAD NEO-HEROIN HAS LEFT THE BUILDING OVER HONG KONG HARBOR.

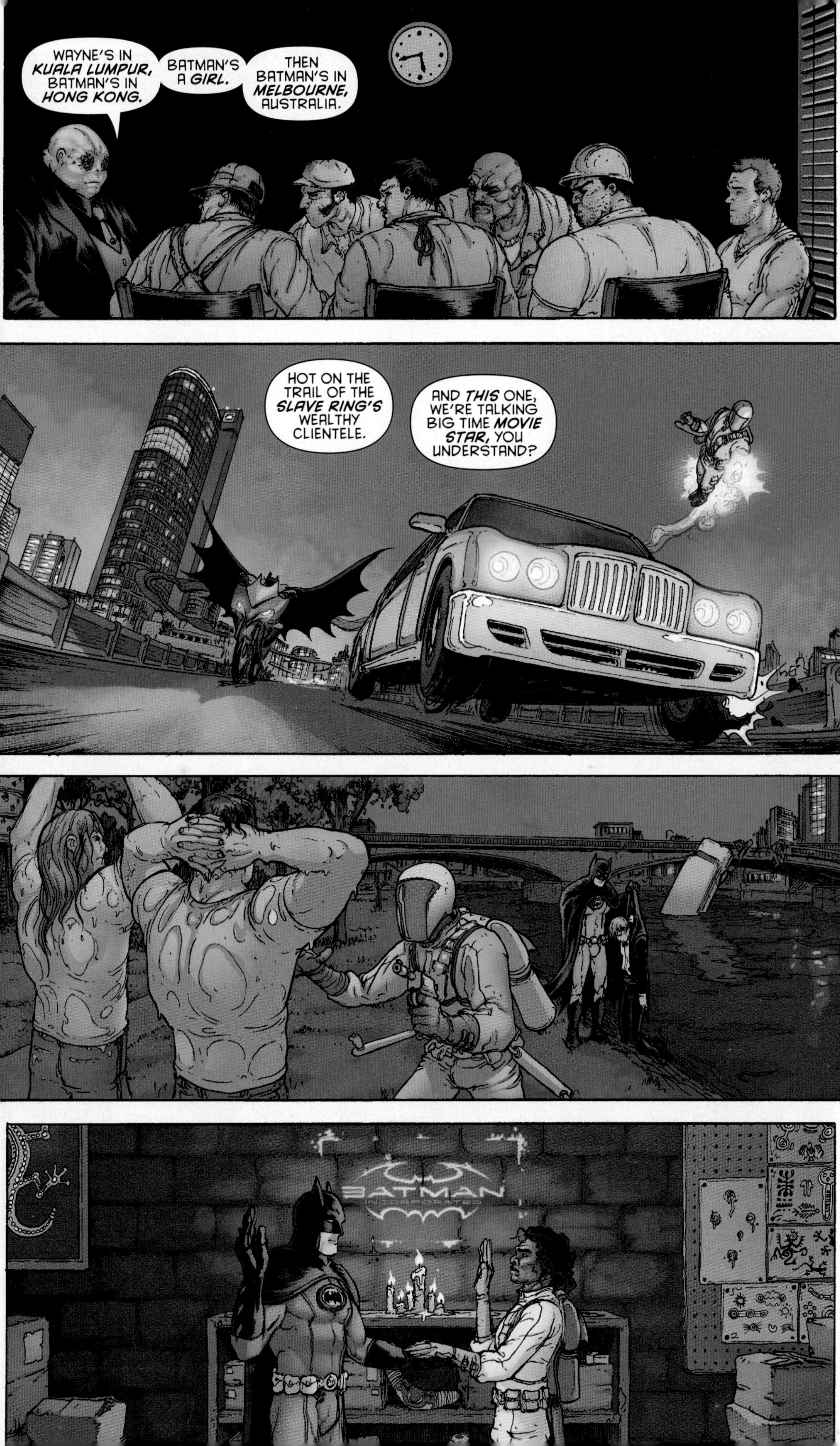
WAYNE'S IN KUALA LUMPUR, BATMAN'S IN HONG KONG.
BATMAN'S A GIRL.
THEN BATMAN'S IN MELBOURNE, AUSTRALIA.
HOT ON THE TRAIL OF THE SLAVE RING'S WEALTHY CLIENTELE.
AND THIS ONE, WE'RE TALKING BIG TIME MOVIE STAR, YOU UNDERSTAND?
BATMAN INCORPORATED

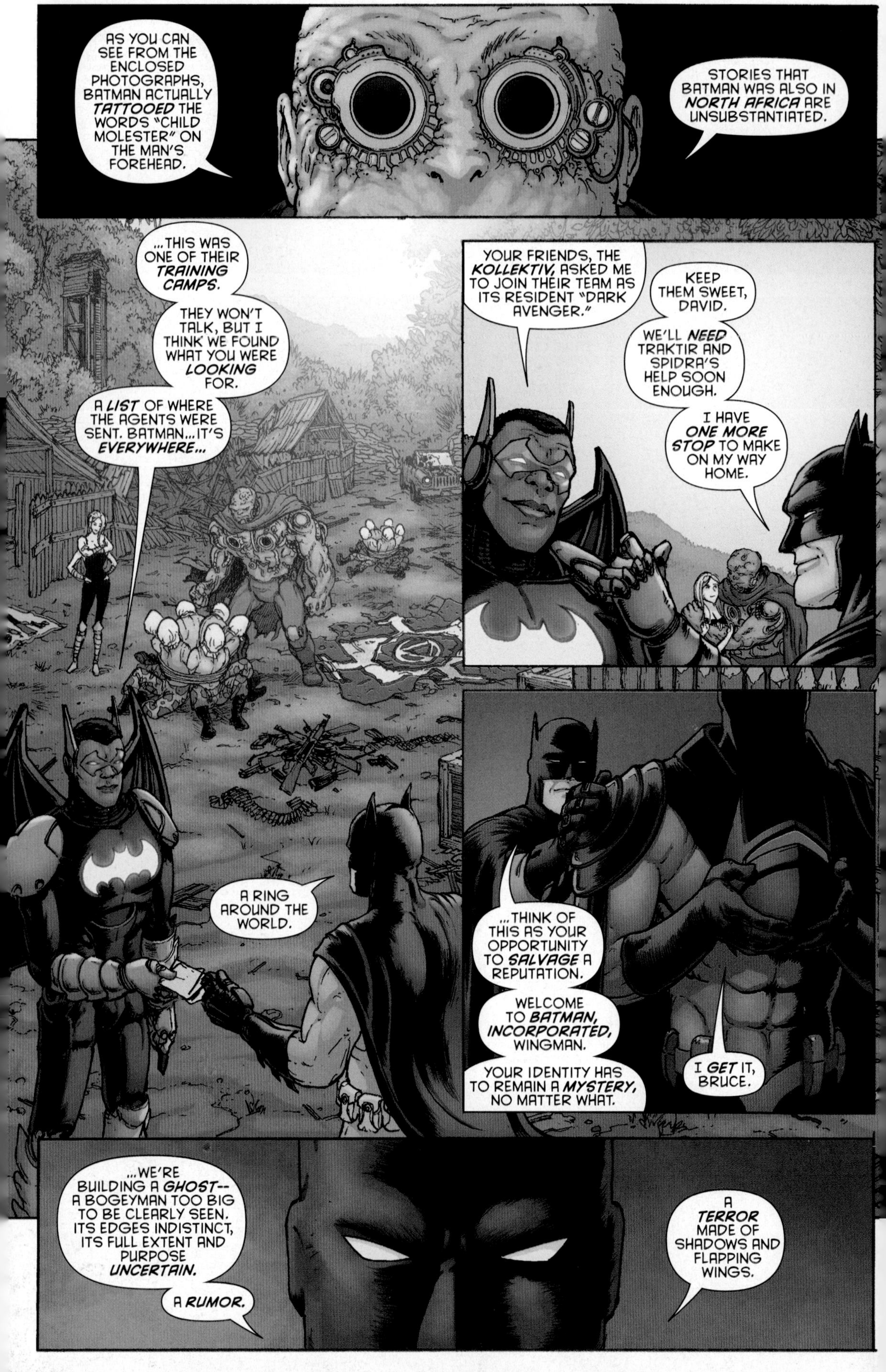
AS YOU CAN SEE FROM THE ENCLOSED PHOTOGRAPHS, BATMAN ACTUALLY TATTOOED THE WORDS "CHILD MOLESTER" ON THE MAN'S FOREHEAD.
STORIES THAT BATMAN WAS ALSO IN NORTH AFRICA ARE UNSUBSTANTIATED.
...THIS WAS ONE OF THEIR TRAINING CAMPS.
THEY WON'T TALK, BUT I THINK WE FOUND WHAT YOU WERE LOOKING FOR.
A LIST OF WHERE THE AGENTS WERE SENT. BATMAN...IT'S EVERYWHERE...
A RING AROUND THE WORLD.
YOUR FRIENDS, THE KOLLEKTIV, ASKED ME TO JOIN THEIR TEAM AS ITS RESIDENT "DARK AVENGER."
KEEP THEM SWEET, DAVID.
WE'LL NEED TRAKTIR AND SPIDRA'S HELP SOON ENOUGH.
I HAVE ONE MORE STOP TO MAKE ON MY WAY HOME.
...THINK OF THIS AS YOUR OPPORTUNITY TO SALVAGE A REPUTATION.
WELCOME TO BATMAN, INCORPORATED, WINGMAN.
YOUR IDENTITY HAS TO REMAIN A MYSTERY, NO MATTER WHAT.
I GET IT, BRUCE.
...WE'RE BUILDING A GHOST-- A BOGEYMAN TOO BIG TO BE CLEARLY SEEN. ITS EDGES INDISTINCT, ITS FULL EXTENT AND PURPOSE UNCERTAIN.
A RUMOR.
A TERROR MADE OF SHADOWS AND FLAPPING WINGS.

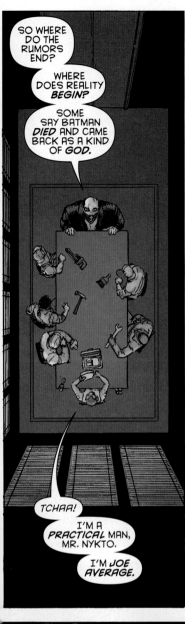

SO WHERE DO THE RUMORS END?

WHERE DOES REALITY *BEGIN?*

SOME SAY BATMAN *DIED* AND CAME BACK AS A KIND OF *GOD.*

TCHAA!

I'M A *PRACTICAL* MAN, MR. NYKTO.

I'M *JOE AVERAGE.*

I PUT MY FAITH IN THE *POWERS-THAT-BE*... AND SO FAR THEY'VE NEVER LET ME DOWN.

NOBODY'S MESSING WITH *WAYNE ENTERPRISES* OR ITS LOONY BOSS BECAUSE SOMEBODY *BIGGER* THAN ALL THIS IS WHISPERIN' *"HANDS OFF."*

BATMAN, HOWEVER, IS A LEGITIMATE TARGET.

YOU *SEE* THAT, YOU SEE THAT *CLOCK* THERE?

6PM EASTERN, WE *JOIN FORCES* WITH BOSSES FROM ALL AROUND THE *WORLD* FOR A GROUNDBREAKING *FLASHCRIME* EVENT.

IF BATMAN'S EVERY-WHERE, LET HIM PROVE IT!

YOU ASKED, JOE.

›KURRF‹

WHAT *IS* THAT STUFF...THAT *SMOKE?*

DWAAA

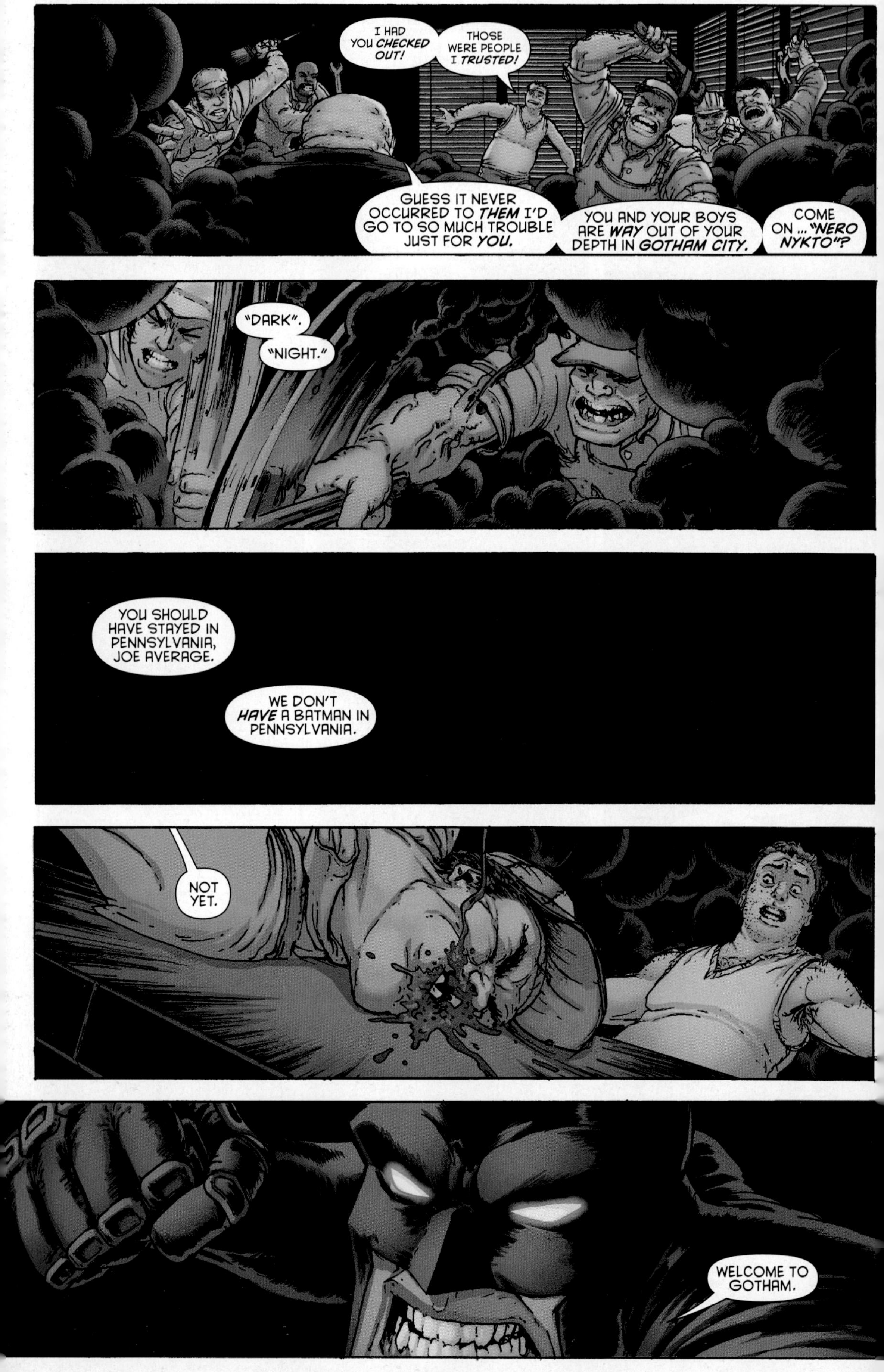
I HAD YOU CHECKED OUT!
THOSE WERE PEOPLE I TRUSTED!
GUESS IT NEVER OCCURRED TO THEM I'D GO TO SO MUCH TROUBLE JUST FOR YOU.
YOU AND YOUR BOYS ARE WAY OUT OF YOUR DEPTH IN GOTHAM CITY.
COME ON ... "NERO NYKTO"?
"DARK".
"NIGHT."
YOU SHOULD HAVE STAYED IN PENNSYLVANIA, JOE AVERAGE.
WE DON'T HAVE A BATMAN IN PENNSYLVANIA.
NOT YET.
WELCOME TO GOTHAM.

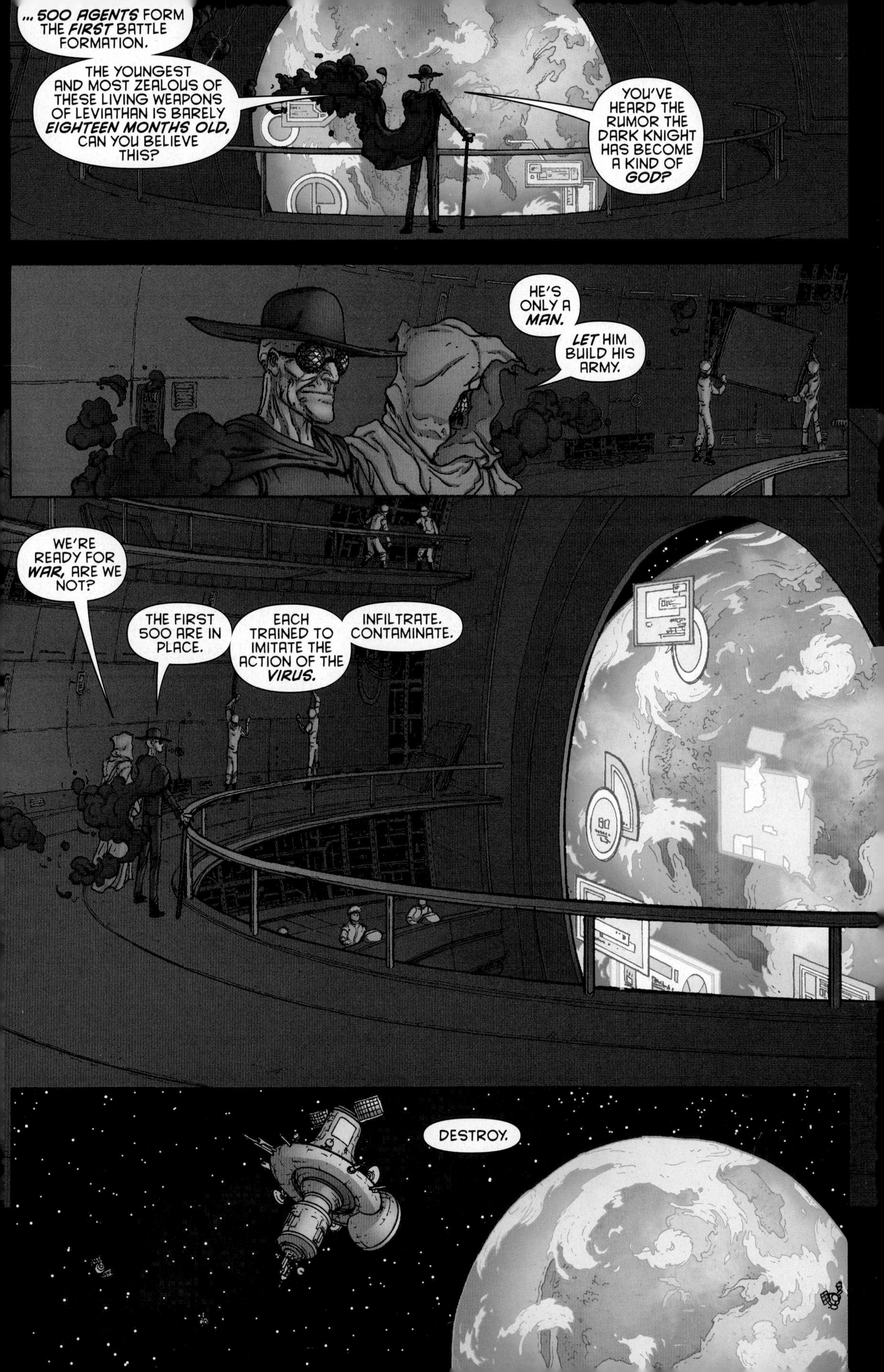
...500 AGENTS FORM THE FIRST BATTLE FORMATION.
THE YOUNGEST AND MOST ZEALOUS OF THESE LIVING WEAPONS OF LEVIATHAN IS BARELY EIGHTEEN MONTHS OLD, CAN YOU BELIEVE THIS?
YOU'VE HEARD THE RUMOR THE DARK KNIGHT HAS BECOME A KIND OF GOD?
HE'S ONLY A MAN.
LET HIM BUILD HIS ARMY.
WE'RE READY FOR WAR, ARE WE NOT?
THE FIRST 500 ARE IN PLACE.
EACH TRAINED TO IMITATE THE ACTION OF THE VIRUS.
INFILTRATE. CONTAMINATE.
DESTROY.

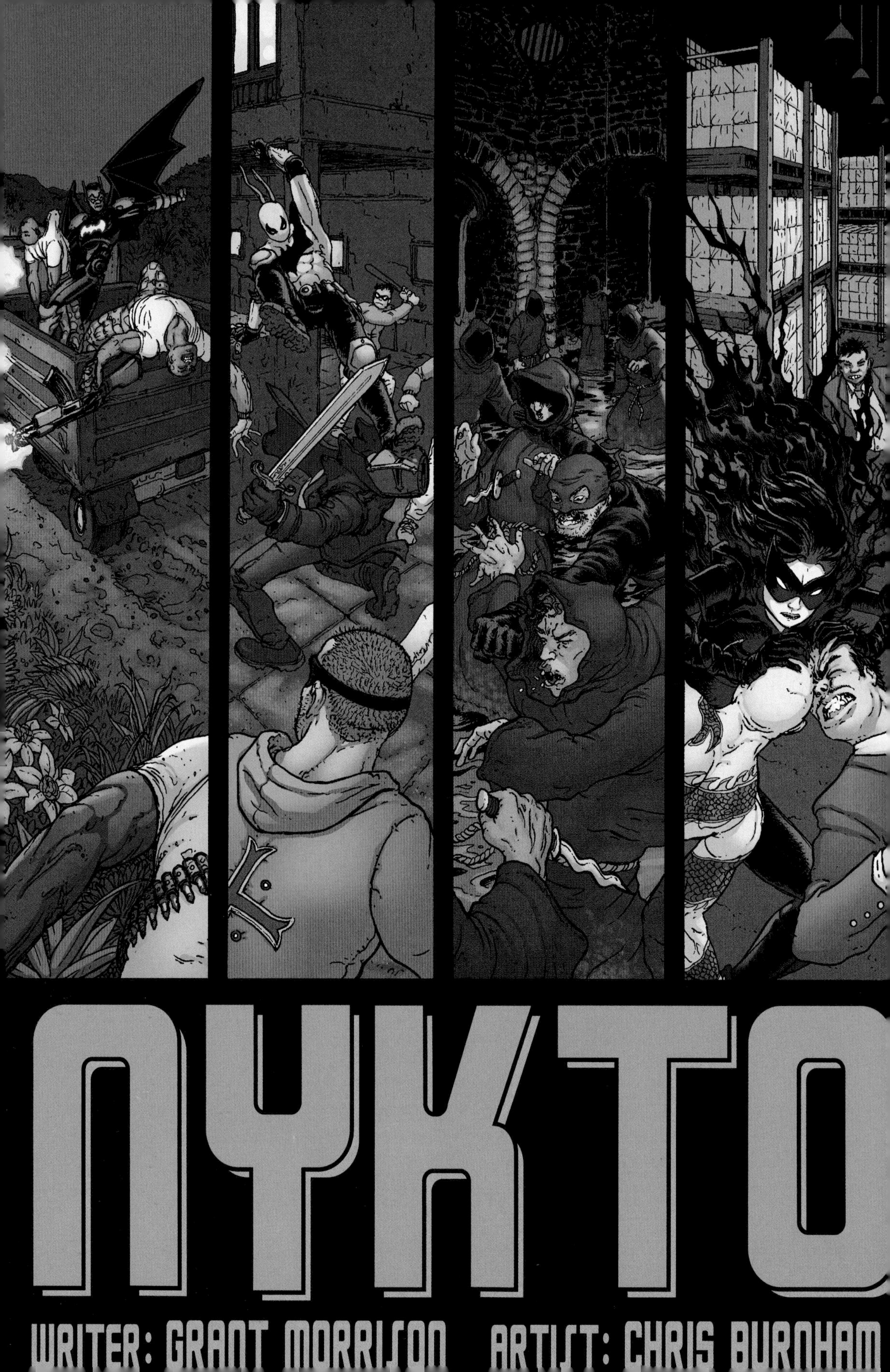

NYKTO

WRITER: GRANT MORRISON ARTIST: CHRIS BURNHAM

MORPH

COLORIST: NATHAN FAIRBAIRN   LETTERER: PAT BROSSEAU

Issue #7 cover art by **CHRIS BURNHAM** (color by **NATHAN FAIRBAIRN**).

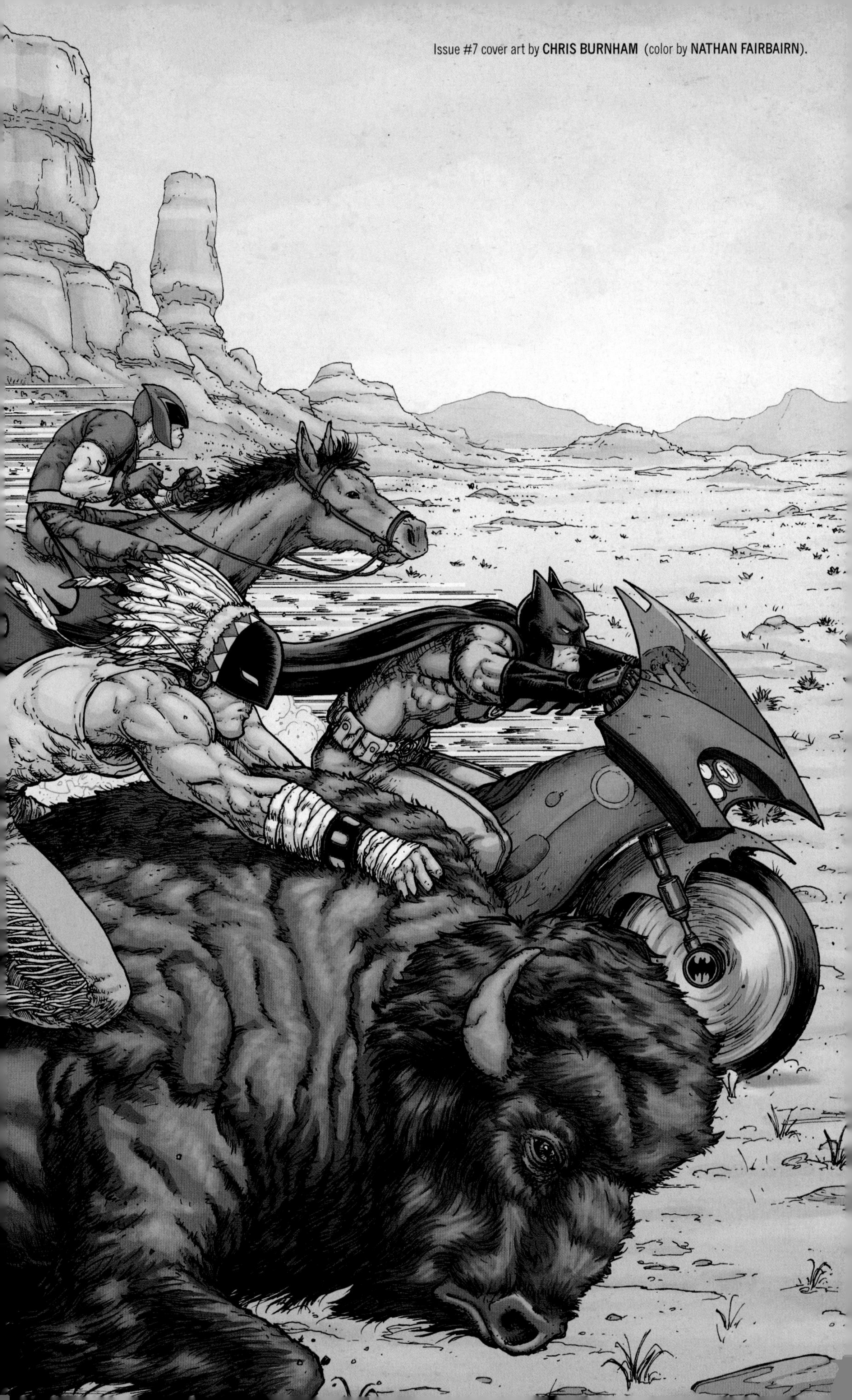

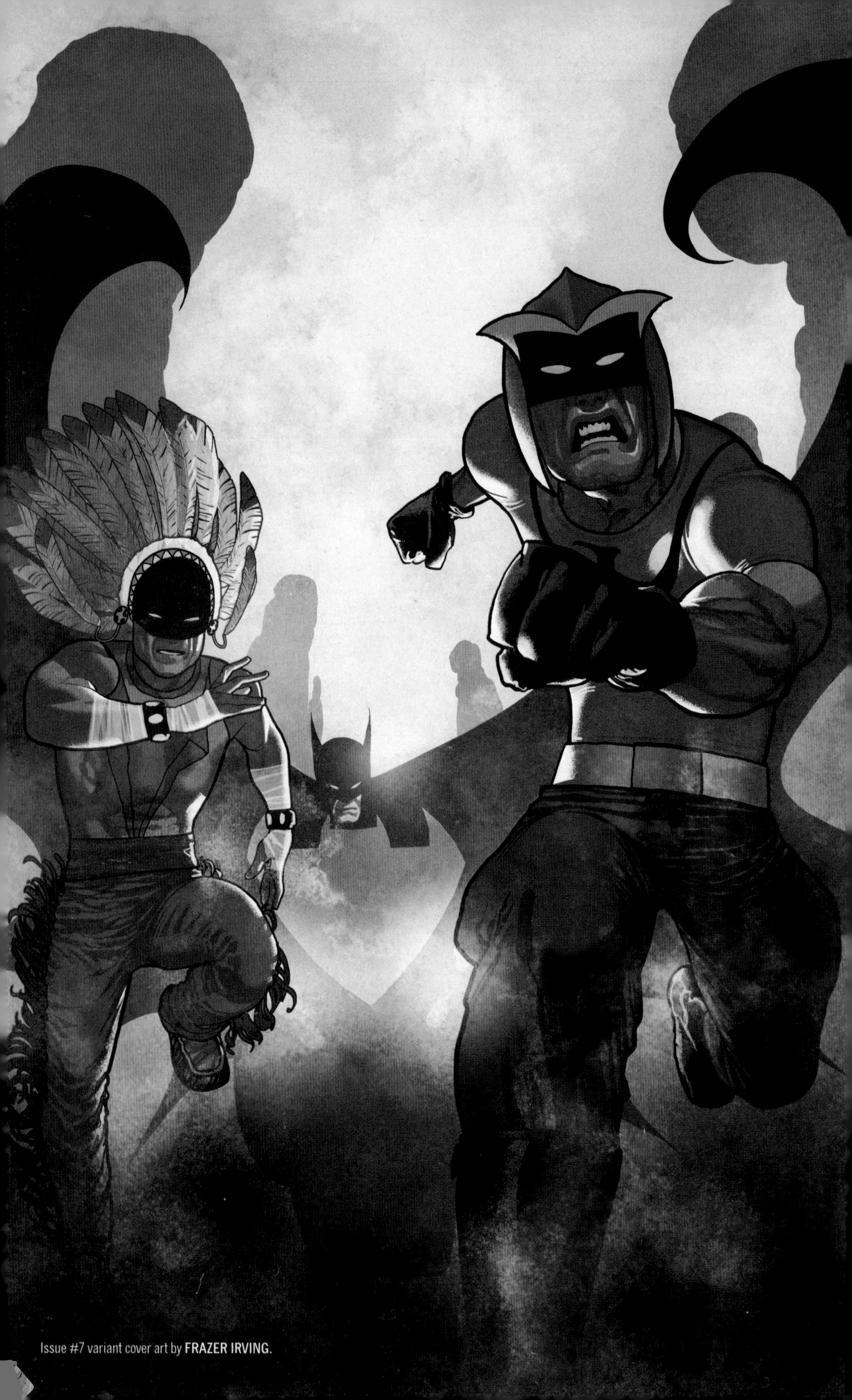

Issue #7 variant cover art by **FRAZER IRVING.**

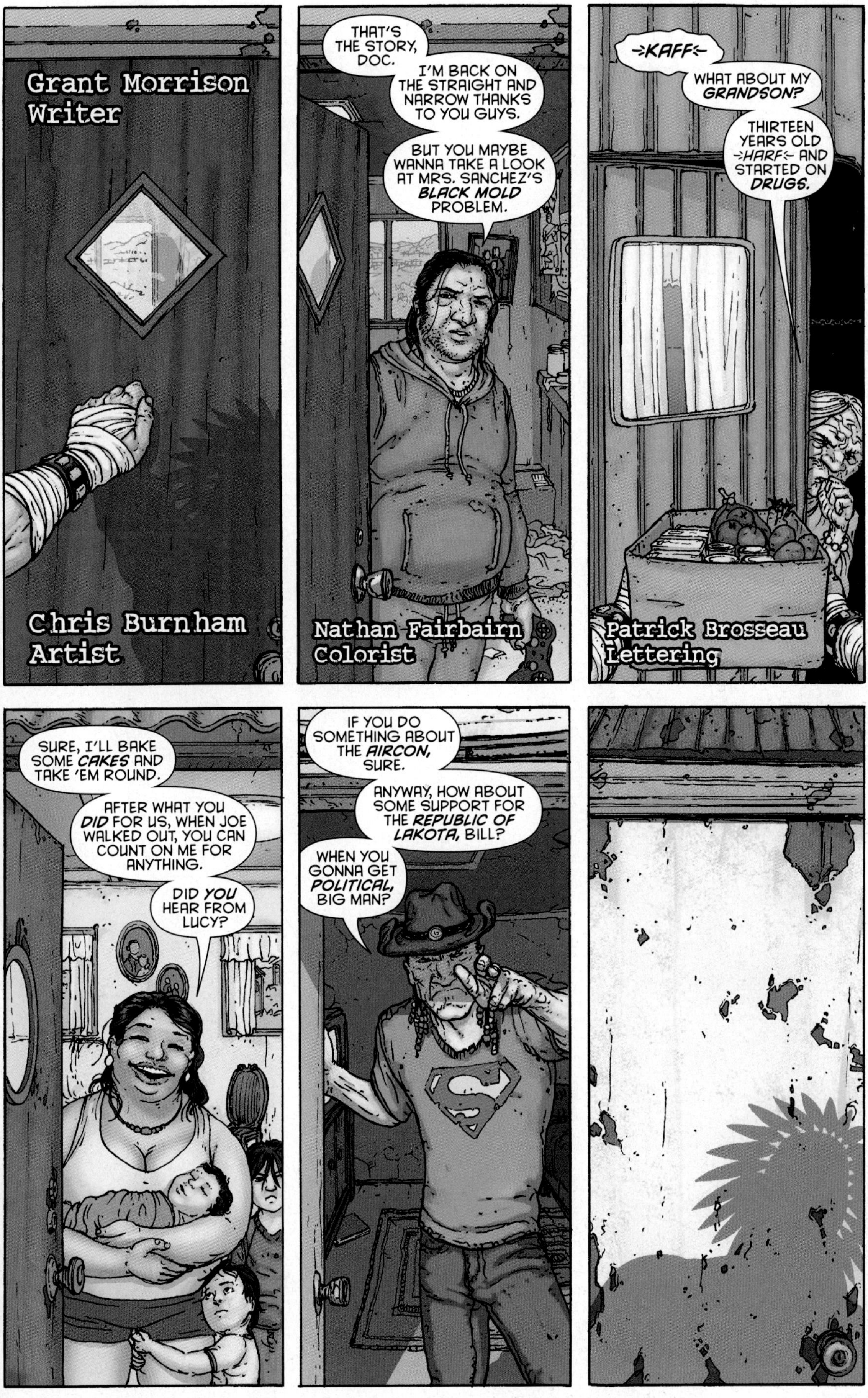
Grant Morrison
Writer
Chris Burnham
Artist
THAT'S THE STORY, DOC.
I'M BACK ON THE STRAIGHT AND NARROW THANKS TO YOU GUYS.
BUT YOU MAYBE WANNA TAKE A LOOK AT MRS. SANCHEZ'S BLACK MOLD PROBLEM.
Nathan Fairbairn
Colorist
KAFF
WHAT ABOUT MY GRANDSON?
THIRTEEN YEARS OLD HARF AND STARTED ON DRUGS.
Patrick Brosseau
Lettering
SURE, I'LL BAKE SOME CAKES AND TAKE 'EM ROUND.
AFTER WHAT YOU DID FOR US, WHEN JOE WALKED OUT, YOU CAN COUNT ON ME FOR ANYTHING.
DID YOU HEAR FROM LUCY?
IF YOU DO SOMETHING ABOUT THE AIRCON, SURE.
ANYWAY, HOW ABOUT SOME SUPPORT FOR THE REPUBLIC OF LAKOTA, BILL?
WHEN YOU GONNA GET POLITICAL, BIG MAN?

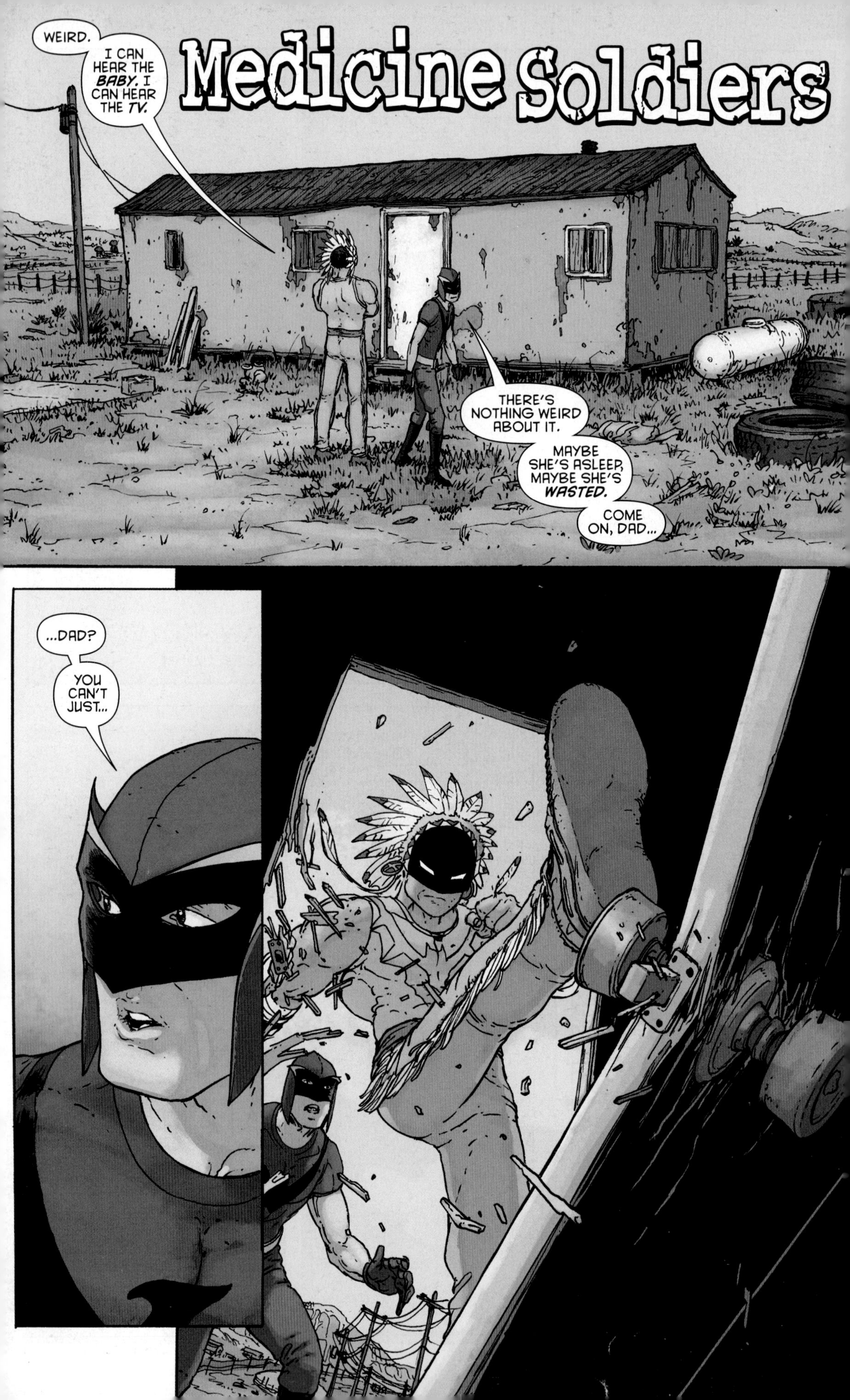
WEIRD.
I CAN HEAR THE *BABY*. I CAN HEAR THE *TV*.
Medicine Soldiers
THERE'S NOTHING WEIRD ABOUT IT.
MAYBE SHE'S ASLEEP, MAYBE SHE'S *WASTED*.
COME ON, DAD...
...DAD?
YOU CAN'T JUST...

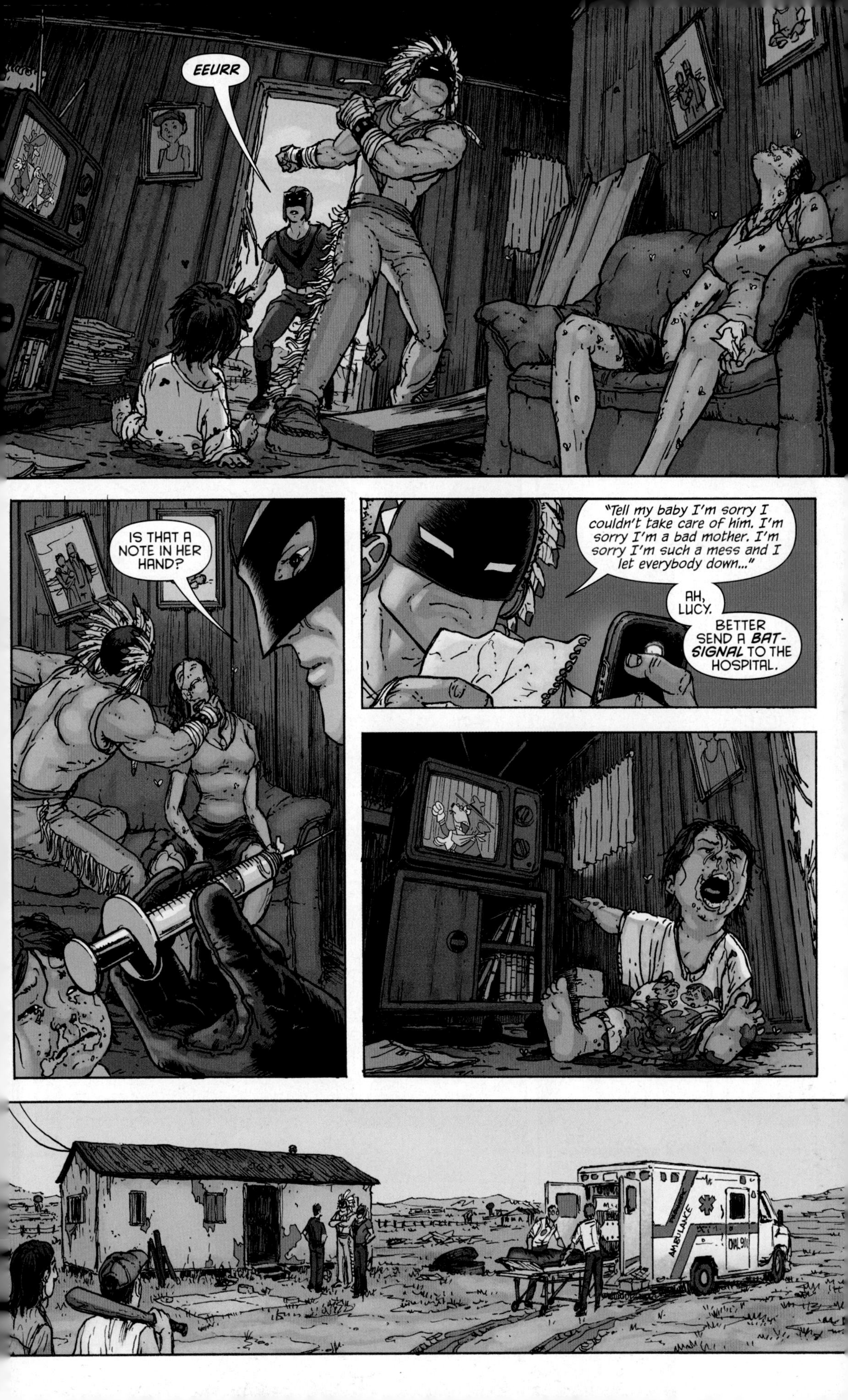
EEURR
IS THAT A NOTE IN HER HAND?
"Tell my baby I'm sorry I couldn't take care of him. I'm sorry I'm a bad mother. I'm sorry I'm such a mess and I let everybody down..."
AH, LUCY.
BETTER SEND A BAT-SIGNAL TO THE HOSPITAL.
AMBULANCE
DIAL 911

...THERE YOU GO, GRAN'MA.

THAT OUGHT TO TAKE THE *PRESSURE* OFF.

BILL, HEY.

NEW *BOSS* WANTS YOU IN HIS OFFICE.

MAN-OF-BATS' PROTES ENDS IN COURT DATE

News from a the Fence to keep you con...

LIQUOR TRADE = GENOCIDE

ONE SHOT AT A TIME

THIS IS *YOU*, DOCTOR?

I KNOW MY *PREDECESSOR* TURNED A BLIND EYE TO THESE ANTICS, BUT THIS MAKES US LOOK LIKE *CARICATURES*.

AND AS FOR THE REST...

...DON'T YOU THINK IT'S RIGHT TO LEAVE *CRIME* TO THE *POLICE*?

WITH FEWER THAN *TWENTY* OFFICERS TO PATROL AN AREA BIGGER THAN *RHODE ISLAND*?

IS THIS ABOUT MY WORK AT THE *HOSPITAL*?

BECAUSE HOW I SPEND MY *NIGHTS* AND *WEEKENDS* IS *MY BUSINESS*.

WHAT I DO AS *MAN-OF-BATS* DOESN'T IMPACT MY WORK AS A *DOCTOR*!

MY *SON* AND I ARE *HELPING* PEOPLE AND *STANDING UP* FOR SOMETHING.

MAYBE YOU DIDN'T *NOTICE*, BUT THE *REDZ GANG'S* BEEN GETTING *BIGGER* AND MORE *ORGANIZED* RECENTLY, AND THEY'RE JUST *ONE* OF OUR PROBLEMS...

YOU NEED TO BE *CAREFUL*, DOCTOR GREAT EAGLE.

THAT'S *ALL* I'M SAYING.

THINGS ARE *CHANGING* 'ROUND HERE.

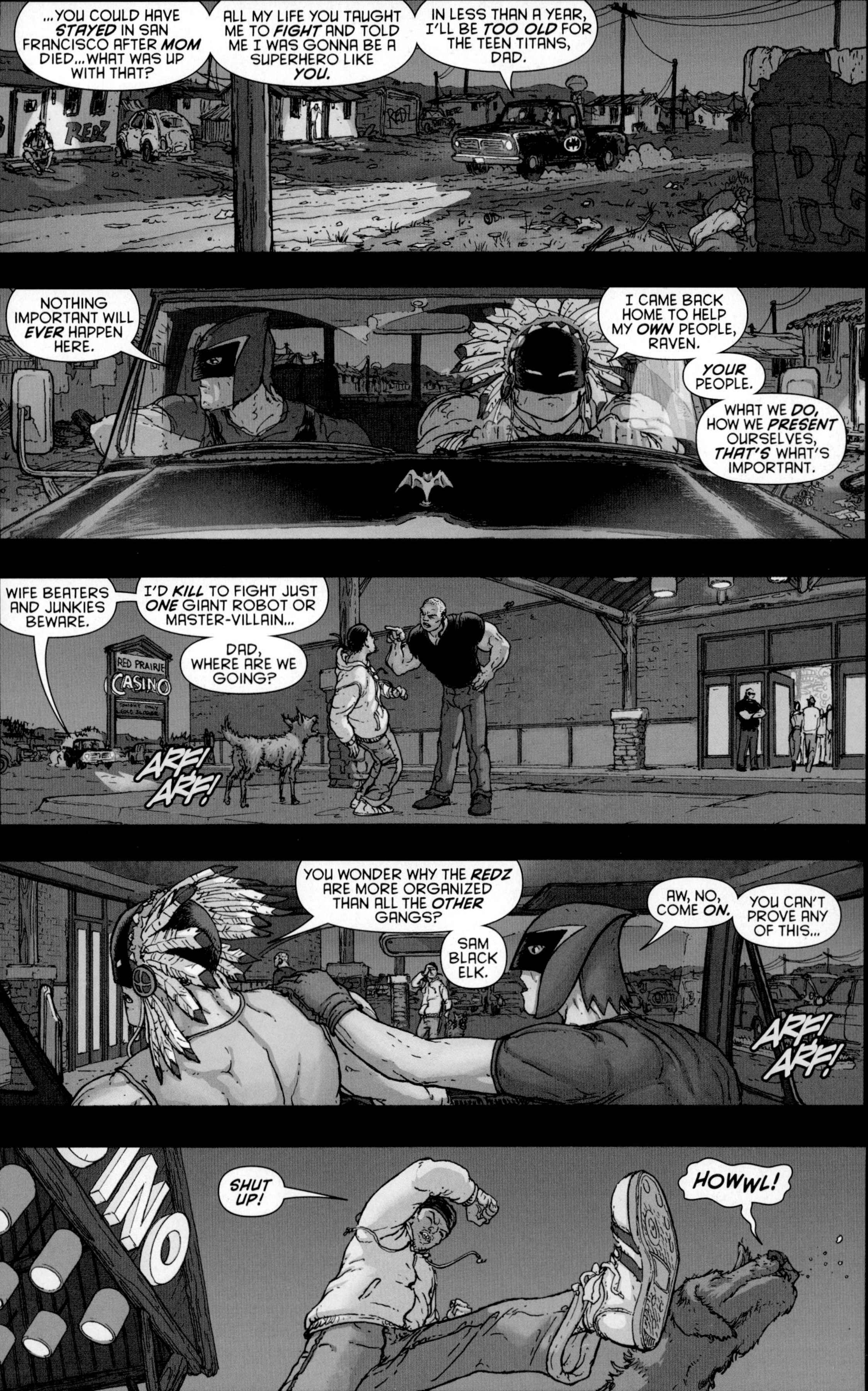

...YOU COULD HAVE STAYED IN SAN FRANCISCO AFTER MOM DIED...WHAT WAS UP WITH THAT?
ALL MY LIFE YOU TAUGHT ME TO FIGHT AND TOLD ME I WAS GONNA BE A SUPERHERO LIKE YOU.
IN LESS THAN A YEAR, I'LL BE TOO OLD FOR THE TEEN TITANS, DAD.
REDZ
NOTHING IMPORTANT WILL EVER HAPPEN HERE.
I CAME BACK HOME TO HELP MY OWN PEOPLE, RAVEN.
YOUR PEOPLE.
WHAT WE DO, HOW WE PRESENT OURSELVES, THAT'S WHAT'S IMPORTANT.
WIFE BEATERS AND JUNKIES BEWARE.
I'D KILL TO FIGHT JUST ONE GIANT ROBOT OR MASTER-VILLAIN...
DAD, WHERE ARE WE GOING?
RED PRAIRIE CASINO
ARF! ARF!
YOU WONDER WHY THE REDZ ARE MORE ORGANIZED THAN ALL THE OTHER GANGS?
SAM BLACK ELK.
AW, NO, COME ON.
YOU CAN'T PROVE ANY OF THIS...
ARF! ARF!
SHUT UP!
HOWWL!

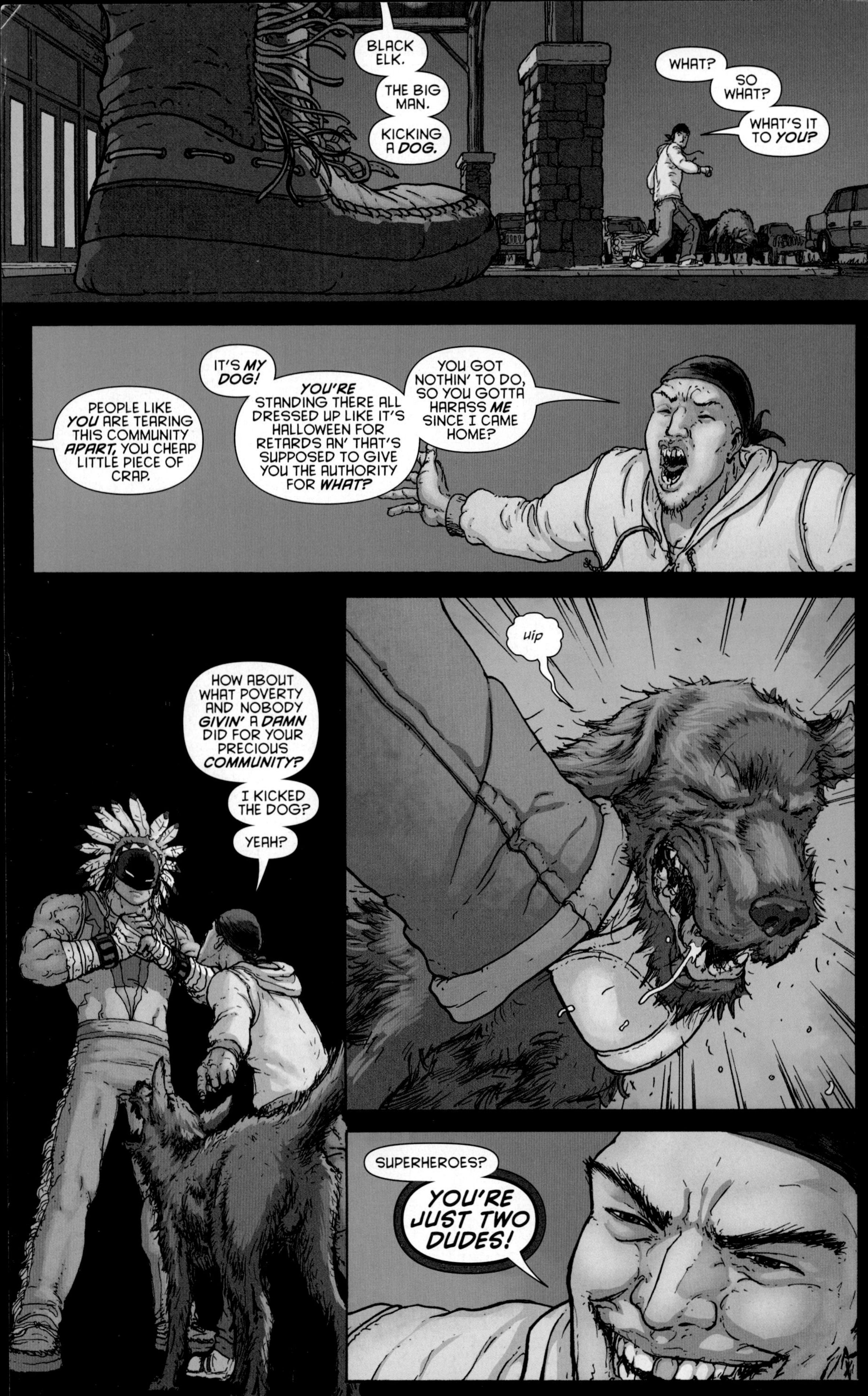
BLACK ELK.
THE BIG MAN.
KICKING A *DOG.*
WHAT?
SO WHAT?
WHAT'S IT TO *YOU?*
YOU GOT NOTHIN' TO DO, SO YOU GOTTA HARASS *ME* SINCE I CAME HOME?
IT'S *MY DOG!*
YOU'RE STANDING THERE ALL DRESSED UP LIKE IT'S HALLOWEEN FOR RETARDS AN' THAT'S SUPPOSED TO GIVE YOU THE AUTHORITY FOR *WHAT?*
PEOPLE LIKE *YOU* ARE TEARING THIS COMMUNITY *APART,* YOU CHEAP LITTLE PIECE OF CRAP.
HOW ABOUT WHAT POVERTY AND NOBODY *GIVIN'* A *DAMN* DID FOR YOUR PRECIOUS *COMMUNITY?*
I KICKED THE DOG?
YEAH?
uip
SUPERHEROES?
YOU'RE JUST TWO DUDES!

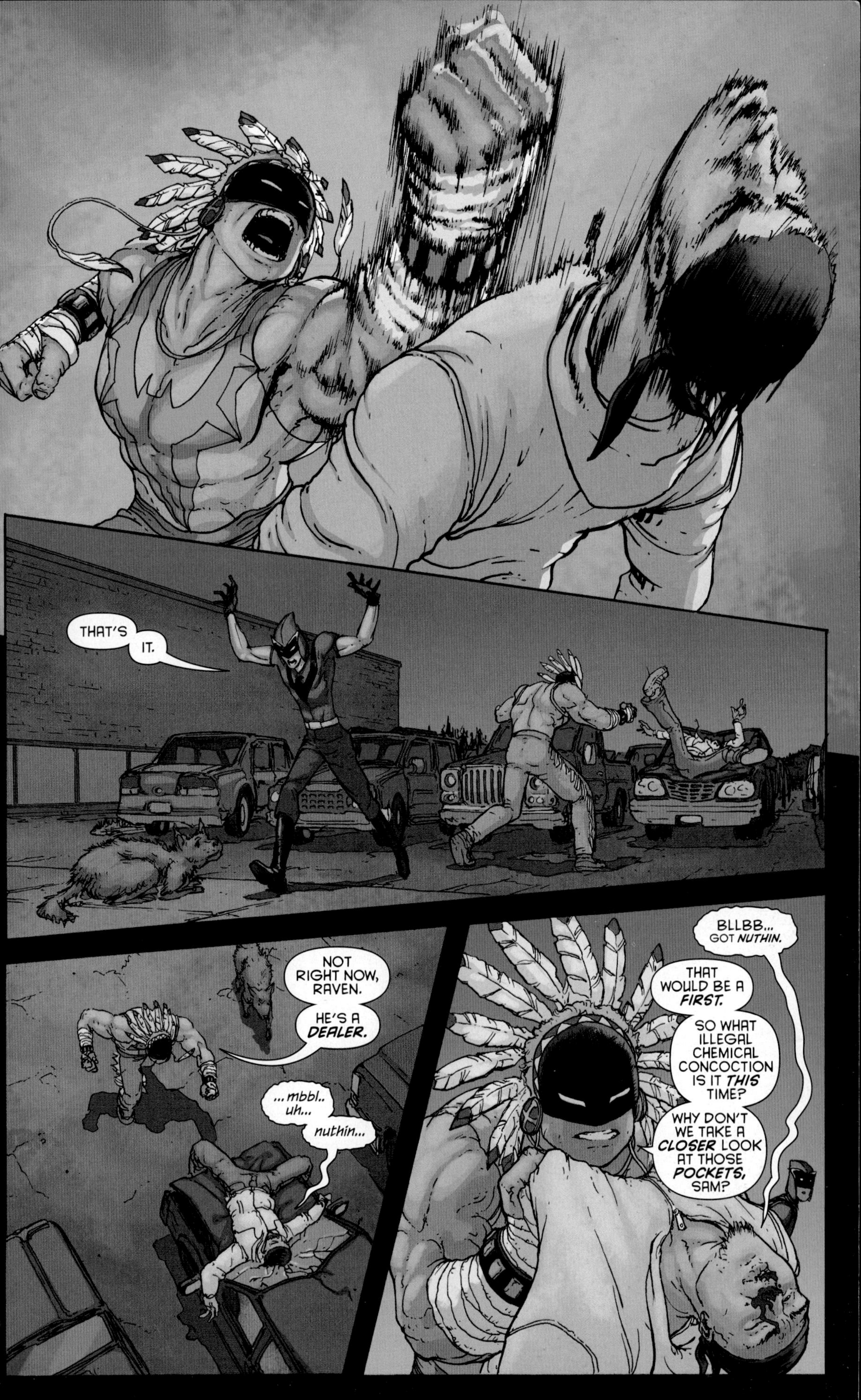

THAT'S IT.
NOT RIGHT NOW, RAVEN.
HE'S A **DEALER.**
...mbbl.. uh... nuthin...
BLLBB... GOT **NUTHIN.**
THAT WOULD BE A **FIRST.**
SO WHAT ILLEGAL CHEMICAL CONCOCTION IS IT **THIS** TIME?
WHY DON'T WE TAKE A **CLOSER** LOOK AT THOSE **POCKETS,** SAM?

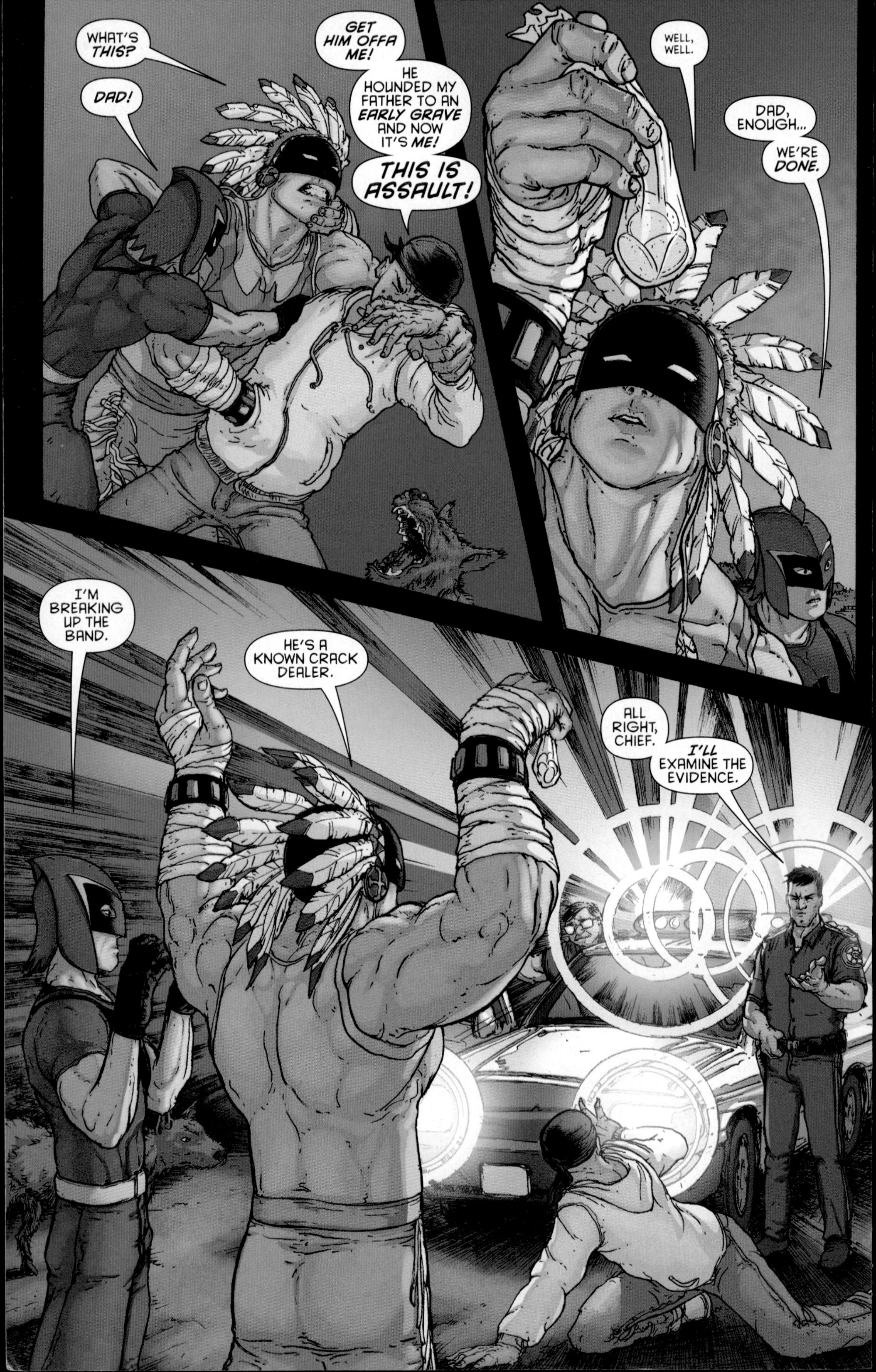
WHAT'S THIS?
DAD!
GET HIM OFFA ME!
HE HOUNDED MY FATHER TO AN EARLY GRAVE AND NOW IT'S ME!
THIS IS ASSAULT!
WELL, WELL.
DAD, ENOUGH...
WE'RE DONE.
I'M BREAKING UP THE BAND.
HE'S A KNOWN CRACK DEALER.
ALL RIGHT, CHIEF.
I'LL EXAMINE THE EVIDENCE.

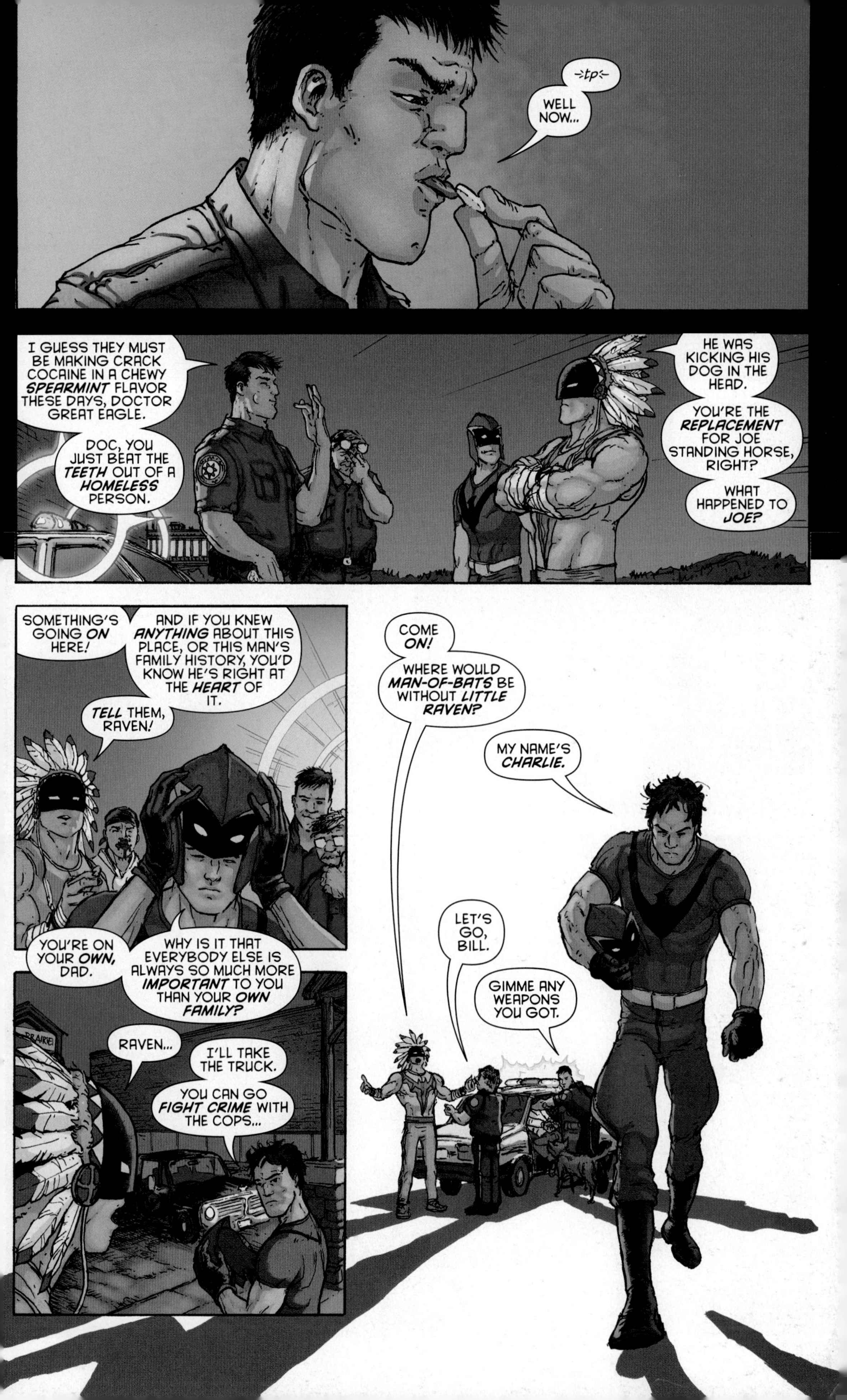

-tp-
WELL NOW...
I GUESS THEY MUST BE MAKING CRACK COCAINE IN A CHEWY SPEARMINT FLAVOR THESE DAYS, DOCTOR GREAT EAGLE.
DOC, YOU JUST BEAT THE TEETH OUT OF A HOMELESS PERSON.
HE WAS KICKING HIS DOG IN THE HEAD.
YOU'RE THE REPLACEMENT FOR JOE STANDING HORSE, RIGHT?
WHAT HAPPENED TO JOE?
SOMETHING'S GOING ON HERE!
AND IF YOU KNEW ANYTHING ABOUT THIS PLACE, OR THIS MAN'S FAMILY HISTORY, YOU'D KNOW HE'S RIGHT AT THE HEART OF IT.
TELL THEM, RAVEN!
YOU'RE ON YOUR OWN, DAD.
WHY IS IT THAT EVERYBODY ELSE IS ALWAYS SO MUCH MORE IMPORTANT TO YOU THAN YOUR OWN FAMILY?
PRAIRIE
RAVEN...
I'LL TAKE THE TRUCK.
YOU CAN GO FIGHT CRIME WITH THE COPS...
COME ON!
WHERE WOULD MAN-OF-BATS BE WITHOUT LITTLE RAVEN?
MY NAME'S CHARLIE.
LET'S GO, BILL.
GIMME ANY WEAPONS YOU GOT.

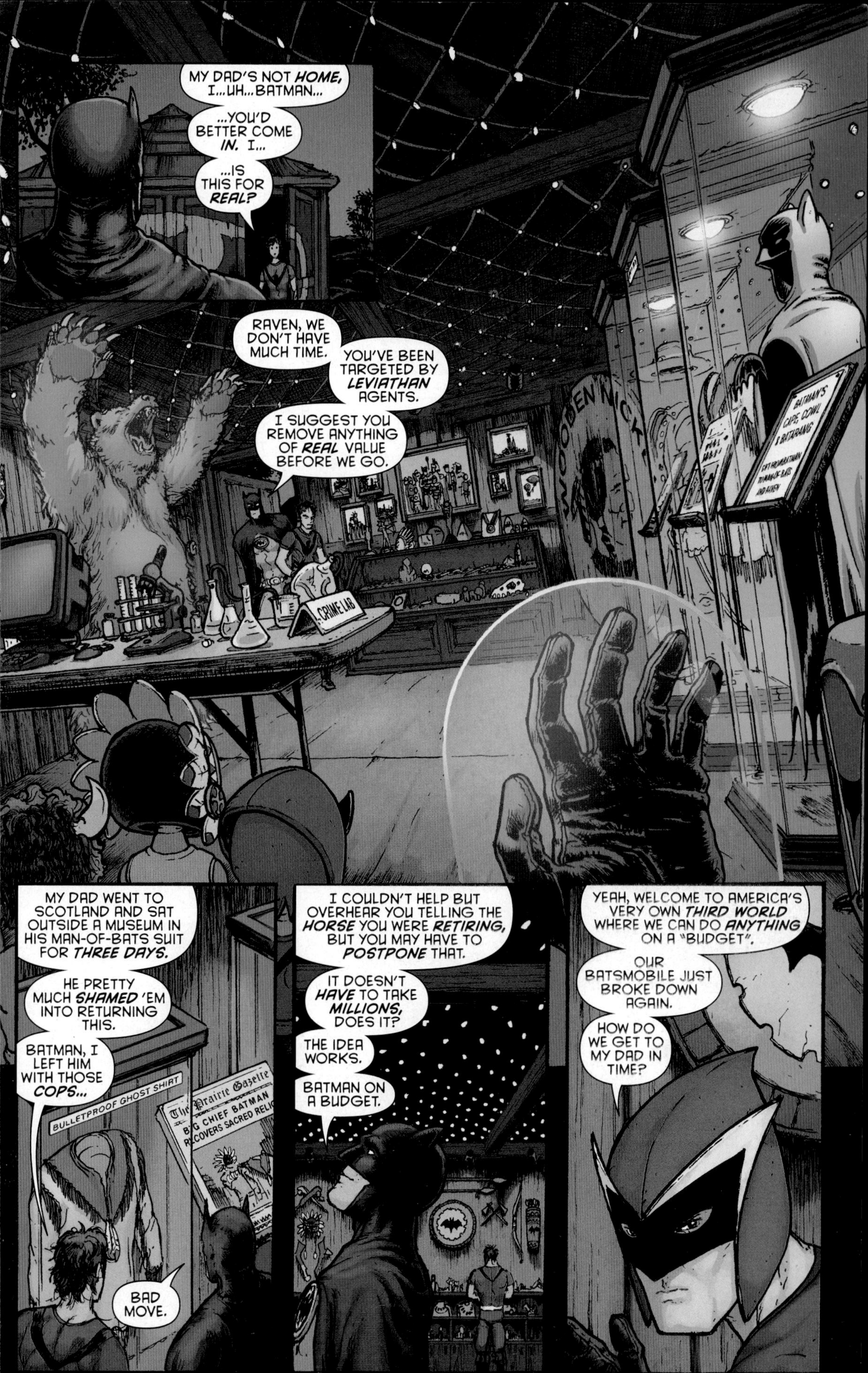
MY DAD'S NOT *HOME,* I...UH...BATMAN...
...YOU'D BETTER COME *IN.* I...
...IS THIS FOR *REAL?*
RAVEN, WE DON'T HAVE MUCH TIME.
YOU'VE BEEN TARGETED BY *LEVIATHAN* AGENTS.
I SUGGEST YOU REMOVE ANYTHING OF *REAL* VALUE BEFORE WE GO.
CRIME LAB
BATMAN'S CAPE, COWL & BATARANG
MY DAD WENT TO SCOTLAND AND SAT OUTSIDE A MUSEUM IN HIS MAN-OF-BATS SUIT FOR *THREE DAYS.*
HE PRETTY MUCH *SHAMED* 'EM INTO RETURNING THIS.
BATMAN, I LEFT HIM WITH THOSE *COPS...*
BULLETPROOF GHOST SHIRT
The Prairie Gazette
BIG CHIEF BATMAN RECOVERS SACRED RELIC
BAD MOVE.
I COULDN'T HELP BUT OVERHEAR YOU TELLING THE *HORSE* YOU WERE *RETIRING,* BUT YOU MAY HAVE TO *POSTPONE* THAT.
IT DOESN'T *HAVE* TO TAKE *MILLIONS,* DOES IT?
THE IDEA WORKS.
BATMAN ON A BUDGET.
YEAH, WELCOME TO AMERICA'S VERY OWN *THIRD WORLD* WHERE WE CAN DO *ANYTHING* ON A "BUDGET".
OUR BATSMOBILE JUST BROKE DOWN AGAIN.
HOW DO WE GET TO MY DAD IN TIME?

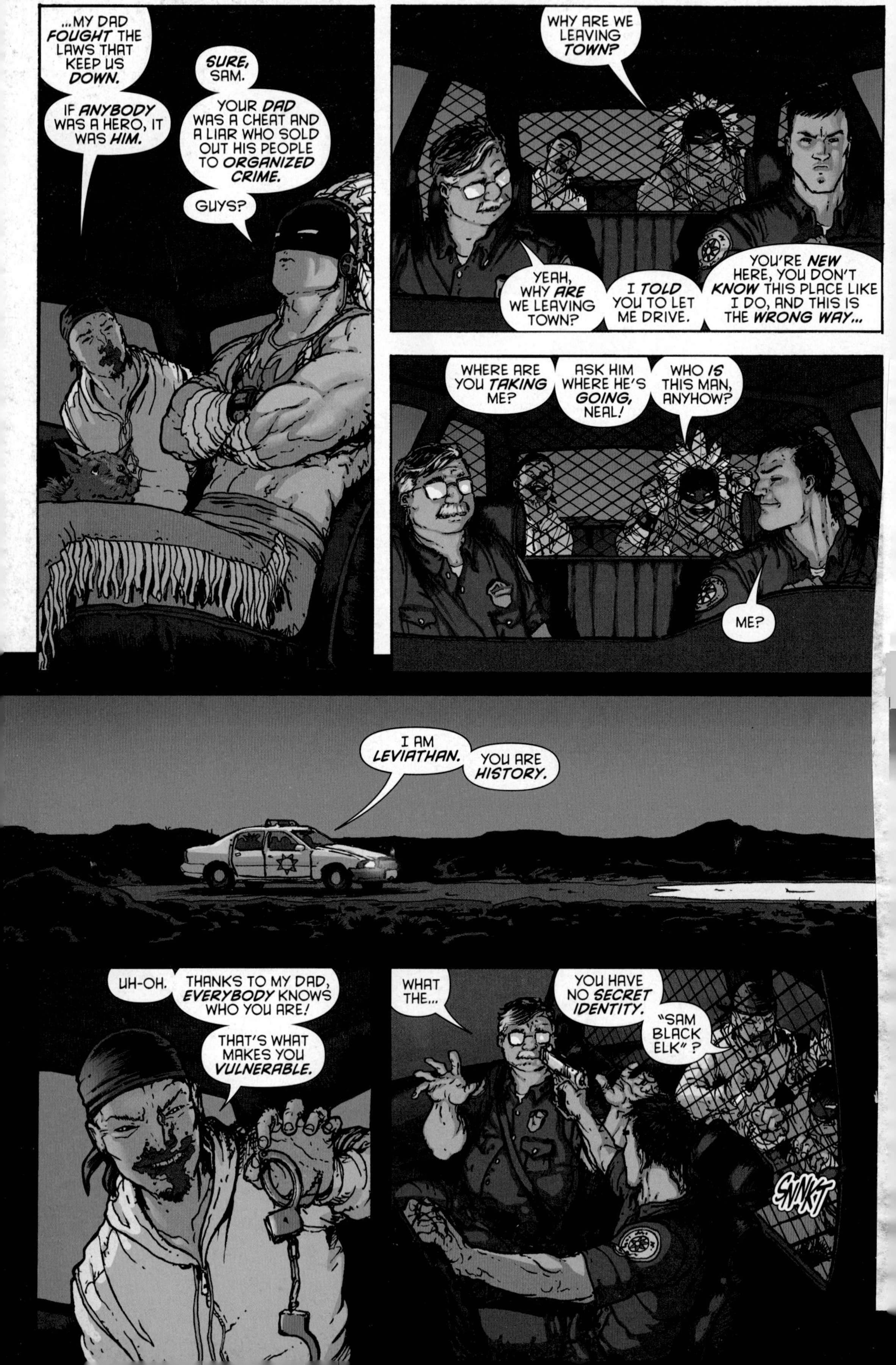

...MY DAD FOUGHT THE LAWS THAT KEEP US DOWN.
IF ANYBODY WAS A HERO, IT WAS HIM.
SURE, SAM.
YOUR DAD WAS A CHEAT AND A LIAR WHO SOLD OUT HIS PEOPLE TO ORGANIZED CRIME.
GUYS?
WHY ARE WE LEAVING TOWN?
YEAH, WHY ARE WE LEAVING TOWN?
I TOLD YOU TO LET ME DRIVE.
YOU'RE NEW HERE, YOU DON'T KNOW THIS PLACE LIKE I DO, AND THIS IS THE WRONG WAY...
WHERE ARE YOU TAKING ME?
ASK HIM WHERE HE'S GOING, NEAL!
WHO IS THIS MAN, ANYHOW?
ME?
I AM LEVIATHAN.
YOU ARE HISTORY.
UH-OH.
THANKS TO MY DAD, EVERYBODY KNOWS WHO YOU ARE!
THAT'S WHAT MAKES YOU VULNERABLE.
WHAT THE...
YOU HAVE NO SECRET IDENTITY.
"SAM BLACK ELK"?
SNIKT

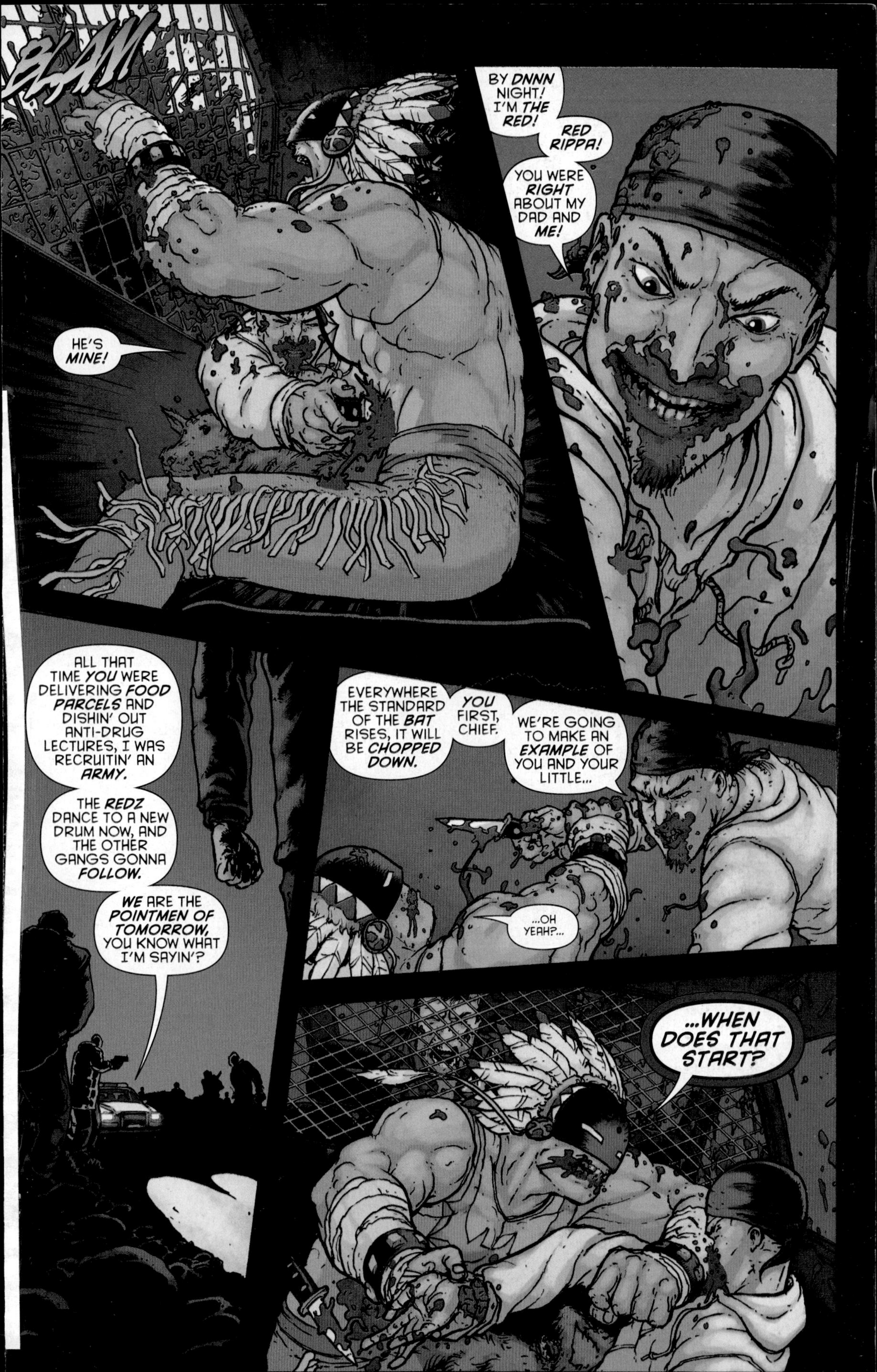
BLAM!
BY DNNN NIGHT! I'M THE RED!
RED RIPPA!
YOU WERE RIGHT ABOUT MY DAD AND ME!
HE'S MINE!
ALL THAT TIME YOU WERE DELIVERING FOOD PARCELS AND DISHIN' OUT ANTI-DRUG LECTURES, I WAS RECRUITIN' AN ARMY.
THE REDZ DANCE TO A NEW DRUM NOW, AND THE OTHER GANGS GONNA FOLLOW.
WE ARE THE POINTMEN OF TOMORROW, YOU KNOW WHAT I'M SAYIN'?
EVERYWHERE THE STANDARD OF THE BAT RISES, IT WILL BE CHOPPED DOWN.
YOU FIRST, CHIEF.
WE'RE GOING TO MAKE AN EXAMPLE OF YOU AND YOUR LITTLE...
...OH YEAH?...
...WHEN DOES THAT START?

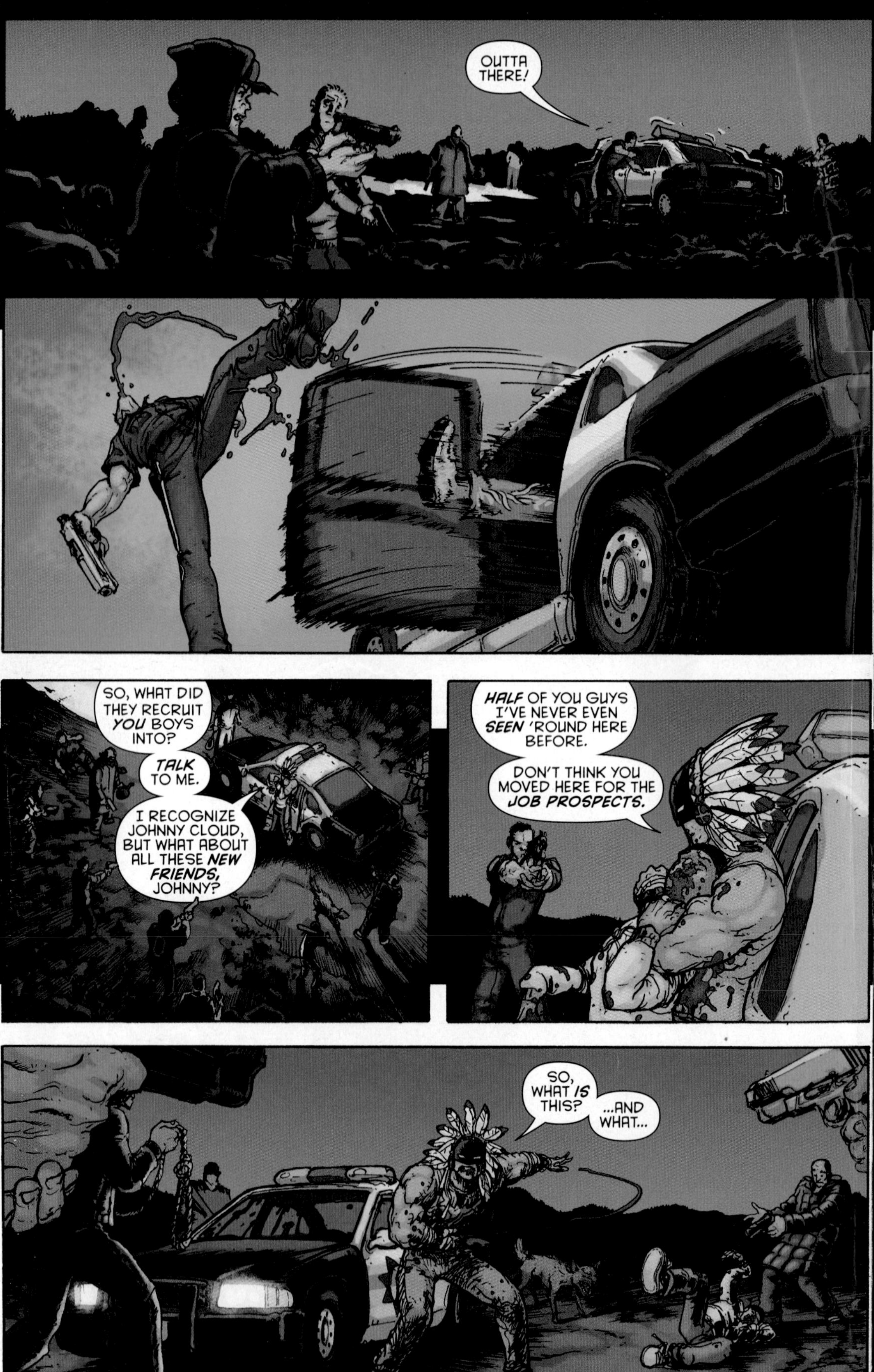
OUTTA THERE!
SO, WHAT DID THEY RECRUIT YOU BOYS INTO?
TALK TO ME.
I RECOGNIZE JOHNNY CLOUD, BUT WHAT ABOUT ALL THESE NEW FRIENDS, JOHNNY?
HALF OF YOU GUYS I'VE NEVER EVEN SEEN 'ROUND HERE BEFORE.
DON'T THINK YOU MOVED HERE FOR THE JOB PROSPECTS.
SO, WHAT IS THIS?
...AND WHAT...

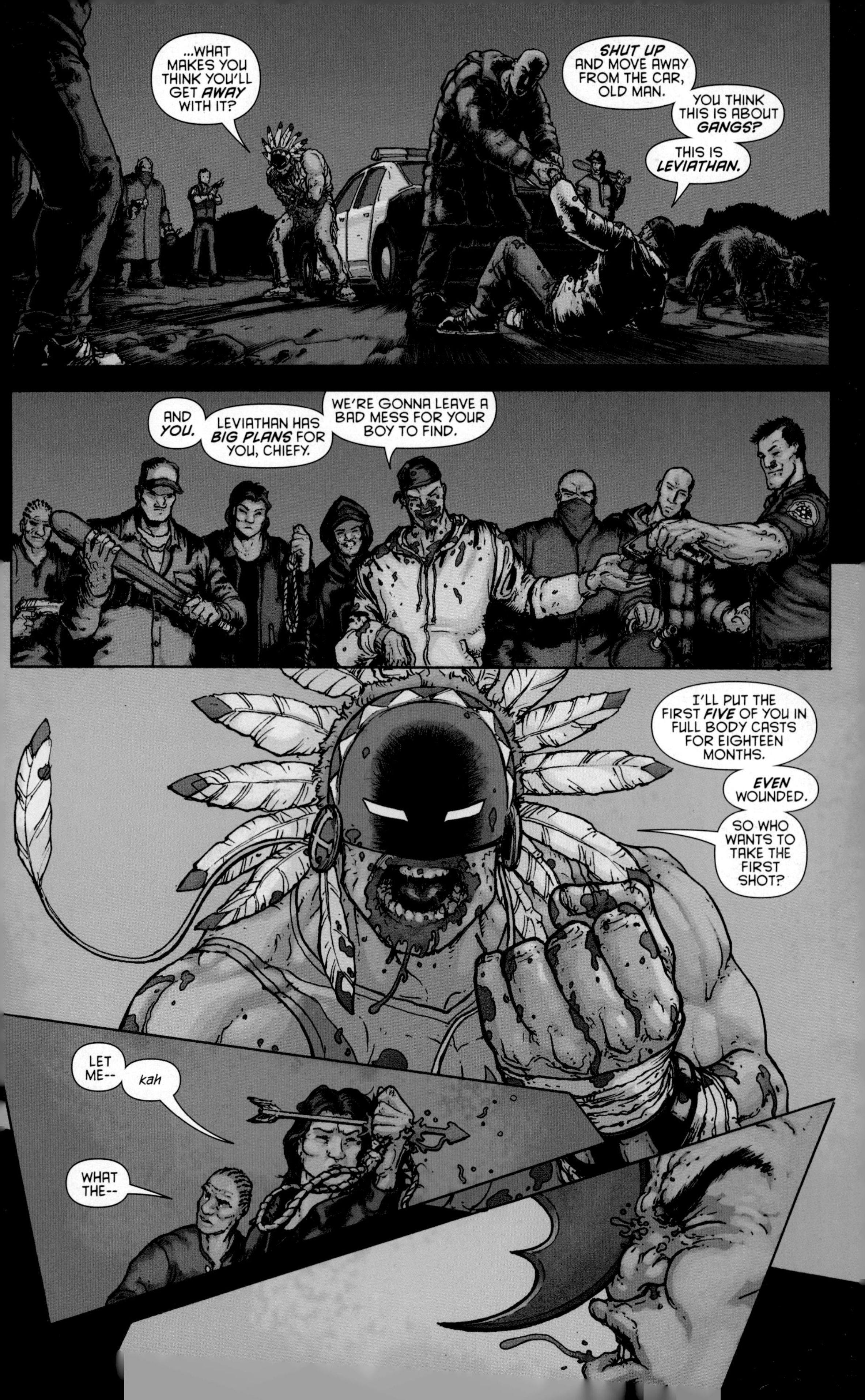
...WHAT MAKES YOU THINK YOU'LL GET *AWAY* WITH IT?
SHUT UP AND MOVE AWAY FROM THE CAR, OLD MAN.
YOU THINK THIS IS ABOUT *GANGS?*
THIS IS *LEVIATHAN.*
AND *YOU.*
LEVIATHAN HAS *BIG PLANS* FOR YOU, CHIEFY.
WE'RE GONNA LEAVE A BAD MESS FOR YOUR BOY TO FIND.
I'LL PUT THE FIRST *FIVE* OF YOU IN FULL BODY CASTS FOR EIGHTEEN MONTHS.
EVEN WOUNDED.
SO WHO WANTS TO TAKE THE FIRST SHOT?
LET ME--
kah
WHAT THE--

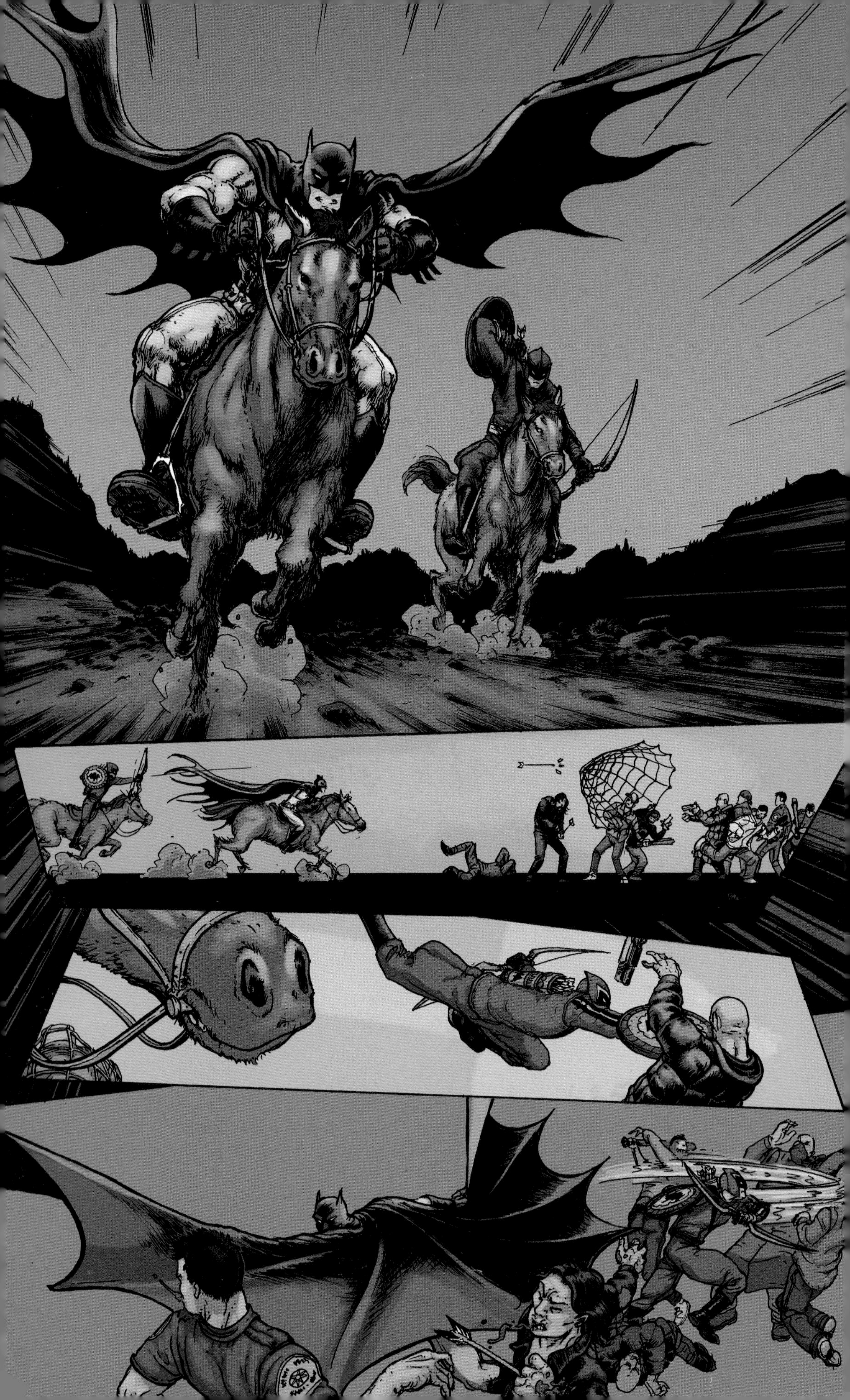

#7

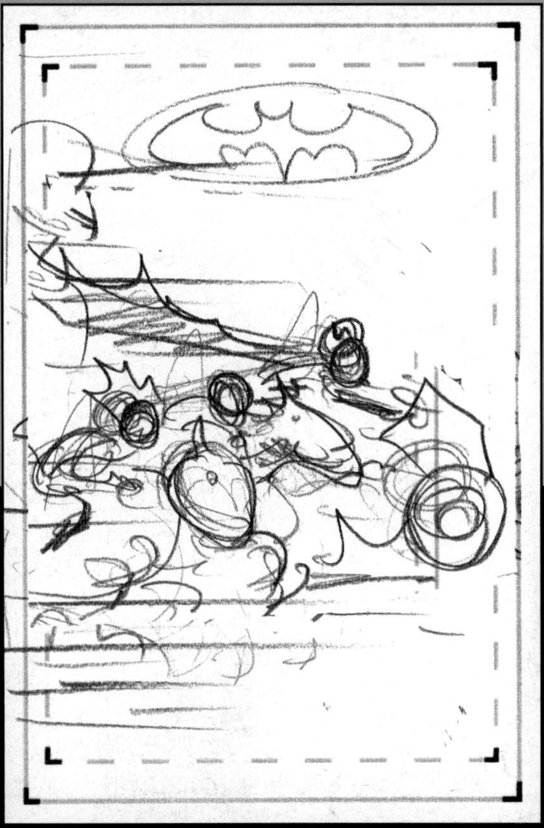

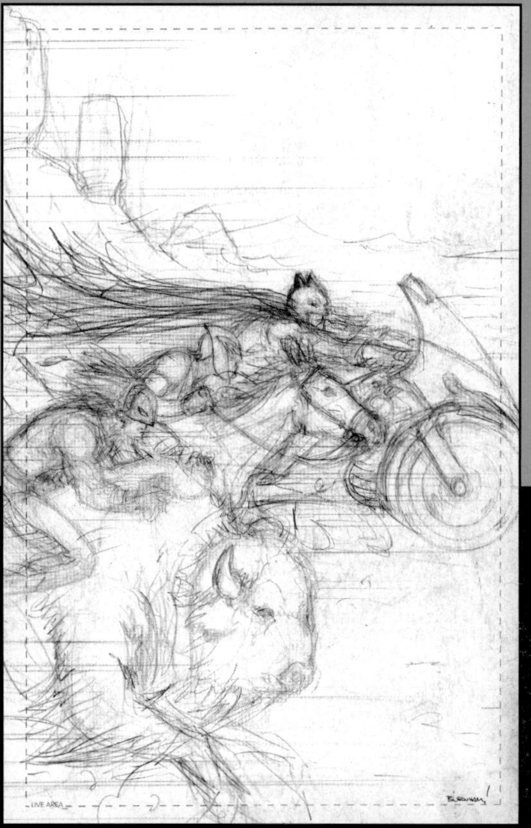

#8

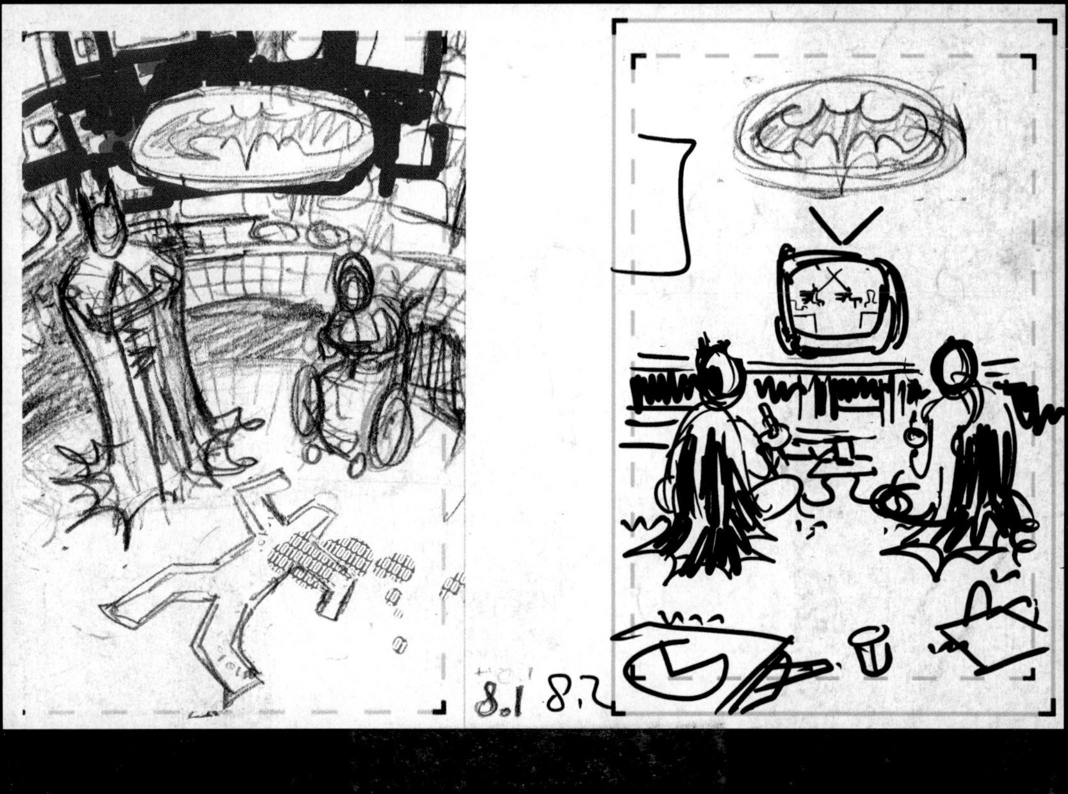
8.1 8.2

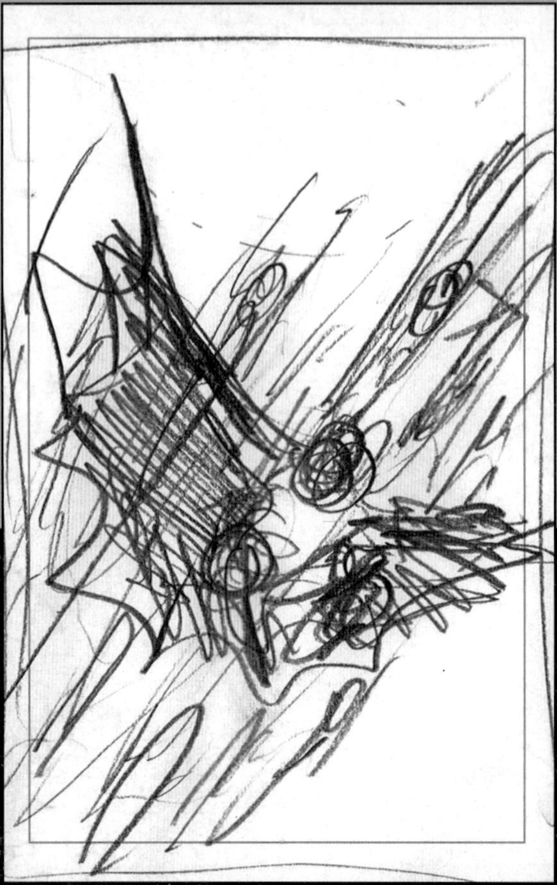

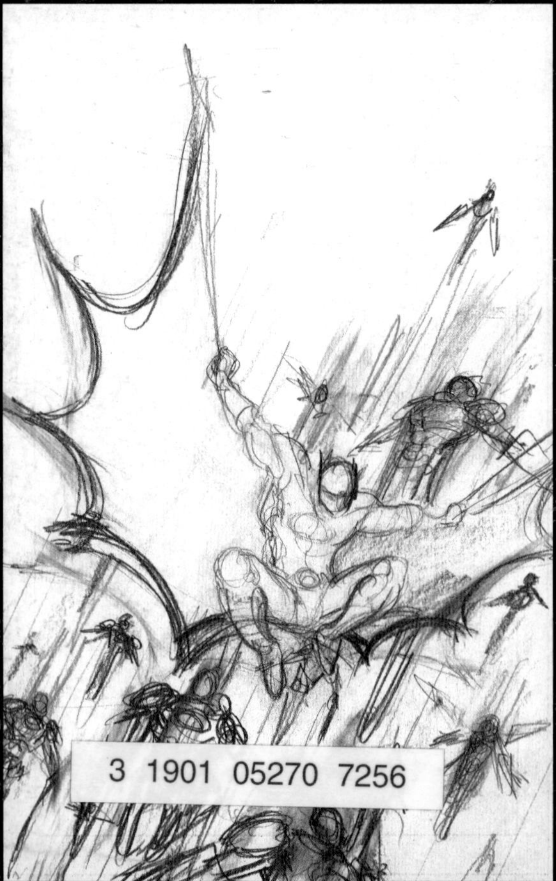

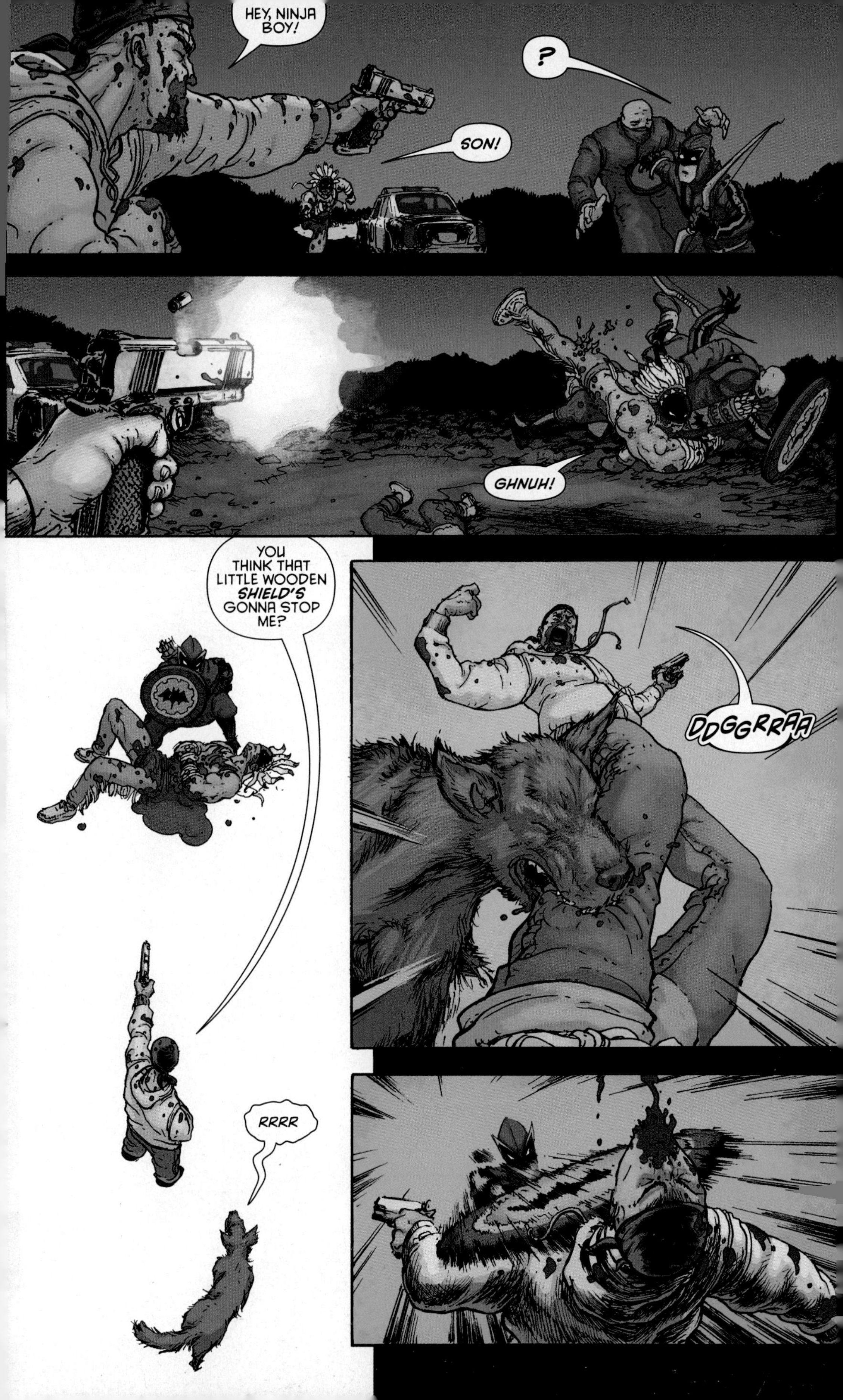
HEY, NINJA BOY!
?
SON!
GHNUH!
YOU THINK THAT LITTLE WOODEN SHIELD'S GONNA STOP ME?
DDGGRRAA
RRRR

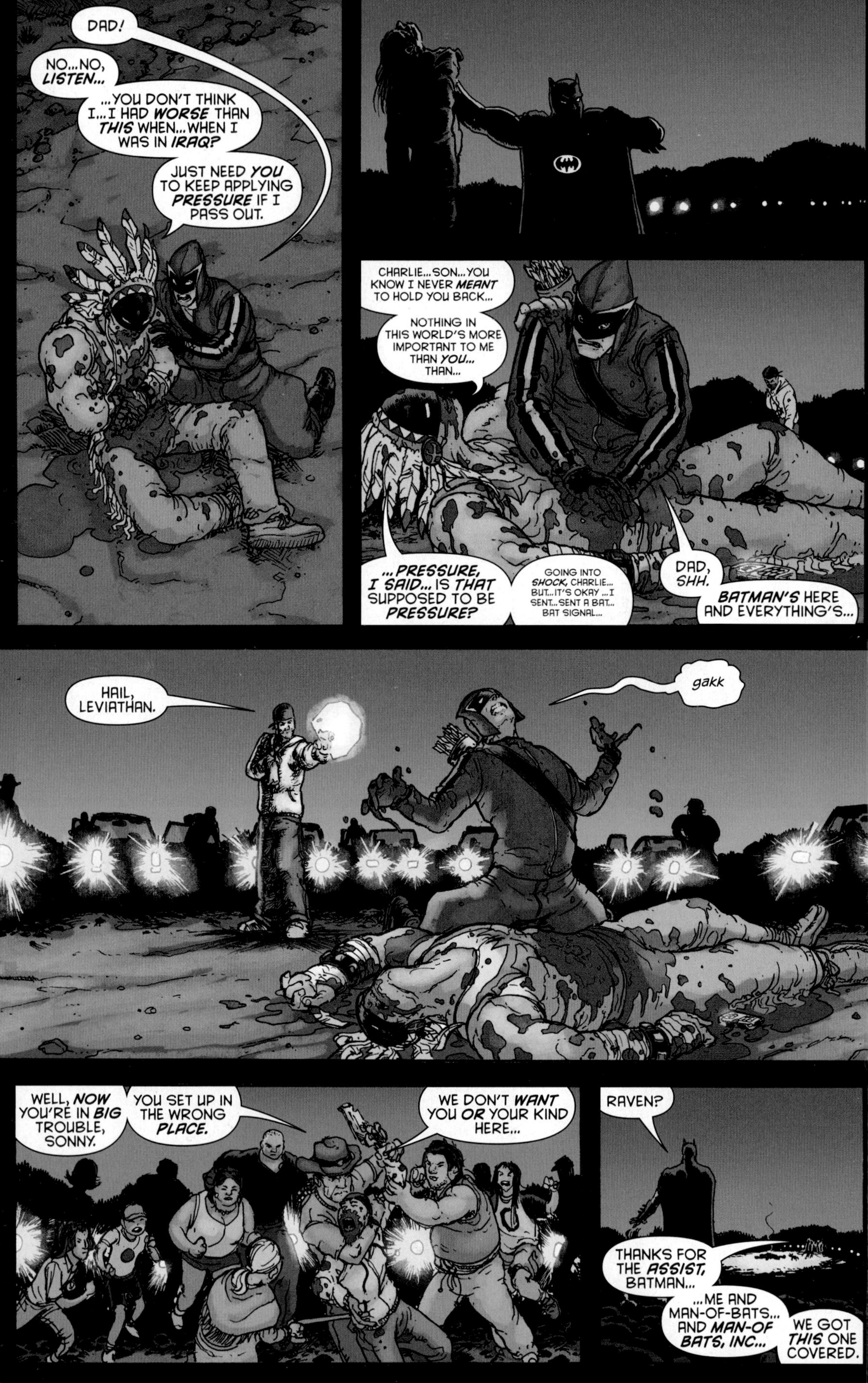
DAD!
NO...NO, LISTEN...
...YOU DON'T THINK I...I HAD WORSE THAN THIS WHEN...WHEN I WAS IN IRAQ?
JUST NEED YOU TO KEEP APPLYING PRESSURE IF I PASS OUT.
CHARLIE...SON...YOU KNOW I NEVER MEANT TO HOLD YOU BACK...
NOTHING IN THIS WORLD'S MORE IMPORTANT TO ME THAN YOU... THAN...
...PRESSURE, I SAID... IS THAT SUPPOSED TO BE PRESSURE?
GOING INTO SHOCK, CHARLIE... BUT...IT'S OKAY ...I SENT...SENT A BAT... BAT SIGNAL...
DAD, SHH.
BATMAN'S HERE AND EVERYTHING'S...
HAIL, LEVIATHAN.
gakk
WELL, NOW YOU'RE IN BIG TROUBLE, SONNY.
YOU SET UP IN THE WRONG PLACE.
WE DON'T WANT YOU OR YOUR KIND HERE...
RAVEN?
THANKS FOR THE ASSIST, BATMAN...
...ME AND MAN-OF-BATS... AND MAN-OF BATS, INC...
WE GOT THIS ONE COVERED.

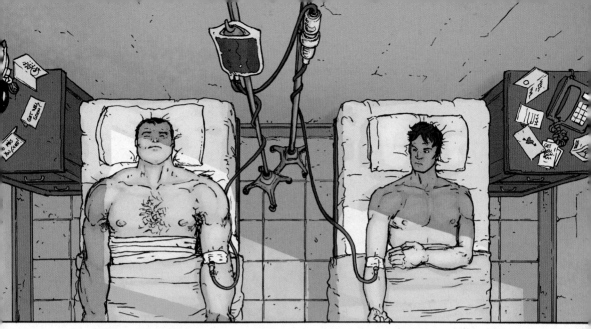

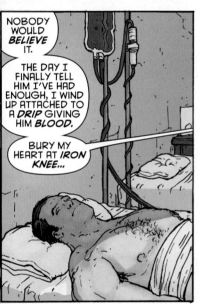

NOBODY WOULD *BELIEVE* IT.

THE DAY I FINALLY TELL HIM I'VE HAD ENOUGH, I WIND UP ATTACHED TO A *DRIP* GIVING HIM *BLOOD*.

BURY MY HEART AT *IRON KNEE*...

...AS FOR THE *GHOST SHIRT,* BEST WAY TO KEEP IT SAFE WAS TO *WEAR* IT.

GUESS IT REALLY *DOES* REPEL BULLETS.

YOU WANT ME TO *STAY* WITH MY DAD?

LEVIATHAN AGENTS HAVE INFILTRATED LAW ENFORCEMENT, EDUCATION *AND* MEDICAL FACILITIES IN YOUR AREA.

I'M HERE TO FIGHT A *WAR,* AND I NEED YOUR *HELP.*

INCORPORATED CAN SUPPLY VEHICLES, EQUIPMENT...

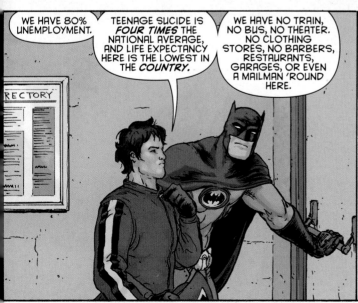

WE HAVE 80% UNEMPLOYMENT.

TEENAGE SUICIDE IS *FOUR TIMES* THE NATIONAL AVERAGE, AND LIFE EXPECTANCY HERE IS THE LOWEST IN THE *COUNTRY.*

WE HAVE NO TRAIN, NO BUS, NO THEATER. NO CLOTHING STORES, NO BARBERS, RESTAURANTS, GARAGES, OR EVEN A MAILMAN 'ROUND HERE.

WE DON'T NEED *BATMOBILES.*

I MEAN, IF YOU *GOT* ANY WE'LL *TAKE* 'EM, BUT WHATEVER YOU GIVE TO *HIM,* HE'S GONNA GIVE BACK TO THE PEOPLE.

WE CAN HANDLE THIS *OUR* WAY, LIKE WE ALWAYS DO.

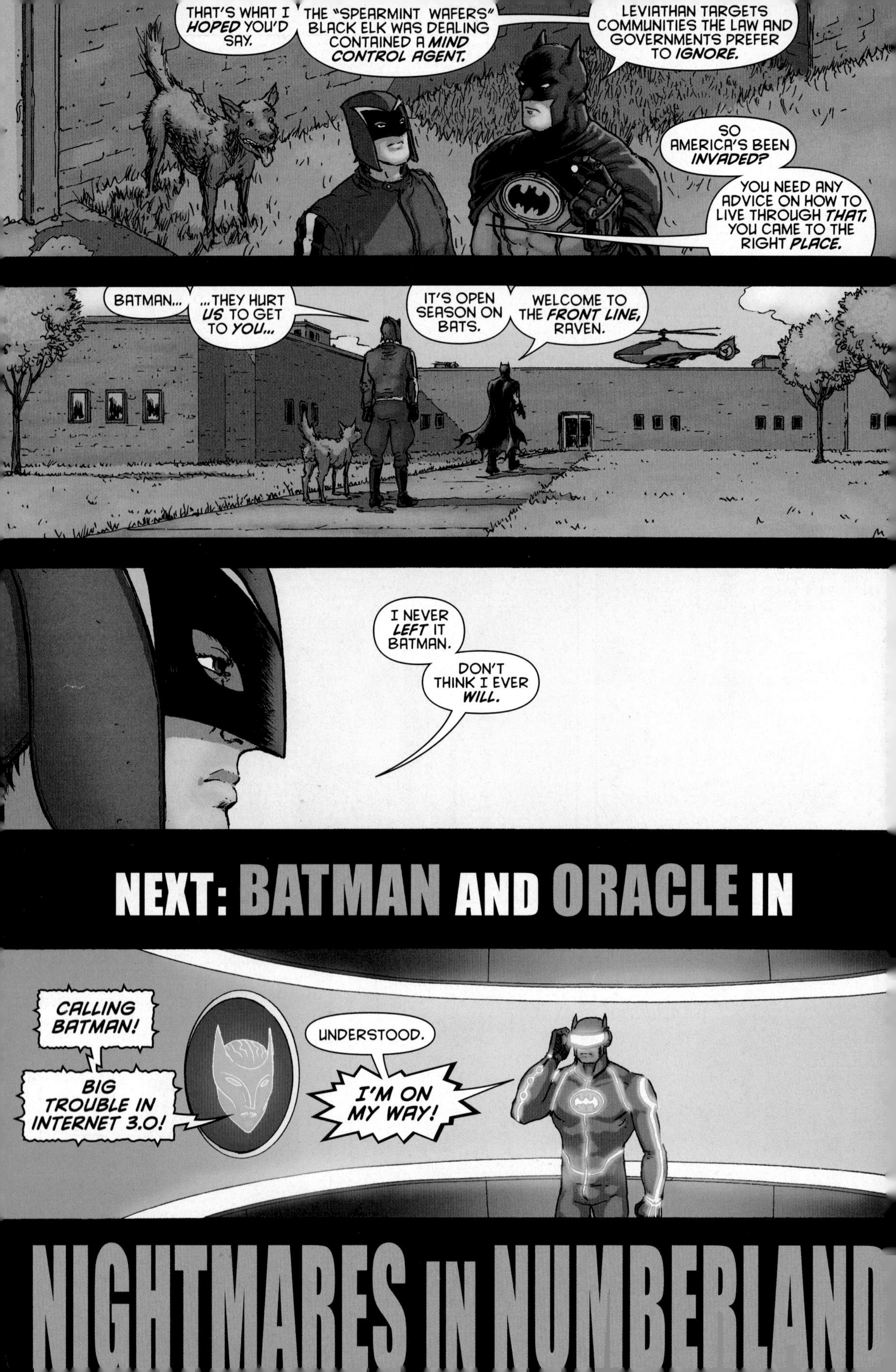
THAT'S WHAT I HOPED YOU'D SAY.
THE "SPEARMINT WAFERS" BLACK ELK WAS DEALING CONTAINED A MIND CONTROL AGENT.
LEVIATHAN TARGETS COMMUNITIES THE LAW AND GOVERNMENTS PREFER TO IGNORE.
SO AMERICA'S BEEN INVADED?
YOU NEED ANY ADVICE ON HOW TO LIVE THROUGH THAT, YOU CAME TO THE RIGHT PLACE.
BATMAN...
...THEY HURT US TO GET TO YOU...
IT'S OPEN SEASON ON BATS.
WELCOME TO THE FRONT LINE, RAVEN.
I NEVER LEFT IT BATMAN.
DON'T THINK I EVER WILL.
NEXT: BATMAN AND ORACLE IN
CALLING BATMAN!
BIG TROUBLE IN INTERNET 3.0!
UNDERSTOOD.
I'M ON MY WAY!
NIGHTMARES IN NUMBERLAND

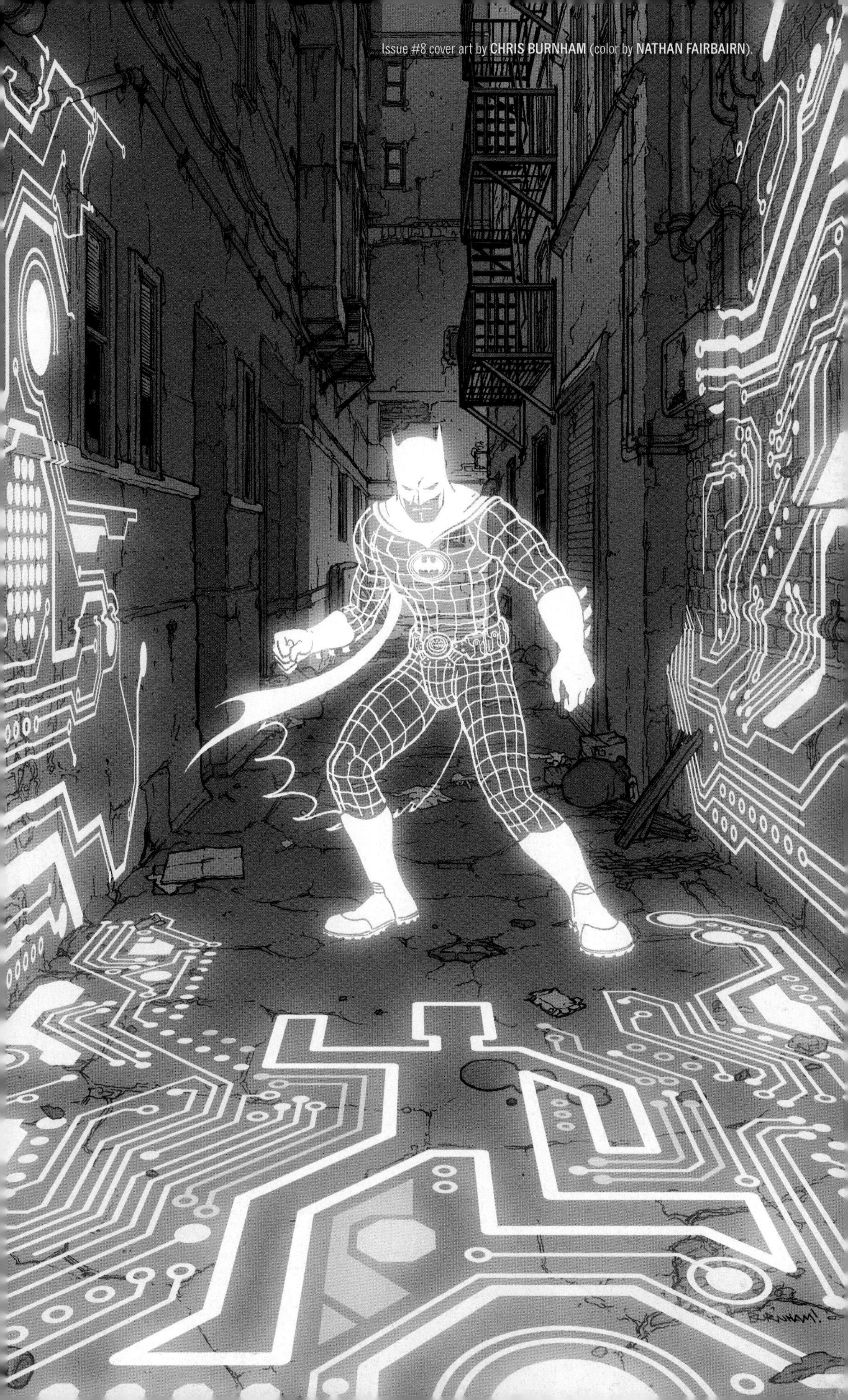
BURNHAM!

Issue #8 cover art by **CHRIS BURNHAM** (color by **NATHAN FAIRBAIRN**).

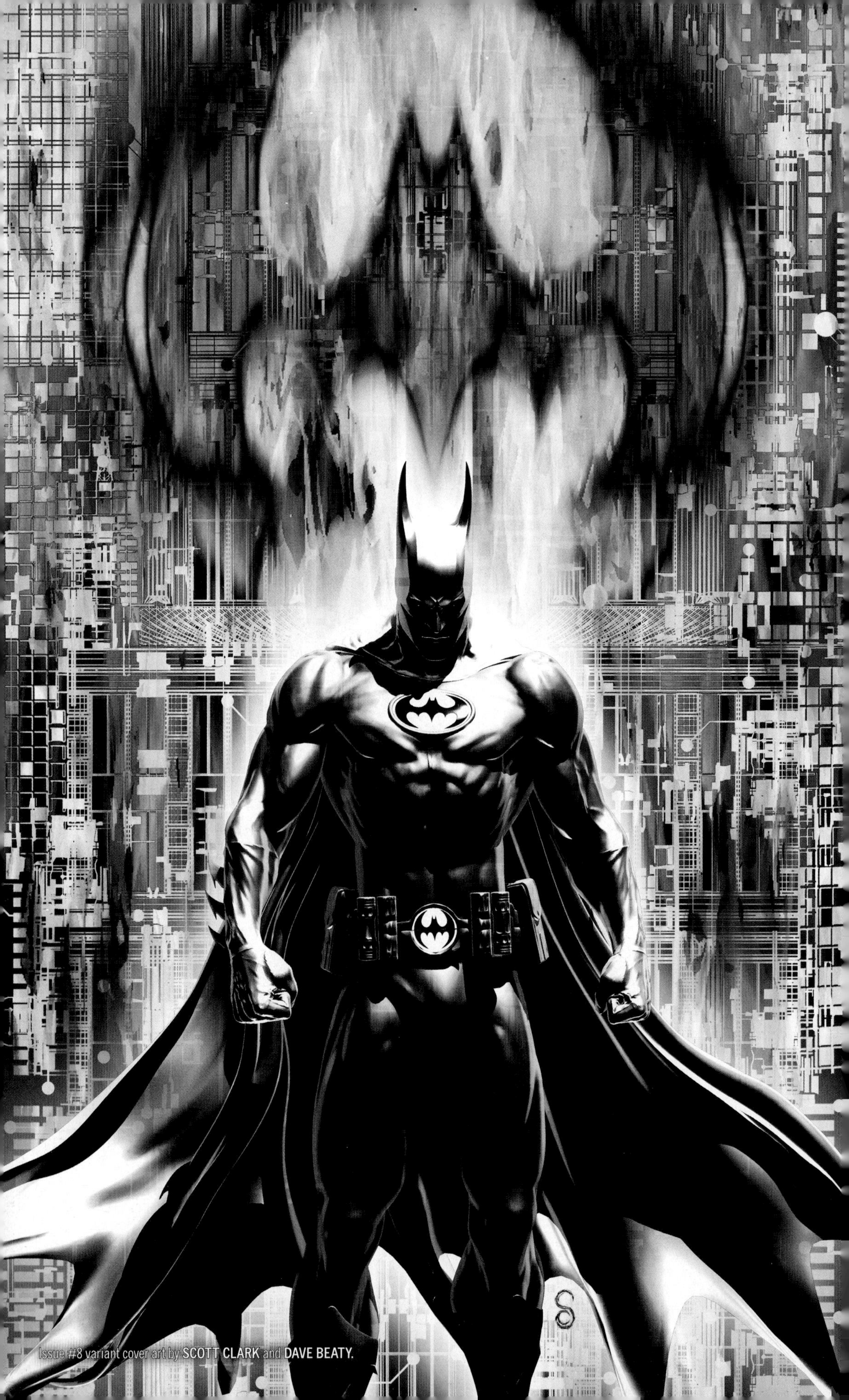

Issue #8 variant cover art by **SCOTT CLARK** and **DAVE BEATY.**

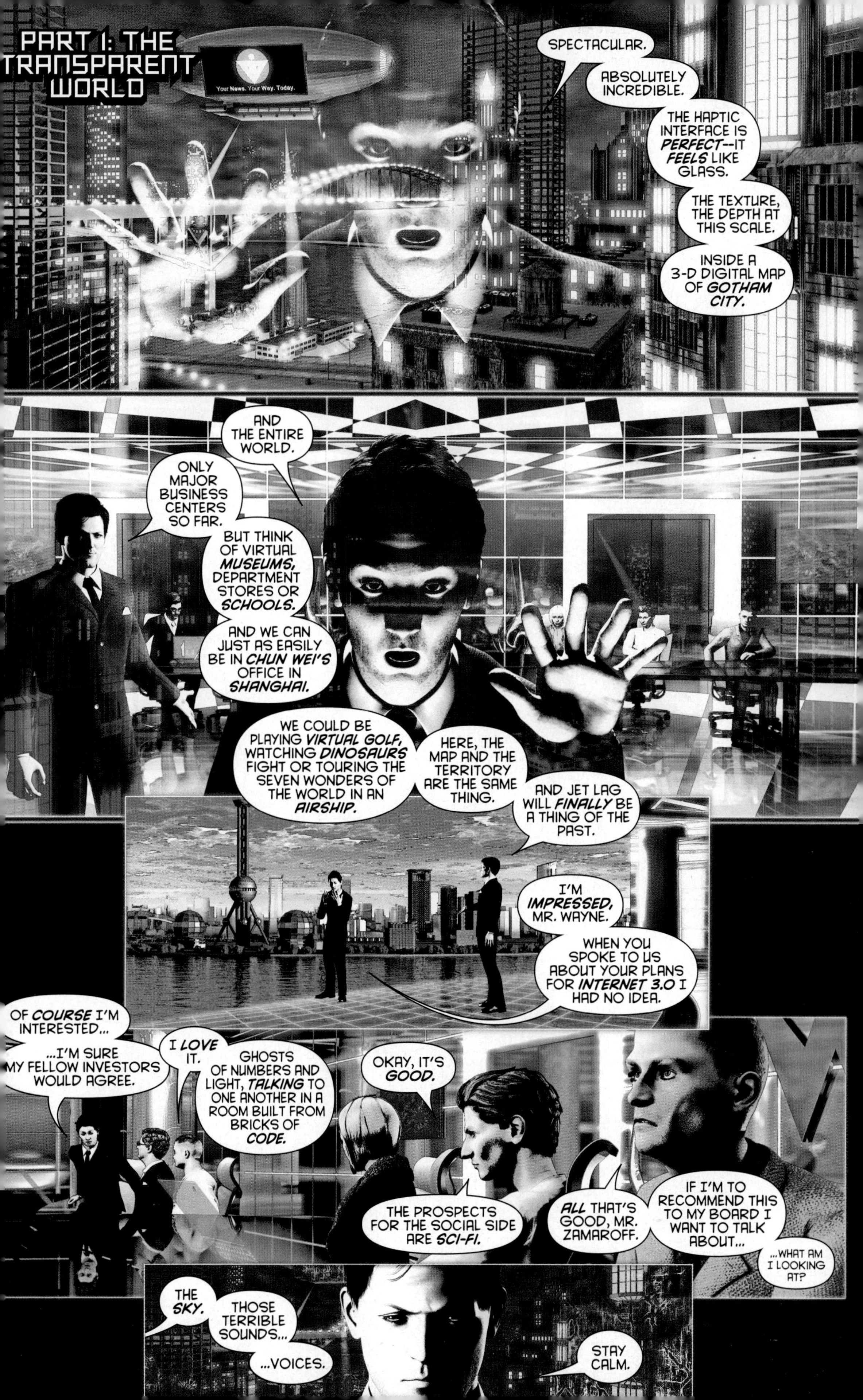
PART 1: THE TRANSPARENT WORLD
Your News. Your Way. Today.
SPECTACULAR.
ABSOLUTELY INCREDIBLE.
THE HAPTIC INTERFACE IS PERFECT--IT FEELS LIKE GLASS.
THE TEXTURE, THE DEPTH AT THIS SCALE.
INSIDE A 3-D DIGITAL MAP OF GOTHAM CITY.
AND THE ENTIRE WORLD.
ONLY MAJOR BUSINESS CENTERS SO FAR.
BUT THINK OF VIRTUAL MUSEUMS, DEPARTMENT STORES OR SCHOOLS.
AND WE CAN JUST AS EASILY BE IN CHUN WEI'S OFFICE IN SHANGHAI.
WE COULD BE PLAYING VIRTUAL GOLF, WATCHING DINOSAURS FIGHT OR TOURING THE SEVEN WONDERS OF THE WORLD IN AN AIRSHIP.
HERE, THE MAP AND THE TERRITORY ARE THE SAME THING.
AND JET LAG WILL FINALLY BE A THING OF THE PAST.
I'M IMPRESSED, MR. WAYNE.
WHEN YOU SPOKE TO US ABOUT YOUR PLANS FOR INTERNET 3.0 I HAD NO IDEA.
OF COURSE I'M INTERESTED...
...I'M SURE MY FELLOW INVESTORS WOULD AGREE.
I LOVE IT.
GHOSTS OF NUMBERS AND LIGHT, TALKING TO ONE ANOTHER IN A ROOM BUILT FROM BRICKS OF CODE.
OKAY, IT'S GOOD.
THE PROSPECTS FOR THE SOCIAL SIDE ARE SCI-FI.
ALL THAT'S GOOD, MR. ZAMAROFF.
IF I'M TO RECOMMEND THIS TO MY BOARD I WANT TO TALK ABOUT...
...WHAT AM I LOOKING AT?
THE SKY.
THOSE TERRIBLE SOUNDS...
...VOICES.
STAY CALM.

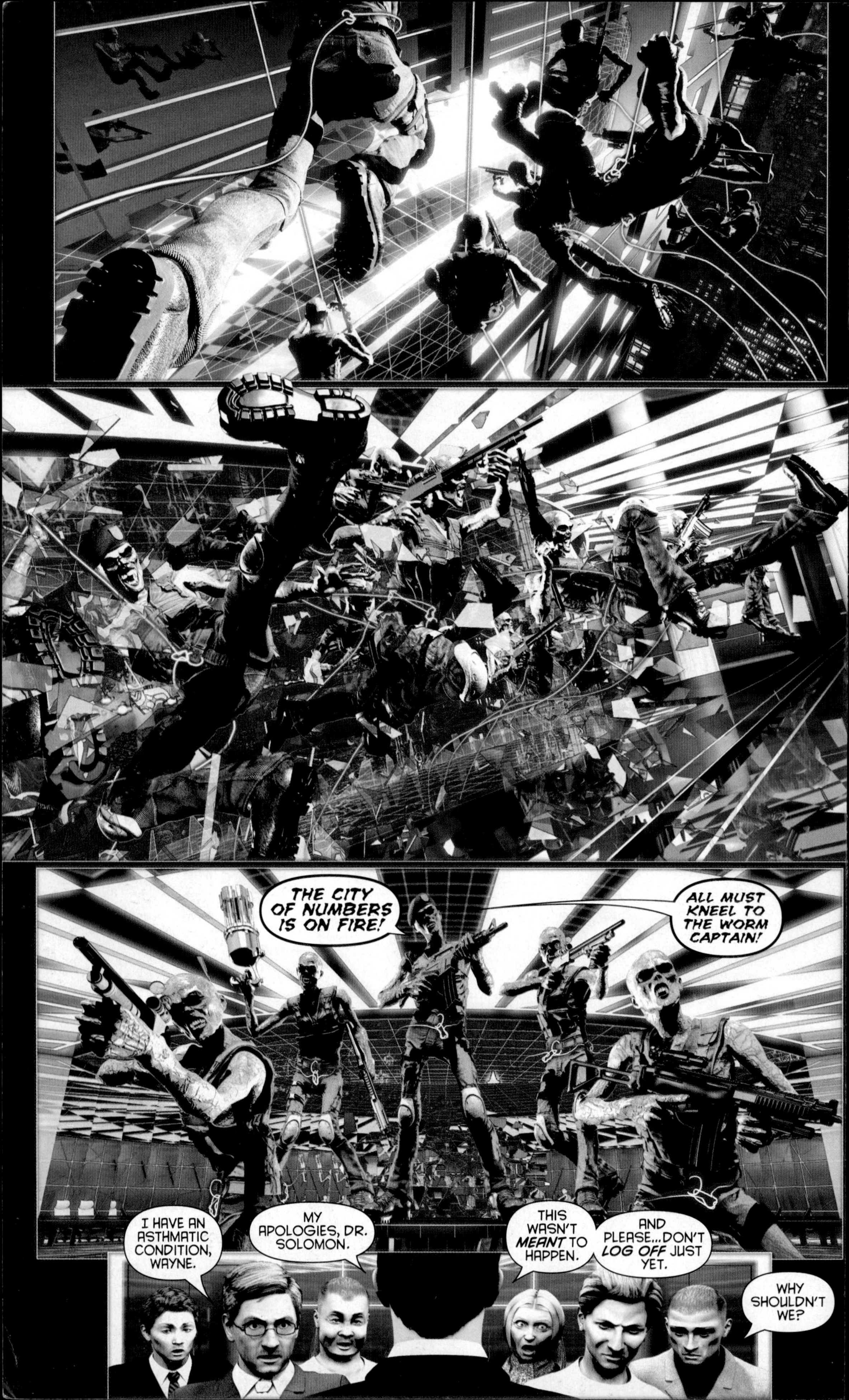
THE CITY OF NUMBERS IS ON FIRE!
ALL MUST KNEEL TO THE WORM CAPTAIN!
I HAVE AN ASTHMATIC CONDITION, WAYNE.
MY APOLOGIES, DR. SOLOMON.
THIS WASN'T *MEANT* TO HAPPEN.
AND PLEASE...DON'T *LOG OFF* JUST YET.
WHY SHOULDN'T WE?

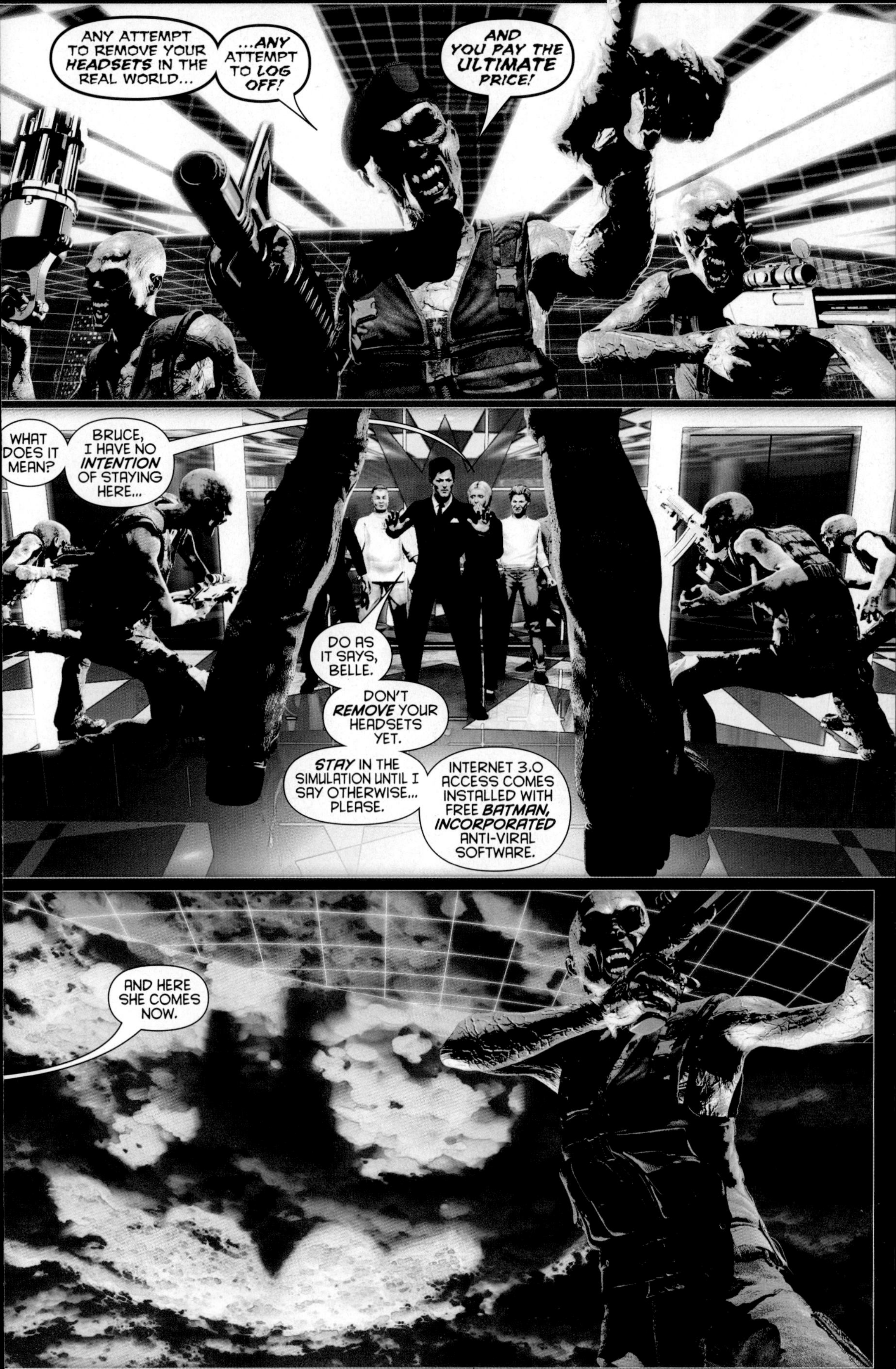
ANY ATTEMPT TO REMOVE YOUR HEADSETS IN THE REAL WORLD...
...ANY ATTEMPT TO LOG OFF!
AND YOU PAY THE ULTIMATE PRICE!
WHAT DOES IT MEAN?
BRUCE, I HAVE NO INTENTION OF STAYING HERE...
DO AS IT SAYS, BELLE.
DON'T REMOVE YOUR HEADSETS YET.
STAY IN THE SIMULATION UNTIL I SAY OTHERWISE... PLEASE.
INTERNET 3.0 ACCESS COMES INSTALLED WITH FREE BATMAN, INCORPORATED ANTI-VIRAL SOFTWARE.
AND HERE SHE COMES NOW.

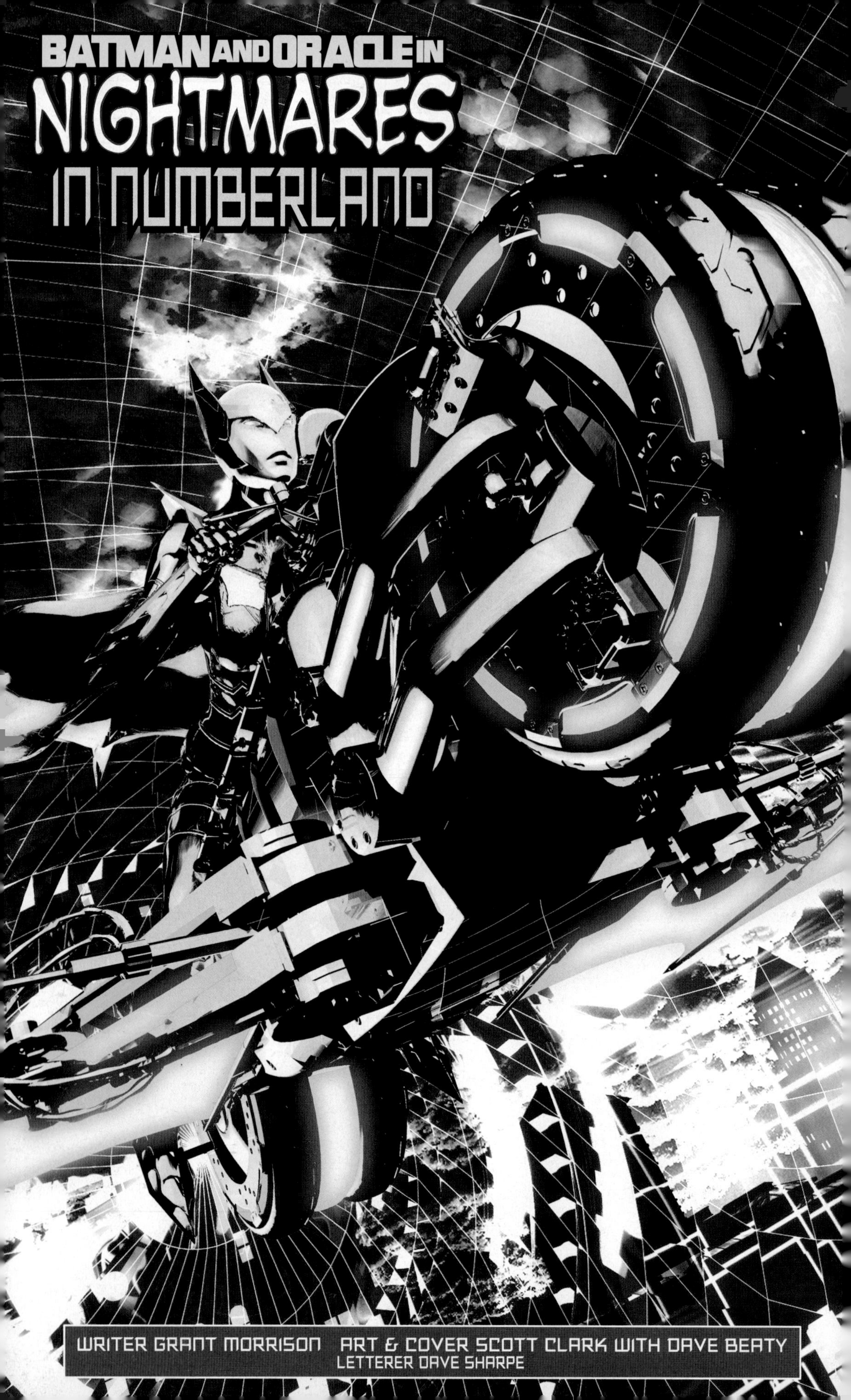
BATMAN AND ORACLE IN
NIGHTMARES
IN NUMBERLAND
WRITER GRANT MORRISON ART & COVER SCOTT CLARK WITH DAVE BEATY
LETTERER DAVE SHARPE

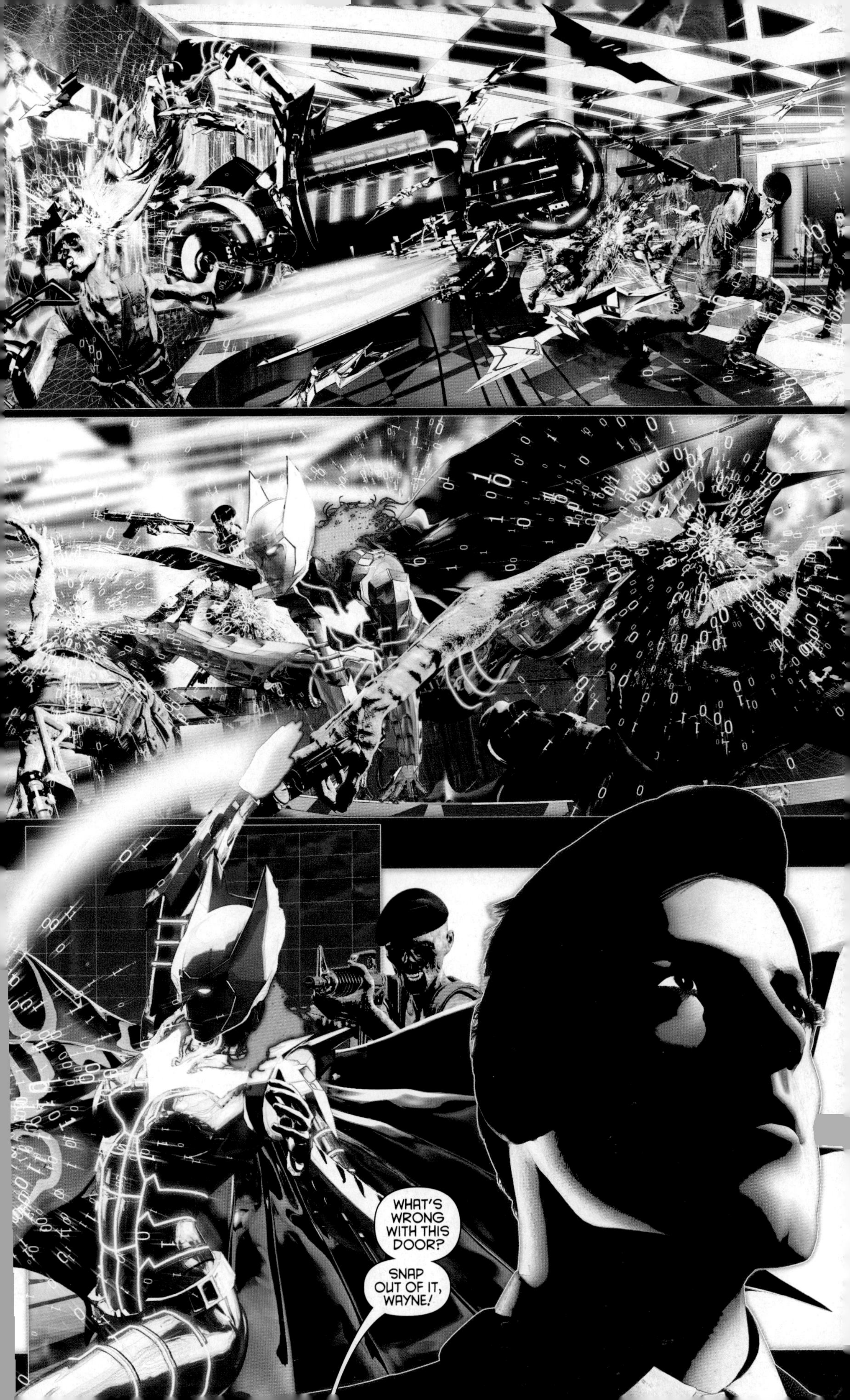
WHAT'S WRONG WITH THIS DOOR?
SNAP OUT OF IT, WAYNE!

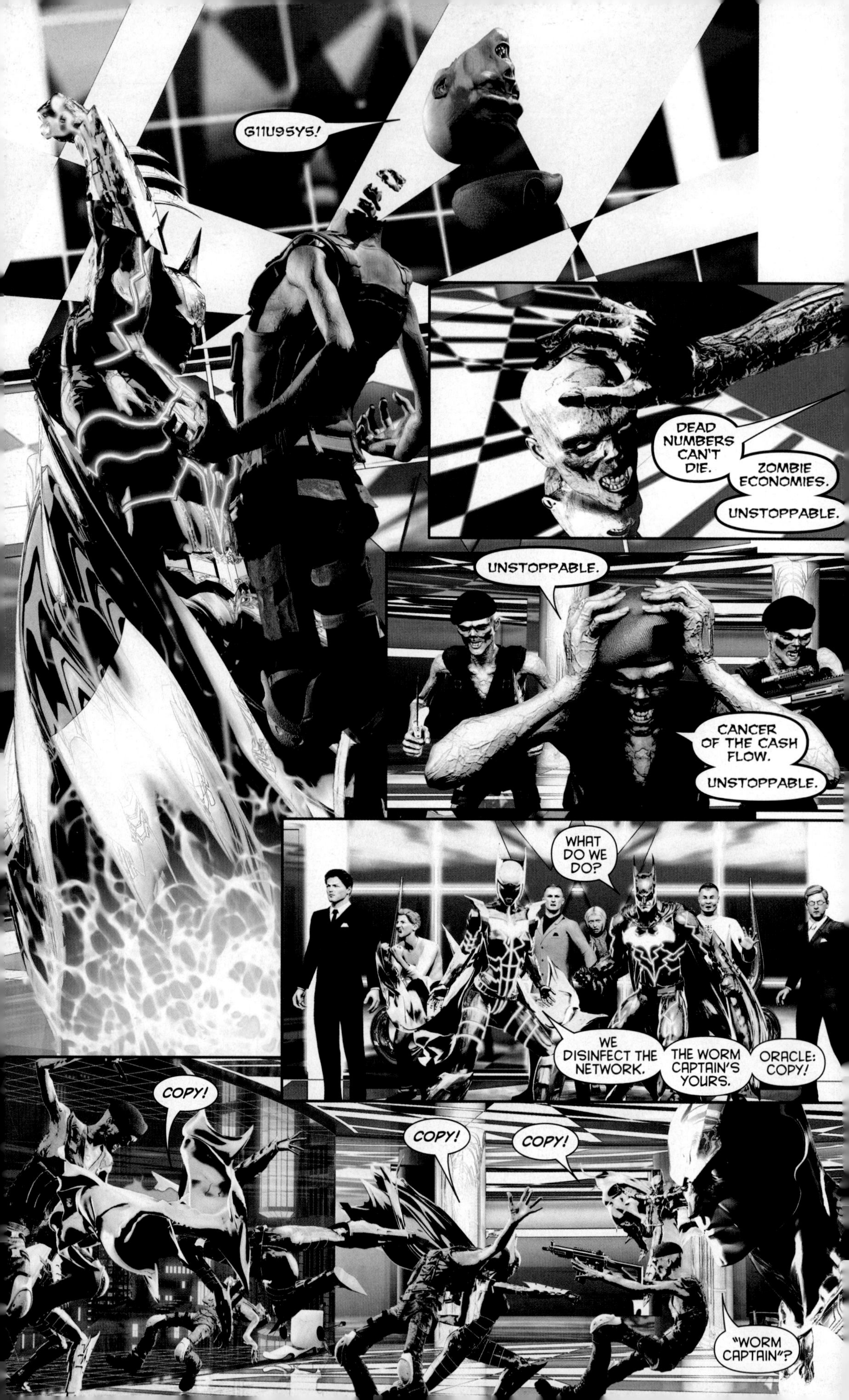
G11U95Y5!
DEAD NUMBERS CAN'T DIE.
ZOMBIE ECONOMIES.
UNSTOPPABLE.
UNSTOPPABLE.
CANCER OF THE CASH FLOW.
UNSTOPPABLE.
WHAT DO WE DO?
WE DISINFECT THE NETWORK.
THE WORM CAPTAIN'S YOURS.
ORACLE: COPY!
COPY!
COPY!
COPY!
"WORM CAPTAIN"?

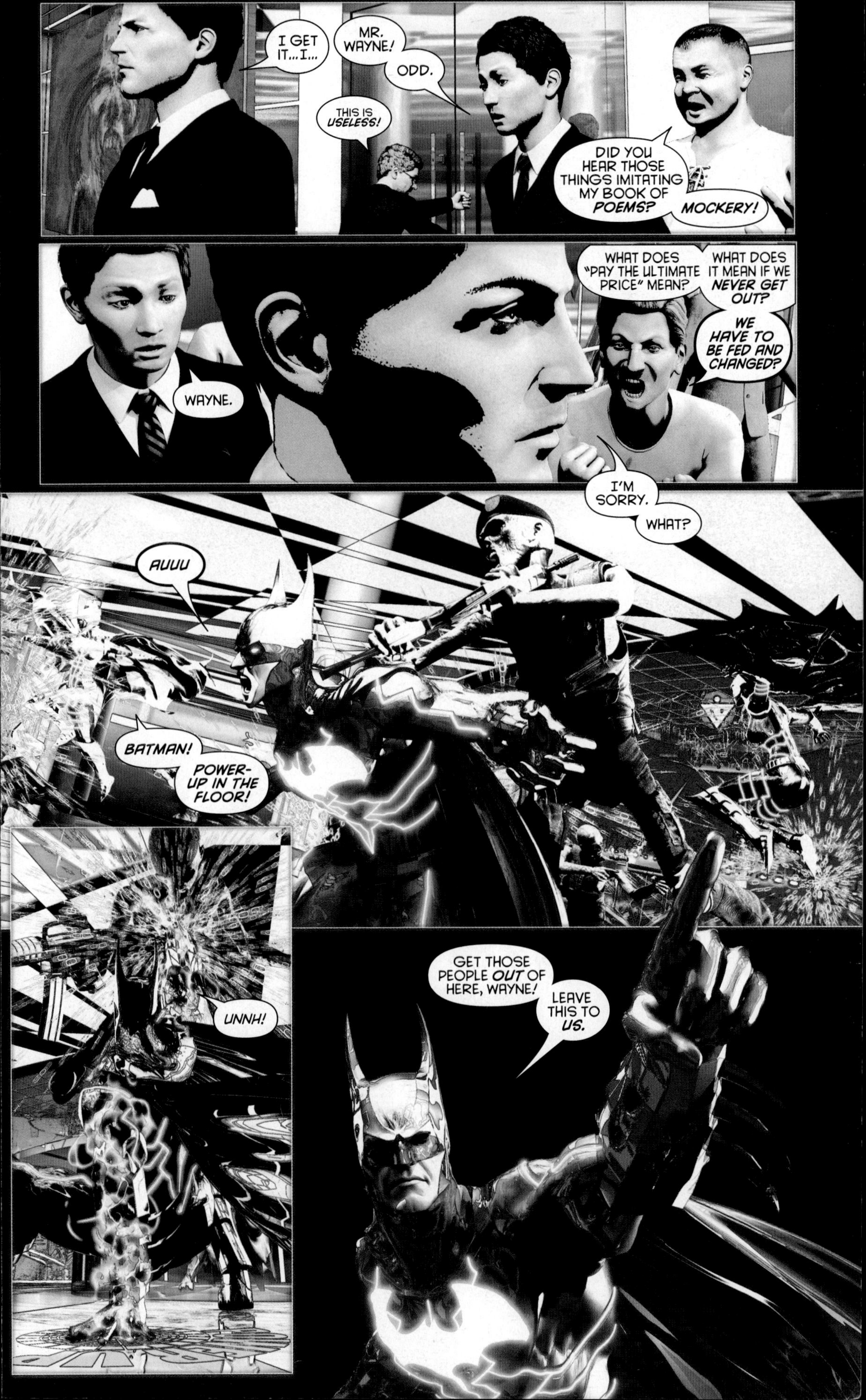
I GET IT...I...
MR. WAYNE!
ODD.
THIS IS *USELESS!*
DID YOU HEAR THOSE THINGS IMITATING MY BOOK OF *POEMS?*
MOCKERY!
WAYNE.
WHAT DOES "PAY THE ULTIMATE PRICE" MEAN?
WHAT DOES IT MEAN IF WE *NEVER GET OUT?*
WE HAVE TO BE FED AND CHANGED?
I'M SORRY.
WHAT?
AUUU
BATMAN!
POWER-UP IN THE FLOOR!
UNNH!
GET THOSE PEOPLE *OUT* OF HERE, WAYNE!
LEAVE THIS TO *US.*

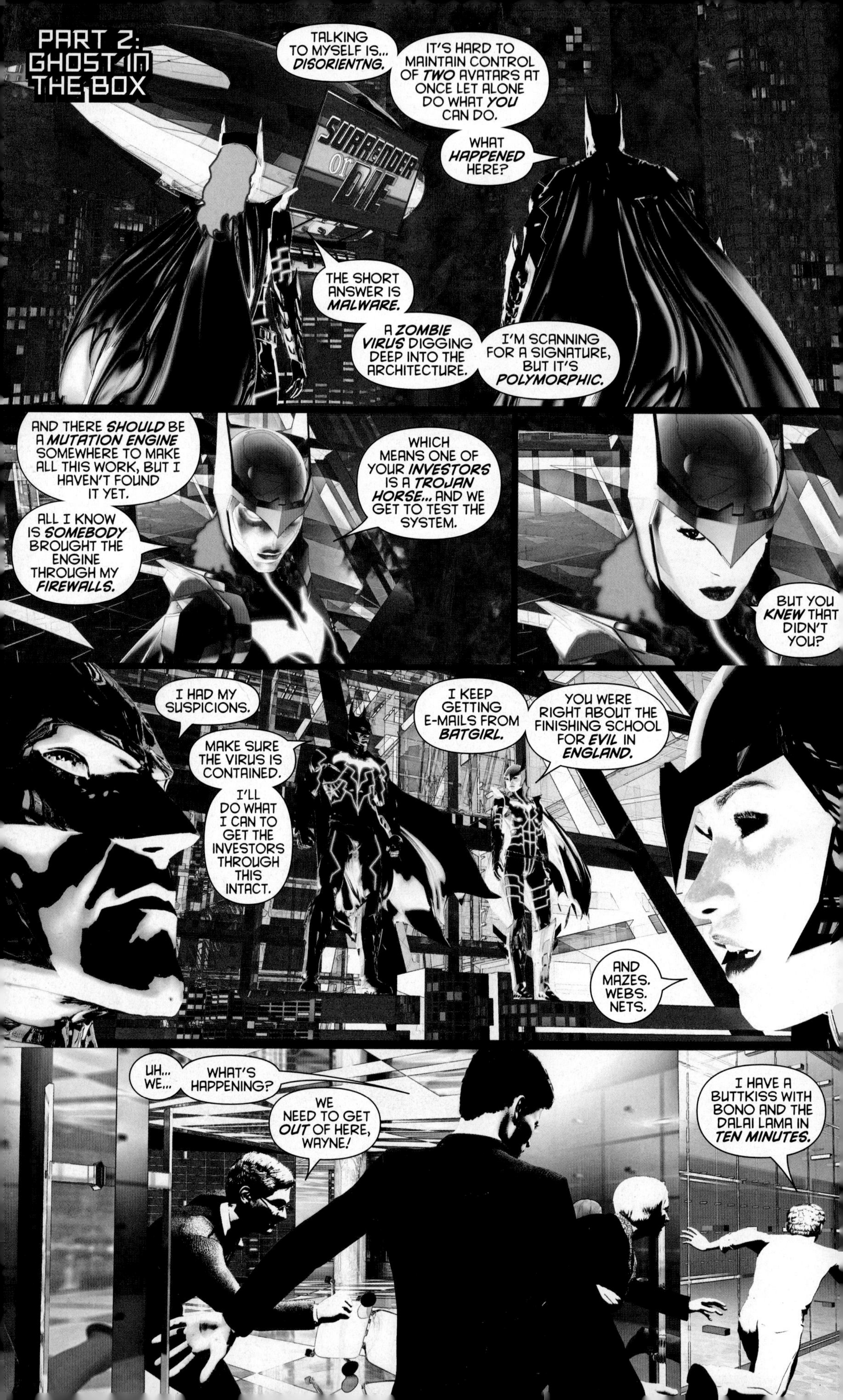
PART 2: GHOST IN THE BOX
TALKING TO MYSELF IS... DISORIENTNG.
IT'S HARD TO MAINTAIN CONTROL OF TWO AVATARS AT ONCE LET ALONE DO WHAT YOU CAN DO.
SURRENDER or DIE
WHAT HAPPENED HERE?
THE SHORT ANSWER IS MALWARE.
A ZOMBIE VIRUS DIGGING DEEP INTO THE ARCHITECTURE.
I'M SCANNING FOR A SIGNATURE, BUT IT'S POLYMORPHIC.
AND THERE SHOULD BE A MUTATION ENGINE SOMEWHERE TO MAKE ALL THIS WORK, BUT I HAVEN'T FOUND IT YET.
ALL I KNOW IS SOMEBODY BROUGHT THE ENGINE THROUGH MY FIREWALLS.
WHICH MEANS ONE OF YOUR INVESTORS IS A TROJAN HORSE... AND WE GET TO TEST THE SYSTEM.
BUT YOU KNEW THAT DIDN'T YOU?
I HAD MY SUSPICIONS.
MAKE SURE THE VIRUS IS CONTAINED.
I'LL DO WHAT I CAN TO GET THE INVESTORS THROUGH THIS INTACT.
I KEEP GETTING E-MAILS FROM BATGIRL.
YOU WERE RIGHT ABOUT THE FINISHING SCHOOL FOR EVIL IN ENGLAND.
AND MAZES. WEBS. NETS.
UH... WE...
WHAT'S HAPPENING?
WE NEED TO GET OUT OF HERE, WAYNE!
I HAVE A BUTTKISS WITH BONO AND THE DALAI LAMA IN TEN MINUTES.

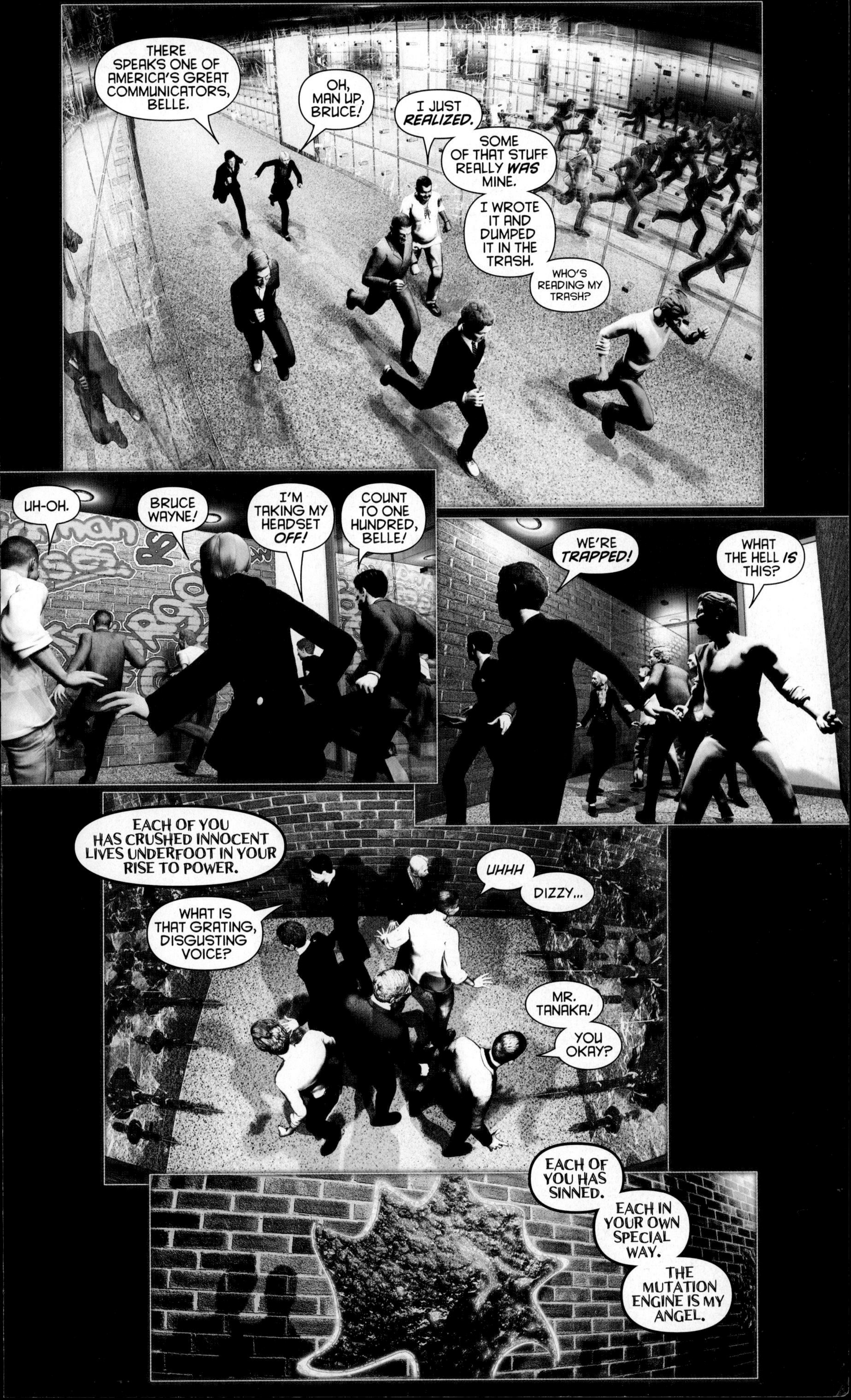
THERE SPEAKS ONE OF AMERICA'S GREAT COMMUNICATORS, BELLE.
OH, MAN UP, BRUCE!
I JUST REALIZED.
SOME OF THAT STUFF REALLY WAS MINE.
I WROTE IT AND DUMPED IT IN THE TRASH.
WHO'S READING MY TRASH?
UH-OH.
BRUCE WAYNE!
I'M TAKING MY HEADSET OFF!
COUNT TO ONE HUNDRED, BELLE!
WE'RE TRAPPED!
WHAT THE HELL IS THIS?
EACH OF YOU HAS CRUSHED INNOCENT LIVES UNDERFOOT IN YOUR RISE TO POWER.
UHHH
DIZZY...
WHAT IS THAT GRATING, DISGUSTING VOICE?
MR. TANAKA!
YOU OKAY?
EACH OF YOU HAS SINNED.
EACH IN YOUR OWN SPECIAL WAY.
THE MUTATION ENGINE IS MY ANGEL.

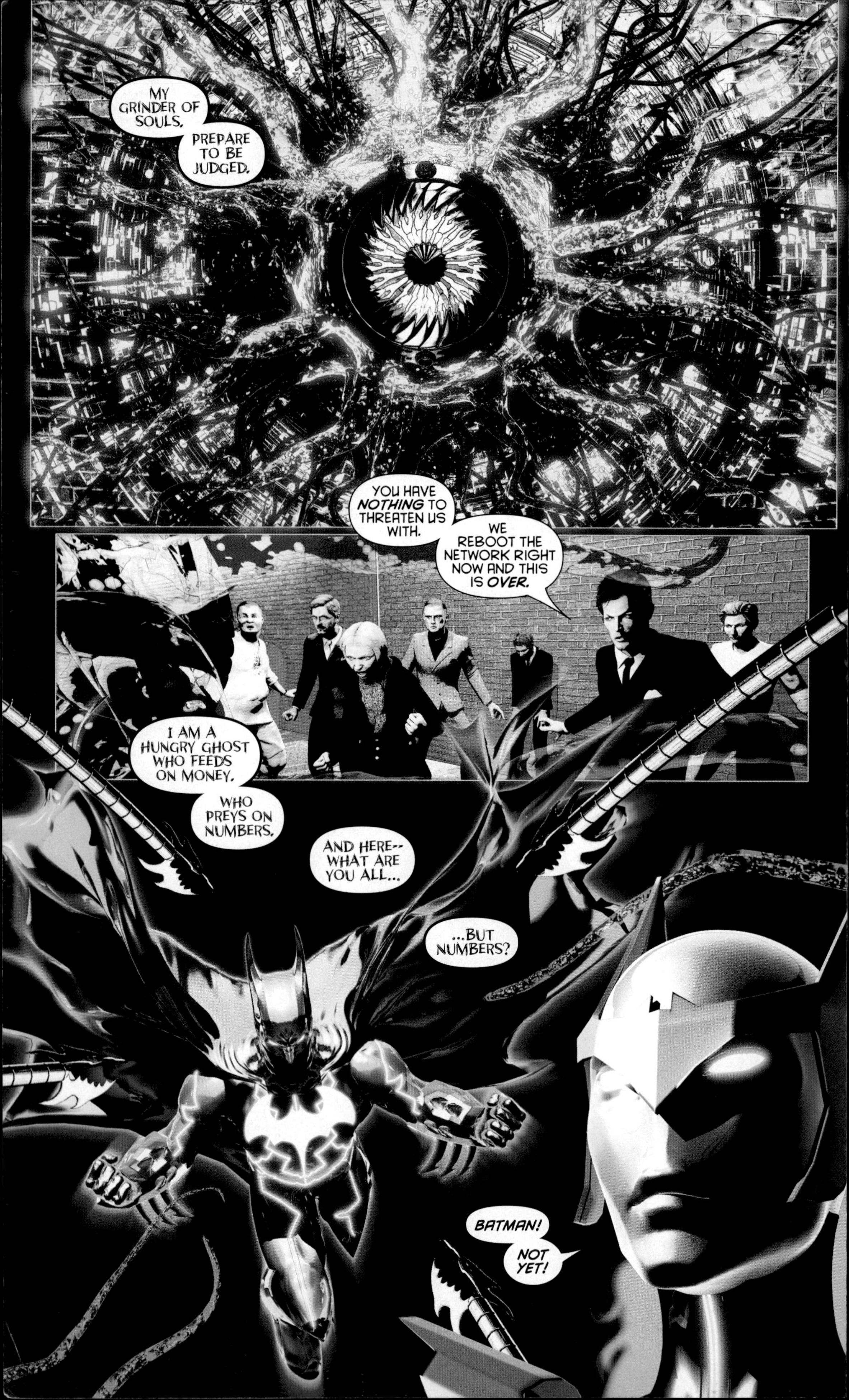
MY GRINDER OF SOULS.
PREPARE TO BE JUDGED.
YOU HAVE NOTHING TO THREATEN US WITH.
WE REBOOT THE NETWORK RIGHT NOW AND THIS IS OVER.
I AM A HUNGRY GHOST WHO FEEDS ON MONEY.
WHO PREYS ON NUMBERS.
AND HERE--WHAT ARE YOU ALL...
...BUT NUMBERS?
BATMAN!
NOT YET!

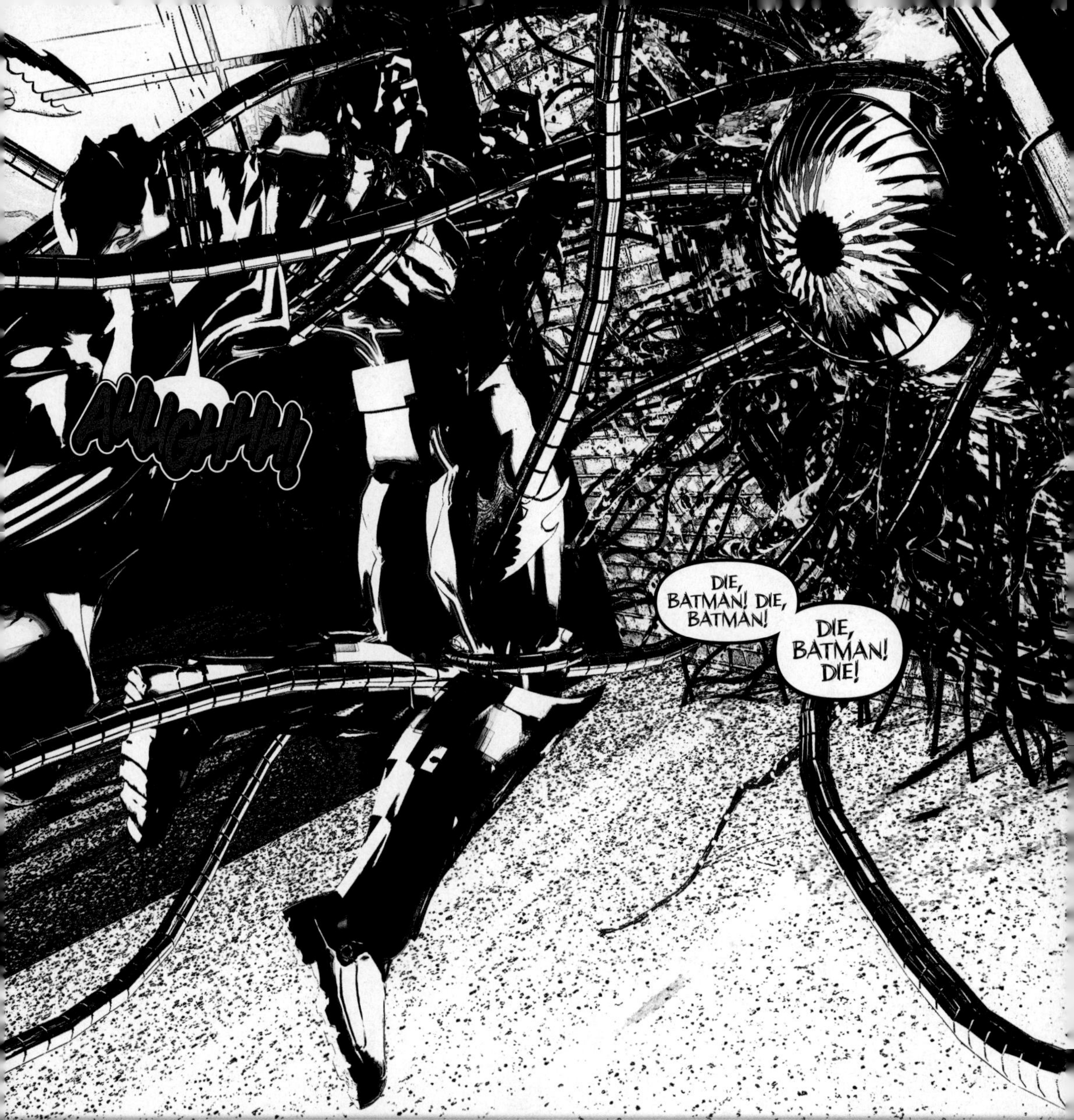
AUUGHHH!
DIE, BATMAN! DIE, BATMAN!
DIE, BATMAN! DIE!

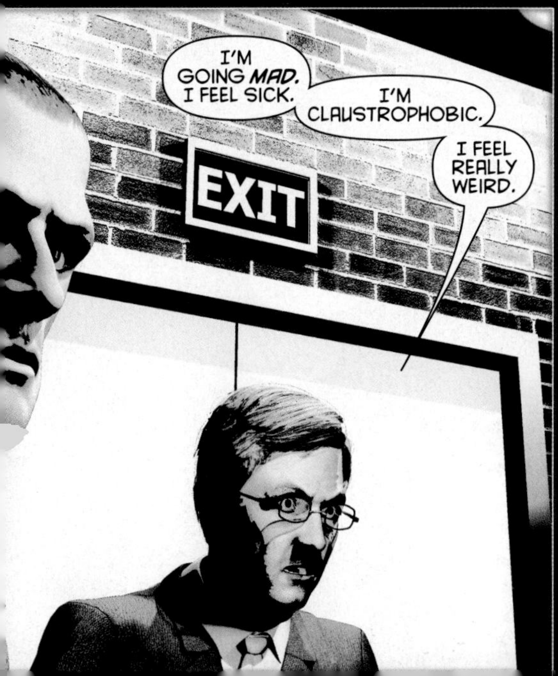
I'M GOING *MAD.* I FEEL SICK.
I'M CLAUSTROPHOBIC.
I FEEL REALLY WEIRD.
EXIT

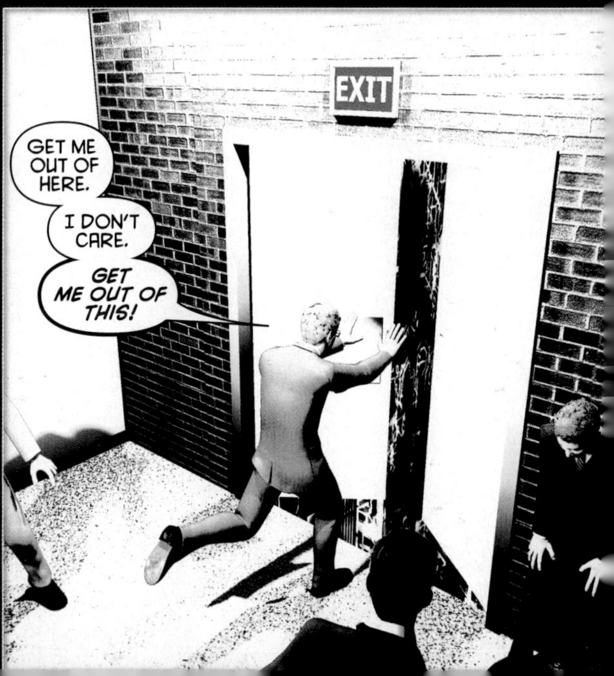
EXIT
GET ME OUT OF HERE.
I DON'T CARE.
GET ME OUT OF THIS!

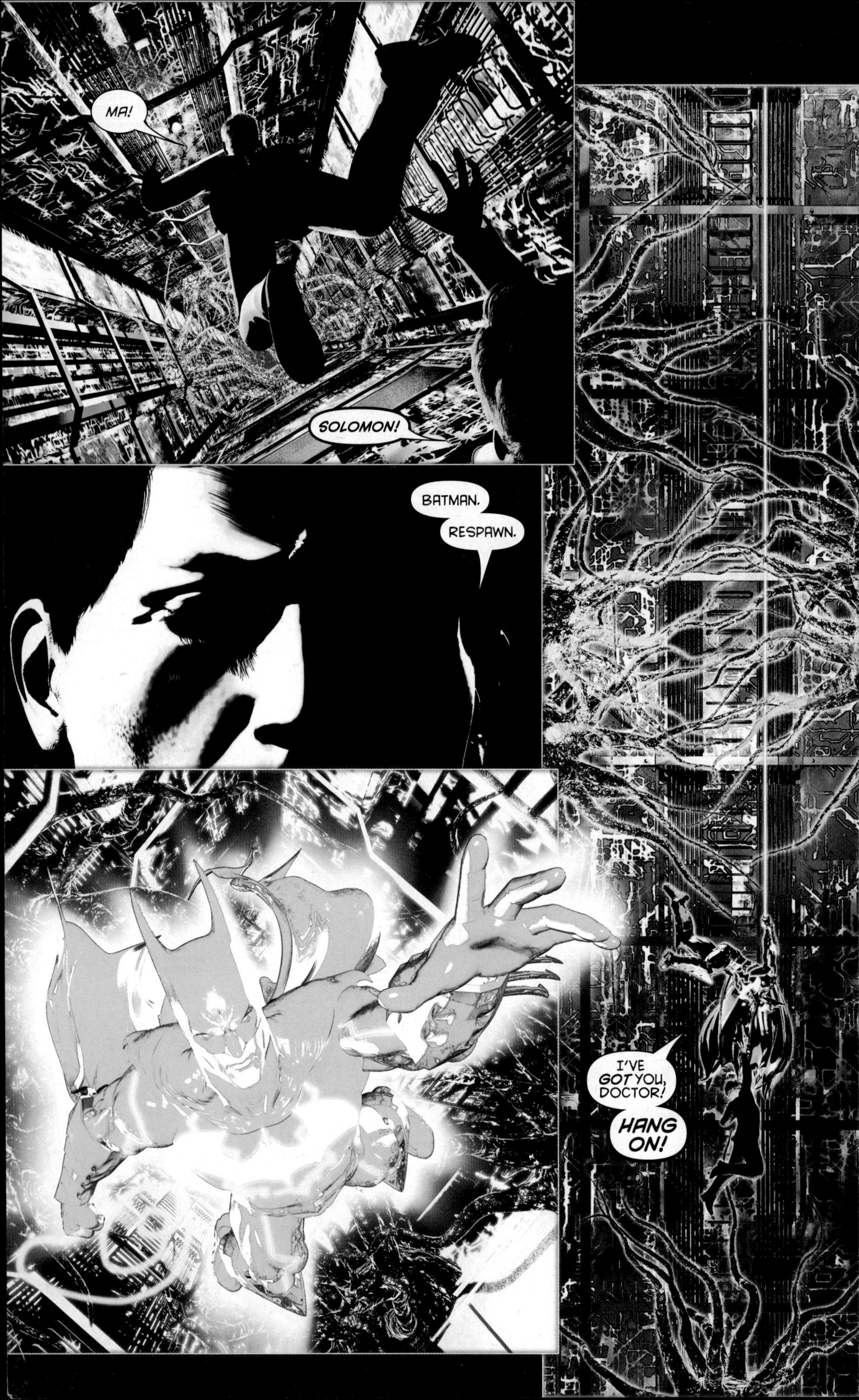
MA!
SOLOMON!
BATMAN.
RESPAWN.
I'VE GOT YOU, DOCTOR!
HANG ON!

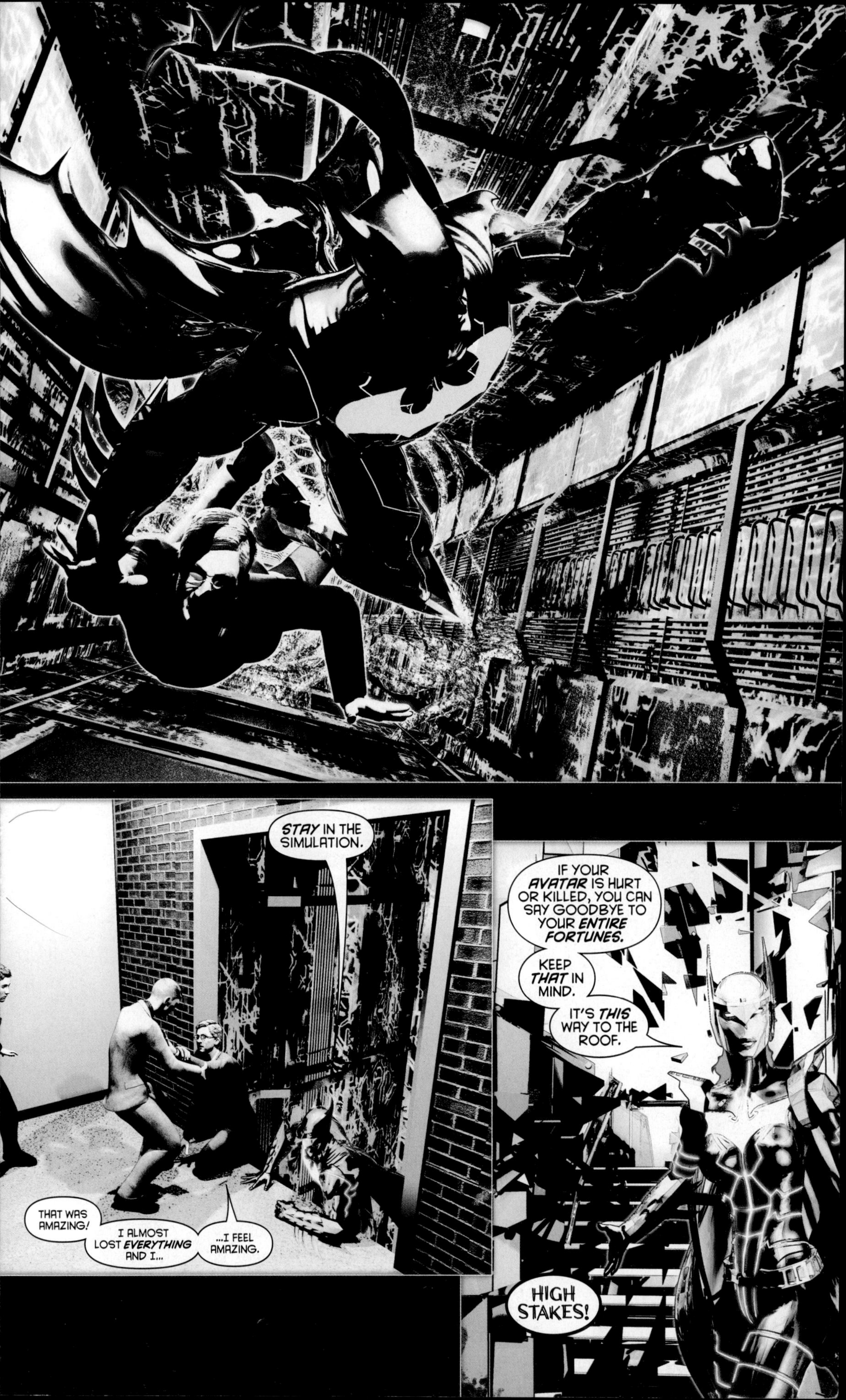
STAY IN THE SIMULATION.
THAT WAS AMAZING!
I ALMOST LOST EVERYTHING AND I...
...I FEEL AMAZING.
IF YOUR AVATAR IS HURT OR KILLED, YOU CAN SAY GOODBYE TO YOUR ENTIRE FORTUNES.
KEEP THAT IN MIND.
IT'S THIS WAY TO THE ROOF.
HIGH STAKES!

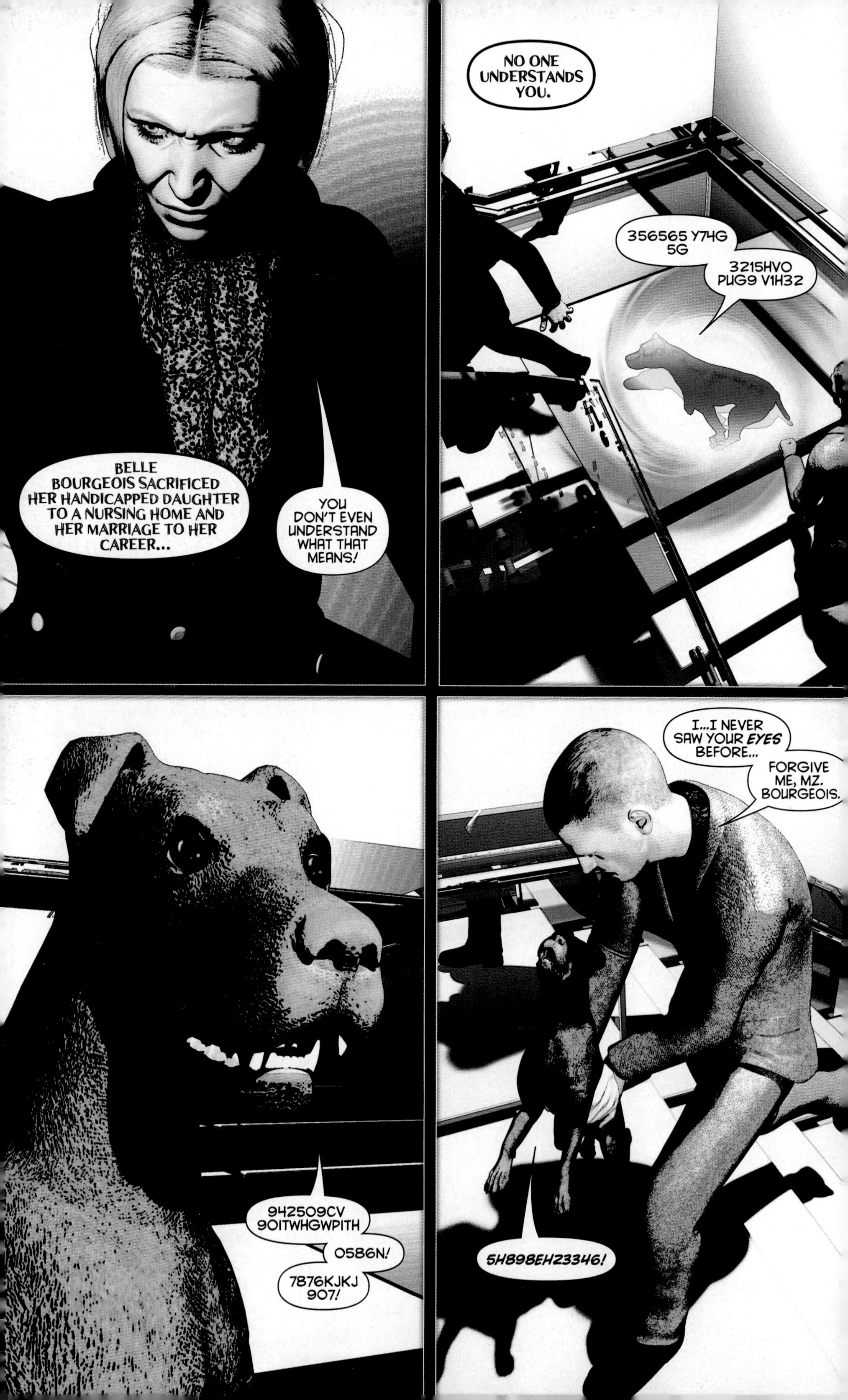
BELLE BOURGEOIS SACRIFICED HER HANDICAPPED DAUGHTER TO A NURSING HOME AND HER MARRIAGE TO HER CAREER...
YOU DON'T EVEN UNDERSTAND WHAT THAT MEANS!
NO ONE UNDERSTANDS YOU.
356565 Y74G 5G
3215HVO PUG9 V1H32
942509CV 90ITWHGWPITH
0586N!
7876KJKJ 907!
I...I NEVER SAW YOUR EYES BEFORE...
FORGIVE ME, MZ. BOURGEOIS.
5H898EH23346!

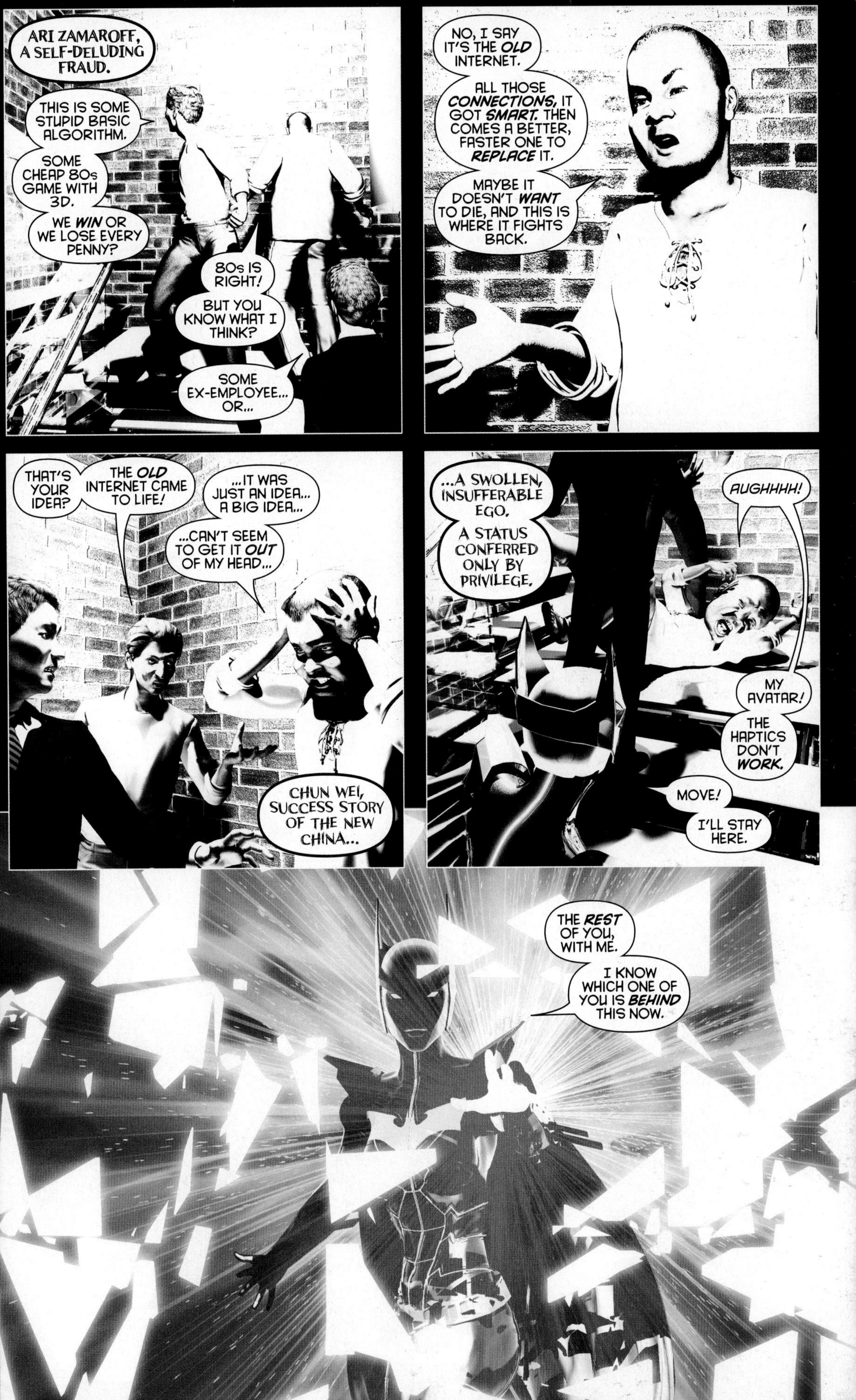
ARI ZAMAROFF, A SELF-DELUDING FRAUD.
THIS IS SOME STUPID BASIC ALGORITHM.
SOME CHEAP 80s GAME WITH 3D.
WE WIN OR WE LOSE EVERY PENNY?
80s IS RIGHT!
BUT YOU KNOW WHAT I THINK?
SOME EX-EMPLOYEE... OR...
NO, I SAY IT'S THE OLD INTERNET.
ALL THOSE CONNECTIONS, IT GOT SMART. THEN COMES A BETTER, FASTER ONE TO REPLACE IT.
MAYBE IT DOESN'T WANT TO DIE, AND THIS IS WHERE IT FIGHTS BACK.
THAT'S YOUR IDEA?
THE OLD INTERNET CAME TO LIFE!
...IT WAS JUST AN IDEA... A BIG IDEA...
...CAN'T SEEM TO GET IT OUT OF MY HEAD...
CHUN WEI, SUCCESS STORY OF THE NEW CHINA...
...A SWOLLEN, INSUFFERABLE EGO.
A STATUS CONFERRED ONLY BY PRIVILEGE.
AUGHHHH!
MY AVATAR!
THE HAPTICS DON'T WORK.
MOVE!
I'LL STAY HERE.
THE REST OF YOU, WITH ME.
I KNOW WHICH ONE OF YOU IS BEHIND THIS NOW.

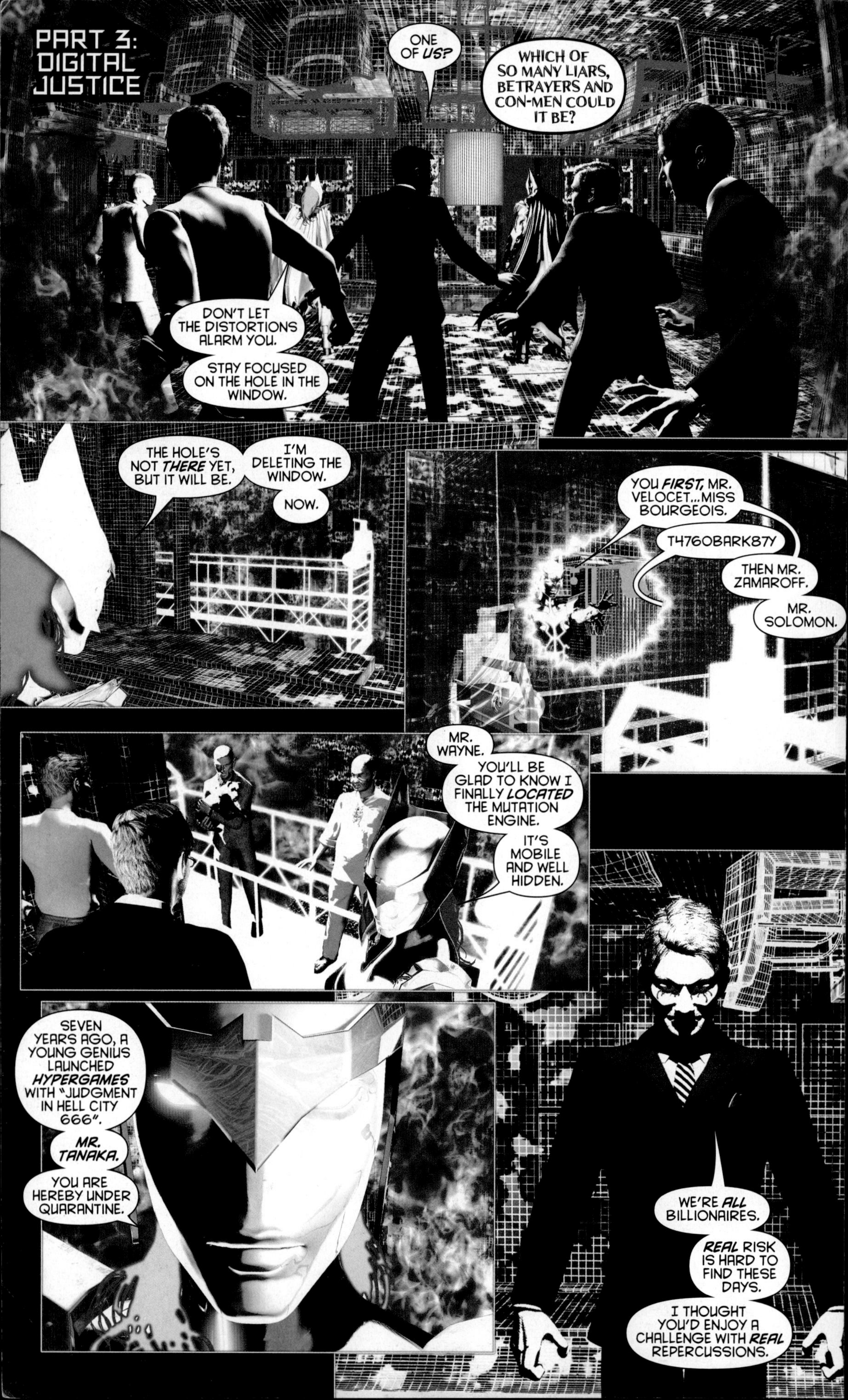
PART 3: DIGITAL JUSTICE
ONE OF US?
WHICH OF SO MANY LIARS, BETRAYERS AND CON-MEN COULD IT BE?
DON'T LET THE DISTORTIONS ALARM YOU.
STAY FOCUSED ON THE HOLE IN THE WINDOW.
THE HOLE'S NOT THERE YET, BUT IT WILL BE.
I'M DELETING THE WINDOW.
NOW.
YOU FIRST, MR. VELOCET...MISS BOURGEOIS.
T4760BARK87Y
THEN MR. ZAMAROFF.
MR. SOLOMON.
MR. WAYNE.
YOU'LL BE GLAD TO KNOW I FINALLY LOCATED THE MUTATION ENGINE.
IT'S MOBILE AND WELL HIDDEN.
SEVEN YEARS AGO, A YOUNG GENIUS LAUNCHED HYPERGAMES WITH "JUDGMENT IN HELL CITY 666".
MR. TANAKA.
YOU ARE HEREBY UNDER QUARANTINE.
WE'RE ALL BILLIONAIRES.
REAL RISK IS HARD TO FIND THESE DAYS.
I THOUGHT YOU'D ENJOY A CHALLENGE WITH REAL REPERCUSSIONS.

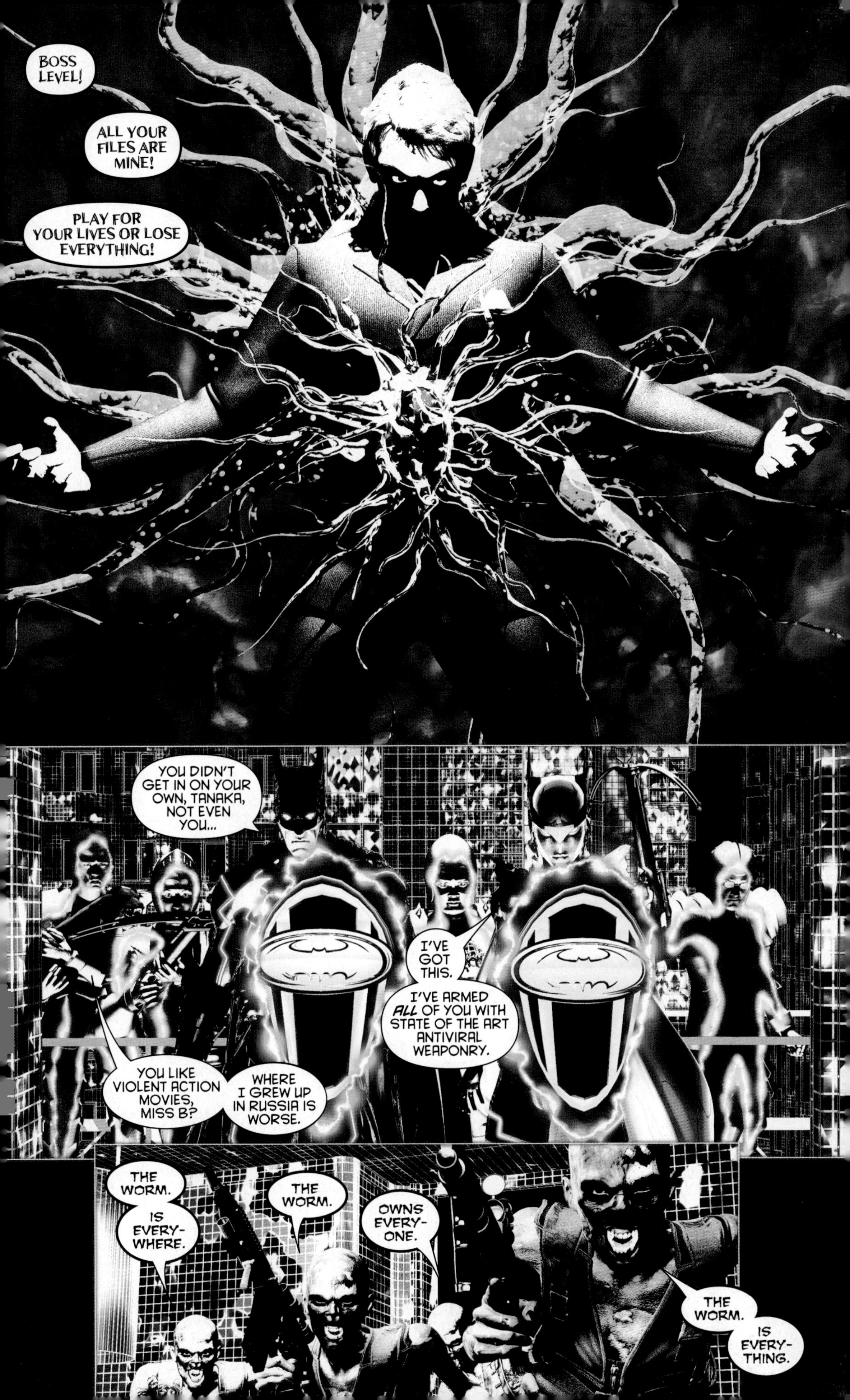
BOSS LEVEL!
ALL YOUR FILES ARE MINE!
PLAY FOR YOUR LIVES OR LOSE EVERYTHING!
YOU DIDN'T GET IN ON YOUR OWN, TANAKA, NOT EVEN YOU...
I'VE GOT THIS.
I'VE ARMED ALL OF YOU WITH STATE OF THE ART ANTIVIRAL WEAPONRY.
YOU LIKE VIOLENT ACTION MOVIES, MISS B?
WHERE I GREW UP IN RUSSIA IS WORSE.
THE WORM.
IS EVERYWHERE.
THE WORM.
OWNS EVERYONE.
THE WORM.
IS EVERYTHING.

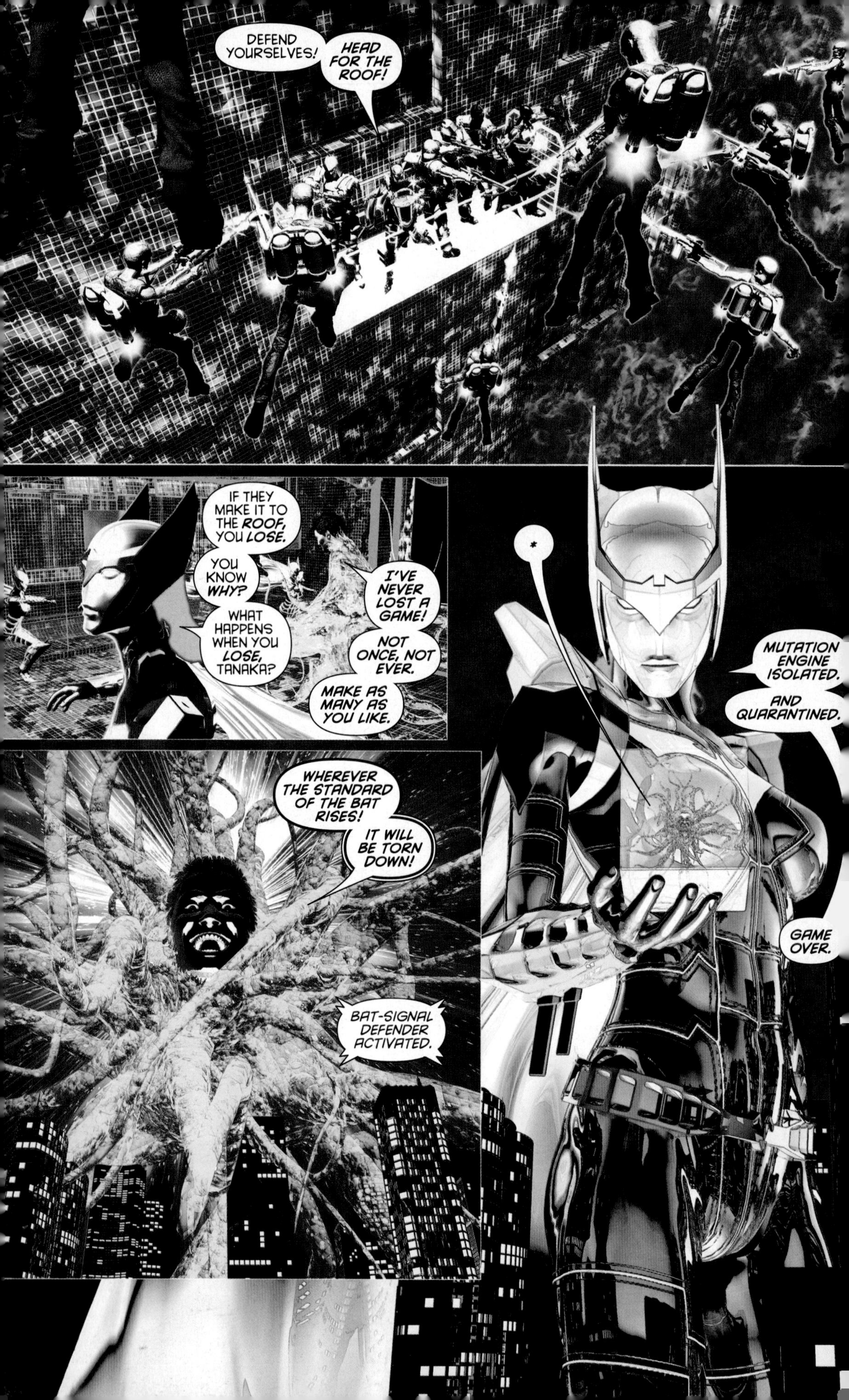
DEFEND YOURSELVES!
HEAD FOR THE ROOF!
IF THEY MAKE IT TO THE ROOF, YOU LOSE.
YOU KNOW WHY?
WHAT HAPPENS WHEN YOU LOSE, TANAKA?
I'VE NEVER LOST A GAME!
NOT ONCE, NOT EVER.
MAKE AS MANY AS YOU LIKE.
WHEREVER THE STANDARD OF THE BAT RISES!
IT WILL BE TORN DOWN!
BAT-SIGNAL DEFENDER ACTIVATED.
*
MUTATION ENGINE ISOLATED.
AND QUARANTINED.
GAME OVER.

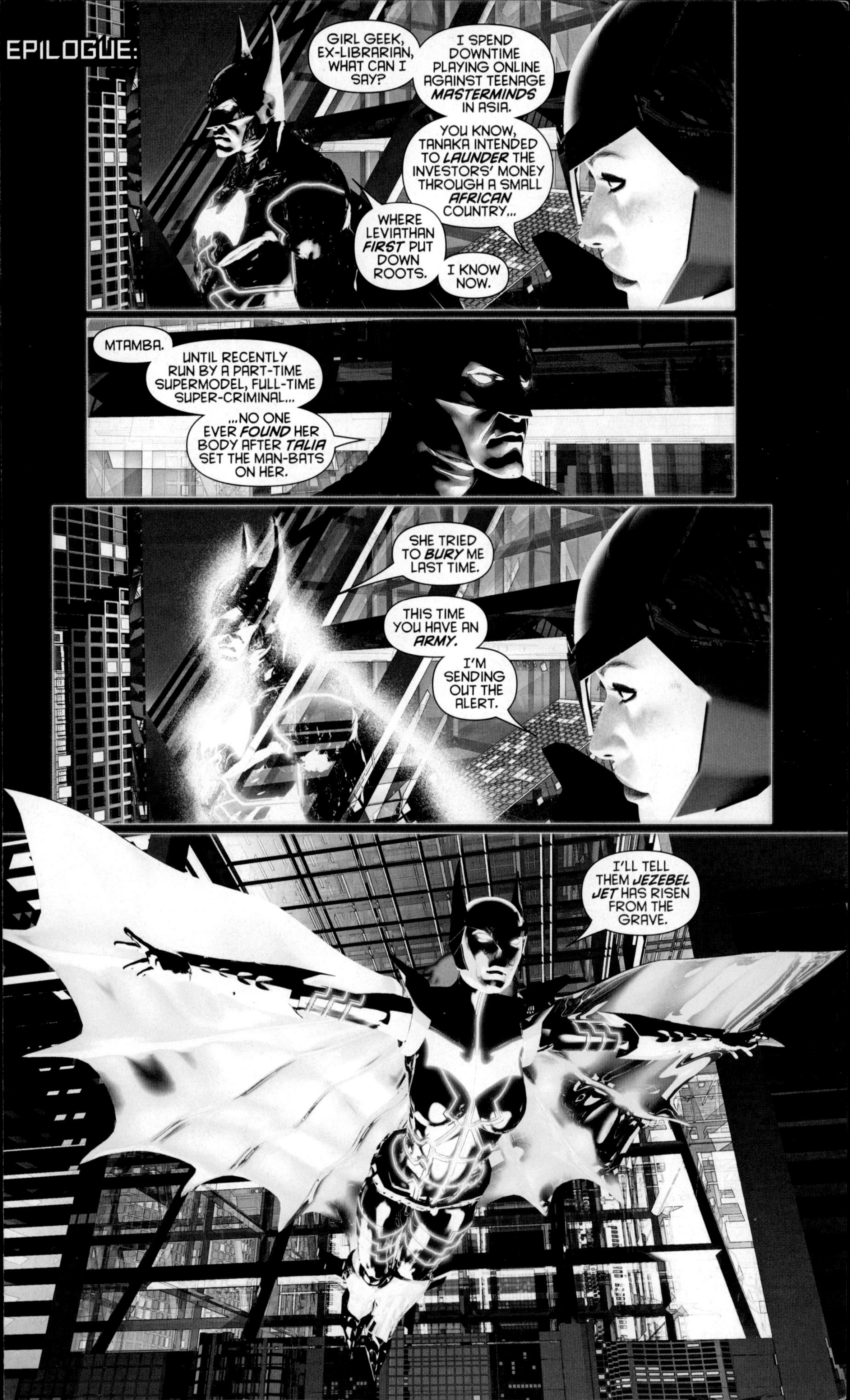
EPILOGUE:
GIRL GEEK, EX-LIBRARIAN, WHAT CAN I SAY?
I SPEND DOWNTIME PLAYING ONLINE AGAINST TEENAGE MASTERMINDS IN ASIA.
YOU KNOW, TANAKA INTENDED TO LAUNDER THE INVESTORS' MONEY THROUGH A SMALL AFRICAN COUNTRY...
WHERE LEVIATHAN FIRST PUT DOWN ROOTS.
I KNOW NOW.
MTAMBA.
UNTIL RECENTLY RUN BY A PART-TIME SUPERMODEL, FULL-TIME SUPER-CRIMINAL...
...NO ONE EVER FOUND HER BODY AFTER TALIA SET THE MAN-BATS ON HER.
SHE TRIED TO BURY ME LAST TIME.
THIS TIME YOU HAVE AN ARMY.
I'M SENDING OUT THE ALERT.
I'LL TELL THEM JEZEBEL JET HAS RISEN FROM THE GRAVE.

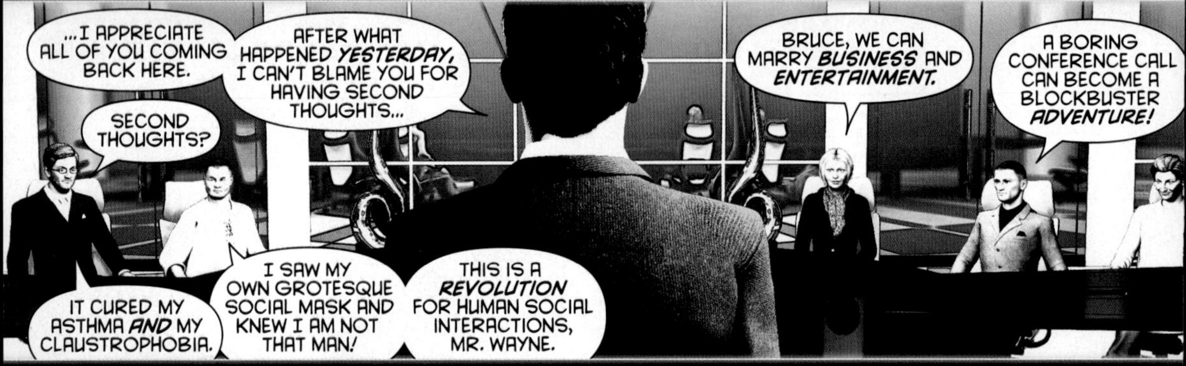
...I APPRECIATE ALL OF YOU COMING BACK HERE.
AFTER WHAT HAPPENED YESTERDAY, I CAN'T BLAME YOU FOR HAVING SECOND THOUGHTS...
SECOND THOUGHTS?
BRUCE, WE CAN MARRY BUSINESS AND ENTERTAINMENT.
A BORING CONFERENCE CALL CAN BECOME A BLOCKBUSTER ADVENTURE!
IT CURED MY ASTHMA AND MY CLAUSTROPHOBIA.
I SAW MY OWN GROTESQUE SOCIAL MASK AND KNEW I AM NOT THAT MAN!
THIS IS A REVOLUTION FOR HUMAN SOCIAL INTERACTIONS, MR. WAYNE.

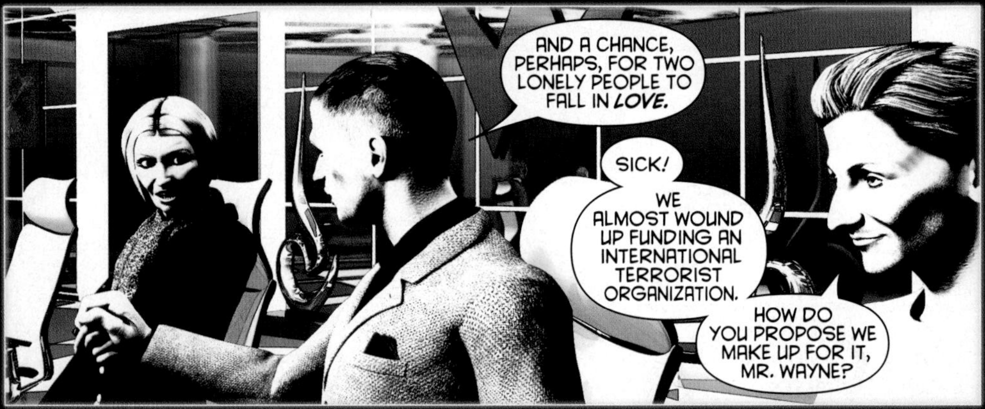
AND A CHANCE, PERHAPS, FOR TWO LONELY PEOPLE TO FALL IN LOVE.
SICK!
WE ALMOST WOUND UP FUNDING AN INTERNATIONAL TERRORIST ORGANIZATION.
HOW DO YOU PROPOSE WE MAKE UP FOR IT, MR. WAYNE?

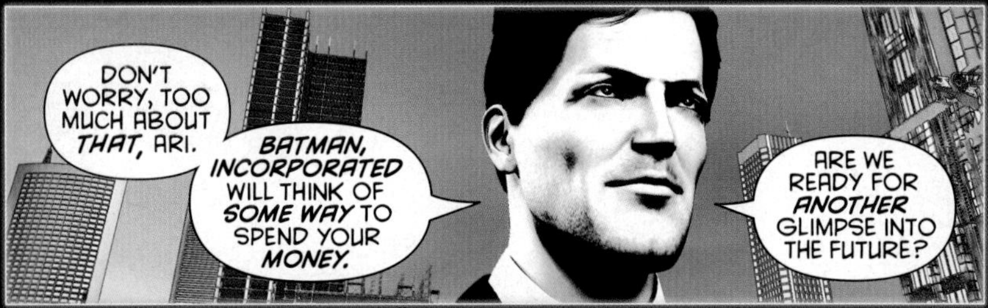
DON'T WORRY, TOO MUCH ABOUT THAT, ARI.
BATMAN, INCORPORATED WILL THINK OF SOME WAY TO SPEND YOUR MONEY.
ARE WE READY FOR ANOTHER GLIMPSE INTO THE FUTURE?

NEXT: BATMAN AND BATGIRL ENTER...

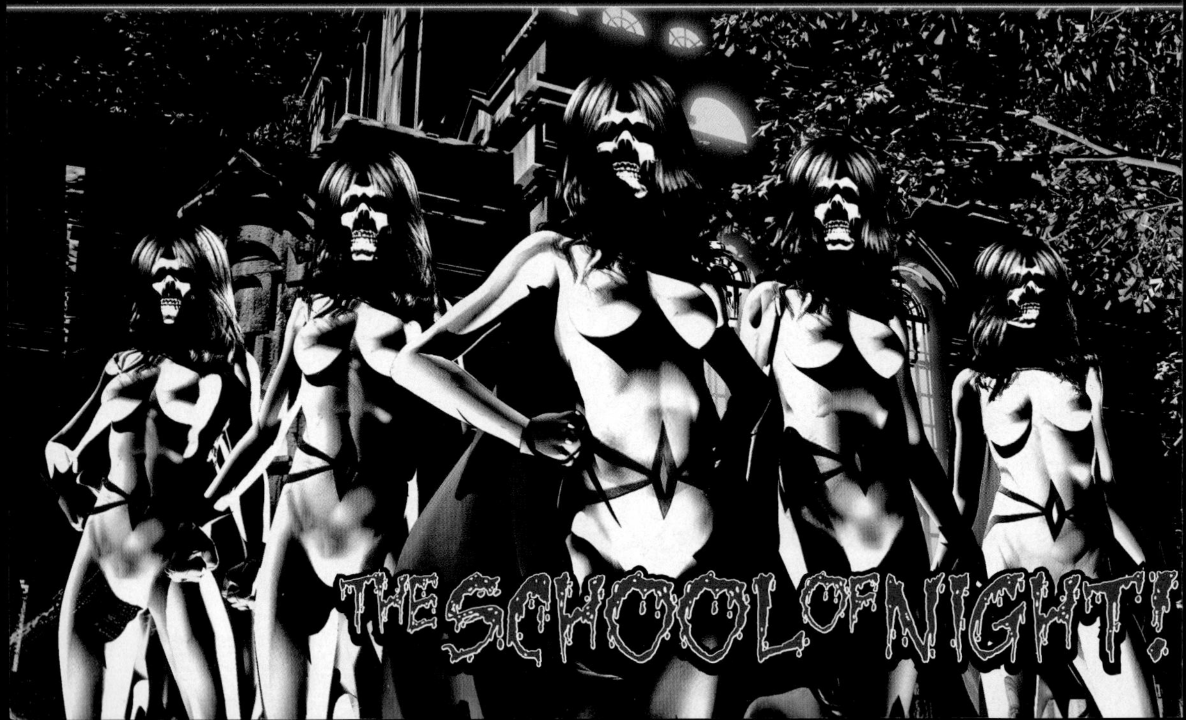
THE SCHOOL OF NIGHT!

Cover art for BATMAN, INCORPORATED: LEVIATHAN STRIKES! by **CHRIS BURNHAM** (color by **NATHAN FAIRBAIRN**).

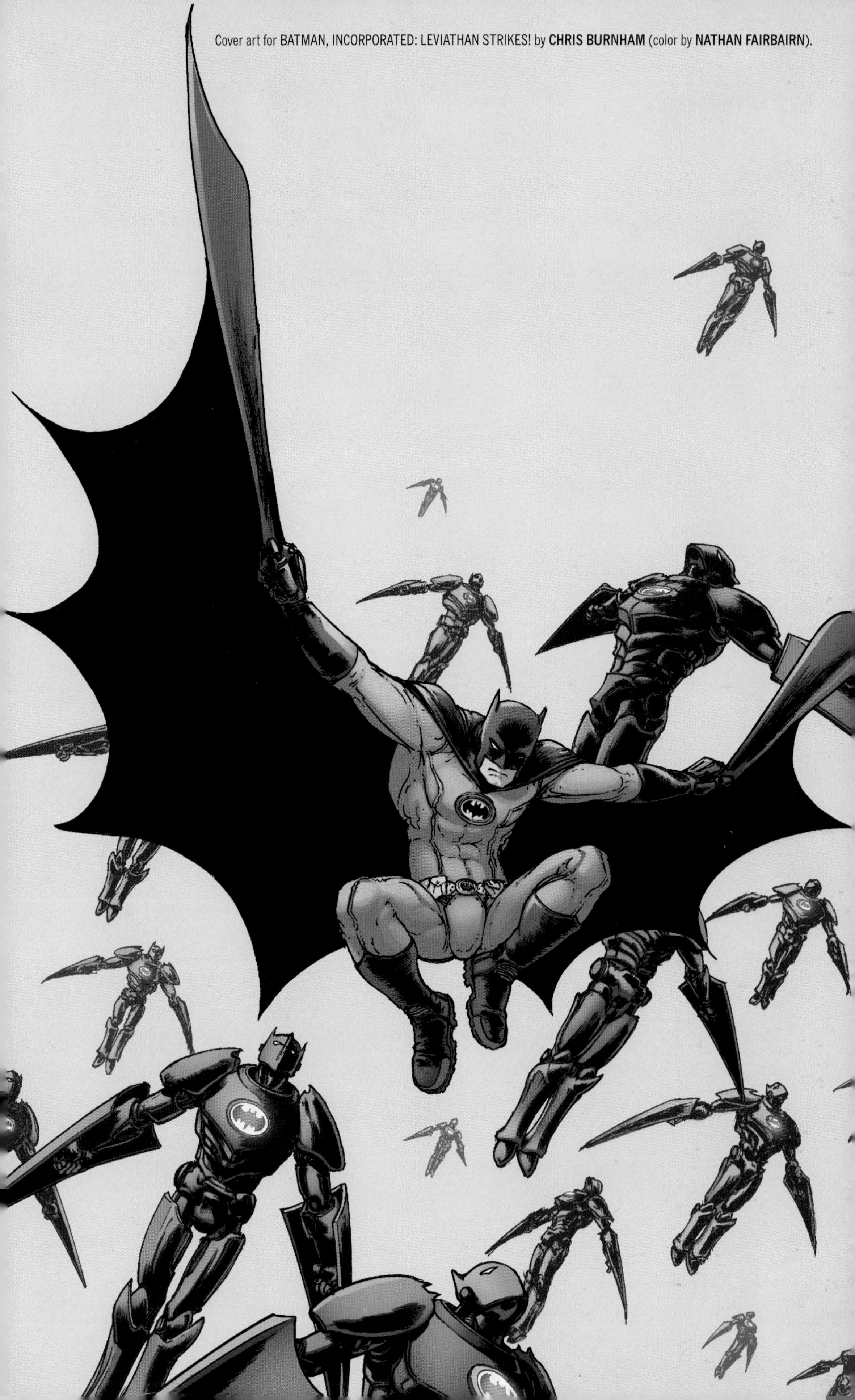

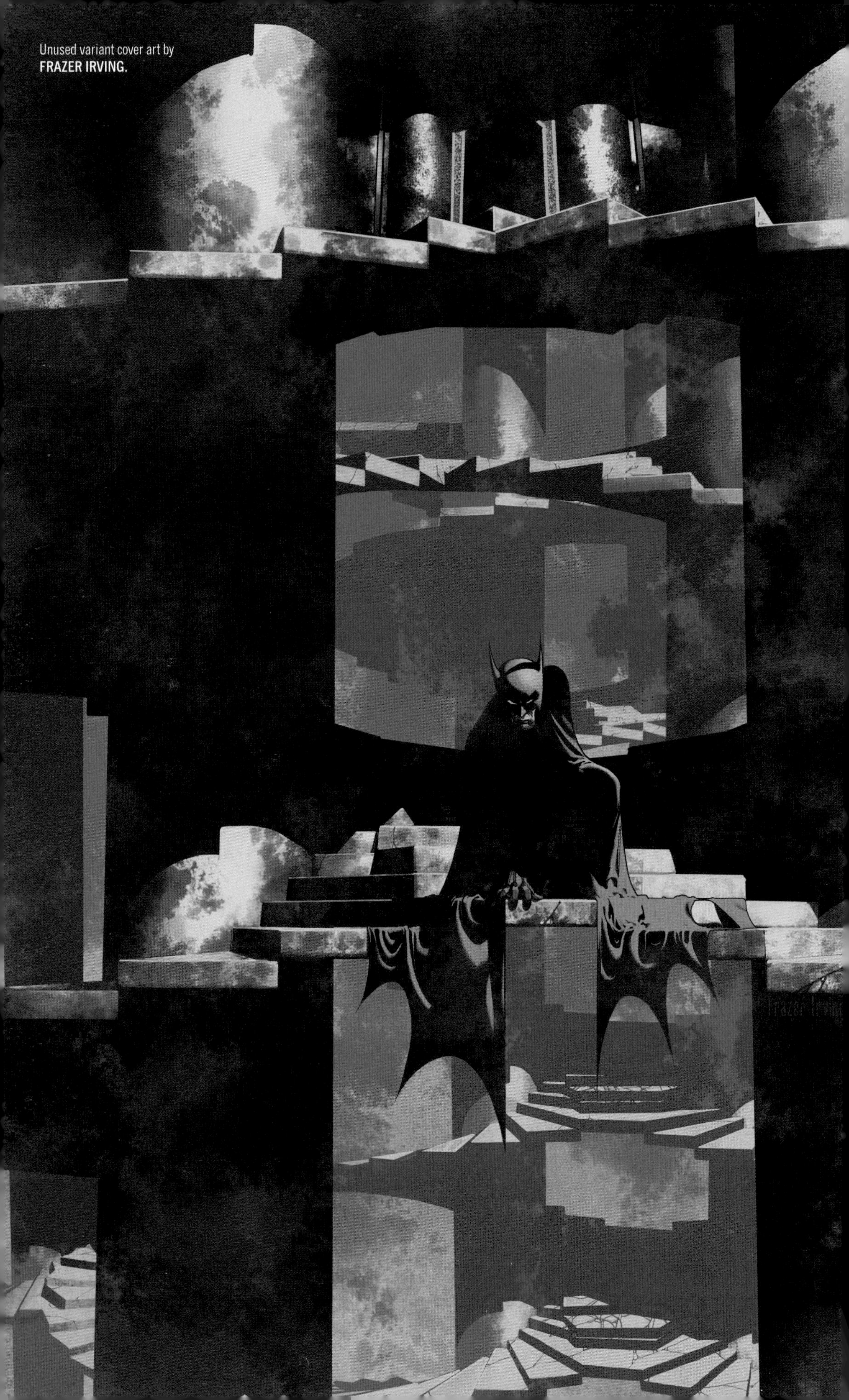

Unused variant cover art by **FRAZER IRVING.**

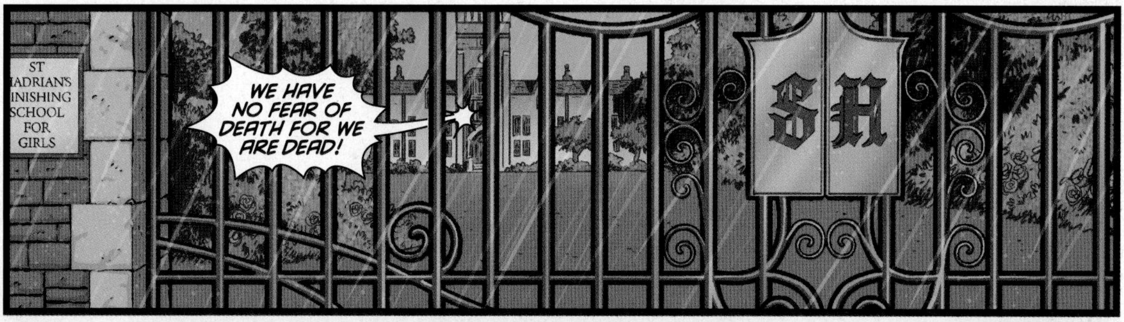
ST HADRIAN'S INISHING SCHOOL FOR GIRLS
SH
WE HAVE NO FEAR OF DEATH FOR WE ARE DEAD!

BATMAN, INCORPORATED: LEVIATHAN STRIKES! Chapter 1
Writer: GRANT MORRISON Artist: CAMERON STEWART

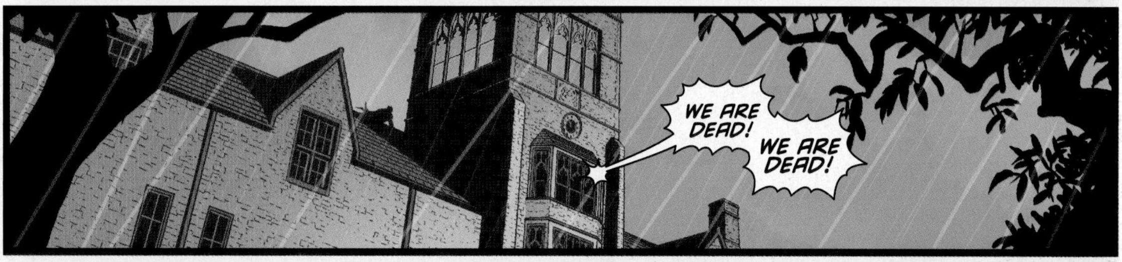
WE ARE DEAD!
WE ARE DEAD!

Color: NATHAN FAIRBAIRN Letters: SAL CIPRIANO

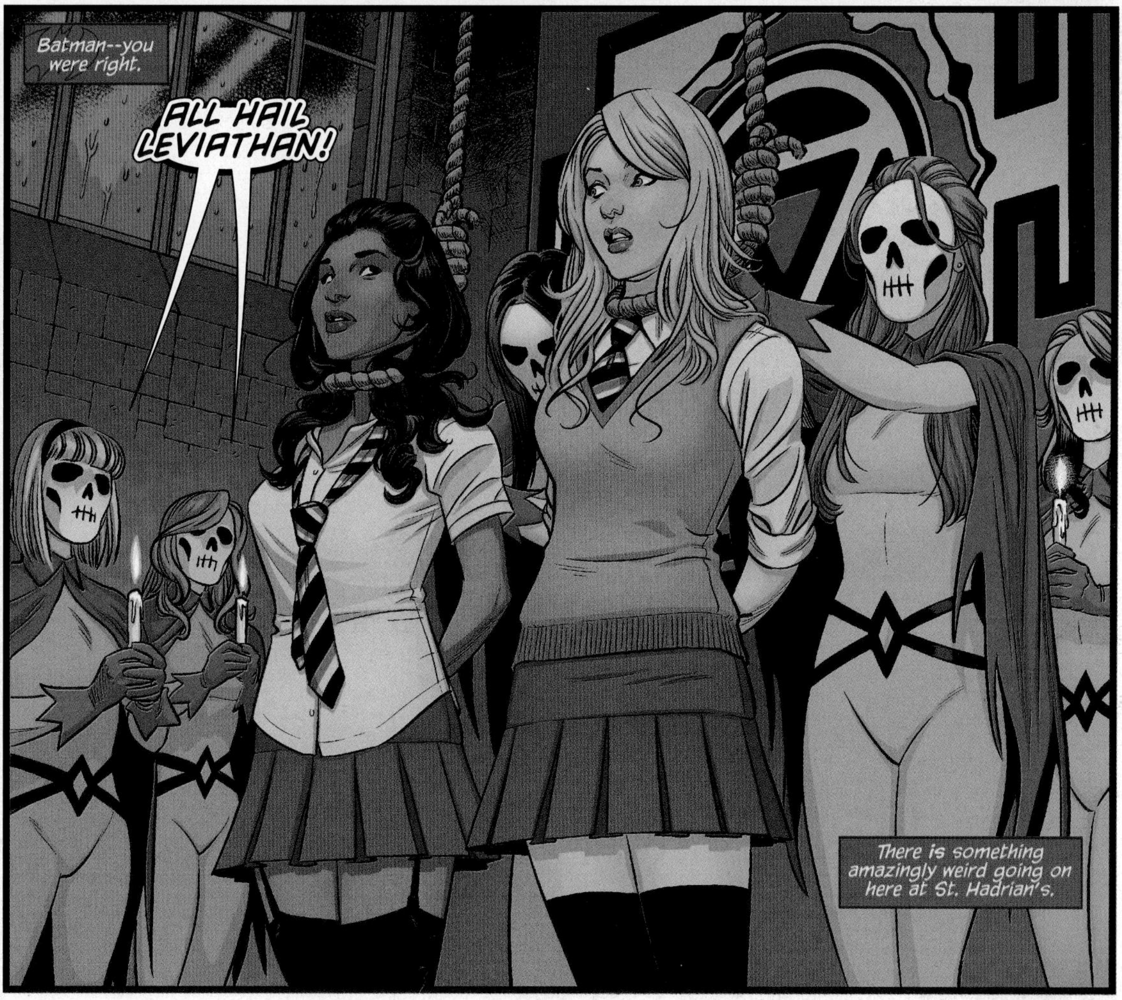
Batman--you were right.
ALL HAIL LEVIATHAN!
There is something amazingly weird going on here at St. Hadrian's.

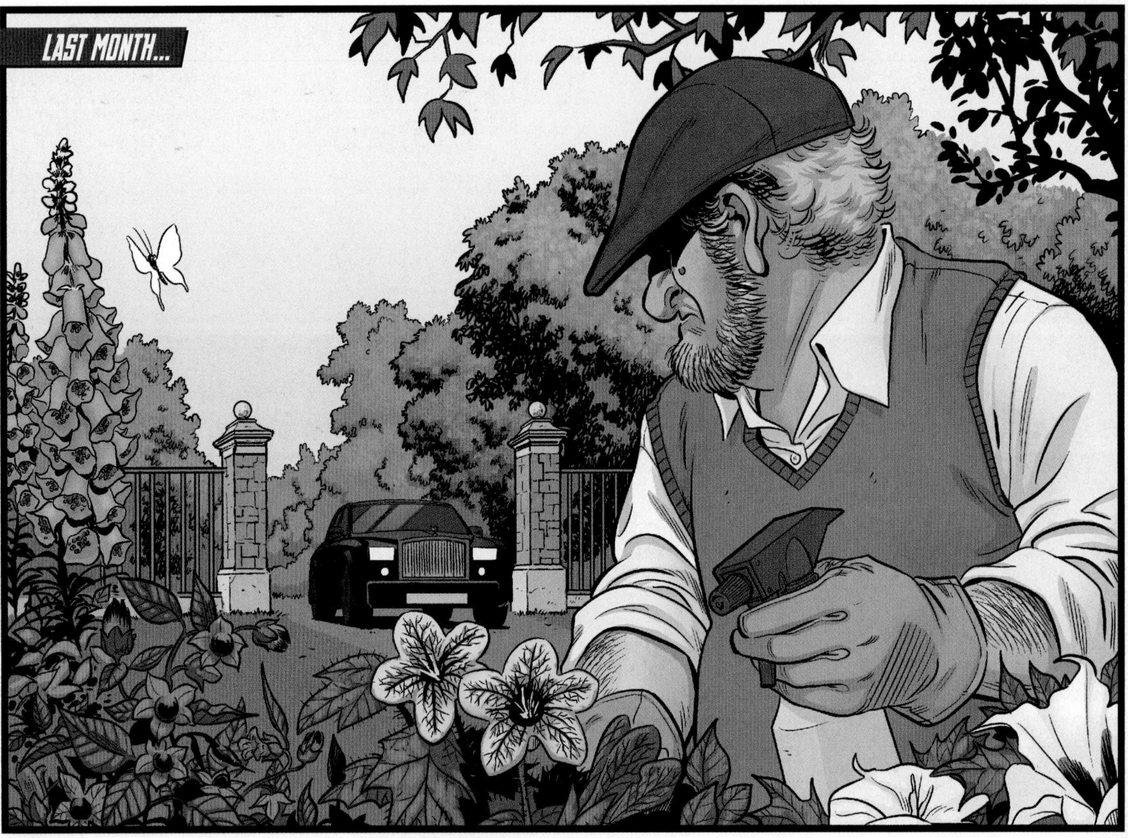
LAST MONTH...
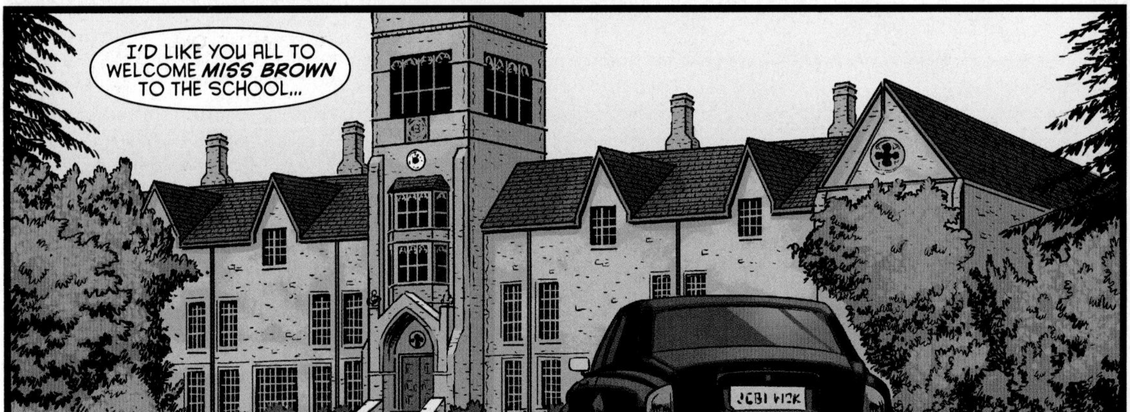
I'D LIKE YOU ALL TO WELCOME MISS BROWN TO THE SCHOOL...
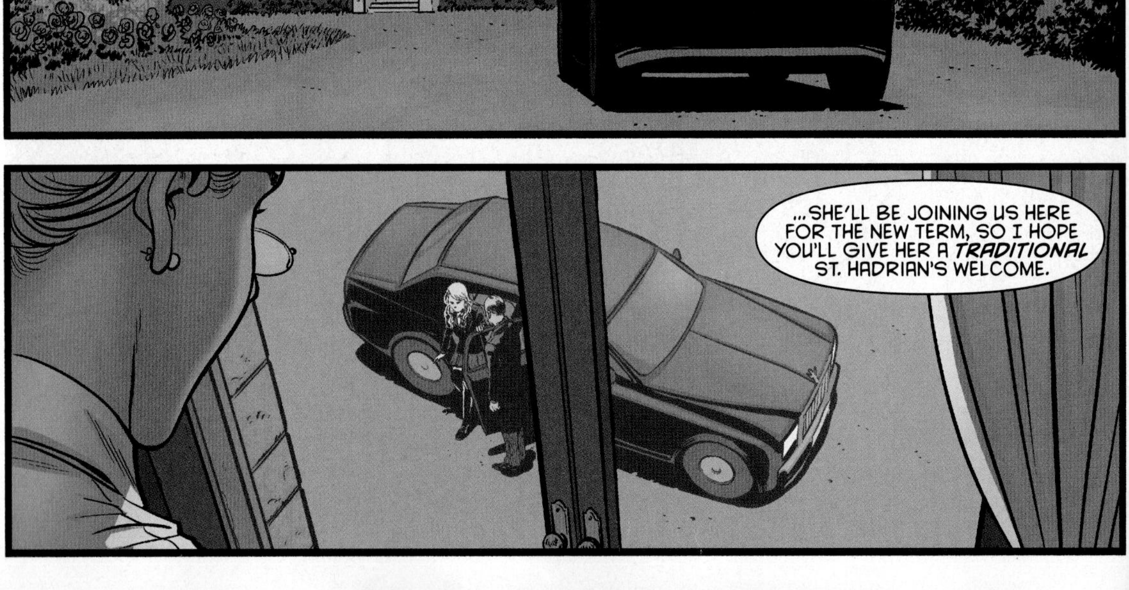
...SHE'LL BE JOINING US HERE FOR THE NEW TERM, SO I HOPE YOU'LL GIVE HER A TRADITIONAL ST. HADRIAN'S WELCOME.

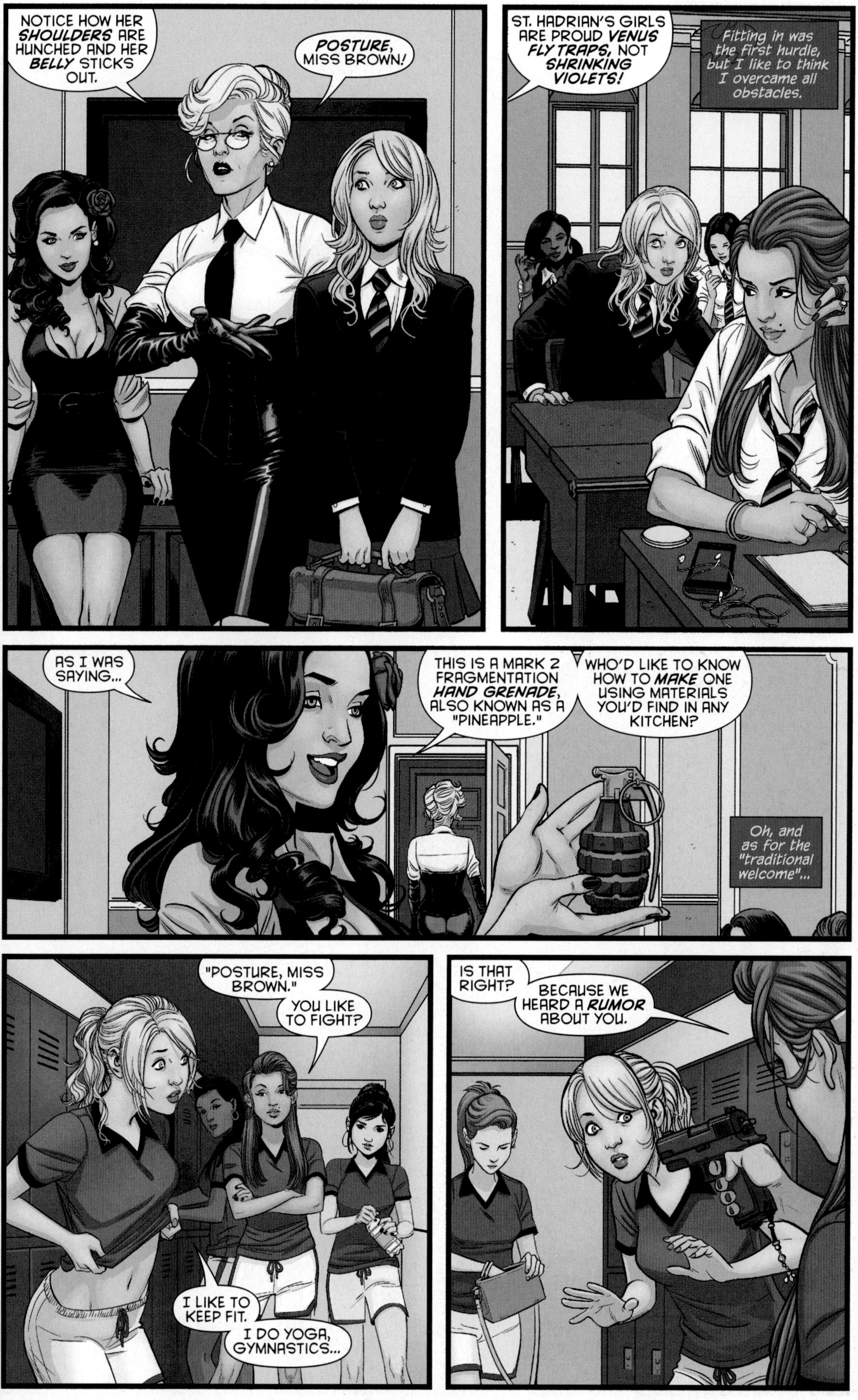
NOTICE HOW HER SHOULDERS ARE HUNCHED AND HER BELLY STICKS OUT.
POSTURE, MISS BROWN!
ST. HADRIAN'S GIRLS ARE PROUD VENUS FLY TRAPS, NOT SHRINKING VIOLETS!
Fitting in was the first hurdle, but I like to think I overcame all obstacles.
AS I WAS SAYING...
THIS IS A MARK 2 FRAGMENTATION HAND GRENADE, ALSO KNOWN AS A "PINEAPPLE."
WHO'D LIKE TO KNOW HOW TO MAKE ONE USING MATERIALS YOU'D FIND IN ANY KITCHEN?
Oh, and as for the "traditional welcome"...
"POSTURE, MISS BROWN."
YOU LIKE TO FIGHT?
I LIKE TO KEEP FIT.
I DO YOGA, GYMNASTICS...
IS THAT RIGHT?
BECAUSE WE HEARD A RUMOR ABOUT YOU.

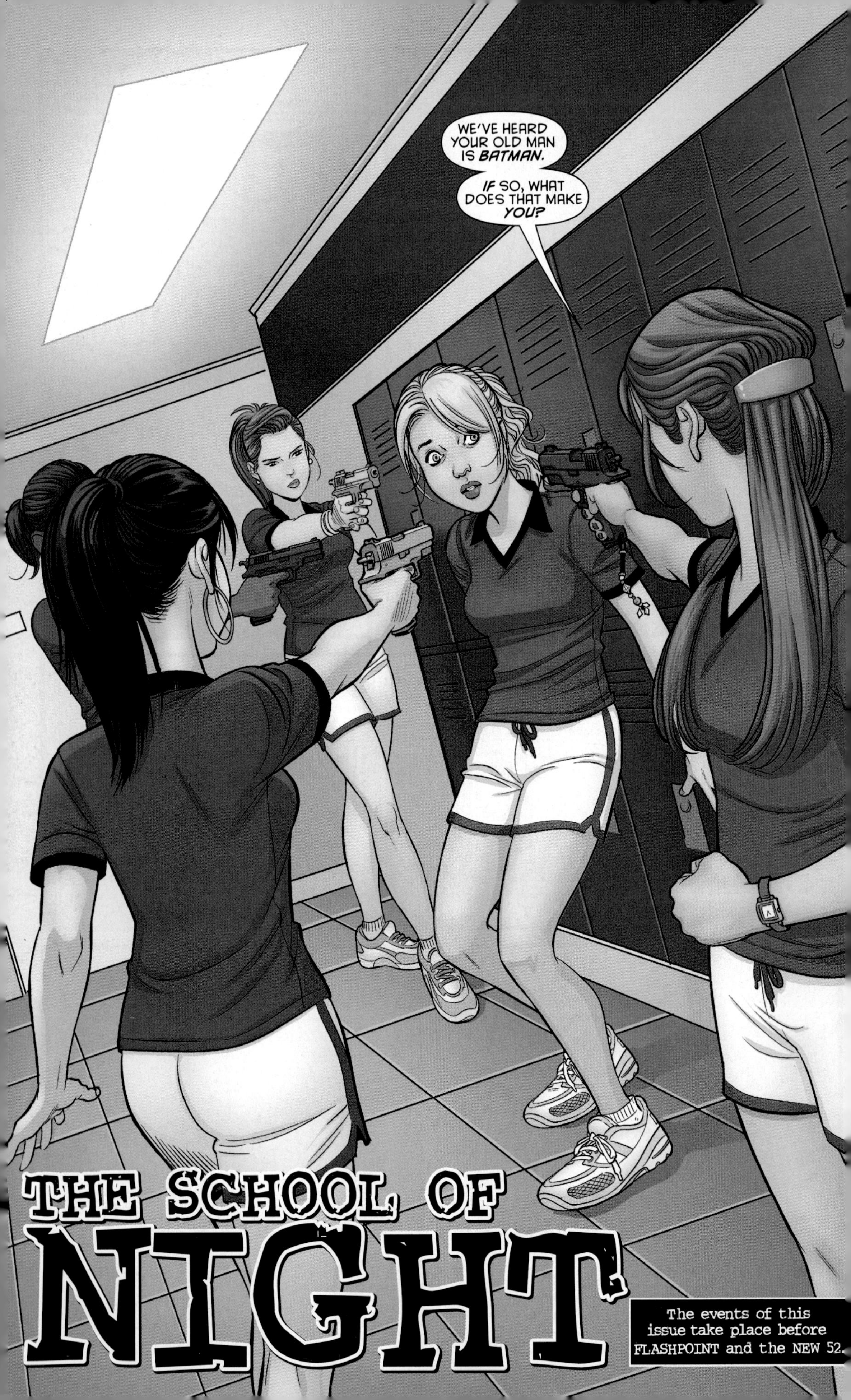
WE'VE HEARD YOUR OLD MAN IS BATMAN.
IF SO, WHAT DOES THAT MAKE YOU?
THE SCHOOL OF NIGHT
The events of this issue take place before FLASHPOINT and the NEW 52.

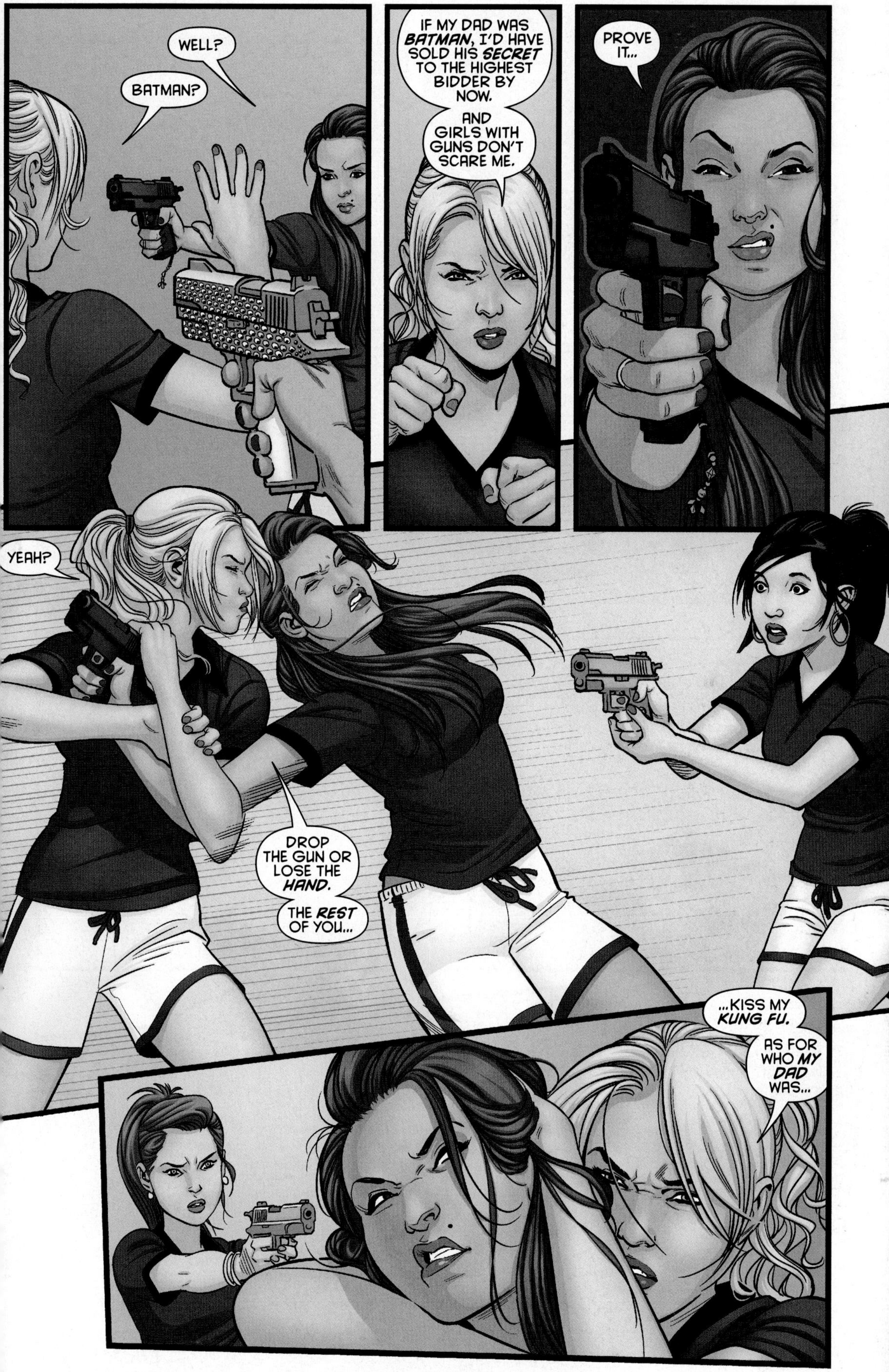
WELL?
BATMAN?
IF MY DAD WAS BATMAN, I'D HAVE SOLD HIS SECRET TO THE HIGHEST BIDDER BY NOW.
AND GIRLS WITH GUNS DON'T SCARE ME.
PROVE IT...
YEAH?
DROP THE GUN OR LOSE THE HAND.
THE REST OF YOU...
...KISS MY KUNG FU.
AS FOR WHO MY DAD WAS...

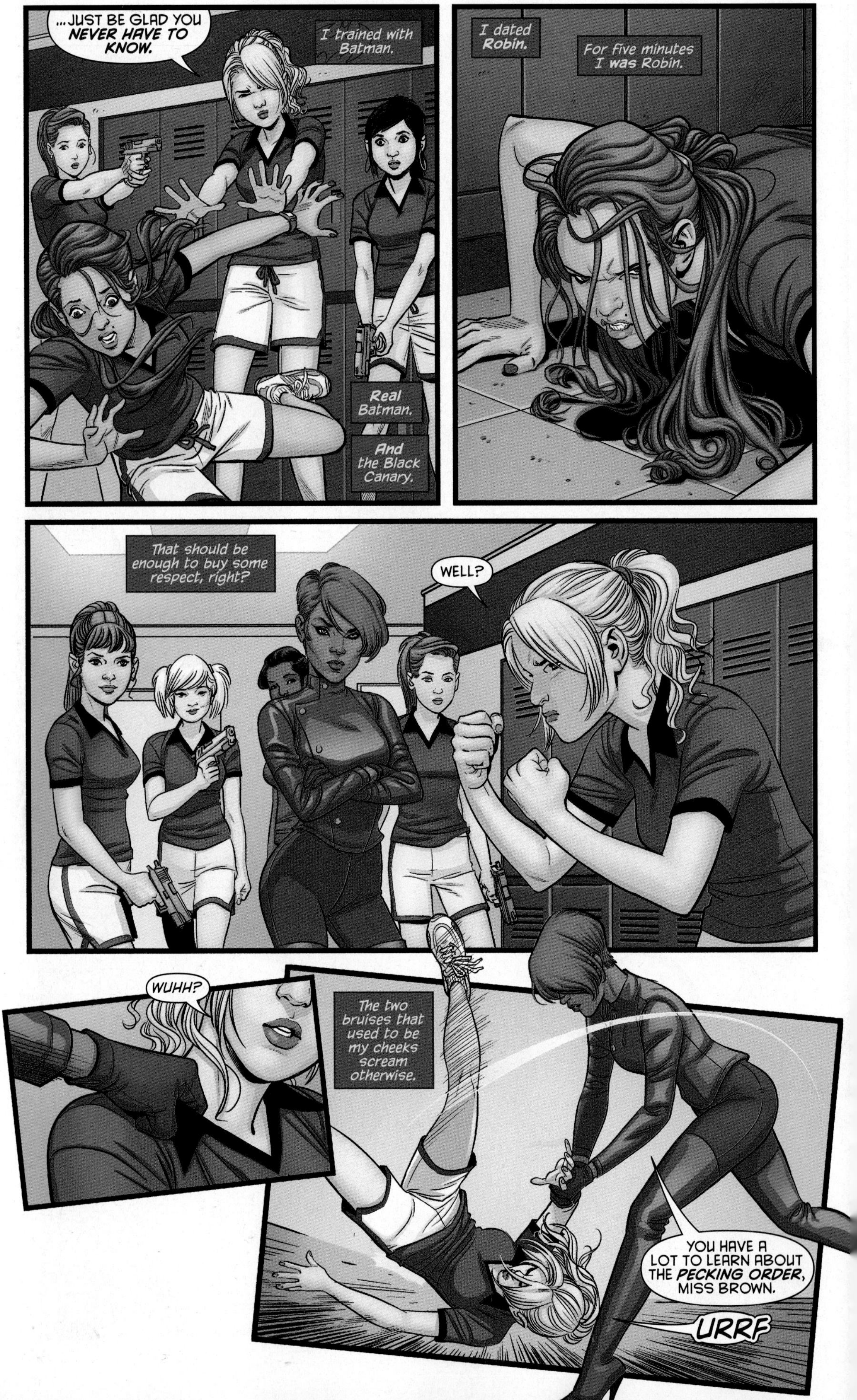

...JUST BE GLAD YOU NEVER HAVE TO KNOW.
I trained with Batman.
Real Batman.
And the Black Canary.
I dated Robin.
For five minutes I was Robin.
That should be enough to buy some respect, right?
WELL?
WUHH?
The two bruises that used to be my cheeks scream otherwise.
YOU HAVE A LOT TO LEARN ABOUT THE PECKING ORDER, MISS BROWN.
URRF

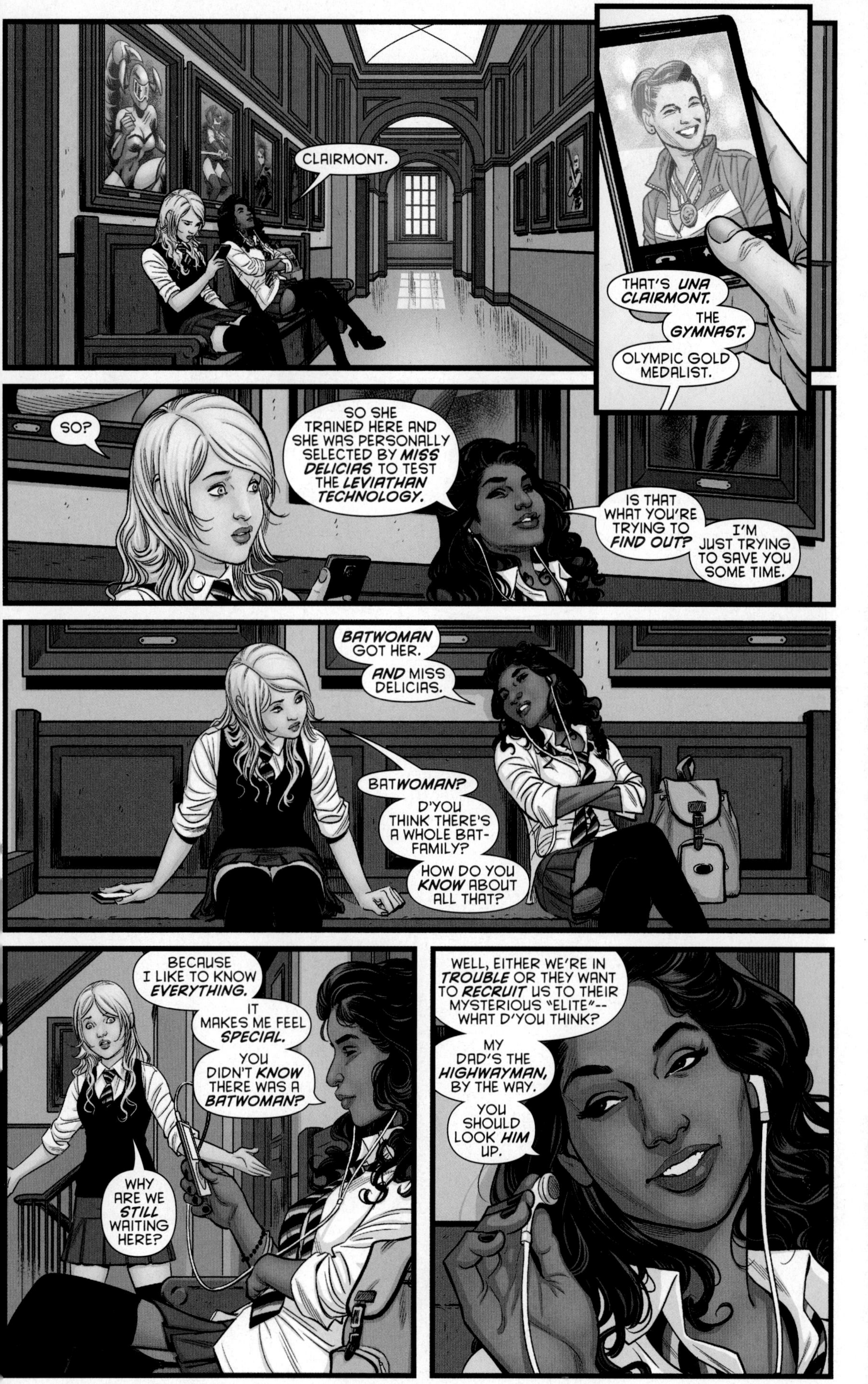

CLAIRMONT.
THAT'S UNA CLAIRMONT.
THE GYMNAST.
OLYMPIC GOLD MEDALIST.
SO?
SO SHE TRAINED HERE AND SHE WAS PERSONALLY SELECTED BY MISS DELICIAS TO TEST THE LEVIATHAN TECHNOLOGY.
IS THAT WHAT YOU'RE TRYING TO FIND OUT?
I'M JUST TRYING TO SAVE YOU SOME TIME.
BATWOMAN GOT HER.
AND MISS DELICIAS.
BATWOMAN?
D'YOU THINK THERE'S A WHOLE BAT-FAMILY?
HOW DO YOU KNOW ABOUT ALL THAT?
BECAUSE I LIKE TO KNOW EVERYTHING.
IT MAKES ME FEEL SPECIAL.
YOU DIDN'T KNOW THERE WAS A BATWOMAN?
WHY ARE WE STILL WAITING HERE?
WELL, EITHER WE'RE IN TROUBLE OR THEY WANT TO RECRUIT US TO THEIR MYSTERIOUS "ELITE"-- WHAT D'YOU THINK?
MY DAD'S THE HIGHWAYMAN, BY THE WAY.
YOU SHOULD LOOK HIM UP.

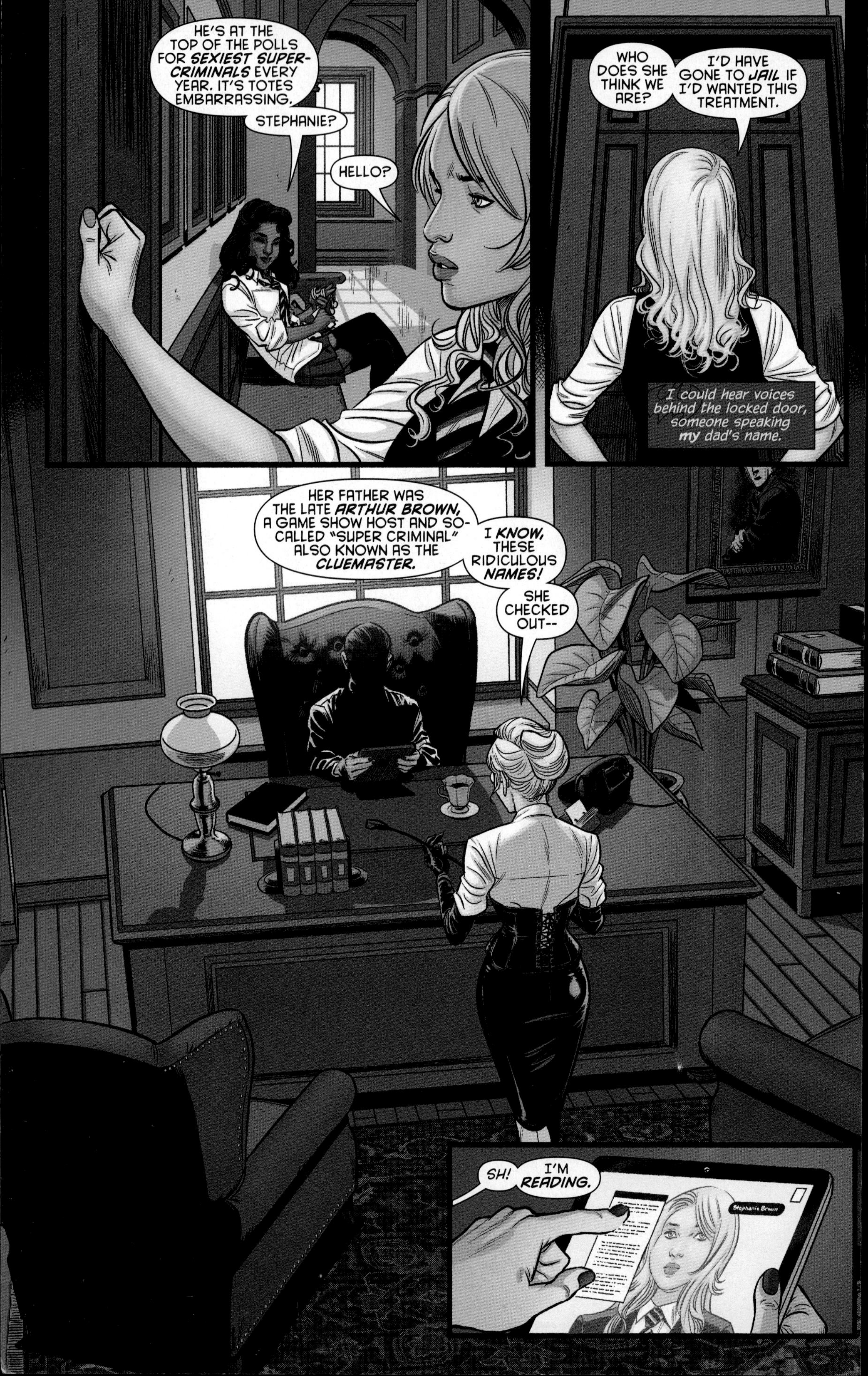

HE'S AT THE TOP OF THE POLLS FOR SEXIEST SUPER-CRIMINALS EVERY YEAR. IT'S TOTES EMBARRASSING.
STEPHANIE?
HELLO?
WHO DOES SHE THINK WE ARE?
I'D HAVE GONE TO JAIL IF I'D WANTED THIS TREATMENT.
I could hear voices behind the locked door, someone speaking my dad's name.
HER FATHER WAS THE LATE ARTHUR BROWN, A GAME SHOW HOST AND SO-CALLED "SUPER CRIMINAL" ALSO KNOWN AS THE CLUEMASTER.
I KNOW, THESE RIDICULOUS NAMES!
SHE CHECKED OUT--
SH!
I'M READING.
Stephanie Brown

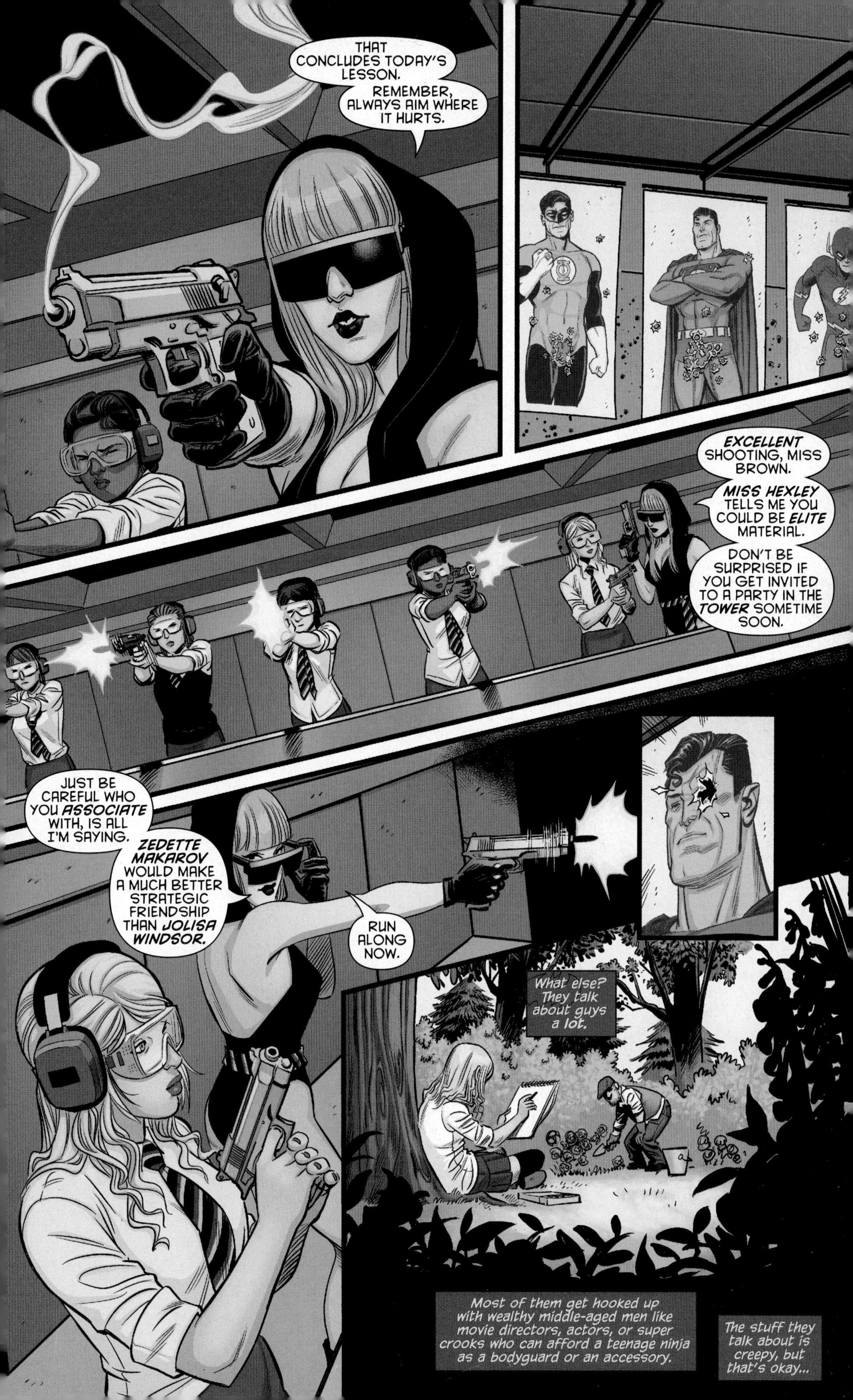
THAT CONCLUDES TODAY'S LESSON.
REMEMBER, ALWAYS AIM WHERE IT HURTS.
EXCELLENT SHOOTING, MISS BROWN.
MISS HEXLEY TELLS ME YOU COULD BE ELITE MATERIAL.
DON'T BE SURPRISED IF YOU GET INVITED TO A PARTY IN THE TOWER SOMETIME SOON.
JUST BE CAREFUL WHO YOU ASSOCIATE WITH, IS ALL I'M SAYING.
ZEDETTE MAKAROV WOULD MAKE A MUCH BETTER STRATEGIC FRIENDSHIP THAN JOLISA WINDSOR.
RUN ALONG NOW.
What else? They talk about guys a lot.
Most of them get hooked up with wealthy middle-aged men like movie directors, actors, or super crooks who can afford a teenage ninja as a bodyguard or an accessory.
The stuff they talk about is creepy, but that's okay...

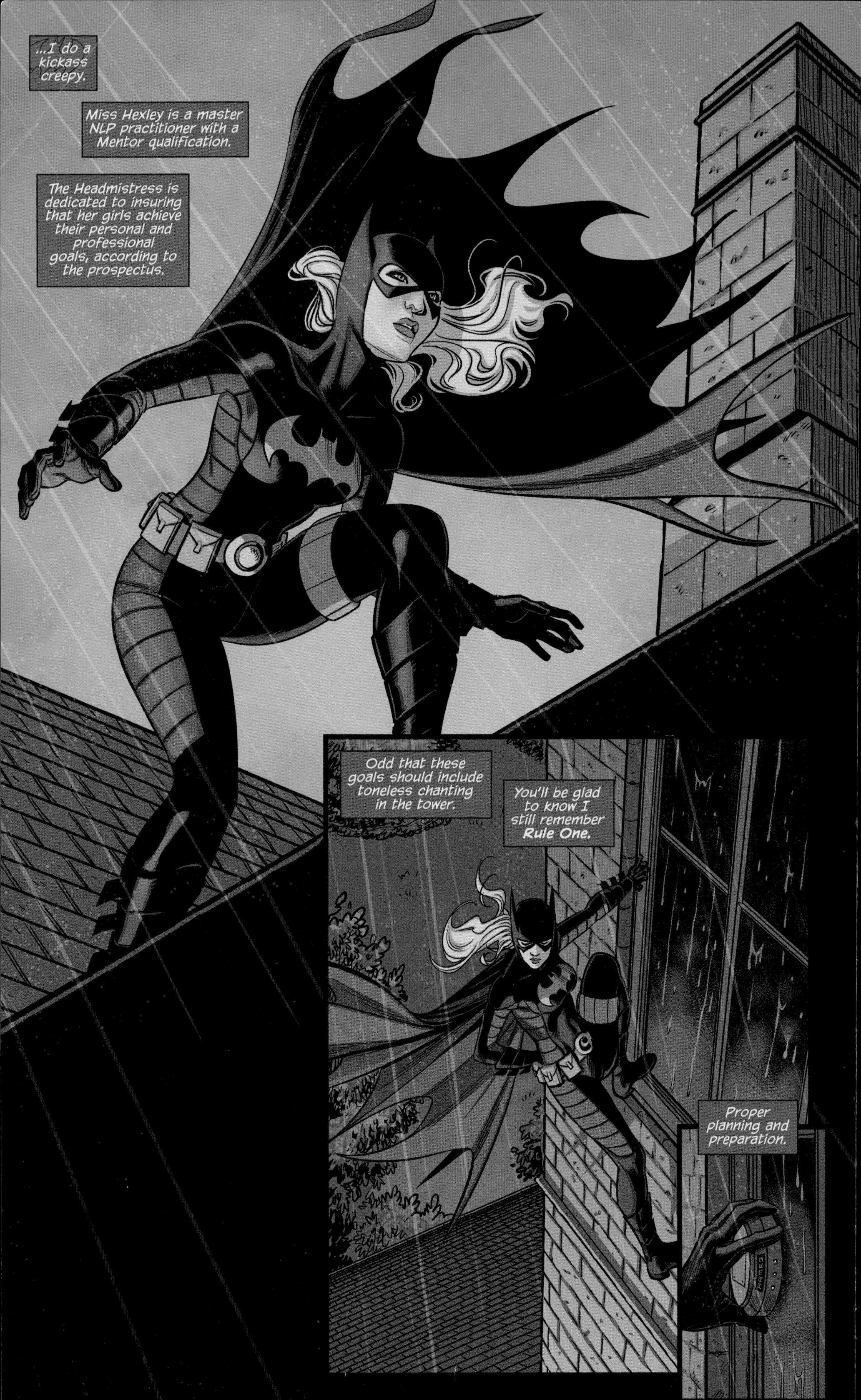
...I do a kickass creepy.
Miss Hexley is a master NLP practitioner with a Mentor qualification.
The Headmistress is dedicated to insuring that her girls achieve their personal and professional goals, according to the prospectus.
Odd that these goals should include toneless chanting in the tower.
You'll be glad to know I still remember Rule One.
Proper planning and preparation.

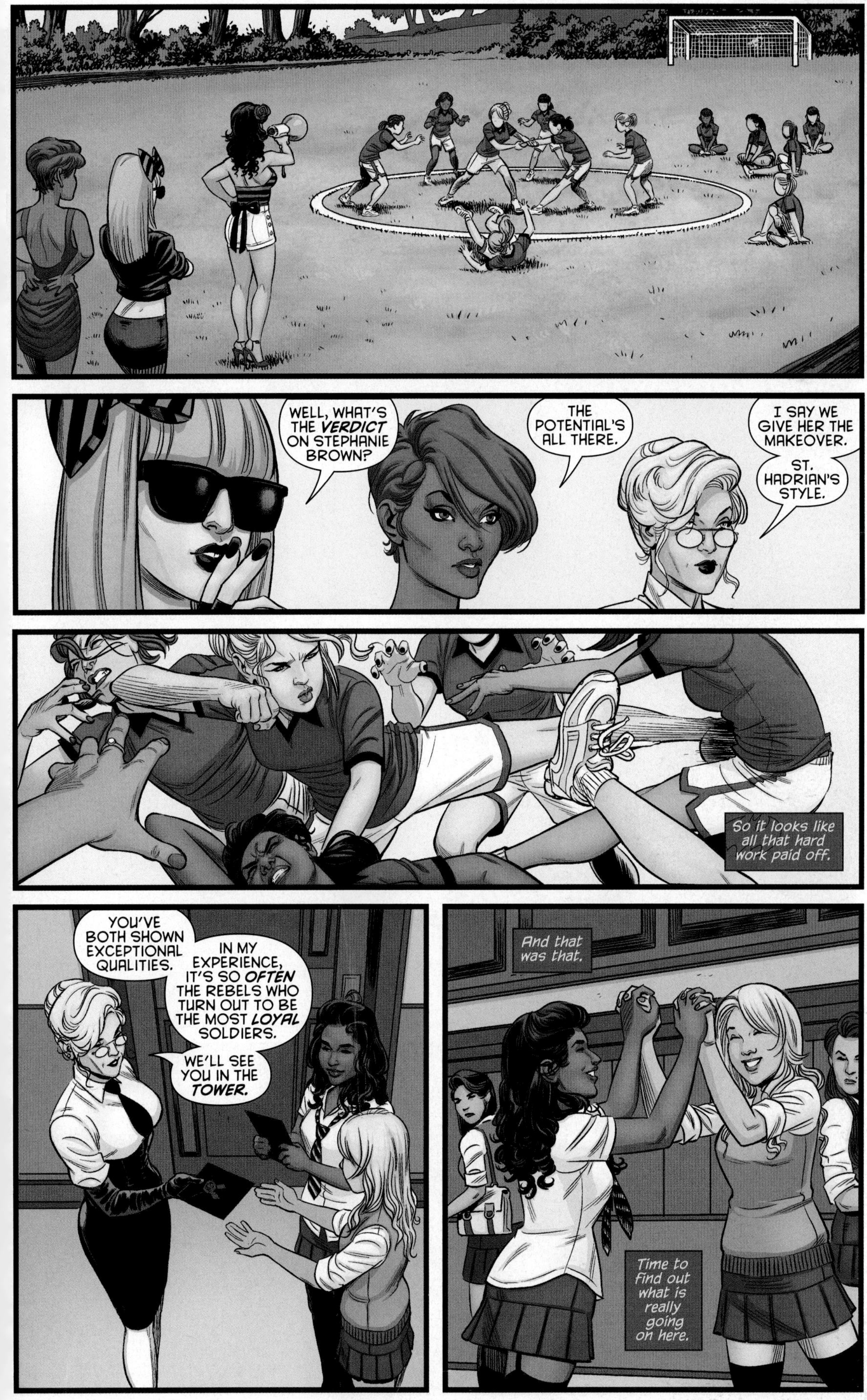
WELL, WHAT'S THE VERDICT ON STEPHANIE BROWN?
THE POTENTIAL'S ALL THERE.
I SAY WE GIVE HER THE MAKEOVER.
ST. HADRIAN'S STYLE.
So it looks like all that hard work paid off.
YOU'VE BOTH SHOWN EXCEPTIONAL QUALITIES.
IN MY EXPERIENCE, IT'S SO OFTEN THE REBELS WHO TURN OUT TO BE THE MOST LOYAL SOLDIERS.
WE'LL SEE YOU IN THE TOWER.
And that was that.
Time to find out what is really going on here.

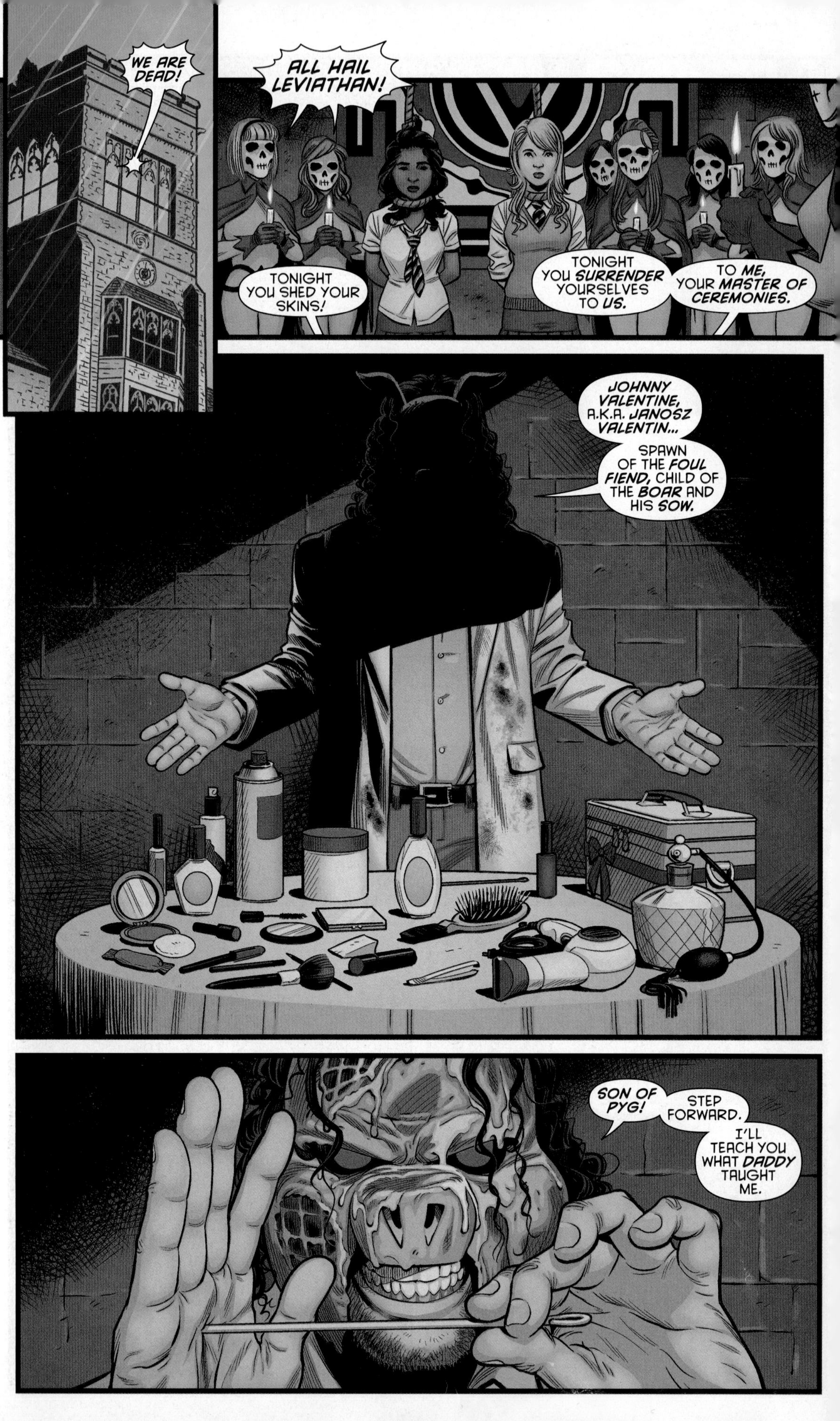
WE ARE DEAD!
ALL HAIL LEVIATHAN!
TONIGHT YOU SHED YOUR SKINS!
TONIGHT YOU SURRENDER YOURSELVES TO US.
TO ME, YOUR MASTER OF CEREMONIES.
JOHNNY VALENTINE, A.K.A. JANOSZ VALENTIN...
SPAWN OF THE FOUL FIEND, CHILD OF THE BOAR AND HIS SOW.
SON OF PYG!
STEP FORWARD.
I'LL TEACH YOU WHAT DADDY TAUGHT ME.

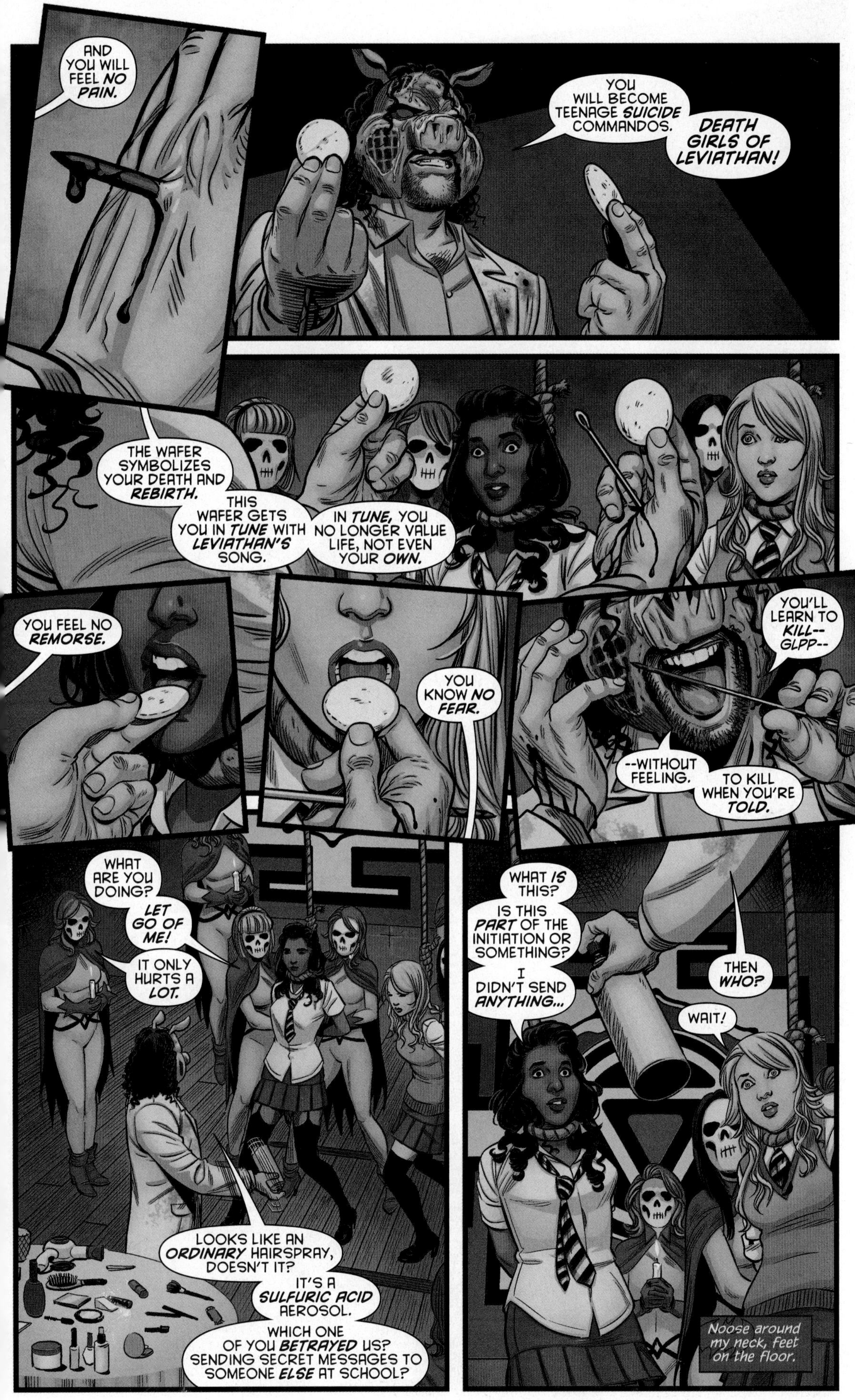
AND YOU WILL FEEL NO PAIN.
YOU WILL BECOME TEENAGE SUICIDE COMMANDOS.
DEATH GIRLS OF LEVIATHAN!
THE WAFER SYMBOLIZES YOUR DEATH AND REBIRTH.
THIS WAFER GETS YOU IN TUNE WITH LEVIATHAN'S SONG.
IN TUNE, YOU NO LONGER VALUE LIFE, NOT EVEN YOUR OWN.
YOU FEEL NO REMORSE.
YOU KNOW NO FEAR.
YOU'LL LEARN TO KILL-- GLPP--
--WITHOUT FEELING.
TO KILL WHEN YOU'RE TOLD.
WHAT ARE YOU DOING?
LET GO OF ME!
IT ONLY HURTS A LOT.
LOOKS LIKE AN ORDINARY HAIRSPRAY, DOESN'T IT?
IT'S A SULFURIC ACID AEROSOL.
WHICH ONE OF YOU BETRAYED US? SENDING SECRET MESSAGES TO SOMEONE ELSE AT SCHOOL?
WHAT IS THIS?
IS THIS PART OF THE INITIATION OR SOMETHING?
I DIDN'T SEND ANYTHING...
THEN WHO?
WAIT!
Noose around my neck, feet on the floor.

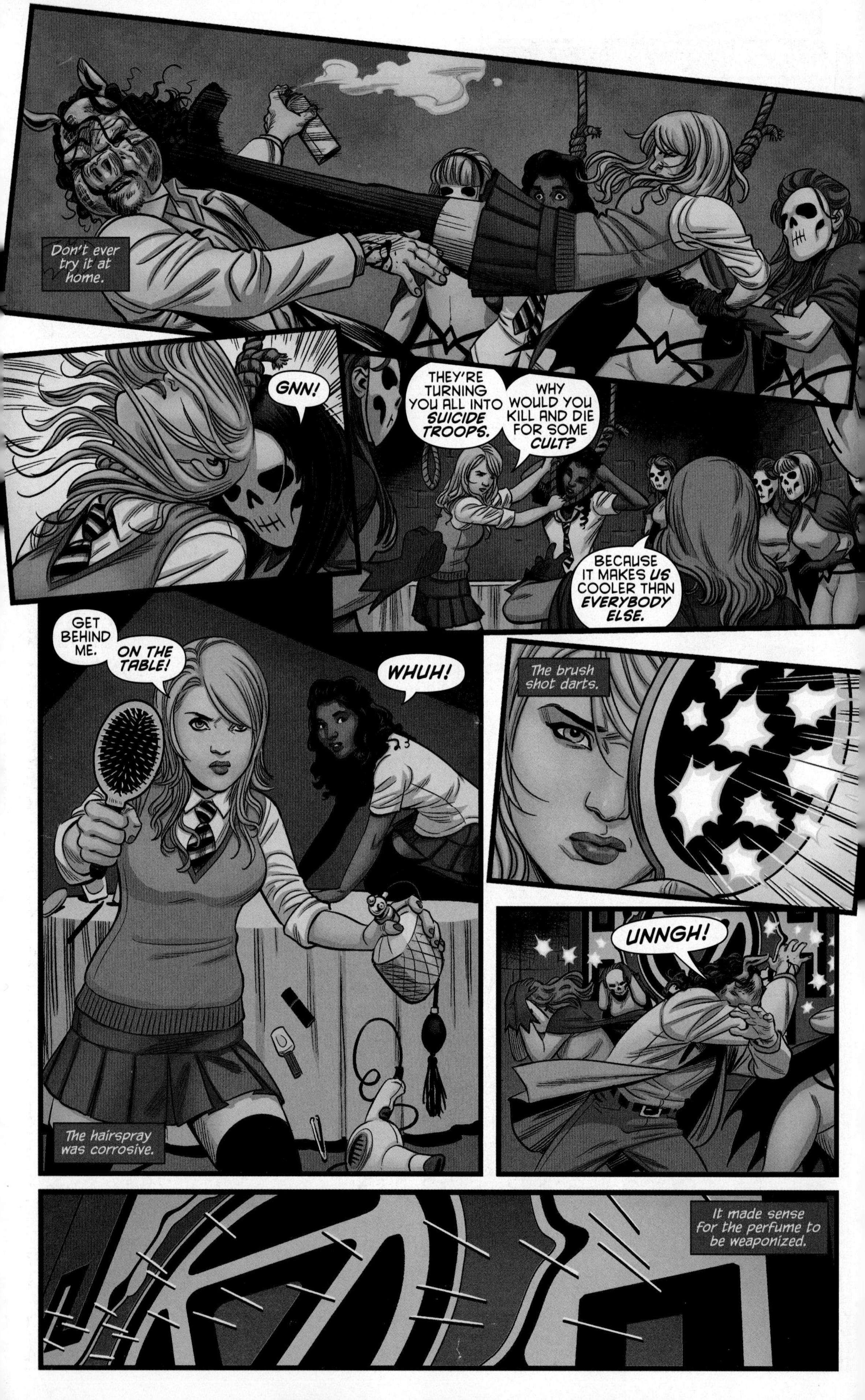
Don't ever try it at home.
GNN!
THEY'RE TURNING YOU ALL INTO SUICIDE TROOPS.
WHY WOULD YOU KILL AND DIE FOR SOME CULT?
BECAUSE IT MAKES US COOLER THAN EVERYBODY ELSE.
GET BEHIND ME.
ON THE TABLE!
WHUH!
The hairspray was corrosive.
The brush shot darts.
UNNGH!
It made sense for the perfume to be weaponized.

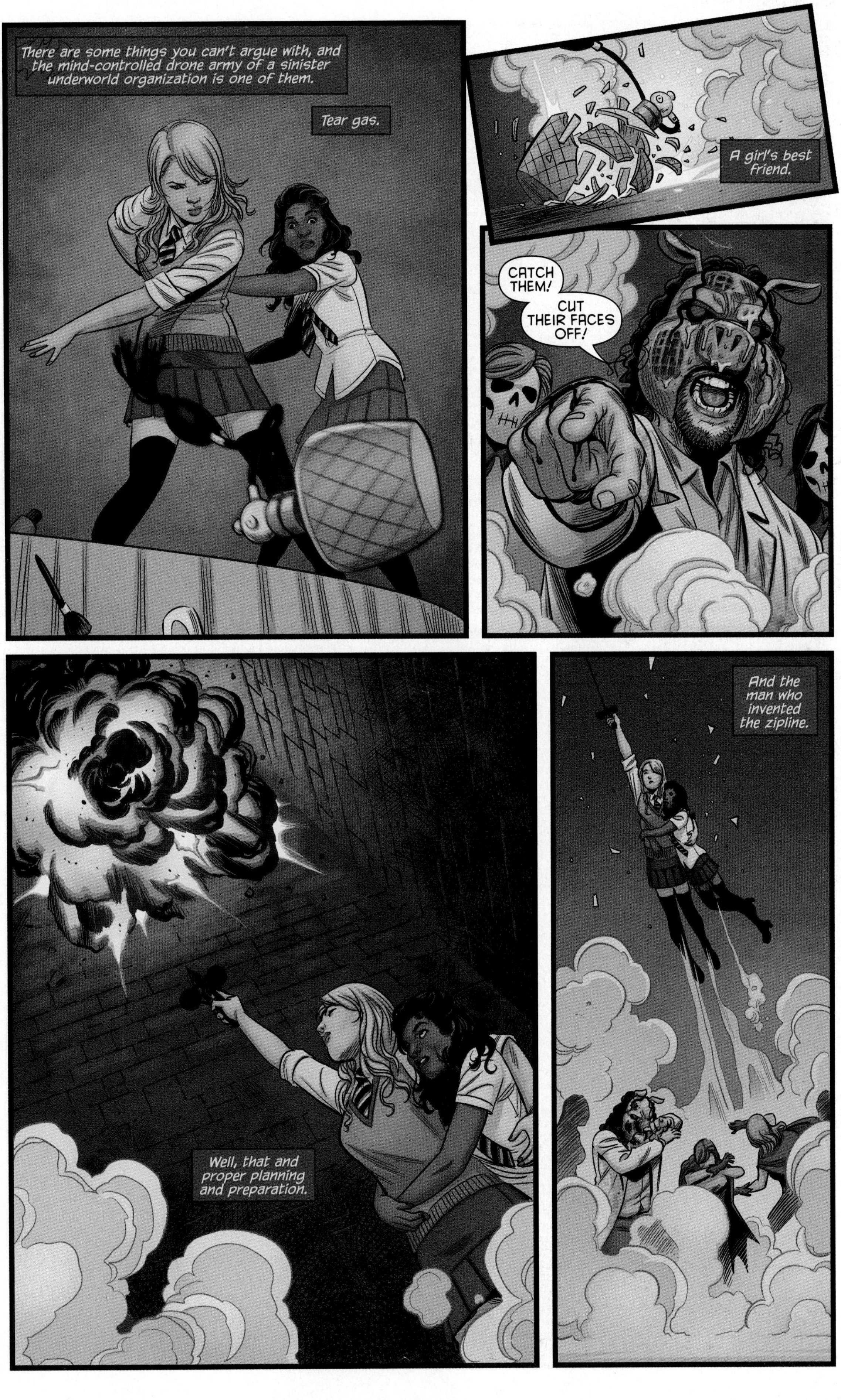
There are some things you can't argue with, and the mind-controlled drone army of a sinister underworld organization is one of them.
Tear gas.
A girl's best friend.
CATCH THEM!
CUT THEIR FACES OFF!
Well, that and proper planning and preparation.
And the man who invented the zipline.

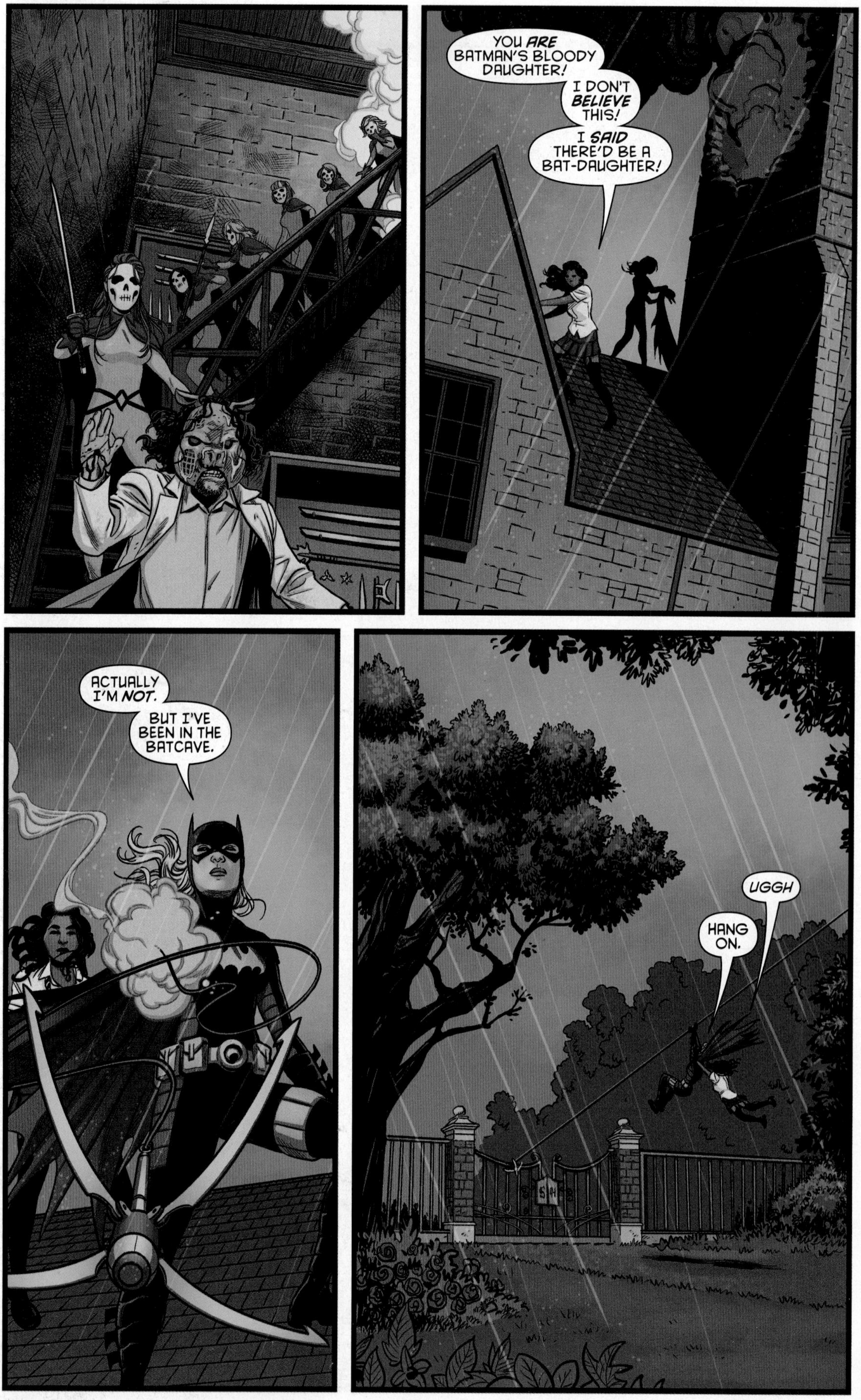
YOU **ARE** BATMAN'S BLOODY DAUGHTER!
I DON'T **BELIEVE** THIS!
I **SAID** THERE'D BE A BAT-DAUGHTER!
ACTUALLY I'M **NOT**.
BUT I'VE BEEN IN THE BATCAVE.
UGGH
HANG ON.

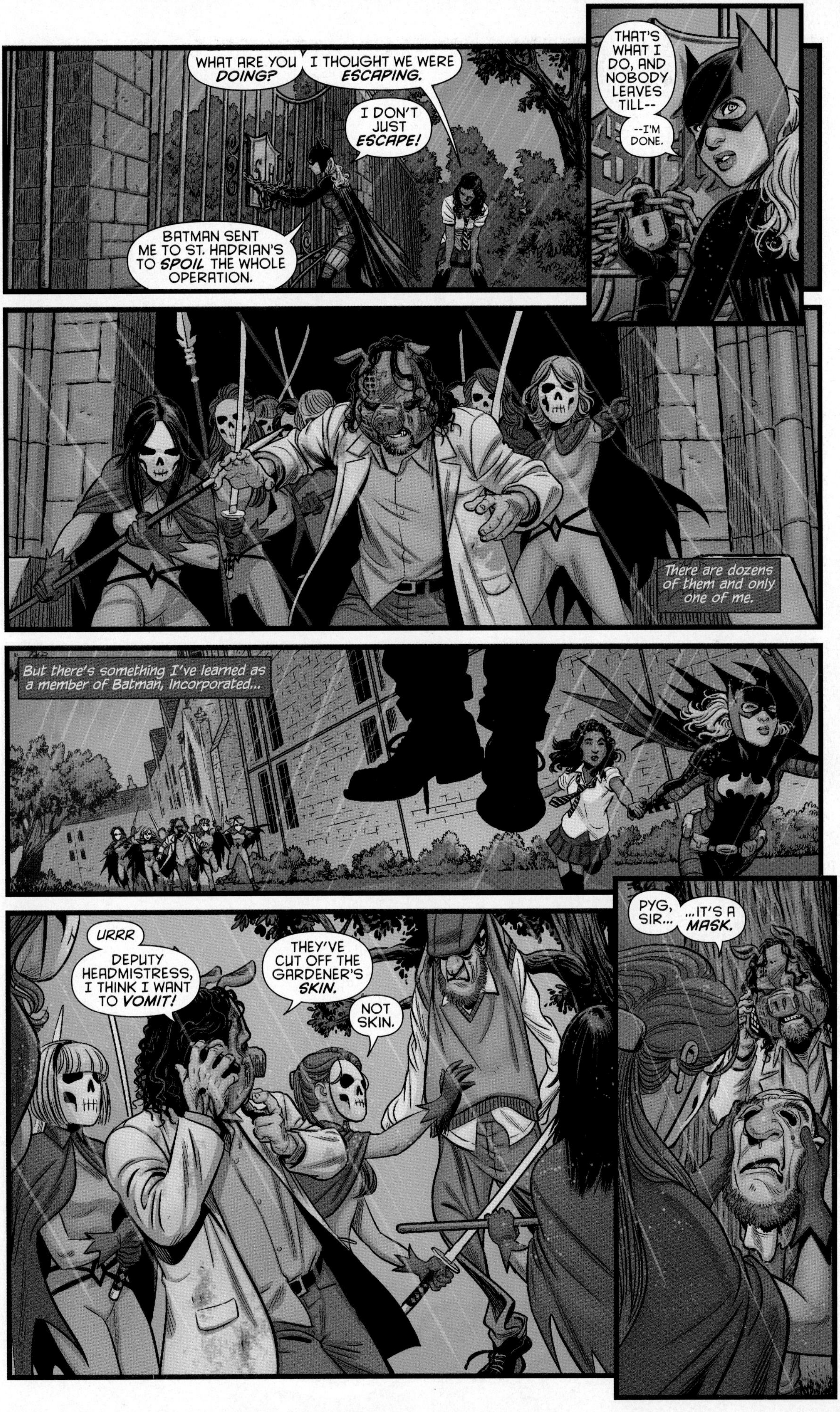

WHAT ARE YOU DOING?
I THOUGHT WE WERE ESCAPING.
I DON'T JUST ESCAPE!
BATMAN SENT ME TO ST. HADRIAN'S TO SPOIL THE WHOLE OPERATION.
THAT'S WHAT I DO, AND NOBODY LEAVES TILL--
--I'M DONE.
There are dozens of them and only one of me.
But there's something I've learned as a member of Batman, Incorporated...
URRR
DEPUTY HEADMISTRESS, I THINK I WANT TO VOMIT!
THEY'VE CUT OFF THE GARDENER'S SKIN.
NOT SKIN.
PYG, SIR...
...IT'S A MASK.

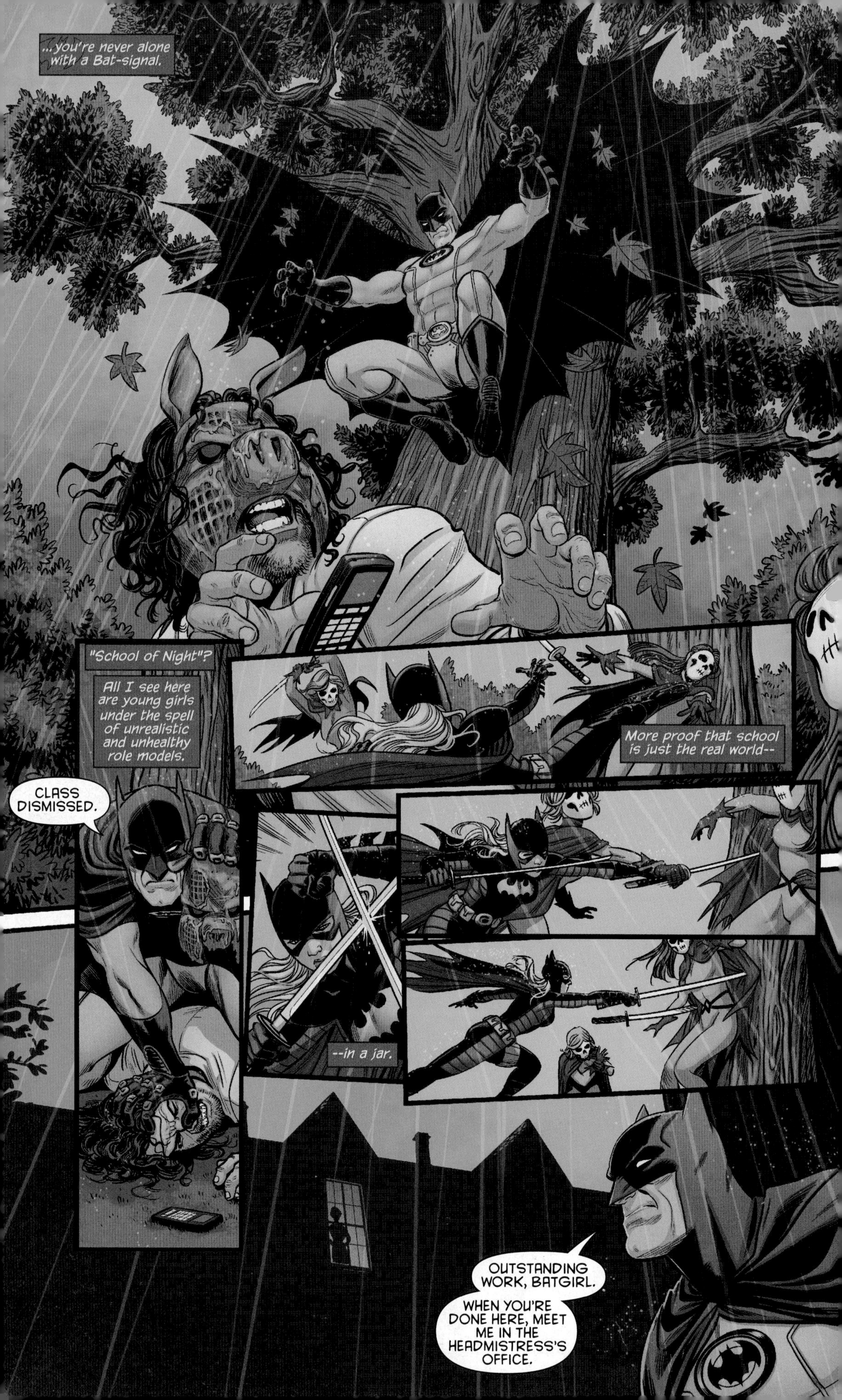

...you're never alone with a Bat-signal.
"School of Night"?
All I see here are young girls under the spell of unrealistic and unhealthy role models.
CLASS DISMISSED.
More proof that school is just the real world--
--in a jar.
OUTSTANDING WORK, BATGIRL.
WHEN YOU'RE DONE HERE, MEET ME IN THE HEADMISTRESS'S OFFICE.

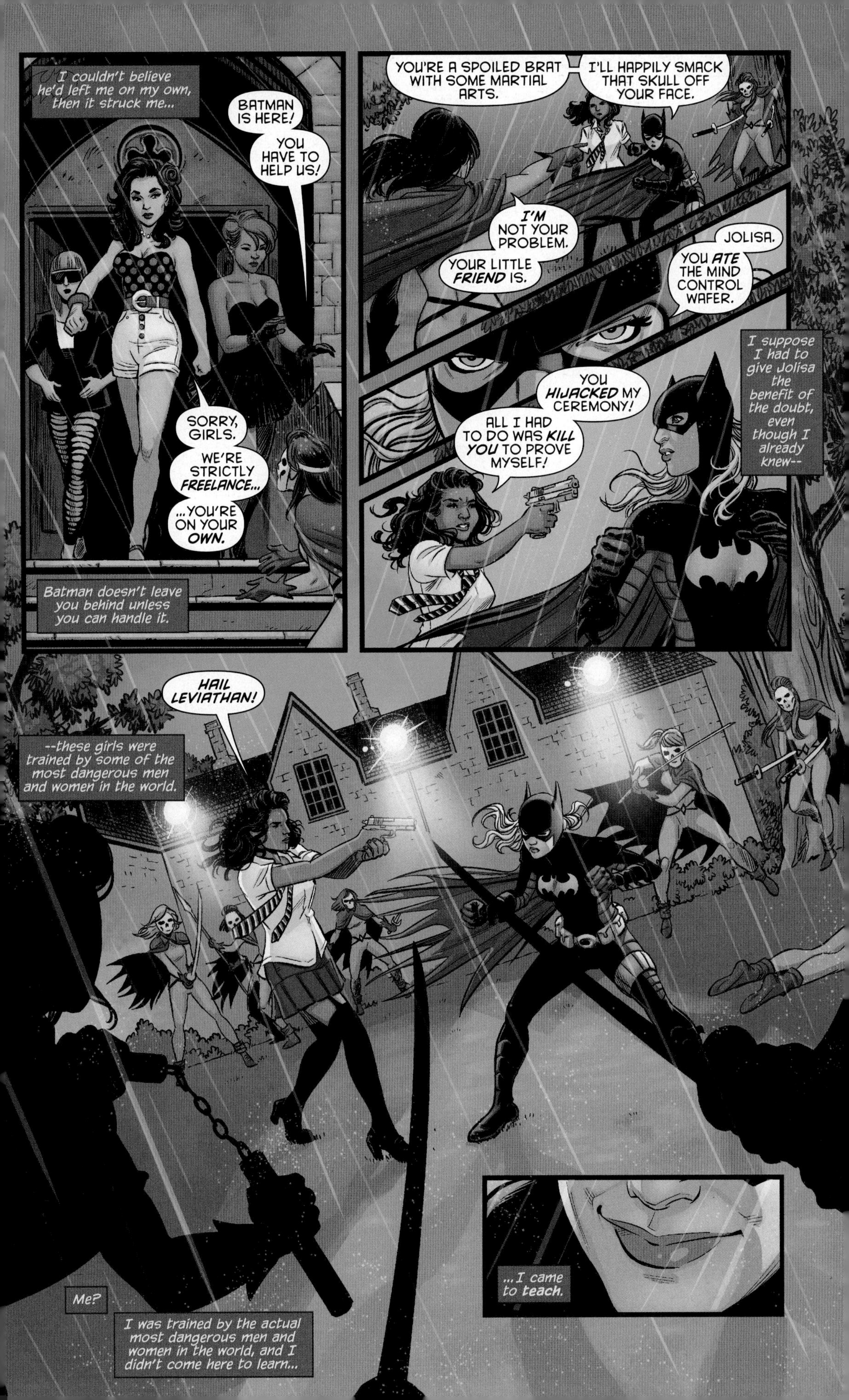

I couldn't believe he'd left me on my own, then it struck me...
BATMAN IS HERE!
YOU HAVE TO HELP US!
SORRY, GIRLS.
WE'RE STRICTLY FREELANCE...
...YOU'RE ON YOUR OWN.
Batman doesn't leave you behind unless you can handle it.
YOU'RE A SPOILED BRAT WITH SOME MARTIAL ARTS.
I'LL HAPPILY SMACK THAT SKULL OFF YOUR FACE.
I'M NOT YOUR PROBLEM.
YOUR LITTLE FRIEND IS.
JOLISA.
YOU ATE THE MIND CONTROL WAFER.
I suppose I had to give Jolisa the benefit of the doubt, even though I already knew--
YOU HIJACKED MY CEREMONY!
ALL I HAD TO DO WAS KILL YOU TO PROVE MYSELF!
HAIL LEVIATHAN!
--these girls were trained by some of the most dangerous men and women in the world.
Me?
I was trained by the actual most dangerous men and women in the world, and I didn't come here to learn...
...I came to teach.

YOU TRAIN AND SUPPLY *SPY GIRLS* FOR INTERNATIONAL CLIENTELE.

YOU SECURED YOUR *BIGGEST* EVER CONTRACT--STREAMING YOUR BEST AND BRIGHTEST GIRLS INTO A *SECRET ORGANIZATION.*

I ALREADY HAVE EVERYTHING I NEED TO KNOW ABOUT YOU *AND* THE SCHOOL RIGHT HERE.

BUT YOU DON'T HAVE *HER,* DO YOU?

THE HEADMISTRESS.

YOU NEVER *DID* AND NEVER WILL.

HEADMISTRESS?

I *KNOW* WHO RUNS THIS PLACE NOW.

YOU SOLD OUT YOUR GIRLS TO A *MIND CONTROL* CULT.

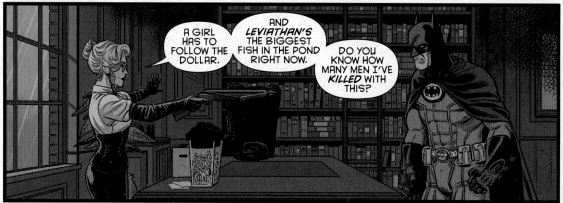

A GIRL HAS TO FOLLOW THE DOLLAR.

AND *LEVIATHAN'S* THE BIGGEST FISH IN THE POND RIGHT NOW.

DO YOU KNOW HOW MANY MEN I'VE *KILLED* WITH THIS?

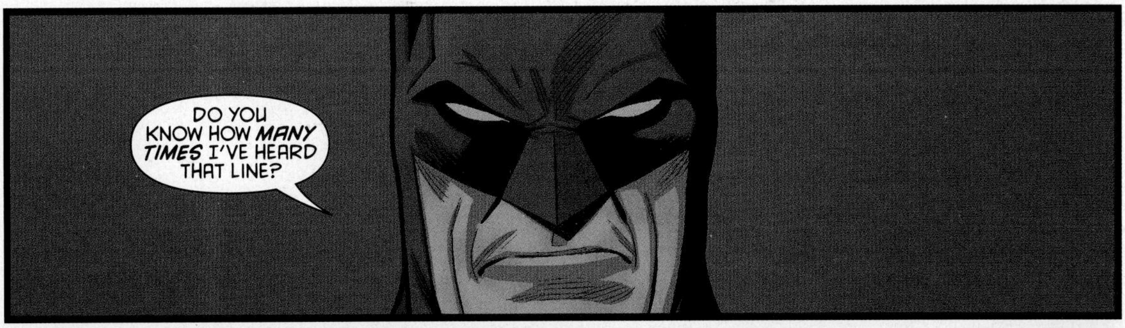
DO YOU KNOW HOW *MANY TIMES* I'VE HEARD THAT LINE?

WHAT IS LEVIATHAN?

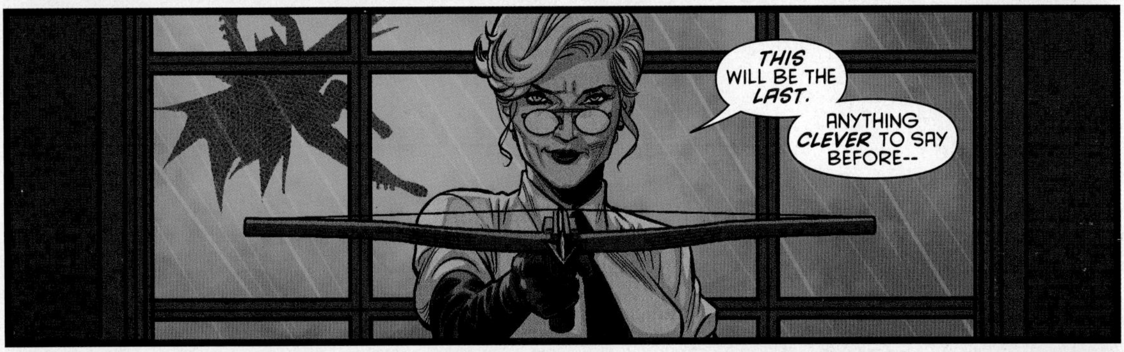
THIS WILL BE THE *LAST.*
ANYTHING *CLEVER* TO SAY BEFORE--

WHO IS LEVIATHAN?

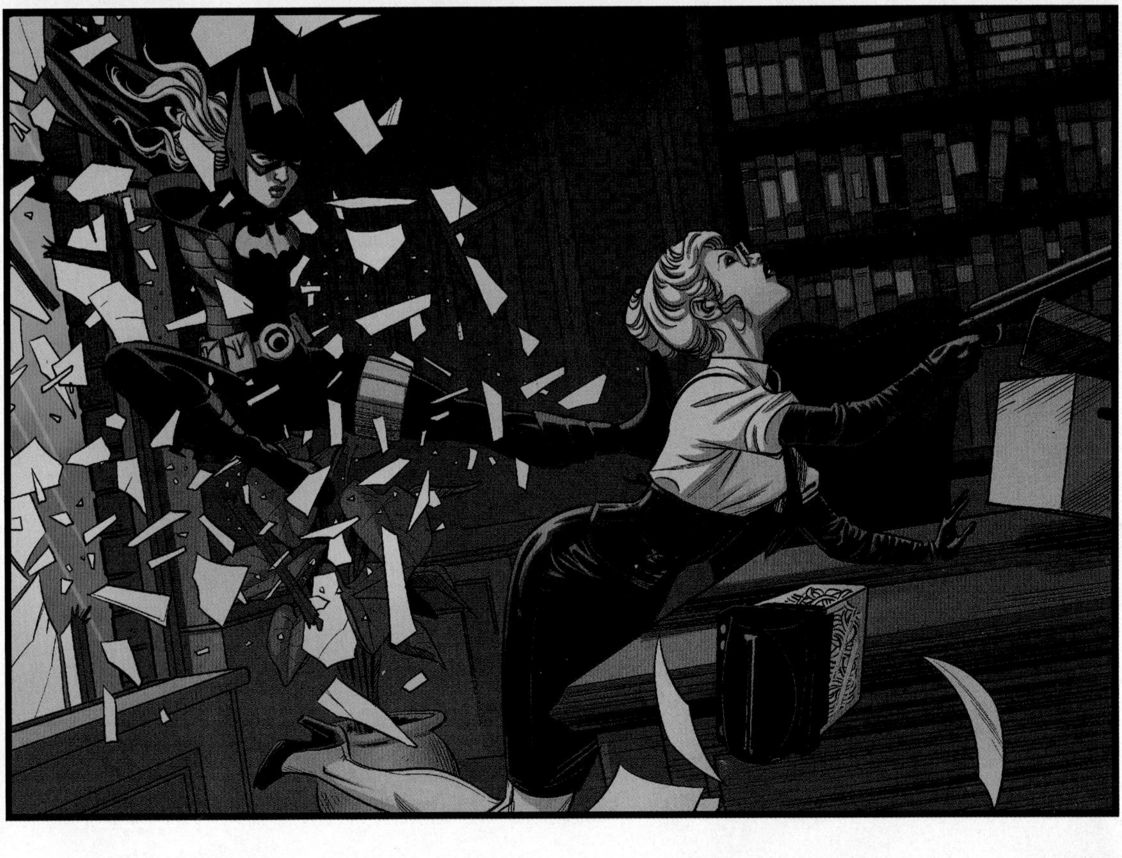

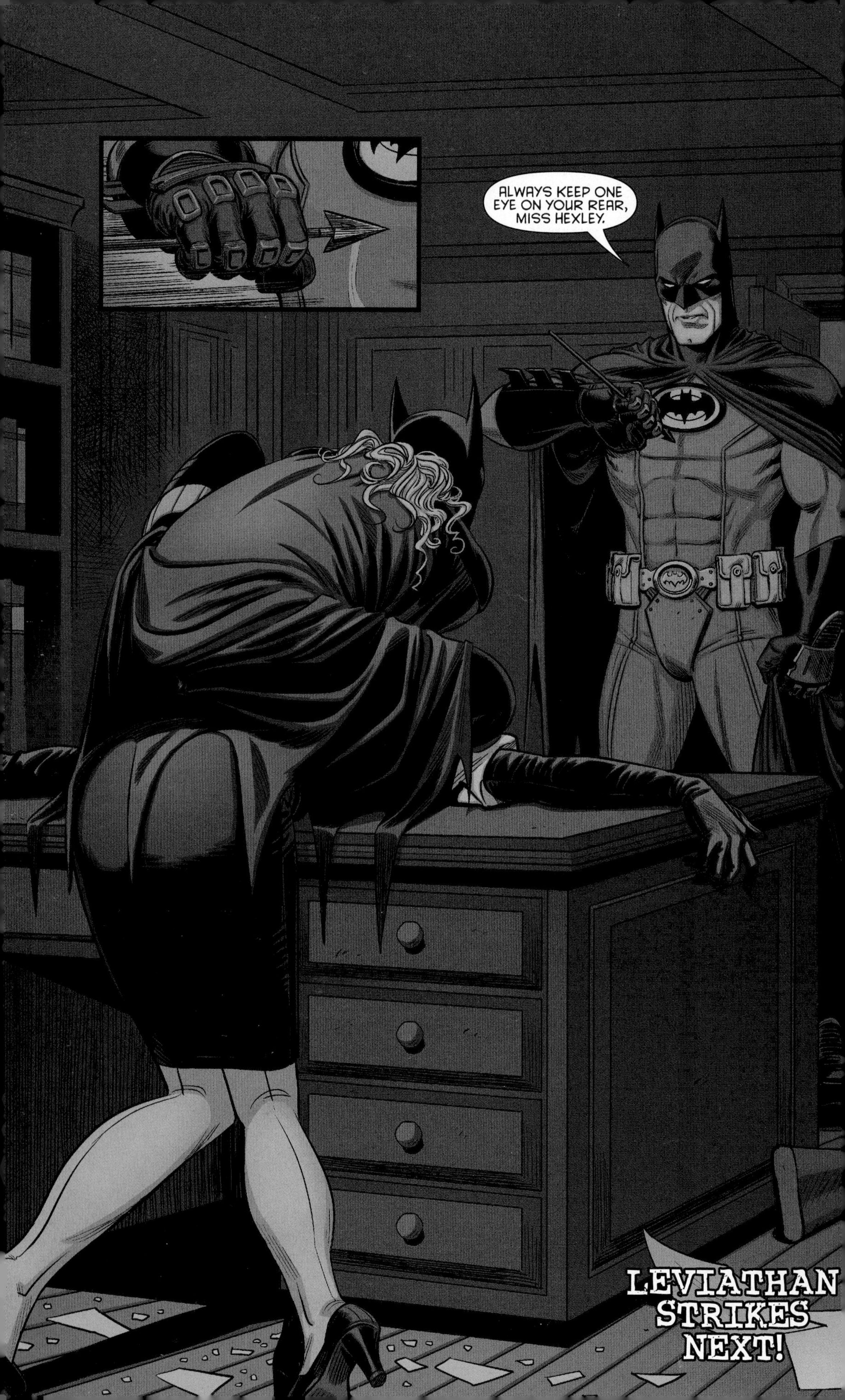
ALWAYS KEEP ONE EYE ON YOUR REAR, MISS HEXLEY.
LEVIATHAN STRIKES NEXT!

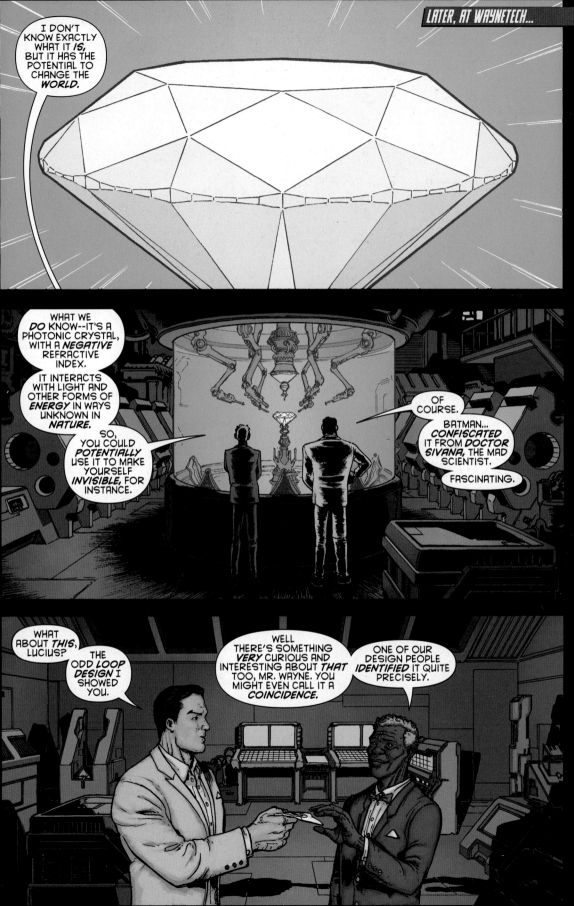

I DON'T KNOW EXACTLY WHAT IT *IS,* BUT IT HAS THE POTENTIAL TO CHANGE THE *WORLD.*

WHAT WE *DO* KNOW--IT'S A PHOTONIC CRYSTAL, WITH A *NEGATIVE* REFRACTIVE INDEX.

IT INTERACTS WITH LIGHT AND OTHER FORMS OF *ENERGY* IN WAYS UNKNOWN IN *NATURE.*

SO, YOU COULD *POTENTIALLY* USE IT TO MAKE YOURSELF *INVISIBLE,* FOR INSTANCE.

OF COURSE.

BATMAN... *CONFISCATED* IT FROM *DOCTOR SIVANA,* THE MAD SCIENTIST.

FASCINATING.

WHAT ABOUT *THIS,* LUCIUS?

THE ODD *LOOP DESIGN* I SHOWED YOU.

WELL THERE'S SOMETHING *VERY* CURIOUS AND INTERESTING ABOUT *THAT* TOO, MR. WAYNE. YOU MIGHT EVEN CALL IT A *COINCIDENCE.*

ONE OF OUR DESIGN PEOPLE *IDENTIFIED* IT QUITE PRECISELY.

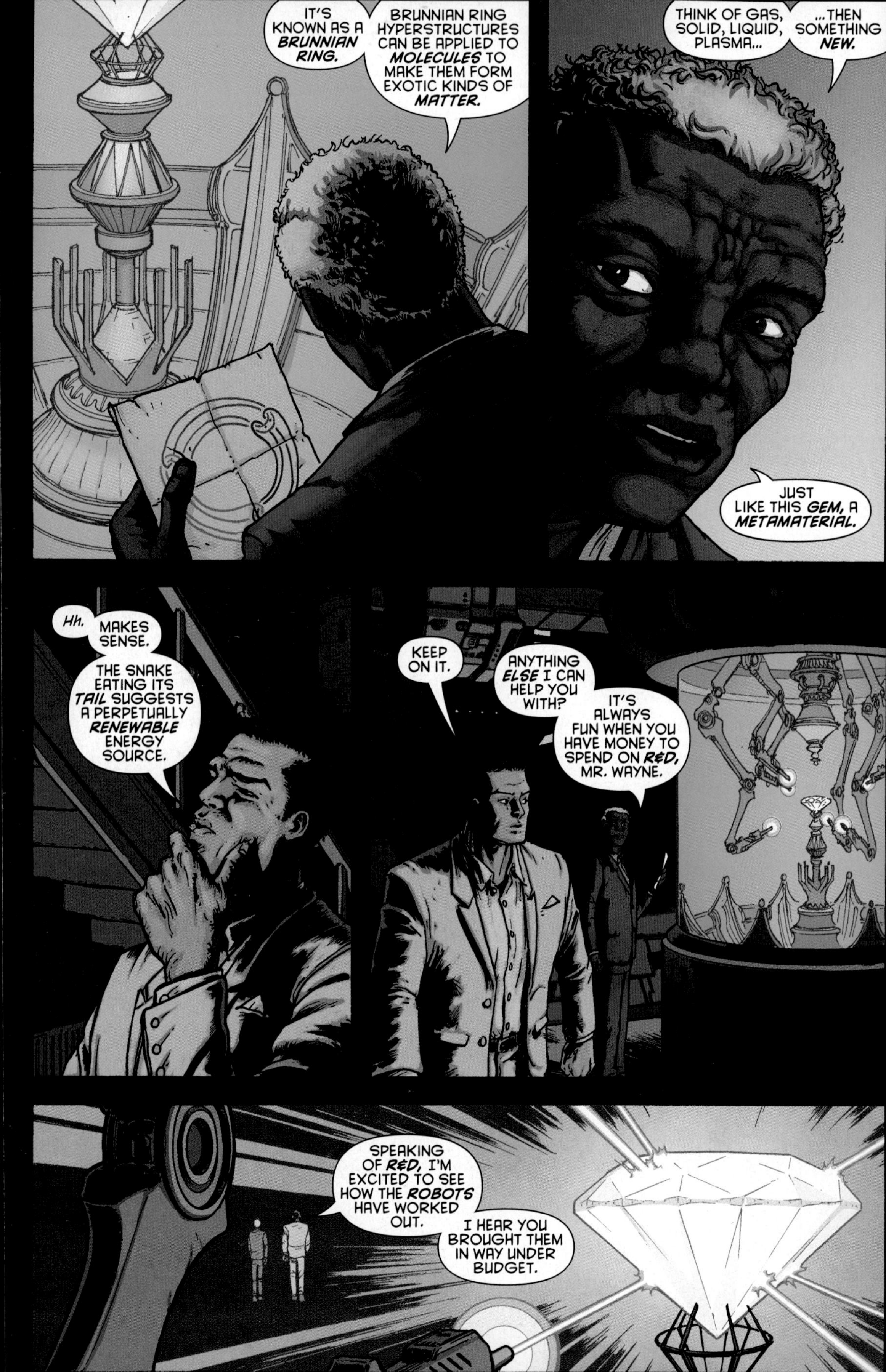
IT'S KNOWN AS A *BRUNNIAN RING.*
BRUNNIAN RING HYPERSTRUCTURES CAN BE APPLIED TO *MOLECULES* TO MAKE THEM FORM EXOTIC KINDS OF *MATTER.*
THINK OF GAS, SOLID, LIQUID, PLASMA...
...THEN SOMETHING *NEW.*
JUST LIKE THIS *GEM,* A *METAMATERIAL.*
Hh. MAKES SENSE.
THE SNAKE EATING ITS *TAIL* SUGGESTS A PERPETUALLY *RENEWABLE* ENERGY SOURCE.
KEEP ON IT.
ANYTHING *ELSE* I CAN HELP YOU WITH?
IT'S ALWAYS FUN WHEN YOU HAVE MONEY TO SPEND ON *R&D,* MR. WAYNE.
SPEAKING OF *R&D,* I'M EXCITED TO SEE HOW THE *ROBOTS* HAVE WORKED OUT.
I HEAR YOU BROUGHT THEM IN WAY UNDER BUDGET.

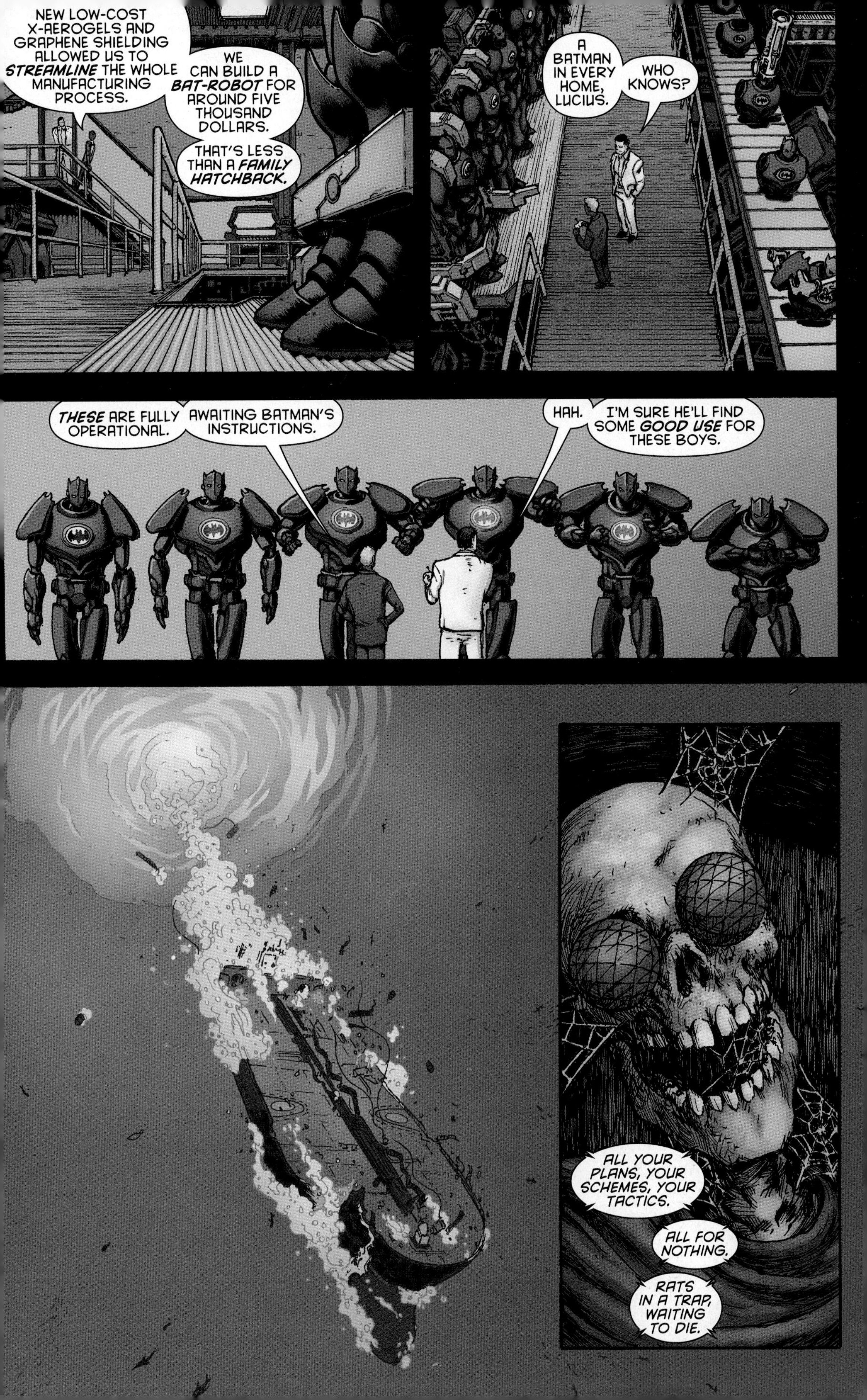
NEW LOW-COST X-AEROGELS AND GRAPHENE SHIELDING ALLOWED US TO STREAMLINE THE WHOLE MANUFACTURING PROCESS.
WE CAN BUILD A BAT-ROBOT FOR AROUND FIVE THOUSAND DOLLARS.
THAT'S LESS THAN A FAMILY HATCHBACK.
A BATMAN IN EVERY HOME, LUCIUS.
WHO KNOWS?
THESE ARE FULLY OPERATIONAL.
AWAITING BATMAN'S INSTRUCTIONS.
HAH.
I'M SURE HE'LL FIND SOME GOOD USE FOR THESE BOYS.
ALL YOUR PLANS, YOUR SCHEMES, YOUR TACTICS.
ALL FOR NOTHING.
RATS IN A TRAP, WAITING TO DIE.

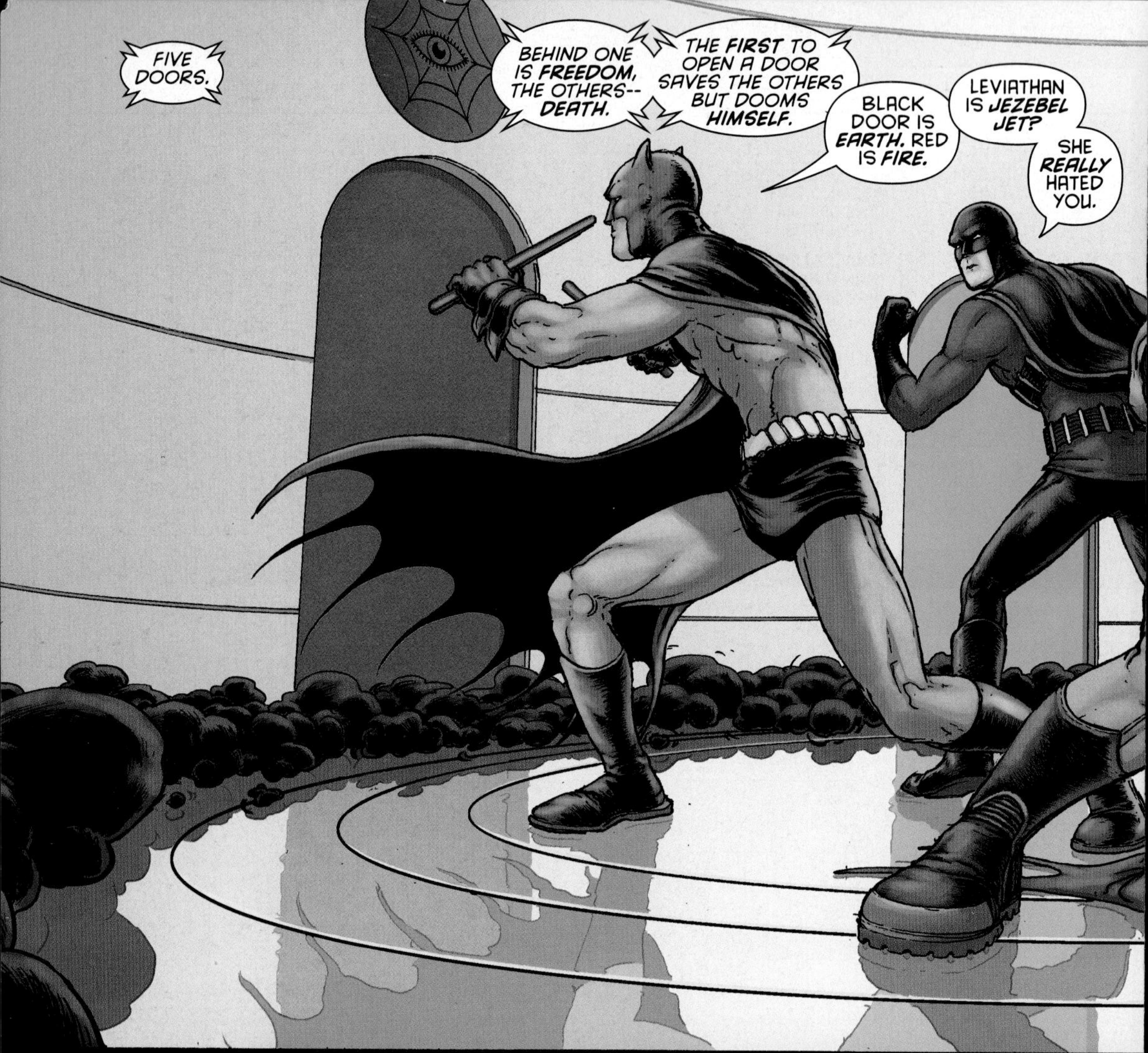
FIVE DOORS.
BEHIND ONE IS FREEDOM, THE OTHERS--DEATH.
THE FIRST TO OPEN A DOOR SAVES THE OTHERS BUT DOOMS HIMSELF.
BLACK DOOR IS EARTH. RED IS FIRE.
LEVIATHAN IS JEZEBEL JET?
SHE REALLY HATED YOU.

BATMAN, INCORPORATED: LEVIATHAN STRIKES!
Chapter 2

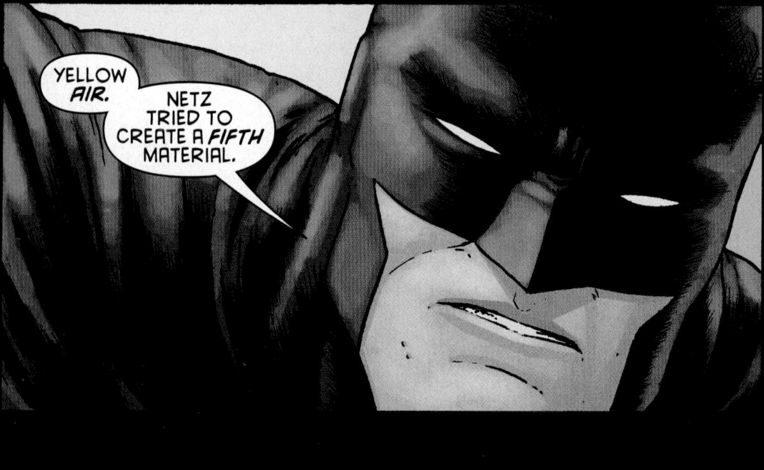
YELLOW AIR.
NETZ TRIED TO CREATE A FIFTH MATERIAL.

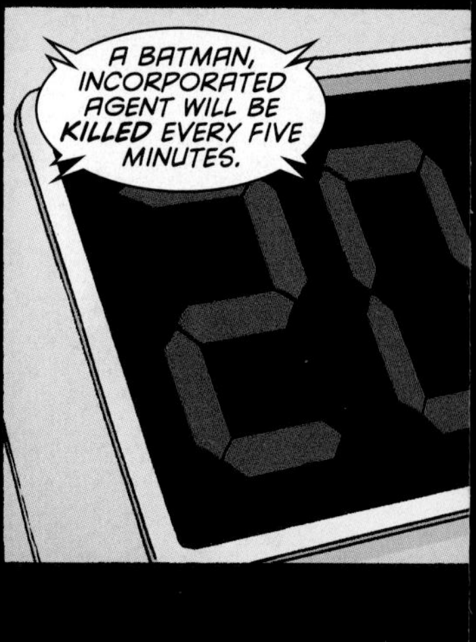
A BATMAN, INCORPORATED AGENT WILL BE KILLED EVERY FIVE MINUTES.

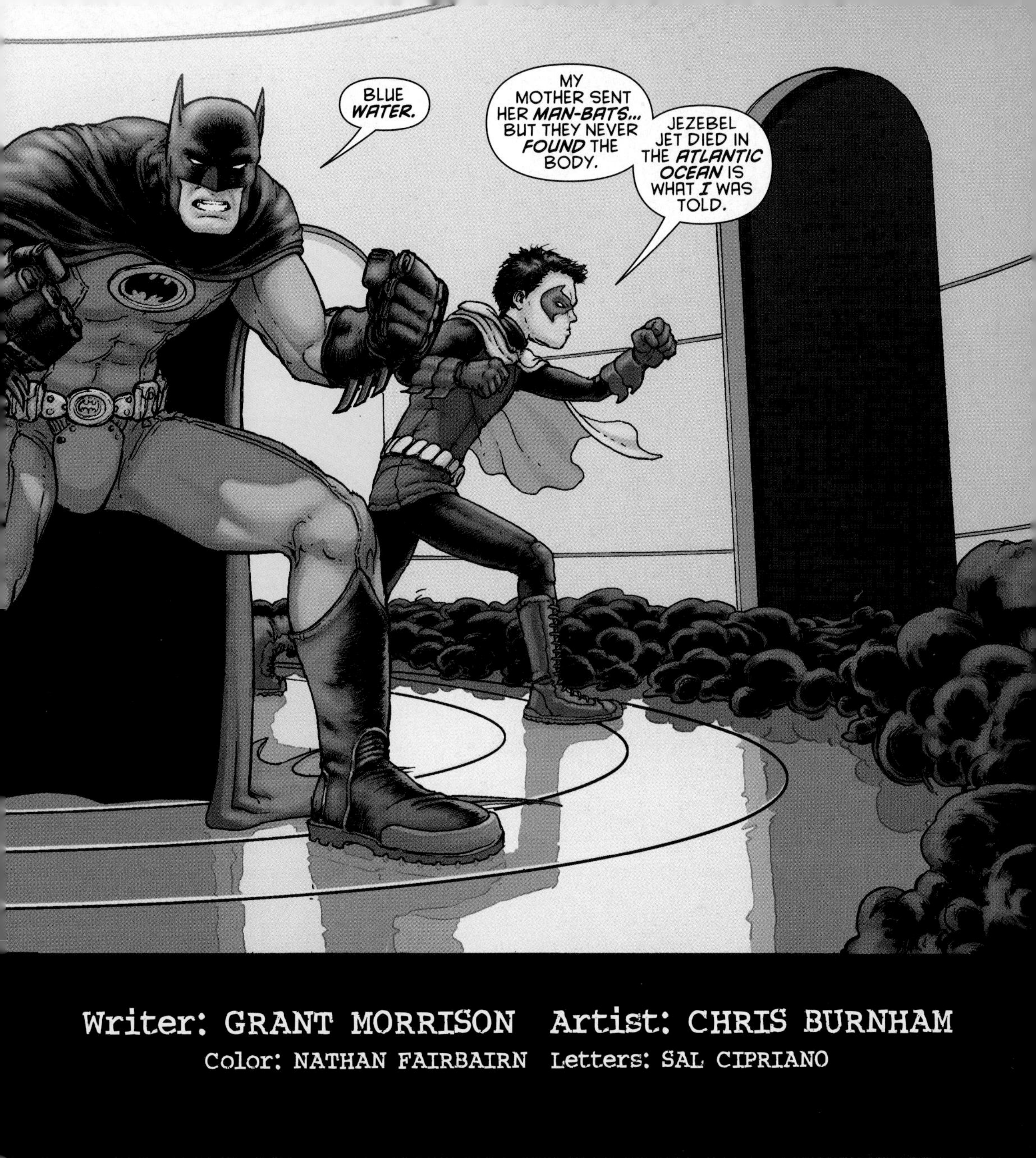
BLUE WATER.
MY MOTHER SENT HER MAN-BATS... BUT THEY NEVER FOUND THE BODY.
JEZEBEL JET DIED IN THE ATLANTIC OCEAN IS WHAT I WAS TOLD.

Writer: GRANT MORRISON Artist: CHRIS BURNHAM

Color: NATHAN FAIRBAIRN Letters: SAL CIPRIANO

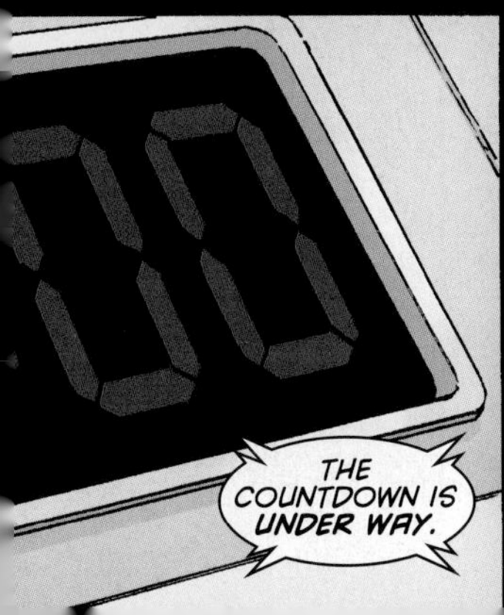
THE COUNTDOWN IS UNDER WAY.

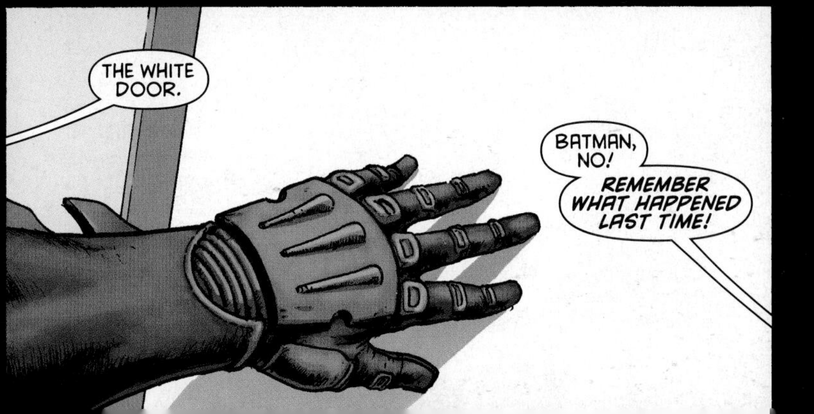
THE WHITE DOOR.
BATMAN, NO! REMEMBER WHAT HAPPENED LAST TIME!

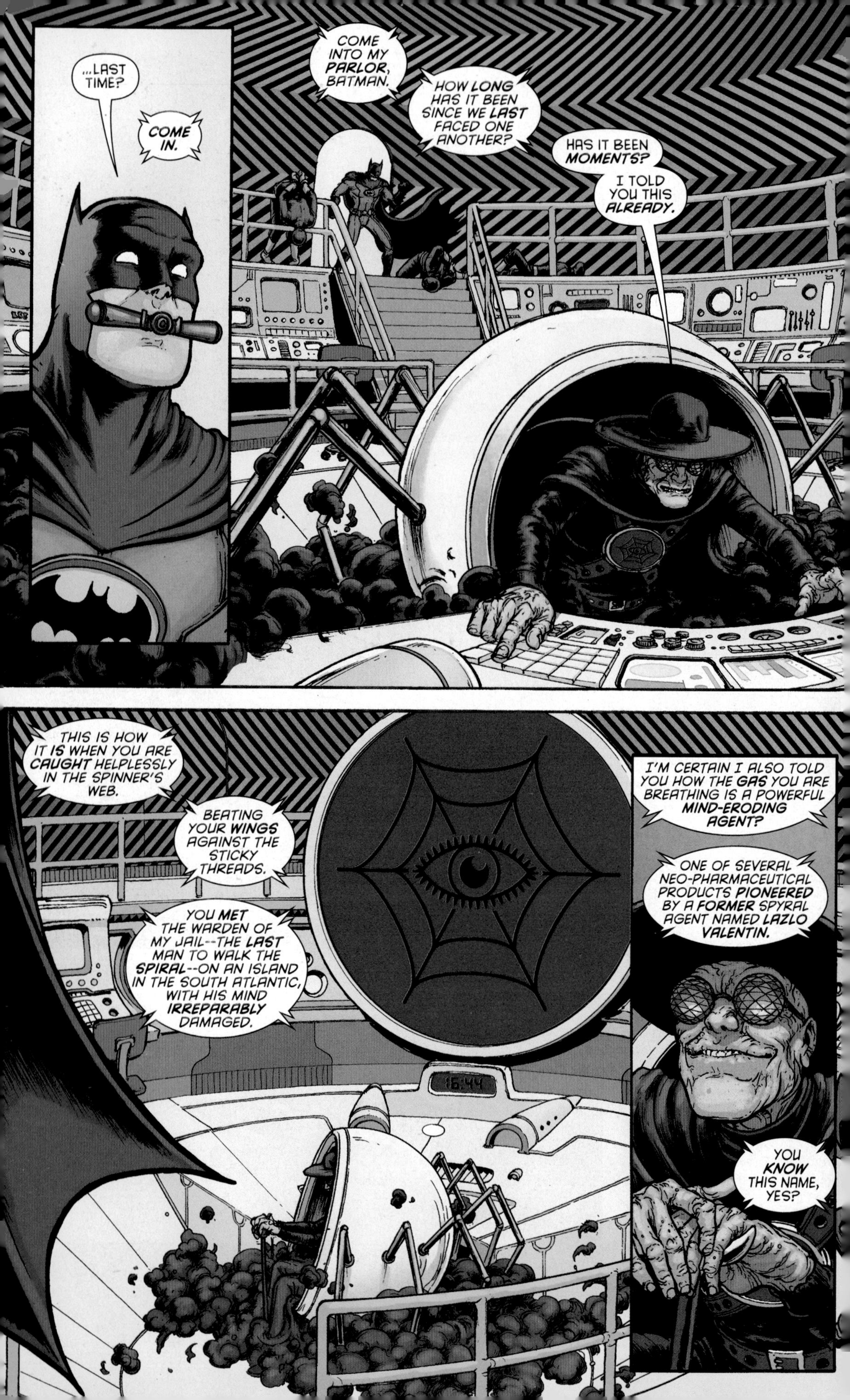
...LAST TIME?
COME IN.
COME INTO MY PARLOR, BATMAN.
HOW LONG HAS IT BEEN SINCE WE LAST FACED ONE ANOTHER?
HAS IT BEEN MOMENTS?
I TOLD YOU THIS ALREADY.
THIS IS HOW IT IS WHEN YOU ARE CAUGHT HELPLESSLY IN THE SPINNER'S WEB.
BEATING YOUR WINGS AGAINST THE STICKY THREADS.
YOU MET THE WARDEN OF MY JAIL--THE LAST MAN TO WALK THE SPIRAL--ON AN ISLAND IN THE SOUTH ATLANTIC, WITH HIS MIND IRREPARABLY DAMAGED.
I'M CERTAIN I ALSO TOLD YOU HOW THE GAS YOU ARE BREATHING IS A POWERFUL MIND-ERODING AGENT?
ONE OF SEVERAL NEO-PHARMACEUTICAL PRODUCTS PIONEERED BY A FORMER SPYRAL AGENT NAMED LAZLO VALENTIN.
YOU KNOW THIS NAME, YES?

THE LABYRINTH WAS DESIGNED TO **BREAK** EVEN THE STRONGEST ENEMY AGENT.

FOR LAZLO VALENTIN, THE ONLY EXIT WAS VIA VIOLENT **PARANOID SCHIZOPHRENIA**, DRUG ABUSE AND **D.I.Y.** SURGERY...

...LAZLO BECAME **PROFESSOR PYG**.

LIKE HIM, YOU BURROW BLINDLY INTO THE **BELLY** OF THE **BEAST**.

ALONE IN THE SPYRAL SINK OF THE **LABYRINTH** OF DEDALUS...

...EVEN IF YOU SURVIVE, YOUR MIND WILL BE FLATTENED, DEFORMED, RUINED BEYOND REPAIR.

WHAT **HAPPENS** TO A MIND WHEN THERE IS **NO** WAY OUT?

WHEN IT KNOWS THERE IS **NO SAFE PLACE** TO RUN AND NEVER WILL BE AGAIN?

SOON **YOU** WILL SEE WHAT **LAZLO VALENTIN** SAW.

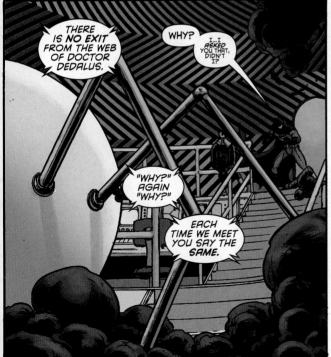

THERE IS **NO EXIT** FROM THE WEB OF DOCTOR DEDALUS.

WHY?

I...I **ASKED** YOU THAT, DIDN'T I?

"WHY?" AGAIN "WHY?"

EACH TIME WE MEET YOU SAY THE **SAME**.

THE **REBREATHER** I'M SURE YOU'LL BE WEARING RAN OUT OF ITS OXYGEN SUPPLY SOME TIME AGO.

THE GAS YOU ARE BREATHING CONTAINS A **MIND-ERODING** FORMULA THAT MIMICS SOME OF THE EFFECTS OF **ALZHEIMER'S DISEASE**.

15:05 15:04 15:03

SO **MTAMBA**. AFRICA.

YOU WERE TELLING ME HOW YOU HAD YOUR **AGENT** THERE AND SO ON...

...AND SO ON AND SO ON...

15:02 15:01 15:00

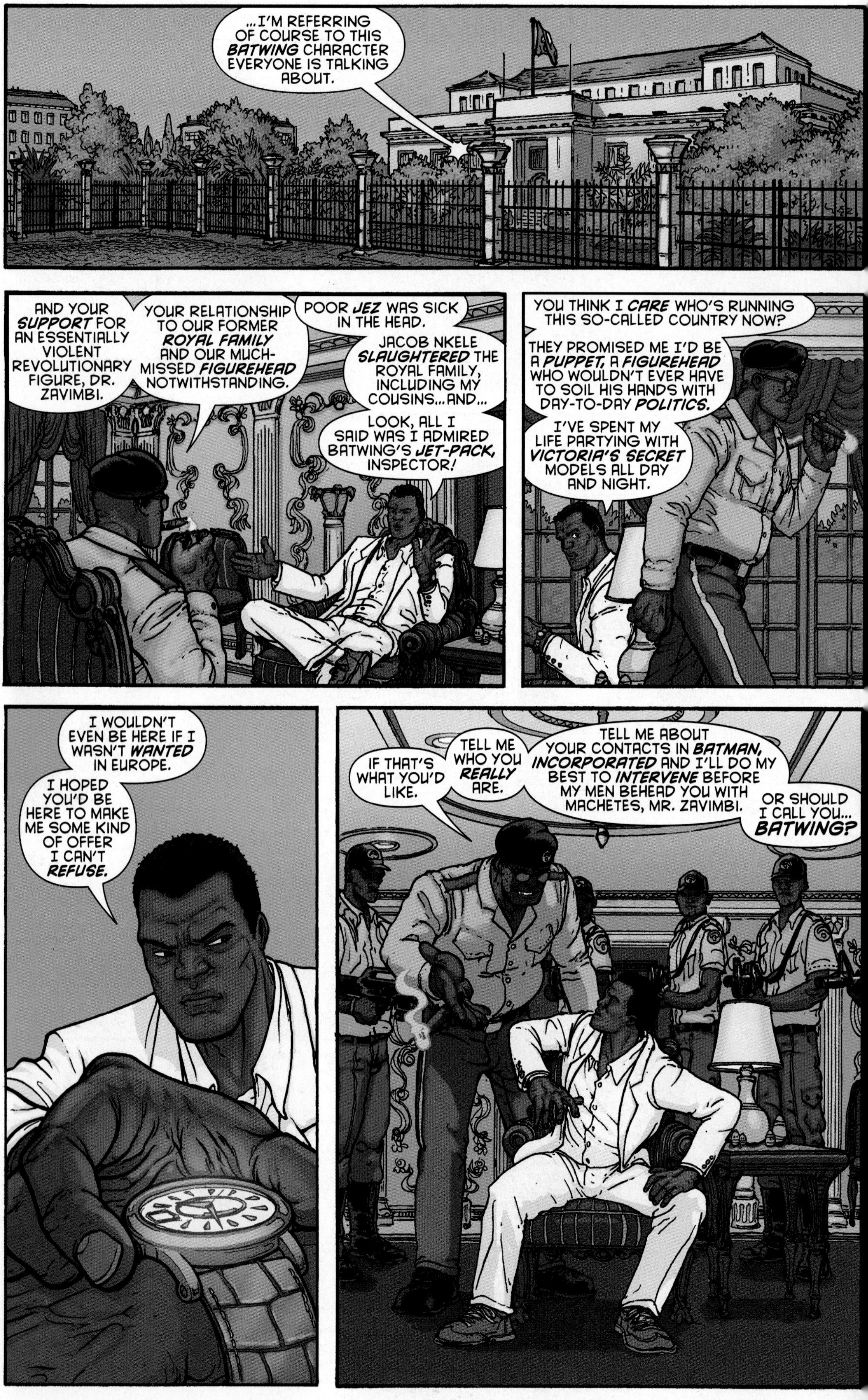
...I'M REFERRING OF COURSE TO THIS BATWING CHARACTER EVERYONE IS TALKING ABOUT.
AND YOUR SUPPORT FOR AN ESSENTIALLY VIOLENT REVOLUTIONARY FIGURE, DR. ZAVIMBI.
YOUR RELATIONSHIP TO OUR FORMER ROYAL FAMILY AND OUR MUCH-MISSED FIGUREHEAD NOTWITHSTANDING.
POOR JEZ WAS SICK IN THE HEAD.
JACOB NKELE SLAUGHTERED THE ROYAL FAMILY, INCLUDING MY COUSINS...AND...
LOOK, ALL I SAID WAS I ADMIRED BATWING'S JET-PACK, INSPECTOR!
YOU THINK I CARE WHO'S RUNNING THIS SO-CALLED COUNTRY NOW?
THEY PROMISED ME I'D BE A PUPPET, A FIGUREHEAD WHO WOULDN'T EVER HAVE TO SOIL HIS HANDS WITH DAY-TO-DAY POLITICS.
I'VE SPENT MY LIFE PARTYING WITH VICTORIA'S SECRET MODELS ALL DAY AND NIGHT.
I WOULDN'T EVEN BE HERE IF I WASN'T WANTED IN EUROPE.
I HOPED YOU'D BE HERE TO MAKE ME SOME KIND OF OFFER I CAN'T REFUSE.
IF THAT'S WHAT YOU'D LIKE.
TELL ME WHO YOU REALLY ARE.
TELL ME ABOUT YOUR CONTACTS IN BATMAN, INCORPORATED AND I'LL DO MY BEST TO INTERVENE BEFORE MY MEN BEHEAD YOU WITH MACHETES, MR. ZAVIMBI.
OR SHOULD I CALL YOU... BATWING?

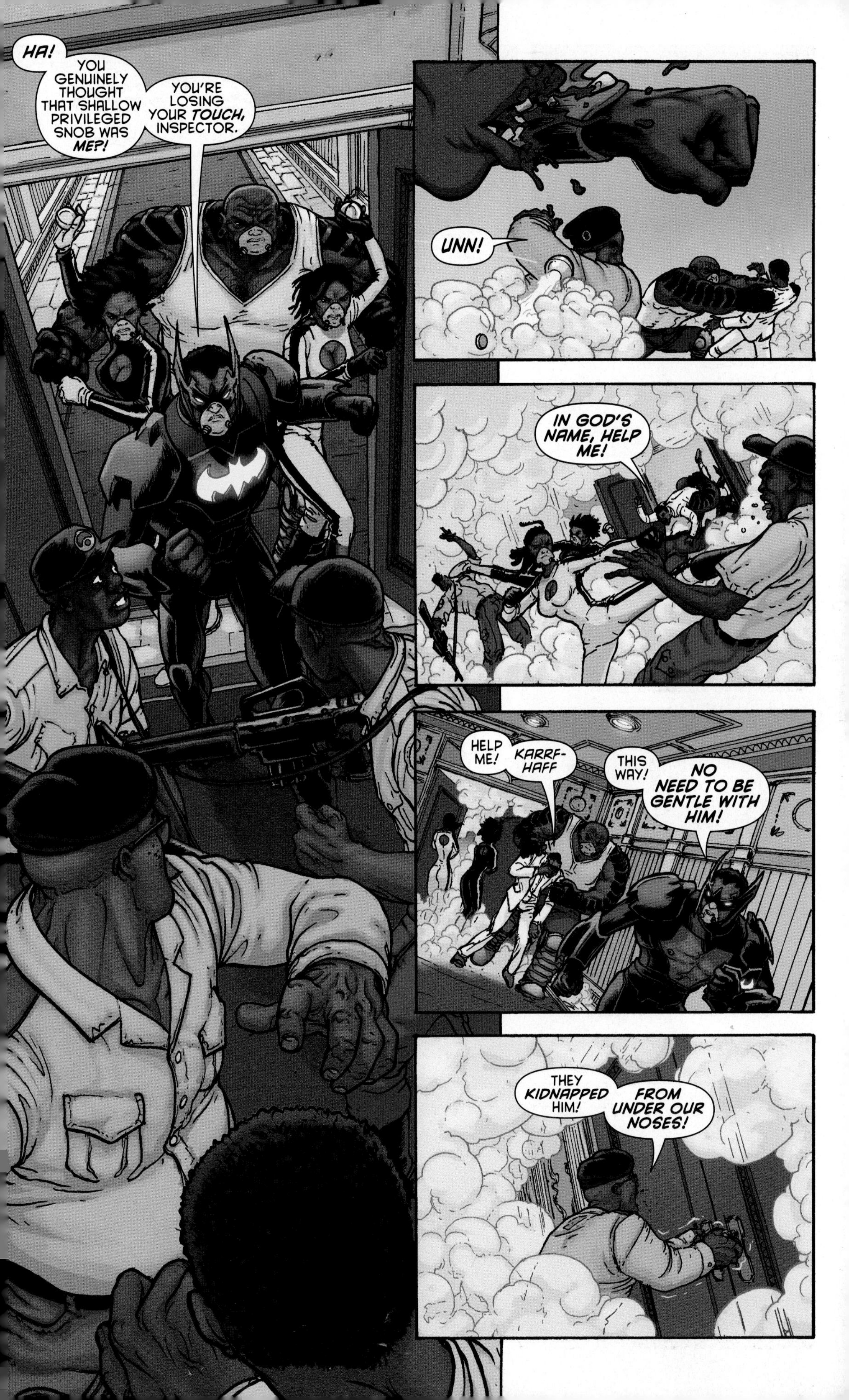
HA!
YOU GENUINELY THOUGHT THAT SHALLOW PRIVILEGED SNOB WAS ME?!
YOU'RE LOSING YOUR TOUCH, INSPECTOR.
UNN!
IN GOD'S NAME, HELP ME!
HELP ME!
KARRF-HAFF
THIS WAY!
NO NEED TO BE GENTLE WITH HIM!
THEY KIDNAPPED HIM!
FROM UNDER OUR NOSES!

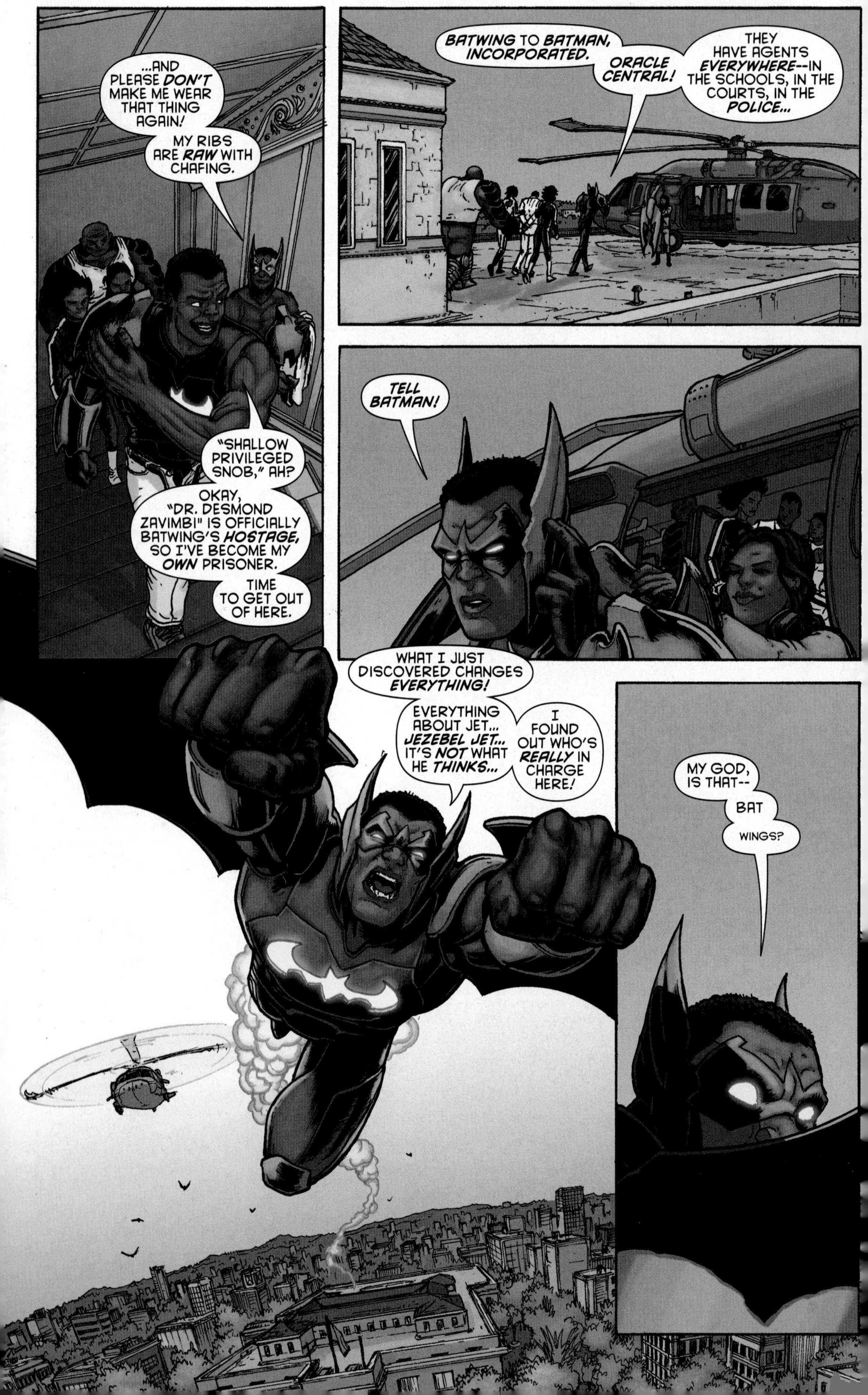
...AND PLEASE DON'T MAKE ME WEAR THAT THING AGAIN!
MY RIBS ARE RAW WITH CHAFING.
"SHALLOW PRIVILEGED SNOB," AH?
OKAY, "DR. DESMOND ZAVIMBI" IS OFFICIALLY BATWING'S HOSTAGE, SO I'VE BECOME MY OWN PRISONER.
TIME TO GET OUT OF HERE.
BATWING TO BATMAN, INCORPORATED.
ORACLE CENTRAL!
THEY HAVE AGENTS EVERYWHERE--IN THE SCHOOLS, IN THE COURTS, IN THE POLICE...
TELL BATMAN!
WHAT I JUST DISCOVERED CHANGES EVERYTHING!
EVERYTHING ABOUT JET... JEZEBEL JET... IT'S NOT WHAT HE THINKS...
I FOUND OUT WHO'S REALLY IN CHARGE HERE!
MY GOD, IS THAT--
BAT
WINGS?

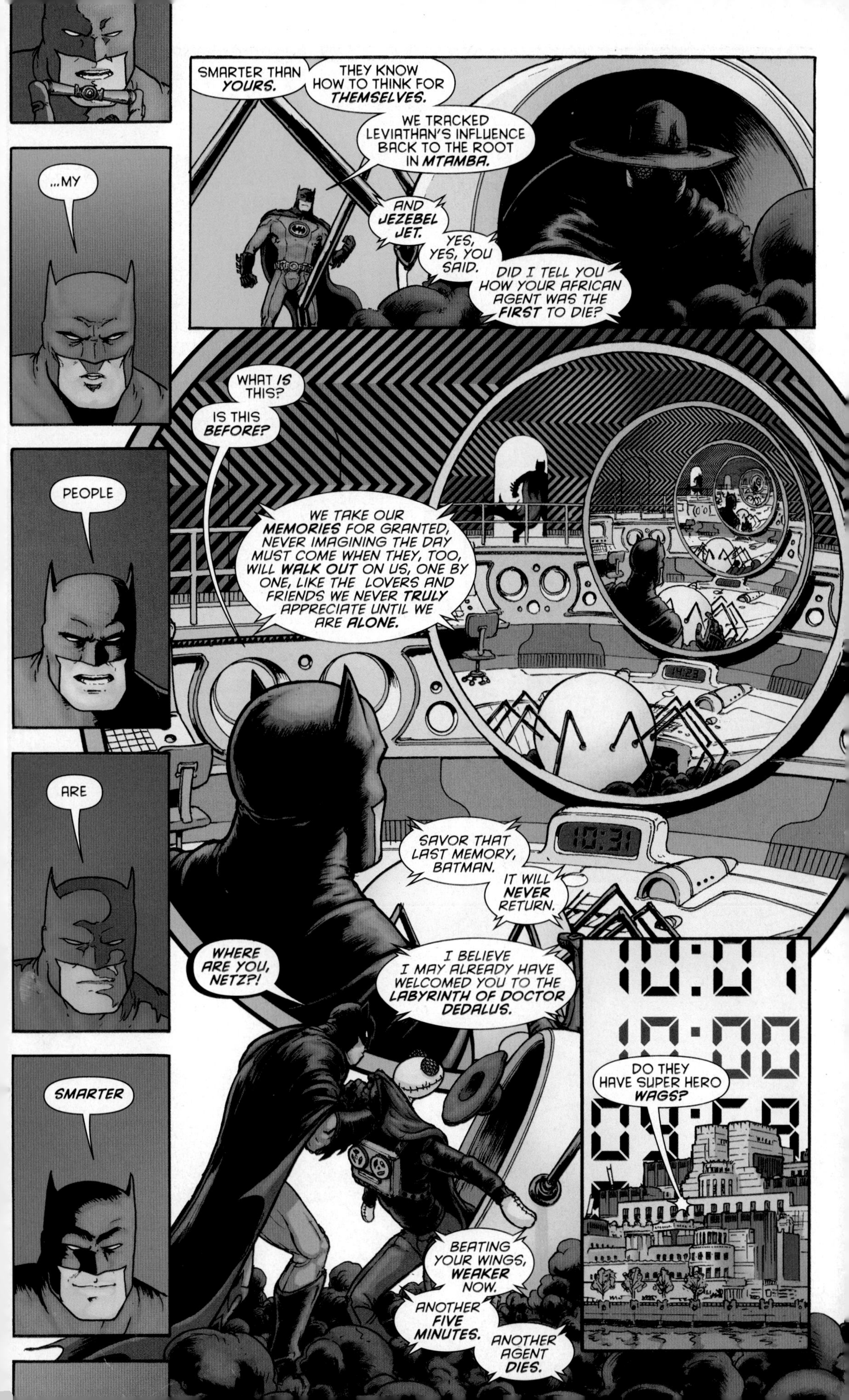
...MY
PEOPLE
ARE
SMARTER
SMARTER THAN YOURS.
THEY KNOW HOW TO THINK FOR THEMSELVES.
WE TRACKED LEVIATHAN'S INFLUENCE BACK TO THE ROOT IN MTAMBA.
AND JEZEBEL JET.
YES, YES, YOU SAID.
DID I TELL YOU HOW YOUR AFRICAN AGENT WAS THE FIRST TO DIE?
WHAT IS THIS?
IS THIS BEFORE?
WE TAKE OUR MEMORIES FOR GRANTED, NEVER IMAGINING THE DAY MUST COME WHEN THEY, TOO, WILL WALK OUT ON US, ONE BY ONE, LIKE THE LOVERS AND FRIENDS WE NEVER TRULY APPRECIATE UNTIL WE ARE ALONE.
SAVOR THAT LAST MEMORY, BATMAN.
IT WILL NEVER RETURN.
WHERE ARE YOU, NETZ?!
I BELIEVE I MAY ALREADY HAVE WELCOMED YOU TO THE LABYRINTH OF DOCTOR DEDALUS.
DO THEY HAVE SUPER HERO WAGS?
BEATING YOUR WINGS, WEAKER NOW.
ANOTHER FIVE MINUTES.
ANOTHER AGENT DIES.

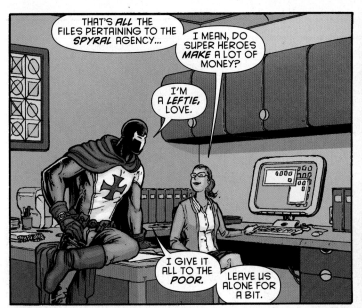

THAT'S *ALL* THE FILES PERTAINING TO THE *SPYRAL* AGENCY...

I MEAN, DO SUPER HEROES *MAKE* A LOT OF MONEY?

I'M A *LEFTIE,* LOVE.

I GIVE IT ALL TO THE *POOR.*

LEAVE US ALONE FOR A BIT.

NOW THEN, LET'S HAVE A LOOK AT--

BLOODY HELL.

THE *HOOD* TO *BATMAN, INC.*

ORACLE, IF YOU'RE ONLINE, CHECK THIS OUT.

LEVIATHAN: AN INESCAPABLE *INTERROGATION FACILITY* SAILING INTERNATIONAL WATERS, ANSWERABLE TO *NO LAWS.*

TELL THEM IT'S A *TRAP*-- THE WHOLE THING IS...

Ah.

MATRON...I CAN *EXPLAIN...*

'*COURSE* YOU CAN, GEORGIE-PORGIE.

WE'RE *TWO OF A KIND, WE DOUBLE AGENTS,* eh?

BUT *MY* TRUE LOYALTY WAS ALWAYS TO *SPYRAL,* AND I ANSWER TO THE HEADMISTRESS *HERSELF.*

CLASSIFIED

SPYRAL SINK

DEUCES HIGH, OLD CHAP.

BAM!

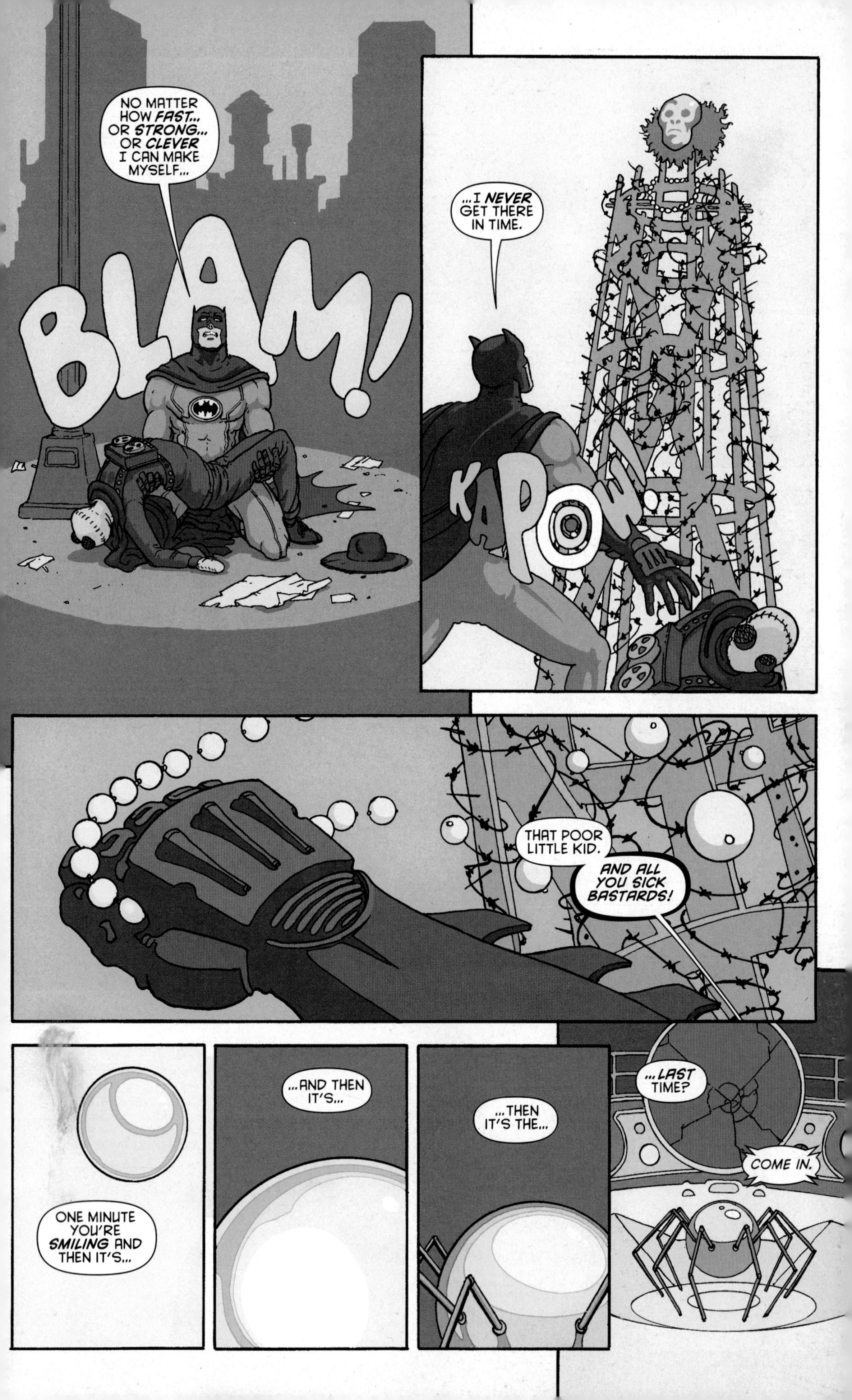
NO MATTER HOW FAST... OR STRONG... OR CLEVER I CAN MAKE MYSELF...
BLAM!
...I NEVER GET THERE IN TIME.
KAPOW
THAT POOR LITTLE KID.
AND ALL YOU SICK BASTARDS!
ONE MINUTE YOU'RE SMILING AND THEN IT'S...
...AND THEN IT'S...
...THEN IT'S THE...
...LAST TIME?
COME IN.

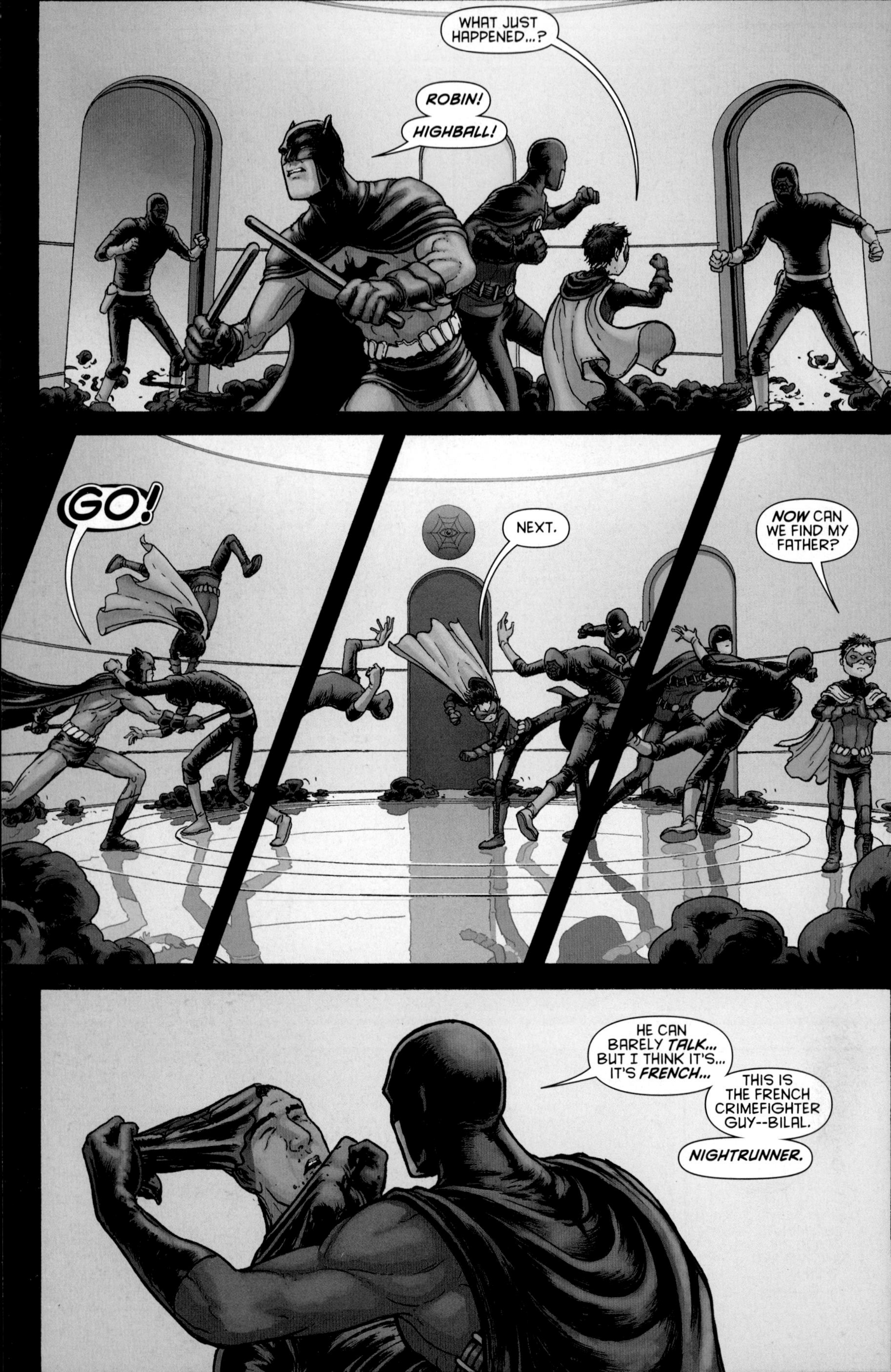

WHAT JUST HAPPENED...?
ROBIN!
HIGHBALL!
GO!
NEXT.
NOW CAN WE FIND MY FATHER?
HE CAN BARELY TALK... BUT I THINK IT'S... IT'S FRENCH...
THIS IS THE FRENCH CRIMEFIGHTER GUY--BILAL.
NIGHTRUNNER.

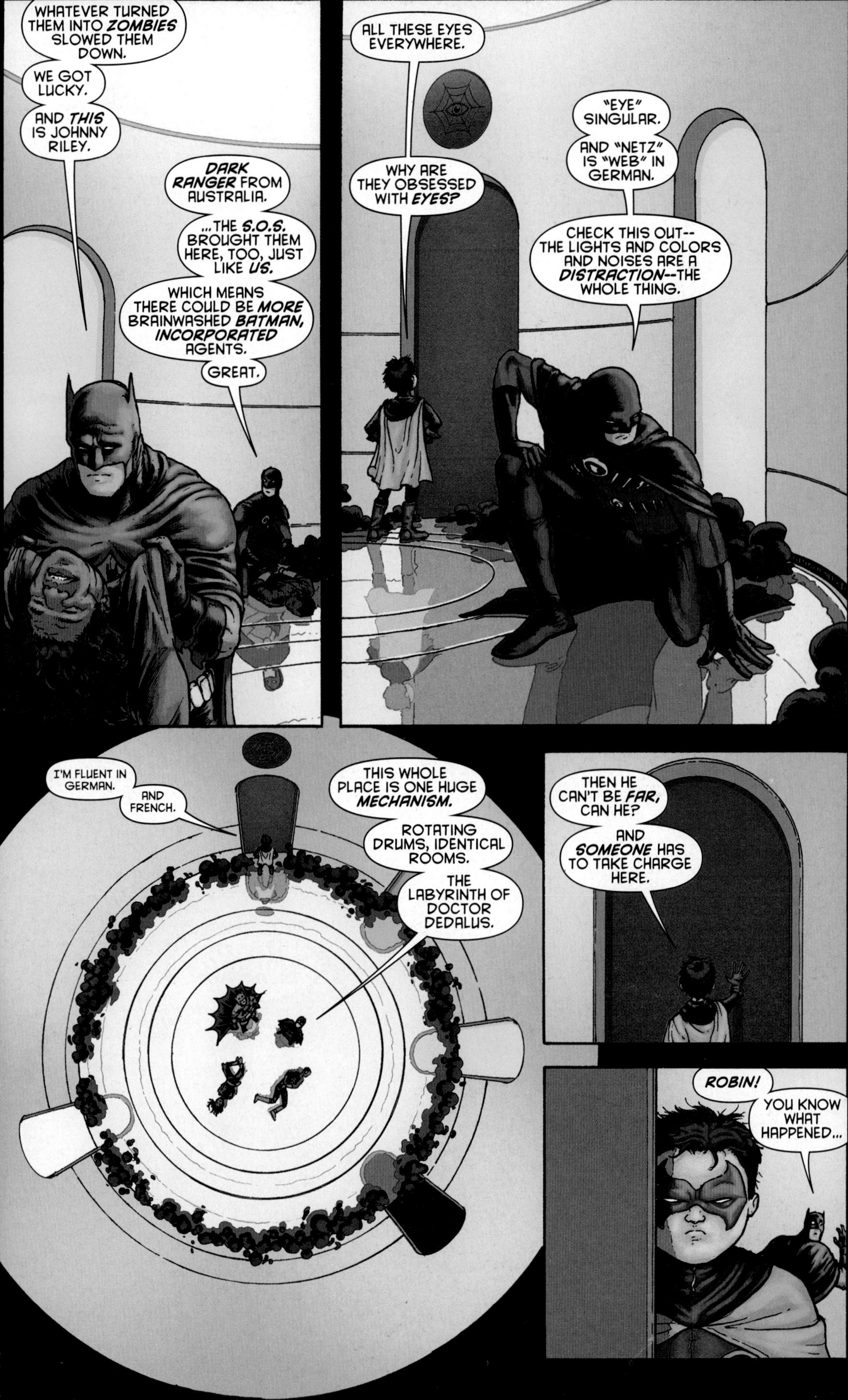
WHATEVER TURNED THEM INTO ZOMBIES SLOWED THEM DOWN.
WE GOT LUCKY.
AND THIS IS JOHNNY RILEY.
DARK RANGER FROM AUSTRALIA.
...THE S.O.S. BROUGHT THEM HERE, TOO, JUST LIKE US.
WHICH MEANS THERE COULD BE MORE BRAINWASHED BATMAN, INCORPORATED AGENTS.
GREAT.
ALL THESE EYES EVERYWHERE.
WHY ARE THEY OBSESSED WITH EYES?
"EYE" SINGULAR.
AND "NETZ" IS "WEB" IN GERMAN.
CHECK THIS OUT-- THE LIGHTS AND COLORS AND NOISES ARE A DISTRACTION--THE WHOLE THING.
I'M FLUENT IN GERMAN.
AND FRENCH.
THIS WHOLE PLACE IS ONE HUGE MECHANISM.
ROTATING DRUMS, IDENTICAL ROOMS.
THE LABYRINTH OF DOCTOR DEDALUS.
THEN HE CAN'T BE FAR, CAN HE?
AND SOMEONE HAS TO TAKE CHARGE HERE.
ROBIN!
YOU KNOW WHAT HAPPENED...

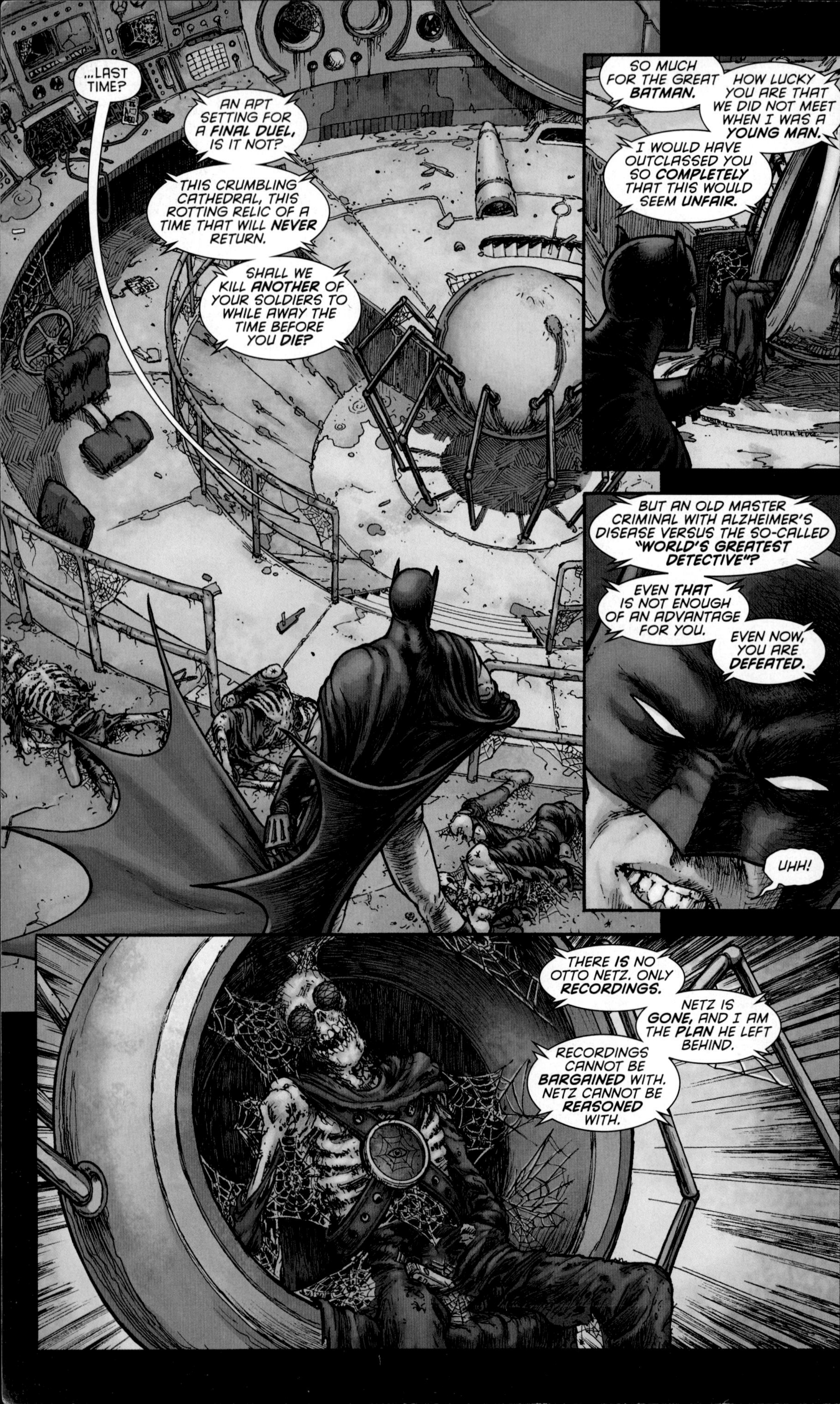
...LAST TIME?
AN APT SETTING FOR A FINAL DUEL, IS IT NOT?
THIS CRUMBLING CATHEDRAL, THIS ROTTING RELIC OF A TIME THAT WILL NEVER RETURN.
SHALL WE KILL ANOTHER OF YOUR SOLDIERS TO WHILE AWAY THE TIME BEFORE YOU DIE?
SO MUCH FOR THE GREAT BATMAN.
HOW LUCKY YOU ARE THAT WE DID NOT MEET WHEN I WAS A YOUNG MAN.
I WOULD HAVE OUTCLASSED YOU SO COMPLETELY THAT THIS WOULD SEEM UNFAIR.
BUT AN OLD MASTER CRIMINAL WITH ALZHEIMER'S DISEASE VERSUS THE SO-CALLED "WORLD'S GREATEST DETECTIVE"?
EVEN THAT IS NOT ENOUGH OF AN ADVANTAGE FOR YOU.
EVEN NOW, YOU ARE DEFEATED.
UHH!
THERE IS NO OTTO NETZ. ONLY RECORDINGS.
NETZ IS GONE, AND I AM THE PLAN HE LEFT BEHIND.
RECORDINGS CANNOT BE BARGAINED WITH. NETZ CANNOT BE REASONED WITH.

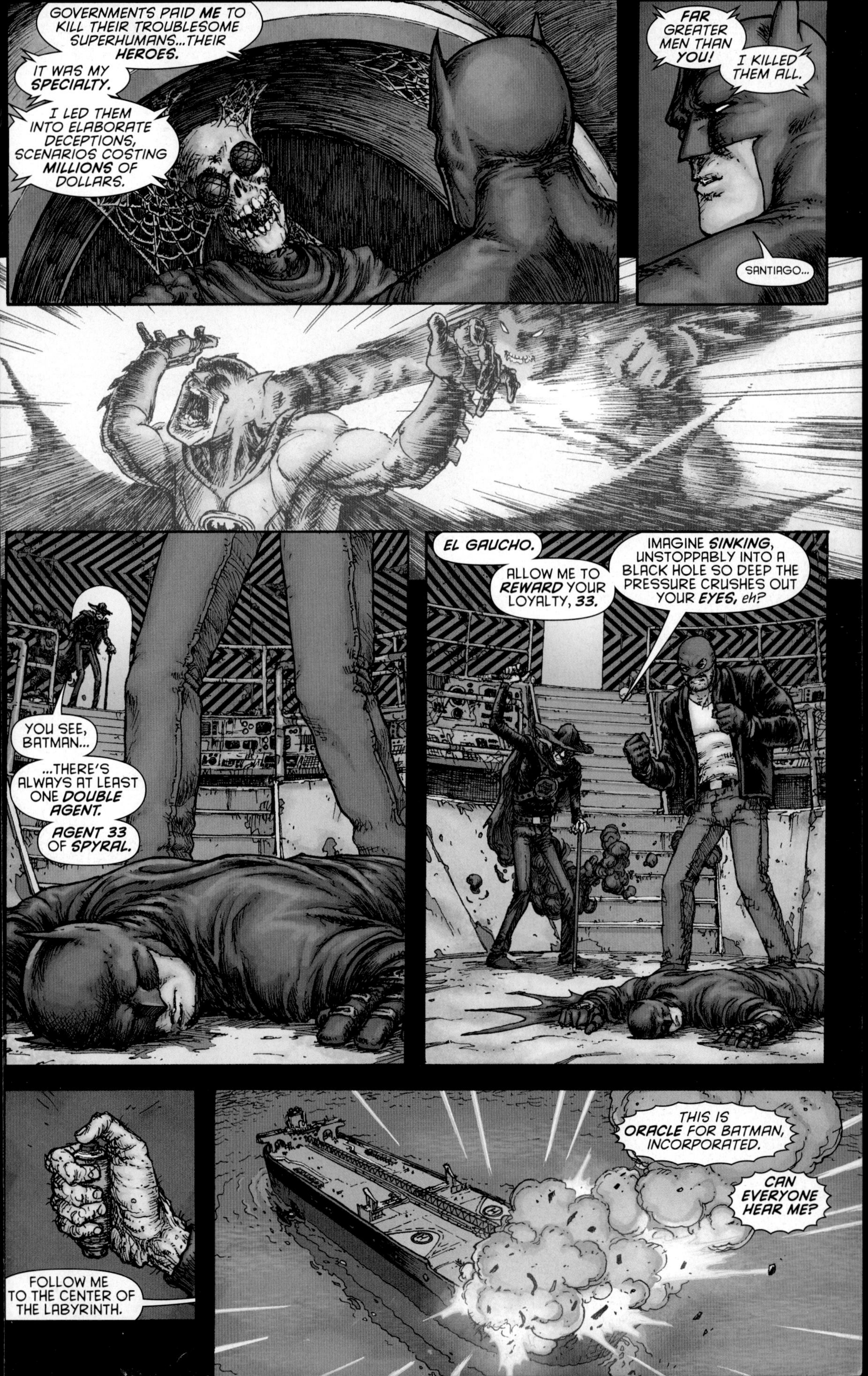
GOVERNMENTS PAID ME TO KILL THEIR TROUBLESOME SUPERHUMANS...THEIR HEROES.
IT WAS MY SPECIALTY.
I LED THEM INTO ELABORATE DECEPTIONS, SCENARIOS COSTING MILLIONS OF DOLLARS.
FAR GREATER MEN THAN YOU!
I KILLED THEM ALL.
SANTIAGO...
YOU SEE, BATMAN...
...THERE'S ALWAYS AT LEAST ONE DOUBLE AGENT.
AGENT 33 OF SPYRAL.
EL GAUCHO.
ALLOW ME TO REWARD YOUR LOYALTY, 33.
IMAGINE SINKING, UNSTOPPABLY INTO A BLACK HOLE SO DEEP THE PRESSURE CRUSHES OUT YOUR EYES, eh?
FOLLOW ME TO THE CENTER OF THE LABYRINTH.
THIS IS ORACLE FOR BATMAN, INCORPORATED.
CAN EVERYONE HEAR ME?

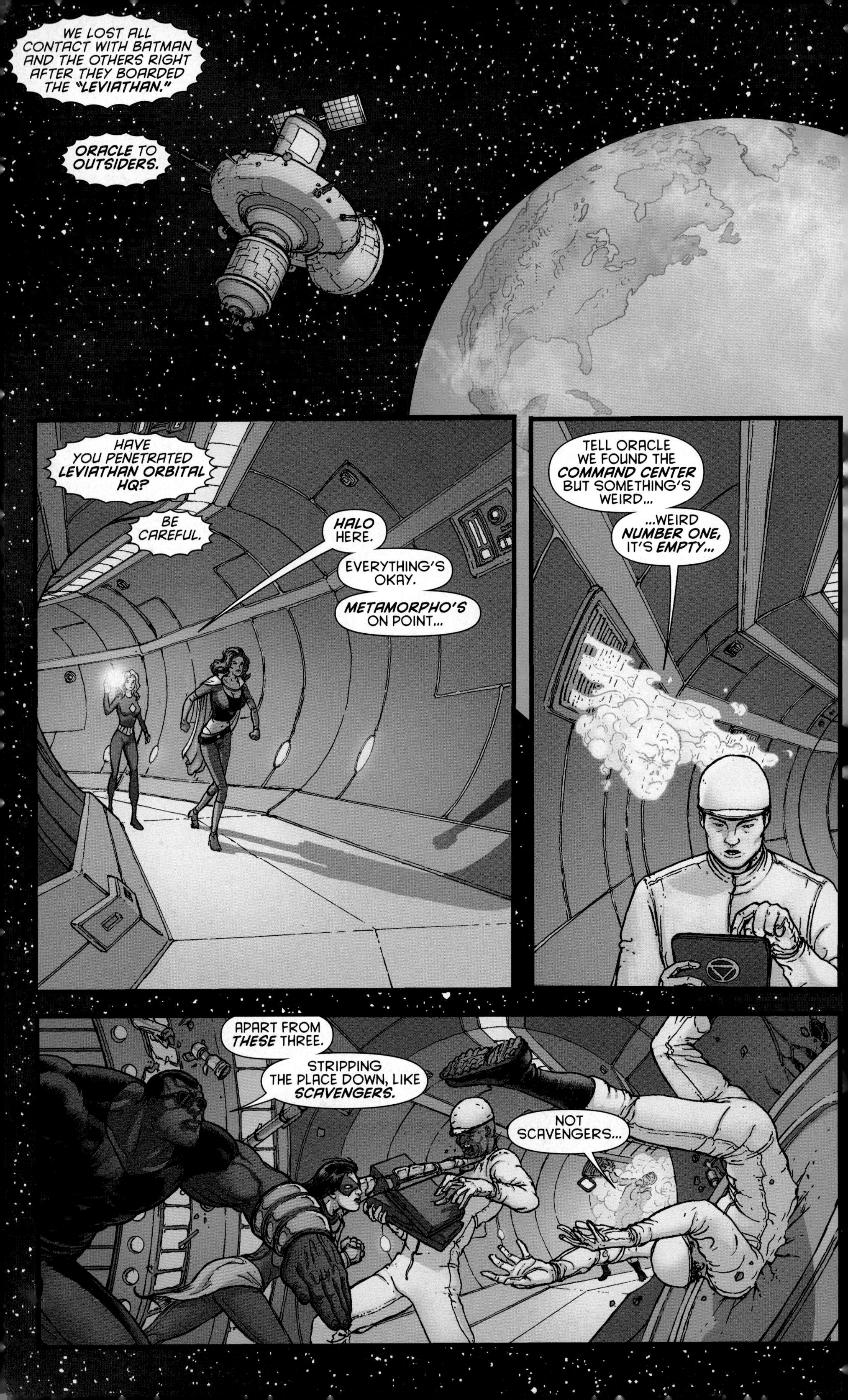
WE LOST ALL CONTACT WITH BATMAN AND THE OTHERS RIGHT AFTER THEY BOARDED THE "LEVIATHAN."
ORACLE TO OUTSIDERS.
HAVE YOU PENETRATED LEVIATHAN ORBITAL HQ?
BE CAREFUL.
HALO HERE.
EVERYTHING'S OKAY.
METAMORPHO'S ON POINT...
TELL ORACLE WE FOUND THE COMMAND CENTER BUT SOMETHING'S WEIRD...
...WEIRD NUMBER ONE, IT'S EMPTY...
APART FROM THESE THREE.
STRIPPING THE PLACE DOWN, LIKE SCAVENGERS.
NOT SCAVENGERS...

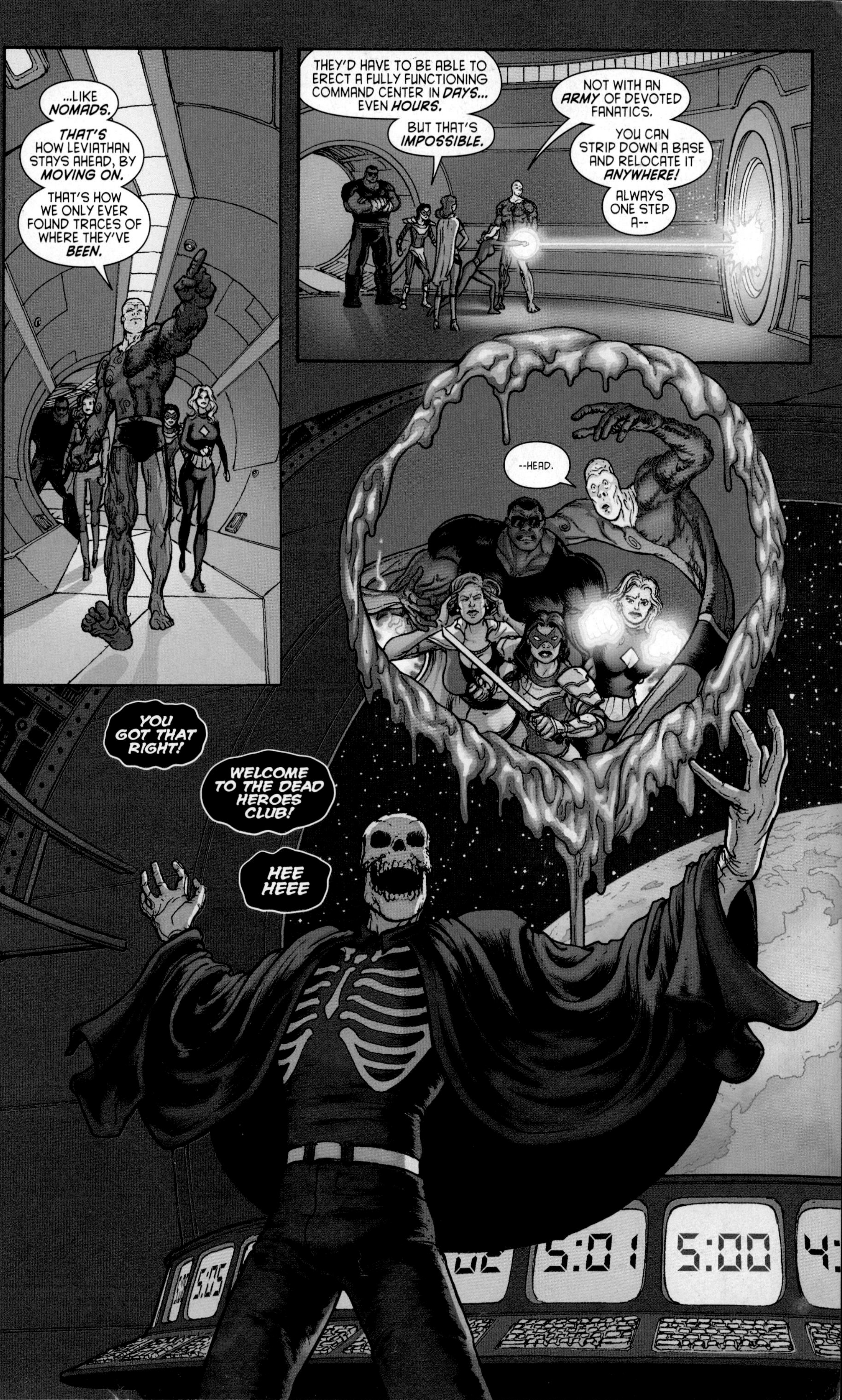
...LIKE NOMADS.
THAT'S HOW LEVIATHAN STAYS AHEAD, BY MOVING ON.
THAT'S HOW WE ONLY EVER FOUND TRACES OF WHERE THEY'VE BEEN.
THEY'D HAVE TO BE ABLE TO ERECT A FULLY FUNCTIONING COMMAND CENTER IN DAYS... EVEN HOURS.
BUT THAT'S IMPOSSIBLE.
NOT WITH AN ARMY OF DEVOTED FANATICS.
YOU CAN STRIP DOWN A BASE AND RELOCATE IT ANYWHERE!
ALWAYS ONE STEP A--
--HEAD.
YOU GOT THAT RIGHT!
WELCOME TO THE DEAD HEROES CLUB!
HEE HEEE
5:01
5:00

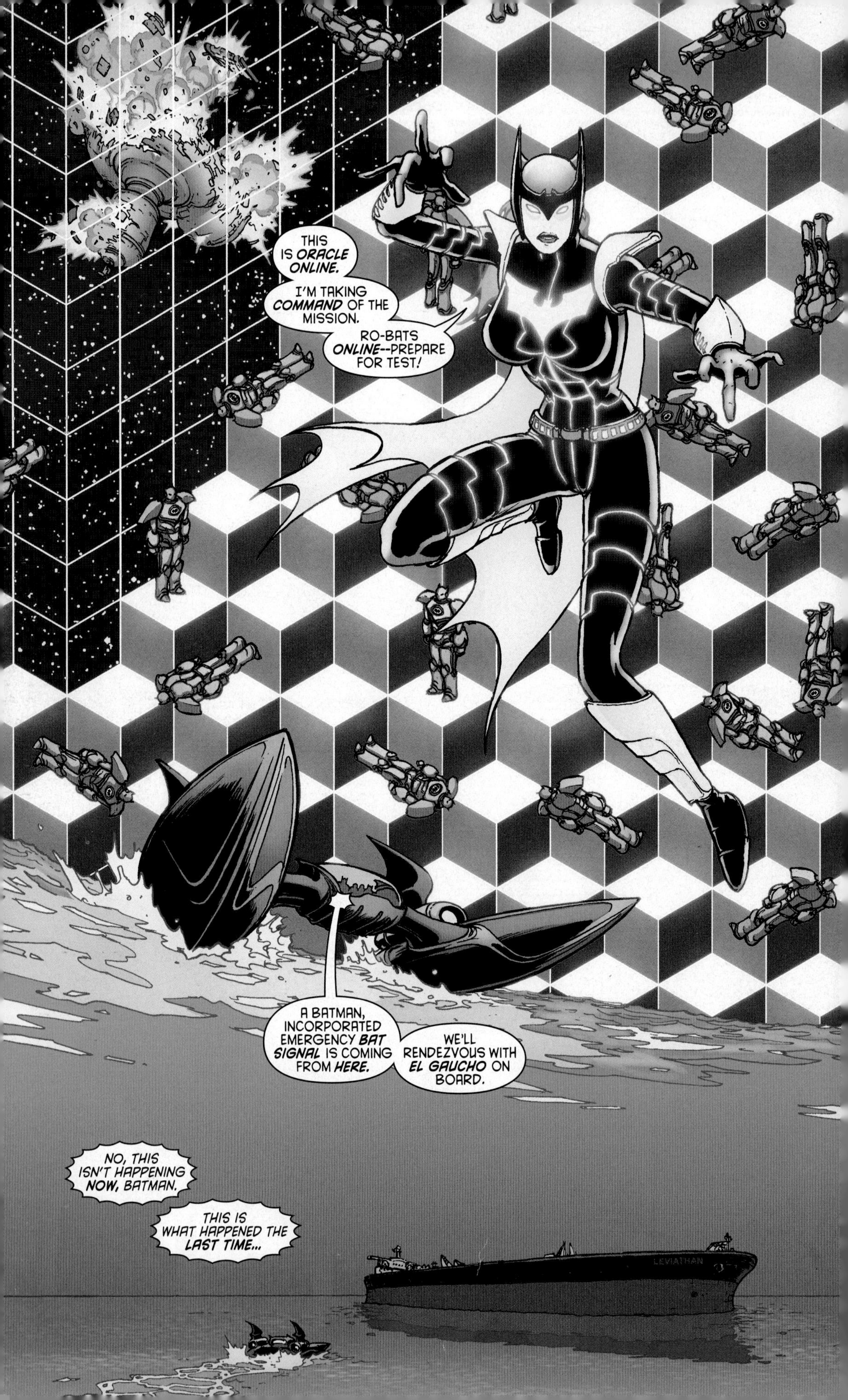
THIS IS ORACLE ONLINE.
I'M TAKING COMMAND OF THE MISSION.
RO-BATS ONLINE--PREPARE FOR TEST!
A BATMAN, INCORPORATED EMERGENCY BAT SIGNAL IS COMING FROM HERE.
WE'LL RENDEZVOUS WITH EL GAUCHO ON BOARD.
NO, THIS ISN'T HAPPENING NOW, BATMAN.
THIS IS WHAT HAPPENED THE LAST TIME...
LEVIATHAN

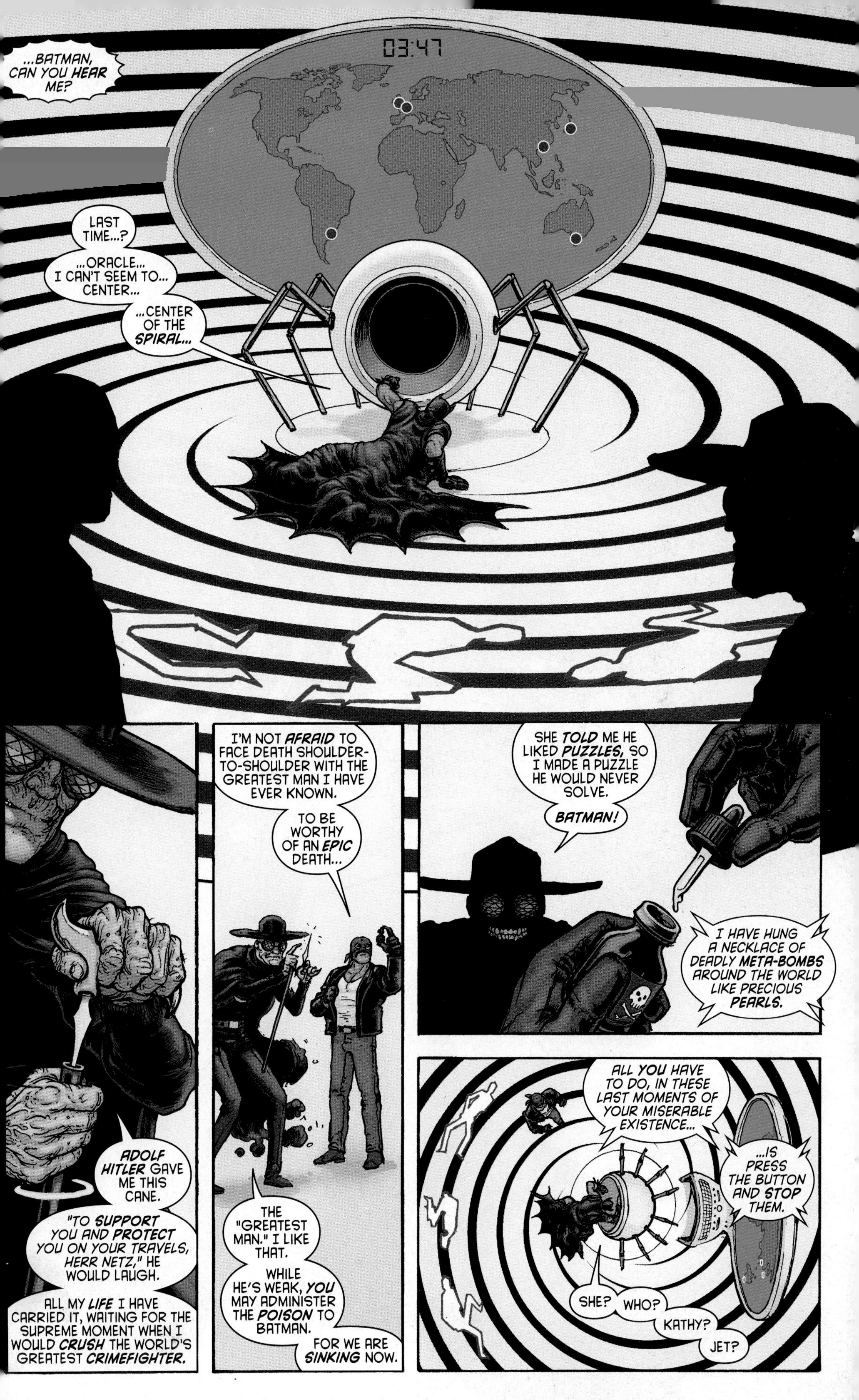
03:47
...BATMAN, CAN YOU HEAR ME?
LAST TIME...?
...ORACLE... I CAN'T SEEM TO... CENTER...
...CENTER OF THE SPIRAL...
ADOLF HITLER GAVE ME THIS CANE.
"TO SUPPORT YOU AND PROTECT YOU ON YOUR TRAVELS, HERR NETZ," HE WOULD LAUGH.
ALL MY LIFE I HAVE CARRIED IT, WAITING FOR THE SUPREME MOMENT WHEN I WOULD CRUSH THE WORLD'S GREATEST CRIMEFIGHTER.
I'M NOT AFRAID TO FACE DEATH SHOULDER-TO-SHOULDER WITH THE GREATEST MAN I HAVE EVER KNOWN.
TO BE WORTHY OF AN EPIC DEATH...
THE "GREATEST MAN." I LIKE THAT.
WHILE HE'S WEAK, YOU MAY ADMINISTER THE POISON TO BATMAN.
FOR WE ARE SINKING NOW.
SHE TOLD ME HE LIKED PUZZLES, SO I MADE A PUZZLE HE WOULD NEVER SOLVE.
BATMAN!
I HAVE HUNG A NECKLACE OF DEADLY META-BOMBS AROUND THE WORLD LIKE PRECIOUS PEARLS.
ALL YOU HAVE TO DO, IN THESE LAST MOMENTS OF YOUR MISERABLE EXISTENCE...
...IS PRESS THE BUTTON AND STOP THEM.
SHE?
WHO?
KATHY?
JET?

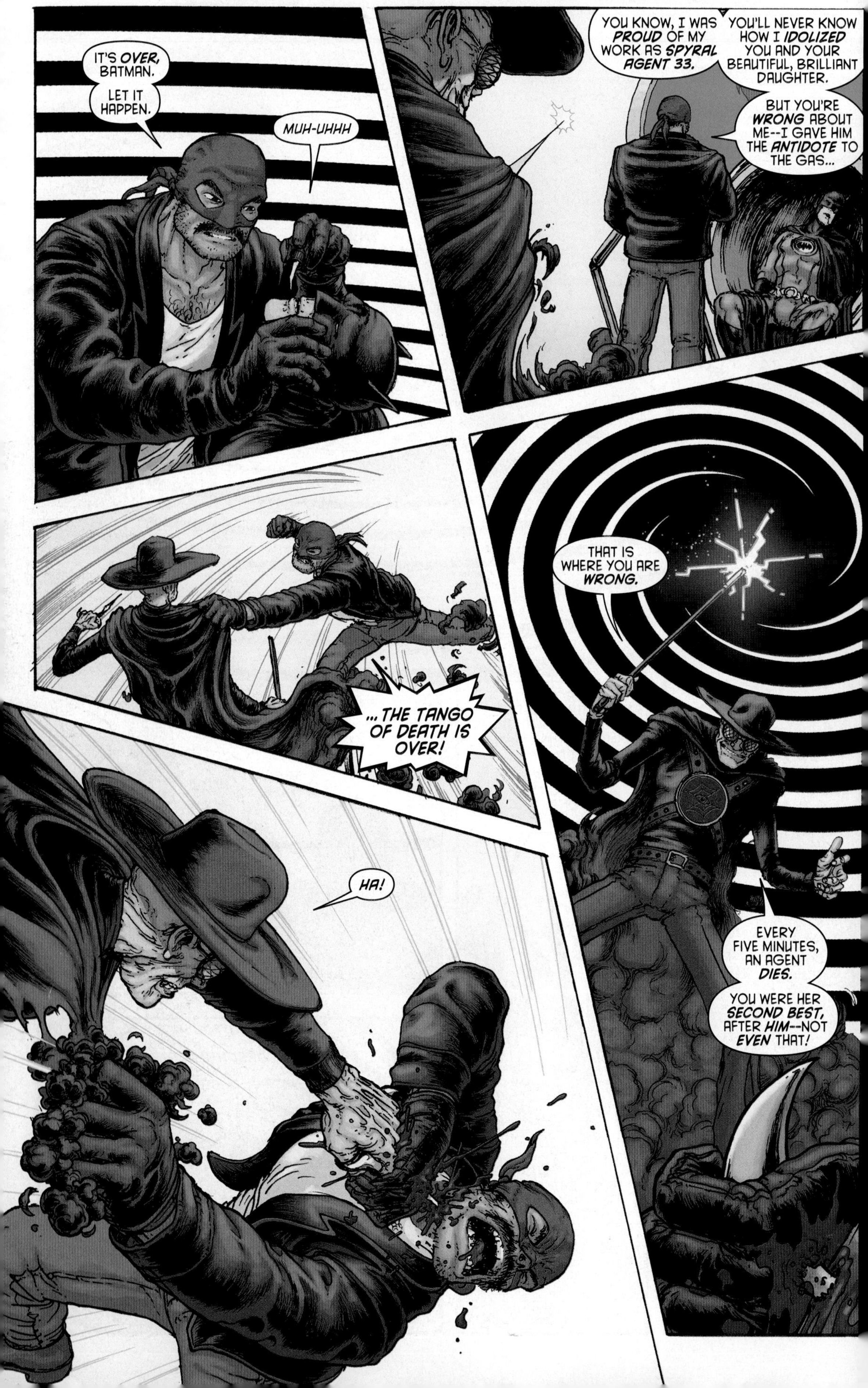
IT'S *OVER*, BATMAN.
LET IT HAPPEN.
MUH-UHHH
YOU KNOW, I WAS *PROUD* OF MY WORK AS *SPYRAL AGENT 33.*
YOU'LL NEVER KNOW HOW I *IDOLIZED* YOU AND YOUR BEAUTIFUL, BRILLIANT DAUGHTER.
BUT YOU'RE *WRONG* ABOUT ME--I GAVE HIM THE *ANTIDOTE* TO THE GAS...
THAT IS WHERE YOU ARE *WRONG.*
...THE TANGO OF DEATH IS OVER!
HA!
EVERY FIVE MINUTES, AN AGENT *DIES.*
YOU WERE HER *SECOND BEST,* AFTER *HIM*--NOT *EVEN* THAT!

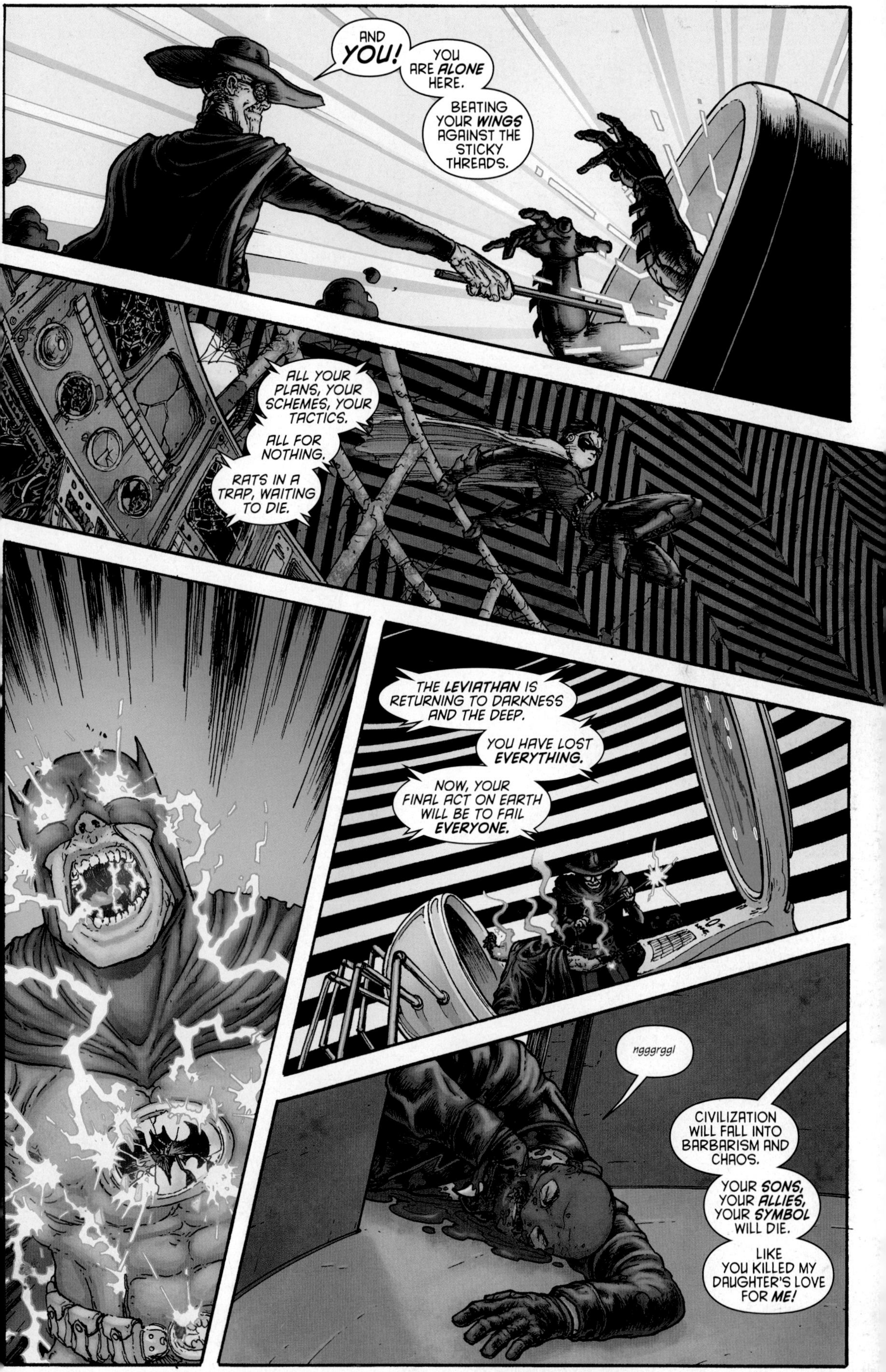
AND YOU!
YOU ARE ALONE HERE.
BEATING YOUR WINGS AGAINST THE STICKY THREADS.
ALL YOUR PLANS, YOUR SCHEMES, YOUR TACTICS.
ALL FOR NOTHING.
RATS IN A TRAP, WAITING TO DIE.
THE LEVIATHAN IS RETURNING TO DARKNESS AND THE DEEP.
YOU HAVE LOST EVERYTHING.
NOW, YOUR FINAL ACT ON EARTH WILL BE TO FAIL EVERYONE.
ngggrggl
CIVILIZATION WILL FALL INTO BARBARISM AND CHAOS.
YOUR SONS, YOUR ALLIES, YOUR SYMBOL WILL DIE.
LIKE YOU KILLED MY DAUGHTER'S LOVE FOR ME!

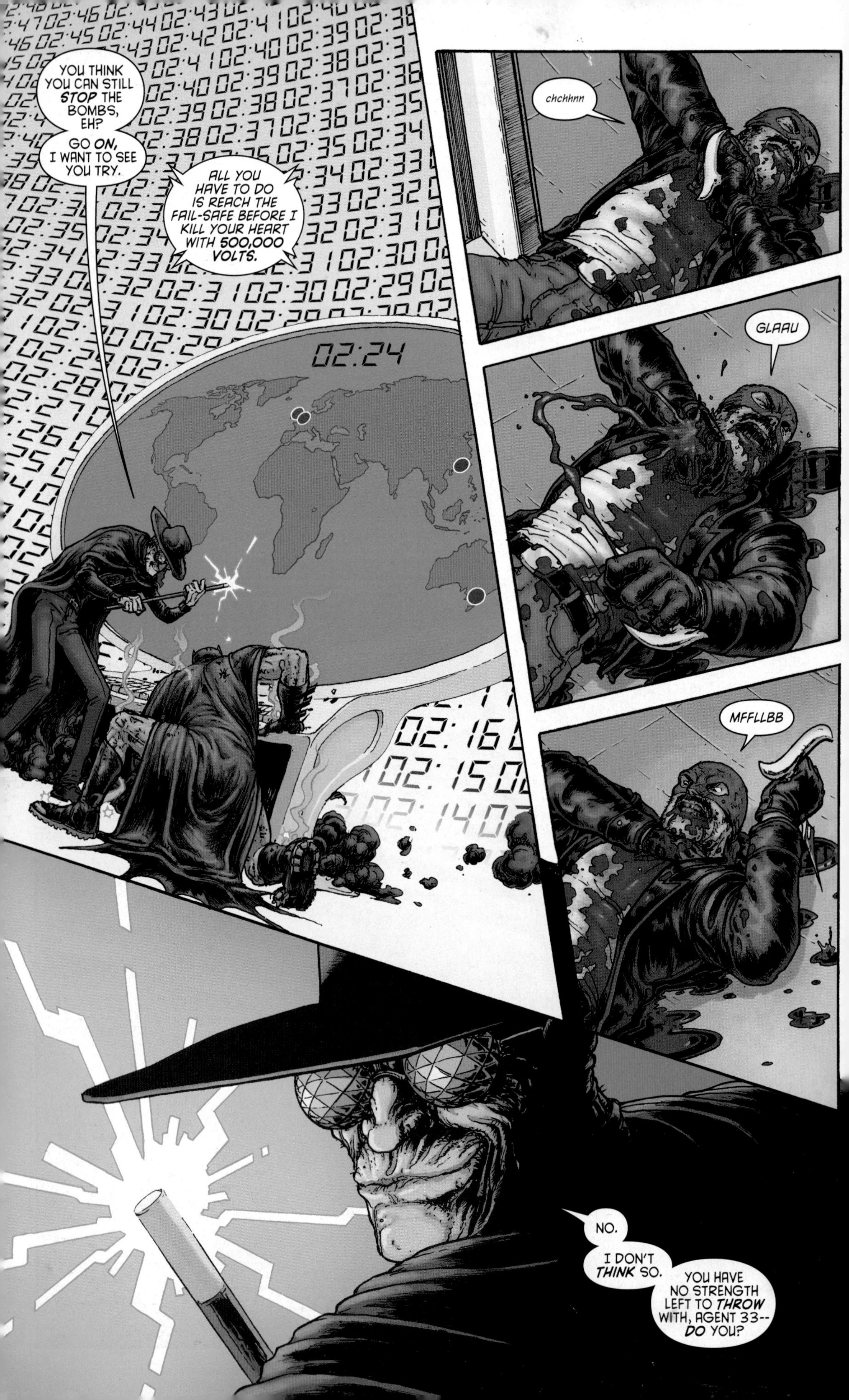
YOU THINK YOU CAN STILL STOP THE BOMBS, EH?
GO ON, I WANT TO SEE YOU TRY.
ALL YOU HAVE TO DO IS REACH THE FAIL-SAFE BEFORE I KILL YOUR HEART WITH 500,000 VOLTS.
02:24
chchhnn
GLAAU
MFFLLBB
NO.
I DON'T THINK SO.
YOU HAVE NO STRENGTH LEFT TO THROW WITH, AGENT 33-- DO YOU?

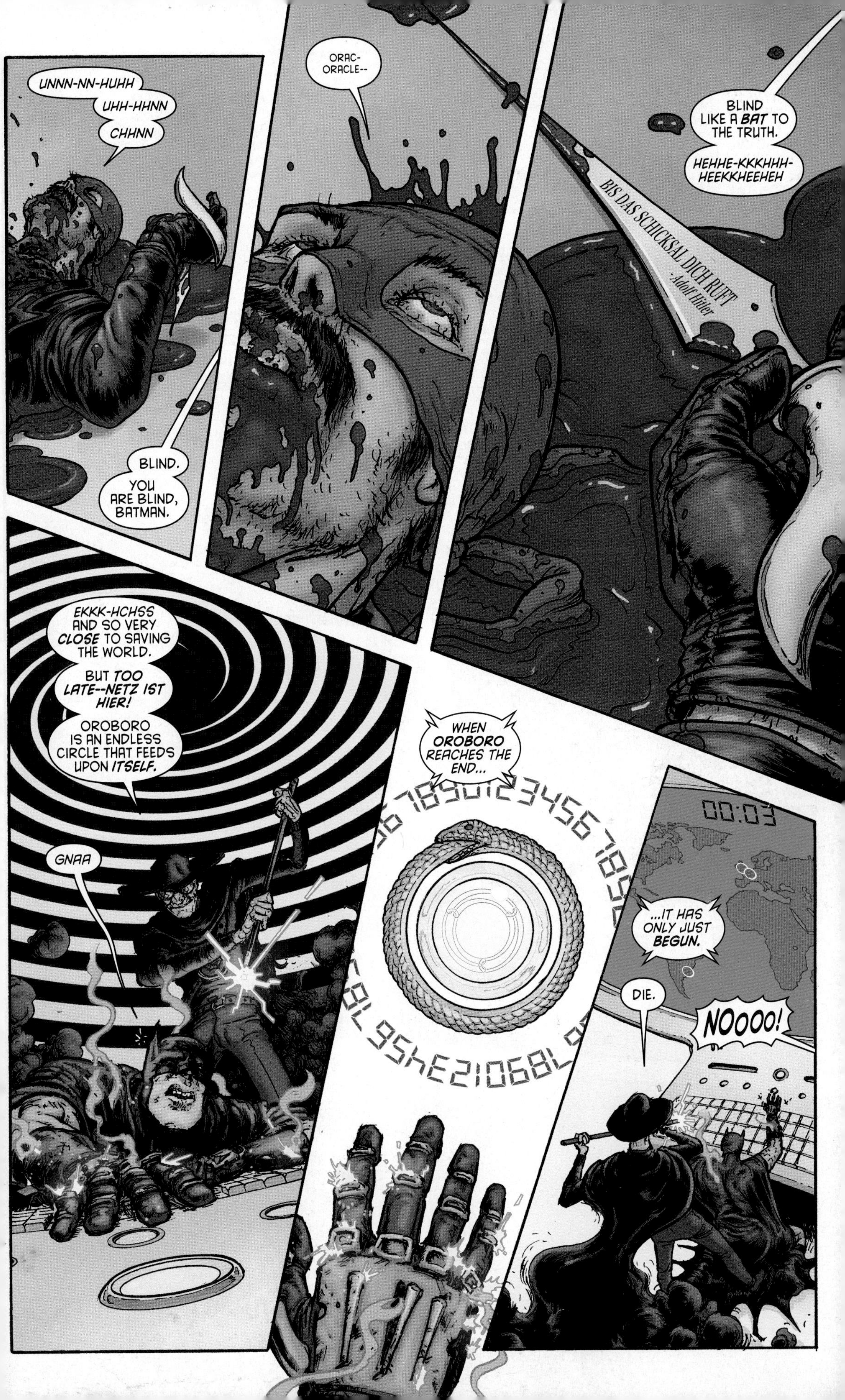
UNNN-NN-HUHH
UHH-HHNN
CHHNN
BLIND.
YOU ARE BLIND, BATMAN.
ORAC-ORACLE--
BLIND LIKE A BAT TO THE TRUTH.
HEHHE-KKKHHH-HEEKKHEEHEH
BIS DAS SCHICKSAL DICH RUFT
-Adolf Hitler
EKKK-HCHSS AND SO VERY CLOSE TO SAVING THE WORLD.
BUT TOO LATE--NETZ IST HIER!
OROBORO IS AN ENDLESS CIRCLE THAT FEEDS UPON ITSELF.
GNAA
WHEN OROBORO REACHES THE END...
...IT HAS ONLY JUST BEGUN.
DIE.
NOOOO!

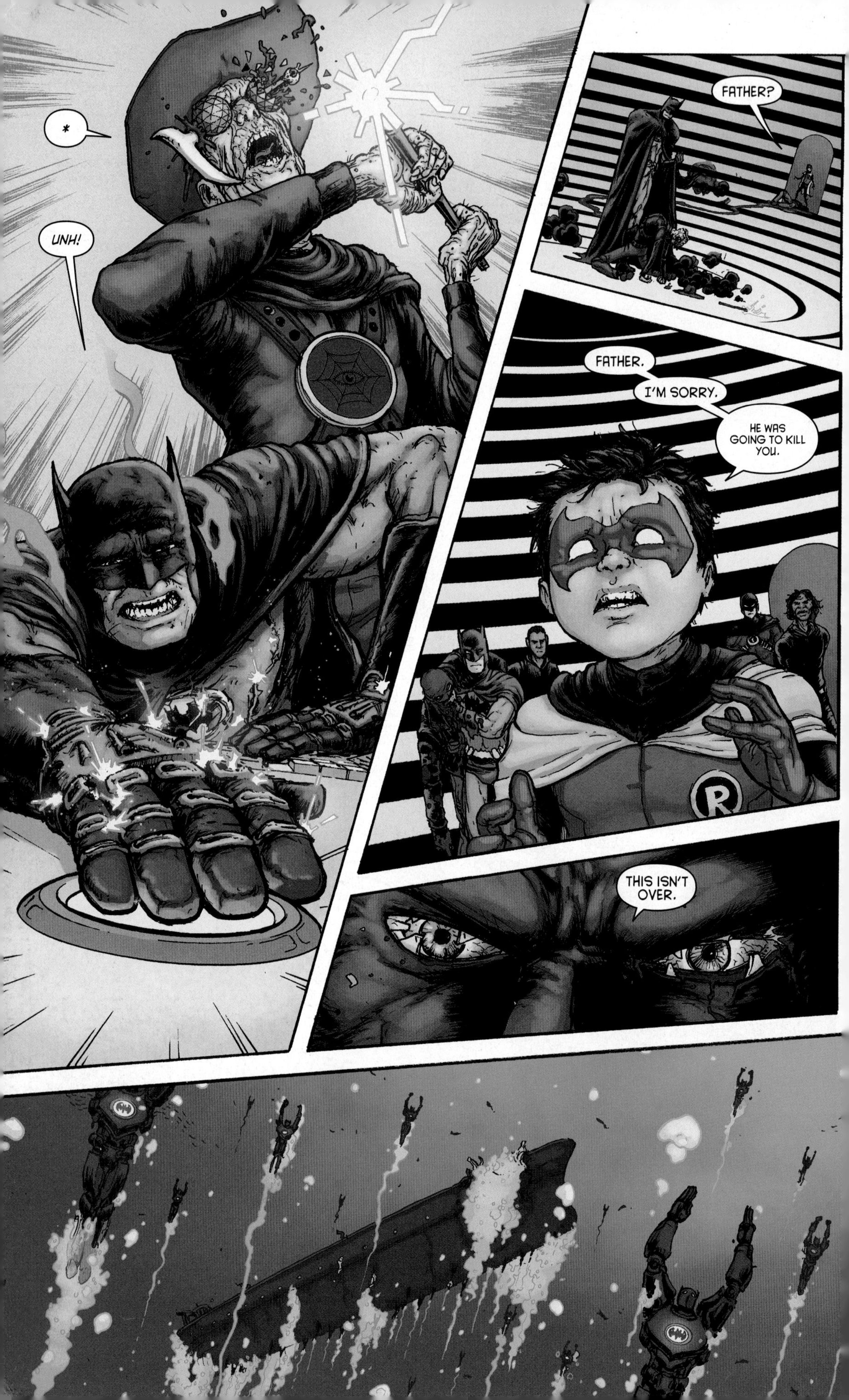

*
UNH!
FATHER?
FATHER.
I'M SORRY.
HE WAS GOING TO KILL YOU.
THIS ISN'T OVER.

...IT'S *NEVER* REALLY OVER, IS IT, MATRON? OROBORO IS A *CIRCLE,* AFTER ALL.

BUT I'LL SEND *FLOWERS,* OF COURSE.

HE *HATED* FLOWERS.

SO WHAT HAPPENED TO *GAUCHO?*

THE BLADE MISSED HIS *CAROTID ARTERY* BY HALF AN INCH.

NETZ WAS *MISDIRECTION,* TO WASTE OUR RESOURCES ON THE EVE OF *WAR.*

WAR WITH *WHO,* BATMAN?

YOU ONLY TOLD US *SOME* OF THE STUFF YOU SAW IN THE *FUTURE.*

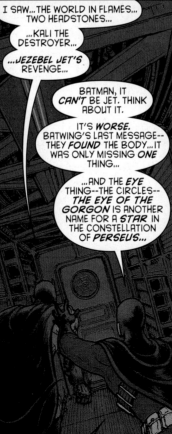

I SAW...THE WORLD IN FLAMES... TWO HEADSTONES...

...KALI THE *DESTROYER...*

...*JEZEBEL JET'S* REVENGE...

BATMAN, IT *CAN'T* BE JET. THINK ABOUT IT.

IT'S *WORSE.* BATWING'S LAST MESSAGE-- THEY *FOUND* THE BODY...IT WAS ONLY MISSING *ONE* THING...

...AND THE *EYE* THING--THE CIRCLES-- *THE EYE OF THE GORGON* IS ANOTHER NAME FOR A *STAR* IN THE CONSTELLATION OF *PERSEUS...*

ALGOL.

THE DEMON'S HEAD.

BUT IT CAN'T BE HER.

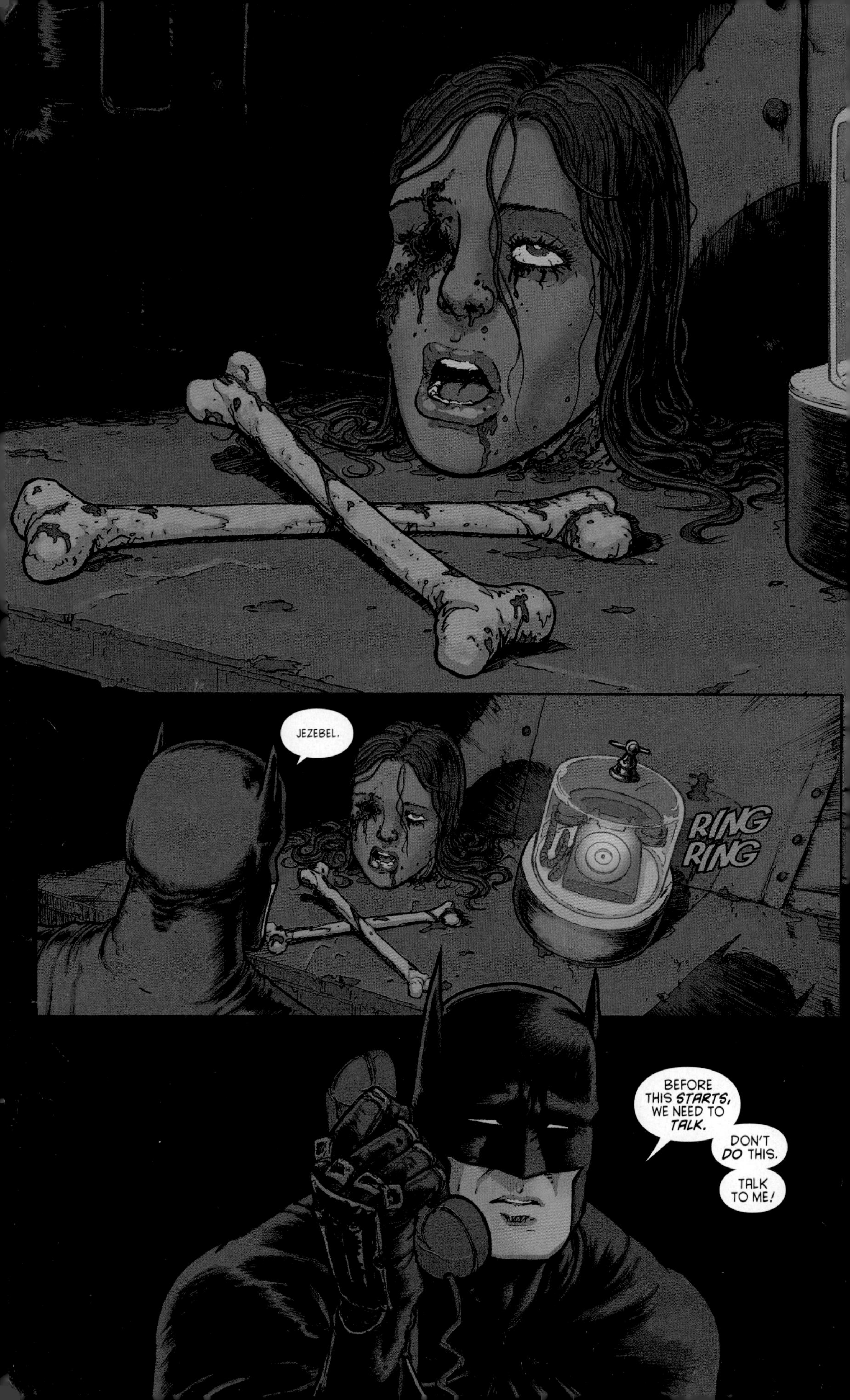
JEZEBEL.
RING RING
BEFORE THIS STARTS, WE NEED TO TALK.
DON'T DO THIS.
TALK TO ME!

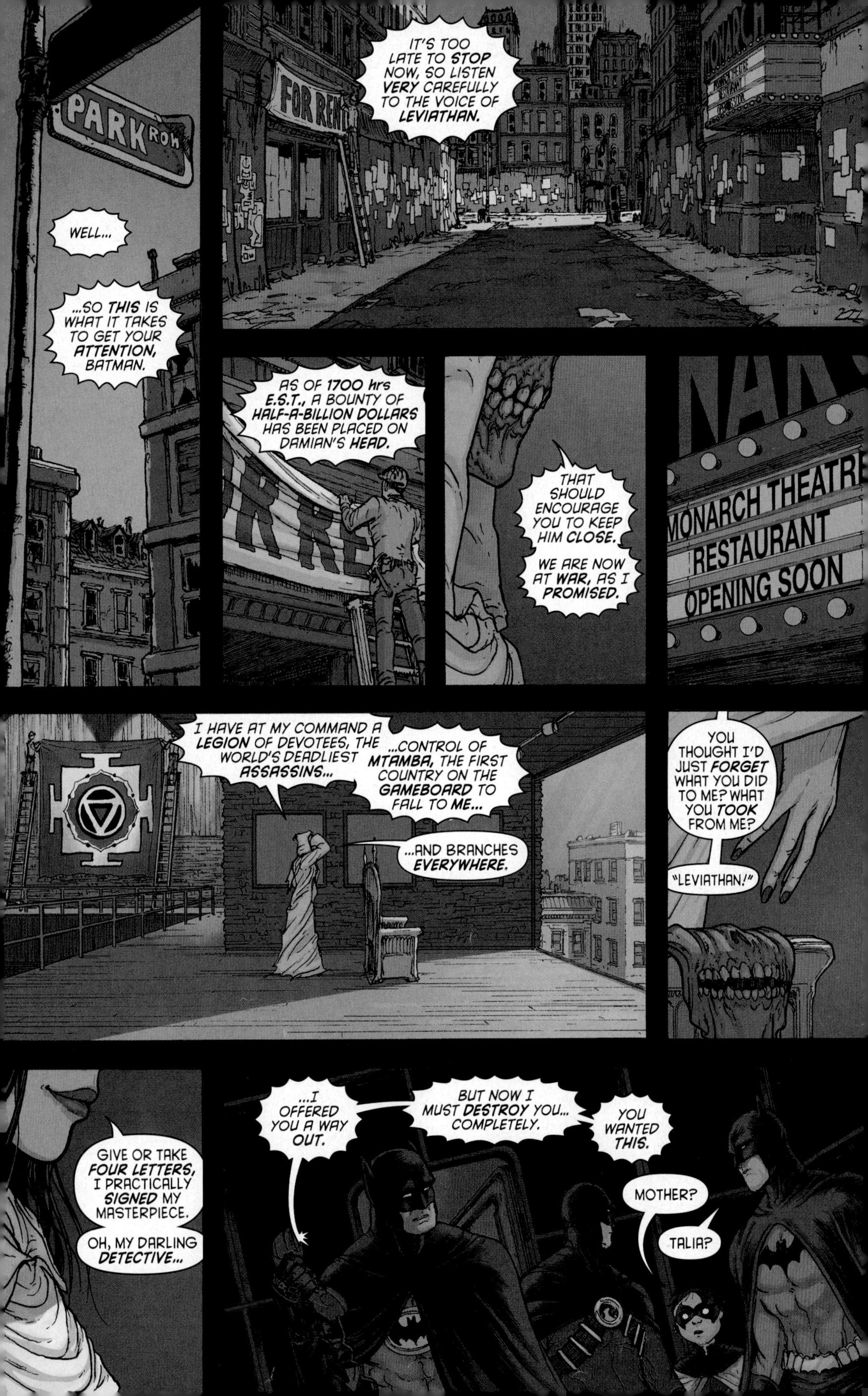
PARK ROW
WELL...
...SO THIS IS WHAT IT TAKES TO GET YOUR ATTENTION, BATMAN.
FOR RENT
MONARCH
IT'S TOO LATE TO STOP NOW, SO LISTEN VERY CAREFULLY TO THE VOICE OF LEVIATHAN.
AS OF 1700 hrs E.S.T., A BOUNTY OF HALF-A-BILLION DOLLARS HAS BEEN PLACED ON DAMIAN'S HEAD.
THAT SHOULD ENCOURAGE YOU TO KEEP HIM CLOSE.
WE ARE NOW AT WAR, AS I PROMISED.
MONARCH THEATRE
RESTAURANT
OPENING SOON
I HAVE AT MY COMMAND A LEGION OF DEVOTEES, THE WORLD'S DEADLIEST ASSASSINS...
...CONTROL OF MTAMBA, THE FIRST COUNTRY ON THE GAMEBOARD TO FALL TO ME...
...AND BRANCHES EVERYWHERE.
YOU THOUGHT I'D JUST FORGET WHAT YOU DID TO ME? WHAT YOU TOOK FROM ME?
"LEVIATHAN!"
GIVE OR TAKE FOUR LETTERS, I PRACTICALLY SIGNED MY MASTERPIECE.
OH, MY DARLING DETECTIVE...
...I OFFERED YOU A WAY OUT.
BUT NOW I MUST DESTROY YOU... COMPLETELY.
YOU WANTED THIS.
MOTHER?
TALIA?

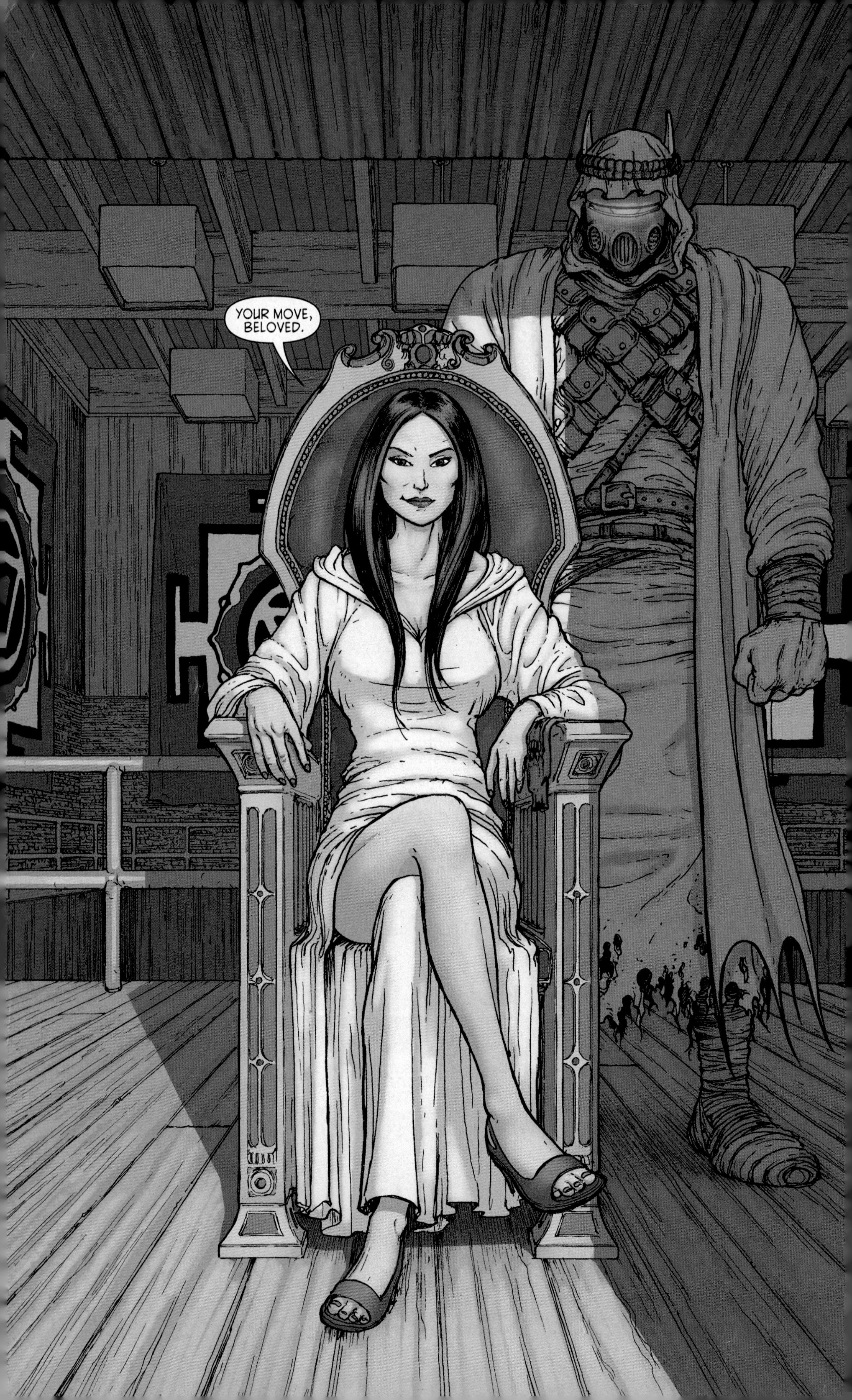
YOUR MOVE, BELOVED.

PAPERWORK

Auditing the books at BATMAN, INCORPORATED
with **Grant Morrison**, **Yanick Paquette** and **Chris Burnham**.

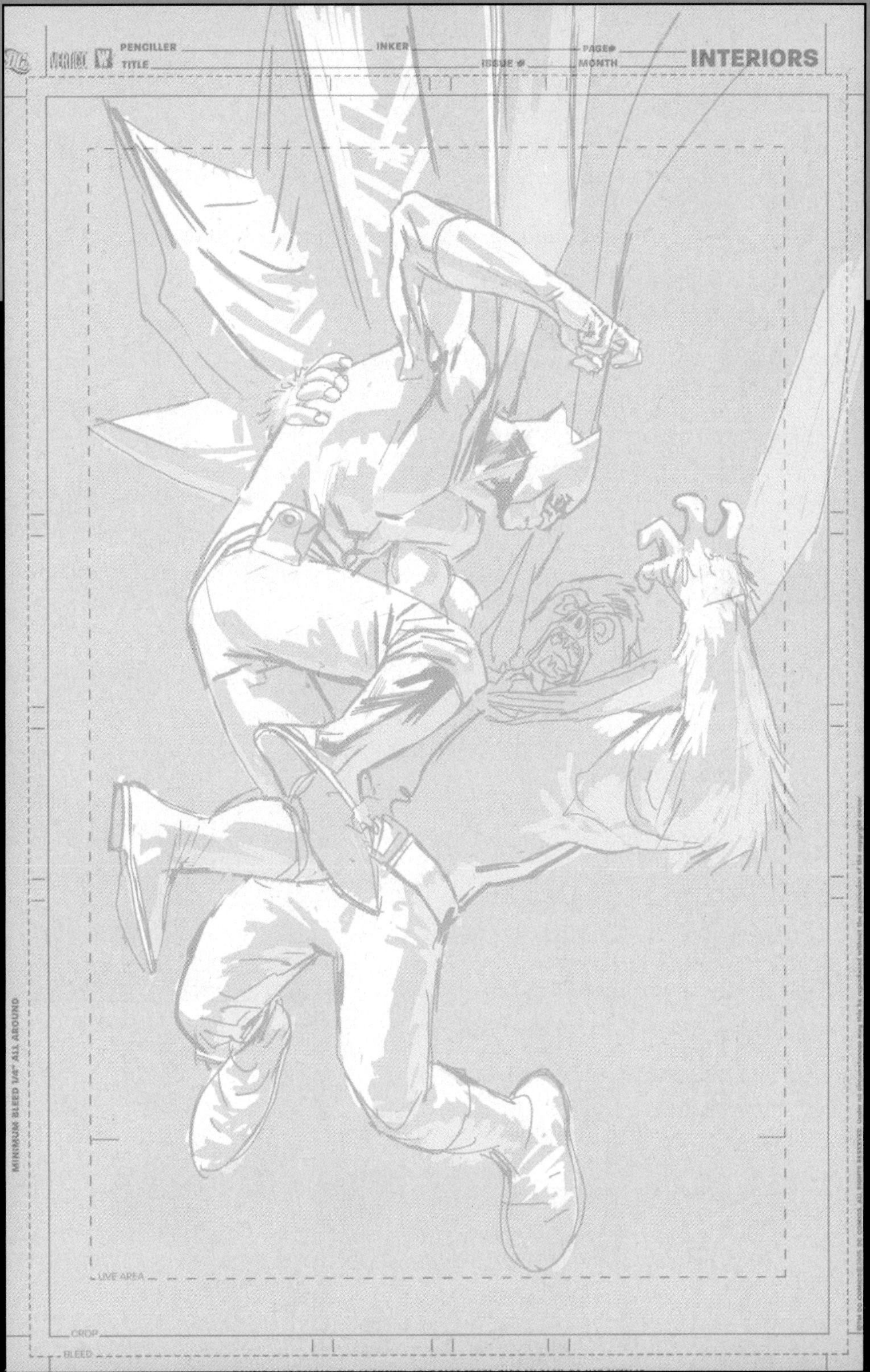
PENCILLER
INKER
PAGE#
TITLE
ISSUE #
MONTH
INTERIORS
LIVE AREA
CROP
BLEED
MINIMUM BLEED 1/4" ALL AROUND

Above: A light source study by Yanick Paquette for issue #2.

THE TEAM-UPS

CATWOMAN

One of Batman's most popular, best-known and long-running adversaries, Catwoman debuted alongside Robin in BATMAN #1 in 1940. Her on/off, love/hate relationship with the Dark Knight has provided fuel for countless stories over the decades and is likely to inspire a whole lot more. Here, the two old sparring partners are in loved-up mode, allowing her to strut her stuff on the right side of the law for once.

The song she's singing is my favorite of several entitled "Felix the Cat." Have fun online finding out which one — and learning to sing along!

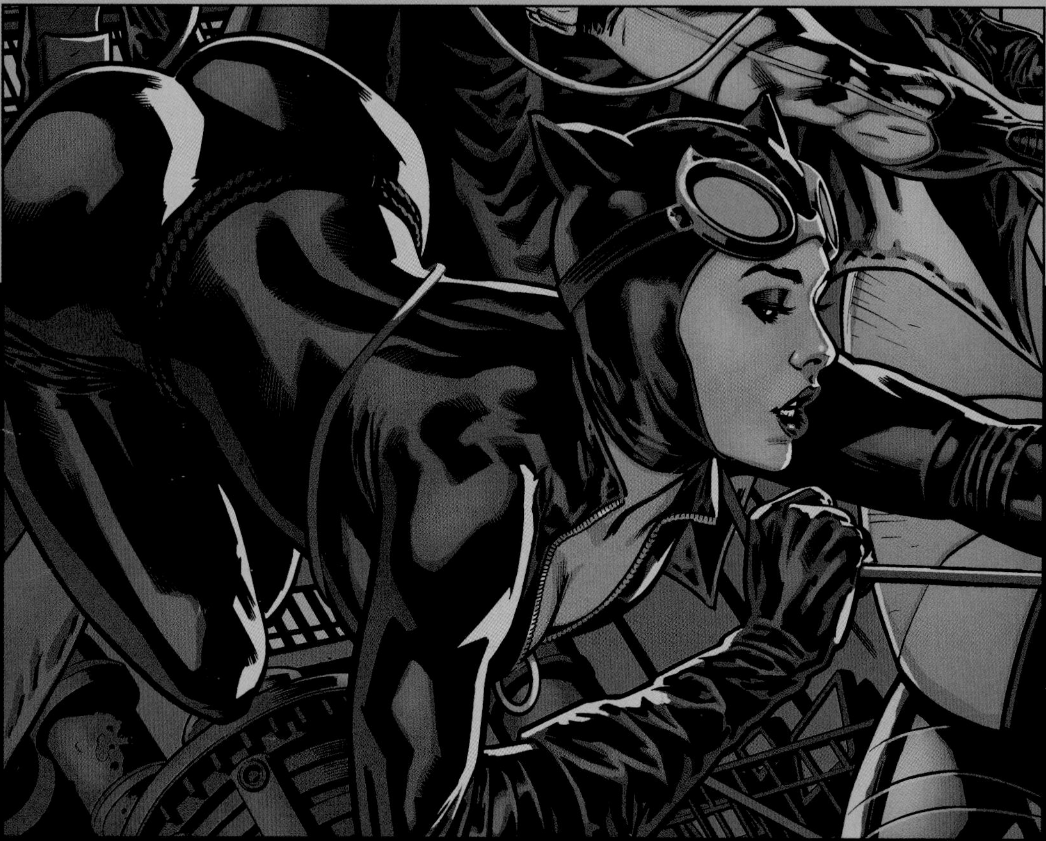

MR. UNKNOWN

Mr. Unknown was a new creation. After reading F. Paul Zehr's book *Becoming Batman* (which takes a hard, real-life look at the kind of diet, training and exercise regimen a crimefighter like Batman would have to endure in order to have a window of peak physical and mental effectiveness that would be barely five years long in a real human life), I wondered what would happen to an action hero past his best and how he would cope with the gradual loss of his strength, speed and reflexes. This led me to the idea of a crimefighting "body double" and Jiro Osamu was born.

The name of the young Mr. Unknown (and future Batman of Japan) combines that of Bat-*manga* artist Jiro Kuwata with that of Kuwata's own artistic hero, the great Osamu Tezuka, known as "the father of *manga*."

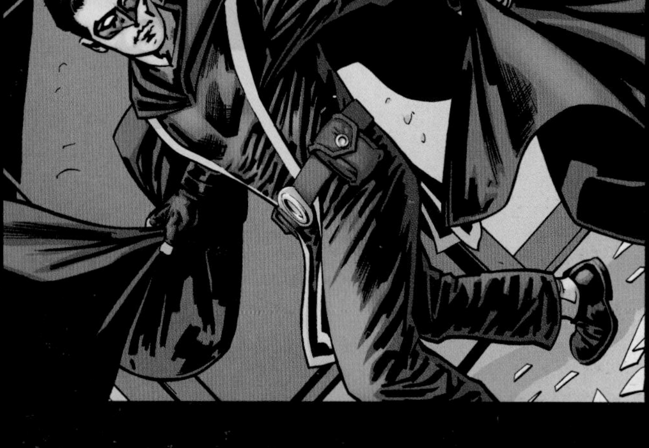

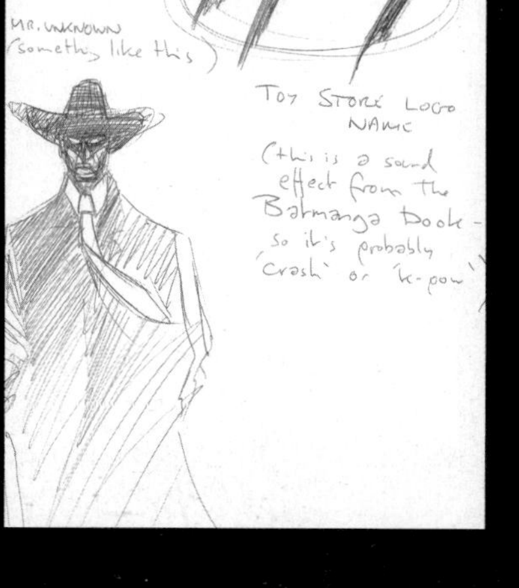
MR. UNKNOWN
(something like this)
TOY STORE LOGO
NAME
(this is a sound effect from the Batmanga book - so it's probably 'crash' or 'k-pow')

EL GAUCHO

The Gaucho made his first appearance in "The Batmen of All Nations" from DETECTIVE COMICS #215 (January 1955). This updated and retooled version of the character — designed by J.H. Williams III — made his return in BATMAN #667 in 2007. For his appearance in BATMAN, INC., I gave Gaucho a secret identity: Santiago Vargas, a wealthy breeder and trainer of racehorses.

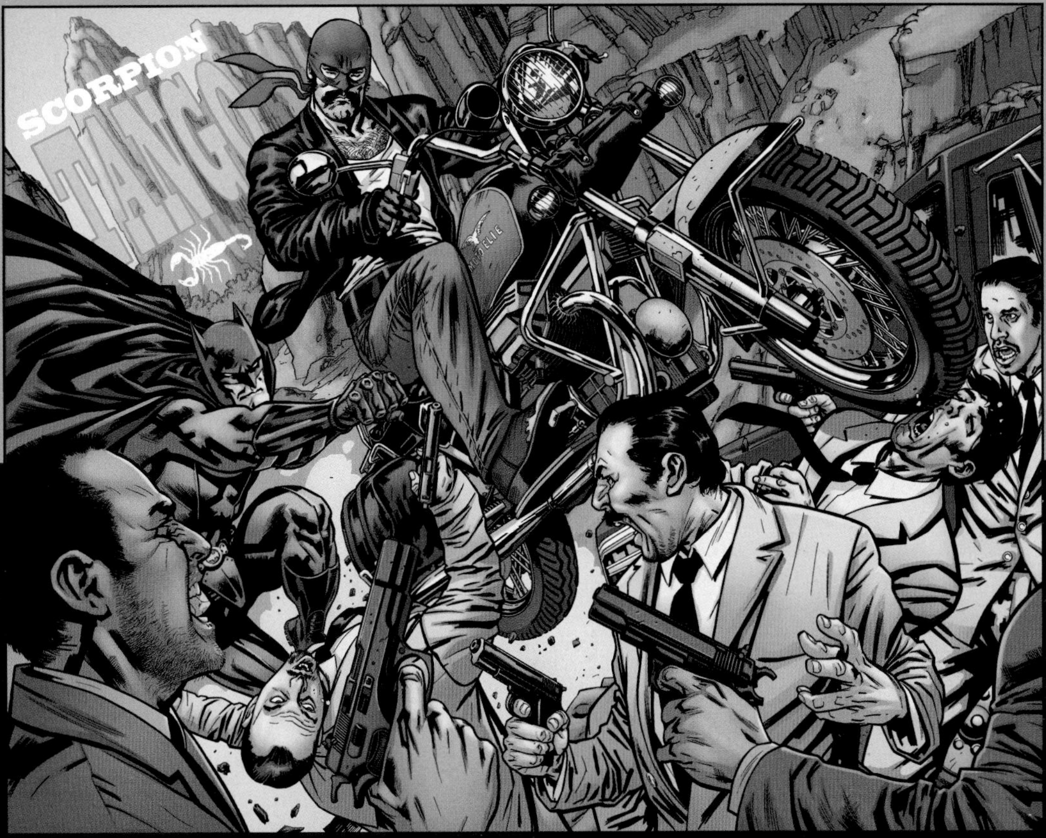
SCORPION
TANGO

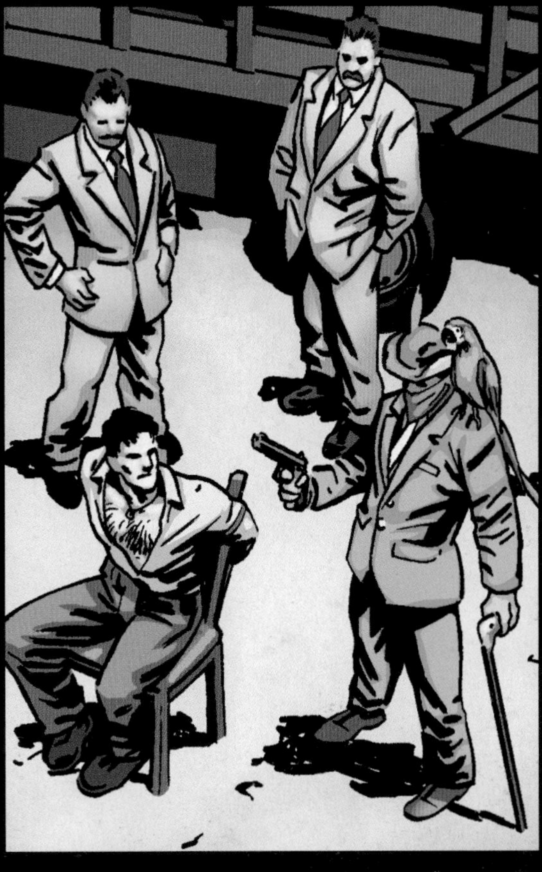

CIMARRON

Cimarron is the swashbuckling adventurer of the Super-Malon, the national super-hero team — the Justice League, if you like — of the DC Universe's Argentina. Appearing in FLASH ANNUAL #13 in the summer of 2000 and featuring such memorable characters as the horseheaded El Bagual, the winged Cachiru, and the genuinely weird-looking super-speedster El Yaguarete, the Super-Malon still operates on the fringes of the DC Universe and is long overdue for a major revival.

BATWOMAN

The original Batwoman first appeared in DETECTIVE COMICS #233 in 1956. The current Batwoman took up the mantle in the weekly 52 series (#9, September 2006). For a long time, the '50s Batwoman was considered non-canonical, but I thought there was a good story to be had by reintroducing her into Batman's history as the first woman he really loved — and the first to break his heart.

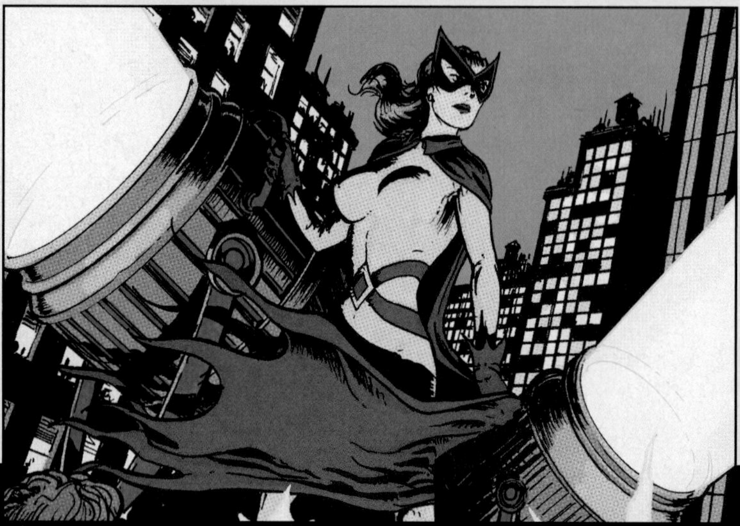

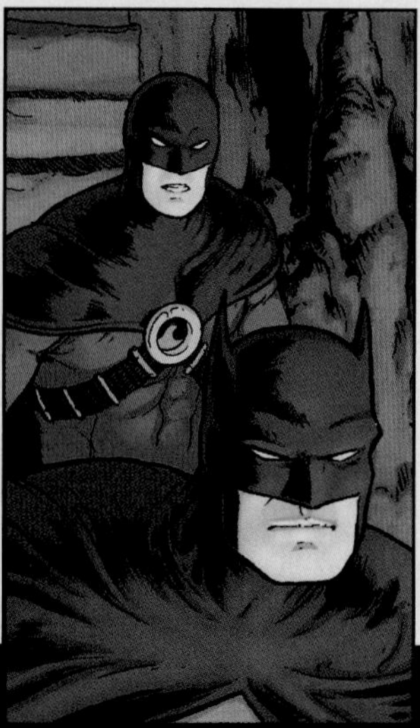

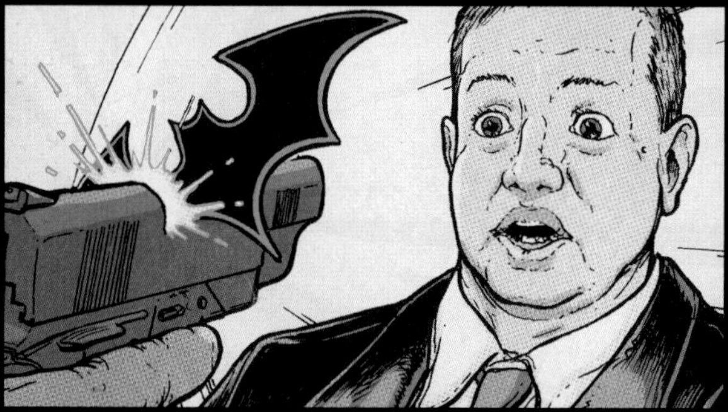

Aldrin Stoja was the generous winner of a charity auction sponsored by the Comic Book Alliance where the prize was an appearance in an issue of BATMAN, INC. He was given the choice to be killed by a villain or rescued by Batman.

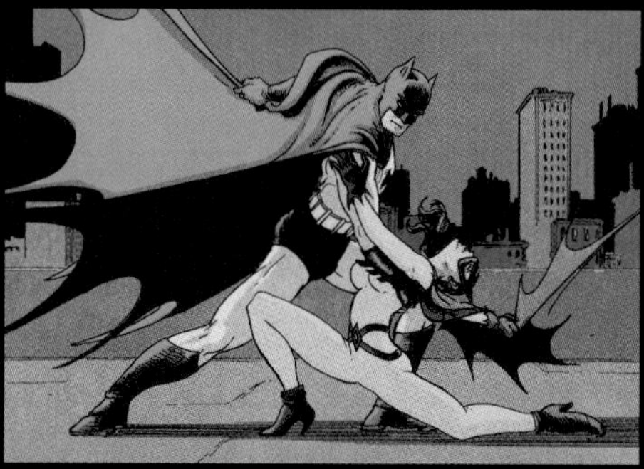

The two double-page flashback sequences were drawn by Chris to recall the work of the great Argentine artist Alberto Breccia.

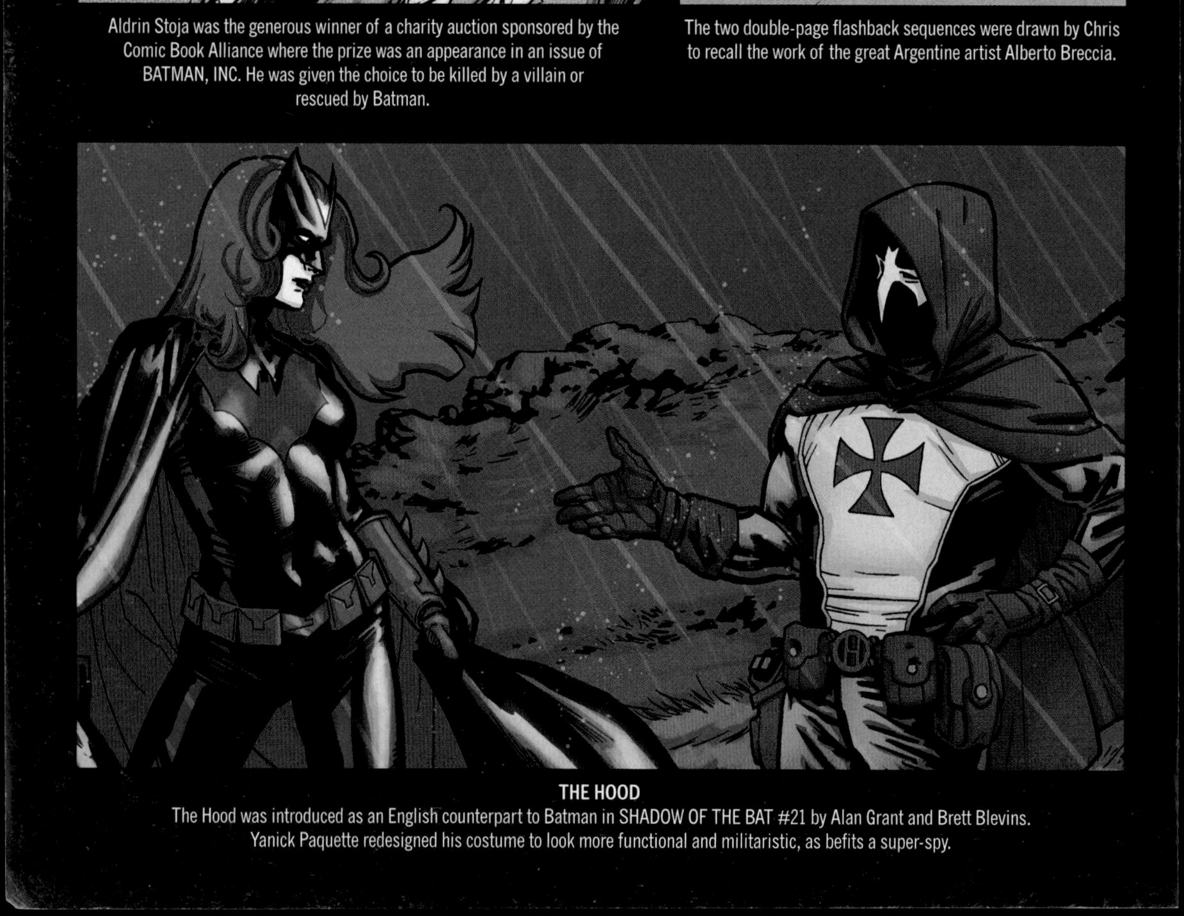

THE HOOD

The Hood was introduced as an English counterpart to Batman in SHADOW OF THE BAT #21 by Alan Grant and Brett Blevins. Yanick Paquette redesigned his costume to look more functional and militaristic, as befits a super-spy.

BATWING

Batwing's look is derived from the classic short story "The Batman Nobody Knows," which appeared in BATMAN #250 in 1973. In this story, Bruce Wayne takes three underprivileged kids on a camping trip and each boy describes his own personal version of the urban legend that is Batman. One of the boys imagines Batman as a high-tech urban crimefighter who is "... MUHAMMED ALI — JIM BROWN — SHAFT AN' SUPER-FLY ROLLED INTO ONE!"

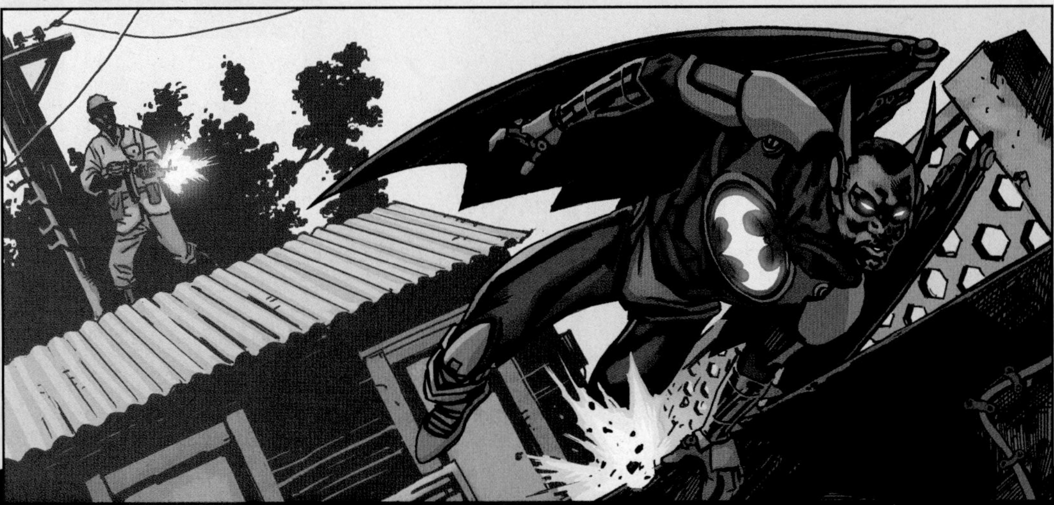

Batwing has since gone on to star in his own comic series written by Judd Winick and drawn by Ben Oliver.

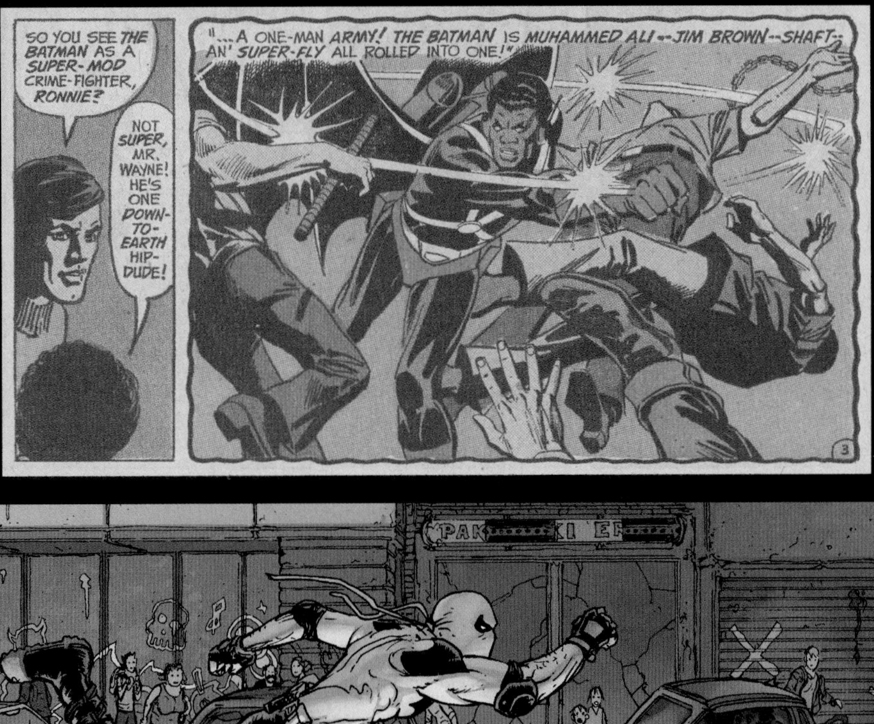
SO YOU SEE THE BATMAN AS A SUPER-MOD CRIME-FIGHTER, RONNIE?
NOT SUPER, MR. WAYNE! HE'S ONE DOWN-TO-EARTH HIP-DUDE!
"...A ONE-MAN ARMY! THE BATMAN IS MUHAMMED ALI--JIM BROWN--SHAFT--AN' SUPER-FLY ALL ROLLED INTO ONE!"
3

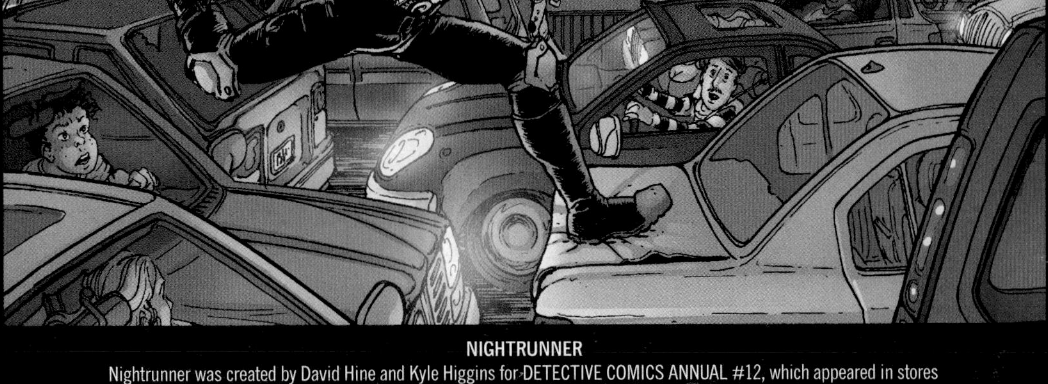

NIGHTRUNNER

Nightrunner was created by David Hine and Kyle Higgins for DETECTIVE COMICS ANNUAL #12, which appeared in stores at the end of 2010. This Muslim master of *le parkour* free-running triggered a media storm in a teacup — go look it up if you don't believe things like this can still happen.

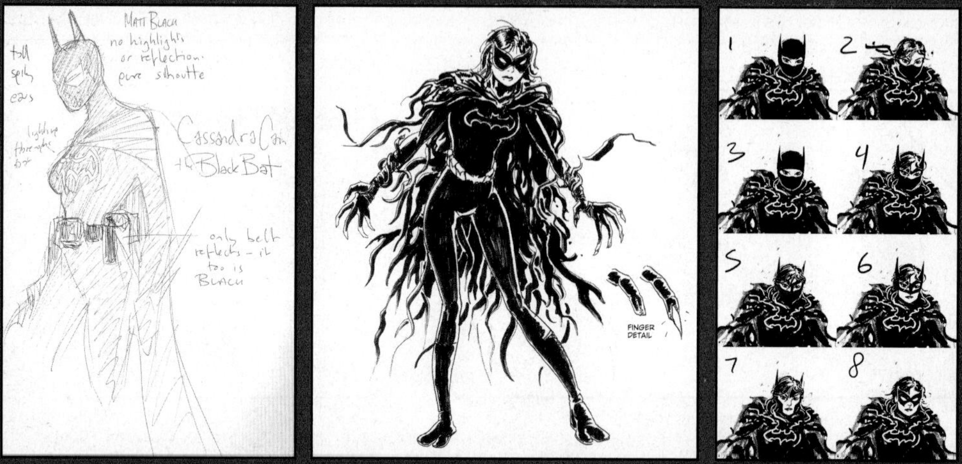

MATT BLACK
no highlights
or reflection.
pure silhoutte
tall
spiky
ears
Cassandra Cain
= Black Bat
only belt
reflects - it
too is
BLACK
FINGER
DETAIL
1
2
3
4
5
6
7
8

BLACK BAT

One of several former (and temporary) Batgirls, the wonderful Cassandra Cain has adopted a new Batman, Inc. identity as the Black Bat operating out of Hong Kong.

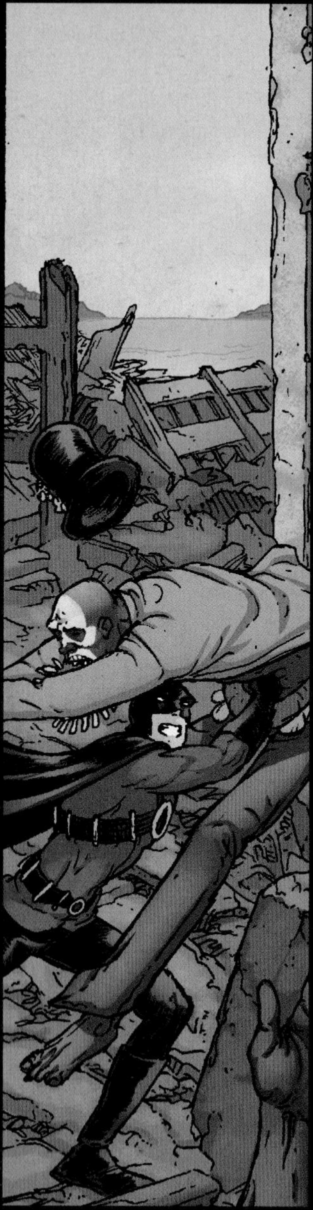

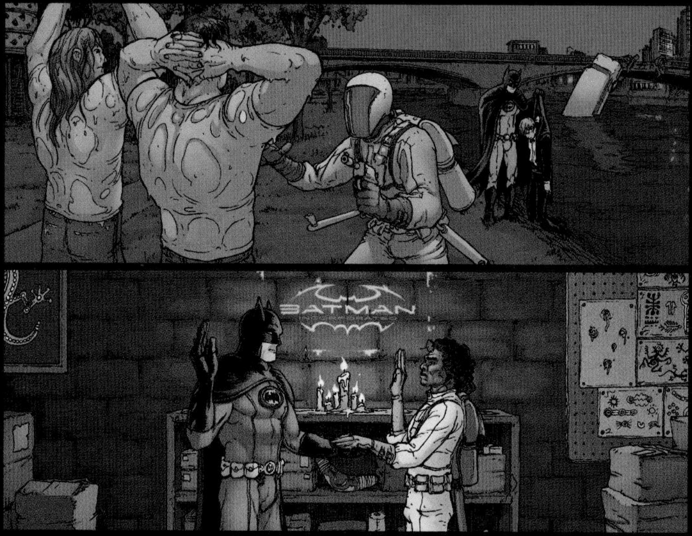

BATMAN

DARK RANGER

Following the murder of the original Ranger by the Black Glove in BATMAN #668, Dark Ranger's former partner, the Scout, has taken up his friend and mentor's mantle to fight crime in Australia's big cities and beyond. The new Dark Ranger is Johnny Riley — a tough, uncompromising, young aboriginal man who works out of a tattoo studio in Melbourne's bohemian St. Kilda district.

As an Easter egg for our Aussie readers, the park where the Dark Knight and the Dark Ranger apprehend the villains is known in real life as Batman Park. This is not, as you may imagine, because Melbourne doubled for Gotham City in Christopher Nolan's *Batman Begins* — although it did — but is instead in honor of explorer John Batman, the founder of Melbourne and the man saddled with only the coolest name in all of history.

The bad guy Red Robin is punching is the OBEAH MAN — he was responsible for the death of Tim (Red Robin) Drake's mother, so we're seeing a little payback here.

MAN-OF-BATS AND RAVEN

Chief Man-of-Bats and his son Little Raven made their first appearance in the 1955 story "Batman — Indian Chief!" in which Lakota culture was portrayed using somewhat stereotypically nostalgic cowboys and injuns images of bat-shaped smoke signals, war bonnets and woven mats. Nevertheless, I was interested in the idea of a "cargo cult" version of Batman's methodology that didn't rely on Bruce Wayne's billions and I became fascinated by the notion of updating these characters into a more contemporary South Dakota setting.

Artist J.H. Williams III and I reintroduced the characters to BATMAN #667 where they were retroactively inducted as members of the Club of Heroes. This story marked the first appearance of Man-of-Bats' secret identity as Doctor William Great Eagle.

The portrayal of Man-of-Bats and Raven was partly inspired by my own dad's social activism and his role as Community Councilor for the deprived working class housing scheme of Corkerhill in Glasgow. While researching the horrendous third world conditions that are endured by men, women and children on reservations in South Dakota, I was not entirely shocked to learn that the only parts of the developed world with similar drug, alcohol, unemployment, poverty and death rate statistics are here in the west of Scotland, where I currently write this piece.

The villain Sam Black Elk, or Red Rippa, is the son of Black Elk, the bad guy in "Batman — Indian Chief!"

ORACLE

Oracle is the online identity of Barbara Gordon, A.K.A. Batgirl — the *original* and the current Batgirl in the New 52.

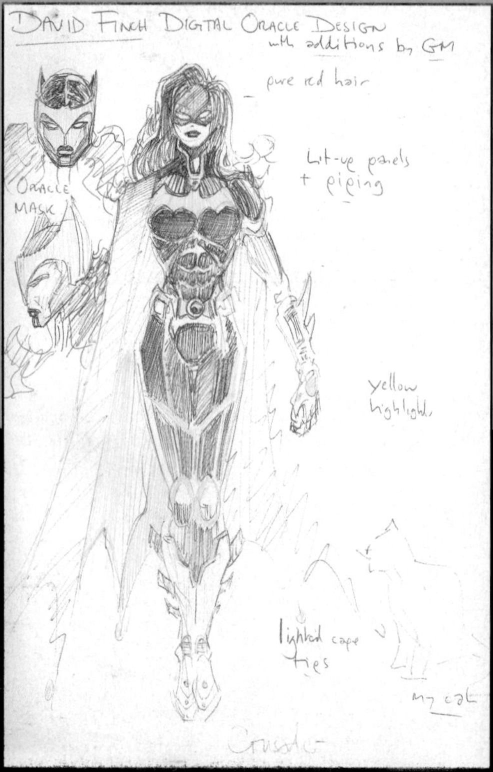
DAVID FINCH DIGITAL ORACLE DESIGN
with additions by GM
pure red hair
ORACLE MASK
Lit-up panels + piping
yellow highlights
lighted cape ties
my cat

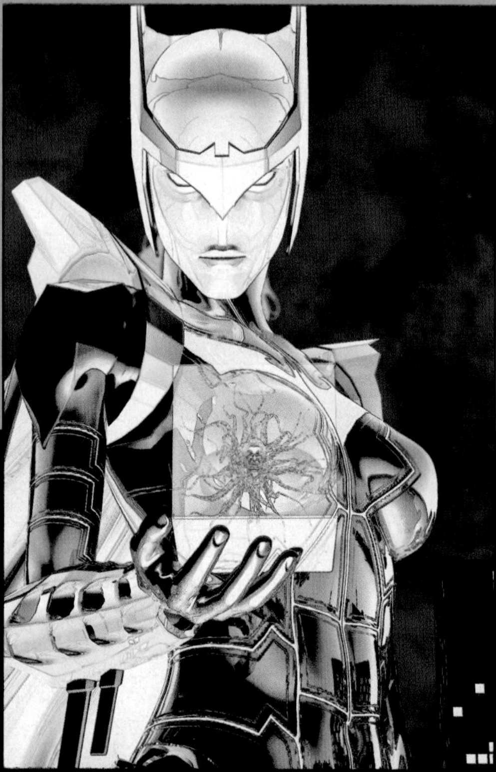

BATGIRL

The part of Batgirl is played in our story by Stephanie Brown, one of Batman's closest crimefighting allies and a former girlfriend of Robin the Boy Wonder, as created by Chuck Dixon and Tom Lyle for a story in DETECTIVE COMICS #647 in 1992. As Stephanie herself says in the story, she was trained by Batman and the Black Canary and even worked at Batman's side as a pinch-hitting Robin for a short time.

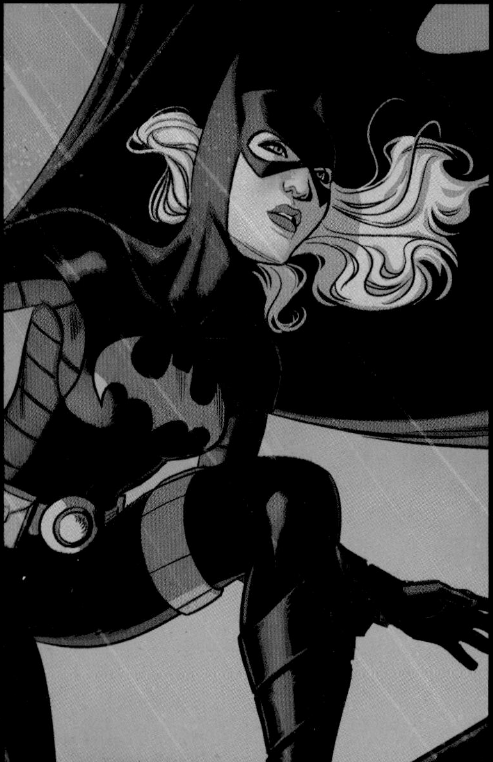

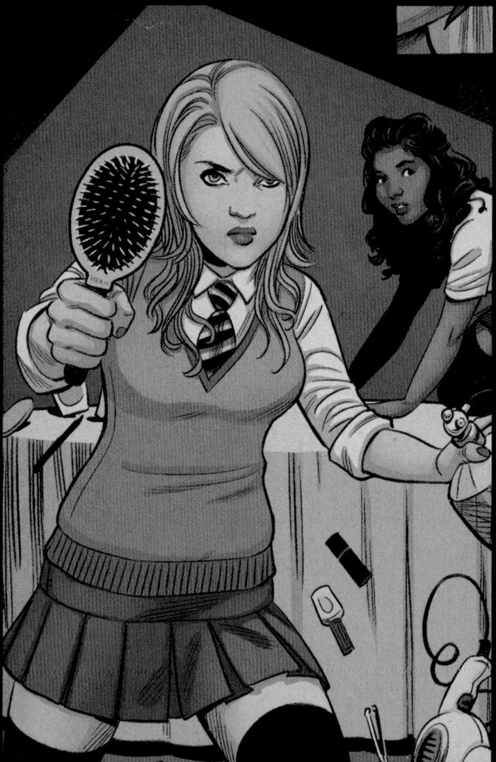

THE VILLAINS

LORD DEATH MAN

Death Man made his debut in DETECTIVE COMICS #180 in 1966. The story and character were recreated for the
Japanese Batman *manga* in which Death Man was re-dubbed Lord Death Man to great effect, and given a cape. He became even more
disturbing and demented as drawn by series artist Jiro Kuwata.

Lord Death Man's portrayal in BATMAN, INC. was inspired by the Italian "*fumetti negri*" adult comics craze of the late '60s which produced
memorable anti-heroes like Diabolik and the infamous skull-masked *Kriminal*. Sadistic, sexual and violent strips like Kriminal eventually
brought down the wrath of the censors, ending the brief, lawless era of the "black comic books" in Italy.

I liked the idea of an unstoppable villain who treats the whole world as a *Grand Theft Auto* videogame playground with the best weapons,
the best cars and the highest body count.

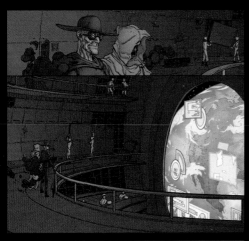

DOCTOR DEDALUS/OTTO NETZ

Doctor Dedalus began as an idea for an aging criminal
mastermind with Alzheimer's disease spinning repetitive,
disconnected schemes. The idea of a Cold War James Bond-
style master villain suffering senile dementia while plotting
to destroy the world appealed to me immensely. I became
fascinated with Netz, and he grew beyond the three issues
I had planned for him to become the principal villain
for the first season of BATMAN, INC.

The op art designs and psychedelic lighting effects in the
Netz HQ were inspired by artists Bridget Riley and Victor Vasarely,
photographer Richard Avedon, and the work of French director
Henri-Georges Clouzot on his never-completed 1964 thriller *Inferno*.
Much credit for the texture, atmosphere and sheer punch of the
book goes to our brilliant, inventive colorist Nathan Fairbairn.

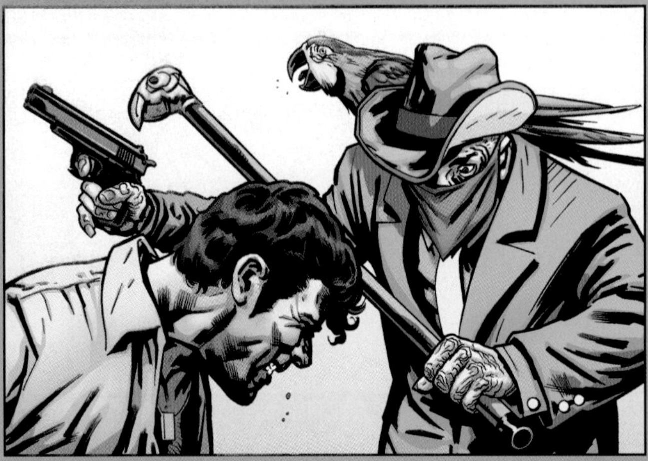

EL PAPAGAYO
"The Parrot" was the villain in a story with the unforgettable title "Ride, Bat-Hombre, Ride!" from BATMAN #56 in 1949. In that story he was a fairly ordinary *bandito*, but here Yanick has made him much more of a super-criminal and more obviously parrot-like, with bright "plumage," a beak-like bandana, and a creeping, unnamable skin disease!

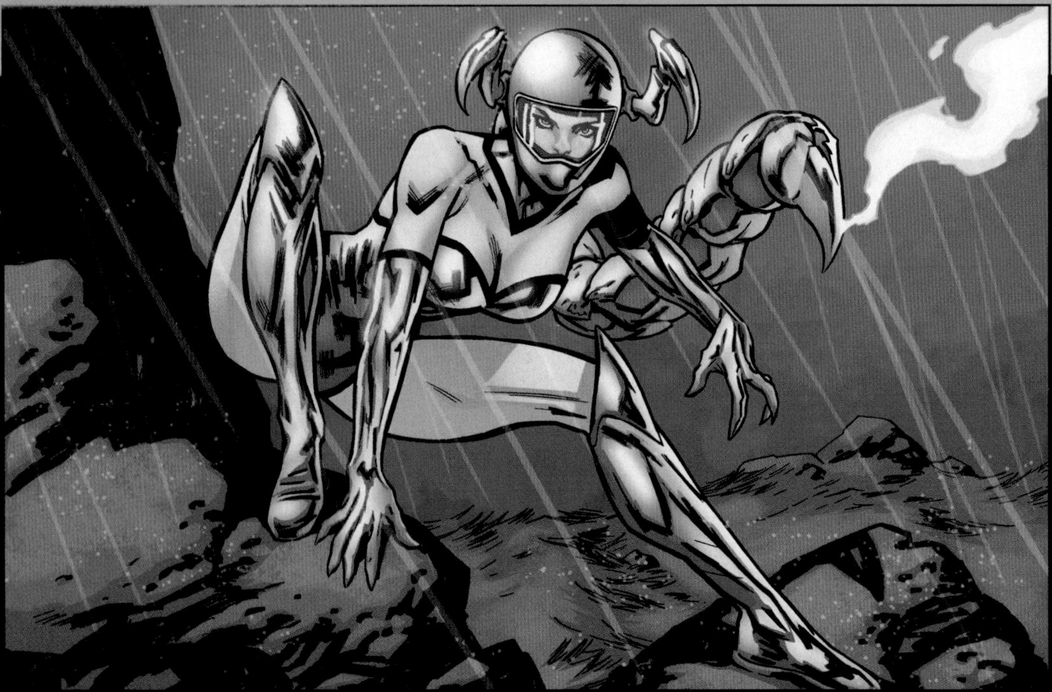

SCORPIANA
Scorpiana is named as one of El Gaucho's adversaries in BATMAN #668, but her first on-panel appearance was in BATMAN #676 as a member of the Club of Villains. I imagined her as El Gaucho's Catwoman counterpart, except much more deranged and far more deadly.

EL SOMBRERO
El Sombrero, like Scorpiana, was mentioned in BATMAN #668 but made his first appearance in BATMAN #676. A Mexican villain in a suit and *luchadore* mask who plagues the countries of Latin America, El Sombrero has been described as "a lunatic who designs and creates fantastic, artistic death traps for crooks who don't have the imagination to make their own."

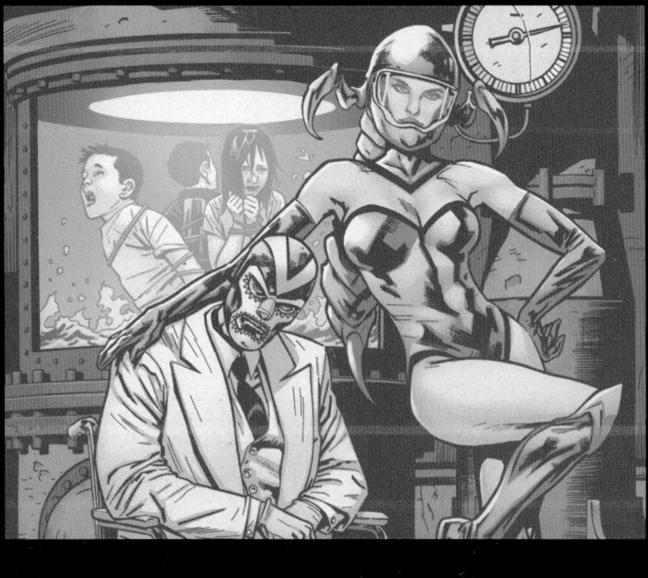

THE VICTORY Vs

The Victory Vs were a British super-team invented for no other reason than to die in this sequence! The action for this section of the story takes place during an ill-defined '80s-like period of DC history corresponding to the war between the UK and Argentina over the Falkland Islands (or the Malvinas, depending on your allegiances). To add to the '80s feel, I created a group of characters that were reminiscent of the British comics characters of that era.

BATMAN INC. 3
'VICTORY V' characters
Grant Morrison
Headdress of Knives
IRON LADY
7½ feet tall
MR ALBION
Hi Yanick - characters a bit like this but better!
FAO YANICK PAQUETTE

BATMAN INC. 3
FAO YANICK PAQUETTE
VICTORY V characters
Grant Morrison
JASPER CHURCHILL
(Adam Ant Prince Charming)
FADAR

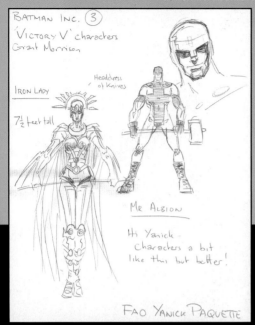

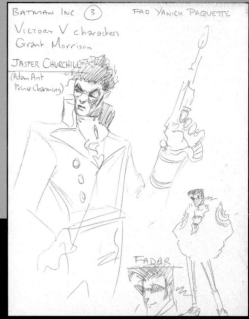

THE KNIGHT

The only member of the Victory Vs who wasn't an original character is Percy Sheldrake, the father of Cyril Sheldrake, the current Knight of England. He's here to represent old school British comics and heroes like General Jumbo. He was created by writer Edmond Hamilton, I believe, for the story "The Batman of England" in BATMAN #62.

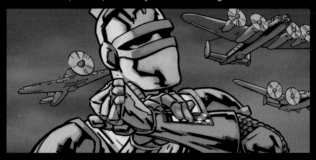

IRON LADY

This was my attempt to prefab a 1980's *2000 AD*-style robot heroine. I imagined "Iron Lady" as a satirical strip written by Pat Mills and drawn by Kevin O'Neill, set in a future world where Margaret Thatcher was worshipped as a god by intelligent machines defending their mecha-Celts-meet-William-Blake civilization against the return of rapacious human explorers from the stars. Her look is inspired by images of Boadicea (Boudicca), the rebel queen who died fighting the Roman occupation of Britain in AD 61, mashed up with Maria the art deco girl-robot from Fritz Lang's 1926 film *Metropolis*.

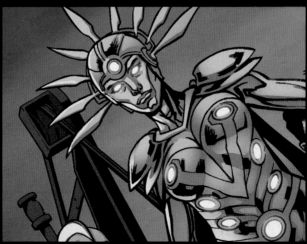

FADAR

This '80s hipster, media-savvy pop star super-hero with his Morrissey quiff was a nod to Brendan McCarthy and Peter Milligan's seminal Paradax character (*Strange Days*, 1982) and also included elements of my own *2000 AD* character Zenith (1987), with a wave in the direction of '80s gay superhero Matt Black, as brought to life by the much-missed Don Melia and Lionel Gracey-Whitman. Fadar's entirely passive super-power is simply to fade and become insubstantial.

MR. ALBION

Mr. Albion echoes Alan Davis's '80s redesign of Captain Britain, with a little dash of Paul Grist's Jack Staff character, to suggest this quintessential English patriot. The red and white of the St. George cross design on his uniform hints at the UK tabloid papers, which use the same color livery to deliver their jingoistic headlines. Wayland Smith is the Saxon god of blacksmiths, a Brit version of the Roman Vulcan.

CAPTAIN CARNATION

Jasper Carnation (originally Jasper Churchill), like Bryan Talbot's influential Luther Arkwright (first appearance: *Brainstorm Comix*, 1976) and my own Gideon Stargrave (from *Near Myths* in 1978) is inspired by Michael Moorcock's Jerry Cornelius character, crossed with Doctor Who. He dresses in New Romantic dandy style and his appearance here quotes '80s pop idol Adam Ant's look from the singer's "Prince Charming" video.

IT ALL MAKES SENSE IN THE END!

— Grant Morrison
Scotland
December 2011

THE COVERS

Preliminary art by **J.H. WILLIAMS III**, **YANICK PAQUETTE** and **CHRIS BURNHAM**.

#1

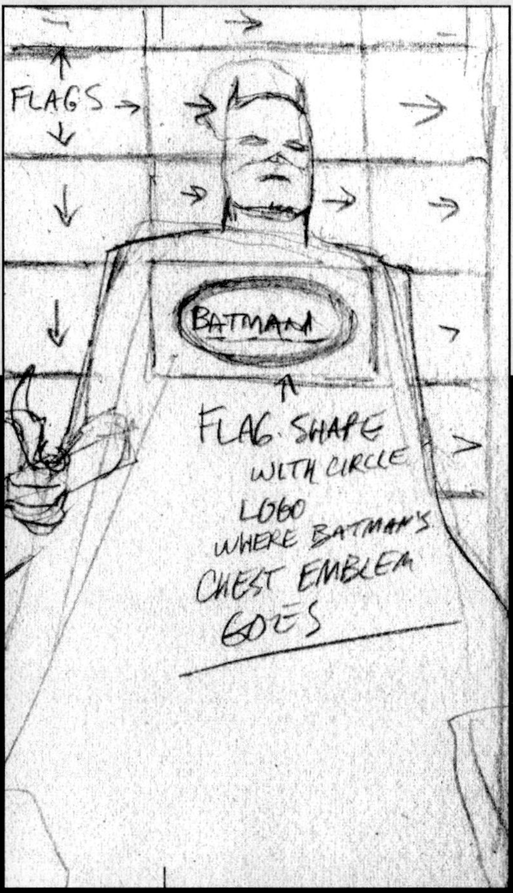
FLAGS
BATMAN
FLAG SHAPE WITH CIRCLE LOGO WHERE BATMAN'S CHEST EMBLEM GOES

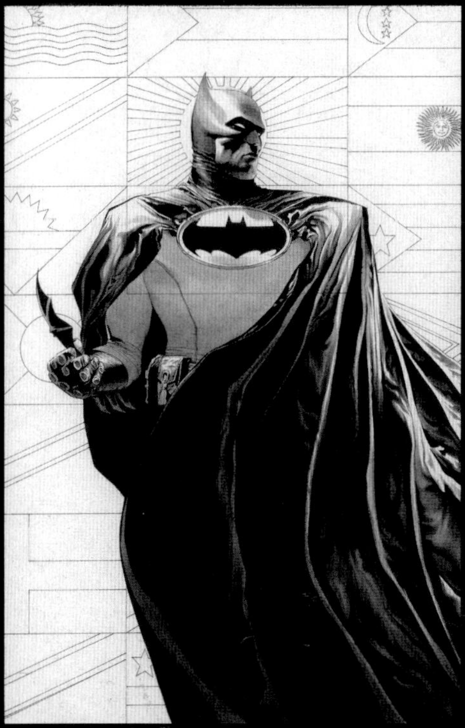

#1 Variant

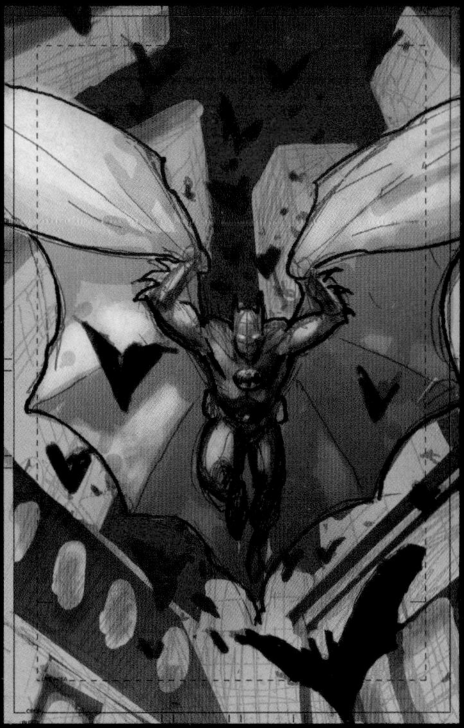

#2

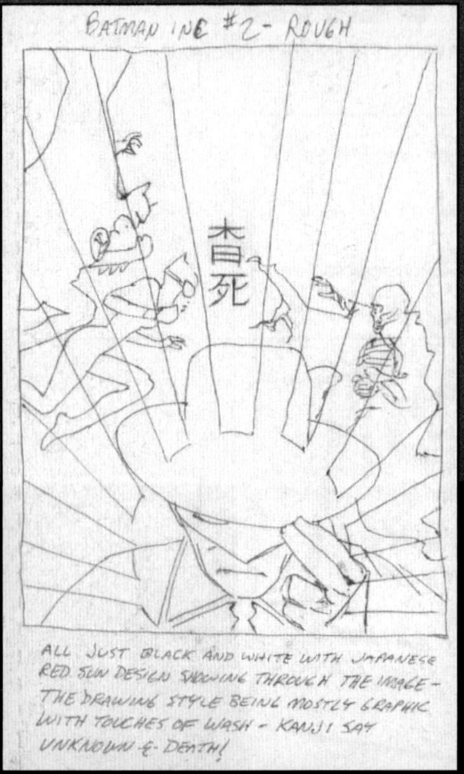
BATMAN INC #2 - ROUGH
ALL JUST BLACK AND WHITE WITH JAPANESE RED SUN DESIGN SHOWING THROUGH THE IMAGE - THE DRAWING STYLE BEING MOSTLY GRAPHIC WITH TOUCHES OF WASH - KANJI SAY UNKNOWN & DEATH!

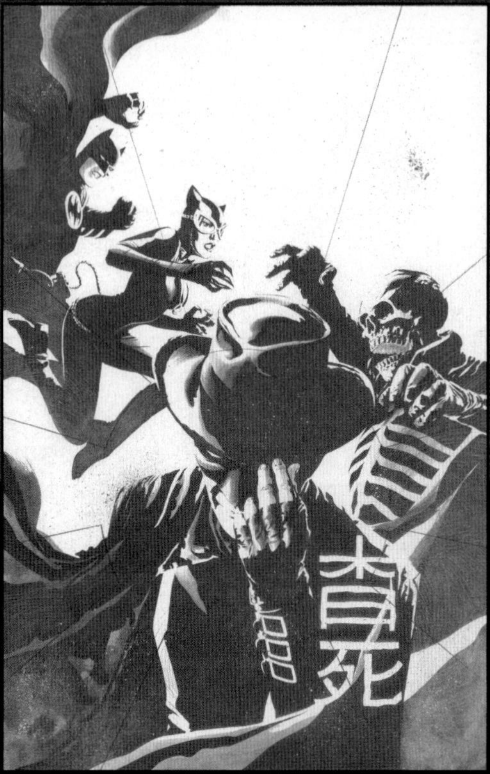

#2 Variant

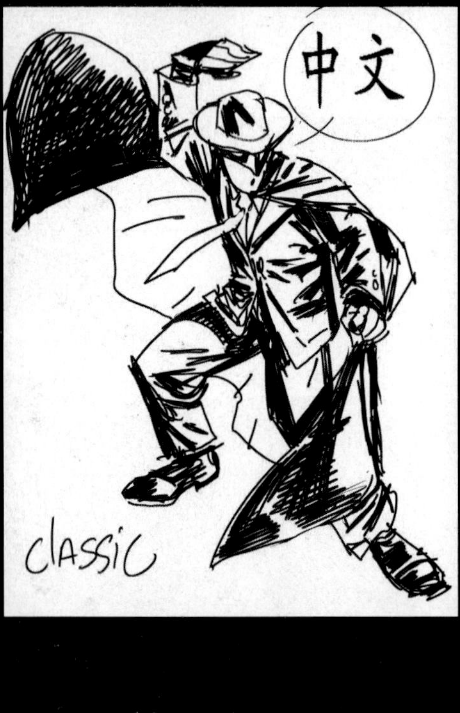
中文
CLASSIC

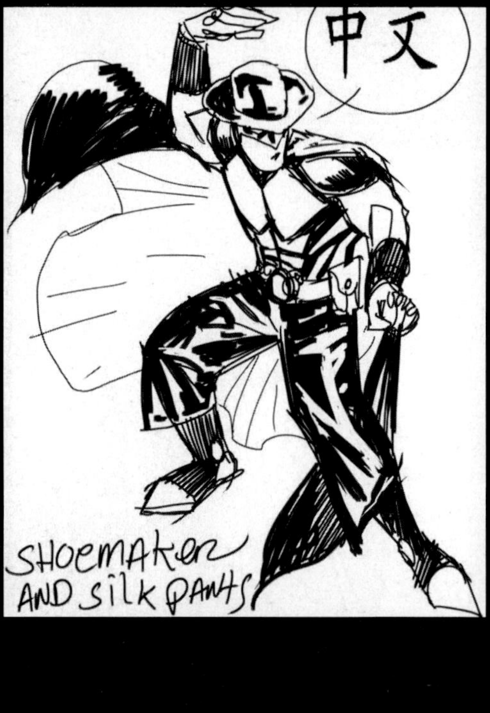
中文
SHOEMAKER AND SILK PANTS

#3

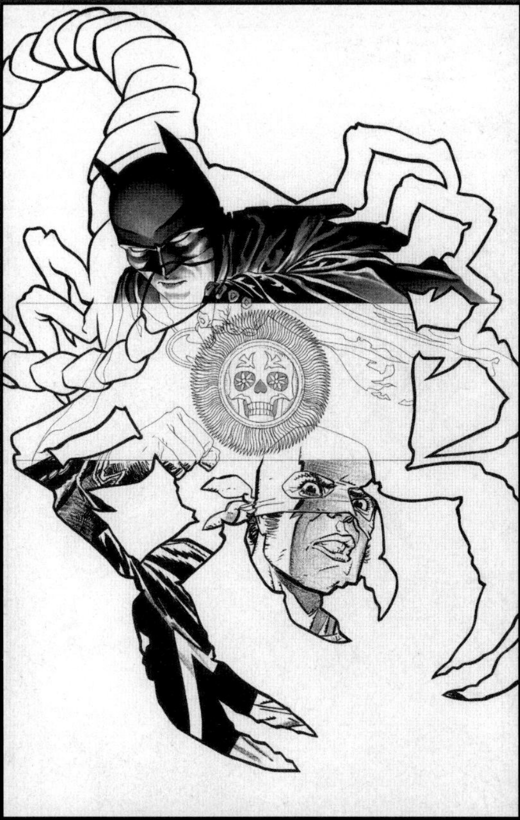

#4

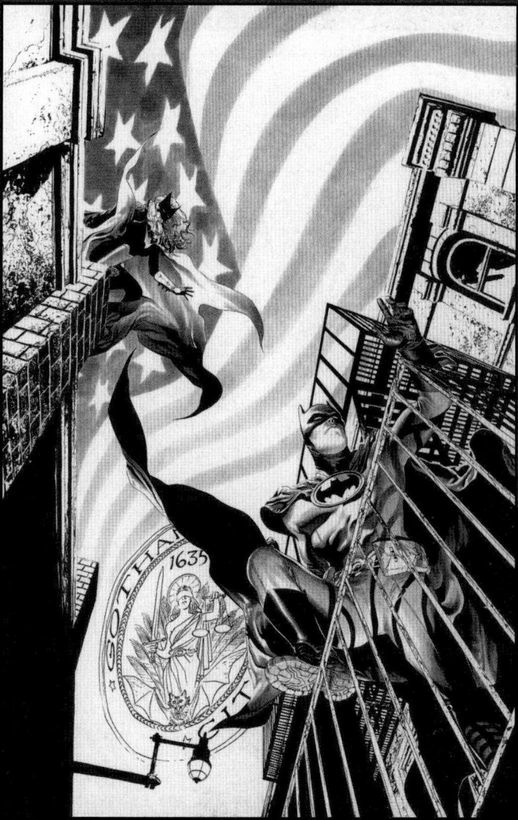

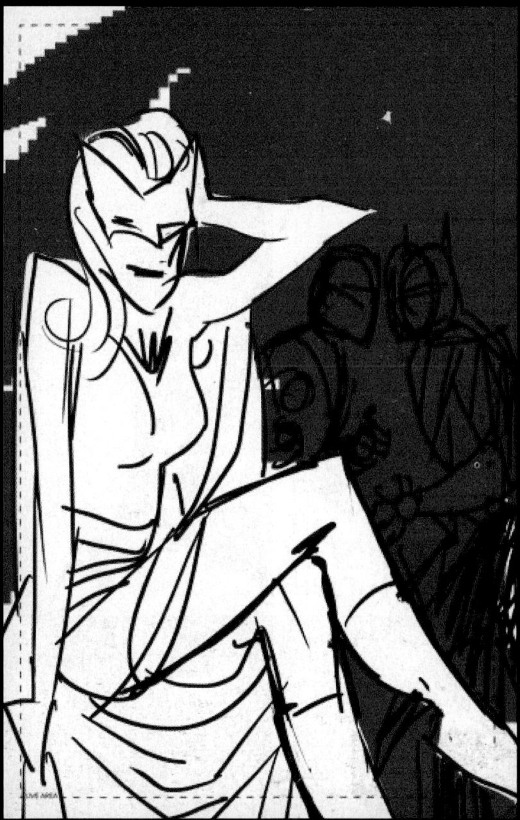

#4 Variant

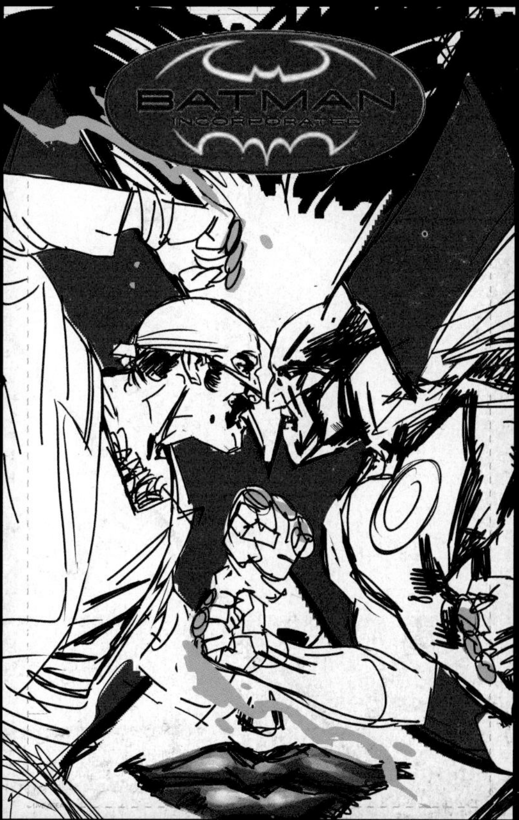
BATMAN
INCORPORATED

#5

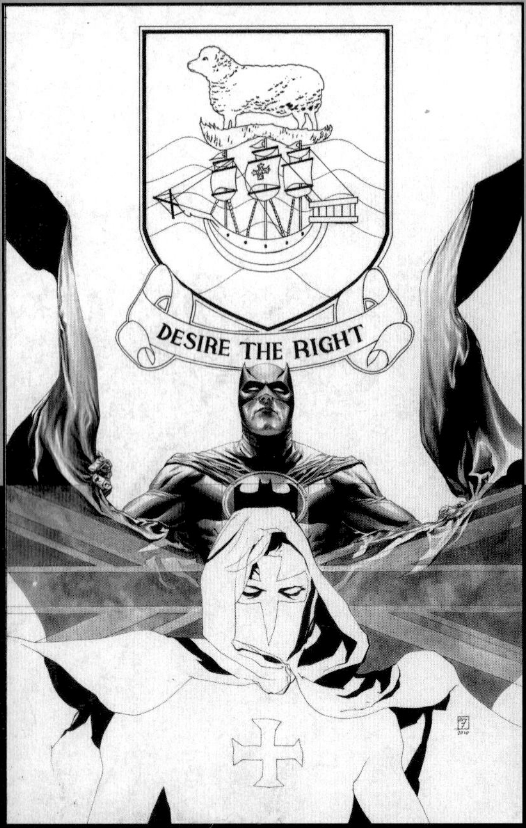
DESIRE THE RIGHT

#5 Variant

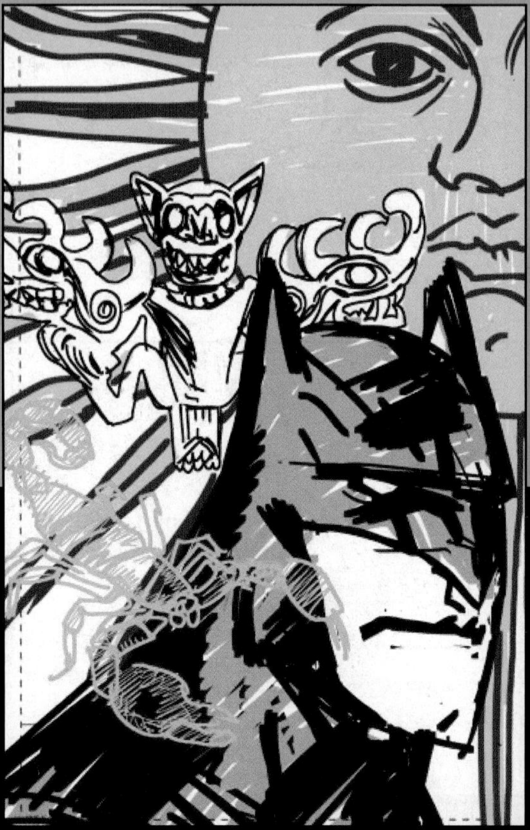

#6

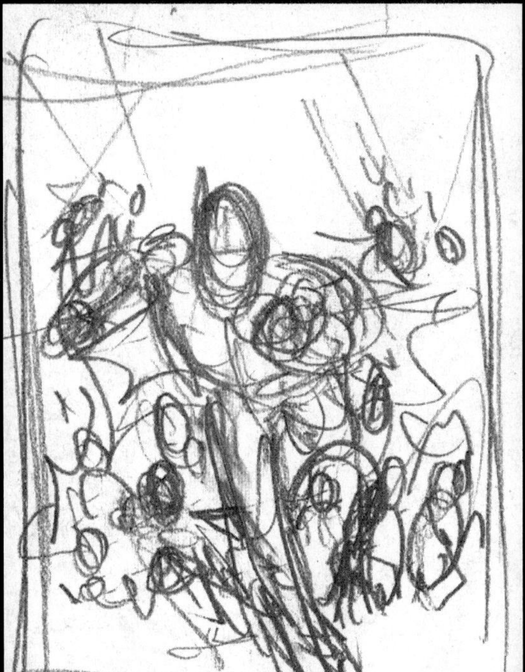